American Settlement Houses and Progressive Social Reform

An Encyclopedia of the American Settlement Movement

Domenica M. Barbuto

ORYX PRESS

1999

The rare Arabian Oryx is believed to have inspired the myth of the unicorn. This desert antelope became virtually extinct in the early 1960s. At that time, several groups of international conservationists arranged to have nine animals sent to the Phoenix Zoo to be the nucleus of a captive breeding herd. Today, the Oryx population is over 1,000, and over 500 have been returned to the Middle East.

Library of Congress Cataloging-in-Publication Data

Barbuto, Domenica M., 1951–
    American settlement houses and progressive social reform : an encyclopedia of the American settlement movement / Domenica M. Barbuto.
        Includes bibliographical references and index.
        ISBN 1-57356-146-0 (alk. paper)
        1. Social settlements—United States—History Encyclopedias.
    2. Progressivism (United States politics) Encyclopedias. 3. Social reformers—United States Encyclopedias. I. Title.
    HV4194.B37 1999
    362.5'57'0973—dc21   99-28054
                                                                          CIP

Contents

Preface   v
Introduction   vii
A–Z entries   1
Bibliography of Resources   241
Index   247

Preface

This reference work brings together in a single source information about the men and women, the institutions, and the events that were part of the American Settlement Movement of the late nineteenth and early twentieth centuries. This encyclopedia focuses on the main currents of the settlement movement and provides only limited descriptions of the settlements founded by religious organizations and by minority groups. It is not intended as a history of the Progressive Era, but some concepts related to this era are discussed to provide context for the settlement movement.

The bulk of the book is an alphabetical listing of more than 230 entries covering a range of topics including biographies of men and women directly involved in the settlement movement as founders of houses or as settlement residents; biographies of women and men who influenced or significantly contributed to the settlement movement; descriptions of the more prominent settlement houses and their programs; explanations of religious, social, or labor movements that influenced those involved in the settlements; accounts of social organizations that influenced or were influenced by the settlement movement; descriptions of significant publications by individuals associated with the settlement movement; and descriptions of legislation related to the work of the settlement movement.

Each entry provides a concise summary of the subject and includes a brief bibliography to guide the reader to additional sources of information. Full citations for works cited in the these bibliographies are available in the Bibliography of Resources, p. 241. Boldface type within an entry is used to indicate that a person, place, or concept has its own entry. (Only the first occurrence of the word within an entry is in boldface.) The accompanying photographs were selected to provide a reader with a visual description of the people, places, and events discussed in the text.

This encyclopedia is intended for individuals researching women's studies, social work, and urban and social history. It is a valuable resource for the American history curriculum for students from high school through college. It is also useful for students and faculty in the social work field who will find it helpful for its insights into the origin of the profession in the United States.

Acknowledgments

I wish to thank Eileen Kennedy and Marguerite Lavin of the Museum of the City of New York; David Klaassen of the Social Welfare History Archives, University of Minnesota; and Marie-Helene Gold of the Arthur & Elizabeth Schlesinger Library on the History of Women in America, Radcliffe College, for their invaluable assistance in locating the photographs.

Thanks also to my colleagues in the Joan & Donald E. Axinn Library of Hofstra University for their interest and encouragement. Finally, and most importantly, I want to acknowledge the support and assistance of my family, Attilia, Ken, Amanda, Kenny, and Bailey Kaplan, and Attilia Barbuto. I am particularly indebted to my sister Frances, who as always, helped me in countless ways.

Introduction

The American Settlement Movement was a late-nineteenth- and early-twentieth-century social movement that took its name from the settlement houses founded by Progressive Era reformers. These college-educated men and women believed that the most effective way for them to bring about significant social reforms was to go live among the poor in large industrial centers and to share in the lives of those whom they hoped to assist. The houses in which they lived were called settlement houses, the name deriving from the fact that they "settled" in the neighborhood. These settlement houses functioned as homes for the reformers and as a type of community center for the neighborhood residents. Settlement houses provided a place for the community to hold social events, supported a neighborhood clinic or dispensary, or furnished a meeting place for local unions. By actually living among the people they were helping, the settlement house workers or settlement house residents had daily contact with their neighbors and worked cooperatively with the poor to bring about social change.

The men and women of the American Settlement Movement were in the vanguard of Progressive Era reformers. The settlement houses they established and then lived and worked in provided them with a network of interlocking directories of reformers in other settlements who made significant contributions to a number of causes, including public health, political reform, public education, protective legislation for women and children, and improved living and working conditions for urban dwellers.

The Progressive Era

The phrase *Progressive Era* itself provokes a wide-ranging and sometimes spirited response from historians. Concerns are voiced not only about what it was, but also when it was. Like the Age of Jackson and the New Deal, the Progressive Era was a distinctive period of reform in America's history. However, it was not a time when reformers could be described as having a clearly defined, single-minded approach. It seemed at times that almost any aspect of society was fair game for reform.

Some date the Progressive period as beginning in 1901, when Theodore Roosevelt became president; others place the origin a decade later when, once again, Roosevelt and the presidency were coupled, this time as he stood as the Progressive Party's candidate in the 1912 presidential election. For the purpose of this encyclopedia, it seems more useful to date the origins of the Progressive Era a decade before Roosevelt was called upon to lead the nation, following William McKinley's assassination.

The 30 years between 1890 and 1920 were characterized by sweeping growth and change in the United States. The advances in technology, the resulting rapid industrialization, and the inundation of immigrants combined to alter the social and economic lives of many

Americans. Although the evils that were present—poverty, disease, crime—in the growing industrial centers were not new, the degree and magnitude of change that urban dwellers experienced exacerbated the impact of relentless industrialization on the existing social order. To a significant degree, reforms instituted during the Progressive Era may be viewed as an attempt to preserve basic human values in the face of a seemingly uncaring urban industrial age.

Life as most Americans knew it changed dramatically during these years. By the end of the second decade of the twentieth century, the United States had emerged as a modern, urban, industrial world power. Almost every aspect of American culture was affected, and a "movement" seemed to be underway for almost everything, including a labor movement, a women's rights movement, a social justice movement, an anti-prostitution movement, a child labor movement, a public health movement, and a child welfare movement. These various causes attracted men and women reformers from different social, ethnic, and economic spheres and brought them together into new kinds of dynamic coalitions that were able to identify problems, propose solutions, and implement courses of action.

Various labels have been applied to the Progressive Era. It has been called a response to a "status revolution" on the part of the old elite who sought to maintain power over the emerging municipal political machines. Others refer to the period as a "triumph of conservatism" engineered by the big business interests, or they characterize it as a "search for order" on the part of the new elite composed of bureaucrats and highly trained technicians and managers. The Progressive Era has also been described as a time characterized by a "search for social justice" on the part of well-meaning clergy, intellectuals, and social workers. What becomes clear is that no single, easily-agreed-upon label can be used to characterize the Progressive Era, and it is not the purpose of this volume to resolve this issue. However, some commonalities were present among the different social reform undertakings, and these commonalities were evident in the work accomplished by the men and women who came to be clearly identified with another prevailing "movement" of the time, the American Settlement Movement.

The History of the Settlement Movement

The settlement concept was first set in motion by Canon Samuel Barnett in England in 1884 as part of an effort to relieve poverty and despair among London's poor, many of whom had been displaced by the rapid pace of industrialization. With the assistance of a group of Oxford University students and tutors, Barnett transformed an old school building into a residence for reformers and a community center for neighborhood residents. Barnett and his followers saw themselves as settlers in the neighborhood, hence the name settlement came to be used to describe the building they lived and worked in. The nomenclature was carried over to the American movement, and those involved in reform efforts were usually identified as settlement workers or residents.

American reformers familiar with Barnett's program and the settlement he established in London, Toynbee Hall, realized that analogous conditions existed in English and American industrial centers and adapted the settlement idea as a way to preserve human integrity in the new urban industrial age.

The growth and development of the settlement movement in the United States is entwined with the growth and development of the American city in the late nineteenth and early twentieth centuries. As larger urban centers such as Boston, Chicago, and New York began to grow in the late nineteenth century, their residents were confronted by myriad problems. Large numbers of migrants from rural areas in the South and Midwest of the United States relocated to Northern cities in search of jobs. They were joined by thousands of immigrants from Europe who came to America in the hope of finding a new life.

Industries located near transportation facilities, people located near their places of work, and cities grew beyond their ability to provide the necessary services and amenities. Very quickly, thousands of people were living in substandard housing, much of it without light and ventilation. As the population increased, housing became scarce and rents were high. Sanitary conditions were primitive and disease spread.

Soon, the poor and needy were very much in evidence, and it became apparent that the municipal authorities and private relief agencies were not equipped to deal with what must have seemed a never-ending stream of requests for assistance. The result was the development of a system of indiscriminate relief. The inequalities of this system were soon apparent as some applicants received aid from several sources simultaneously while others received little or nothing at all.

Charity Organization Societies and the Settlement Movement

A concept called the Charity Organization Society (COS) came into being to control indiscriminate relief by organizing the work of public and private relief agencies. The COS workers, primarily drawn from the middle class, concentrated their efforts on investigating requests for aid, a process that involved their assessing whether the applicants were "worthy" or "unworthy" of receiving assistance.

Generally, Charity Organization Societies frowned on the distribution of relief. Instead, they saw their responsibility as twofold: to detect fraud in the relief system and to promote the idea of self-help among those deemed worthy of assistance. The COS approach reflected the prevailing belief that poverty was a manifestation of a personal flaw; correct the flaw—intemperance, laziness—and eliminate the need for assistance. Simply put, in their minds society was functioning; some families were broken.

The men and women who elected to become settlement workers witnessed the same situation and came to a very different solution. They had different goals than their COS counterparts and pursued them using alternative techniques and programs. For the most part, they operated from the perspective that families were not at fault. They believed that people were moving from a known to an unknown culture and needed assistance adjusting to their new environment. When families could not cope, it was society that was at fault, and therein lay the need for reform. To accomplish this change, they became involved in a variety of the reform crusades that defined the Progressive Era, often serving as leaders, always providing support.

Despite good intentions, these men and women reformers were not free of personal prejudices, nor could they entirely overcome the ethnic and racial stereotypes of their age. Much of the good they accomplished was offset by an apparent attempt to set up social and economic controls that would check the impact of the new immigrants. In addition, settlements largely ignored the significant number of blacks who found their way into Northern urban centers, rationalizing their racial prejudice by claiming that these emigrants could better progress on their own. Like much of history, the settlement movement defies any attempt to label it as entirely good or bad. Every attempt has been made in this encyclopedia to provide a balanced picture of both aspects of settlement work.

In addition to the many programs and services that the settlement workers developed for their urban neighbors, the settlement movement also provided opportunities for the reform workers themselves. For example, educated middle-class women who joined the movement were given a chance to move beyond the traditional confines of the home and to enter the working world in positions of leadership, achieving a level of equality with their male colleagues. Another lasting legacy of the settlement movement was the growth and development of the modern profession of social work, whose foundations were established by the settlement workers.

Abbott, Edith

researcher, social work educator and
administrator, reformer
b. September 26, 1876; d. July 28, 1957.

Edith Abbott was associated with **Hull House**
and its circle of reformers, which allowed her
to become involved with a number of social
welfare reform efforts. She used her training
as an economist to work for a variety of social,
legal, and political causes. In addition, she made
a significant contribution to the developing field
of social work education.

Abbott was born and raised in Grand Island, Nebraska. The Abbott family's precarious
financial situation delayed her entry to college,
but by combining correspondence courses, summer sessions, and full-time study, Abbott was
able to earn an A.B. degree from the University
of Nebraska in 1901. The following summer she
attended the University of Chicago, coming to
the attention of the economists Thorstein
Veblen and James L. Laughlin. With their assistance, she secured a fellowship in political
economy, entered the University of Chicago
(1903), and earned a Ph.D. in economics (1905).

Based on her achievements and reputation
in Chicago, Abbott was offered a dual position
in 1905. She lived for a time at **Denison House**,
a settlement in Boston, working as the secretary of the **Women's Trade Union League**, a
coalition of middle-class and working-class
women which tried to organize women into
trade unions. She also spent time in Washing-

ton, DC, as a researcher for the American Economic Association, working on an industrial
history of the United States which was funded
by the Carnegie Institution. These positions
were followed in early 1906 by another assignment for Carnegie in New York City, where she
lived at the **College Settlement** on the city's
Lower East Side and studied working conditions
in the cigar factories and the garment industry.
This research was published in her book, *Women
in Industry* (1910).

Toward the end of 1906, Abbott won a competition for a Foreign Fellowship of the
Association of Collegiate Alumnae and studied
at the University of London. While in England,
she met the social activists Beatrice and Sidney
Webb who encouraged her to become a social
investigator with an interest in poor law reform.
She also spent some time living and working at
St. Hilda's settlement house in Bethnal Green
in London's East End. This experience brought
Abbott into personal contact with the people
behind the economic statistics she had studied
for so long, and it played a pivotal role in deter-
mining the future direction of her professional
life.

Returning to the United States in 1907,
Abbott accepted a position as an instructor of
economics at Wellesley College. After one year,
she returned to Chicago to work as an assistant
to **Sophonisba Breckinridge**, then the director of social research at the Chicago School of
Civics and Philanthropy and a friend and re-

search collaborator from her days at the University of Chicago.

For most of the next decade Abbott and her sister **Grace Abbott** lived and worked at Hull House, the settlement founded by **Jane Addams,** which they considered a center for social research. The sisters were involved in a number of social, legal, and political campaigns such as housing, child labor, woman suffrage, and protective labor legislation. Her residency at Hull House along with her position at the Chicago School presented Abbott with an excellent opportunity to investigate many aspects of urban life and resulted in the publication of more than 100 books and articles.

Abbott was also committed to the field of social work education, and during the 1920s, she contributed significantly to its development. In 1920, she and Breckinridge were instrumental in the transfer of the Chicago School of Civics and Philanthropy (*see* **Graduate School of Social Service Administration**) to the University of Chicago, making it the first graduate school of social work to be part of a coeducational university. By 1924, when the school had been renamed the Graduate School of Social Service Administration, Abbott was dean, a position she held until 1942.

During her years as dean, Abbott emphasized social reform and public social service administration. She established a broad-based, scholarly curriculum, incorporating a number of disciplines including law, economics, and political science. Students were required to gain practical experience in the community, applying the scientifically based methods of social investigation to bring about public policy reform. Breckinridge and Abbott established the University of Chicago Social Service Series of books and monographs, and in 1927, they founded an important professional journal, the *Social Service Review*.

In addition to her academic work, throughout the 1930s and 1940s Abbott was actively involved in formulating public policy regarding assistance for the poor. She wrote and spoke out in favor of the federal government assuming a leadership role in providing economic relief to individuals and the desirability of a comprehensive social insurance program, much of which was realized by the New Deal legislation.

In 1954, Abbott retired after dedicating more than 50 years to social work research and education and to a variety of social justice reform efforts including working for protective legislation for women and children workers and safeguarding the rights of immigrants.

Bibliography

Carson, *Settlement Folk: Social Thought and the American Settlement Movement, 1885–1930*; Costin, *Two Sisters for Social Justice: A Biography of Grace and Edith Abbott*; Davis, *Spearheads for Reform: The Social Settlements and the Progressive Movement, 1890–1914*; *Dictionary of American Biography*, supl. 2, pp. 1–2; Sicherman, *Notable American Women, The Modern Period*, pp. 2–4; Trattner, *Biographical Dictionary of Social Welfare in America*, pp. 6–10.

Abbott, Grace
social reformer, public administrator, social work educator
b. November 17, 1878; d. June 19, 1939.

As the head of the Immigrants' Protective League (*see* **Immigrants' Service League**), Grace Abbott devoted most of her adult life to protecting the thousands of immigrants who settled in urban centers like Chicago during the opening decades of the twentieth century. Living and working at the Chicago-based **Hull House**, she was drawn into the local community of social welfare reformers and went on to become a leading national advocate of the rights of women and children through her work with the **United States Children's Bureau**.

Grace Abbott earned a B.A. from Grand Island College in 1898. Between 1899 and 1907, Abbott taught at Grand Island High School. During this time, she completed a semester of graduate study at the University of Nebraska (fall, 1902). Abbott spent the summer of 1904 at the University of Chicago and continued her graduate studies intermittently during the next few years. In 1907, she moved to Chicago where she completed her graduate work, earning a master's degree in political science later that year.

Influenced in part by her sister Edith, Abbott joined Chicago's active reform community. The sisters became residents at Hull House in 1908 and during the following nine years cooperated with other residents such as **Jane Addams**, **Florence Kelley**, and **Julia Lathrop** on a variety of reform campaigns.

The residents at Hull House were keenly aware of the problems encountered by the newly arrived as they made their way to Chicago. Many new immigrants were easy targets for exploitation by unscrupulous ticket agencies and employment bureaus. Most did not speak English and arrived in a strange city with little money and without the prospect of securing employment. Single immigrant women without friends or relatives to meet them and assist in their transition to a new culture were exposed to a variety of physical and moral hazards, which frequently resulted in their working in dangerous factories or in becoming prostitutes.

To assist these immigrants, **Sophonisba Breckinridge** and a number of Hull House residents established the Immigrants' Protective League to combat these abuses. Grace Abbott was selected to head the league. She conducted investigations and wrote articles about the abuses she uncovered and lobbied the Illinois State Legislature for the passage of protective legislation. In 1911, Abbott spent four months in Eastern Europe studying the background and culture of the men and women whom she was trying to help in Chicago. She even taught a course on immigration at the Chicago School of Civics and Philanthropy. In 1914, while on a leave of absence from the league, Abbott served as secretary of the Massachusetts Immigration Commission. Her work resulted in the passage of protective legislation for immigrants in Massachusetts.

In addition to her immigration-related work, Abbott was also active in a number of other social reform initiatives. She supported local workers during the garment strike (1910–1911), campaigned for Theodore Roosevelt in 1912, and was active in the woman suffrage campaign in Illinois the following year. In 1915, Abbott accompanied Addams to the International Congress of Women at The Hague. She also served as a faculty member of the Chicago School of Civics and Philanthropy from 1910 to 1917.

In 1917, Lathrop, then the director of the United States Children's Bureau, recruited Abbott to go to Washington and administer the first Child Labor Act. The act was only in force for nine months when it was declared unconstitutional by the United States Supreme Court in June 1918. However, during its short duration, Abbott successfully enforced its provisions. After the law was invalidated, she still made an effort to apply its principles. As a consultant to the Labor Policies Board, Abbott succeeded in having a child labor clause written into U.S. government war contracts, and she conducted site inspections to be sure that this clause was honored.

In October 1919, Abbott returned to Illinois when she was appointed director of the new State Immigrants Commission by Governor Frank O. Lowden. Two years later, she succeeded Lathrop as head of the Children's Bureau. During the next 13 years, Abbott worked to establish the bureau on a solid, scientific footing. She conducted a number of special studies of child labor and examined the effects of unemployment and industrial accidents on children.

Abbott's interest in children extended to mothers. She studied maternal mortality and examined the nutritional status of both mothers and children. In 1921, the Children's Bureau was charged with administering the **Sheppard-Towner Act**, which established a federal grants-in-aid program for maternal and infant health.

Besides her domestic interests, Abbott was involved in a number of international initiatives during the 1920s and 1930s. In 1919, she served as secretary of the Children's Committee of the First International Labor Conference, which was held in Washington, DC. From 1922 to 1934, she served in an unofficial capacity as the United States representative on the League of Nations Advisory Committee on Traffic in Women and Children. In 1935, Abbott served as the American delegate to the International Labor Organization, and she successfully sponsored a recommendation raising the minimum age for leaving school to enter the job market to 15 years old.

In 1934, Abbott left the Children's Bureau to become a professor of public welfare at the University of Chicago's **Graduate School of Social Service Administration**. In this capacity, she developed standards and methodologies for educating and training social workers. Despite her declining health, Abbott continued her active career in public service as a member of the Textile Industry Committee of the Wage and Hours Division of the Department of Labor. As a member of President Franklin Roosevelt's Council on Economic Security, she helped draft the provisions of the Social Security Act which were related to children. Additionally, at the time of her death in 1939, Abbott was serving as the editor of the *Social Service Review*, an influential social work professional journal.

Grace Abbott was a tireless worker who used her connection with the American Settlement Movement to accomplish substantive social reform goals including the passage of protective legislation for immigrants and the establishment of social welfare programs for women and children.

Bibliography

Costin, *Two Sisters for Social Justice: A Biography of Grace and Edith Abbott*; *Dictionary of American Biography*, supl. 6, pp. 1–2; James, *Notable American Women: 1607–1950*, vol. 1, pp. 1–3 ; Trattner, *Biographical Dictionary of Social Welfare in America*, pp. 3–6.

Abbott, Lyman

attorney, clergyman, editor of social welfare-related periodicals
b. December 18, 1835; d. October 22, 1922.

Lyman Abbott enlarged the scope of the primarily religious periodical *The Outlook* to include coverage of the labor and social reform efforts that were gaining momentum during the 1890s. His editorial policy provided many settlement workers a forum in which to publish articles describing the conditions in their neighborhoods and the programs they were undertaking to improve them.

Abbott did not begin his career as a social welfare advocate. After graduating from New York University in 1853, Abbott joined the law firm of his brothers, Austin and Vaughn, in New York City. His law practice grew steadily, but after considerable deliberation, Abbott pursued his boyhood desire and abandoned the law to study for the ministry. Ordained in 1860, he moved to Terre Haute, Indiana, to become pastor of the Congregationalist Church. Like so many of his fellow citizens, Abbott was deeply affected by the Civil War. As the hostilities subsided, he moved to work toward the physical and spiritual healing of the South. In February 1865, Abbott resigned his pastorate to become corresponding secretary of the American Union Commission, a group of New York clergy and lay people committed to working with the federal government to rebuild the Southern states.

During his four years with the commission, Abbott also served as pastor of the newly established New England Congregational Church in New York City. In addition, he was in charge of a church in Cornwall-on-Hudson. He became a book reviewer for *Harper's Magazine*, and over time, Abbott's journalistic endeavors became quite successful.

In 1870, Abbott was appointed editor of the American Tract Society's new publication, *The Illustrated Christian Weekly*. Six years later, he joined Henry Ward Beecher as an editor on the *Christian Union,* and in 1881, he succeeded Beecher as editor-in-chief. When Beecher died in 1887, Abbott succeeded him once again, this time as pastor of the Plymouth Congregational Church in Brooklyn, New York. Abbott continued in his dual role as pastor and editor until 1899, when he retired from his pastorate to devote himself full time to his editorial work.

In 1893, the *Christian Union* became *The Outlook*, and under Abbott's guidance it enjoyed a wide circulation. Socially and spiritually moderate, Abbott subscribed to the **Social Gospel** doctrine that called on the churches to interpret the teachings of Christ in a manner that would ease the social problems of industrialization. Abbott opened the pages of *The Outlook*, which previously was primarily a religious periodical, to include general discussions of labor and social problems of the day, and the work of many social reformers appeared in *The Outlook*. In addition to biographical and autobiographical features, Abbott also published literary criticism and political commentaries.

Under Abbott's editorship, *The Outlook* became a powerful and respected journal of public affairs. Circulation reached 100,000 and remained steady for almost 20 years. When he died in 1922, Abbott was succeeded as editor by his son, E.H. Abbott. Four years later *The Outlook* was sold to the journalist and writer Francis A. Bellamy who merged it with another publication, the *Independent*.

As the editor of *The Outlook,* Abbott provided a wide-ranging and respected forum for reformers, religious leaders, and politicians to voice their concerns and to propose solutions to a variety of public affairs issues as well as industrial and social problems.

Bibliography

Brown, *Lyman Abbott: Christian Evolutionist: A Study in Religious Liberalism*; *Dictionary of American Biography,* vol. 1, pt. 1, pp. 24–25; Seligman, *Encyclopedia of the Social Sciences,* vol. 1, pp. 355–56.

Addams, Jane

settlement house founder, social reformer, peace activist
b. September 6, 1860; d. May 21, 1935.

Jane Addams
Social Welfare History Archives, University of Minnesota

Jane Addams was for many the symbol of the settlement movement in the United States. She and her colleague **Ellen Gates Starr** founded **Hull House** in 1889, which became a center for social reform in Chicago and perhaps the best-known social settlement in the United States. Addams served as both an inspiration and mentor to a generation of young college-educated women who became involved in social welfare work as a means both to do good and to find a meaningful occupation for themselves beyond the traditional confines of home and family. As a result of her work in the international peace movement, her inspiration and reputation extended beyond the United States.

Addams was born in Cedarville, Illinois, where she attended the local public schools. She completed her course work for an A.B. degree at Rockford College in 1881. That same year, Addams enrolled at the Woman's Medical College in Philadelphia but after six months was forced to abandon her studies due to illness. In August 1883, Addams embarked on a two-year European tour, but she found her travels and studies unfulfilling; she returned home dissatisfied with her life and her prospects.

Addams's second European tour, undertaken in 1887 with Ellen Gates Starr, a Rockford classmate, proved to be pivotal. While in London, Addams and Starr visited **Toynbee Hall**, the first English settlement house, which had been established by **Samuel Barnett**. Based on what she observed and what she read about the English Settlement Movement, Addams resolved to open a settlement of her own.

In September 1889, Addams and Starr moved into the old Hull Mansion on South Halsted Street in Chicago. This was the beginning of **Hull House**. The settlement sponsored clubs, worked for housing and sanitary reforms, provided medical assistance, and opened a kindergarten, a nursery, and a gymnasium.

As a result of the work accomplished at Hull House, Addams was soon recognized as a leader of the American Settlement Movement. **Florence Kelley**, **Alice Hamilton**, **Grace** and **Edith Abbott**, **Julia Lathrop**, **Mary Kenney O'Sullivan,** and **Alzina Stevens** were among the settlement leaders who spent time as residents at Hull House.

Addams was personally involved in a wide range of reform activities. She was particularly interested in labor issues and supported local striking workers on a number of occasions, including the building trades strike (1900), the national anthracite coal strike (1902), the Chicago Stockyards strike (1902), and the textile workers strike (1910).

Addams's role in establishing Hull House and in promoting the settlement movement was recognized nationally and resulted in leadership positions in a number of national organizations. In 1909, Addams became the first woman to be elected president of the National Conference of Charities and Correction (*see* **National Conference on Social Welfare**), the influential organization composed of leaders from both public and private charitable relief organizations and correctional institutions. Two years later, she became head of the **National Federation of Settlements**, the national coalition of settlement houses that promoted cooperation and coordination among its members, a position she held until her death in 1935. Her national reputation also kept her in demand as a lecturer.

Addams became involved in national politics when she seconded Theodore Roosevelt's nomination for president at the Progressive Party convention in 1912 and then campaigned for him. She was also active in the woman suffrage campaign on the national level, serving as first vice president of the National American Woman Suffrage Association (1911–1914).

In addition to her settlement and reform work, the cause of international peace had long been dear to Addams's heart. With the outbreak of the war in Europe in 1914, she focused her attention more and more on the issue. In 1915, she was elected chair of the newly organized Woman's Peace Party in the United States. That same year, she became president of the International Congress of Women at The Hague. Prior to the United States' entry into World War I, Addams worked to persuade President Woodrow Wilson to initiate a mediation conference to end the hostilities.

Addams opposed America's entry into World War I in 1917, a position that isolated her from many of her settlement colleagues. She continued her peace efforts following the end of the war. She was elected the first president of the **Women's International League for Peace and Freedom** in 1919 and undertook a world tour in 1923 to promote the cause of international peace. In 1931, Addams shared the Nobel Peace Prize with Nicholas Murray Butler of Columbia University. Addams continued her work into the 1930s despite her declining health. She died of cancer in May 1935.

Throughout her career, Addams served as a role model and inspiration for many women and men interested in careers in social reform. She opened the doors of Hull House to provide others with opportunities and facilities to pursue a wide range of social welfare causes including protective legislation for women and children, labor and industrial reform, protection for newly arrived immigrants, juvenile court reform, woman suffrage, and the international peace crusade.

Bibliography

Davis, *American Heroine: The Life and Legend of Jane Addams*; *Dictionary of American Biography*, supl. 1, pp. 10–13; Melvin, *American Community Organizations: An Historical Dictionary*, pp. 2–4 ; James, *Notable American Women, 1607–1950*, pp. 16–22; Trattner, *Biographical Dictionary of Social Welfare in America*, pp. 13–15.

Adler, Felix

founder Ethical Culture Society, social reformer
b. August 13, 1851; d. April 24, 1933.

Felix Adler's impassioned spirituality inspired him to found the **Ethical Culture Society**, which was devoted to the concept of the inherent worth of every individual. His concern for his fellow humans extended beyond meeting their spiritual needs, however, and he became a central figure in the social welfare efforts undertaken by settlement workers and other reformers on the local, state, and national levels.

Born in Alzei in the Rhineland, Adler was six years old in 1857 when he, his parents, and his older brother emigrated to the United States so that his father could take up his responsibilities as rabbi of the Temple Emanu-El in New York City. Felix attended Columbia Grammar School and in 1870 graduated Phi Beta Kappa from Columbia College. Study in Europe followed, first at the University of Berlin and then at Heidelberg where he earned a Ph.D., summa cum laude. Adler studied Semitics in preparation for the rabbinate, but his studies awoke in him a new awareness of the intellectual and moral issues of the day. He eventually re-evaluated his commitment to traditional religious values and attempted to synthesize his new ethical idealism and religious convictions with the traditional view of Judaism held by his father's generation.

Once he had decided that he would not succeed his father as the leader of the Temple Emanu-El congregation, Adler attempted to find the continuity he was seeking in teaching. Between 1873 and 1875, he held the chair of Hebrew and Oriental Literatures at Cornell. But he soon realized that an academic life could not provide him with a satisfactory focus for his fervent spirituality.

At about this time, Adler began reading Emerson and was attracted to, but not entirely satisfied with, the liberalism of the Free Religious Association, which had been inspired by the New England Transcendentalists. In 1876 at a meeting held in Standard Hall in New York City, Adler and a group of associates founded the Society for Ethical Culture, which was centered on the concept that every human being has worth; the society's motto was "deed not creed." The society was to be both practical and spiritual, unimpeded by religious dogma. Between 1876 and 1908, Adler elaborated on his views through weekly addresses delivered to large crowds assembled in meeting halls around the city. In 1908, the society constructed its own meeting house.

Adler and the members of the society did more than just talk, however. In 1877, the society opened the first free kindergarten in New York City and established a visiting nurse service, a Sunday school, and a sewing club to make clothing for the poor. Soon, affiliated Ethical Culture Societies were established in other cities in the United States, including Boston, Chicago, St. Louis, and Philadelphia as well as outside of the country in Berlin, London, and Vienna.

One of Adler's primary interests was education. In 1880, under his direction, the society established the Workingman's School, which offered manual training and later became the Ethical Culture School (1895). Adler also established the Summer School of Applied Ethics at Plymouth, which was concerned with labor issues and attracted the settlement leader **Jane Addams** and the philosopher William James, among others, as lecturers. Each of these educational endeavors emphasized the value that the Ethical Culture Movement placed on the concept of individual difference and was devoted to the ideal of providing moral instruction adapted to various age levels.

In addition to his work with the Ethical Culture Society, Adler was a well-respected participant in many of the social reform movements of the day. He organized a Tenement House Building Company to erect model tenements, promoted cooperative shops, and was instrumental in the establishment of a settlement house, the **Hudson Guild**, which was founded by **John L. Elliott** in 1895. He served as a member of the **New York State Tenement House Commission of 1884** and was chair of the **National Child Labor Committee** from 1904 to 1921.

Beside his participation in social welfare concerns, Adler maintained an active and productive academic life. In 1890, he founded the *International Journal of Ethics*, and between 1902 and 1933, he was professor of Social and Political Ethics at Columbia University. In 1906, he was named the third Theodore Roosevelt Professor of American History and Institutions at the University of Berlin, and in 1928, Adler became president of the Eastern Division of the American Philosophical Association.

At his death in 1933, Adler was still actively involved in the Ethical Culture Society. The society's work, which continues up to the present day, is a testament to his vision and dedication.

Bibliography

Dictionary of American Biography, supl. 1, pp. 13–14; *Fiftieth Anniversary of the Ethical Movement, 1876–1926*; Guttchen, *Felix Adler*.

Alfred, Helen
settlement worker, public housing advocate
b. [n.d]; d. [n.d.].

Helen Alfred may not be as well known as some of her colleagues in the settlement movement; nevertheless, she contributed significantly to the campaign for better housing that so many settlement workers waged during the opening decades of the twentieth century.

Alfred spent most of her career as a settlement worker at **Madison House** on New York City's Lower East Side. During the late 1920s, she worked in New Jersey as a field agent for the American Association of Old Age Security. This group was committed to promoting security for the elderly and later on to working for the adoption of comprehensive social insurance.

In addition to her settlement work, Alfred was particularly interested in housing reform. Like many of her settlement colleagues, Alfred witnessed the negative impact of substandard, overcrowded housing. She recognized the need for slum clearance and the need for the construction of government-sponsored public housing that would put improved dwellings within the reach of the city's poorer residents. To accomplish these initatives, Alfred worked with a number of housing reform organizations. On the municipal level, she served as chair of the Housing Committee of the City Affairs Committee of New York. In 1931, she co-founded the Public Housing Conference (later the National Public Housing Conference and then the **National Housing Conference**), the most significant organization working to secure housing legislation in the 1930s. **Mary K. Simkhovitch** of **Greenwich House** was president of the Public Housing Conference, and Alfred served as the organization's secretary and executive director. She was also a member of the conference's policy committee.

Alfred was an energetic woman who wrote well and was a capable public speaker. As part of her work for the Housing Conference, she published articles about the housing situation in the United States in a variety of magazines including *The New Republic*, *Public Health Nursing*, and *The Journal of Home Economics*. Alfred also attended housing-related conferences and made periodic speaking tours across the United States.

Alfred worked with the other members of the conference to draft housing legislation, testified before congressional committees, and lobbied members of Congress. Public relations and public education were important components of the work of the Public Housing Conference. To accomplish these charges, the group began publishing a monthly newsletter, *Public Housing Progress,* in November 1934. Alfred served as editor. Through the pages of this publication, she coordinated the efforts of the various pressure groups and social service agencies that were involved in slum clearance and public housing campaigns.

During the 1930s, Alfred remained active in the campaign for better housing, and her major contribution to this effort was her ability to effectively communicate the goals and initatives of the movement to government officials and to the American public, both as a writer and as a public speaker.

Bibliography

Chambers, *Seedtime of Reform: American Social Justice and Social Action, 1918–1923*; McDonnell, *The Wagner Housing Act: A Case Study of the Legislative Process*; Trolander, *Settlement Houses and the Great Depression*.

Almy, Frederic
Charity Organization Society administrator, reformer, social work educator
b. 1858; d. 1935.

Frederic Almy was a leader in the **Charity Organization Society** (COS) movement, serving as secretary of the Buffalo, New York, COS for more than 20 years. His social welfare reform activities bridged the gap between the work of the charity organization and settlement movements.

In his work, Almy stressed the importance of applying casework standards to social welfare work, and he advocated using trained professionals to investigate requests for relief. Although he favored the use of public money for relief work, Almy believed that the funds should be administered by voluntary relief organizations. For Almy, administering relief without professional assistance was worse than doing nothing to meet the needs of the poor.

While serving as the secretary of the Buffalo COS, Almy established close ties with the national network of social reformers. He was particularly familiar with the work of his colleagues in New York City. To remain active and current, Almy was a frequent resident at both the **University Settlement** and **Greenwich House** in New York City. Along with **Edward Devine**, **Robert W. DeForest**, and **Mary Richmond**, he lectured at the New York Charity Organization Society Summer School of Philanthropy. Like many settlement workers, Almy supported the Progressive Party in the 1912 presidential election. Following the election, he served as a member of the Progressive Service's committee on social insurance, which was chaired by **Paul U. Kellogg**, the editor of the social reform journal the *Survey*.

Almy remained active in social welfare reform efforts during the opening decades of the twentieth century. To a degree, Almy's career illustrates the transition between the Charity Organization Society philosophy that emphasized the moral condition of the poor and the approach taken by settlement workers and professionally trained social workers which emphasized the social and economic causes of poverty.

Bibliography

Axinn, *Social Welfare: A History of the American Response to Need*; Chambers, *Paul U. Kellogg and the Survey: Voices for Social Welfare and Social Justice*; Davis, *Spearheads for Reform: The Social Settlements and the Progressive Movement, 1890–1914*.

Altgeld, John Peter

attorney, social-reform-minded politician
b. December 30, 1847; d. March 12, 1902.

John Peter Altgeld was an elected official whose reputation as a reformer gained him the support of men and women of the American Settlement Movement. After supporting Altgeld in his successful campaign for governor of Illinois, a number of Chicago-based settlement workers were given the opportunity to work toward significant labor-related reforms. Altgeld gained a national reputation based on a number of controversial decisions he made while serving as governor of Illinois in the 1890s; however, many of his less-controversial actions related to labor and social issues contributed significantly to the social reform efforts of settlement workers.

Born in the village of Nieder Selters in southern Germany, Altgeld was only three months old when his parents emigrated to the United States and settled in Richland County, Ohio. As a boy, Altgeld received little formal education because he had to work on the family farm. In 1864, at the age of 16, he enlisted in an Ohio volunteer regiment and saw action in the closing battles of the Civil War.

In 1869, Altgeld left Ohio and journeyed west. During the next five years, he worked as a farm laborer and taught school, eventually settling in St. Louis where he read law and opened a law office. In 1874, Altgeld was elected state's attorney for Andrew County, Missouri. The following year he moved to Chicago.

Over the next several years, Altgeld practiced law and amassed a fortune by buying and selling Chicago real estate and by investing in street-railways. Although he was unsuccessful in his bid for a congressional seat in 1884, two years later Altgeld was elected superior judge of Cook County. He rose to the position of chief justice of the Superior Court before resigning in 1891. During this period, Altgeld had become an influential member of the Illinois State Democratic party. At the party's convention in 1892, he was nominated as the gubernatorial candidate on the first ballot and went on to win the election.

Not long after assuming office, Altgeld, in response to appeals for clemency, pardoned three anarchistic agitators who had been jailed after being convicted of complicity in the Haymarket Riot of May 1886. Based on his examination of the proceedings, Altgeld concluded that the men had not received a fair trial. Although it had been more than six years since the riot, public opinion was still strong, and Altgeld was branded as an anarchist sympathizer and criminal advocate because of his action.

The following year Altgeld bore the brunt of negative public opinion once again when he protested President Cleveland's decision to send federal troops to keep the peace during the Pullman strike. Altgeld's protest was based on constitutional grounds, but his Republican opponents took the opportunity to once more portray him as soft on law and order issues.

While he was attracting a good deal of negative publicity on the national level, Altgeld's attention on the state level was occupied by a number of pioneering endeavors that identified him as a moderate advocate of legislative and labor reforms. His reputation earned him the support and cooperation of social reformers, especially residents of the Chicago settlement **Hull House** such as **Florence Kelley** whom he appointed as a special investigator for the Illinois State Bureau of Labor, assigned to study child labor in sweatshops.

During the 1892 gubernatorial campaign, Altgeld opposed the trusts, championed the working person's right to organize and strike, supported the eight-hour workday, and called for the abolition of sweatshops. As governor he fulfilled a number of these campaign promises, in part due to the efforts of settlement workers who supported his agenda, although the courts soon reversed much of the progress that the Altgeld-sponsored legislation promised.

One significant piece of labor reform legislation passed during Altgeld's administration was the Illinois Factory Act of 1893, which prohibited the employment of children under the age of 14 at night and established the eight-hour day for women and children. The act also provided for regular inspections of factories and for the establishment of a new position of state factory inspector. When the writer and social reformer **Henry Demarest Lloyd** declined the position, Altgeld turned to Hull House resident Florence Kelley to lead the effort. Two other women from the settlement were also called upon; **Alzina Stevens** was made an assistant factory inspector and **Mary Kenney O'Sullivan** a deputy factory inspector. Although the Illinois Supreme Court ruled some provisions of the act unconstitutional in 1895, Altgeld had helped to bring the issue of child labor to the public's attention, and provided the settlement workers with an ally in their fight to end child labor abuses.

Renominated for governor in 1896, Altgeld was defeated by the Republican candidate, John R. Tanner. After leaving office, Altgeld continued to speak out publicly regarding social issues. He died suddenly in 1902 while delivering a speech in support of Boer independence.

Altgeld was a pioneer in social and political reforms who used his office to fight corruption and graft in government and to broaden the participation of women in public service. Chicago-based settlement workers benefited from his assistance and gained insight and experience in how to work with public officials to bring about social reforms.

Bibliography

Barnard, *"Eagle Forgotten": The Life of John Peter Altgeld*; Browne, *Altgeld of Illinois: A Record of His Life and Work*; *Dictionary of American Biography*, vol. 1, p. 231; Seligman, *Encyclopedia of the Social Sciences*, vol. 1, pp. 12–13.

American Association of Social Workers

The men and women involved in the American Settlement Movement realized the value of forming working committees and societies that would reinforce their informal social and professional reform networks. Often these groups evolved into professional organizations. The American Association of Social Workers (AASW) was an example of this phenomenon.

The AASW had its origins in the Intercollegiate Bureau of Occupations (IBO), which was founded in 1911 in New York City by a group of women's college alumnae. It was created to provide young women with information about jobs and careers. In response to the large number of inquiries it received about the new field of social work, the IBO created a special department for social workers in 1913. **John M. Glenn** and **Mary Van Kleeck** of the **Russell Sage Foundation** and **Edward T. Devine** of the New York **Charity Organization Society** were members of the social work department's executive committee. A number of social welfare workers, including **Homer Folks**, **Lillian Wald**, **Owen Lovejoy**, and **Mary Richmond,** were members of the advisory committee.

The Russell Sage Foundation and the New York School of Philanthropy (*see* **Columbia University Graduate School of Social Work**) each contributed $1,000 toward the social work department's annual budget, and over time both organizations developed even closer ties with the department. Sigrid V. Wynbladh of the New York School of Philanthropy supervised the department's operations. Under her guidance, the department developed into a clearinghouse for information about employment opportunities in the field of social welfare reform. Through its work it also established the need for employment standards for social welfare workers, including setting standards for accreditation of professional schools, determining qualifications for certifying trained personnel, recruiting qualified candidates for positions as social workers, and ensuring adequate financial compensation.

In 1917, the department for social workers became an independent agency known as the National Social Workers Exchange (NSWE). Its offices were located in the Russell Sage Foundation building, and a number of New York social welfare workers were on the new organization's board of directors. They were joined by colleagues from other parts of the country including **Robert A. Woods** of Boston and **Sophonisba Breckinridge** of Chicago.

During the 1920s, the NSWE worked to clarify its goals and to consolidate its operations. It focused its attention on two particular issues: job placement and the establishment of educational standards for professional certification. To accomplish these goals, the board of directors formed a central council that appointed committees on job placement and analysis, training and education, and public relations. **Graham Taylor**, founder and head resident of the settlement **Chicago Commons**, became the organization's chief executive officer in 1921. Although the NSWE continued to operate as a nonprofit employment service, many of its members believed that social workers needed a professional organization to represent their interests.

In response to these needs the American Association of Social Workers was established in 1921. Owen Lovejoy served as the organization's first president. During the 1920s and 1930s, the AASW underwent a number of organizational changes that reflected the growing professionalization of the field of social work. For example, to consolidate its organizational structure, AASW's council became the national council in June 1922. Later that same year, the association adopted new requirements for establishing local chapters which required at least 10 charter members for recognition. The so-called Providence resolution adopted in 1923 required that only members' dues and contributions be used to support the AASW, thereby limiting the influence of foundations and other organizations. By 1926, an executive committee of the national council was charged with assuming administrative responsibility for the association on a full-time basis. When this structure became unwieldy in the early 1930s, the AASW adopted a decentralized structure that distributed responsibility and authority among a number of divisions including one for government and social work and another for personnel standards. Dissatisfaction with this governance structure led the membership to call for yet another reorganization by 1939. A new national board of directors was established and the divisional structure was phased out.

During the 1940s and 1950s, the AASW merged with a number of related social welfare professional organizations including the American Association of Group Workers and the American Association of Medical Social Workers. Today, the AASW remains an important professional organization dedicated to serving the needs of social welfare professionals.

Bibliography

Romanofsky, *The Greenwood Encyclopedia of American Institutions: Social Service Organizations*, vol. 1, pp. 22–27.

American Civil Liberties Union

The American Civil Liberties Union and its predecessor, the **National Civil Liberties Bureau**, can trace their roots to the American Settlement Movement. Many settlement workers were active in the anti-preparedness and peace movements and formed pressure groups to persuade the U.S. government to remain neutral before and during World War I.

Several of the most prominent leaders of the American Settlement Movement, including **Lillian Wald** of the **Henry Street Settlement**, **Jane Addams** of **Hull House**, and **Paul U. Kellogg** of the social welfare journal the *Survey* formed one of these groups, the **American Union Against Militarism** (AUAM). They were joined by younger settlement worker colleagues and other social welfare reformers, many of whom had different ideas about how best to proceed in their campaign to prevent America entering the war. Wald and some of the other founding members of the AUAM were unwilling to appear to be opposed to the federal government. This desire not to appear disloyal brought about sharp divisions within the settlement movement and eventually led Addams to break with many of her colleagues when she continued to oppose U.S. involvement in the hostilities. In the AUAM, the younger settlement workers and their peace activist colleagues withdrew from the organization and formed their own anti-war pressure groups. The National Civil Liberties Bureau (NCLB), which later became the American Civil Liberties Union, was one of the groups.

In the years immediately following World War I, many leaders of the NCLB became concerned that their organization was too closely associated with the cause of conscientious objectors and pacifists. As part of their effort to reposition the bureau in the postwar years, in 1920 a group of NCLB board members, including **Roger Baldwin**, proposed reorganizing and renaming the NCLB as the American Civil Liberties Union (ACLU).

Under the reorganization plan that was finally adopted, the ACLU was based in New York City and was composed of two directing committees. The National Executive Committee included members from across the United States. The smaller Directing Committee was composed of those members of the National Executive Committee who lived in New York and who were available to attend meetings regularly. Overall policy was controlled by the National Executive Committee.

As reorganized, the ACLU continued to concern itself with defending free speech, free press, and right of assembly. In addition, the ACLU began to turn its attention to labor issues. This shift reflected Baldwin's interest in the labor movement and in many ways parallels the settlement workers' interest in helping to organize labor unions years earlier. Although the ACLU was not part of the labor movement, during the anti-union crusade of the 1920s it defended the workers' rights of freedom of speech and assembly when management obtained court orders prohibiting public meetings and picketing. During the 1930s when the Wagner Act established labor's right to organize, the ACLU turned its attention to other issues such as censorship and free speech in much the same way that the early settlement workers turned their attention to other social reform issues as the unions they helped to organize became more established, independent entities.

Still active today, the ACLU was the first national organization committed to defending the civil liberties of all citizens rather than representing the special interests of a particular group.

Bibliography

Jackson, *Encyclopedia of New York City*, p. 22; Johnson, *The Challenge to American Freedoms: World War I and the Rise of the American Civil Liberties Union.*

American Union Against Militarism

Social welfare reform efforts on the domestic front were not the only issues that concerned settlement workers. Many became involved in the international peace movement, and using their established networks, they formed pressure groups to persuade the U.S. government not to enter World War I in Europe. One of the best known and most influential of these groups was the American Union Against Militarism (AUAM).

In the fall of 1914, **Lillian Wald** of the **Henry Street Settlement**; **Jane Addams** of **Hull House**; and **Paul U. Kellogg**, editor of the social work magazine the *Survey* called together a group of social workers, academicians, clergy, and newspaper reporters to discuss the war in Europe. Although they had no specific agenda at the time, these individuals, who referred to themselves as the Henry Street Group, were resolved to publicly denounce the war. Additionally, they decided that if necessary, their informal organization could serve as a focus for the establishment of a more systematic antimilitarism campaign in America.

Over the next several months, similar groups were formed around the United States. Wald of the Henry Street Group went a step further; she organized the American League for the Limitation of Armament (ALLA) in New York City along with Nicholas Murray Butler, president of Columbia University; Oswald Garrison Villard, the editor of the *New York Evening Post* and the *Nation*; Hamilton Hold, editor of the *Independent*; and Frederic C. Howe, the commissioner of Immigration. The members of ALLA moved beyond the stand taken by the Henry Street Group with their call for an international congress and an international court to mediate disputes among nations. ALLA's call for a preparedness for peace rather than for war inspired the formation of other groups such as the League to Enforce Peace and the Woman's Peace Party.

With the introduction of the National Defense Bill in Congress on December 7, 1915, it soon became clear that the war-preparedness movement was gaining momentum, particularly because the bill included a provision for compulsory military training. In response, the Henry Street Group called for a national conference in December 1915. One result of this meeting was the establishment of the Anti-Preparedness Committee (APC), which, in addition to Wald and Kellogg, included John Haynes Holmes, a Unitarian minister; the Socialists, **Crystal Eastman** and her brother Max; L. Hollingsword Wood, a Quaker attorney; Rabbi Stephen S. Wise; the pacifist Louis P. Lochner; **Florence Kelley**; and Alice Lewisohn.

Drawing on its congressional contacts, the APC hoped to kill the National Defense Bill, to outlaw profits from the manufacture of armaments, and to create a League of Neutral American Nations dedicated to peace and republican ideals. In the spring of 1916, the APC changed its name to the American Union Against Militarism. Within a year, the AUAM boasted an active membership of more than 1,500, organized in branches in virtually every major city in the United States.

The AUAM mounted a nationwide anti-preparedness crusade and held public meetings in New York City, Buffalo, Cleveland, Detroit, Chicago, Minneapolis, St. Louis, and Pittsburgh. In April 1916, representatives of the AUAM met in Washington, DC, with President Woodrow Wilson.

Early in 1917, **Roger Baldwin**, a social reformer from St. Louis, joined the board of directors of the AUAM. Baldwin quickly put his personal stamp on the organization and its activities, including organizing a Bureau for Conscientious Objectors. The creation of this group was opposed by some AUAM board members, particularly Kellogg and Wald, who did not want the AUAM to appear to be in opposition to the federal government. In response to this disapproval, the Bureau of Conscientious Objectors was renamed the Civil Liberties Bureau in the summer of 1917.

Relations among the AUAM board members remained uneasy and reached a crisis when the board voted to participate in a conference sponsored by the predominantly socialist antiwar organization, the People's Council. This particular decision alienated Wald and led to the Civil Liberties Bureau becoming a separate organization in October 1917. After the separation, the AUAM declined in size and in influence until it officially ceased operations in February 1922.

In its heyday the AUAM was probably the largest peace pressure group in the United States with a membership of almost 6,000. It was a significant component of the Progressive reform movement because its opposition to war was grounded in part in the belief that military conflict would prevent further social progress, a goal that settlement workers and their reformer colleagues had long been working to achieve. The AUAM also galvanized the efforts of those in the peace movement, and it provided settlement workers who were interested in the peace movement with an established network of like-minded colleagues.

Bibliography

Duffus, *Lillian Wald: Neighbors and Crusader*; Johnson, *The Challenge to American Freedoms: World War I and the Rise of the American Civil Liberties Union*.

Americanization

Americanization describes the process of social assimilation whereby immigrants gradually identify with the everyday life in their new community. In the years between the establishment of the first settlements in the United States in the 1890s and the passage of the Immigration Restriction Acts in the 1920s, the settlements occupied a central position in the Americanization movement.

An important part of the settlement's function in the Americanization process was its role as intermediary, interpreting America to its new residents, and the immigrants to their new country. This intermediary role was a double-edged one. While some settlement workers were more tolerant of the newly arrived and more positive about their potential contributions to American life, others were less open to the possibilities. They were more concerned with the immigrants leaving their old ways behind in favor of the settlement workers' own white, middle-class values.

For most new immigrants, the transition from their old way of life to the new was difficult and confusing. People sounded different, dressed differently, and looked different in the United States. Gradually, the new American environment exerted a conforming pressure until, through a process of accommodation and adjustment, the new arrival ultimately became an integral part of American society.

For many settlement workers, Americanization was a problematic concept and process. In their dealings with their immigrant neighbors, they were often engaged in a seemingly contradictory enterprise. Some settlement workers shared the fears and prejudices of many Americans. While most genuinely wanted to help the immigrants, they were also anxious to exercise a degree of control over the newly arrived, and they encouraged the immigrants to learn English, to eat American food, and to wear American clothing.

The assimilation of the foreign born into the mainstream of American society quickly became a priority once the United States entered World War I in 1917. Many reform groups, organizations, and agencies became involved in the campaign. Anti-immigration sentiment grew during this time, and efforts to teach English and to encourage naturalization increased. Classes were offered at public schools, night schools, and by agencies such as the YMCA. At the same time, in some quarters, fear and suspicion of foreign immigrants led to the passage of restrictive immigration legislation.

Some settlement workers soon realized that they had to make an effort to overcome their prejudices if they did not want to alienate their neighbors. They were committed to the idea of cultural pluralism; at the same time they were anxious to have the newly arrived set aside their native language, customs, and dress, and to embrace the culture of the new world. The more accommodating settlement residents believed that it was not necessary for a new immigrant to reject the past to become an American. They wanted to provide a common experience for their neighbors, to encourage a sense of social unity, and to encourage their assimilation. During the 1890s, many settlement houses sponsored ethnic festivals and pageants. In an effort to preserve native handicrafts, some houses sponsored sewing and craft classes.

Part of the Americanization process involved protecting the newly arrived from some of the darker aspects of American culture. For example, immigrants were often the victims of unscrupulous ticket agents who charged them exorbitant rates leaving them little or no money for room and board once they reached their destination. Some new arrivals were taken advantage of by employment bureaus that promised good jobs and then failed to deliver. Many young women who were unable to support themselves were unwittingly lured into **prostitution**. Organizations such as the Immigrants' Protective League (*see* **Immigrants' Service League**), which was organized in Chicago in 1908, met new immigrants at the train stations, arranged housing for them, and helped them to locate friends and relatives. The league's director, **Grace Abbott**, a social reformer and settlement resident, worked to ease their social and economic assimilation.

The Americanization process was somewhat controversial at the time and is more so today. Individuals coming to a new culture realize to a greater or lesser degree that they must adopt the mores of the new society they want to join, setting old ways aside so that new ways can take their place. At the same time, people still want to retain particular customs and adapt them to their new environment. This process enables them to survive in a new world and has enriched American culture. A true cultural give and take can help a newly arrived immigrant make a smoother transition to a new culture, and when it is permitted to work, the new immigrants can gradually and confidently become fully realized citizens of their new country or local community.

However, for those who are already established in American society, the influx of new immigrants can be threatening. The response to this perceived threat is to attempt to force the newcomers to abandon their "old" ways in favor of the "American" way. The Americanization process forces one to walk a fine line between assimilation and suppression of the parent culture, and the settlement workers and their reformer colleagues were not always able to come to a satisfactory comprise in the process. Ethnic neighborhoods and cultural enclaves exist up to the present time, a fact that indicates that assimilation is a long-term process. *See also* **Athletics; Clubs.**

Bibliography
Carson, *Settlement Folk: Social Thought and the American Settlement Movement, 1885–1930*; Davis, *Spearheads for Reform: The Social Settlements and the Progressive Movement, 1890–1914*; Seligman, *Encyclopedia of the Social Sciences*, vol. 2, pp. 33–35.

Americans in Process (1902)

In an effort to draw the general public's attention to urban living conditions, many settlement workers spent a significant amount of time preparing detailed social surveys of their neighborhoods and the surrounding areas. These studies often involved compiling a wide variety of statistics, interviewing residents, and documenting the location of various structures and industrial zones.

Americans in Process: A Settlement Study, North and West Ends, Boston, which was written by the residents of the Boston social settlement **South End House** and was edited by the house's head resident, **Robert A. Woods**, is an example of this type of social survey. It is a companion volume to *The City Wilderness*, which was published in 1898 and presented a social survey of the South End of Boston.

Woods and the other residents believed that a thorough study of the other two major downtown working-class districts of Boston would benefit them in their work at the settlement. As was true with *The City Wilderness*, the purpose of *Americans in Process* was to present a picture of the city and to lay the groundwork for social and municipal reform efforts.

The residents of South End House were assisted in their efforts by agents of the **Boston Associated Charities** and by school and church leaders. The text is supplemented by detailed maps that depict nationalities, types of tenements, industrial grades, and chief institutions and meeting places in both the North and West Ends.

Reports such as *Americans in Process* drew attention to the political corruption in urban centers and to overcrowded conditions. By doing so, these reports sometimes prompted municipal officials to clean up slum areas or to improve public transportation networks. Many progressive reformers believed that if the public was informed of the substandard conditions, that a way could be found to bring about improvements. The technique of conducting an in-depth social survey of a community was used by later social workers.

Bibliography

Woods, *Americans in Process: A Settlement Study: North and West Ends, Boston*.

Andover House *See* South End House

Association for Improving the Condition of the Poor

Settlement workers did not discover poverty and urban overcrowding. What they did have was a different approach to solving these and other social welfare problems that was based in part on the work that had been proposed and accomplished by the reformers who came before them. The work of the Association for Improving the Condition of the Poor (AICP) provides a context for understanding the efforts undertaken by the men and women who later established and worked in social settlements.

The financial panic of 1837 strained the resources of many public and private relief agencies as they attempted to meet the needs of the working-class men, women, and children living in crowded urban centers such as New York City. During the winter of 1842–1843, a group of concerned New Yorkers investigated the city's existing relief agencies. Their report concluded that the resources of the public agencies were inadequate and that in many instances, private aid was dispensed indiscriminately, a situation that often resulted in a duplication of effort.

To address this situation, the New York Association for Improving the Condition of the Poor, a private benevolent society, was organized by a group of wealthy business owners in 1843. In the decades before the Civil War, the AICP led the fight against the substandard housing, disease, and crime that characterized the New York City slums. The social and economic situation of New York City and the response of social

reformers in founding the AICP was repeated in other urban centers.

Robert M. Hartley served as the association's general secretary from its inception until his retirement in 1876. The founders of the New York AICP, who were primarily white, middle-class Protestants, subscribed to the then-popular belief that poverty was the manifestation of a defective character. They believed if all the bad influences were eliminated, the better nature of the poor would emerge and that they would pull themselves up out of their squalor. The primary objective of the AICP was, therefore, to elevate the moral condition of the needy, which the members believed could bring about an improvement in their physical condition. More than relief, the organizers of the AICP believed the poor needed supervision and moral exhortation.

To carry out this work, the association divided Manhattan into districts that corresponded to the city's wards. Each district was headed by an advisory committee that was responsible for recruiting **friendly visitors** and, if found necessary, for dispensing relief. At first, only men served as visitors, but in 1879, the New York AICP became one of the first organizations of its kind to employ women as visitors.

It was the responsibility of the friendly visitors to investigate requests for assistance and to distinguish between the worthy poor who were willing but unable to work, perhaps due to illness, and the unworthy who chose not to work and to live off the charity of public and private relief agencies. The AICP regarded itself as the coordinator of New York City's many charitable agencies. Through its program of friendly visits it attempted to eliminate duplication of effort on the part of public and private agencies. In this way, the AICP anticipated the concept of the **Charity Organization Society**.

In addition to this moral interpretation of the causes of poverty, the association also recognized that environment had an impact on poverty. Overcrowding was considered a particular evil. Not only did it have a detrimental effect on the health of the inhabitants of the cities, but it also, in the minds of the middle class, posed a substantial threat to the safety of the whole community when poor, unskilled immigrants were thrown together and could at any time rise up and threaten the general peace and prosperity. Thus, the benevolence of the AICP was tempered by a desire for social control.

One solution that the AICP proposed to the overcrowding problem was the construction of model tenements built by private companies who, inspired by humanitarian motives, agreed to limit their profits in order to observe higher sanitary and structural construction standards. In 1854, the AICP sponsored a model tenement, the Working Men's Home for Black Men, that was constructed near Elizabeth and Mott Streets on New York's Lower East Side. This building, which included 87 apartments, eventually became one of the worst slums in the city and was sold in 1867. However, the failure of this project did not dissuade the AICP from fighting for improved housing and carrying on other work such as assisting the unemployed in finding jobs.

The AICP also fought for municipal legislation such as the Metropolitan Health Act of 1866. It worked to clean up existing housing and to improve the construction of new units. The AICP established dispensaries, such as the Neponsit Beach Hospital for nonpulmonary tuberculosis patients, and baths including the People's Bath (1852) and the Milbank Memorial Bath (1904).

Although the settlement house movement and the AICP shared a common goal of helping the needy, their fundamental approach to the problem of poverty was different. The AICP stressed that poverty was the result of a moral deficiency while the reformers in the settlement house movement believed that the prevailing economic and social conditions contributed to poverty. The two groups maintained their separate orientations and co-existed for some time. Some of the men and women who lived and worked in settlement houses began their careers as social reformers in the AICP organization. The AICP also borrowed ideas and techniques from the settlement movement as witnessed by **Hartley House**, a settlement the AICP established on the west side of Manhattan in 1893. The AICP merged with the Charity Organization Society in 1939 to form the Community Service Society, which continues to operate as an important social service agency.

Bibliography

Davis, *Spearheads for Reform: The Social Settlements and the Progressive Movement, 1890–1914*; Jackson, *The Encyclopedia of New York City*, p. 61; Lubove, "The New York Association for Improving the Condition of the Poor: The Formative Years"; Lubove, *The Progressives and the Slums: Tenement House Reform in New York City, 1890–1917*; Romanofsky, *The Greenwood Encyclopedia of American Institutions: Social Service Organizations*, vol. 2, pp. 623–28; Trattner, *From Poor Law to Welfare State: A History of Social Welfare in America*.

Association of Neighborhood Workers (Chicago)

Workers in different settlement houses in many urban areas recognized the benefits of coming together in formal organizations to share their experiences and their approaches to solving problems. In addition, they realized that this approach could expedite the sharing of resources and help to eliminate the duplication of efforts.

One example of this type of organization was the Chicago Association of Neighborhood Workers, formed in May 1908 to bring about more effective cooperation among the various settlements in the city. The association continued the work of the Federation of Social Settlements in Chicago, which was formed at **Hull House** in October 1894. In addition to Hull House, the other members of the old federation were **Northwestern University Settlement**, Maxwell Street Settlement, **University of Chicago Settlement**, Epworth House, and **Chicago Commons**.

The association included a number of standing committees: legislation, tenement houses, education, membership, local industrial conditions, public health, and publicity. The officers and chairs of the standing committees also served as the association's council. Ad hoc committees were formed to investigate and report on selected issues. Monthly meetings were held at Hull House between October and June.

The association's meetings focused on a variety of settlement and social work topics, such as municipal politics, vacation work, and neighborhood centers. Although the Association did not frequently act as a unified body, its meetings provided the members the opportunity to discuss issues and formulate policies for cooperative effort.

The Association of Neighborhood Workers continues to serve the needs of the Chicago reform community up to the present.

Bibliography

Woods, *Handbook of Settlements*.

Association of Neighborhood Workers (New York) *See* United Neighborhood Houses

Athletics

From the beginning, settlement workers recognized that sports and games were a drawing card to entice neighborhood residents, particularly children, to become involved in and to benefit from settlement-sponsored activities, and by extension to gain acceptance for themselves by those they sought to help. Reformers also recognized a connection between participation in sports activities and character building, and they were anxious to use any methods that would improve the neighborhood's quality of life. To meet the needs of their tenement neighborhoods, settlement workers understood they needed to provide libraries, assembly rooms, meeting rooms for small groups, playgrounds, and gymnasiums.

Many settlements started out by providing small playgrounds in their backyards and by working with municipal authorities to secure playgrounds and park space for outdoor activities. One New York City settlement, **Greenwich House**, requested certain streets be closed to traffic at specified times for additional play space.

Settlement residents were assisted in their efforts to provide open-air recreation facilities by other social reform organizations such as the **Outdoor Recreation League**, which worked to secure, among other things, public parks in New York City, and the National Playground Association of America, which carried the campaign to the national level.

Settlement workers also recognized the need to provide appropriate indoor recreation facilities. To accomplish this, they often converted the settlement house cellar or a nearby shed into a makeshift gymnasium. Up to this time, fully equipped gymnasiums were primarily available only in colleges or in private clubs open to those of a particular religion or by subscription. The settlements sought to provide access to all community residents.

At first, donors were hesitant to provide funding, but after 1900, some settlements were successful in obtaining funding for the construction of fully equipped gymnasiums. In many neighborhoods, settlement workers requested that gymnasiums be included when new public school buildings were being constructed, and after the schools were open, they lobbied to have the gymnasiums open after hours for use by the neighborhood residents.

Settlement-sponsored athletic programs did more than just provide much-needed recreation for the community. Athletic directors in the settlements and in community gymnasiums instructed those participating in sporting activities about personal hygiene and the importance of bathing, diet, and exercise. Athletic leagues provided an opportunity to build relationships via intra- and inter-settlement tournaments. The New York **United Neighborhood Houses** organization held citywide tournaments in a local armory.

Following World War I, social reformers looked to athletic programs to provide an antidote to the dance halls and motion pictures, which they believed contributed to the new permissive society.

Overall, athletic programs were a positive component of the settlement house movement. They provided a common ground where children and adults of different ethnic backgrounds could meet to share experiences and build relationships. To a degree settlement-sponsored athletic programs may be considered part of the **Americanization** process since they often encouraged young people to play American games. However, in many respects this negative aspect was offset because the settlement athletic programs encouraged neighborhood residents to develop their personal skills thereby giving them a sense of individual pride and acomplishment.

Bibliography
Carson, *Settlement Folk: Social Thought and the American Settlement Movement, 1885–1930*; Woods, *The Settlement Horizon*.

B

Balch, Emily
settlement house founder, educator, economist, peace activist
b. January 8, 1867; d. January 9, 1961.

Through her writings, teaching, and active participation in various causes, Emily Balch made significant contributions to the American Settlement Movement and to various related reform efforts. She co-founded a settlement house and served as its head resident. Through her teaching, she inspired others to join the settlement house movement. Additionally, her study of economics encouraged her to become involved in a number of labor crusades.

For many college-educated young women the settlement movement provided an opportunity to build productive careers. Balch was a member of the first graduating class of Bryn Mawr in 1889, where she majored in economics and sociology. She wanted to gain some practical experience after her academic training and went to work with Charles W. Birtwell of the **Boston Children's Aid Society**. Balch also spent a year studying privately with the sociologist Franklin H. Giddings. She then won a Bryn Mawr European Fellowship, which she used to study poor relief in Paris.

While attending a summer institute sponsored by the **Ethical Culture Society** Summer School of Applied Ethics, Balch met **Vida Scudder**, **Jane Addams**, and **Katherine Coman**. That same year, 1892, Balch co-founded **Denison House**, the first Boston

settlement established by the **College Settlements Association**. Balch served as the first head resident of Denison House until **Helena S. Dudley** could take up this responsibility.

Although she was interested in the work of the settlements, Balch believed that she could have a more significant impact as a teacher who could excite others to become involved in reform work. Her contact with labor leaders at Denison House also intensified Balch's interest in economics. She formed the Federal Labor Union, which was part of the American Federation of Labor, and attended meetings as a representative of the Cigar Makers' Union.

In 1895, Balch began preparing for a teaching career by attending the Harvard Annex and the University of Chicago. She spent a year at the University of Berlin (1896), after which she joined the faculty of Wellesley as an assistant of Katherine Coman. Balch taught courses on socialism, labor movements, and immigration. She often took her students to immigrant neighborhoods and to sweatshops.

In 1903, Balch co-founded the Boston branch of the **Women's Trade Union League**. She served on a number of labor-related state commissions and helped to draft a Massachusetts minimum wage bill. Balch was one of the organizers of the First State Conference of Charities in Massachusetts.

Balch was also interested in child welfare. She served on the Boston Municipal Board of Trustees, which was responsible for the care of delinquent and neglected children (1897–1898). She also was a member of the Massachusetts State Commission on Industrial Education (1908–1909).

While on a two-year leave from Wellesley, Balch spent part of her time studying emigration in Austria-Hungary and the remaining time visiting Slavic communities across the United States. Her book *Our Slavic Fellow Citizens* (1910) was the result of this research.

Like many reformers of her time, Balch was active in the international peace movement, and in 1915, she joined Jane Addams and more than 40 other women from the United States at the International Congress of Women at The Hague. In 1916, she participated in an unofficial Neutral Conference for Continuous Mediation, and she was active in the work of the Committee against Militarism, the Collegiate Anti-Militarism League, and the Fellowship of Reconciliation. Because of her pacifist activities, the Wellesley trustees declined to reappoint Balch in 1918. She spent the next year as a member of the editorial staff of the *Nation*, while maintaining an active interest in the international peace movement. She served as secretary-treasurer of the **Women's International League for Peace and Freedom** from the time it established its headquarters in Geneva in 1919 until 1922.

In 1927, Balch represented the league on a fact-finding mission to Haiti. Her aversion to fascist aggression caused her to reluctantly support World War II. She concentrated her efforts on helping European refugees relocate to the United States and worked for the release of interned Japanese-Americans from relocation camps. In 1946, Balch shared the Nobel Peace Prize with John R. Mott of the YMCA. She donated the $17,500 prize to the Women's International League for Peace and Freedom.

Settlement house founder, teacher, scholar, labor reformer, and peace advocate, Balch was outspoken and committed to social reform, and she was not afraid to take risks in pursuit of what she believed to be right. Although she moved into a nursing home in December 1956, she continued to take an active interest in the work of the International League for Peace and Freedom up to her death in 1961.

Bibliography

Dictionary of American Biography, supl. 7, pp. 28–29; Randall, *Improper Bostonian: Emily Greene Balch*; Sicherman, *Notable American Women: The Modern Period*, pp. 41–45; Trattner, *Biographical Dictionary of Social Welfare in America*, pp. 46–48.

Baldwin, Roger

social worker, educator, political organizer, civil libertarian
b. January 21, 1884; d. August 26, 1981.

Roger Baldwin's experience as a settlement worker eventually led him to other causes, particularly free speech and civil rights issues. He began his career by working for a number of social welfare reform causes including civil rights, labor-management relations, and social work education. His commitment to free speech led him to adopt a more radical approach than that of many other social reformers of his time.

A native of Wellesley, Massachusetts, Baldwin was raised a Unitarian. His father was a successful businessman, and the family's comfortable lifestyle insulated Roger from the problems faced by the working class. While a student at Harvard, Baldwin participated in social services projects, but when he graduated 1905, he had no clear idea of what he wanted to do with his life.

Baldwin was influenced by his uncle, William Baldwin, the president of the Long Island Railroad, who was involved in a number of reform efforts in New York City. William Baldwin was one of the founders of the National Urban League, was a member of the **National Child Labor Committee,** and was chair of the Committee of Fifteen, which had been formed to investigate **prostitution** in New York City. Through his uncle, Roger Baldwin met many prominent social reformers such as **Lillian Wald**, **Felix Adler**, **Jacob Riis**, **Paul U. Kellogg**, and **Owen Lovejoy**.

Another significant influence on Baldwin's life was his family's attorney, Louis D. Brandeis. It was Brandeis who steered Baldwin toward a social service career. After earning a master's degree at Harvard, Baldwin moved to St. Louis where he taught the first classes in sociology at Washington University and worked in a local settlement house.

While in St. Louis, Baldwin became involved in a number of social organizations. In 1908, he was appointed chief probation officer to the St. Louis Juvenile Court. He also helped to organize the National Probation Association. Two years later he became secretary of the St. Louis Civic League. The league was sponsored by business and professional men and women who supported community causes. Baldwin organized the City Club, a discussion group concerned with fostering good government. He was also a member of the Joint Committee for Social Service among Colored People. As a result of the racial segregation he encountered in St. Louis, Baldwin became interested in racial civil rights and in free speech. These interests led him to have a more radical perspective than many of his reformer colleagues.

Although he favored the broader approach of **Jane Addams** and others to social welfare work, Baldwin recognized the popularity of the individual case study method in social work, which advocated focusing on naturally occuring events and relationships rather than on survey data or formal laboratory experiments. Case studies generally employ extensive inverviews and direct observation to gather data. Toward this end, Baldwin co-founded the School of Social Economy at Washington University, which offered counseling training to social workers. He also established a strong national reputation by publishing his views in the social reform magazine, the *Survey*.

After reading a report of the United States Industrial Commission on labor-management relations, Baldwin became interested in labor concerns, particularly the issue of free speech for workers. At the 1916 meeting of the National Conference of Social Work, Baldwin organized the Division on Industrial and Economic Problems. He authored the division's report, which urged social workers to challenge the existing economic order.

Baldwin's interests gradually moved away from the field of social work toward the issue of free speech. By 1917, he had become concerned that America's entry into World War I would destroy all hope of social reform. In conjunction with the Socialist Party, the Women's Peace Party, and the **American Union Against Militarism** (AUAM), Baldwin organized a rally in St. Louis in February 1917. He called on the AUAM to sponsor similar protests in other cities.

In March 1917, Baldwin moved to New York City to work for the AUAM. Shortly after he arrived, he joined with the reformer **Crystal Eastman** in working to have the AUAM Executive Committee pressure Congress to stop the creation of the military draft. When this effort failed, they established the Bureau of Conscientious Objectors, which advised noncompliance with the draft law.

Baldwin and Eastman were also concerned that the pending Espionage Act would limit free speech and assembly. When the act was signed into law in June 1917, Baldwin and Eastman split with two other members of the AUAM executive board, Wald and Kellogg, over the role of the AUAM vis-a-vis the Espionage Act. As a compromise, Eastman proposed that the work of the AUAM be divided into three subcommittees: civil liberties, wartime labor conditions, and international peace. This compromise led to the creation of the **National Civil Liberties Bureau** (NCLB) in 1917, which Baldwin headed.

When the draft age was raised to 35, Baldwin notified his draft board that he would refuse induction. He resigned from the NCLB and was tried and sentenced to time in jail. When he was released in July 1919, Baldwin committed himself to working for radical social change. In August he married fellow reformer Madeline Doty, and then he embarked on a three-month trip through the Midwest as a laborer to investigate conditions firsthand. After working in a restaurant, in a steel mill, and in a brick yard, Baldwin returned to New York City and agreed to lead a reorganized NCLB now called the **American Civil Liberties Union** (ACLU).

Unlike other civil rights organizations, such as the National Association for the Advancement of Colored People, the Anti-Defamation League, and the American Jewish Congress, the ACLU did not serve a specific interest group. Rather, it adopted a policy of impartially defending civil liberties, particularly free speech.

Baldwin extended his civil-liberties-related work beyond the United States. In 1947, at the invitation of General Douglas MacArthur, he visited Japan and investigated the state of civil liberties under the American occupation. Based on his recommendations, a Japanese Civil Liberties Union was established in 1948.

In 1950, Baldwin retired from the ACLU, but he did not stop working on behalf of a number of causes that were important to him. For the next five years, he served as chair of the ACLU National Advisory Committee. In 1955, Baldwin chaired the International League for the Rights of Man. This group coordinated civil liberties groups in 18 countries and worked with the United Nations to secure the passage of an International Bill of Rights.

Baldwin started his long and varied career in the settlements and went on to earn a reputation as a dedicated and controversial political activist, social worker, teacher, and civil libertarian.

Bibliography

Lamson, *Roger Baldwin, Founder of the American Civil Liberties Union: A Portrait*; Trattner, *Biographical Dictionary of Social Welfare in America*, pp. 48–51; Walker, *In Defense of American Liberties: A History of the ACLU*.

Barnett, Samuel Augustus

clergyman, social reformer, settlement house founder

b. February 8, 1844; d. June 17, 1913.

Samuel Barnett was an English clergyman whose interest in parishioners extended beyond their spiritual well-being. His efforts to establish a church-centered parish community involved him in the founding of the first English social settlement, **Toynbee Hall**. Barnett's social welfare work in London became the inspiration for the American Settlement Movement.

Barnett was born in Bristol in 1844, where his father, Francis, was a wealthy businessman and the first manufacturer of iron bedsteads. Samuel was educated at home and grew up in the midst of a large, extended family. In 1862, he left home to attend Wadham College, Oxford, whose warden, Benjamin Parsons Symons, was a strong Tory supporter. Influenced by Symons and the general atmosphere at Wadham, Barnnett soon embraced the conservative Tory political philosophy. Barnett took a second class in law and modern history (1865) and spent the next two years as a teacher at Winchester to earn enough money to go to the United States.

During his travels in the United States, Barnett observed young freed slaves who were educated, and he was inspired by their ability to improve their lives. Based on this experience, Barnett came to believe that education at an early age would make a difference in a person's life. Gradually he abandoned his Toryism, which he came to view as support of the status quo.

When he returned to England in 1867, Barnett was ordained a deacon, and he became curate at St. Mary's, Bryanston Square, London. The rector of St. Mary's, W. H. Freemantle, was among the church leaders and nonconformists who believed that Christians had an obligation to provide more than just spiritual comfort to the poor. In his work, Freemantle tried to create a church-centered parish community. He had Barnett teach school and manage a workingman's club in addition to his other duties.

During his first five years at St. Mary's, Barnett became acquainted with the housing reformer **Octavia Hill**, whom Freemantle had invited to work in the parish dispensing relief. Barnett worked with Hill to investigate parishioners' applications for assistance. Through Hill, Barnett met Henrietta Rowland, a rent collector in one of Hill's tenement developments who would become his wife in 1873.

That same year, through Hill's influence, Barnett secured an appointment as the vicar of the Parish of St. Jude's, Whitechapel in London's East End. At the time, the bishop of London, John Jackson, described St. Jude's as the worst parish in the diocese. Although most of his parishioners were criminals, Barnett was determined to use his church as an instrument of community regeneration. During the next decade, he worked to attract the residents to church services. He established an art gallery and a library, and he introduced art classes into the parish school. Barnett established an education reform league in 1884 and supported the Association for Promoting Technical Education (1887).

Although a strong supporter of education, Barnett understood that education alone could not change the lives of the poor; their general living conditions had to be improved. As a result, he was active in housing reform, encouraged the demolition of unsanitary buildings, and was a supporter of the Artisan's Dwellings Act of 1875. In addition to this work, he established a children's country holiday fund in 1877 to enable children to escape the squalor of the city for even a short time. Barnett's system of dispensing poor relief in the Parish of St. Jude's served as a model for other communities.

After 10 years, Barnett had made some progress, but he had doubts about the effectiveness of using the parish structure as a solution to the community's problems. During the late 1870s, he and Henrietta began to make contact with a group of reform-minded young men and women at Oxford. Gradually, Barnett began to see the value of blending together the spiritual and the secular in his work.

Henrietta Barnett was acquainted with Gertrude Toynbee whose brother Arnold was an Oxford undergraduate interested in social reform work. He and Samuel Barnett began to correspond. Toynbee had started a club at Oxford devoted to spiritual and secular unification. He became a frequent visitor at St. Jude's, often bringing his Oxford friends along with him to work in the community.

In November 1883, Barnett read a paper at Oxford entitled "University Settlements in East London." In it he set forth his ideas for the establishment of a nondenominational settlement in a parish community that was headed by a chief who was a qualified teacher. This man would be assisted by recent university graduates who were interested in living and working in a poor area to improve the lives of the community residents. Barnett carefully distinguished between a settlement, which was nondenominational and a mission, which was established to proselytize for a particular sect or dogma.

In 1884, a group of Oxford tutors, who were joined by tutors from Cambridge and by members of Parliament, established a joint-stock undertaking called the **Universities Settlement Association**. This association provided the initial funding for a settlement house in the Parish of St. Jude's, which was named Toynbee Hall in honor of Arnold Toynbee who had recently died. Barnett was named warden. The settlement served as a residence and also contained lecture and reception rooms as well as a library.

Although he was connected with the Whitechapel community for the rest of his life, Barnett resigned from St. Jude's in 1894 when he was made a canon of Bristol. He was a select preacher at Oxford (1895) and at Cambridge (1889 and 1905). From 1906 until his death in 1913, Barnett served as canon and then as sub-dean of Westminster.

Barnett's influence extended far beyond the diverse communities of Whitechapel and Westminister. His belief in the value of the community and the responsibility that the educated had to assist their poorer neighbors led him to establish Toynbee Hall. This settlement house proved to be the model for the settlement house movement and was adopted by men and women in communities across the United States.

Bibliography

Dictionary of National Biography, 1812–1921, pp. 31–32; Meacham, *Toynbee Hall and Social Reform, 1880–1914: The Search for Community*; Seligman, *The Encyclopedia of the Social Sciences*, vol. 2, pp. 464.

Baths

Settlement workers were concerned with all aspects of their neighbors' lives. They fought for better and safer working conditions and for healthier living conditions. Life in a congested urban center presented a number of challenges to new immigrants including the need to modify the personal hygiene regimen to help avoid a number of debilitating, possibly deadly, diseases that flourished in grossly overcrowded cities that lacked even the most rudimentary sanitary facilities. The campaign for personal cleanliness became a priority for many settlement workers.

Public baths were a feature of civilized society beginning in ancient Egypt. They were an integral part of the gymnasiums of Greece and in Rome were centers of luxury and amusement. Beginning in the 1840s and 1850s, cleanliness

Public Bath House, Rivington Street, 1912.
Museum of the City of New York

was considered an indication of moral superiority among the middle and upper classes. By the late nineteenth century, public baths were a common feature of city life in most of the larger cities of Europe. Health problems were an integral part of life in the crowded slums of the industrial cities of the late nineteenth and early twentieth centuries, and although initially settlement workers may not have intended to become involved in neighborhood health care, their interest in housing and economic reforms were soon linked with public health appeals. They understood the relationship between personal hygiene and the spread of disease, and many of them also believed that personal cleanliness had a favorable effect on an individual's character.

The rapid growth of American cities in the decades following the Civil War strained available resources and introduced new varieties of health-related anxieties. An extensive study conducted by the Department of Labor of the slum districts of four large cities noted that in 1893 more than 90 percent of the populations of Baltimore, New York, and Chicago were living in tenements that did not have bathrooms; conditions were only slightly better in Philadelphia where approximately 80 percent of the residents were without bathroom facilities. Uneasiness about the cleanliness of those living in the slum districts of cities escalated as immigration, especially from countries in eastern and southern Europe, increased.

During the 1890s, many American municipalities followed the European example and made provisions for public bath facilities. In some cities, New York among them, these were augmented by bathhouses operated by private philanthropic organizations such as the **Association for Improving the Condition of the Poor**. In many instances, one of the first accomplishments cited by the residents of a new settlement house was the construction of a neighborhood bathhouse.

Five types of municipal baths were provided: the beach bath, the floating bath, the pool bath, the shower bath, and the combined shower and pool bath. Boston established a beach bath, the simplest convenience, as early as 1866. In 1870, New York was among the first cities to provide floating baths, which were wooden structures installed in the Hudson and East Rivers that formed large pools which residents could make use of during the warmer months. When pollution became an issue, floating baths were replaced by pools located at various sites around the city; Philadelphia led the way when it constructed a municipal pool in 1885. While these three types of facilities provided recreation and an opportunity for the populace to achieve a measure of cleanliness, they were only useful during the warmer months. Beginning in the 1890s, many municipalities began constructing bathhouses that provided showers or a combination of pool baths and showers. Settlement workers were strong supporters of the movement to secure public baths. Many settlement houses maintained shower baths, and they cooperated with sanitary reformers in their cities by organizing the neighborhood residents to put pressure on the municipal authorities to supply public baths. Although some of these facilities charged a fee, they provided at least some time when baths were given free of charge.

Use of public baths declined following improvements in housing legislation in the opening years of the twentieth century which required that running water be supplied to the apartments of all tenants.

Bibliography

Bushman, "The Early History of Cleanliness in America"; Jackson, *Encyclopedia of New York City*, pp. 87–88; Williams, M. *Washing "The Great Unwashed": Public Baths in Urban America, 1840–1920*.

Bauer, Catherine Krouse
social reformer, housing expert, city planner
b. May 11,1905; d. November 22, 1964.

Catherine Bauer's career as a housing expert and city planner brought her into contact with a number of settlement workers and housing reformers. In addition to advocating her own ideas about providing adequate housing for all segments of society, she worked to introduce European housing reform efforts into the United States. She was part of a new generation of social reformers whose careers bridged the period between the early settlement volunteers and the professionally trained social workers. Her belief that adequate housing was a fundamental right of all citizens echoed the call of the inner city settlement workers who prevailed on municipal authorities to carry out slum clearance projects and to provide all citizens with clean, adequate housing.

After attending the Vail-Deane School in her hometown of Elizabeth, New Jersey, Bauer entered Vassar College. She spent a year at Cornell University studying architecture and then graduated from Vassar in 1926. While traveling after finishing college, Bauer became interested in housing reform efforts in Europe, and she wrote a series of articles based on her observations.

After returning to the United States, Bauer obtained a job in the advertising department at Harcourt Brace Publishers. In 1929, she met Lewis Mumford with whom she had a personal and professional relationship. Under Mumford's guidance, Bauer began to turn her attention to social reform issues.

In 1931, Bauer became executive director of the Regional Planning Association of America. She also published articles about housing, and in 1934, she completed her first book, *Modern Housing*. In the book, Bauer advocated eliminating housing problems within a sociopolitical context that would bring together social workers, intellectuals, consumers, and workers into a working coalition that would recognize housing as a fundamental right of all citizens and that would work to accomplish this goal.

In 1934 under the auspices of the National Association of Housing Reformers, Bauer became involved in the campaign to develop effective housing legislation. She spoke in favor of public housing and of the **Wagner-Steagall Housing Bill**. She also served as the executive director of the Labor Housing Conference. After the United States Housing Authority was created in 1937, Bauer was selected to head the agency's research office.

In 1940 Bauer resigned from her position with the Housing Authority to pursue an academic career. During the 1950s, she served on the advisory committee of the Housing and Home Finance Agency's Division of Slum Clearance and Urban Redevelopment and as vice president of the **National Housing Conference**.

Even though most of Bauer's work was accomplished after the peak of the settlment period, she built on many of the ideas about housing and community planning put forward by settlement workers and housing reformers who came before her.

Bibliography

Notable American Women: The Modern Period, pp. 66–68; Trattner, *Biographical Dictionary of Social Welfare in America*, pp. 72–75.

Bellamy, George Albert
settlement founder, social reformer
b. September 29, 1872; d. July 8, 1960.

George Bellamy devoted half a century of service to the people of Cleveland, Ohio, through the work of **Hiram House**, the settlement he founded. Like settlement workers in other cities, Bellamy used his work on the local level as a springboard to become involved in reform work on the national level. In his case, it was his work in the field of recreation that drew him beyond Cleveland.

Born and raised in Cascade, Michigan, Bellamy earned a B.A. from Hiram College in Ohio in 1896. That same year, he founded Hiram House, which he named in recognition of the support the faculty and students at Hiram College gave his venture. Bellamy served as director and as a member of the settlement's board of trustees for a total of 50 years until his retirement in 1946.

Bellamy started his settlement house in temporary quarters in one of Cleveland's poorest neighborhoods, which was populated by recently arrived immigrants. His first benefactors were the local churches. Bellamy soon made contact with a number of prominent citizens who established a fund-raising committee and who eventually became members of the house's board of trustees.

By 1900, Bellamy and his supporters had raised sufficient capital to construct a four-story brick building on the lower east side of Cleveland which provided space for the clubs, kindergarten, and **Americanization** classes that the settlement residents offered.

In addition to these activities, Hiram House also operated Hiram House Camp in Chagrin Falls, Ohio, which was used by the children in the nursery and kindergarten. Once the settlement was established in its permanent location, Bellamy opened the first playground in the United States that was illuminated for night activities and that was equipped for year-round use.

Bellamy also secured a branch of the Cleveland Public Library for Hiram House and opened an infants' dispensary and a day nursery. Initially, the house employed a nurse who provided care to the residents of the surrounding neighborhood. Once a visiting nurse association was established in Cleveland, a branch was opened at Hiram House.

Like their counterparts in other cities, Bellamy and the settlement workers at Hiram House also worked to secure pure milk stations and public baths. They lobbied the state legislature to establish a juvenile court system and to regulate the personal loan operations of both individuals and private companies. Bellamy was also active in a campaign to regulate Cleveland's public dance halls. Eventually, Bellamy advocated decentralization of many of the activities and services sponsored by Hiram House. For example, he encouraged children to clean up vacant lots in their neighborhoods in order to establish small neighborhood playgrounds that could be operated by municipal authorities.

Bellamy was particularly interested in promoting the benefits of recreation. During World War I, Secretary of War Newton D. Baker appointed Bellamy to head the Committee on Training Camp Activities, which was responsible for organizing recreational resources for the troops in camps and cantonments. Bellamy was also active in the National War Fund Campaign and later raised money in support of the League of Nations. From 1931 to 1946, Bellamy served as a special representative of the Playground and Recreation Association of America (*see* **National Recreation and Park Association**), and during this time he was also a playground consultant working to establish playgrounds in 40 communities.

In addition to his work at Hiram House, Bellamy was involved in a number of professional and civic associations including the **National Federation of Settlements**, the **American Association of Social Workers**, and the Chamber of Commerce and the City and Union Clubs of Cleveland.

Bibliography

Davis, *Spearheads for Reform: The Social Settlements and the Progressive Movement, 1890–1914; The National Cyclopaedia of American Biography*, vol. XLIX, pp. 29–30.

Bing, Alexander Maximillian

attorney, real estate developer, urban planner
b. June 22, 1878; d. November 28, 1959.

Bing's involvement with the **Hudson Guild** and with the **Survey Associates**, the financing organization for the publication of the social work journal the *Survey*, provided him with firsthand knowledge of the social welfare work being accomplished by settlement workers and other reformers. He combined this experience with an interest in housing to become a leader in the urban planning and planned community movements of the early twentieth century.

Born in New York City, Bing attended the local public schools before earning an A.B. degree (1897) and an A.M. degree (1898) from the City College of New York. In 1900, he graduated from Columbia University with an L.L.B. degree. Later that year, he was admitted to the New York Bar and established a partnership with his brother Leo. By 1906, the brothers had abandoned their law practice to devote them-

selves full-time to the real estate development business.

At first, the Bings concentrated on erecting and operating apartment buildings. In 1917, Alexander took a leave of absence from the firm to devote time to war-related work, first in the U.S. Shipping Board's housing department and then in the industrial service section of the U.S. Army Ordnance Department. During this time, Bing began researching and writing about wartime industrial problems. His most significant publication was *War-Time Strikes and Their Adjustment,* which was published in 1921. The same year Bing resigned from the family firm to devote his attention to solving the problem of low-cost housing in the United States.

Bing founded the City Housing Corporation in 1924 along with a group of philanthropists, financiers, and business professionals. He served as the corporation's president until 1952. In its first year of existence, the corporation purchased 70 acres in Long Island City, New York. Four years later the planned community of Sunnyside Gardens was completed. In addition to retail establishments, Sunnyside Gardens included small apartment buildings as well as one- and two-family homes. When it was completed, it was hailed as a model development for the use of commonly shared open space.

In 1928 and 1929, the City Housing Corporation purchased 1,200 acres in Bergen County, New Jersey, where it built the Radburn development. Radburn was a planned community designed to accommodate 500 families. It included a 100-apartment house as well as detached and semi-detached homes. All living units faced central park areas that were bordered by pedestrian paths. Vehicular traffic was confined to streets that ran between the rows of houses.

In addition to his work with the City Housing Corporation, Bing was president of the Hudson Guild settlement (1915–1925), was a director of the Survey Associates, and was a member of the executive committee of the New York Building Congress. On several occasions Bing represented the United States as vice president of the International Federation for Housing and Town Planning.

Bing was a forward-thinking realtor whose interaction with the settlement community in New York City inspired him to seek a workable solution to the problems of urban congestion and overcrowding. While settlement residents were working to re-create their inner-city neighborhoods, Bing was working on an alternative solution to construct self-contained neighborhoods that would entice people into the suburbs. Even though the two planned communities he built, Sunnyside Gardens and Radburn, were not overwhelming successes, they provided a workable alternative to the urban housing dilemma.

Bibliography

Davis, *Spearheads for Reform: The Social Settlements and the Progressive Movement, 1890–1914; The National Cyclopaedia of American Biography*, vol. XVIII, p. 544; Scott, *American City Planning Since 1890*.

Blaine, Anita Eugenie McCormick

philanthropist, reformer
b. July 4, 1866; d. February 12, 1954.

Anita Blaine was a wealthy socialite who drew on her family's commitment to philanthropy as a way to overcome her personal sense of loss. Her interest in education, housing, and world peace drew her into the circle of reformers at the Chicago-based **Hull House** settlement. Her involvement in reform work was such that during her lifetime Blaine contributed more than $10 million to philanthropic causes.

Born in Manchester, Vermont, Anita McCormick was the daughter of Cyrus Hall McCormick, the inventor of the mechanical reaper. She enjoyed all of the privileges of wealth and was a popular debutante. Cyrus McCormick and his wife, Nancy, were very religious Presbyterians, deeply committed to a variety of charitable causes. They encouraged their seven children to develop their own philanthropic interests, and from an early age, Anita was aware of the needs of those less fortunate than she.

In 1889, Anita McCormick married Emmons Blaine, the son of Secretary of State James G. Blaine. The following year Emmons, Jr., was born. In 1892, Emmons Blaine died of blood poisoning, and Anita turned to the family's charity work as a way to come to terms with her grief.

Blaine developed an interest in education when she began investigating schools for her son in 1897. Before making a selection, she consulted John Dewey and Colonel Francis Wayland Parker, two well-known educational reformers. Blaine favored the progressive theories of Parker who had achieved a national reputation as superintendent of schools in Quincy, Massachusetts, and she enrolled young Emmons in the laboratory school of the Cook County Normal School. Parker stressed creativity, personal freedom, self-control, and individuality, and he emphasized the importance of teacher training.

Blaine became interested in Parker's teacher training efforts, but before she committed any money to the enterprise, she consulted **Jane Addams**, the founder of Hull House; **Graham Taylor**, the founder of **Chicago Commons;** and William Rainey Harper, the president of the University of Chicago. Based on their recommendations, Blaine donated $1 million to fund the Chicago Institute, a model teacher training institute that Parker directed between 1899 and 1901.

In 1901, Blaine established the Francis W. Parker School in Chicago, eventually donating a total of $3 million to this institution. Three years later she donated $2 million toward the founding of the School of Education at the University of Chicago. In addition, Blaine was a member of the Chicago Board of Education from 1905 to 1907.

Blaine's interest in education brought her into contact with many of Chicago's social welfare reformers. In 1899, she became a member of the executive committee of the Chicago Bureau of Charities (*see* **Chicago Relief Society**), and eventually donated more than $100,000 to it and its successor, United Charities. In 1900 along with Addams, Blaine founded the City Homes Association and served as the chair of its executive committee. The next year she became a member of the University Settlement Association.

In addition to her work in education, child welfare, and other social reform movements in the United States, Blaine supported the international peace movement and the League of Nations. Following the death of her son in 1918, she established a trust fund for the league on the condition that the United States was active in its work. Blaine contributed more than $1 million to the Foundation for World Peace in 1948.

Blaine's generosity continued after her death in 1954. In her will she left the New World Foundation a $20 million endowment to be distributed among various institutions. Through her philanthropic donations and her personal involvement in a variety of activities, Blaine made significant contributions to many of the causes championed by those involved in settlement work.

Bibliography

Dictionary of American Biography, supl. 5, pp. 60–61; McCarthy, *Noblesse Oblige: Charity and Cultural Philanthropy in Chicago, 1849–1929*.

Bliss, William Dwight Porter

clergyman, social and political activist
b. August 20, 1856; d. October 8, 1926.

William Dwight Porter Bliss's advocacy of the doctrine of **Christian Socialism**, which called upon men and women to apply the doctrines of Christianity to correct social problems, provided a powerful stimulus for many people to become involved in social welfare activities, including settlement work. Through his ministry and his work as a writer and editor during the last decades of the nineteenth century, he called attention to social and economic injustices and provided inspiration and practical advice on constructive approaches to social reform.

The son of missionaries, Bliss was born in Constantinople (now Istanbul), Turkey, where he received his early education before emigrating to the United States and attending Phillips Academy and Amherst College in Massachusetts. In 1882, he graduated from the Hartford Theological Seminary. Shortly after he was ordained a Congregationalist minister, Bliss was assigned to a parish in a working-class district of South Natick, Massachusetts. Moved by the economic and social plight of his parishioners, he soon identified with the cause of labor and became interested in socialism through reading the *Christian Union* and the works of Henry George, the journalist and single-tax advocate.

Devoutly religious, Bliss was concerned with more than just the spiritual well-being of his parishioners. He believed that he must care for the whole person, and this meant that he must also minister to his congregation members' physical needs. He also believed that the church itself had an obligation to alleviate the harsh living conditions of the working class. To Bliss, capitalism, with its emphasis on the individual and the accumulation of wealth by a few at the expense of many, was the antithesis of Christianity. To truly gain God's Kingdom, society must gradually move toward complete cooperation. Bliss thought the established churches were too concerned with dogma, and that this preoccupation resulted in their being indifferent to social justice. Progress toward achieving the ultimate goal of cooperation could only be realized when the churches began to accept their social responsibilities, especially toward the working class.

By 1886, Bliss had become increasingly dissatisfied with Congregationalism, and he joined the Episcopal Church. While working in a parish in Lee, Massachusetts, he joined the Knights of Labor to demonstrate his solidarity with his parishioners. He served as Master Workman of the Assembly at Lee and was a delegate at the Knights of Labor convention in Cincinnati in 1887. Later that same year, Bliss and an associate, Father Huntington, started the Church Association for the Advancement of the Interests of Labor.

In 1888, Bliss assumed responsibility for Grace Church in South Boston. At about this time he became interested in Christian Socialism, a movement that had originated in England during the 1840s and that was enjoying a revival during the 1880s and 1890s. The term *Christian Socialism* was first used around 1848 by a small group of young men in London including **Frederick Denison Maurice**, John Malcolm Ludlow, and **Charles Kingsley**. For them, socialism was primarily a religious movement, and they focused their attention and efforts on what they considered neglected aspects of the church's social responsibilities. Their aim was not to reform society along socialist principles but to realign socialism to make it conform to Christian principles.

This marriage of Christianity and socialism was taken up by Bliss and his American followers in the late 1880s. Many reformers associated with the settlement movement were attracted to the doctrines of Christian Socialism. Bliss, like most later Christian Socialists, and especially those in the United States where the concept of class struggle was never fully embraced, was more concerned with the sentimental aspects of socialism—cooperation and brotherhood—than with its more radical aspects—collective ownership of land and capital. In 1889, along with a number of fellow clergymen, Bliss helped to organize the Society of Christian Socialists in the United States. The following year he established the Church of the Carpenter in Boston and served as rector for four years. **Vida Scudder**, **Mary Simkhovitch**, and other reformers associated with **Denison House** were frequent visitors. Bliss was also the founder and editor of the society's propagandist magazine, *The Dawn*. Bliss served as editor for six years and used the pages of the magazine to illustrate the need for reform in the church in theological matters and in its relationship to society.

Bliss's other pastorates included San Gabriel, California (1898); Amityville, Long Island (1902–1906), and West Orange, New Jersey (1910–1914). In addition, Bliss traveled across the United States delivering lectures on social reform issues. In 1894, he lectured for the Christian Socialist Union. Bliss served as president of the National Social Reform Union (1899), and he worked as an investigator for the U.S. Bureau of Labor (1907–1909).

In addition to his church-related responsibilities and his reform work, Bliss was a prolific writer, editor, and compiler. He published collections of the writings of John Ruskin and John Stuart Mill and produced the *Handbook of Socialism* (1895) and the *Encyclopedia of Social Reform* (1897), which was revised and enlarged in 1908.

During World War I, Bliss taught French and Belgian soldiers interned in Switzerland. After returning to the United States he served as rector of St. Martha's Church in New York City (1921–1925). He died in 1926 after a long illness.

Although he never lived in a settlement, Bliss's ideals of Christian Socialism, which called for cooperation between social classes for mutual benefit, influenced many of the young men and women who became involved in the settlement movement and in various other social reforms.

Bibliography

Dictionary of American Biography, vol. 1, pt. 2, pp. 377–78; Mott, *A History of American Magazines*, vol. 4; Seligman, *Encyclopedia of the Social Sciences*, vol. 2, pp. 590–91.

Booth, Charles

social researcher, reformer

b. March 30, 1840; d. November 23, 1916.

Charles Booth, the English social reformer and pioneering social survey investigator, influenced the work of many of the women and men who were active in the American Settlement Movement. His methodology and use of statistics are evident in the pioneering study entitled *Hull-House Maps and Papers*, published by **Florence Kelley** and other residents of the Chicago-based **Hull House** settlement, and in the social survey works published by **Robert A. Woods** and the residents of the **South End House** settlement in Boston, such as *The City Wilderness* and *Americans in Process*.

Born into a wealthy Liverpool shipping family, Booth enjoyed an active and successful business career for most of his adult life. He was educated at the Royal Institute School and then trained in the office of the Lamport and Holt Steamship Company. In 1862, he joined his brother Alfred's steamship company, Alfred Booth & Company, as a partner. Sometime later the Booth Steamship company was formed, and Booth served as its chair until 1912.

Booth had a scholarly temperament and his interest in the welfare of working men and women was stimulated by the general concern regarding the condition of the urban poor that characterized the 1880s. Works such as W.C. Preston's *The Bitter Cry of Outcast London* (1883) prompted strong reactions, and accounts of deplorable conditions led some to doubt if a benevolent charitable approach was the answer to the evils of poverty. Many believed that a more scientific approach toward relief would be a more effective way to bring about the necessary reforms.

In response to these prevailing conditions, Booth undertook a study of various occupations, which he hoped would provide an effective statistical solution to London's poverty. His initial study of industrial conditions in Britain and Ireland, which he published in 1868, was based on census records, but it proved to be too large an undertaking. He refocused his study and then spent the next 16 years conducting an in-depth inquiry into the lives and occupations of London's poor.

In the course of his work, Booth utilized detailed field investigation methodology based on, among other sources, the records of school attendance officers. He also secured the cooperation of various public and private philanthropic organizations, such as London Charity Organization Society, and of trade union officials.

To assist him with his research, Booth brought together a corps of investigators that included the housing reformer **Octavia Hill**. Booth's researchers culled data related to a number of aspects of the life and occupations of London's working class. The results were published in two volumes and an appendix entitled *Labour and Life of the People* (1889–1891). The objective of Booth's pioneering study was to demonstrate a statistical relationship between employment and poverty. The text was supplemented by regional maps of London which indicated various income groups. Booth's study was significant because it marked the first time that the social survey method had been used to systematically investigate urban conditions. This methodology, which emphasized a more scientific approach to social problems, was adopted by other social welfare reformers both in England and America.

Booth's next undertaking was an examination of the influence of religion on the population of London. Then in 1903, he revised his initial research and issued an 18-volume series entitled *Life and Labour of the People in London*.

As a result of his research, Booth developed a particular interest in the condition of the poor. He conducted a public campaign, writing and speaking in favor of old age pensions. His efforts were a contributing factor in the passage of the Old Age Pensions Act of 1906 in England. In addition to his social research, Booth served as president of the Royal Statistical Society (1892–1894), was a fellow of the Royal Society (1899), and was named a Privy Councillor in 1904. He also served on the Poor Law Commission of 1905–1909. Booth also maintained his connection with his family's steamship company until shortly before his death in 1916.

Booth's pioneering use of the social survey method introduced a more scientific approach to the study of social problems. His research served as a model for settlement workers in the United States as they undertook systematic social surveys in their own communities.

Bibliography

Dictionary of National Biography, 1912–1921, pp. 48–50; O'Day, *Mr. Charles Booth's Inquiry: Life and Labour of the Peoples in London Reconsidered*; Seligman, *Encyclopedia of the Social Sciences*, vol. 2, p. 642.

Boston Associated Charities

During the latter part of the nineteenth century, municipal authorities became increasingly concerned about the cost, both in time and money, of indiscriminate charitable giving. In response, cooperative societies were organized in many cities to coordinate relief efforts on behalf of the poor. The organization that eventually became the Boston Associated Charities is representative of this type of relief society.

In 1875, two wealthy Boston women, Mrs. James T. **(Annie) Fields** and Mrs. James Lodge, formed the Cooperative Society of Visitors. Lodge served as president and Fields was vice president. This society, which was based on the work accomplished by the London-based relief worker **Octavia Hill**, coordinated the efforts of **friendly visitors** who visited the poor in their homes to investigate requests for assistance.

The founders of the Cooperative Society were reluctant to simply give money to the poor. Instead, they established workrooms and devised other methods of helping the poor to find work. They also realized that the friendly visitors would be more effective if they were trained in how to carry out their investigations. Once again, Lodge and Fields looked to Hill for inspiration. They developed the idea of a district committee, which brought together visitors at regular intervals so they could share their experiences and learn from one another.

In 1879, the Cooperative Society of Visitors was absorbed by the Boston Associated Charities, and Fields became one of the latter's most active and creative directors. The aim of the new society was to raise the needy above the need for relief, not to give alms. Its main principle was cooperation. The visitors of the Associated Charities would investigate calls for assistance and then make individuals, charitable associations, and government agencies aware of the need. The group's ultimate aim was to secure employment for those in need.

To accomplish its work, the Associated Charities established district conferences that corresponded to the Boston City Wards. The membership of each conference represented a wide range of public and private agencies. Conferences held weekly meetings to discuss cases. Each conference elected an executive committee that organized and advised volunteer visitors, passed reports onto the central office, and hired a paid agent to oversee the day-to-day operations. This system of investigation and careful record keeping marked the beginning of the application of scientific principles to the field of charity work in Boston.

Convinced that charity work required training as well as good intentions, the Associated Charities offered a training program for district agents and a series of study classes for agents and volunteers. This program was developed by **Zilpha D. Smith**, secretary of the Associated Charities from 1879–1903. Smith believed that social workers needed help and guidance, just like their clients. The training program she developed was based on the assumption that the knowledge, skills, and techniques of social work could be transmitted from teacher to student through the technique of casework supervision. Smith transformed the district conference into a learning forum in which paid agents and volunteers shared their experiences and supported each other in their attempts to help the needy.

Over the years the Boston Associated Charities evolved into a leader in the national charity organization movement. Its strength lay in its ability to combine the traditional moralistic concept of charity and public service with a more scientific approach that emphasized training for professional social welfare workers. The organization is still active today.

Bibliography
Huggins, *Protestants against Poverty: Boston's Charities, 1870–1900*; Lubove, *The Professional Altruist: The Emergence of Social Work as a Career, 1880–1930.*

Boston Children's Aid Society

During the nineteenth century, social reformers became increasingly concerned about the welfare of children, particularly those children arrested for committing minor offenses and sent to institutions and held in the company of adult offenders. Social welfare workers were aware of the need to intercede on behalf of these youthful offenders and to provide them with an opportunity for rehabilitation. The Boston Children's Aid Society (BCAS), which was founded in 1865, is representative of this type of social agency. Later, settlement workers established similar types of agencies such as the Juvenile Court Committee, which was organized by the residents of the Chicago-based settlement **Hull House.**

Rufus R. Cook, the chaplain of the Suffolk County, Massachusetts, Jail was the first agent working for the Boston Children's Aid Society. At first, Cook would attend the police court and offer to take responsibility for boys who had been arrested. To avoid being sent to jail, the boys agreed to report to Cook at least once per week. Gradually, Cook and other reformers, such as the philanthropist and social reformer **Robert Treat Paine**, came to believe that the city offered too many temptations to young people and that the best way to save a city youth in trouble was to send him to the country.

Toward this end, a representative from the BCAS would obtain the release of a boy from the court and from his parents, who agreed to let the society assume responsibility for a certain number of years. The boy was then sent to the society's farm, Pine Farm, in West Newton, where he received preliminary training. The society's next step was to transfer responsibility for the boy to a local farmer. Under this "cottage plan," the boy lived and worked on the farm for a specified period of time. The farmer assumed responsibility for the youth's food, clothing, and schooling. At the end of this probationary period, the boy was returned to his own family.

Eventually, the BCAS expanded its program to include a home for girls (1866). It also experimented with an industrial home in Ludlow, Massachusetts, that provided employment for delinquent boys in a factory. However, this program was not successful and was discontinued after a short time.

During the 1880s, Charles W. Birtwell joined the Boston Children's Aid Society as an outside agent. When Cook became ill, Birtwell began to assume responsibility for the society's operations, and he gradually introduced measures to broaden its effectiveness.

One innovation that Birtwell introduced was working with children after they returned to their old neighborhoods. Members of the BCAS acted as visitors and sometimes as probation officers, counseling children and their parents to take advantage of existing relief programs. Birtwell stressed the need to tailor the society's action to the individual child's needs. Under his guidance, the society offered three approaches in its work with children: working with them in their own homes, providing reformatory work in a society-sponsored farm, and placing the child in another home setting. By 1900, the society began to rely on the use of foster homes instead of sending children to farms.

The work of the Boston Children's Aid Society, particularly its program of counseling children and their families in the neighborhood setting, provided a model for settlement house workers and other social welfare reformers. The society's workers and leaders introduced innovative methods of dealing with dependent and delinquent children, a function the society performs up to the present day. *See also* **Child Welfare.**

Bibliography
Huggins, *Protestants against Poverty: Boston's Charities, 1870–1900.* Lubove, *The Professional Altruist: The Emergence of Social Work as a Career, 1880–1930.*

Boston Cooperative Society of Visitors *See* Boston Associated Charities

Boston School for Social Workers

Settlement residents and other social welfare workers recognized the importance of professional training, both theoretical and practical, to assist them in their work. In 1897, **Mary Richmond** of the Baltimore Charity Organization called for the establishment of training schools in applied philanthropy. Richmond's idea was taken up by social welfare reformers in Boston and in other large cities such as Chicago and New York. The Boston School for Social Workers was one of the first institutions of its type and served as a model for other schools because of its innovative practices such as inviting specialists to teach advanced course work and establishing a medical social work course.

Founded in 1904 by **Jeffrey R. Brackett** and **Zilpha D. Smith**, the Boston School for Social Workers immediately sought a university affiliation, which it received from Simmons College and Harvard University. Women students registered at Simmons, men at Harvard.

Twenty-seven students were in the first class, some of whom were already involved in social welfare work. All students met as a group at least twice per week to discuss assigned readings. An additional meeting each week was devoted to the discussion of a particular method. Occasionally, students visited institutions to observe certain activities or methodologies.

Brackett and Smith taught most of the introductory course work. Specialists were invited to offer more advanced level work. Among those who taught at the Boston School for Social Workers were **Robert A. Woods**, head resident of the Boston-based **South End House** settlement, who also served on the school's board of directors; **Florence Kelley**, a resident of the **Henry Street Settlement**; and **Mary E. McDowell**, founder of the **University of Chicago Settlement**. Many of the students also gained practical experience working in Boston-area settlements.

The directors of the Boston School for Social Workers were interested in pursuing a variety of innovative approaches to the professional training of social welfare workers. Toward this end the school enlisted the assistance of Dr. Richard C. Cabot, who in 1899 was appointed physician to outpatients at the Massachusetts General Hospital. He was a director of the **Boston Children's Aid Society** and in 1905 established a social service department at the Massachusetts General Hospital. Cabot hoped to use this facility to overcome the sense of depersonalization that many felt when they entered the hospital. He believed that trained social workers could assist physicians in ensuring that a full, accurate diagnosis was achieved for all patients. In 1913, the Boston School for Social Workers teamed up with the Massachusetts General Hospital to offer a one-year course in medical social work, the first of its kind in the United States.

Attendance at the Boston School for Social Workers increased steadily over the years. Local settlement houses benefited from the program since students were required to work in settlements and other social welfare agencies to gain practical experience. Eventually a four-

year degree program was adopted at Simmons College under the new name—The School of Social Work.

Bibliography

Carson, *Settlement Folk: Social Thought and the American Settlement Movement, 1885–1930*; "Encouraging Opening of the Boston School for Social Workers"; Lubove, *The Professional Altruist: The Emergence of Social Work as a Career, 1880–1930*; "The School for Social Workers, Boston"; Trattner, *From Poor Law to Welfare State: A History of Social Welfare in America*.

Boston Social Union

During the first half of the nineteenth century, relief organizations such as the New York **Association for Improving the Condition of the Poor** were formed to coordinate the relief services of local charities and to control the cost of indiscriminate charitable giving. In a similar way, settlement workers in larger urban centers with several settlement houses also realized the need to eliminate competition and to reduce the duplication of efforts.

Settlement workers in Chicago were the first to unite in a common organization in 1894. Their Boston colleagues soon followed their example. In November 1908, the Boston Social Union (BSU) was founded by representatives of the South End Social Union (organized November 1899) and the Social Union of the North and West Ends (organized March 1905).

The union of these two organizations was viewed as a way to bring about a program of broad, united action among social welfare workers in the city. Settlements and clubs that had been continually engaged in social work for at least three years were eligible for membership in the union. Members of the BSU could not offer religious instruction or attempt to influence the religious beliefs of anyone. They were encouraged to support any undertaking and to ally themselves with any organization whose purpose was to improve the education, sanitation, housing, or political situation of Boston. Individual members of the union were not bound to support any action of other members with which they disagreed.

The union was maintained by a number of committees including juvenile protection, playgrounds, inter-settlement concerts, and athletic events. It sponsored conferences for specialized settlement workers such as nurses and cooking teachers to assist them in meeting the challenges of their jobs. The union also maintained a Bureau of Registration to assist men and women looking for positions as settlement workers.

The Boston Social Union continued to operate during the opening decades of the twentieth century. It provided a valuable service to organizations involved in social welfare work by helping to avoid duplication of efforts. This was particularly important during difficult economic times when funding for programs and services was reduced. The union also assisted settlement workers by sponsoring meetings and conferences and by enabling its membership to present a strong, united front when dealing with the local authorities.

Bibliography

Carson, *Settlement Folk: Social Thought and the American Settlement Movement, 1885-1930*; Woods, *The Settlement Horizon*.

Bowen, Louise DeKoven
philanthropist, social reformer, settlement house supporter, suffragist
b. February 26, 1859; d. November 9, 1953.

Louise DeKoven Bowen was a wealthy Chicago philanthropist whose friendship with **Jane Addams**, the founder of **Hull House**, drew her into the Chicago reform community. Bowen not only provided funding for social welfare causes, but she also gave freely of her time by serving as an officer and active member of a number of social service and reform agencies such as the **Visiting Nurse Association** of Chicago, the **Juvenile Protective Association**, and the Chicago Equal Suffrage Association.

As the daughter of a successful Chicago businessman, Louise DeKoven enjoyed a privileged upbringing. At 16, she graduated from the fashionable Dearborn Seminary. Energetic and intelligent, Louise resisted her parents' attempts to mold her into an appropriately feminine young woman whose life revolved around family and church. Instead, she looked to charity work for a sense of personal fulfillment.

DeKoven's first exposure to the lives of Chicago's poor involved home visiting and teaching Sunday School classes at St. James Episcopal Church. In addition, she used her own money to open a clubhouse on Huron Street to relieve the isolation of the boys who had come to the city in search of work. With the help of her friend Eleanor Ryerson, DeKoven established a Kitchen Garden Association in the 1880s to teach poor young women the finer points of housekeeping.

In 1886, Louise DeKoven married Joseph Tilton Bowen, a well-known banker from Providence, Rhode Island. The Bowens, who eventually had four children, divided their time between their 40-room mansion in Chicago and their summer home in Bar Harbor, Maine. During the early years of her marriage (1886–1896), Bowen served on the boards of three Chicago hospitals.

In 1893, Bowen met Jane Addams. This encounter marked the beginning of a 60-year friendship between the two women during which Bowen donated almost one million dollars to the settlement house. In 1903, Bowen became a trustee of Hull House. The following year, she funded the construction of Bowen Hall, a women's club building. Several years later, she paid for a five-story building to be used for men's and boys' activities. Bowen's husband died in 1911. The following year she established the Bowen Country Club in his memory, donating 72 acres of land and 10 buildings in Waukegan, Illinois, for use as a summer camp for Hull House.

Bowen was active in the Hull House Woman's Club and in the Juvenile Protective Association. She served as head of the association, which was formed to address the environmental causes of juvenile delinquency. In 1899, Bowen and other Hull House residents, including **Julia Lathrop**, were successful in their campaign to establish the Chicago Juvenile Court, the first of its kind in the United States. The Hull House residents also organized a Juvenile Court Committee to assist the court in its work. Lathrop served as the committee's first president. She was succeeded by Bowen who served for seven years and was successful in obtaining salaries for court probation officers.

In addition to her work at the settlement, Bowen was also active in other social and political movements. She was one of the founders of the Visiting Nurse Service of Chicago and a member of the Committee for School Nurses. She served as president of the Chicago Equal Suffrage Association, and in 1912, she campaigned for Theodore Roosevelt and the Progressive Party. Bowen was the only woman member of the Illinois State Council of Defense (1917–1919), which coordinated local welfare programs during World War I. In 1922, she served as an official delegate to the Pan-American Congress of Women, which was held in Baltimore, Maryland.

In addition to these activities, Bowen helped establish the Woman's Roosevelt Republican Club, which supported reform candidates in state and local elections. She served as president of the club, which on four occasions during the 1920s sponsored Woman's World Fairs in Chicago to highlight various accomplishments of women. During the 1930s, Bowen served as vice president of the United Charities of Chicago. (*See* **Chicago Relief Society**.)

Following Addams's death in 1935, Bowen visited Hull House daily, playing an active role in the settlement's activities and engaging in frequent clashes with Addams's successors, Adena Miller Rich and Charlotte Carr. Bowen acted as treasurer of Hull House until 1952, the year before her death.

More than just a philanthropist with deep pockets, Bowen was an active participant in the work of Hull House and the Chicago social welfare community. She not only funded settlement workers' programs, particularly those benefiting women and children, but she also worked to bring these programs to fruition.

Bibliography

Dictionary of American Biography, supl. 5, pp. 84–85; McCarthy, *Noblesse Oblige: Charity and Cultural Philanthropy in Chicago, 1849–1929*; Trattner, *Biographical Dictionary of Social Welfare in America*, pp. 111–14.

Brace, Charles Loring
engineer, child welfare worker, social reformer
b. June 2, 1855; d. May 24, 1938.

Charles Loring Brace's career as a social reformer began as the result of his fulfilling a promise to his father to continue the work of the Children's Aid Society. Building on the tradition established by his father of providing assistance to homeless and orphaned children, Brace used his connection to the New York City reform community to work with settlement workers and other reformers to expand the services of the Children's Aid Society and to make an important contribution to child welfare reform.

Born in Hastings-on-Hudson, New York, Brace attended the Phillips Andover Academy. He graduated from the Sheffield Scientific School at Yale with a Ph.D. in 1876. For the next 13 years, Brace was employed as a construction engineer for a number of railroad companies in the Midwest, including the Chicago, St. Paul, Minneapolis, and Omaha Railway at Hudson, Wisconsin (1880–1883), and the Minneapolis and St. Louis Railway in Minneapolis, Minnesota (1883–1890).

In 1890, Brace returned to New York after his father's death to fulfill his promise to continue the elder Brace's work as secretary of the Children's Aid Society. The elder Brace founded the society in 1853 and had initiated the practice of placing homeless children in families rather than in orphanages or as indentured laborers. The younger Brace carried on his father's work, rescuing homeless children from the streets of New York City. Under his leadership, the Children's Aid Society arranged for homeless children to live with families in the Midwest, where they would benefit from the fresh air and the opportunity of growing up in a more supportive family atmosphere.

Over time, the use of this type of placement declined, in part because of a change in the attitudes of social workers. Rather than continuing with the wholesale evacuation of children, Brace instituted a program of individualized study and diagnosis that was designed to consider each individual child. At first, children were placed in a boarding home program close to New York City. Gradually, Brace expanded and enhanced these activities to provide assistance to the entire family and to create an environment that would enable children to remain with their own families.

Brace also concentrated his efforts on ways to improve the health and education of children. In 1893, the Children's Aid Society supported programs for school nurses, school lunches, and playgrounds. It established a day school for crippled children in 1900 and arranged for special classes for mentally ill children and for children with cardiac ailments. Many of these programs were eventually taken over by the public authorities. The Children's Aid Society programs helped establish the Brace Memorial Farm in Valhalla, New York (1900), to provide children with a summer respite from the city streets. In 1909, the society opened a convalescent children's home in Chappaqua, New York, which by the early 1940s had cared for more than 30,000 children.

By the time he retired due to ill health, Brace had made significant progress toward individualizing child welfare reform work. He established a foster home department that emphasized family care and the preservation of the family unit and also assisted in the permanent adoption of homeless children. Brace participated in a variety of child-welfare-related reform activities on the national level as well. He played an active role in the work of the **White House Conference on Dependent Children** (1909), which was organized by **Lillian Wald** of the **Henry Street Settlement** in New York and other reformers to call national attention to the social and economic problems of children. Brace also wrote numerous pamphlets, papers, and reports during his 37 years in the Children's Aid Society. During his tenure, the society spent $20 million on the care of children.

Bibliography

Dictionary of American Biography, supl. 2, pp. 57–58; *The National Cyclopaedia of American Biography*, vol. XXXI, p. 127.

Brackett, Jeffrey Richardson

social welfare administrator, social work educator, political activist

b. October 20, 1860; d. December 4, 1949.

Jeffrey Brackett's career illustrates how social welfare reform changed during the settlement movement. Active in the **Charity Organization Society** movement, which relied on volunteer **friendly visitors**, Brackett also played a significant role in the professionalization of social work as a career through his work with the **Boston School for Social Workers**, which trained many women and men active in the settlements.

A native of Massachusetts, Brackett established his reputation as a public welfare and charity worker in Baltimore, where he earned a Ph.D. from Johns Hopkins University in 1889. Between 1897 and 1904, he was actively involved in a number of local relief agencies. He served as chair of the Baltimore Charity Organization's executive committee, head of the Department of Charities and Correction, and chair of the City Relief Committee, which was established to coordinate relief efforts after fire swept through the city in 1904. During this time, Brackett also lectured on public aid, charity, and correction at Johns Hopkins.

For the most part, Brackett subscribed to the charity organization movement tenet that celebrated the moral virtue of work over public relief. In addition, he also acknowledged the value of applying a scientific, data-gathering approach to social welfare work that emphasized the casework method in an attempt to more fully understand the individual situation under consideration. Brackett , however, moved a step further in his own philosophy of social welfare work. As a result of his association with the Baltimore Central Relief Committee, Brackett recognized that individual casework had to be supplemented with programs that attacked the fundamental social, industrial, and economic origins of poverty. He concluded that the solution to many social ills lay in closer cooperation between public and private philanthropic agencies.

In 1897, Brackett chaired a committee charged with formulating recommendations to reform Baltimore's public welfare programs. As a result of this committee's work, a Board of Supervisors of City Charities was created. In 1900, Brackett was named chair of this board. That same year he headed the Department of Charities and Corrections. Brackett held these two appointments until 1904, when, in recognition of the leadership role he occupied in the Baltimore charity organization movement and his cooperative endeavors with other social reformers on the national level, he was elected president of the National Conference of Charities and Correction (*See* **National Conference on Social Welfare**), an influential organization composed of leaders from both public and private charitable relief organizations and correctional institutions.

Like his Baltimore Charity Organization Society colleague **Mary Richmond**, Brackett believed that the future of scientific professional social work depended upon its ability to provide formal training for prospective social workers that included a broad academic foundation in addition to more specialized training in the methodology of scientific charity. To accomplish this goal, Brackett organized the **Boston School for Social Workers** in cooperation with members of the **Boston Associated Charities** in 1904. This school, which was jointly sponsored by Harvard University and Simmons College, was the first of its kind and offered a curriculum that combined traditional academic training with practical field work. Brackett served as director of the Boston School until his retirement in 1920. He was assisted in his work by **Zilpha D. Smith** who held the position of associate director.

While in Massachusetts, Brackett did not restrict his social reform efforts to the Boston School. He was a member of the Massachusetts State Board of Charity (1906–1919) and sat on the advisory board of the Massachusetts Board of Public Welfare from 1920 to 1934. In 1911, he was one of the incorporators of the American Red Cross, and two years later served as chair of the Boston Associated Charities. Brackett also channeled his energies into the political arena, helping to secure the passage of a mother's aid law in 1912 and an old-age assistance law in 1931.

After his retirement from the Boston School for Social Workers, Brackett remained active in a number of social work causes. He continued his work with the Red Cross and with the Protestant Episcopal Diocese of Massachusetts. When he died in 1949, he left behind an important legacy in his pioneering work to establish social work as a career through the development of social work education.

Bibliography
Dictionary of American Biography, supl 4, pp. 100–01;
Lubove, *The Professional Altruist: The Emergence of
Social Work as a Career, 1880–1930*.

Bradford, Cornelia Foster

settlement house founder, social reformer,
nativist sympathizer

b. December 4, 1847; d. January 15, 1935.

Cornelia Foster Bradford's life changed forever
when in 1892, at the age of 45, she visited
Toynbee Hall in London's East End. Until this
time, she had lived the quiet life of a middle-
class, college-educated woman whose interests
and activities were centered around home and
family. Like so many other men and women who
became interested in the American Settlement
Movement, she was inspired by the work being
accomplished by **Jane Addams** and her **Hull
House** colleagues. For the energetic Bradford,
establishing her own settlement seemed the
natural thing to do.

The daughter of a Congregationalist minister who, along with his wife, was a supporter
of a number of reform causes such as abolition,
women's rights, and temperance, Bradford grew
up in the Finger Lakes region of New York State.
After graduating from the Houghton Seminary
in Clinton, New York, she attended Olivet College in Michigan. After leaving college, she
taught Sunday school, studied independently,
and traveled. From time to time, she lectured
on history, travel, and literature.

But it was her visit to London to study the
settlement house movement that galvanized
Bradford's interests and energies. In addition
to visiting Toynbee Hall, she lived for a short
time at another London settlement, Mansfield
House. When she returned to the United States,
Bradford became a resident of Hull House in
Chicago. The following year, 1893, she established her own settlement in Jersey City, New
Jersey, where her father and brother were then
residing.

The neighborhood Bradford selected was
populated by Italian, Irish, and Eastern European immigrants, many of whom found employment on the city's waterfront. As an
introduction to the neighborhood, Bradford took
a room at a local working-class cultural center,
the People's Palace, and set about meeting the
residents and organizing sports and club activities. With the financial assistance of her brother,
Amory Howe Bradford, she purchased a large
house in Jersey City. In May 1894, she opened
the door of New Jersey's first social settlement,

Whittier House, named for the poet John
Greenleaf Whittier.

Like many other settlement workers at this
time, Bradford believed that she and her fellow
residents could instill their working-class neighbors with their own middle-class values by forg-
ing personal relationships and bonds that would
transcend their class and ethnic differences.
Toward this end, Whittier House, which was
clean and well-furnished, offered literature,
dance, and art classes, as well as academic and
vocational study programs. In addition to this
cultural agenda, the settlement sponsored
health clinics, and in the early 1920s, the house
opened both a Babies' Hospital to aid mothers
and babies and a Diet Kitchen to prepare food
for underweight babies and children.

Bradford possessed a forceful personality,
and her influence was felt beyond the walls of
her settlement. In 1898, the New Jersey Consumers' League, a branch of the National **Consumers' League**, was formed at Whittier
House, and Bradford served as its vice president and as a lobbyist. On behalf of the league,
she investigated the working conditions of child
laborers in New Jersey's bottle-blowing industry. Based on this work, Bradford led a number
of campaigns that resulted in the passage of
child labor laws in New Jersey in 1903. Bradford
was also one of the founders of the Children's
Protective League.

After a housing investigation undertaken
in 1902 by Mary Sayles, another Whittier House
resident and College Settlement Association
fellow, Governor Franklin Murphy appointed a
Tenement House Protective League in 1903.
Bradford became a member of the league and
encouraged it to meet regularly at Whittier
House. As a show of support, she invited housing inspectors who were working for the New
Jersey Tenement House Commission to reside
at Whittier House during their investigations.

Bradford also helped to organize the New
Jersey Neighborhood Workers' Association and
went on to serve both as its president and as
chair of its legislation committee. She was also
president of the New Jersey Conference for Social Welfare and was an appointee to the State
Board of Charities, Aids, and Corrections and
the State Board of Children's Guardians.

The war years brought major changes to
Bradford's life. A member of the **Women's International League for Peace and Freedom** and the Woman's Peace Party, Bradford
eventually modified her pacifist stance and supported the United States entry into World War

I. For a time, Whittier House even served as a home for displaced soldiers. But the war had other consequences for Bradford. As more and more Eastern European immigrants moved into the neighborhood, she resented what she considered their "cliquish" behavior and their indifference to Whittier House's offerings. These feelings of distrust and resentment led her to become involved with the **Americanization** movement and with a nativist organization, the North American Civic League for Immigrants.

After the war, Whittier House, like so many other settlements, faced severe financial difficulties, and in a strange twist of fate, had become a victim of its own success. Bradford and her colleagues had launched a number of thriving initiatives and had succeeded in having the municipal authorities of Jersey City assume responsibility for them. With the city running most of Whittier House's old programs, it seemed that the settlement had outlived its usefulness. When Bradford retired in 1925, however, she could look back on a career in which she had successfully translated many of the reform efforts of her settlement colleagues into practical programs and initiatives that benefited the state of New Jersey.

Bibliography

Davis, *Spearheads for Reform: The Social Settlements and the Progressive Movement, 1890–1914*; Handen, "In Liberty's Shadow: Cornelia Bradford and Whittier House"; James, *Notable American Women*, vol. 1, pp. 218–19; Trattner, *Biographical Dictionary of Social Welfare in America*, pp. 119–22.

Brandt, Lilian

educator, social welfare researcher, author
b. May 15, 1873; d. June 4, 1951.

Lilian Brandt contributed to the social welfare reform efforts of the first half of the twentieth century through her association with the New York **Charity Organization Society** (COS) and its School of Philanthropy (*See* **Columbia University Graduate School of Social Work**). Her research was vital to settlement workers who were concerned with issues such as preventative health care campaigns. Additionally, as an instructor at the School of Philanthropy, she taught social welfare workers how to carry out their professional responsibilities.

Brandt graduated from Wellesley College in 1895. She secured positions at Lindewood College, St. Charles, Missouri, and at Bradford Academy, Bradford, Massachusetts, teaching history and classical languages before returning to Wellesley to earn an M.A. in economics

in 1901. During the 1901–1902 academic year, Brandt taught history and economics at National Parks Seminary in Forest Glen, Maryland.

During the summer of 1902, Brandt attended the New York Charity Organization Society's Summer School of Philanthropy. Brandt's ability to interpret the factual material she collected for her research brought her to the attention of **Edward T. Devine**, the general secretary of New York Charity Organization Society. When the School of Philanthropy became a full-year program two years later, Devine, now its director, selected Brandt to serve as secretary of the Committee on Social Research for both the Charity Organization Society and the School of Philanthropy.

During this time, Brandt worked on a number of projects. She published a pioneering study on tuberculosis, "Social Aspects of Tuberculosis" (1903), and along with Devine and **Paul U. Kellogg**, who was a classmate at the Summer School of Philanthropy and who later became editor of the *Survey*, she helped to develop the preventative aspects of the COS's anti-tuberculosis campaign. In addition, Brandt was also an instructor at the School of Philanthropy.

Her social welfare work took a more practical turn when Brandt participated in disaster relief activities following the San Francisco earthquake (1906) and the Dayton, Ohio, flood (1913). In 1931, Brandt left the COS to join the Welfare Council of New York, a state-run agency. She also was involved in a number of social welfare-related special projects sponsored by the Community Service Society of New York and the **Russell Sage Foundation**.

Following her retirement, Brandt continued her research and writing and published histories of a number of social service organizations including the New York School of Social Work and the **Russell Sage Foundation**. Brandt was involved in several aspects of social welfare work, but perhaps her most significant contribution was her ability to compile and interpret statistical and factual information, which she made available to settlement workers and other social work professionals.

Bibliography

Trattner, *Biographical Dictionary of Social Welfare in America*, pp. 124–26.

Breckinridge, Sophonisba Preston

educator, social worker, political activist, author
b. April 1, 1866; d. July 30, 1948

Breckinridge was a central figure in the social welfare reform community that flourished in the Chicago area in the late nineteenth and early twentieth centuries. A resident of the Chicago settlement **Hull House**, she was involved in a number of reform crusades. Her career exemplified the ways in which research, social reform, and philanthropy were woven together during the Progressive Era. This convergence of scholarship and social action forms a leitmotiv in the career of Sophonisba Breckinridge, a key figure in transforming social work into a professional career.

Descended from a prominent Kentucky family, Breckinridge graduated from Wellesley College in 1888 and worked for a short time as a high school mathematics teacher. In 1894, she became the first woman to successfully pass Kentucky's bar examination. However, her law practice did not flourish, and this failure only added to her general sense of unhappiness and discontent. At the suggestion of a former Wellesley classmate, she accepted a position as secretary to Marion Talbot, dean of women at the University of Chicago, which offered scholarships to women graduate students and provided a supportive environment. Breckinridge won a fellowship in political science, and in 1901, she became the first woman in the United States to be awarded a Ph.D. in political science.

Three years later, Breckinridge graduated from the university's law school and began teaching family law and family economics in the newly founded Department of Household Administration, which Talbot headed. By 1907, she was also teaching at the Chicago School of Civics and Philanthropy, a private training school for social workers that was founded by **Graham Taylor**, the head resident of the **Chicago Commons** settlement.

As a result of her research into the legal aspects of the employment of women, Breckinridge had become interested in the work of the **Women's Trade Union League** around 1907. This association brought her into contact with Chicago's busy social reform community, which was based at Hull House, and until 1920, she spent at least part of each year as a resident at the settlement.

Her association with Hull House influenced Breckinridge's research interests, which became increasingly concerned with social conditions and with the impact of the urban environment on the family. Working as a Chicago city health inspector, Breckinridge investigated tenement conditions, and as a probation officer for the Chicago Juvenile Court, she re-

searched the juvenile court movement. Breckinridge served on the executive committee of the Illinois **Consumers' League** and as an advisor to both **Julia Lathrop** and **Grace Abbott** when they each headed up the **United States Children's Bureau**. She was also a member of the National Association for the Advancement of Colored People (NAACP) and the secretary of Chicago's Immigrants' Protection League. (*See* **Immigrants' Service League**.)

Breckinridge also found time in her busy schedule to devote herself to a variety of causes related to women. In 1911, she served as vice-president of the National American Woman Suffrage Association. She fought for economic equality for women and helped to draft bills that would regulate women's wages and hours of employment. In 1912, she worked to ensure the Progressive Party's endorsement of these same issues.

By 1920, Breckinridge and her associate **Edith Abbott** had assumed control of the Chicago School of Civics and Philanthropy and made arrangements for the school to be absorbed by the University of Chicago as its new **Graduate School of Social Service Administration**. Abbott served as dean and Breckinridge held the position of Samuel Deutsch Professor of Public Welfare Administration. The two women worked to fashion the school into a bridge between the university and the community, and they made it into a model professional school for the emerging field of social work.

During this period, Breckinridge concentrated on her scholarly research and teaching. Her writings of the late 1920s and early 1930s reflected her belief that if comprehensive social welfare programs were to succeed, the federal and state governments must play a prominent role. This position gained favor during the New Deal. Beginning in the mid–1930s, enrollment at the Chicago School of Social Service Administration increased as graduates fanned out across the United States to work in flourishing public welfare programs.

It was through her teaching that Breckinridge exerted her greatest influence on the field of social work. She and Edith Abbott believed that social workers must be professionally trained. Toward this end, they created a broad-based curriculum designed to move social workers beyond the narrowly conceived role they occupied as charity technicians into a broader arena in which they could function in the dual capacity of social researchers and social welfare administrators. The two women contributed to the social work literature by writing books and articles; through the professional journal they started in 1927, the *Social Service Review;* and by editing a series of books on social service which were published by the University of Chicago Press.

Breckinridge officially retired from the University of Chicago in 1942, but she continued to write and edit scholarly journals until shortly before her death in 1948. Although Breckinridge made a number of contributions to the social welfare efforts of her time, perhaps her most important contribution was preparing young women and men for social work professions.

Bibliography

Costin, *Two Sisters for Social Justice; Notable American Women, 1607–1950*, vol. 1, pp. 111–12; Trattner, *Biographical Dictionary of Social Welfare in America*, pp. 126–29; Wade, *Graham Taylor: Pioneer for Social Justice, 1851–1938.*

Brewster, Mary Maud
nurse, social reformer
b. [n.d.] ; d. 1895

Mary Brewster may not be as well known as her colleague **Lillian Wald**, but she made a significant contribution to the field of public health nursing. She and Wald established the **Visiting Nurse Service** of New York, and although she died shortly after the Nurses' Settlement (*see* **Henry Street Settlement**) was opened, Brewster served as an inspiration to other young women.

Tall, fair-haired, and blue-eyed, Mary Brewster was a descendant of the Pilgrim leader, the Reverend William Brewster. She was raised in Montrose, New Jersey, where her father, Andrew Jackson Brewster, was a blacksmith and a church elder.

Brewster was a classmate of Lillian Wald at the School of Nursing of New York Hospital. During their 18-month training program, the two women became close friends. Although she was not a robust individual (she was frequently described as "fragile"), Brewster shared Wald's enthusiasm and her desire to be of use to others.

It was Wald who actually convinced Brewster to become involved in reform efforts. After graduating from nursing school, Wald taught a class for immigrant women on home health care and hygiene. This teaching experience brought Wald face-to-face with the shocking conditions that so many immigrants were forced to endure in the filthy, overcrowded tenements. Although she was appalled at what she witnessed, Wald was also energized by the possibility of being able to do something to improve the situation.

Once she made up her mind to improve the lives of the poor, Wald recruited Brewster to her cause. The two women decided that the best way for them to accomplish their goal was to live among the poor and nurse them in their own homes. After securing the financial backing of Mrs. Solomon Loeb and her son-in-law, **Jacob Schiff**, Brewster and Wald went to live at the **College Settlement** on Rivington Street on New York's Lower East Side early in 1893. By September of that year, they had moved to the top floor of a tenement on nearby Jefferson Street.

Every morning Wald and Brewster set out from their small apartment to visit the homes of their neighbors. They attended to the sick, often making arrangements for the gravely ill to be seen by a doctor or admitted to a nearby hospital. At night they wrote up their case files. Although others joined Wald and Brewster, it was primarily the two of them who made the daily visits to their sick neighbors to care for them and to train their families to do the same.

Sometime in 1894, Brewster broke down from the strain of the work. Wald attempted to care for her colleague in addition to her other responsibilities. However, Brewster's condition worsened, and she was forced to spend some time in the hospital to regain her health.

Brewster was able to return to work in 1895, shortly after the nursing service had acquired larger quarters and established itself as the Nurses' Settlement at 265 Henry Street. Although she and Wald now had a staff of 11 nurses at the settlement, Brewster's health was too fragile for her to resume her responsibilities, and she was forced to retire only a few months after the Henry Street headquarters opened. Brewster died a few months later, but in her short life she managed to make a major improvement in the provision of health care to the poor.

Bibliography

Daniels, *Always a Sister: The Feminism of Lillian D. Wald*; Duffus, *Lillian Wald: Neighbor and Crusader*; Siegel, *Lillian Wald of Henry Street*; Williams, *Lillian Wald: Angel of Henry Street*; Woods, *The Settlement Horizon*.

Brooks, John Graham
clergyman, social science researcher, author, social reformer
b. July 19, 1846; d. February 8, 1938.

Like many other clergymen of his time, John Graham Brooks was concerned with more than just the spiritual well-being of his parishioners. This interest led him into a career in social welfare reform. Brooks took a practical approach to social reform efforts and recognized the value of employing organizations such as settlements, labor unions, and consumers' leagues to accomplish change.

Born and raised in Acworth, New Hampshire, Brooks graduated from Kimball Union Academy of Meriden, New Hampshire, in 1866 and intent on a career in the law, enrolled in the University of Michigan Law School. After only one year he left Michigan to attend Oberlin College (1869–1871) before going on to the Harvard Divinity School to prepare for the Unitarian Ministry. Brooks earned the S.T.B. degree in 1875 and was ordained the same year. Until 1882 he served the First Religious Society in Roxbury, Massachusetts, as a Unitarian minister.

While a student at Harvard, Brooks attended a lecture on the eight-hour day by the labor organizer George E. McNeill which aroused an interest in economics and labor issues. Although he was committed to his ministerial responsibilities, Brooks felt compelled to understand more than just the spiritual aspects of people's lives. Toward this end, he organized economics and history classes for workers in 1878. Two years later, he married Helen Lawrence Washburn, who also shared his interest in social reform work.

Brooks left Massachusetts in 1882 and spent the next three years in Europe. He attended the universities of Berlin, Jena, and Freiburg. He also had contact with various labor groups in France, Belgium, England, and Germany. After returning to the United States, Brooks assumed a pastorate in Brockton, Massachusetts, and once again, he organized discussion classes for workers. In addition, he lectured on socialism at Harvard. In 1887, Brooks delivered a lecture, "Labor Organizations, Their Political and Economic Service to Society" at a meeting of the American Social Science Association.

Eventually, Brooks's interest in labor and economics became dominant, and he left the ministry in 1891 to devote himself to the study of labor relations. He lived in Boston, and over the next 40 years he was in demand as a lecturer as he traveled across the United States investigating labor issues. In his work, Brooks emphasized the value of personal interviews and firsthand observation in working with labor issues.

In addition to his investigative work, Brooks published a number of books including *Compulsory Insurance in Germany* (1893), a study of the growth of Germany's social security legislation; *The Social Unrest* (1903), the story of the growth of American socialism; *American Syndicalism* (1913), an examination of the background of the Industrial Workers of the World (IWW) movement; and *Labor's Challenge to the Social Order* (1920), which advocated accepting unskilled workers into trade unions.

Brooks was impressed with the work being accomplished by the New York **Consumers' League**, which was organized in 1891. He was instrumental in establishing consumers' leagues in Boston and Chicago in 1897. The following year a call came for members of the Boston League to form a federation that would help ensure uniform safety and sanitary standards for women and children workers in the garment trade and in retail stores. In May 1898, representatives from the Chicago, Boston, New York, and Philadelphia leagues met in New York City to lay the groundwork for a national organization, including drawing up a constitution and agreeing on the basics of labeling goods.

The following year the representatives met in New York again to ratify the proposals presented at the previous meeting. The group agreed to call itself the National Consumers' League. **Florence Kelley**, formerly the chief factory inspector for the state of Illinois, was elected general secretary. Brooks became president of the organization, a position he held until 1915.

After stepping down as president, Brooks remained active in the National Consumers' League. He also continued to write and to deliver lectures for special interest groups such as the League for Political Education in New York City and at the University of California. After 1920, health problems compelled him to limit his activities. He died in 1938 after a long illness.

Bibliography

Dictionary of American Biography, supl. 2, pp. 66–67; Trattner, *Biographical Dictionary of Social Welfare in America*, pp. 140–42.

Brooks, Phillips
clergyman, social activist
b. December 13, 1835; d. January 23, 1893.

Many young men and women were drawn to the settlement movement and to other social reform crusades by a religious impulse to assist the needy. Phillips Brooks was one of the most dynamic spiritual leaders of the time, and his call for the recognition of one's social responsibility inspired many people to become actively involved in social reform.

A descendant of two prominent Massachusetts families, Brooks was born in Boston and studied at the Boston Latin School. He graduated from Harvard in 1854 and took a job as a teacher at the Latin School. His teaching career was short and disastrous. An intensely spiritual young man, he decided to enter the Episcopal seminary in Alexandria, Virginia.

Ordained in the summer of 1859, Brooks began his ministry as a deacon at the Church of the Advent in Philadelphia. From the beginning, the parishioners were impressed with his oratory. Three years later Brooks became rector of Holy Trinity in Philadelphia. He attained prominence as a result of two sermons he preached in 1865—both of which were commented on in the local press. One was delivered in Philadelphia, where the body of Abraham Lincoln was lying in state at Independence Hall, and the second was delivered at Harvard on commemoration day to honor graduates who had died during the Civil War.

In 1869 after traveling in Europe, Brooks became rector of Trinity Church in Boston. A commanding figure who stood over six feet three inches tall and was an insightful and powerful orator, Brooks soon aroused public interest, and during his years in Boston, large crowds came to hear him preach. In October 1891, Brooks was consecrated Bishop of the Diocese of Boston; he died only 15 months later after a short illness.

Sensitive to the spiritual currents of the time, Brooks was influenced by the work of the Christian Socialist **Frederick Denison Maurice** among others. In the tradition of the Christian Socialists, he preached the **Social Gospel,** urging business owners to adopt a more Christian attitude toward their employees. He called on churches to realize the importance of their worldly duties as well as their spiritual obligations.

Brooks had an important influence on many social reformers including **Vida Scudder** and **Mary Simkhovitch**. Both of these women had heard Brooks preach at Trinity Church and were personally inspired by him to become involved in settlement house work. In fact, Brooks's biggest contribution to the settlement movement was the spiritual dimension he inspired in those who dedicated themselves to settlement work and to other social welfare reform efforts.

Bibliography
Dictionary of American Biography, vol. 2, pp. 83–88.

C

Charities *See* The *Survey*

Charities and The Commons
See The *Survey*

Charities Review *See* The *Survey*

Charity Organization Society

With the advent of the Charity Organization Society (COS) movement in the United States in the 1880s, philanthropy began to emerge as what one historian has described as a "science of therapeutics." Sentimental alms-giving was gradually replaced by a more scientific, systematic approach that provided for registration, investigation, and cooperation among relief agencies.

In the United States, this new age of philanthropy began in Buffalo, New York, when in December 1877, S. Humphries Gurteen, an English Episcopal clergyman, organized the Buffalo Charity Organization Society. Conceived in response to the economic crisis of the 1870s and the social dislocation occasioned by the growth of industrial centers after the Civil War, Gurteen's relief agency was intended to eliminate the existing system of chaotic relief policies of municipal and private charities that, according to many, encouraged dependency and

fraud. These new organizations did not dispense relief themselves. Instead, they served as clearinghouses for the charitable organizations already at work in the community. Their goal was self-sufficiency as a way to eliminate poverty.

The Buffalo society was modeled after the London Society for Organizing Charitable Relief and Repressing Mendicancy, which had been established in 1869. The London society evolved out of social experiments and church-related programs that had been organized in the opening decades of the nineteenth century. In the 1820s, the Scottish clergyman Thomas Chalmers divided his Glasgow parish into districts, each under the supervision of a deacon. The poor were encouraged to cultivate thrifty habits and to use the example of the deacons and middle-class visitors who went out among them. This concept of a **friendly visitor** was employed in other countries as well.

The New York **Association for Improving the Condition of the Poor** (AICP) founded in 1843, for example, relied on the services of friendly visitors who investigated and evaluated appeals for assistance. The AICP viewed itself in some measure as a regulatory body, although it was never entirely successful in coordinating the relief services of all of New York City's charities. With the institution of the poor-relief program in Elberfeld, Germany, in the 1850s, another important element of the later COS philosophy was initiated. In this instance, visiting was considered a compulsory civic responsibility, and visitors met regularly to discuss their charges. These meetings anticipated the case conference approach eventually employed by later Charity Organization Societies.

A final important influence on the COS movement was the work of **Edward Denison** and **Octavia Hill** in England during the 1860s. Denison gave witness to his ideal of personal service by going to live among the London poor and trying to reform them by his example. Hill's rent collection program employed both paid and volunteer workers as friendly visitors.

Key elements from all of these previous efforts found their way into the Charity Organization Society approach to relief work in the United States. The systematic application of the more business-like objective principles of investigation, evaluation, and coordination was coupled with the concept of the individual worker, either paid or voluntary, whose friendly visits served as a manifestation of individual duty. These visitors provided the personal contact between the rich and the poor that the leaders of the COS movement considered vital. This contact was intended to influence the character of the poor and to stimulate their ambition to improve their lives. Character building, in their minds, should take precedence over almsgiving. Most COS workers believed that poverty was due to a moral deficit and that once this deficit was corrected, the poor could become productive members of society.

The COS concept was quickly adopted by other communities in the United States that were experiencing a similar social relief crisis. Within five years of the founding of the Buffalo society, similar agencies were established in New Haven and Philadelphia (1878); Boston, Cincinnati, and Brooklyn (1879); and New York (1882). Twenty years later, 92 societies were servicing more than 11 million people in large urban centers along the East Coast and in the Midwest.

Organized charity not only was a more efficient mechanism for ensuring that the deserving poor received the assistance they needed, but it also functioned as an instrument of social control, providing the middle and upper classes with a safeguard against the possibility of violent class antagonism and urban anarchy. The COS ideal was to duplicate the social patterns of a small village in which the primary group exercised powerful social controls. Later on, settlement workers pursued a similar path and worked to reestablish the neighborhood, which they believed had been destroyed by the growth of industrial cities.

Gradually, the COS point of view regarding the moral condition of the poor was replaced by a realization on the part of many charitable agencies that the social and economic causes of poverty were much more significant than any personal inadequacies. By the late 1880s, the emphasis in relief work began to shift away from reliance on voluntary friendly visitors.

At about this time, settlement houses were being established in larger cities such as Boston, Chicago, and New York. In contrast to COS volunteers, settlement workers tended to look at the social and economic conditions in large industrialized cities for an explanation of the substandard conditions people were living in, rather than at the moral condition of the individuals. Settlement workers wanted to improve living and working conditions by actually sharing in the lives of the poor, not by just providing a good moral example as the friendly visitors had. The work of the settlement residents may be characterized as a transitional phase in social welfare work between the COS volunteer and the professionally trained social worker. Settlement workers employed some of the techniques used by the COS workers such as investigating conditions, evaluating requests for assistance, and coordinating their efforts; however, they also took the process one step further, and eventually, many settlement workers were involved in the campaign to create a cadre of professionally educated social workers who were better equipped to deal with the real causes of poverty.

For a time, Charity Organization Society workers, settlement workers, and trained social workers coexisted, each supplying services to those in need and often combining their efforts. In some cities Charity Organization Societies continued to operate well into the 1930s.

Bibliography

Jackson, *Encyclopedia of New York City*, p. 201; Lubove, *The Professional Altruist: The Emergence of Social Work as a Career, 1880–1930*; Trattner, *From Poor Law to Welfare State: A History of Social Welfare in America*.

Chicago Association of Neighborhood Workers *See* Association of Neighborhood Workers (Chicago)

Chicago Bureau of Charities

See Chicago Relief Society

Chicago Central Relief
Association *See* Chicago Relief Society

Chicago Civic Federation *See*
Civic Federation of Chicago

Chicago Commons
Modeled on **Hull House**, the settlement founded by **Jane Addams** and **Ellen Gates Starr** in 1889, Chicago Commons, which was also located in Chicago, was both representative of and unique among American settlement houses: representative because it offered a wide range of services to the neighborhood; unique because its residents were particularly active in local politics, and because its founder and first head resident, **Graham Taylor**, and his family lived in the settlement.

In 1894, Graham Taylor was a professor of Christian Sociology at the Chicago Theological Seminary. He was aware of the work being accomplished by Jane Addams and her colleagues at Hull House, and he was interested in establishing a settlement to provide his students with practical experience in social welfare reform work.

In May 1894, Taylor and three of his students established a settlement called Chicago Commons on Union Street in the northwest section of Chicago. The people in the neighborhood surrounding Chicago Commons were primarily Irish, German, and Scandinavian immigrants. Within five months, the house had a staff of eight men and four women. The following June, Taylor, his wife, and their children went to live in the settlement house. Eventually, two of the Taylor children became active in the settlement movement. **Graham Romeyn Taylor** joined the editorial staff of the social welfare journal the *Survey*, and **Lea Demarest Taylor** succeeded her father as head resident of Chicago Commons in 1922.

In addition to providing a kindergarten and a day nursery, the settlement offered an array of clubs and classes. Chicago Commons opened a playground and secured a municipal bath for the community. The residents worked for better street lighting and refuse collection. The house also served as a site for the Chicago **Visiting Nurse Association**.

Taylor and the other residents of Chicago Commons were very interested in local politics. The settlement house served as a branch of the Municipal Voter's League and offered meeting space to a variety of municipal and political reform organizations. Its residents organized a nonpartisan political club, the Seventeenth Ward Civic Federation, later know as the Seventeenth Ward Community Club. They worked to defeat the local ward bosses in various elections by sponsoring and supporting reform candidates.

Many of the settlement residents served as ward inspectors, public school teachers, and probation officers. Among his many other activities, Taylor served on the board of directors of the Chicago Public Library. Within five years, Chicago Commons outgrew its original quarters. A new L-shaped, five-story brick building, equipped with a modern gymnasium and a large auditorium, was constructed.

In the opening decades of the twentieth century, the Chicago Commons settlement responded to the changing ethnic makeup of the surrounding neighborhood as Italians and Poles, Mexicans, and blacks moved to the area and called upon the staff for assistance. During these years, the house modified the focus of its offerings as it moved away from traditional clubs and classes toward group activities and family service programs. By instituting these changes, each responding to the needs of its neighbors, Chicago Commons was able to continue to serve the local community, which it continues to do up to the present, thus providing an example of what a settlement was intended to be—an integral element of the community.

Bibliography
Melvin, *American Community Organizations: An Historical Dictionary*, pp. 26-28; Wade, *Graham Taylor: Pioneer for Social Justice, 1851–1938*; Woods, *The Handbook of Settlements*.

Chicago Institute of Social Science *See* Graduate School of Social
Service Administration (Chicago)

Chicago Relief Society
Like the **Association for Improving the Condition of the Poor** (AICP) in New York City, the Chicago Relief Society (CRS) was formed to control the duplication of effort among relief programs. The work of the CRS reflected the unique way in which the city of Chicago responded to the need to assist its poorer citizens.

In the middle of the nineteenth century, a cholera epidemic and the demands of an ever-increasing number of new immigrants placed a severe strain on the resources of the Chicago municipal authorities who eventually refused to provide any relief grants. In response, a group of private citizens established the Chicago Relief Society, which was founded in December 1850 and was intended to provide temporary relief and advice to those whom it determined were among the worthy poor. Assistance was provided in the form of clothing, food, and fuel. The society's founders forbade the distribution of money under any circumstances.

Like similar organizations operating in other urban centers at the time, such as the New York AICP, the society attempted to systematize the work of Chicago's various charities. Toward this end, it divided the city into districts and sections, each of which was under the direction of a volunteer who was charged with investigating applications for aid.

Although the CRS was initially a success, it was discontinued in 1851 when county relief payments were reinstated. During the financial panic of 1857, the society was reactivated as the Chicago Relief and Aid Society (CRA) and provided assistance only to the sick and those who were temporarily in need. As soon as the immediate crisis subsided, the CRA became inactive again.

Even though relief agencies such as the CRS and the CRA received the support and financial backing of prominent citizens, they were not as long-lived as relief agencies in other cities such as the New York AICP. Rather, they were activated in response to a crisis and allowed to suspend operations once the immediate need had been met. However, this did not mean that the organizations were allowed to suspend operations completely. They continued at a minimal operating level until the next crisis.

In response to the movement for scientific philanthropy, the first **Charity Organization Society** (COS) in Chicago was established in 1883. Four years later, the COS merged with the Chicago Relief and Aid Society (CRA). The director of the CRA, Charles Trusdale, did not subscribe to one of the fundamental tenets of the COS's approach to relief—cooperation among philanthropic organizations. He viewed the COS as a rival organization and when he realized that he could not gain control of the COS, he withheld his cooperation. As a result of Trusdale's attitude, for several years Chicago had no active Charity Organization Society.

Members of the Chicago Central Relief Association Philanthropic Department established the Central Relief Association in the winter of 1893–1894 as a stopgap measure to meet the crisis of the depression of that year. The Central Relief Association was guided by Mrs. **Lucy Flower**, a member of the Chicago school board and an advocate of industrial training schools.

Over the course of five months, the association processed almost 28,000 applications for relief. **Graham Taylor**, head resident of the **Chicago Commons** settlement, was a member of the Philanthropic Department of the **Civic Federation**, and he participated in the claims processing procedure. The Central Relief Association raised and distributed $135,000 in addition to distributing food and coal. In addition to dispensing aid, the association also established sewing rooms for women and gave men jobs as street sweepers. An effort was made to place qualified workers in a variety of jobs. Its operations were conducted according to the principles of scientific charity, and the association kept careful records to avoid duplication with other city relief agencies.

Three years later, the Central Relief Association became a permanent organization and was renamed the Bureau of Associated Charities. Over the next decade the bureau's operations were expanded. After Trusdale's death in 1903, the remaining directors of the Chicago Relief and Aid Society were more amenable to sharing their resources, and in 1909, the Chicago Relief and Aid Society merged with the Bureau of Associated Charities to form the United Charities of Chicago.

This new agency was headed by Sherman Kingsley, who involved the United Charities in a number of preventative crusades such as the pure milk movement and the antituberculosis campaign. The organization's new board included **Jane Addams**, **Louise DeKoven Bowen**, and **Anita McCormick Blaine**. United Charities encouraged cooperation among Chicago's existing charities. It emphasized the need for personal involvement and stressed the need for careful investigation and meticulous record keeping. To accomplish its work, the United Charities relied on a corps of **friendly visitors** who, like their counterparts in other cities, spent time getting to know those who requested aid.

Like its predecessor the Chicago Relief Society, the United Charities was concerned with coordinating relief efforts throughout the city. The formulation of a more permanent relief agency such as the United Charities illustrates the way in which the city of Chicago modified its views regarding the provision of relief services. The United Charities was a permanent, consistently active organization that did not come to life only in times of crisis. Rather it attempted to provide consistent service to the citizens of Chicago.

Bibliography

Brown, James, *The History of Public Assistance in Chicago, 1833–1893*; Kusmer, "The Functions of Organized Charity in the Progressive Era: Chicago as a Case Study"; McCarthy, *Noblesse Oblige: Charity and Cultural Philanthropy in Chicago, 1849–1929*; Small, "The Civic Federation of Chicago, A Study in Social Dynamics"; Sutherland, *Fifty Years on the Civic Front*.

Chicago School of Civics and Philanthropy *See* Graduate School of Social Service Administration (Chicago)

Child Welfare

During the nineteenth century a variety of "child-saving" initiatives were undertaken in the United States, particularly in cities, to rescue children from poverty. Some of these efforts were concerned with the child's spiritual well-being, and city missions and Sunday schools were established to develop this well-being. Other efforts dealt with children's physical needs and included denominational orphanages, children's aid societies, and social settlements.

By the 1890s the welfare of the nation's children had become a central concern of social reformers. Up to this time, the various child-saving activities had been the responsibility of religious organizations, which sponsored orphanages or foster care programs, but the care was often inadequate. Children in orphanages were frequently subjected to harsh discipline, and those in foster care were often accepted only if they could work for the families with whom they were placed.

Reformers, however, began to question these methods and looked for alternatives. One such alternative in foster care placement was developed by the **Boston Children's Aid Society** under the direction of Charles Birtwell. Birtwell's philosophy of foster care focused on the particular needs of the individual child. His child-centered approach was adopted by **Homer Folks** when Folks was serving as the general agent of the Children's Aid Society of Pennsylvania. Gradually, others followed the example of Birtwell and Folks, and the emphasis turned from placing children in institutional care such as orphanages toward placing them in foster homes, which were carefully selected and monitored to meet the needs of the child.

The methods for dealing with dependent children were eventually extended to delinquent children. Reformers were increasingly concerned about the negative impact of placing delinquent children in facilities with adult offenders, and special courts were set up to handle juvenile offenders. The establishment of the Chicago Juvenile Court is an example of this modified approach. In 1899, members of the Chicago Women's Club secured a separate juvenile court system for youthful offenders. This system did not operate as a criminal court. Instead, whenever possible, children were returned to the care of their parents under the condition that they worked with a court-appointed probation officer. The settlement workers at the Chicago settlement **Hull House** were intimately involved in the creation of the juvenile court system. Additionally, they were members of the Juvenile Court Committee, which was established under the guidance of **Julia Lathrop**, a Hull House resident. This committee helped to raise funds to pay the salaries of juvenile court probation officers. Eventually, juvenile court systems based on this model were established in other cities

Child welfare reformers were particularly active in the child labor reform crusade. One settlement worker who took a leading role in this area was **Florence Kelley**, who had witnessed firsthand the cost of child labor in terms of sickness, disability, crime, and pauperism. Kelley drew attention to child labor issues while working as a factory inspector in Illinois. At this time, she fought to prohibit the employment of children under 14 at night and to restrict the total number of hours they worked per day to eight.

Kelley continued to fight for child workers when she became head of the National **Consumers' League** in 1899. Under the league's regulations, the manufacturers had to prohibit child labor to earn the right to display the prestigious Consumers' League Label in their garments.

Reformers' interest in child welfare led to a number of social investigations. One example was the survey of settlement club leaders that resulted in the publication of *Young Working Girls* by the **National Federation of Settlements** in 1913.

Eventually, all the reformers' research and the community organizations they formed created enough interest in child welfare that it became an issue on the national level. A number of prominent social workers, including Kelley, **Lillian Wald**, and **Jane Addams**, were involved in the **White House Conference on Dependent Children**, which was called by President Theodore Roosevelt in 1909. This conference was significant because it brought the work of child welfare workers into the national spotlight and acknowledged that the federal government was responsible in matters related to the social welfare of all citizens, including children.

Another significant outcome of the child welfare efforts of settlement workers and other social reformers was the establishment of the **United States Children's Bureau** in 1912. The bureau was a national commission intended to collect, analyze, and interpret information related to children. Under the guidance of Julia Lathrop and the social activist **Grace Abbott**, it conducted extensive social investigations whose findings contributed to the passage of the **Sheppard-Towner Act** (1921), which provided funding for maternal and infant health care.

Settlement workers and other Progressive Era reformers made significant strides toward raising the standard of living of children in the United States. The care and treatment of children in orphanages and in foster care was more carefully maintained as the child-centered approach to care gained acceptance. In addition, delinquent children were no longer treated as adults by the court system and were provided with a juvenile court system that sought to reform children rather than incarcerate them. Significant strides were made in regard to child labor as well. New laws prohibited children from working in certain trades, and the number of hours they could work was curtailed. Perhaps most important, settlement workers and their reformer colleagues pressured the federal government to acknowledge its responsibility for the social welfare of children through the White House Conference on Dependent Children and the establishment of the United States Children's Bureau. *See also* **Boston Children's Aid Society; Juvenile Protective Association; National Child Labor Committee; New York Child Labor Committee.**

Bibliography

Axinn, *Social Welfare: A History of the American Response to Need*; Bremner, *From the Depths: The Discovery of Poverty in the United States*; Davis, *Spearheads for Reform: The Social Settlements and the Progressive Movement, 1890–1914*; Leiby, *A History of Social Welfare and Social Work in the United States*.

Christian Socialism

The English and American Settlement Movements evolved from the heterogeneous reform crusades of the nineteenth century. Anxious about the disruption and the emphasis on materialism that industrialization wrought, particularly in urban centers, many reformers sought ways to restore a sense of spiritual value to people's lives. The Christian Socialist revival of the 1880s seemed to many to provide a blueprint for action.

In simplest terms, the doctrine of Christian Socialism advocated applying Christianity to social problems. The term *Christian Socialism* was first used around 1848 by a small group of young men in London who recognized **Frederick Denison Maurice** as their spiritual guide. Maurice entered the Church of England in 1831 and was ordained three years later. He wrote a number of articles on religious and social questions which attracted the attention of a wide audience and laid the foundation for his later theology. Maurice served as chaplain of Lincoln's Inn between 1846 and 1859, and during this time he became acquainted with a young English lawyer named John Malcolm Ludlow.

Ludlow, considered the originator of the Christian Socialist Movement in England, held strong religious convictions that he combined with an interest in solving social problems. He lived for a time in Paris and was acquainted with French Socialism. As a result, Ludlow became interested in the relationship between socialism and Christianity.

While they were both associated with Lincoln's Inn, Ludlow had a number of discussions with Maurice. One result of their interaction was the establishment of a system of visiting poor neighborhoods and distributing relief, which was undertaken by a group of students from Lincoln's Inn. Eventually, elementary day and evening schools were established. This was an independent program undertaken by the students and not related to any existing religious charity organization. Those involved in the visiting and relief work met at Maurice's home each week for discussion and religious fellowship.

Ludlow and Maurice were joined by **Charles Kingsley**, an author and clergyman from Eversley, Hampshire, whose social reform sentiments had been awakened by the Chartist movements (1836–1848), which called for democratic social and political reform in England, including equal participation by all adult males in the affairs of state. During the 1850s, the three men formed study clubs, conducted classes in slum areas, worked for sanitary reforms, formed a society for promoting workingmen's associations, and established a workingmen's college.

For Ludlow, Kingsley, and Maurice, socialism was primarily a religious movement. They focused their attention on what they considered were neglected aspects of the church's social responsibilities. Their aim was not to reform society according to socialist principles but to realign socialism with Christian principles.

The late 1880s witnessed a renewed interest in the doctrines of Christian Socialism. This revival was dominated by the high church clergy through the work of a number of organizations, the most powerful of which was the Christian Social Union founded in 1889 by Charles Gore and **Henry Scott Holland**. The union's objectives included proclaiming Christian law as the ultimate authority over social practice and applying the moral truths and principles of Christianity to the social and economic difficulties of the present time. It emphasized that reformers must anchor their convictions in a strong faith, which could then be translated into direct social action. It carefully distanced itself from other socialist doctrines that emphasized state ownership or worker control.

The marriage of Christianity and socialism was taken up in the United States by Reverend **William Dwight Porter Bliss**. Bliss, like most later Christian Socialists and especially those in the United States, where the concept of class struggle was never fully embraced, was more concerned with the sentimental aspects of socialism—cooperation and brotherhood—than with the more radical aspects—collective ownership of land and capital.

The Christian Socialist doctrine was especially appealing to the young women and men who became active in the American Settlement Movement. Although they may not have identified themselves as Christian Socialists, they subscribed to many of the doctrines that Maurice, Ludlow, Kingsley, and later Gore and Holland espoused. These settlement workers also believed that it was their Christian duty to help those who were less fortunate, not only by distributing immediate relief but also by working to change the social and economic systems that had produced the inequalities between the rich and the poor. In this way, the doctrines of the Christian Socialists first inspired and then became an integral part of the philosophy of the settlement movement, both in the United States and in England. *See also* **Social Gospel**.

Bibliography

Meacham, *Toynbee Hall and Social Reform, 1880–1914: The Search for Community*; Seligman, *Encyclopedia of the Social Sciences*, vol. 3, pp. 449–52.

The City Wilderness (1898)

Like the ***Hull-House Maps and Papers*** (1895) published by the residents of **Hull House** in Chicago, *The City Wilderness* was a pioneering study of American urban sociology that called attention to the work being accomplished in the settlement houses and that inspired many to become part of the urban social reform crusade. Published in 1898, *The City Wilderness* was a collection of reports and statements that provided a comprehensive evaluation and analysis of the first seven years of operation of the **South End House** settlement in Boston.

Founded in 1891, South End House, originally called Andover House, was Boston's first settlement. **Robert A. Woods** was the house's first head resident and remained in the position until his death in 1925. Woods considered South End House a social science laboratory, and he encouraged the residents to study and record the social and economic conditions of the surrounding community. Later these studies became the basis of the book, for which Woods served both as editor and contributor. The other contributors had all lived in the South End of Boston for a considerable period of time, and all but one were residents of South End House.

Like his English social researcher counterpart **Charles Booth**, Woods studied urban sociology and wrote several books on the subject. His first book, *English Social Movements* (1891), was based on his observations during the year he spent studying English reform movements and settlement houses. *The City Wilderness* was his second book. It includes chapters on population, public health, politics, work and wages, education, religion, crime, and amusements. The text is supplemented by several maps and a diagram. The maps include information on land use and types of buildings and the location of chief institutions (schools, libraries, health facilities) and meeting places (amusements, churches). The diagram includes information on race and nationality. The information for the text and maps which supplement the text was obtained primarily from personal investigation. Official sources, such as the state census, were also consulted.

Overall, these types of works served several purposes. In *The City Wilderness*, for example, Woods and his collaborators exposed the overcrowding and generally unsanitary conditions that the residents of the area were forced to endure. They discussed the corruption of the political bosses and its effect on the city as well as the corrupting influence of certain popular amusements. However, even though much of what is discussed is negative, Woods and the others noted that their work had produced some hope. Thus, *The City Wilderness* served as a model for settlement workers to emulate.

Bibliography

Davis, *Spearheads for Reform: The Social Settlements and the Progressive Movement, 1890–1914*; Melvin, *American Community Organizations: An Historical Dictionary*, pp. 196–98; Woods, *The City Wilderness*.

The City Workers' World in America (1917)

Many settlement workers published studies that provided detailed accounts of the neighborhoods they lived in and of the efforts they made to help the people who lived and worked there. Some of these studies relied on statistics and in-depth surveys. Others were more impressionistic, relying on the retelling of anecdotes and the setting forth of personal philosophies. Regardless of the approach, these studies provide valuable insight into the thought and motivation of settlement workers.

The City Workers' World in America was written in 1917 after **Mary Simkhovitch** had been living and working at **Greenwich House** for 15 years. She describes the book's purpose as an attempt to furnish a "plain description of the facts of the city dweller's life, together with some indication of the evolutionary process going on at the city's heart." Simkhovitch identifies the industrial family as wage earners whose family income is $1,500 annually or less. In the book's 10 chapters she describes the various immigrant groups living in her neighborhood and then goes on to discuss their housing, standard of living, education, work, leisure, politics, and religion.

The purpose of the book was not only to provide factual descriptions based on the author's personal observations, but also to present to the reader some idea of the social values of various immigrant groups. Simkhovitch was interested in discovering these values, working to preserve them, and at the same time, incorporating them into the mainstream of American life. Unlike earlier accounts of the hardships endured by city dwellers such as *How the Other Half Lives* by **Jacob Riis**, *The City Worker's World* was not an attempt to evoke sympathy for its subjects. Rather, Simkhovitch demonstrated a high degree of respect for the working poor.

Bibliography

Simkhovitch, *The City Worker's World in America.*

Civic Federation of Chicago

Like their counterparts in other urban centers, the residents of Chicago were hit hard by the economic depression of 1893. Political corruption and the widespread tolerance of vice seemed to be acceptable to many as essential services and relief assistance to those most in need were not forthcoming. The impact was particularly strong in the overcrowded city neighborhoods where thousands of newly arrived immigrants lived and worked. However, social reformers, particularly those active in the city's settlement community, were grimly aware of the problems of the poor and of the shortcomings of the municipal authorities.

In 1894, a group of concerned Chicago citizens established the Civic Federation to investigate and correct abuses in municipal government and to increase citizens' interest in municipal affairs. Lyman J. Gage served as president of the Civic Federation; Mrs. Potter Palmer was the vice president. **Jane Addams**, the founder of the settlement **Hull House**, was one of the trustees.

The Civic Federation was composed of six principal committees: political, municipal, industrial, moral, education and social, and philanthropic matters. The work of the Civic Federation was carried out by councils, which were established in each of the city's 34 wards.

The federation concentrated its efforts on conducting a campaign for good government. Toward this end, it investigated **prostitution** and saloons in the city, gathered evidence of political corruption, and worked for the passage of laws to regulate elections and to ensure equitable labor practices. In addition, the federation led a campaign to revise the Chicago City Charter and to reform the procedure for the procurement of city contracts. With the assistance of settlement workers and other social reformers in Chicago, the federation achieved a moderate degree of success in eliminating the worst of the corrupt practices that plagued city government.

Bibliography

Small, "The Civic Federation of Chicago: A Study in Social Dynamics."

Civil Liberties Bureau *See*

National Civil Liberties Bureau

Clinics and Dispensaries

The reformers who established settlement houses were concerned with all aspects of the lives of their neighbors, including their health. The influx of new immigrants and the impact of rapid industrialization left cities congested and unsanitary, and these unsafe conditions were further hampered by a lack of adequate health care facilities, especially for the poor. Because of these problems, one of the primary interests for settlement workers and other reformers was providing health care for the neighborhood's residents.

The reformers' approach was two-fold. The settlement workers wanted to institute sanitary improvements in the neighborhoods, such as cleaner streets, adequate light and ventilation in the tenements, and public baths. They were also worried about the physical vitality of their neighbors. Settlement residents cooperated with local health officials to identify individuals with contagious diseases such as tuberculosis and to ensure that they received the proper care. They were also concerned about their neighbors' diets, whether or not they had sufficient exercise, and if their places of employment were safe to work in. Combining the settlement residents' neighborhood work with health care proved to be extremely beneficial to all neighborhood residents.

During the 1890s when settlements were first opening, the residents concentrated their efforts on the most pressing problem—identifying cases of contagious diseases and ensuring that the patients were quarantined and were receiving adequate care. Assisting those most in need was one way the settlement workers could win the trust of their neighbors. To accomplish this, many settlements opened first-aid rooms and referrals were made to nearby clinics, dispensaries, and hospitals.

In some cases, physicians opened offices in or near settlements, often donating several hours of their time each week to settlement-sponsored neighborhood clinics. To meet the needs of their neighbors who worked, many settlements established evening medical and dental clinics.

Settlement workers also realized the importance of carrying out the prescribed treatment after a patient had seen a physician. They were often called upon to assist in childbirth or to supply food or medicine. However, they knew their limitations and recognized the need for employing trained visiting nurses who could ensure adequate follow-up care. The idea of these nursing services was not new, however. In many cities, visiting nurse services pre-dated the settlements and were affiliated with missions and dispensaries. The first visiting nurse service was established in the United States by the women's branch of the New York City Mission in 1877, 10 years before the establishment of the first settlement in the United States.

The Nurses' Settlement (later the **Henry Street Settlement**) was one of the first attempts to coordinate settlement work with health services. Founded by **Lillian Wald** and **Mary Brewster** in New York City in 1895, the Nurses' Settlement was a significant step forward in the provision of home-based health care. Trained nurses from the settlement were dispatched to neighborhoods all over the city. As a result of the success of the Nurses' Settlement and the obvious need for nursing services in most neighborhoods, many other settlements either invited nurses to live in the settlement house or established a formal relationship with the local visiting nurse association to function as a branch office.

Besides providing nursing services and free or low-cost clinics, settlements were at the forefront of the movement to ensure the health of infants and children. They realized the importance of clean milk in the diet, and in fact, one of the first services that most settlements offered their neighbors was a milk station. An important promoter in the crusade for clean milk was the New York City retailer Nathan Straus who established the city's first chain of clean milk stations in 1893. Straus's stations provided pasteurized milk at cost, or gratis when necessary, to tenement residents. Four years later, Dr. George W. Galen, the Rochester, New York Health Officer, organized a series of municipal milk stations in that city. That same year, 1897, the **Northwestern University Settlement** in Chicago purchased milk pasteurizing equipment that enabled the settlement to provide a supply of clean milk to other settlements in the city. In connection with milk stations, many settlements established well baby clinics and clinics specifically intended to treat women and small children.

Settlements also provided classes in first aid and in the elementary care of the sick to assist neighborhood residents in caring for relatives at home. In addition, many settlement clubs sponsored lectures on personal and family hygiene, household management, proper food handling and preparation, and the importance of recreation and exercise.

Providing health care to the residents in their neighborhoods was one of the settlement houses' most vital roles. Initially, the settlements were the only place that many people could turn to for help when they became ill. In addition to nursing the sick and often providing them with a place to stay until they had recovered, the settlement workers arranged for referrals to doctors and hospitals. In this way they established a health care network that their neighbors came to rely upon. Settlement workers also played another important role in the provision of health care by conducting sanitary surveys in their neighborhoods and documenting hazards such as extreme overcrowding, garbage in the streets, inadequate ventilation, and polluted water supplies. They also kept careful records of the incidence of disease and worked with health authorities in times of crisis. These health-related programs were among the most important services sponsored by the settlement houses.

Bibliography

Seligman, *Encyclopedia of the Social Sciences*, vol. 3, pp. 562–67; Woods, *The Settlement Horizon*.

Clubs

It was not enough for young, college-educated men and women to just live among the poor to assist them in improving their lives. To accomplish their goals, the settlement workers had to engage the neighborhood residents in their work. They realized that they could not hope to help people until they earned their trust and respect. One way to become acquainted with the people in the neighborhood was to sponsor a club that would bring residents together in a nonthreatening, social encounter. Thus, the primary purpose of settlement-sponsored clubs was to provide an opportunity for positive social interaction. Secondarily, they provided opportunities for character building by emphasizing discipline, cooperation, and self-respect.

Often, settlements began as informal outreach programs in which a man or woman would move into a neighborhood and open his or her apartment for use by a group of neighborhood children as a clubhouse or as a classroom where particular skills were taught. **John L. Elliott** started the **Hudson Guild** in New York City by sponsoring boys' clubs out of his Chelsea apartment. **Jean Fine** and **Jane E. Robbins** organized girls' clubs when they first moved to New York City's Lower East Side to establish the **College Settlement** on Rivington Street.

Many settlements started their outreach efforts by targeting the boys in the community. At first, settlement workers attempted to assign neighborhood boys more or less arbitrarily to small groups. This was done in part to permit group leaders to get to know the boys better and perhaps more importantly, to prevent the clubs from turning into organized gangs. As settlement-sponsored clubs became more successful, many boys wanted to invite their friends to join. Eventually, the settlement workers realized that it was better to accept the boys' natural alliances and to assign a club leader to work with them and participate in their activities. Club leaders often visited the boys' homes to meet their families and get to know them better. Some settlements extended house privileges only to those clubs that established formal rules and elected officers.

Athletics were central to settlement-sponsored activities for boys. Many settlements maintained a gymnasium, and membership in a club gave one access to these facilities. Settlement clubs for young men in their late teens and early twenties frequently focused more on social activities such as public dances. Although many settlements offered men's clubs that combined recreation and civic activities, for the most part the fathers of families had little time to devote to club activities.

At first, girls seemed to receive less attention from the settlements than boys. Those girls' clubs that were organized were basically classes that taught cooking, sewing, and housekeeping skills. After the **National Federation of Settlements**'s study of girls' clubs, *Young Working Girls: A Summary of Evidence from Two Thousand Social Workers*, appeared in 1913, settlements began to devote more attention to the needs of young girls.

Settlements also sponsored women's clubs, which were particularly useful for the dissemination of information about childbearing, nutrition, and housekeeping. Many of the settlement houses in New York City sponsored a mother's club, which served both a social and an educational function. Many settlements used these clubs to exercise a measure of control over their neighbors and to Americanize the new immigrants. For example, clubs sponsored cooking classes that emphasized the preparation of "American" food. But the clubs also offered neighborhood women an opportunity to come together to discuss common problems and mutual concerns. By working with these women, settlement residents were able to identify their concerns and needs. Through the contacts they established with mothers, the settlement residents were often able to interest the rest of the family in the settlement's other programs.

On May 1912, John L. Elliott of the Hudson Guild called together representatives from the mother's clubs in New York City to form a League of Mother's Clubs. This organization was intended to promote opportunities for friendship, education, and recreation; to provide an understanding of various social reform efforts; and to encourage efforts for securing necessary social welfare legislation.

Working in tandem with the New York Association of Neighborhood Workers (*see* **United Neighborhood Houses**), the League of Mother's Clubs was active in a number of crusades such as public dance hall supervision, the construction of model tenements, the establishment of a minimum wage for women workers, and the enactment of laws to regulate child labor.

Overall, clubs were a vital aspect of settlement work. They provided an opportunity for different groups within the community to take advantage of the settlement house's offerings, and they allowed the settlement workers to get to know the men, women, and children in the neighborhood as individuals. In addition, clubs were a source of individual and community pride and a manifestation of one of the central principles of settlement work: to discover ways in which all members of the community can come together for the collective good. *See also* **Americanization.**

Bibliography

Carson, *Settlement Folk: Social Thought and the American Settlement Movement, 1885–1930*; Woods, *The Settlement Horizon.*

Coit, Stanton

settlement house founder, Ethical Culture Society leader, social reformer
b. August 11, 1857; d. February 15, 1944.

Stanton Coit's primary interest was his involvement in the **Ethical Culture Society** Movement, however, it would not be inaccurate to say that Coit was the founder of the American Settlement Movement even though he himself spent very little time as an active participant in the effort. Coit established the first American settlement house, which he named the Neighborhood Guild (*see* **University Settlement**), and he introduced the idea of making all the residents in the community responsible for their neighborhood.

Born in Columbus, Ohio, Coit was particularly influenced by his mother who abandoned her orthodox Episcopal faith and became an ardent Spiritualist. As a teenager, Coit exhibited an interest in philosophy and was especially drawn to the writings of Ralph Waldo Emerson. Although he was described by some as a pious man, Coit disassociated himself from formal religion while a college student and eventually refined his own synthesis of Emerson, Kant, Coleridge, socialism, and the natural sciences.

After graduating from Amherst College in 1879, Coit joined the faculty there as an English instructor. Two years later, he traveled to New York City to hear **Felix Adler**, the founder of the Ethical Culture Society, deliver a lecture. Coit felt an immediate attachment both to Adler, who was to be an important influence in his life, and to the Ethical Culture Movement. He volunteered his services as a lecturer straightaway and moved to New York City, where he enrolled in Columbia University to prepare himself for his new career.

In 1883 at Adler's suggestion and expense, Coit enrolled at the University of Berlin. There he studied German society and culture, becoming particularly interested in the concept of the positivist state which advanced the idea of the state employing its power to promote the general welfare of people.

In December 1885, Coit earned a Ph.D. He spent the next three months working as a volunteer at **Toynbee Hall** in London before returning to New York to become Adler's assistant. The Ethical Culture philosophy stressed the importance of expressing personal virtue through social service. Coit believed that he could manifest his moral worthiness by engaging in social reform activities such as settlement work even though he was critical of Toynbee Hall for not having more clearly defined goals. Once again he worked out a synthesis of ideas and decided to introduce the settlement concept, in modified form, to the United States.

In 1886, Coit purchased a tenement on New York's Lower East Side and established the Neighborhood Guild. The name Neighborhood Guild described both a physical building and Coit's concept of social reform. Unlike many other reformers at the time, he believed that the potential for leadership was present in the community, and he advocated a system in which residents were organized into guilds of approximately 100 families. These social units could assist residents in developing organizational skills and experiencing the benefits of cooperative activity and social solidarity.

Coit was soon joined by other reformers, among them **Charles B. Stover** and Edward King. They established connections with local labor groups, organized lectures and theatricals, instituted clubs for boys and girls, and established a kindergarten and a gymnasium. At the same time, Coit maintained an active interest in the Ethical Culture Society, which had always been his primary commitment. He was so successful in his efforts on behalf of that movement that he was offered the principal Ethical Culture ministry in England at South Place Chapel, Finsbury, London, and he accepted. While in England, Coit introduced the guild concept, but once again he eventually redirected his energies into the Ethical Culture Society. Coit remained in England for the rest of his life, devoting himself to Ethical Culture work and to encouraging the Church of England to reform itself according to Ethical Culture principles. From time to time, Coit returned to the United States to lecture on social issues.

After he left New York in 1888 to take up his new position, the Neighborhood Guild almost collapsed. However, Stover and King successfully reorganized the guild as the University Settlement in 1891. Although he was not an active participant in the American Settlement Movement for very long, Coit was instrumental in introducing the idea of settlement work to the United States and in providing an organizational construct that provided a place for local residents in the decision-making process.

Bibliography

Blackham, *Stanton Coit, 1857–1944: Selections from his Writings with a Prefatory Memoir*; *Dictionary of American Biography*, supl. 3, pp. 175–76; Melvin, *American Community Organizations: An Historical Dictionary*, pp. 34–35; Trattner, *Biographical Dictionary of Social Welfare in America*, pp. 186–87.

College Settlement (New York)

The women who founded the **College Settlements Association** (CSA) were interested in establishing a network of settlements in urban centers whose work would be coordinated by a national organization. The College Settlement, which was located in a primarily Jewish neighborhood on New York City's Lower East Side, was the first settlement house opened by the association.

The College Settlement opened on September 1, 1889. Modeled after London's **Toynbee Hall**, its purpose was to establish "a home in a neighborhood of working people in which educated women might live, in order to furnish a common meeting ground for all classes for their mutual benefit and education" (*Handbook of Settlements,* p. 193). The first residents were seven recent graduates of Smith, Wellesley, and Vassar. The head resident was **Jean Fine**, who over the course of the next 25 years was succeeded by a number of women who gained prominence in the American Settlement Movement: **Jane E. Robbins**, **Mary Simkhovitch**, and **Elizabeth S. Williams**. The settlement, which was sometimes referred to as the Rivington Street Settlement, was maintained by an annual donation from its sponsoring agency, the College Settlements Association, and by funds raised by the settlement's executive committee. During its first year, more than 80 women applied for residency.

As was true with most settlements, the process of investigation preceded any form of action, and shortly after arriving, the residents initiated a number of inquiries into neighborhood conditions, including a series of sociological studies of the living and working conditions of women and children. These were followed by an analysis of unemployment in 1894, a data collection project on behalf of the **New York City Tenement House Committee** (1894–1900), and an extensive investigation of housing and health conditions for the **Committee on Congestion of Population**'s exhibit, which was organized in 1908 to illustrate the dangers of overcrowding.

Among other projects, the residents of the College Settlement lobbied for better sanitary conditions, provided public baths for women, and set up small libraries in neighborhood public schools. They established a playground in the settlement's rear yard, and between 1897 and 1898, the College Settlement served as the headquarters of the East Side Recreation Society. The house's music school evolved into the Music School Settlement.

The working conditions of neighborhood residents were always a primary concern to the settlement residents. In 1894, the College Settlement provided moral and financial support to local striking garment workers, and for many years fought for enforcement of labor laws in stores and factories.

By 1930, the College Settlement had closed partly because of the changing population in the neighborhood and partly because many pro-

Cooking School in College Settlement (New York)
Museum of the City of New York

grams that it started had been taken over by the municipal and state governments. A decision was made to modify the settlement's mission to provide leisure activities such as teaching art and dramatics, and it eventually reopened uptown as an arts workshop.

Bibliography

Davis, *Spearheads for Reform: The Social Settlements and the Progressive Movement, 1890–1914*; Jackson, *Encyclopedia of New York City*, p. 254; Woods, *The Handbook of Settlements*.

College Settlement (Philadelphia)

The College Settlement in Philadelphia was the second settlement house established by the **College Settlements Association** (CSA). From the time it opened in September 1899, the College Settlement had a significant influence on reform in Philadelphia. The work of the settlement was supported by a grant from the College Settlements Association and by subscriptions (donations or pledges from individuals). **Helena S. Dudley** and **Katherine B. Davis** served as head residents.

The residents of the settlement were active in various crusades throughout their neighborhood of Polish, Italian, and Russian immigrants. One of their campaigns was to secure better housing for the neighborhood and to have the streets paved. They worked closely with the local public school, and several residents were elected to the school board. In addition, the settlement workers took an interest in the work of the city's juvenile courts. They carried on probation work, and through friends of the settlement, provided salaries for probation officers. The settlement workers were also active in local politics, and they took an interest in local labor issues. For example, the house served as strike headquarters during the 1909–1910 shirtwaist makers' strike.

In addition to the reform campaigns, the College Settlement maintained a kindergarten and a bank. It also provided the services of a doctor to the neighborhood residents and offered classes in sewing, cooking, drawing, and gymnastics.

In 1900, the College Settlement was reorganized as the Starr Center. It continued to serve the community by providing a range of services including opening the Casa Ravello Branch in 1907, which was specifically intended to meet the needs of the growing Italian population within the area. In addition, in the fall of 1908, a music school was established. Over time, the settlement's mission was modified to provide for more leisure activities as some of its services such as the library and the bank were taken over by municipal and private agencies.

Bibliography
The College Settlement of Philadelphia: A History; Woods, *The Handbook of Settlements*.

College Settlements Association

In the latter part of the nineteenth century many members of the first generation of college-educated young women were interested in finding meaningful work outside the traditional confines of home and family. Involvement in one of the many social reform crusades of the time promised an opportunity both to enjoy a constructive career and to help others. As a result of traveling and studying abroad, some young women were aware of the developing English Settlement Movement, and they saw the potential for a similar undertaking in the United States.

One young American woman who had observed the work of the English social reformers was **Vida Scudder**, who attended a meeting of the Association of Collegiate Alumni at Smith College in 1885 at which she discussed the idea of establishing a social settlement with two of her former classmates Helen Rand and **Jean Fine**. Two years later, the women founded the College Settlements Association (CSA). They were interested in opening a social settlement that would not only provide assistance to the poor, but would also provide women college graduates with an opportunity to further their education and to engage in meaningful work.

Scudder, Rand, and Fine were joined by other women interested in their project including **Katherine Coman**, Katherine Lee Bates, Cornelia Warren, **Jane E. Robbins**, and **Helena S. Dudley**. In 1889, the CSA established its first settlement, the **College Settlement (New York)**, which was located on Rivington Street on the Lower East Side of New York City. During its first year of operations, 80 women applied to be residents. In 1899, the CSA established the **College Settlement (Philadelphia)**, and three years later, **Denison House** was opened under its auspices in Boston.

In addition to these settlements, the CSA established chapters at other colleges including Wellesley, Vassar, Bryn Mawr, and Harvard Annex (Radcliffe) as well as in girls' finishing schools. It offered fellowships to men and women ranging from $300 to $500 per year to cover the cost of room and lodging at selected settlements. This program was designed to encourage college graduates to become settlement residents and to engage in various social welfare research projects.

One of the most significant features of the College Settlements Association was its intention to oversee and coordinate the work of its various settlements through a national organization. In this capacity, it provided a support network for settlement workers who could share problems and solutions and advise each other on various approaches in dealing with local authorities and other community organizations. The CSA continued to operate during the opening decades of the twentieth century, and although it sponsored a limited number of settlement houses, its fellowship program was highly successfully in financing a variety of important research projects in various settlements.

Bibliography
Carson, *Settlement Folk: Social Thought and the American Settlement Movement, 1885–1930*; Davis, *Spearheads for Reform: The Social Settlements and the Progressive Movement, 1890–1914*; Woods, *The Settlement Horizon*.

Columbia University Graduate School of Social Work

As the belief in the importance of scientific charity gained acceptance in the nineteenth century, reformers sought ways to effectively organize the philanthropic resources of their communities. The acceptance of the scientific casework approach to charity work led to the need to organize a cadre of trained professionals who possessed the necessary specialized knowledge, skills, and techniques to carry out their responsibilities. The development of this professional subculture was made possible in part by the growth of professional training schools. The school that eventually became the Columbia University Graduate School of Social Work is an example of this type of institution.

At the 1897 meeting of the National Conference of Charities and Correction (*see* **National Conference on Social Welfare**), **Mary Richmond** of the Baltimore **Charity Organization Society** read a paper entitled "The Need of a Training School in Applied Philanthropy." In this paper, Richmond maintained that educational opportunities were the way to interest college-educated men and women in social work. Richmond recommended that a school be established in a large city and that, if possible, it have an affiliation with a college or university. Richmond maintained that the school's curriculum should emphasize the practical aspects of social work. To accomplish this goal, the school should cultivate a close working relationship with public and private charities in the surrounding community so that students could engage in social reform work under the supervision of experienced professionals.

Heeding Richmond's call, the New York Charity Organization Society's Committee on Philanthropic Education established the first school of social work in 1898 when it offered a six-week summer School of Philanthropy. The school's program of study was designed to increase the knowledge and efficiency of those in the field, and it included lectures, site visits to public and private agencies, and opportunities for field work.

Philip W. Ayres served as the first director of the school. He was assisted by **Edward T. Devine**, the secretary of the New York Charity Organization Society. A short time later, Devine assumed responsibility for the program, and he introduced a number of modifications. In the fall of 1903, the school offered a three-month course with sessions that met in the late afternoon. The following spring it offered a six-month, full-time training program in social work, which was well received. The New York Charity Organization Society then contributed $250,000 to establish a full-time, permanent training school, which it named the New York School of Philanthropy, and Devine became its first director.

The newly established **Russell Sage Foundation**, which provided funding for social welfare-related projects, was interested in encouraging investigations and research into social problems. Beginning in 1907, the foundation instituted a program offering grants of $10,000 per year to training schools to fund this type of research. The New York School of Philanthropy received annual grants from the Russell Sage Foundation until 1912. During this time the school expanded its program to two years, with the second year providing an opportunity for supervised field work. Students spent 12 hours per week for five months in a clinical experience. They then worked for two months in the district office of the Charity Organization Society before selecting a specialty they wanted to examine.

Following the lead of the **Boston School of Social Work**, the New York School introduced medical social training into the curriculum after 1912. In 1919, the school's name was changed to the New York School of Social Work.

During the 1920s, the school's curriculum moved more and more in the direction of specialization and casework. Although the School of Social Work offered courses in sociology, economics, and political science, these courses were all related to social work methods and techniques. In 1940, the School became the Columbia University Graduate School of Social Work, and it is recognized today as one of the leading institutions of its kind. *See also* **Graduate School of Social Service Administration (Chicago).**

Bibliography

Lubove, *The Professional Altruist: The Emergence of Social Work as a Career, 1880–1930*; Trattner, *From Poor Law to Welfare State: A History of Social Welfare in America.*

Coman, Katherine
educator, social reformer, political activist
b. November 23, 1857; d. January 11, 1915.

Katherine Coman helped to initiate the American Settlement Movement and was responsible for encouraging many young college graduates to become involved in the social welfare crusades of the time. Although she was primarily an academician, her close association with the founders of the **College Settlements Association** (CSA) drew her into the mainstream of settlement work and into a number of allied concerns such as labor reform and social insurance.

Coman's father, Levi Parson Coman, believed in educating his daughter as well as his sons. As a result, Coman was enrolled in the Steubenville (Ohio) Female Seminary in 1873, but when the principal refused to provide her with more advanced work, her father transferred her to the high school of the University of Michigan. The next year she entered the university itself and earned a Ph.D. degree in the spring of 1880. The following fall Coman accepted a position as an instructor of rhetoric at Wellesley College. However, her real interest was in economics, and in 1893, she secured an appointment as a professor of political economy at Wellesley. Seven years later she organized a new department of economics and became professor of economics and sociology, a position she retained until her retirement in 1913.

An author as well as a successful teacher, Coman was deeply religious, having joined **Phillips Brooks**'s Trinity Church when she first moved to Boston. Although she regularly attended socialist meetings, she never joined the Socialist Party. Encouraged by some of her Wellesley colleagues, notably **Vida Scudder** and **Emily Balch**, Coman participated in the social reform movements of her day, employing her organizational and administrative skills for the good of the College Settlements Association in particular.

After the CSA was organized in 1887 by Scudder, Katherine Bates, Helen C. Rand, and **Jean Fine**, Coman proved to be an enthusiastic supporter. She arranged for a close friend, Mrs. Cornelia P. Warren of Boston, to become the association's first major financial contributor. Coman chaired the Boston Settlement Committee, which opened **Denison House** in 1892. Although she was never a resident, she served the house first as secretary, then as chair, and later as a member of the executive committee. Coman enjoyed a close working relationship with **Helena S. Dudley**, the head resident of Denison House.

Coman served as president of the electoral board and chair of the standing committee of the CSA between 1900 and 1907. During this time she was instrumental in the development of the fellowship program that enabled young college graduates to spend a year or more in one of the settlement houses sponsored by the CSA. Coman was also an associate director of CSA from 1911 until 1914.

Coman's participation in the settlement house movement dovetailed with her interest in labor. In 1890, she and Cornelia Warren organized the Thursday Evening Club for women tailors, and she served as the group's first president. An attempt was even made to organize a cooperative tailor shop with Warren, but it failed after only a few months. After Denison House opened, Dudley supported Coman's efforts to make it a center for labor organizing activities.

Coman's interest in improving workers' conditions led her to become involved in a number of other labor-related concerns. She was a charter member of the National **Consumers' League** and was a strong advocate of the league's policy of applying consumer pressure to influence manufacturers. Coman was honorary vice president of the league until her death in 1915. She also served on the executive committee of the league's Boston branch from its inception in 1889 until 1905. While on a visit to Chicago in 1910, Coman supported striking members of the United Garment Workers by writing articles to clarify the basis for the strike and by serving as chair of the Grievance Committee of the **Women's Trade Union League**.

Coman was also interested in the concept of social justice. She volunteered with the **Na-tional Progressive Service** and helped organize the social justice planks of the Progressive Party platform. After retiring from Wellesley, Coman acted on the suggestion of **Jane Addams**, founder of **Hull House**, that she spend the following year (1913–1914) conducting a study of social insurance programs in England, Denmark, Spain, and Sweden. Coman published the results of this study in a series of nine articles on social insurance that appeared in the social welfare journal the *Survey*. In addition, she adapted her findings to American conditions and drafted preliminary social insurance legislation. Her posthumous book, *Unemployment Insurance: A Summary of European Systems* (1918), provides a more comprehensive account of her research.

Coman left a large legacy when she died in 1915. She had helped to initiate the settlement movement and to direct a generation of young college graduates into settlement work.

Bibliography
Davis, *Spearheads for Reform: The Social Settlements and the Progressive Movement, 1890–1914*; James, *Notable American Women*, vol. 1, pp. 365–67; Trattner, *Biographical Dictionary of Social Welfare in America*, pp. 194–97.

Committee on Congestion of Population

Rapid industrialization during the nineteenth century led to unprecedented growth in urban centers such as New York City. This growth, combined with the influx of large numbers of immigrants, caused a range of problems. Settlement workers and other social reformers took on the responsibility for finding solutions to these difficulties.

Many reformers, **Florence Kelley** among them, believed that urban congestion was responsible for a variety of the other problems they were working to alleviate. Social welfare workers from many different perspectives—housing, recreation, city planning, child labor—joined together in the crusade to find a solution to the problem of population density. It is not surprising that reformers in New York City, the most densely populated urban center in the United States, were at the forefront of this effort. Once her own interest in the problem was aroused, Kelley set about involving her reformer colleagues, including **Lillian Wald** of the **Henry Street Settlement**, **Mary Simkhovitch** of Greenwich House, and Gaylord White of the Union Settlement, in finding a solution.

In 1907, Kelley and the others formed the Committee on the Congestion of Population (CCP). Dr. Herman C. Bumpus, director of the American Museum of Natural History, also joined the group. Simkhovitch served as president, and the committee hired **Benjamin C. Marsh**, a Greenwich House resident, as secretary. The CCP was formed to arouse public interest in the causes and consequences of congestion and to propose possible solutions to the congestion problem. In all, representatives from more than 35 civic and philanthropic organizations participated in the work of the CCP. Greenwich House served as the committee's headquarters. George Ford, an architect and a Greenwich House volunteer, served as the CCP's technical advisor.

Marsh spent the summer of 1907 in Europe gathering information about city planning. He visited Germany, France, and England, where he attended an international conference on housing. When he returned to the United States, Marsh and the other members of the CCP decided that an exhibit that graphically portrayed the existing conditions would be the most powerful way to capture the attention of both the residents of New York City and their elected officials.

Toward this end, Marsh set about organizing New York City's first exhibit about urban congestion. He modeled the exhibit on the housing and tuberculosis exhibits that the housing reformer **Lawrence T. Veiller** arranged for the New York **Charity Organization Society**.

Dubbed the "Congestion Show" by Marsh and his colleagues, the exhibition was staged at the American Museum of Natural History and opened in March 1908. Each of the displays was intended to show the wisdom of the CCP's goal of long-range city planning that included investigating ways to distribute the population over wider areas. An array of maps, charts, diagrams, models, and photographs were supplemented with statistics to graphically portray the social and economic price of overcrowding. The New York City Tenement House Department, the National **Consumers' League**, the New York Charity Organization Society, the **Association for Improving the Condition of the Poor**, and the **New York Child Labor Committee** were among the welfare and reform organizations and agencies who contributed displays.

The exhibition was extremely popular, and the CCP capitalized on the public interest by pressuring New York's Governor Hughes and the New York State Legislature to create a State Commission on Congestion of Population. The CCP also persuaded New York City Mayor Gaynor to appoint the New York Congestion Commission. Marsh served as secretary of this group. In 1911, the commission published a comprehensive report that examined the causes and consequences of overcrowding and that also proposed possible solutions. This report echoed the concerns of many housing reformers by stating that many social and physical problems were the direct result of population overcrowding.

The commission's report included a number of recommendations that it believed would help to reduce the current congestion and also to discourage overcrowding in the future. Among the most significant recommendations were calls for a more efficient distribution of industry, restrictions on the height and lot coverage of buildings, and extension of the rapid transit system to encourage development of surrounding suburban areas.

The New York CCP also sponsored a conference in connection with a city planning exhibit held in Washington, DC, in 1909. The members of the CCP hoped that their conference would generate interest in the formation of a national planning association, and in fact, the National Conference on City Planning was a significant outcome of the CCP's meeting. The conference served as an important link between the housing and city planning reform movements.

The Committee on Congestion of Population was formed to arouse public interest regarding the immediate and pressing problem of overcrowding in New York City. It fulfilled its charge admirably by sponsoring a successful exhibition, by having state and municipal congestion commissions appointed, and by sponsoring a city planning exhibition. Having done all this, the committee disbanded. **See also New York Charity Organization Society Tenement House Exhibition.**

Bibliography

Davis, *Spearheads for Reform: The Social Settlements and the Progressive Movement, 1890–1914*; Lubove, *The Professional Altruist: The Emergence of Social Work as a Career 1880–1930*; Lubove, *The Progressives and the Slums: Tenement House Reform in New York City, 1890–1917*; Scott, *American City Planing Since 1890: A History Commemorating the Fiftieth Anniversary of the American Institute of Planners.*

The Commons See The *Survey*

Conference of Boards of Public Charities *See* National

Conference on Social Welfare

Conference of Charities *See*

National Conference on Social Welfare

Congestion Exhibition *See*

Committee on Congestion of Population

Consumers' Leagues

Child labor and women's working conditions were an important concern for many reformers during the late nineteenth and early twentieth centuries. The existing laws were in most cases inadequate and unable to protect these vulnerable groups. The women who worked in the garment trades and their counterparts in the burgeoning retail stores were often exploited, working long hours under dangerous conditions. When reform activists learned of these conditions, they quickly took up the cause. They organized consumers' leagues on the local, state, and national levels to galvanize public opinion and to pressure authorities to bring about change.

In 1890, a study by Alice Woodbridge, a young New York City woman, served as the catalyst for forming the first consumers' league. Woodbridge was concerned about the terrible working conditions she witnessed in many fashionable retail stores and prepared a report detailing the unfair labor practices for the New York City-based Working Women's Society. These practices included requiring young women clerks in retail stores to work from 7:45 in the morning until 11 in the evening with only short breaks for meals and no compensation for overtime work and no paid vacation time. The young women were required to stand at all times and were disciplined if found leaning against a counter or a pile of boxes. Dirty, inadequate eating facilities were made available to employees, and toilets and dressing rooms had no doors to discourage employees from stealing. Additionally young children were often employed for long hours in store packing rooms to prepare purchases for delivery.

When Woodbridge's report was brought to the attention of **Josephine S. Lowell**, the founder of the New York **Charity Organization Society**, Lowell arranged for a mass meeting in December 1890 and revealed the contents of Woodbridge's report. This meeting aroused the public's interest and concern, and in January 1891, the New York Consumer's League (NYCL) was formally organized with Lowell as the league's first president.

The league's founders hoped to convince consumers they had a responsibility to ensure the goods they purchased were made under safe, sanitary conditions. The NYCL members pressured factory and retail store owners to improve working conditions for women and children or risk having the public boycott their products or stores. To accomplish this, the New York League published a "white list" of stores that met its minimum standards and recommended only these establishments to the public.

The white lists were not the New York league's only resource. It undertook a successful lobbying campaign that resulted in the passage of the Mercantile Inspection Law of 1896. Enforced by the New York City Board of Health, this legislation limited sales clerks to 60 hours per week and required that store owners supply employees with chairs. When the city board proved to be less than effective in enforcing the regulations, the NYCL fought successfully to have that responsibility transferred to the New York State Department of Labor in 1908.

The ethical idealism of the New York organization soon spread to other cities, and consumers' leagues were established in Philadelphia, Boston, and Chicago. In 1899 delegates from the four leagues came together to establish a National Consumers' League. **Florence Kelley**, formerly the chief factory inspector for Illinois, agreed to serve as the organization's executive secretary. To fulfill this duty, Kelley went to live at the **Henry Street Settlement** on New York City's Lower East Side, nearby the league's headquarters in the United Charities Building.

Kelley was a powerful and dynamic leader. Using the New York league as a model, she had established more than 60 leagues in 21 states by 1909. Branches were also opened on college campuses. The national and local leagues conducted a continuing campaign of consumer education. In 1901, the National Consumers' League organized a traveling exhibition to advertise the "white list," and the National Consumers' League label, which manufacturers who met league standards were entitled to sew into their garments. By 1914, 70 manufacturers had earned this right.

While the national league prospered, the local leagues expanded their concerns. When **Maud Nathan** assumed responsibility for the New York Consumers' League in 1906, she combined forces with the New York Child Labor Committee and the New York Women's Trade Union League to conduct a campaign to raise wages and lower the number of hours for women and children workers. Although the wage campaign was not successful in New York, leagues in other states managed to secure raises for women workers.

In 1905, the New York Consumers' League launched a pure food campaign as part of the league's broader crusade to raise living standards. The leadership appointed a Committee on Food Inspection which sent out its own inspectors. The committee called for better monitoring of the preparation and distribution of food products citywide and also worked for the regulation of pushcarts.

The National Consumers' League often joined forces with local branches. In 1913, the New York and national leagues came together to lobby for legislation that prohibited the employment of children under 14. The proposed law, which was never passed, also prohibited the manufacture of babies' and children's clothing and all food products in tenements. In addition to working for the passage of specific laws, the national league encouraged the state-level groups to constantly monitor legislative activity.

During World War I, the national league worked to ensure that minimum age and maximum hour standards were maintained during wartime conditions. After the hostilities ended in 1919, the National Consumers' League embarked on a 10-year legislative program to win passage of the eight-hour day and the elimination of night work for women. It also lobbied for child labor laws, minimum wage commissions in all states, and compulsory health insurance.

In the following years, the Consumers' League faced new challenges, including the campaign for the Equal Right Amendment. Many league supporters feared that women would lose the benefit of protective legislation if this amendment passed. In addition, some courts ruled unfavorably regarding child labor laws, and the U.S. Supreme Court overturned state minimum wage laws, weakening some of the protection the league had secured.

Bibliography

Goldmark, *Impatient Crusader: Florence Kelley's Life Story*; Jackson, *Encyclopedia of New York City*, p. 801; Lubove, *The Progressives and the Slums: Tenement House Reform in New York City, 1890–1917*; O'Neill, *Everyone Was Brave: A History of Feminism in America*; Romanofsky, *The Greenwood Encyclopedia of American Institutions: Social Service Organizations*, vol. 2 , pp. 488–92.

Cooperative Society of Visitors (Boston) *See* Boston Associated Charities

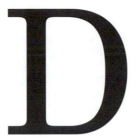

D

Davis, Katharine Bement

social reformer, settlement resident,
penologist
b. January 15, 1860; d. December 10, 1935.

Although she began her career as a settlement worker, Katharine Davis's interest in social welfare reform took her beyond the settlement movement. She became involved in penal reform and broke new ground by becoming the first female superintendent of a women's reformatory and the first woman to head a municipal department of corrections.

Davis graduated from the Free Academy in Rochester, New York, in 1879. Because her family was unable to finance her college education, she became a science teacher at the local high school in Dunkirk, New York. By studying at night and saving her salary, Davis was able to enroll in Vassar College in 1890. She graduated with honors two years later.

While studying food chemistry on the graduate level at Columbia University, Davis also taught science at the Brooklyn Heights Seminary (1892–1893). Based on her work at Columbia, Davis was selected as director of the workingman's home exhibit at the World's Columbian Exposition in Chicago in 1893. Her exposure from this position led to her being invited to become the head resident at St. Mary's College Settlement in a Russian-Jewish neighborhood in Philadelphia.

Four years later, Davis left the settlement to pursue additional graduate study, this time in political economy and sociology at the University of Chicago. In 1898, she received a European Fellowship from the New England Women's Educational Association. She used this opportunity to travel in Europe and to study at the universities of Vienna and Berlin. Her dissertation, which she completed in 1900, compared the socioeconomic status of Bohemians in Chicago and in Europe.

After she returned to the United States, Davis used her connections at the University of Chicago to secure an appointment as the first superintendent of the Bedford Hills, New York, women's reformatory. She operated Bedford Hills as an educational institution and earned the praise of her peers for the work she accomplished. Based on Davis's accomplishments, John D. Rockefeller, Jr., provided a five-year contract, starting in 1912, for funding a Laboratory of Social Hygiene at Bedford Hills.

Davis's experience at Bedford Hills led to other positions in corrections. In 1914, she became New York City Commissioner of Corrections. Davis was the first woman to head a city department, and her tenure in office was marked by controversy. A 1915 State Prisons Commission investigation upheld charges that her administration was too repressive, but the Prison Association of New York, the Office of the Mayor of New York City, and a number of other social reformers came to her defense. The investigation did not permanently harm Davis's career, and in 1916, she left the Department of

Corrections to become the chair of New York City's first parole commission.

Two years later Davis was named general secretary of the Bureau of Social Hygiene, a position she held until her retirement in 1928. The bureau, which was Rockefeller-funded, was established to eliminate **prostitution**. Under Davis's leadership, it enlarged its scope to include work related to the international white slave trade, sex education, and public health.

Although Davis was best known as a corrections officer, she was interested in a range of social reform initiatives beyond her corrections and settlement work. She performed relief work in Italy following a 1908 earthquake, and she was active in the woman suffrage movement and in the Progressive Party.

In 1930, Davis moved to California to live with family members. She died five years later after a long illness. Although Davis started out as a settlement worker, her most important contribution was breaking new ground in penal reform and showing that women were more than capable of running a correctional facility.

Bibliography

Dictionary of American Biography, supl. 1, pp. 227-28; James, *Notable American Women, 1607–1950*, vol. 1, pp. 439–41; Trattner, *Biographical Dictionary of Social Welfare in America*, pp. 207–10

DeForest, Robert Weeks
attorney, businessman, social reformer
b. April 25, 1848; d. May 6, 1931.

Robert Weeks DeForest
Museum of the City of New York

Robert Weeks DeForest was a successful attorney who became involved in an eclectic array of social reform crusades. Over the later years of his life, he used his personal wealth and social contacts to further the work of a variety of social reform causes and organizations. DeForest founded, helped to finance, and served as an officer of organizations or commissions concerned with prison reform, child labor, state parks, health and hospitals, and the arts.

Educated at Yale, the University of Bonn in Germany, and Columbia University Law School, DeForest was descended from a wealthy and distinguished family. He reinforced both his social and financial standing by his marriage to Emily Johnson whose father, John Taylor Johnson, was the president of a railroad and a founder of the Metropolitan Museum of Art in New York City.

For more than 50 years, DeForest served as general counsel for the Central Railroad of New Jersey. In addition, he was on the board of a number of corporations. His legal work and interests in a variety of businesses helped DeForest to become one of the wealthiest men in the United States.

Motivated by the patrician sense of *noblesse oblige*, DeForest also shared the belief of other social reformers of his time that the most effective way to secure the social and economic position of the upper and middle classes was to use social welfare programs to exert some control over the growing number of immigrants who found their way into America's growing industrial cities. Reflecting his own background and interests, DeForest was especially drawn to charitable undertakings operated according to sound business methods.

In 1882, working with **Josephine Shaw Lowell** and a number of others, DeForest helped to organize the New York **Charity Organization Society (COS)**. Five years later, he became its president, a position he held until his death 43 years later.

His work with the COS led DeForest to assume a leading role in the housing reform movement in New York City. Following the COS's highly successful Congestion Exhibition, which was intended to demonstrate the negative impact of overpopulation, New York Governor Theodore Roosevelt created the **New York State Tenement House Commission** (1900) and appointed DeForest its chair. One of the laws drawn up by the commission established a Tenement Department for New York City charged with regulating the lighting, ventilation, and sanitary standards in tenement houses. DeForest was appointed by New York City Mayor Seth Low to serve as the city's first

Tenement House Commissioner (1902–1903). Various reports of the commission along with other information on tenement house reform initiatives were included in *The Tenement House Problem* (1903), a book edited by DeForest and the housing reformer Lawrence Veiller.

DeForest was also involved with reform at the national and regional levels. In 1910, he joined a group of housing reformers, including settlement workers, in establishing the **National Housing Association**. He later served as the group's president. DeForest also helped to organize the Committee on the Regional Plan of New York and Its Environs, later known as the Regional Plan Association, which was charged with planning the future growth of the city. He also served as president of the **National Conference of Charities and Correction** (*see* **National Conference on Social Welfare**) and was a member of the Prison Association of New York, the National Employment Exchange, and the New York State Charities Association.

Besides his reform efforts, DeForest favored and supported education, particularly the training of social workers. He chaired the COS's Committee on Philanthropic Education and in 1898 helped found what became the New York School of Social Work, the first institution of higher education in the United States dedicated to the training of professional social workers.

DeForest was also key in the development of the *Survey*, which was a national magazine that offered professional social workers and other reformers a vehicle for examining a broad range of social welfare issues. In 1891, the COS's Committee on Publications began issuing the *Charities Review*, one of the first social work journals in the United States. DeForest provided some of the necessary capital and helped guide this publication through several name changes until it evolved into the *Survey*. DeForest served as president of **Survey Associates**, a core group of supporters of the *Survey*, from 1912 until his death in 1931.

DeForest's influence extended to other philanthropic interests as well. In 1907 in his capacity as legal advisor to **Margaret Olivia Sage**, DeForest was instrumental in establishing the **Russell Sage Foundation**. He served as the foundation's principal officer and exercised substantial influence over which organizations and projects received funding. A number of projects that DeForest was involved with benefited from grants from the foundation, including the New York School of Social Work (*see* **Columbia University Graduate School of Social Work**) and the Survey Associates. The foundation also provided funding for the continuance of the **Pittsburgh Survey**, an extensive social and economic investigation of Pittsburgh, Pennsylvania, which was originally sponsored by the COS.

Although he was basically a conservative businessman, DeForest was committed to social welfare projects. By maintaining an open mind and generally optimistic point of view, he recruited dedicated social reformers to become involved in a variety of causes and projects and was able to provide the funding necessary to see many projects through to completion, including many efforts of interest to those in the settlement movement.

Bibliography

Dictionary of American Biography, supl. 1, pp. 236–37; Jackson, *Encyclopedia of New York City*, p. 323; *National Cyclopedia of American Biography*, vol. X:II, pp. 15–16; Trattner, *Biographical Dictionary of Social Welfare in America*, pp. 220–22.

Denison, Edward
social activist, social reformer
b. [n.d.], 1840; d. January 26, 1870.

Edward Denison was an English social reformer who believed that more than just food or money, the poor needed moral regeneration. To accomplish this, he went to live among the poor in Stepney in London's East End during the 1860s. Denison's approach to social welfare work, which stressed personal contact and moral suasion, anticipated the methods used by settlement workers both in England and in the United States.

At the time that Denison became interested in social welfare work, London officials were attempting to deal with the city's economic distress via a system of indiscriminate charitable giving. Anyone who asked for assistance received it. Denison was one of a number of social reformers who believed that this type of assistance was detrimental both to the giver and to the receiver. They believed that doling out food and money only demoralized the poor and needy. What was really needed was the benefit of personal contact to bring about the regeneration of the community.

To accomplish this personal contact, Denison advocated that reformers go and live among the poor while delivering assistance. While an undergraduate at Oxford, Denison lived and worked in a poor area of London under the auspices of the London Society for the Relief of Distress. Denison and others hoped that by doing this, a general sense of community that had existed in smaller scale social units such as towns and villages could replace the sense of demoralized dependence that prevailed in larger urban areas. Denison acknowledged that to accomplish their work reformers needed support from the state such as programs to reduce the number of unemployed, but he did not want the government to blindly provide money. As a result of his social reform work, he hoped the poor would look to him for moral inspiration, not money.

Denison did not enjoy good health, and he died in 1870 at the age of 30. Two years later a volume of his letters and addresses was published by his friends. This volume inspired other like-minded reformers to take up Denison's work. For example, another Oxford undergraduate influenced by Denison's work was Arnold Toynbee. Canon **Samuel Barnett**, the founder of **Toynbee Hall**, the first English settlement house, was inspired by both Denison and Toynbee and in turn inspired many Americans to become involved in settlement work. Denison's reputation spread to the United States, and **Denison House**, the first settlement established in Boston by the **College Settlements Association** was named in his honor.

Bibliography

Meacham, *Toynbee Hall and Social Reform, 1880–1914: The Search for Community*; Pacey, *Readings in the Development of Settlement Work*.

Denison House

The founders of the **College Settlements Association** (CSA) planned to open settlements in different cities which were to be administered by a central national organization. Denison House, the Boston College Settlement, was established by the CSA in 1892. The house was named in honor of **Edward Denison,** an Oxford University undergraduate who lived and worked among the poor of London's East End. Denison's work inspired other Oxford students and many Americans, including the founders of the CSA, to become involved in social welfare work.

Helena S. Dudley was to have been the first head resident of the settlement, but when she was not immediately available because of her work at the **College Settlement** in Philadelphia, **Emily Greene Balch**, a Wellesley graduate interested in social reform, assumed the job for one year so that the house's opening would not be delayed. Denison House was maintained by an appropriation from the College Settlements Association and by subscriptions (donations or pledges from individuals).

In their efforts to assist the neighborhood residents, who at first were predominately Irish, but were gradually replaced by Syrians, Greeks, and Italians, the settlement workers established a public library and a reading room, public **baths**, and a gymnasium. They also opened a milk station, a baby clinic, and a dispensary.

Founders of Denison House and Staff. (Emily Greene Balch is seated to the left of the small child.)
The Schlesinger Library, Radcliffe College

Denison House offered other activities including clubs for men and women, summer camps for boys and girls, dramatics, concerts, and lectures.

Besides providing services to their neighborhood, the residents of Denison House also took a keen interest in trade unionism and other social issues. The Boston Trade Union was established at Denison House as were several women's unions. While she was head resident, Helena Dudley also served as a delegate to the Central Labor Union. In 1893, Dudley organized a Social Service Club. Each week 40 or 50 business owners, professionals, workers, and students gathered at Denison House to hear lectures on various social reform topics. Although this formal group lasted for only three years, Denison House continued to sponsor public conferences on a variety of topics including trade unionism and Social Christianity.

Although many settlement workers were interested in the **Americanization** of immigrants, Denison House workers made efforts to celebrate their neighbors' cultures. One of the settlement's better-known residents, **Vida Scudder**, was instrumental in founding the Circolo-Italo-Americano in 1904. This organization promoted understanding of the new immigrants in the neighborhood by, among other activities, encouraging a revival of native Italian arts and crafts. The group held regular meetings that were conducted in Italian and sponsored lectures and debates that appealed primarily to local intellectuals and professionals.

Like many of its counterparts, Denison House modified its offerings and programs over the years to meet the changing needs of the residents in the surrounding area. The present day Denison House, located in Dorchester, Massachusetts, continues the settlement's tradition of community service.

Bibliography

Carson, *Settlement Folk: Social Thought and the American Settlement Movement, 1885–1930*; Davis, *Spearheads for Reform: The Social Settlements and the Progressive Movement, 1890–1914*; Woods, *The Handbook of Settlements*; Woods, *The Settlement Horizon*.

Devine, Edward Thomas

educator, social services administrator, writer
b. May 6, 1867; d. February 27, 1948.

Edward Devine's varied career as a social reformer was anchored in his work as general secretary of the New York **Charity Organization Society** (COS). Through the COS, he became involved in the movement to profession-

alize social work and in a number of campaigns to secure social welfare legislation. Through his editorial work, teaching, and involvement in government service, Devine made other significant contributions to the reform efforts of the first half of the twentieth century.

Born and raised on his family's farm near Union in Harden County, Iowa, Devine received a classical education in preparation for a teaching career. He attended the Methodist Albion Seminary and then moved on to Cornell College in Mount Vernon, Iowa, in 1883. During the next four years he attended classes, taught school, and served as the principal of a public school in Albion. Devine earned an A.B. degree in 1887. The following year he accepted a position at the local high school in Marshalltown, Iowa. Eventually he became the principal of the Mount Vernon, Iowa, public schools.

While teaching in Marshalltown, Devine became acquainted with Simon Nelson Patten, a fellow teacher who went on to become a professor of political economy at the University of Pennsylvania. Patten convinced Devine to pursue a graduate degree, and in 1890, Devine spent a year studying at the University of Halle in Germany. The following year he enrolled at the University of Pennsylvania where he studied with Patten and Edmund James. In 1893, Devine earned the Ph.D.

While a student at the University of Pennsylvania, Devine worked as a lecturer for the American Society of Extension of University Teaching. He served as secretary of the society from 1894 to 1896. At Patten's suggestion, Devine arranged for a summer school for economists in 1896. His organizational skills were recognized by one of the attendees, Franklin H. Giddings, a member of the Central Council of the New York Charity Organization Society. Giddings recruited Devine to join the COS as the organization's general secretary.

Under Devine's guidance, the COS became a leader in the field of social work and in the crusade for social reform legislation. In 1898, the COS established a Summer School of Philanthropy. Six years later the school expanded to offer a full-year course of study as the New York School of Philanthropy. It eventually became the **Columbia University School of Social Work**. Devine served as the school's director from 1904 to 1907 and again from 1912 to 1917.

Devine's influence in the field of social reform extended beyond New York City. In 1897 he founded and served as editor of *Charities*, an official publication of the COS that eventually became the *Survey*, which was recognized as the leading social welfare journal of the time. In 1904, Devine helped establish the **National Child Labor Committee** and the National Association for the Study and Prevention of Tuberculosis. He was a member of the advisory committee of the International Prison Congress (1910), and in 1912, he led a group of social workers who lobbied for the passage of the act that created the federal **Industrial Relations Commission**. To keep in touch with social reform activities, Devine often spent short periods as a resident in various settlements including **Greenwich House** and the **University Settlement**.

Devine was also active in the American Red Cross, participating in disaster relief missions following the San Francisco earthquake (1906) and the Dayton, Ohio, flood (1913). In 1917, Devine served as chief of the Bureau of Refugees and Relief of the American Red Cross Commission in France.

When he returned to the United States in 1917, Devine resigned from the Charity Organization Society. However, his resignation did not mark an end to his involvement in social reform, but marked only a change in focus. He remained active as an author and an administrator. During the 1920s, Devine was a member of the United States Coal Commission (1922–1923), a professor of social economy and dean of the graduate school at American University in Washington, DC (1926–1928), and director of the Bellevue-Yorkville Health Demonstration, which was sponsored by the Milbank Memorial Fund.

In 1930, Devine became director of the Housing Association of New York. The following year he served as vice chair of the New York Committee of 1,000, a private reform group created to investigate corruption in New York City. He also spent two years (1931–1933) as the executive director of the Nassau County (Long Island) Emergency Work Bureau, and from 1933 to 1935 he directed the county's Emergency Relief Bureau.

Devine retired in 1935 after years dedicated to social welfare reform as a researcher, writer, agency administrator, and innovator for social action. He continued to write and during his lifetime published 14 books and a large number of reports regarding the evolution of social thought. He was an outspoken critic of the New Deal and was particularly vocal in his criticism of the Roosevelt administration's relief and Social Security programs.

Bibliography

Chambers, *Paul U. Kellogg and the Survey: Voices for Social Welfare and Social Justice; Dictionary of American Biography*, supl. 4, pp. 236–38; Trattner, *Biographical Dictionary of Social Welfare in America*, pp. 228–31.

Dock, Lavina Lloyd

nurse, nursing educator, social reformer, suffragist, peace activist
b. February 26, 1858; d. April 17, 1956.

Lavina Dock was an experienced nurse and nursing education administrator before becoming involved in settlement work as a visiting nurse at the **Henry Street Settlement**. Her interaction with the reformers at Henry Street drew Dock into other reform crusades such as the suffrage campaign and the international peace movement.

Dock's family was well-to-do, and after graduating from a private school in her hometown of Harrisburg, Pennsylvania, she lived at home like other young women of her class and devoted herself to family and social concerns. However, when she was in her mid-twenties, Dock read an article about nursing in the *New Century* magazine and decided to enroll in the Bellevue Training School for Nurses in New York City.

Following her graduation in 1886, Dock found employment with an organization called United Workers, which operated in the Norwich, Connecticut, area and provided trained nurses. During the next few years, she volunteered to work for a number of disaster services including caring for the sick during a yellow fever epidemic in Jacksonville, Florida, and helping victims of the 1889 Johnstown, Pennsylvania, flood. During this time Dock also worked as a night supervisor at Bellevue Hospital and as a visiting nurse for the New York City Mission.

In addition to her nursing work, Dock was also interested in the field of nursing education. In 1890, she published *Materia Medica for Nurses*, a reference that detailed the correct dosage of drugs and explained the preferred method of administering them. The same year she became assistant director at the recently opened school of nursing at Johns Hopkins Hospital in Baltimore, Maryland. In 1893, Dock was named secretary of the first national nursing association, the American Society for Superintendents of Training Schools for Nurses. Three years later she resigned from the Johns Hopkins School of Nursing.

In 1898, Dock returned to active service when she joined **Lillian Wald** as a visiting nurse at the Henry Street Settlement on New York City's Lower East Side. Living and working in a settlement house aroused her interest in other social reform endeavors such as the international peace movement. Dock's pacifism inspired her to find a way to make nursing an international profession. Toward this end, she was one of the founders of the International Council of Nurses, and she served as the council's first secretary from 1899 to 1922. Dock would not accept a salary for her work and financed her own trips to Europe for council business. Dock's dedication to her pacifist principles was so deep-rooted that she forbade any mention of World War I in the section of the *American Journal of Nursing* that she edited.

Dock also became a militant suffragist; she was jailed three times for her activities, which included picketing the White House, participating in pro-suffragist demonstrations, and causing a disturbance at the polls. In addition, she was active in the campaign for stricter anti-prostitution laws and was an advocate of birth control for women.

In 1922, Dock stopped participating in the various organizations that had meant so much to her both personally and professionally. She retired to her family farm in Pennsylvania to care for family members who were ill.

Dock left an indelible mark on the nursing profession. Her dedication, willingness to serve, and her research made her a well-respected leader of her profession and the settlement movement.

Bibliography
Dictionary of American Biography, Supl. 6, pp. 166–68; Duffus, *Lillian Wald: Neighbor and Crusader*.

Down Town Ethical Society *See*

Madison House

Dreier, Mary Elisabeth
labor organizer, social reformer, suffragist
b. September 26, 1875; d. August 15, 1963.

Mary Dreier's search for meaningful work led her to a Brooklyn, New York, settlement house where she became involved in the **Women's Trade Union League** (WTUL). Through her association with the WTUL, Dreier worked with a number of social reformers and politicians who were active in the crusade to obtain better working conditions for women.

Dreier's father, Theodor, settled in Brooklyn after emigrating from Bremen, Germany. He worked his way up to become a partner in

the New York branch of Naylor, Benson and Company, an English iron firm, and provided his family with a comfortable lifestyle. The Dreiers were civic-minded and instilled the same values in their children. They were an extraordinary family. Their four daughters each went on to distinguished careers in the fine arts or in social reform. Mary and Margaret were pioneers in the labor movement in the United States, Dorothea was a painter, and Katherine a benefactor of modern art.

Mary and her sisters were educated by tutors and at a local private school. The Dreiers did not encourage their children to attend college; however, Mary Dreier did take some classes at the New York School of Philanthropy in 1904. (*See* **Columbia University Graduate School of Social Work**.) Dreier was not particularly interested in the contemporary social life, and by the time she was in her early twenties, she was actively looking for meaningful work.

In 1899 while working at a settlement house in Brooklyn, Asacog House, Dreier met Leonora O'Reilly, a garment worker who at the time was also the head worker at the house. O'Reilly soon recruited Dreier and her sisters as members of the Women's Trade Union League, which brought together employed working-class women and middle- and upper-class women in an association devoted to organizing working women into unions.

Her association with the WTUL seemed to provide Dreier with the purposeful work she sought. She served as president of the New York chapter of the league from 1906 to 1914. In 1909, she was arrested during the shirtwaist makers' strike, and it was this experience that galvanized her commitment to the labor movement.

During her tenure at the WTUL, Dreier became a strong advocate for women workers, especially those in the garment trade. She led the WTUL in organizing unskilled workers and in fighting for legislation to curb abuses. In addition, she also wrote articles advocating unionization in the WTUL's journal, *Life & Labor*.

Dreier worked closely with her sister **Margaret Dreier Robins** during her years at the WTUL. Margaret began her career with the New York chapter of the WTUL before moving to Chicago to work with the league's branch there and to serve as president of the national league.

Mary Dreier was active in other causes besides the WTUL. She was a member of the **New York State Factory Investigating Commission**, which was established after the **Triangle**

Shirtwaist Company Fire in 1911 in which 146 women garment workers died. Between 1911 and 1915 Dreier also worked with New York State Senator **Robert Wagner** and New York State Assemblyman **Alfred Smith** on the most comprehensive study of industrial conditions in the United States up to that time. The nine-member committee on which they served investigated and made recommendations regarding fire prevention, hours and wages, safety standards, and the prevention of industrial diseases.

Following her work with the factory commission, Dreier became involved in the woman suffrage campaign, chairing the New York City Woman Suffrage Party. In addition, she served as head of the industrial section of the New York State Woman Suffrage Party and on the Americanization Committee for New York State.

In 1917, Dreier became the chair of the New York State Committee on Women in Industry of the Advisory Commission of the Council of National Defense. Following World War I, she devoted a considerable amount of time and money to the peace movement and to other international concerns including working for stronger United States-Soviet relations and mobilizing public opinion against Nazism. Dreier continued her work for international cooperation after World War II. However, the labor movement remained a central concern in Dreier's life, and she remained active in the National Women's Trade Union League until its demise in 1950.

Bibliography

Dictionary of American Biography, supl. 7, pp. 196–97; *Notable American Women, The Modern Period*, pp. 204–06.

Dudley, Helena Stuart
settlement worker, labor reformer, pacifist
b. August 31, 1858; d. September 29, 1932.

Although not as well known as some of her contemporaries in the American Settlement Movement, Helena Stuart Dudley nevertheless made significant contributions to the fields of social and labor reform and to the world peace movement. As the head resident of the Boston-based settlement **Denison House**, she focused her attention on helping her neighbors earn a living that would provide them with economic security.

Dudley's early life was unsettled. Her father, Judson H. Dudley, was one of the original settlers of Denver, Colorado, and although he prospered in various mining and real estate ven-

tures, the family moved frequently. Helena worked at a variety of jobs before entering the Massachusetts Institute of Technology in 1884 to pursue an interest in science. The following year she transferred to Bryn Mawr, where she majored in biology and was a member of the first graduating class in 1889. She found employment as a biology teacher, and during the next three years taught at the Pratt Institute and at Packer Institute, both in Brooklyn, New York.

Dudley's involvement with the settlements began while she was a student when she and her classmate **Emily Greene Balch** heard **Vida Scudder**, **Jean Fine**, and Helen Rand discuss the new social settlement movement. Dudley then served as one of Bryn Mawr's representatives at the May 1890 meeting of the **College Settlements Association** (CSA), which was founded by a group of college alumnae to establish settlements in several American cities. In 1892, she resigned her teaching position to become the head worker at one of the CSA's settlements, the College Settlement in Philadelphia. The following year Dudley left for Boston to replace Balch as head of Denison House, the CSA-sponsored settlement in that city's South End.

When Dudley arrived, the neighborhood around Denison House was suffering through the economic hardships of the Panic of 1893. She immediately organized the house as a relief agency, a new role for a settlement. In addition to the aid dispensed, Dudley opened a sewing room at Denison House, providing work for 300 neighborhood women. She also urged municipal authorities to establish relief stations.

During her tenure at Denison House, Dudley was involved in a wide range of activities similar to those offered by other settlements. Under her guidance Denison House opened one of the first public gymnasiums in Boston. In cooperation with **Robert Woods** and the other residents of **South End House**, another Boston settlement, Dudley and her colleagues investigated local housing conditions, sponsored exhibits, and campaigned for public **baths**. In her first year at Denison House, she and Scudder organized a Social Science Club that brought together professionals, business owners, students, and workers to listen to lectures and engage in discussions.

Although she believed the neighborhood residents could learn from the settlement workers, Dudley understood that no amount of education or relief services could take the place of assisting the men and women in the surrounding neighborhood to earn a living wage. She devoted much of her time and efforts toward achieving this goal. Union meetings were held regularly at Denison House, and Dudley became a member of Federal Labor Union 5915, American Federation of Labor. In 1894, she and other Denison House residents successfully organized the women garment workers of Boston through the union. Along with Scudder, Dudley served as a union delegate to the Boston Central Labor Union. In 1903, Dudley, Balch, **Mary Morton Kehew**, **William English Walling**, and **Mary Kenney O'Sullivan** organized the National **Women's Trade Union League**. Dudley served for a time as the vice-president of the Boston branch.

Although Dudley was opposed to labor violence, she, unlike some of her colleagues in the settlement movement, was sympathetic to the more militant approach of the Industrial Workers of the World (IWW). Her support of the IWW's cause during the 1912 textile workers' strike in Lawrence, Massachusetts, forced Dudley to resign as head resident of Denison House, because she believed that her support of radical causes might alienate potential benefactors for the settlement.

Following her departure from Denison House, Dudley became even more active in radical causes, including the peace movement. She remained in the Boston area and joined the board of the Massachusetts branch of the **Women's International League for Peace and Freedom**. She was also a member of another pacifist group, the Fellowship of Reconciliation. Dudley maintained her pacifist stance even after the United States entered World War I. After the armistice, she actively promoted the League of Nations by, among other activities, making several trips to Europe to deliver speeches before various groups.

Eventually, Dudley became impatient with what appeared to her to be a lack of progress on the part of the peace movement, and she joined the Socialist Party. She died in Geneva, Switzerland, after attending a meeting of the Women's International League in 1932.

Bibliography

James, *Notable American Women 1607–1950*, vol. 1, pp. 526–27; Randall, *Improper Bostonian: Emily Greene Balch*; Scudder, *On Journey*; Trattner, *Biographical Dictionary of Social Welfare in America*, pp. 252–54.

Dumbbell Tenements

The tremendous influx of new immigrants into New York City in the closing decades of the nineteenth century precipitated a serious housing crisis. Architects, engineers, and housing reformers were hard-pressed to devise a quick, workable solution to providing housing within the confines of an overcrowded city. The dumbbell-style tenement was hailed by some as a solution, but it was quickly condemned by many, including settlement workers and other reformers, as an even more serious housing problem.

In 1878, the publisher of the newspaper *Sanitary Engineer* sponsored a competition for the best architectural design for a tenement to be constructed on an average city lot of 25 feet wide by 100 feet deep. One hundred and ninety architects from the United States, Great Britain, and Canada submitted a total of 206 plans in the hope of winning the top prize of $500. An award jury, which included Robert Hoe; the architect R.S. Hatfield; the president of the Board of Health, Charles F. Chandrel; and two clergymen, the Reverend John Hall and the Reverend Henry C. Potter, evaluated the plans.

The competition attracted widespread interest. The *Sanitary Engineer* reproduced the plans for the top 10 entries, accompanied by a series of articles that described each design in detail. The winning design was submitted by James E. Ware and consisted of two tenements, which were one behind the other and connected by a hallway. The name *dumbbell* was assigned to this design because the outline of the building was tapered in the middle, giving it the appearance of the handle of a dumbbell.

These tenements were generally six or seven stories high with 14 rooms per floor. Each floor contained four apartments, two four-room units at the front and two three-room units at the rear. The four apartments shared two toilets. The building was usually 90 feet long, which meant that the back of the lot had ten feet of unoccupied space. This space allowed for some air and light to enter the rooms at the back of the house. The rooms at the front of the house received direct light and air from the street. The windows in the rest of the rooms opened out onto a narrow airshaft that was formed by the abutting tenements and which was enclosed on all sides.

Shortly after the competition ended, critics began to discuss the problems inherent in the winning design, which did not provide adequate light and ventilation and occupied too much of the lot, thereby eliminating any recreation space around the house, but it was too late. The dumbbell model was adopted in many New York City neighborhoods. By the time this type of housing was outlawed by the **Tenement House Law of 1901**, two-thirds of the population of New York City were housed in dumbbell tenements. *See also* **New York City Tene-** **ment House Department; Tenement Houses.**

Bibliography

DeForest, *The Tenement House Problem*; Jackson, *The Encyclopedia of New York City*, pp. 161–63.

E

Eastman, Crystal

attorney, social researcher, peace activist, writer

b. June 25, 1881; d. July 8, 1928.

Crystal Eastman pursued her interest in social reform through a career as an attorney. She established a reputation as an expert in industrial safety and workers' compensation and served on a number of committees that sponsored worker's compensation legislation. In addition, Eastman maintained an interest in woman suffrage and the crusade to protect civil liberties.

Eastman was born in Marlborough, Massachusetts, where her parents were both ordained Congregationalist ministers. Her mother, who emphasized the equality of men and women to her children, and her younger brother Max Eastman, the well-known editor, writer, and socialist, proved to be the two most powerful influences on Eastman. After graduating from Vassar in 1903, Eastman moved to New York City. She earned an M.A. in Sociology from Columbia University the following year. While living in New York, Eastman came into contact with the city's dynamic settlement community and decided that she could best serve the cause of social reform by becoming a lawyer. She enrolled in New York University Law School, and to support herself while in school, Eastman ran a recreation center in **Mary Simkhovitch**'s settlement, **Greenwich House** in nearby Greenwich Village.

She was admitted to the bar in 1907, and that same year Eastman joined the staff of the **Pittsburgh Survey**, the in-depth social and economic investigation that was being conducted under the direction of **Paul U. Kellogg**, the editor of the social welfare journal *Charities and the Commons* (*See* the **Survey**.) For the next two years she investigated and analyzed more than 1,000 industrial accidents. Her findings were published as part of the six-volume Pittsburgh Survey under the title *Work Accidents and the Law* (1910). Eastman's research was useful in advancing the campaign for worker's compensation legislation and identified her as a pioneer in the fields of industrial safety and workers' compensation.

As a result of her work on the Pittsburgh Survey, Eastman was appointed secretary and treasurer of the New York branch of the American Association for Labor Legislation in 1909. That same year Charles Evans Hughes, governor of New York, appointed her secretary of the New York State Commission on Employers' Liability and Causes of Industrial Accidents, Unemployment and Lack of Farm Labor. Eastman was the only woman on this 14-member commission, and she was the principal author of its report which appeared in 1911. As a result of this appointment, she was instrumental in securing the passage of a worker's compensation law for New York State.

While a member of the New York State Commission, Eastman delivered a paper at the

1910 annual meeting of the **National Conference of Charities and Correction** (NCCC), an influential organization composed of leaders from both public and private charitable relief organizations and correctional institutions. Her paper was entitled "Work-Accidents and Employers' Liability." The next year she was invited to speak to the American Academy of Political and Social Science on ways to create an ideal factory that would minimize work-related accidents.

A turning point in Eastman's career came two years later, when she served on the NCCC's Committee on Standards of Living and Labor. As her work on this committee exposed her to other reform issues, she gradually began to turn her attention from social welfare issues to embrace other causes such as woman suffrage, pacifism, and civil liberties. Along with **Roger Baldwin** and other social reformers, Eastman played a significant role in the establishment of the **American Civil Liberties Union**.

In 1921, Eastman moved to London where her husband took a job with the British Broadcasting Company. She continued her reform activities and was involved in establishing a London branch of the National Woman's Party and was active in the Conference of Labor Women, which was a group of birth control advocates and socialist suffragists. Eastman returned to the United States in 1927 and died the following year of nephritis, closing an industrious career as an ardent industrial reformer, suffragist, and pacifist.

Bibliography

James, *Notable American Women, 1607–1950*, vol. 1, pp. 543–45; Trattner, *Biographical Dictionary of Social Welfare in America*, pp. 264–67.

Elliott, John Lovejoy

settlement founder, Ethical Culture Society leader, social reformer

b. December 2, 1868; d. April 12, 1942.

John Elliott combined a career as a leader in the Ethical Culture Society with a second, equally challenging one as the founder and head resident of the **Hudson Guild** settlement. As a leader in the New York City reform community, Elliot cooperated with other settlement workers to organize and participate in the work of a number of organizations and community groups.

Elliott grew up in an atmosphere of genteel poverty on his family's farm in Princeton, Illinois. His mother, Elizabeth Denham Lovejoy, the stepdaughter of the noted abolitionist **Owen Lovejoy**, was an important influence on Elliott

as was his father's friend Robert Ingersoll, the noted orator and agnostic. After attending local schools, Elliott continued his education at Cornell University in Ithaca, New York, where as a freshman in 1889, he attended a lecture by **Felix Adler**, founder of the **Ethical Culture Society**. Adler's lecture changed the course of Elliott's life. Elliott was particularly taken with Adler's idea that it was the deeds that a person performed and the ethical motivation to perform good deeds that led a person to lead a worthy life. This emphasis on the ethical underpinning of life appealed to Elliott. After graduating from Cornell in 1892, Elliott attended the University of Halle in Germany, where he earned his Ph.D. in philosophy.

When he returned to the United States in 1894, Elliott settled in New York City. He became Adler's assistant, working as a lecturer and organizer for the Ethical Culture Society. Through his work with the Ethical Culture Movement, Elliott met many of the men and women who lived and worked in the various New York City settlement houses. He developed close friendships with many prominent settlement activists including **Mary Simkhovitch**, **Lillian Wald**, **Helen Hall**, **Paul U. Kellogg**, and **Jane Addams**. Like them, Elliott was committed to social reform, and this commitment led him to become personally involved in the lives of the poor. Although he was deeply involved in the work of the Ethical Culture Society, Elliott went a step further than Adler in his efforts to alleviate the hardships and sufferings of the poverty-stricken residents of the inner city, many of whom were recently arrived immigrants.

Elliott worked as a volunteer with the New York **Charity Organization Society** for a short time, but he did not agree with that organization's philosophy of relief work. Nor did he wish to align himself with any existing settlement. In 1895, he founded a settlement of his own, the **Hudson Guild** in Chelsea, a mostly Irish section on Manhattan's West Side.

Elliott was dedicated to improving the lives of the people his settlement served, and he undertook his work carefully and deliberately. He started out with a single room and began offering clubs for boys of various ages. He then expanded his offerings to include a kindergarten for the children of working mothers, places for recreation and gymnastics, and a mother's club. Eventually, the Hudson Guild also established a printshop (1912) for training apprentices, an employment bureau for unskilled women, and a 500-acre farm in New Jersey which was worked by neighborhood residents. A dramatic group, the Cellar Players, presented professional-quality productions. More than many other settlement founders, Elliott encouraged the neighborhood residents to participate in the governance of the guild, often at the expense of his temper and patience.

Besides his commitment to the settlement enterprise, Elliott also devoted his time to various social service enterprises. Along with Mary Simkhovitch of **Greenwich House**, he organized the New York **Association of Neighborhood Workers** (1900), later the **United Neighborhood Houses**; served as the president of the **National Federation of Settlements** (1919–1923); was one of the founding members of the **American Civil Liberties Union** (1920); and was a member of the New York State Committee on Education and the New York City Council of Social Agencies.

In addition to his work at the Hudson Guild, Elliott continued to fulfill his obligations to the Ethical Culture Society. In 1933, after the death of Felix Adler, Elliott became the senior leader of the society, teaching classes, performing marriages, and officiating at burials.

Elliott's interest in social reform extended into the international arena. In 1938, he founded and served as chair of the Good Neighbor Commission, an organization that assisted refugees from central Europe in finding homes and jobs in the United States. Elliott's efforts on behalf of refugees occupied much of his attention during the last years of his life. He died after a short illness in 1942.

Throughout his long career, Elliott made many significant contributions both to the Ethical Culture Movement and to the American Settlement Movement. He was particularly active in the New York City social reform community and effectively encouraged cooperation among the city's settlements.

Bibliography

Artera, *Living in Chelsea: A Study of Human Relations in the Area Served by the Hudson Guild*; Carson, *Settlement Folk: Social Thought and the American Settlement Movement, 1885–1930*; Melvin, *American Community Organizations: An Historical Dictionary*; pp. 58–60; Trattner, *Biographical Dictionary of Social Welfare in America*, pp. 271–73.

Ely, Richard Theodore

political economist, author, educator
b. April 13, 1854; d. October 4, 1943.

Richard Ely was an influential political economist who wrote and lectured on a variety of social and economic issues. Through his friendship with the social reformer **Florence Kelley**, Ely was introduced to **Jane Addams** and the work she and her settlement colleagues were accomplishing at the **Hull House** settlement in Chicago. Ely encouraged the settlement's residents to pursue in-depth social research projects and to publish their findings. He was instrumental in the publication of the settlement's first book, *Hull-House Maps and Papers*.

A graduate of Columbia University (1876), Ely went on to study economics in Germany at the University of Halle and the University of Heidelberg where he earned a Ph.D. in 1879. He remained in Europe for post-graduate study at the Universities of Geneva and Berlin before returning to the United States in 1881 to join the faculty of Johns Hopkins University as a lecturer on political economy.

Gradually, Ely emerged as a forerunner among the advocates of the new economics. Ely and other new economists held that economic principles were not governed by natural law. Rather, they believed these principles should be grounded in the needs of society at a particular time and place and that they must respond to the society as it changes. Ely was confident that if the inductive method of modern science was applied to economics, it would help correct the errors of the classical school. Along with other like-minded new economists, Ely founded the American Economic Association in 1885. He served as the association's secretary from 1885 to 1892 and as president from 1900 to 1901.

According to Ely, society was an organic whole in which all the elements were interdependent. He believed that the state played a pivotal role in the workings of society and that gradually a cooperative commonwealth would be achieved. Toward this end, he supported a number of social reform causes including slum clearance, factory regulation, and labor unions' rights.

Religious-ethical beliefs were also important elements in Ely's social and economic philosophy. Although he had been raised in a strict Presbyterian household, Ely eventually became an Episcopalian. He embraced the **Social Gospel** Movement and counted among his personal friends most of the prominent social gospel ministers of the time. Through his addresses to religious groups, Ely popularized the ideas of the English **Christian Socialists Frederick Denison Maurice** and **Charles Kingsley**. Along with the Reverend **William Dwight Porter Bliss**, he formed the Episcopal Church's

Christian Social Union and served as its first secretary from 1891 to 1894.

Ely believed that the Christian concept of brotherhood was a central tenet of human nature. In applying his economic and religious beliefs to the labor movement, he stressed the idea that peaceful unionism, such as that advocated by the Knights of Labor, served to bring members of the working class into a more equitable relationship with their employers. For Ely, an important component of labor unions was their emphasis on brotherhood which he considered a potential mainstay of social harmony.

In his later life, Ely turned his attention to the field of urban land studies, and toward this end, he organized the Institute for Research in Land Economics to encourage research into the way land is utilized and the economic and tax implications of land improvement.

Ely retired in the mid-1930s and died after a long illness in 1943. While primarily an academic economist, Ely did have an influence on the American Settlement Movement by encouraging Florence Kelley and her Hull House colleagues to undertake social research projects; their work served as a model for other settlements.

Bibliography

Dictionary of American Biography, supl. 3, pp. 248–51; Garraty, *Encyclopedia of American Biography*, pp. 347–49; Rader, *The Academic Mind and Reform: The Influence of Richard T. Ely in American Life*.

Ethical Culture Society

In general, ethical culture societies promoted the understanding of moral law, of the sense of duty, and of the infinite human worth. One of the earliest and most significant ethical culture societies was the Society for Ethical Culture founded in 1876 in New York City by **Felix Adler**. The society welcomed anyone who was willing to commit to a religious moral life, regardless of creed and free of theological dogmatism.

The roots of ethical culture societies can be traced to Adler's own religious training. While studying for the rabbinate, Adler began to question his personal commitment to traditional religious values. Although he abandoned what he considered were limitations of Jewish theology, he maintained a strong religious faith in moral law. Adler was also influenced by the writings of the New England Transcendentalists, particularly Ralph Waldo Emerson, and by his own study of Christian ethics.

The basic principle of the Ethical Culture Society was that morality should be nurtured in its own terms without reference to any external sanctions or motives. Members of the society emphasized the importance of the ethical component in all relationships—personal, social, national, and international. The society's unifying force was the members' participation in practical endeavors to solve moral problems.

Under Adler's leadership, the New York Society for Ethical Culture played a leading role in many philanthropic endeavors. The society was one of the first organizations to provide a free kindergarten. Its members were active in the campaigns for tenement house reform and the abolition of child labor. The society also provided a visiting nurse service and sponsored the establishment of two New York City settlement houses, the **Hudson Guild** and **Madison House**.

Affiliated societies were organized in the United States in Chicago, St. Louis, Philadelphia, and Brooklyn. In addition, societies were established in England, Germany, Switzerland, France, Austria, Italy, and Japan.

The Ethical Culture Movement is a strong and viable source for social welfare up to the present. The movement had a direct influence on the American Settlement Movement, particularly in New York City where it established two settlement houses. Although it is not possible to identify a precise number of settlement workers who were members of the movement, it is reasonable to assume that a significant number of them subscribed to the movement's doctrines of ethical action, and both groups shared a belief in the importance of undertaking practical endeavors to solve moral problems.

Bibliography

The Fiftieth Anniversary of the Ethical Movement, 1876–1926; Guttchen, *Felix Adler*; Jackson, *Encyclopedia of New York City*, p. 384; Seligman, *Encyclopedia of the Social Sciences*. vol. 5, pp. 600–02.

Exploring the Dangerous Trades (1943)

Published in 1943 when she was 74 years old, **Alice Hamilton**'s autobiography, *Exploring the Dangerous Trades,* reveals both her own character and the character of her generation of reformers. Like her Progressive colleagues at the Chicago-based settlement **Hull House**, Hamilton believed that if individuals were confronted with a problem, and if they were given the necessary information, they could bring about positive change.

In many ways, *Exploring the Dangerous Trades* is an impersonal autobiography. In its pages Hamilton does not disclose details of her private life, nor does she focus on her personal feelings. Rather, the book records Hamilton's professional progress as she worked to develop and institute industrial safety standards and to make employers more accountable to their employees by providing for medical programs and by eliminating dangerous substances in the manufacturing process.

In addition to being the record of a woman's life, *Exploring the Dangerous Trades* is also a record of the changes that took place in industrial medicine during the 30 years in which Hamilton was an active participant. Besides the insights into her work, Hamilton also provides information about her life and work at Hull House, her involvement in the international peace movement, and her travels in Europe.

Exploring the Dangerous Trades is a typical example of the literature of the American Settlement Movement. It graphically portrays the hazardous working conditions endured by men, women, and children and the effects of these conditions on the individuals' lives and their communities.

Bibliography

Hamilton, *Exploring the Dangerous Trades*; Sicherman, *Alice Hamilton: A Life in Letters*.

F

Fields, Annie Adams
philanthropist, social reformer, author
b. June 6, 1834; d. January 5, 1915.

Annie Fields was a wealthy Bostonian whose husband's social position and wealth allowed her to embark on a philanthropic career that blossomed following his death. Fields was one of the relief workers who steered the course of organized charity work in Boston away from a reliance on almsgiving toward a more scientific approach that emphasized the training of social welfare workers and the systematic investigation of requests for aid.

In 1854 at the age of 20, Annie Adams married James Thomas Fields, a family friend almost 17 years her senior. James Fields was a minor poet and popular lecturer who achieved renown as a partner in the well-known Boston publishing house of Ticknor & Fields and later on as editor of the *Atlantic* magazine. The couple traveled widely, and the vibrant and energetic Annie was drawn into literary circles on both sides of the Atlantic which included Longfellow, Whittier, Hawthorne, Dickens, Thackeray, and Trollope. The couple's home on Charles Street in Boston became a literary salon. Fields published some poetry and wrote a novel, but her more important literary contribution may have been the advice she gave her husband when called upon to evaluate manuscripts for publication.

This exhilarating and rewarding period of Fields's life came to an end with the death of her husband in 1881. Well provided for, she maintained both her Charles Street home and her ties to many old friends, but she also redirected her energies into the social welfare work that had been a parallel interest in her life since the 1870s, when she became involved in an effort to sponsor coffeehouses in poor neighborhoods to support temperance reform.

An early, direct encounter with Boston's poor occurred when Fields became involved in a rehousing effort following a fire that destroyed a large number of tenement dwellings in 1872. Three years later, she and Mrs. James Lodge founded the Co-operative Society of Visitors among the Poor, a group that was grounded in the charity organization principles of the British social reformer **Octavia Hill**. These principles, emphasizing the training of social welfare workers and the systematic investigation of aid requests, were a departure from the almsgiving approach previously used in Boston.

In 1879, Fields co-founded the Cooperative Society of Visitors, which was later absorbed by the **Boston Associated Charities**. She was connected with this organization for more than 25 years, serving as director from 1879 to 1894 and as vice president from 1894 to 1906. Her handbook for charity workers, *How to Help the Poor* (1883), sold more than 22,000 copies in two years.

Fields remained active in the Associated Charities until shortly before her death in 1915. In addition to work that she did while she was alive, Fields ensured that the Associated Charities would continue to serve the Boston community after her death by leaving the organization a bequest of $40,000.00

Bibliography

Huggins, *Protestants against Poverty: Boston Charities, 1870–1900; Notable American Women, 1607–1950*, vol. 1, pp. 615–17; Tryon, *Parnassus Corner: The Life of James T. Fields, Publisher to the Victorians*.

Fine, Jean
settlement house worker
b.[n.d.]; d. [n.d.].

Jean Fine was a founding member of the **College Settlements Association** (CSA). Like many other young women who worked in the settlement houses, Fine did not continue as an active participant after her marriage. Yet, she made an important contribution to the movement through her efforts to establish the CSA-sponsored **College Settlement** in New York City.

Her parents, the Reverend Lambert S. Fine and Mary Burchard, encouraged Jean to pursue an interest in social reform. She traveled in Europe after graduating from college and was familiar with the work of the early English settlement houses such as **Toynbee Hall**. Like many young college-educated women of her generation, Fine was anxious to find meaningful work for herself. In 1887, she and other members of the Smith College Graduating classes of 1883 and 1884 formed the College Settlements Association. The other participants were Clara French, Mary H. Mather, Helen C. Rand, and **Vida Scudder**.

The members of the CSA wanted to establish a network of settlement houses in a number of cities including New York, Philadelphia, and Boston. In November 1888, Fine and **Jane Robbins** made an initial effort on behalf of the CSA to establish a settlement in New York City. They worked with **Stanton Coit** of the **Neighborhood Guild** to locate accommodations in a working-class neighborhood so that the two women could engage in social settlement work. Eventually they rented furnished rooms at 130 Forsyth Street on New York's Lower East Side. Robbins remained in the neighborhood all week long, and Fine, who was teaching at a school further uptown, joined her on weekends. At first, the two women only sponsored social clubs for girls. Their efforts were successful, and shortly after they began their work, Robbins and Fine began looking for larger, more permanent quarters.

On September 1, 1889, Robbins and Fine moved their operation to the house at 95 Rivington Street, not far from Coit's Neighborhood Guild, and their settlement became known as the College Settlement, the first one established in New York under the auspices of the College Settlements Association. During its first year of operation 80 applications were received from men and women interested in working at the College Settlement.

Fine was selected as the settlement's first head resident in 1889, and she assumed responsibility for the girls' clubs that she and Robbins had started while living on Forsyth Street. At first, the settlement was to devote itself to programs and services for the women and girls in the neighborhood, but the settlement was soon offering a full range of programs to both women and men.

Among the first projects undertaken by Fine and the other residents was to establish a small library in the settlement house and to provide two **baths** for use by women and children in the neighborhood.

Fine resigned her position in July 1892, when she married Charles B. Spahr, an economist who was on the editorial staff of the *Outlook*. The couple were married in Princeton, New Jersey. Although she was no longer as active, Fine maintained an interest in social welfare reform.

Bibliography

Carson, *Settlement Folk: Social Thought and the American Settlement Movement, 1885–1930*; Davis, *Spearheads for Reform: the Social Settlements and the Progressive Movement, 1890–1914*.

Flower, Lucy Louisa
educational reformer, child welfare advocate
b. May 10, 1837; d. April 27, 1921.

Lucy Flower was a wealthy Chicagoan whose interest in social welfare extended beyond providing the funds to reform causes. She had a particular interest in child welfare reform and allied herself with the settlement workers of **Hull House** to significantly change the way in which delinquent children were treated by the Chicago municipal authorities.

Born Lucy Coues, she attended the local public school in Portsmouth, New Hampshire, and completed a year of study at the Packer Collegiate Institute in Brooklyn, New York. After the Coues family moved to Washington, DC, she worked at the United States Patent Office. However, she did not find this work fulfilling, and in 1859, Coues moved to Madison, Wisconsin, where she became an instructor in the preparatory department of the state university.

In 1863, Lucy Coues married James Monroe Flower, an attorney. Ten years later they moved to Chicago with their three children. James Flower became a successful lawyer and achieved a measure of influence in Republican Party political circles.

Like many women of her social class, Lucy Flower interested herself in social reform. She became involved in a variety of causes to aid slum children and orphans, including working with the Lake Geneva Fresh Air Association, which provided a summer recreation program for city children. In 1880, Flower joined forces with a number of other local women to establish the Illinois Training School for Nurses. Four years later she helped establish the Chicago Board of Charities.

Flower's interest in child welfare extended to education. She was appointed to the Chicago Board of Education in 1891. She immediately and enthusiastically set about reforming the public school curriculum. She advocated focusing on the needs of the individual child and having the child become an active participant in the education process. Flower also worked to develop a manual training program that would offer a practical education to those young men and women who did not continue their formal education by attending college.

The interest Flower had in children was not confined to their time in the classroom. She was also concerned about the prevailing policy under which young children who broke the law were imprisoned with older, more seasoned criminals. Flower persuaded the Chicago municipal authorities to build a training school for youthful offenders, and she raised the funds to build a dormitory so that the children would not have to spend time in jail with the adult inmates.

Flower was also instrumental in the establishment of the Cook County juvenile court, the first of its kind in the United States. Working with settlement residents from Hull House, including **Jane Addams** and **Julia Lathrop**, Flower successfully campaigned to have the city authorities institute a separate juvenile court in the summer of 1899. She also founded the Juvenile Court Committee, which was headed by Julia Lathrop, and she raised funds to pay the salaries of juvenile court probation officers.

In 1902, Flower moved to California in search of a more suitable climate for her husband, who was in poor health. Despite her contributions to various social welfare reform causes advocated by the resident of Hull House, Flower did not fit the mold of the "typical" progressive era reformer. Unlike many of the college educated women who entered social reform work in search of something meaningful in their lives, Flower found meaning in her home and family. She became involved in social reform because it was expected that women of her social class would do so, but her practical personality and willingness to get involved led her to go beyond the role of patron and to become involved in reform work on a personal level.

Bibliography

McCarthy, *Noblesse Oblige: Charity and Cultural Philanthropy in Chicago, 1849–1929*; Trattner, *Biographical Dictionary of Social Welfare in America*, pp. 293–395.

Folks, Homer
social welfare pioneer, child welfare advocate, public health reformer
b. February 18, 1867; d. February 13, 1963.

Most of Homer Folks's career was devoted to working for reforms that would benefit children. As secretary of the New York State Charities Aid Association and as a co-founder of **National Child Labor Committee**, he occupied a significant place in both the state- and national-level reform communities. He worked closely with settlement workers on a variety of child-related reform crusades. In addition, Folks contributed to the work of the American Red Cross and served as an advisor to President Franklin D. Roosevelt.

Born in Hanover, Michigan, where his father supported the family by working as a farmer, Folks attended a one-room country school until he was 12 years old. His parents instilled Folks with an unusually strong sense of social responsibility that would guide many of his future career choices. He graduated from the local high school in 1893, and two years later enrolled at Albion College. Folks earned a B.A. degree from Albion in 1889 and a second bachelor's degree the following year from Harvard College.

Based on his academic achievements and his concern for social issues, Folks became general superintendent of the Children's Aid Society of Pennsylvania. The society had been formed in 1882, and its program advocated placing children whose families could no longer care for them in foster homes rather than in public institutions. Folks extended this program of home placement to delinquent children. His effort was so successful that in 1891 he was invited to speak about it at the annual meeting of the National Conference of Charities and Correction (*see* **National Conference on Social Welfare**), an influential organization composed of leaders from both public and private charitable relief organizations and correctional institutions.

While working for the Children's Aid Society, Folks campaigned to secure legislation that would prevent the placement of children in almshouses and other similar institutions where they were exposed to adult criminals and to mentally ill people. Eventually, Folks became dissatisfied with his situation at the Children's Aid Society, and he resigned in 1893 to become the secretary of the State Charities Aid Association of New York, a position he held until his retirement in 1947.

His new assignment provided Folks with a broader scope of activities. He served as a welfare expert during the New York State Constitutional Convention (1894) and as a member of the New York City Board of Alderman (1897). He also served as commissioner of Public Charities for New York City from 1902 to 1903.

Folks's work brought him into contact with many of the social reformers of his day, particularly with settlement workers. In 1904, he was one of the founders of the **National Child Labor Committee**, along with **Florence Kelley** and **Lillian Wald**. He worked with Wald again in 1909 to arrange the **White House Conference on Dependent Children**, and then years later, was involved in the formation of the **United States Children's Bureau**.

While maintaining his position at the State Charities Aid Association of New York through 1947, Folks held a number of positions on the national level. Toward the end of World War I, Folks served as director of the American Red Cross Department of Civil Affairs in France. During the 1930s, he served as an advisor on welfare matters to President Franklin Roosevelt. Folks was also the only individual to be elected president of the National Conference of Charities and Correction for two terms.

Bibliography

Trattner, *Biographical Dictionary of Social Welfare in America*, pp. 295–98; Trattner, *Homer Folks: Pioneer in Social Welfare*.

Frederick Douglass Center

The mainstream American Settlement Movement largely ignored the needs of the large black population in America's cities. In some cases, this lack of attention reflected the personal bias of the settlement workers. In other instances, the settlement workers were responding to the prevailing prejudice in the society at large. For example, settlement workers feared losing the support of their benefactors if they worked with black people, and as a result, they often made little or no effort to reach out to the black residents in their neighborhoods. Some settlements operated branch houses that were located nearby, but little effort was made to truly integrate the settlements' programs and services. The Chicago-based Frederick Douglass Center was an exception to this norm.

Located on the periphery of the south-side, black ghetto of Chicago, the Frederick Douglass Center was established on April 26, 1904. The center promoted ethical and friendly relations between the races by providing assistance to both blacks and whites. **Jane Addams** of **Hull House** was instrumental in raising funds for the creation of the center, and after it was established, it was supported by subscriptions (donations or pledges from individuals).

The founder of the Frederick Douglass Center, the white Unitarian Minister **Celia Parker Woolley**, worked to make the house a symbol of interracial cooperation. Woolley and her small cadre of staff provided meeting rooms for organizations, maintained a library and reading rooms, and offered sewing and cooking classes. In addition, clubs were organized for boys and girls of various ages, and a playground and an athletic association were established as well. As was true at other settlements, the staff of the Frederick Douglass Center worked for better housing and sanitary conditions in the neighborhood, but they also tried to eliminate the prejudice that blacks encountered in their social and work lives. Advocates of equal opportunity, Woolley and the other residents encouraged the blacks who used the settlement to organize so that they could be better able to avail themselves of opportunities.

Although the Frederick Douglass Center is no longer in operation today, it played an important role in the delivery of social welfare services to the community it served. The men and women involved in this settlement not only worked for better housing, sanitary, and educational services for their neighbors, they also demonstrated the significant work that could be achieved through interracial cooperation. *See also* **Robert Gould Shaw House**.

Bibliography

Woods, *The Handbook of Settlements*.

Friendly Visitors

Charity organization societies were established to help to coordinate the work of public and private relief agencies, to promote efficiency, and to eliminate the duplication of effort. The **Charity Organization Society** (COS) movement that began in England in the early 1800s served as a prototype for a similar movement that gained momentum in the United States later in the century. It was based upon the belief that poverty was a manifestation of some moral deficit; people were poor because they were intemperate or lazy. Leaders of the American movement, such as **Josephine Shaw Lowell**, founder of the New York Charity Organization Society, believed that the poor needed to be exposed to the good example of their economic and social betters to overcome their poverty.

To accomplish its mission, the COS employed a cadre of volunteer agents sometimes called moral guardians or, most often, friendly visitors, whose role was to investigate appeals for assistance and to distinguish between the worthy poor, those who were too ill or disabled to work, and the unworthy poor, those who chose not to work. After categorizing the plea for assistance, the primary responsibility of the friendly visitor was to provide moral exhortation.

In urban centers such as Boston and New York, the local COS divided the city into wards that were then subdivided into districts. Each district was supervised by a paid agent who was responsible for recruiting and training volunteer visitors. At first, only men worked as friendly visitors, but by the late 1870s, middle-class women had become the mainstay of the effort.

Friendly visitors were dispatched to the homes of the poor in an effort to re-establish the social interaction patterns that had existed in small towns and villages before institutional almsgiving had replaced the concept that each member of society was personally responsible for the needy. The leaders of the COS movement did not believe that friendly visiting could eliminate class differences, but they did believe that it would eliminate friction and misunderstanding.

Once an applicant was deemed deserving of aid, it was the responsibility of the friendly visitors to get to know the individual or family. The visitors would not dispense relief. Rather, they would help someone find employment, ensure that children were enrolled in school, or teach the fundamentals of good housekeeping. The concept of personal service and a strong faith in the power of personal influence were central to the work of the friendly visitor.

While carrying out their responsibilities, the friendly visitors compiled a comprehensive amount of data on the social and economic problems of the poor. This information was shared with various relief agencies and with other social welfare reformers. Over time, this data was instrumental in changing the attitudes of many social welfare groups. As friendly visitors uncovered information about involuntary unemployment, low wages, and industrial accidents, they gradually broadened their views of the causes of poverty and came to see that it often took more than just the good example of the friendly visitor to provide the poor with the necessary means to achieve a measure of economic independence. ***See also* Octavia Hill.**

Bibliography

Carson, *Settlement Folk: Social Thought and the American Settlement Movement, 1885-1930*; Huggins, *Protestants against Poverty: Boston's Charities, 1870–1900*; Lubove, *The Professional Altruist: The Emergence of Social Work as a Career, 1880–1930*.

G

Garden Cities

The growth of cities during the second half of the nineteenth century, and the attendant problems of overcrowding, pollution, and disease, led many people to long for a return to what they remembered as the idyllic rural lifestyle. Since they could not turn back the clock, they sought ways to accommodate the growth and advances of industrialization and at the same time to recapture the peace and sense of community of the small town or village. The concept of neighborhood, which was advocated by many settlement workers, was an attempt in some ways to return to the type of social organization in which people felt a sense of belonging to a community.

One approach that attempted to construct a more acceptable physical environment was the concept of the Garden City, which was put forward by Sir Ebeneezer Howard in his book *Tomorrow: The Peaceful Path to Real Reform* (1898), which was reissued in 1902 as *Garden Cities of Tomorrow*. Howard's book inspired a worldwide movement.

Howard believed that the dual problems of the depopulation of rural areas and the over-population of urban areas could be solved harmoniously through the construction of small urban units that provided the advantages of both city and country life. According to Howard's plan, limited dividend companies would be formed to purchase a substantial amount of land. The companies' profits would

be limited to a maximum of five or six percent. Any additional earnings would be set aside to be used for the benefit of the community. Each garden city constructed would be a self-contained unit surrounded by a belt of agricultural land. Careful planning would be employed to ensure that a balance was maintained among the various elements—space for industrial facilities, for commercial venues, and for workers' homes and recreation areas.

At the time that Howard published his book, two English manufacturers had already constructed model villages for their employees, Cadbury at Bournville and Lever at Port Sunlight. The garden city concept was revived in England in the years following World War I. In 1918, the First Garden City Ltd. Company built the first English garden city at Letchworth, 34 miles north of London. A second community was constructed in 1919 at Welwyn, Hertfordshire.

In 1906, Howard and a group of American clergy and financiers came together to form the Garden City Association of America. In addition to Howard, the group included the Episcopal Bishop Henry C. Potter; August Belmont, a New York banker; **William Dwight Porter Bliss**, Episcopal Minister and Christian Socialist; and **Elgin R.L. Gould**, president of the City and Suburban Homes Company. The association did not construct model towns itself. Rather, it advised planners and builders on how to incorporate Howard's ideas into their communities.

The association consulted with firms in Long Island, Pennsylvania, New Jersey, and Connecticut, but the financial panic of 1907 prevented any of the planned construction projects from going forward. Even though the garden city concept was not very popular, it was an important and creative example of the reforms proposed to come to terms with the changes brought about by industrialization.

Bibliography

Davis, *Spearheads for Reform: The Social Settlements and the Progressive Movement, 1890–1914*; Scott, *American City Planning Since 1890: A History Commemorating the Fiftieth Anniversary of the American Institute of Planners*; Seligman, *Encyclopedia of the Social Sciences*, vol. 6, pp. 569–71.

Gilder, Richard Watson

writer, editor, reformer, housing advocate
b. February 8, 1844; d. November 18, 1909.

Richard Watson Gilder was a writer and magazine editor whose personal sense of moral responsibility led him to join the crusade for better housing that was being waged by settlement workers and their colleagues in the housing and sanitary reform movements.

Born in Bordentown, New Jersey, Gilder received his early education in the school his father, Henry Watson Gilder, a Methodist minister, operated in Flushing, New York. The younger Gilder read law before enlisting in the First Philadelphia Artillery in 1863. After the death of his father the following year, Gilder helped support the family by working as paymaster of the Camden and Amboy Railroad. He also worked as a reporter for the *Newark Daily Advertiser*.

The association with journalism led Gilder to a career in that field. Gilder was one of the founders of the *Newark Morning Register* newspaper (1868). In addition, he edited a magazine called *Hours at Home* for one year until it merged with the *Scribner's Monthly* in 1870. Gilder then became the periodical's managing editor with special responsibility for art features. In 1881, the *Scribner's Monthly* was succeeded by the *Century*, and Gilder became its editor.

Gilder's influence went far beyond journalism, however. Gilder's father imbued him with a strong sense of moral obligation, and while he was a young man, his father had taken him to see housing conditions in some of the worst areas of New York City. It was not surprising, therefore, that while Gilder continued his publishing work as an adult, he also became involved in social reform work.

Civil service and municipal reform were of particular interest to Gilder, and he served as chair of the **New York Tenement House Committee of 1894**. This committee focused its attention on the structural and sanitary deficiencies of the tenements, the effects of overcrowding, and the lack of parks and playgrounds in tenement neighborhoods. Gilder's work with the committee brought him into contact with a variety of social welfare reformers, including settlement workers who cooperated with the committee by compiling information about conditions in their neighborhoods.

Gilder took his responsibility as chair of this committee seriously. He personally inspected tenement houses in various city neighborhoods and then lobbied the New York State Legislature for the passage of the committee-sponsored bills related to adequate light and ventilation, sanitation, and fire prevention.

After his work as chair of the Tenement House Committee ended, Gilder resumed editing and writing, but he also maintained his association with the New York reform community and was active in various reform campaigns throughout the rest of his life.

Bibliography

Dictionary of American Biography, vol. 4, pp. 275–78; *National Cyclopedia of American Biography*, vol. 1, p. 312.

Glenn, John Mark

social work administrator, foundation director
b. October 28, 1858; d. April 20, 1950.

John Glenn's successful work with the Baltimore Charity Organization Society prepared him for his role as the director of the **Russell Sage Foundation**. In this capacity, he was able to make significant contributions to many of the reform campaigns that were spearheaded by settlement workers.

Glenn was a member of one of Baltimore's most prominent families. He earned a B.A. Degree (1873) and an M.A. Degree (1879) from Washington and Lee University; he graduated from the University of Maryland Law School in 1882.

For several years, Glenn was involved in his family's business concerns but soon his interests expanded. His uncle, also named John Glenn, was a leading figure in the **Charity Organization Society** movement of the time. In addition, Glenn was a devout Episcopalian and was actively involved in church-sponsored social welfare work.

In 1887, Glenn began a 20-year association with the Baltimore reform community. His involvement in the Baltimore social reform community was further strengthened by the fact that his wife, Mary Wilson (Brown) Glenn, whom he married in 1902, served for a time as general secretary of the Baltimore Charity Organization Society. He later became chair of the executive committee of the Baltimore Charity Organization Society and served as president of the city's board of supervisors for city charities. Glenn's national reputation was firmly established after he became president of the National Conference of Charities and Correction. (*See* **National Conference on Social Welfare**.)

In 1907, **Olivia Slocum Sage** established the **Russell Sage Foundation** (RSF) in honor of her husband, Russell Sage. The foundation was established with an initial endowment of $10 million. Glenn was appointed the first director of the RSF, and under his leadership, the foundation became a major national social welfare resource.

Glenn believed that effective social reform must be based on solid research by well-trained workers. He therefore considered that the major functions of the RSF should be research, demonstration, and consultation. He organized the RSF into divisions, such as child welfare, housing, and recreation, and he hired trained social workers to oversee the foundation's operations. During his tenure, the RSF also provided five-year grants to pioneering social work schools in New York, Chicago, Boston, and St. Louis. It also financed the **Pittsburgh Survey**, a major social study of the social and economic conditions of Pittsburgh, Pennsylvania's working poor.

Glenn also developed the RSF's library and publications program. During the years that he directed the foundation, 84 books were published in addition to hundreds of pamphlets on health, housing, and recreation. The library of the RSF became the most comprehensive social work library in the United States.

Glenn retired as director in 1931, but he remained active in the work of the Russell Sage Foundation as a member of the board of trustees until 1948.

Bibliography

Dictionary of American Biography, supl. 4, pp. 332–34; Lubove, *The Professional Altruist: The Emergence of Social Work as a Career, 1880–1930*; Trattner, *Biographical Dictionary of Social Welfare in America*, pp. 321–23.

Goldmark, Josephine Clara
social reformer, researcher, labor advocate, nursing administrator
b. October 13, 1877; d. December 15, 1950.

Josephine Goldmark's sister Pauline introduced her to the New York City reform community, and Josephine quickly established a reputation as a researcher with a particular interest in the effects of worker fatigue on safety and productivity.

After graduating from Bryn Mawr (1898) and completing a year of graduate work in education at Barnard College, Goldmark was introduced to **Florence Kelley**, the head of the National **Consumers' League**, by her sister **Pauline Goldmark** who at the time was assistant secretary of the New York Consumers' League. Josephine worked as a volunteer at the league's New York Office, and she served as publications secretary of the national league (1903–1908).

Goldmark became chair of the National Consumers' League's Committee on Legislation and Legal Defense of Labor Laws in 1908. That same year she and Pauline worked with Kelley to collect the economic, social, and medical data needed to support the Boston lawyer and future U.S. Supreme Court Justice Lewis Brandeis's case in *Miller v. Oregon* in which the Supreme Court ruled that states had the right to regulate the number of hours that women could work. Over the next few years, Goldmark worked with Brandeis on several other occasions as he fought to win legal protection for women and children workers.

Josephine and Pauline Goldmark were also members of the **New York State Factory Investigating Commission** that was established to look into safety conditions in factories in the aftermath of the **Triangle Shirtwaist Company Fire** of March 1911, in which more than 140 young women were killed. The following year Josephine Goldmark published *Fatigue and Efficiency*, a study in which she established that fatigue had an adverse effect on industrial productivity and efficiency. The results of her research were used by reformers to secure shorter working hours and safer working conditions.

Goldmark pursued her studies of working conditions and other reform concerns throughout the rest of her career. During World War I, Goldmark continued her research while working as a member of the Committee on Industrial Fatigue of the Council of National Defense. In this official capacity, she studied the effects of eight- and 10-hour shifts on workers in war-time factories. Goldmark also conducted a health and hospital survey for the city of Cleveland. Based on this research, she secured an appointment as secretary for the Rockefeller Foundation's Committee for the Study of Nursing Education in 1919. Goldmark also served as director of the **New York Visiting Nurse Service** for 20 years.

Goldmark spent the last 10 years of her life in Hartsdale, New York, with her sister, Pauline, where the two women pursued a mutual interest in nature, and Goldmark completed work on a biography of Florence Kelley entitled *Impatient Crusader: Florence Kelley's Life Story*, which was published posthumously in 1953.

Bibliography

Notable American Women, 1607–1950, vol. 2, pp. 60–61; Trattner, *Biographical Dictionary of Social Welfare in America*, pp. 328–30.

Goldmark, Pauline Dorothea
social reformer, labor advocate, author
b. February 21, 1874; d. October 18, 1962.

Pauline Goldmark directed her reform efforts toward improving the working conditions of women and children. Among other interests, she was active in the New York **Consumer's League**, which mobilized consumer pressure to improve working conditions for women in retail stores. Like her sister **Josephine Goldmark**, she also researched women's working conditions and published the results of her findings.

Pauline Goldmark graduated from Bryn Mawr with a degree in biology (1896) and then completed two years (1896–1898) of graduate study in botany, sociology, and zoology at Columbia University and Barnard College. Like many young women of her class, Goldmark was interested in social reform work, which was considered an acceptable activity for young women. Additionally, Goldmark was most probably acquainted with the work being accomplished by the very active New York City reform community since her sister Helen was married to **Felix Adler**, the founder of the **Ethical Culture Society** and an active participant in many reform crusades.

Goldmark's most significant legacy was her work with the New York Consumers' League, which she was active in during most of the first half of the twentieth century. Goldmark joined its staff as an assistant secretary in 1899, and six years later she became the league's executive head, a position she held until 1909. In ad-

dition, she chaired its legislative and investigative committee from 1909 to 1911 and served on its governing board for the next 40 years (1909–1949).

Like her sister Josephine, Goldmark was interested in the working conditions of women and children. In 1902 she co-founded the **New York Child Labor Committee**. When the **New York State Factory Investigating Commission** was formed to investigate safety conditions in the workplace following the **Triangle Shirtwaist Company Fire** of 1911, Goldmark joined its staff and authored two of the commission's reports: one dealing with sanitary conditions in factories, the other with the working conditions of women workers in retail stores. Goldmark was also a member of the New York State Labor Department's Industrial Board (1913–1915), and she served as research secretary of the New York Consumers' League from 1915 to 1918.

After the United States entered World War I in 1917, Goldmark served as chair of the Women in Industry Committee of the State Defense Council. She was also secretary of the Council of National Defense's State Committee on Women in Industry; both these committees were charged with overseeing safety and sanitary conditions of women working in war-related industries. Between 1918 and 1920 in her capacity as the national manager of the Women's Services Section of the United States Railroad Administration's Division of Labor, Goldmark supervised the more than 100,000 women who worked in the railroad industry

In addition to her practical work in the field, Goldmark maintained an interest in research and writing and the training of social workers. She was member of the faculty of the New York School of Philanthropy (*see* **Columbia University Graduate School of Social Work**), and between 1910 and 1912, she served as the head of its Bureau of Social Research. During that time, she supervised the research and writing of a number of studies including *West Side Studies* (1914), an examination of New York City neighborhoods, and *The Longshoremen* (1915), which reported on working conditions on the New York City docks.

During the 1920s, Goldmark worked as a consultant for the American Telegraph and Telephone Company in New York City where she conducted time and motion studies and investigated the causes and effects of fatigue.

Goldmark retired in 1939 and moved to Hartsdale, New York, where she shared a home with her sister Josephine, who died in 1950.

Pauline Goldmark died in 1962 after a long career dedicated to the social reform efforts of the early twentieth century. A long-time activist in the work of the Consumers' League, she was a principal participant in the Factory Investigating Commission, a social work educator, and a pioneering industrial researcher.

Bibliography

Bremner: *From the Depths: The Discovery of Poverty in the United States*; Trattner, *Biographical Dictionary of Social Welfare in America*, pp. 330–32.

Gould, Elgin Ralston Lovell
urban reformer, political economist, housing advocate
b. August 15, 1860; d. August 18, 1915.

Elgin Gould was an urban reformer whose knowledge of housing and urban planning brought him to the attention of settlement workers and other social reformers, particularly in New York City where overcrowding and substandard construction made housing reform a priority. As head of the City and Suburban Homes Company, he successfully introduced the concept of model tenements and provided shelter for thousands of New Yorkers while also earning a profit for the company's investors.

Born in Oshawa, Ontario, Gould earned an A.B. degree from Victoria College in 1881; five years later he received his Ph.D. from Johns Hopkins University. While a graduate student, Gould published articles based on his original research in history and economics, and he compiled data for Lord Bryce's "American Commonwealth." After earning his degree, Gould taught in Washington, DC, and he also obtained a position as an expert assistant to the U.S. Commissioner of Labor, Carroll D. Wright.

Between 1888 and 1892, Gould headed a Bureau of Labor Commission, which was sent to Europe to study production costs, wages, housing conditions, and family budgets. The results of these inquiries appeared in the sixth and seventh Annual Reports of the Commissioner of Labor. While abroad, Gould also studied working-class housing conditions, and shortly after he returned to the United States, he published a comprehensive analysis of housing conditions in Europe and America which was entitled *The Housing of the Working Poor* (1895). This report, which helped to establish Gould's reputation among reformers, provided an in-depth analysis of the initiatives that had been undertaken to solve the housing crisis including sanitary regulations, the provision of model tenements, and initiatives by the private sector to house the poor.

Upon his return, Gould resumed his teaching career at Johns Hopkins (1892–1897) and later taught at the University of Chicago, but he remained active in various reform efforts. After delivering a speech at a housing reform conference sponsored by the New York **Association for Improving the Condition of the Poor**, he was invited in 1896 to organize the City and Suburban Homes Company of New York. This limited-dividend corporation built model tenements designed to make comfortable homes available to the poor at a reasonable price. Gould was president of the City and Suburban Homes Company until his death in 1913. Other housing-related work included Gould's role as a charter member of the New York Charity Organization Society Tenement House Committee and his efforts with settlement workers and other reformers to secure housing reform legislation. Their efforts culminated in the passage of the **New York State Tenement House Law of 1901**.

Gould was also interested in political reform. Along with Robert Fulton Cutting, he organized the Citizen's Union to promote reforms in municipal governments (1897). Gould played a prominent role in Seth Low's election as mayor of New York City, and he was subsequently appointed city chamberlain in Low's reform-minded administration. From 1907 to 1908, Gould was vice-chair of the commission to revise the New York City Charter. Gould also served as chair of the board of trustees of the League for Political Education (1904–1915).

At the height of his career, Gould died unexpectedly in 1915 after a riding accident. He was a competent businessman and administrator whose practical abilities were complimented by a sound theoretical understanding of housing problems. This combination of skill and ability, widely acknowledged by his social reformer colleagues, allowed Gould to make a significant contribution to the campaign to provide quality low-cost housing for the poor.

Bibliography

Dictionary of American Biography, vol. 4, pp. 449–50; *National Cyclopedia of American Biography*, vol.23, pp. 449–50; Trattner; *Biographical Dictionary of Social Reform in America*, pp. 332–34.

Graduate School of Social Service Administration (Chicago)

The consequences of industrialization such as the growth of crowded urban centers and the accompanying health, economic, and social control problems strained existing voluntary philanthropic efforts in many cities. It became apparent that social welfare programs needed to be more efficiently organized and staffed by trained personnel, and volunteers were gradually replaced by paid social welfare workers. The effort to train social workers made it necessary to provide them with specialized schools. Toward this end, professional training schools were established in large urban centers such as Boston, New York, and Chicago, all of which had significant social reform communities.

At the 1897 meeting of the National Conference of Charities and Correction (*see* **National Conference on Social Welfare**), an influential organization composed of leaders from both public and private charitable relief organizations and correctional institutions, **Mary Richmond** of the Baltimore Charity Organization Society called for the establishment of a school of applied philanthropy to offer training for social welfare reformers. **Graham Taylor**, the founder of the **Chicago Commons** settlement house, was aware of Richmond's suggestion. In 1903, after spending six weeks in England visiting settlements and investigating training programs established by the London Charity Organization Society, Taylor decided to establish a training program for social workers in Chicago.

He approached the administration of the University of Chicago with his idea, and its President William Rainey Harper agreed to permit him to offer a series of lectures through a downtown extension program in the fall of 1903, under the name Social Service Center for Practical Training in Philanthropic and Social Work.

Taylor and **Charles R. Henderson**, a colleague, taught the first course, which met weekly for three months. During the winter/spring session of 1903/1904, two additional courses were added. Taylor and Henderson also arranged for occasional lectures by settlement, labor, and reform leaders. During the program's second year of operation, 1904–1905, seven classes were offered.

The University of Chicago assumed financial responsibility for the program, and by the fall of 1905, its name had been changed to the Institute of Social Science and Arts. Offerings were expanded to include summer classes. However, the University of Chicago withdrew its financial backing that same year, forcing the trustees of Chicago Commons to assume this responsibility. They did so, and they also gave the program a new name, the Chicago Institute of Social Science.

In 1907, the **Russell Sage Foundation** began providing grants to pioneering social work schools, and the Chicago Institute of Social Science received a grant of $10,000 each year for the next several years. Taylor hired **Julia Lathrop**, a resident of **Hull House** with a particular interest in social work education, as director of research. **Sophonisba Breckinridge**, a social worker and member of the faculty of the University of Chicago, was named her assistant. The following year the institute was incorporated as an independent corporation called the Chicago School of Civics and Philanthropy. The new school offered two programs—one for general training and a second called the Department of Social Investigation, which emphasized field work.

The Department of Social Investigation made a significant contribution to the success of the school. **Edith Abbott**, another Hull House resident and social work researcher, joined the staff of this department and was instrumental in the development of studies on housing, delinquency, and truancy. After the Russell Sage grant ended in 1915, the Chicago School of Civics and Philanthropy was able to secure government contracts for social investigations which helped it to meet its expenses. Taylor began to investigate the possibility of an academic affiliation again, and after several years of negotiating, the University of Chicago agreed to establish a professional school for social workers. The Chicago School of Civics and Philanthropy merged with the University of Chicago, and in 1920 became known as the University of Chicago School of Social Work. A short time later, the name was changed to the Graduate School of Social Service Administration.

The training program for social workers that Graham Taylor and his colleagues established at the University of Chicago was a pioneering effort in the movement to professionalize the field of social work The program offered students both theoretical and practical learning experiences and took advantage of the well-established Chicago social reform community to enrich the students' learning experiences. The Graduate School of Social Services Administration at the University of Chicago remains active in training social workers up to the present. *See also* **Columbia University Graduate School of Social Work.**

Bibliography

Lubove, *The Professional Altruist: The Emergence of Social Work as a Career, 1880–1930*; Wade, *Graham Taylor: Pioneer for Social Justice, 1851–1938.*

Greenwich House

Prior to establishing Greenwich House in 1902, **Mary Kingsbury Simkhovitch** had been the head resident at two other New York City settlements, the **College Settlement** and the Friendly Aid House. She and her husband, Vladimir Simkhovitch, and a number of colleagues from the Friendly Aid House joined forces with a group of prominent New York City-based social reformers, including **Felix Adler** and **Jacob Riis**, to form the Cooperative Social Settlement Society.

Simkhovitch secured a building on Jones Street on New York's Lower West Side in an area known as the Old American Quarter. This building became the Greenwich House settlement. The people in the neighborhood were primarily second- and third-generation Irish and Germans. A growing population of Italian immigrants and a number of blacks also lived in the area.

Simkhovitch was a determined and energetic woman, and she involved the residents of Greenwich House in a variety of reform efforts. They worked for better housing and sanitation and for adequate recreation facilities. They established a school visiting program, sponsored a baby clinic, and provided a medical and nursing service. The settlement organized the Greenwich Village Improvement Society in 1903, secured a branch of the public library, and opened a public bath (*see* **baths**) that included a gymnasium and a roof garden. In January 1917, Greenwich House moved into larger quarters on nearby Barrow Street. Simkhovitch wrote about her life and work at Greenwich House in her autobiographical account, ***Neighborhood: My Story of Greenwich House*** (1938).

Besides its public services and support of a variety of reform causes, Greenwich House provided fellowships to encourage young women and men to become involved in settlement work and to undertake social research projects. **Mary White Ovington** was the recipient of one such Greenwich House Fellowship, which she used to conduct a groundbreaking study on the condition of blacks in New York City. Greenwich House also served for a time as the headquarters of the New York Association of Neighborhood Workers. (*See* **United Neighborhood Houses.**)

A flourishing community center today, Greenwich House has modified and expanded its offerings and now sponsors a music school and an active drama program.

Bibliography

Simkhovitch, *Neighborhood: My Story of Greenwich House*; Woods and Kennedy, *The Settlement Handbook*.

H

Half a Man: The Status of the Negro in New York (1911)

Mary White Ovington is best known for her book *Half a Man: The Status of the Negro in New York*. Ovington came from a family of ardent abolitionists, an environment that encouraged her egalitarian attitudes. While working at the Greenpoint Settlement on Twenty-third Street in New York City, she witnessed the difficult conditions that black residents of the city were forced to endure. In 1903, Ovington attended a lecture by Booker T. Washington at the **Social Reform Club** in New York City, which further stimulated her interest in the social and economic condition of blacks living in urban centers. These experiences inspired Ovington to undertake a detailed study of New York City's black inhabitants in an effort to arouse interest in their living and working conditions and to bring about significant improvements by establishing a settlement for blacks.

After leaving the Greenpoint Settlement, Ovington was appointed a Greenwich House Fellow in 1904. During the term of her fellowship she lived and worked at **Greenwich House**, the social settlement that had been founded by **Mary Simkhovitch** on Manhattan's Lower West Side in 1902. The neighborhood around Greenwich House had a significant black community, and Ovington spent her time at the settlement learning about the lives of these residents. She eventually became convinced that the best approach to improving race relations was to establish a settlement for blacks.

Although she was interested in the economic situation of blacks, she realized that she needed to examine all aspects of their lives if the settlement she planned to establish was to succeed. Toward this end, she traveled throughout the South studying the social, cultural, and economic conditions that many of the blacks living in New York City had left behind. She then returned to survey almost every black family living in New York City at the time, using census materials, juvenile court records, and personal interviews.

The title of Ovington's book was prompted by a comment made by a black man she interviewed who said that in the North he was considered only "half a man." In it, she describes the home life, education, occupations, and amusements of black people living in New York City during the first decade of the twentieth century.

Ovington's work was well received by contemporary reviewers who described it as an honest assessment that revealed an appreciation for the difficulties under which black men, women, and children lived.

Bibliography

Ovington, *Half a Man: The Status of the Negro in New York*.

Hall, Helen
settlement house leader, consumer advocate, recreation activist
b. January 5, 1892; d. August 31, 1982.

Helen Hall had a varied career in social reform. She entered the field as a child welfare worker and went on to serve in the American Red Cross during both World Wars I and II. She also directed settlements in Philadelphia and New York City, was active in consumer-related campaigns, and conducted research on the standard of living both in the United States and in selected foreign countries.

Born in Kansas City, Missouri, Hall was raised in Port Chester, New York, where she attended the local public schools. Intent on becoming a sculptor, she studied art at Columbia University (1912–1913). Like many young women of her generation, Hall was drawn to a career in social welfare, and in 1915, she enrolled in the New York School of Philanthropy. Afterward, she became involved in settlement work when she organized the Eastchester Neighborhood House in Westchester County and worked as a caseworker for the Westchester County Department of Child Welfare.

Hall joined the American Red Cross during World War I and was stationed in Chateaureux and Solesmes, France, where she administered recreation units in base hospitals operated by the American Expeditionary Force. At the end of the hostilities, she remained in Europe to organize a YWCA girls' club in Mulhouse, Alsace. Before returning to the United States, Hall spent two years (1920–1922) supervising women's relations and organizing recreation services for enlisted men for the U.S. Army in China and in the Philippines.

When she arrived back home, Hall resumed settlement work. She spent 11 years (1922–1933) as director of the University Settlement in Philadelphia. In 1928, Hall became chair of the Unemployment Committee of the **National Federation of Settlements**, the national coalition of settlement houses that promoted cooperation and coordination among its members. Under her direction the committee investigated the impact of unemployment on workers and their families, and issued two publications: *Some Folks Won't Work* by Clinch Calkins and *Case Studies of Unemployment* by Hall.

The decade of the 1930s was a busy one for Hall. In 1932, she traveled to Europe to study unemployment and relief programs in England. The following year she moved to New York City's Lower East Side to succeed **Lillian Wald** as head resident of the **Henry Street Settlement**. In 1934, she served on the Advisory Council to the Committee on Economic Security, which drafted the Social Security Act. In February of the following year, Hall married **Paul U. Kellogg**, the editor of the social welfare journal the *Survey*.

Social welfare reform was not Hall's only concern at this time. She was also interested in consumer-related issues and helped to organize the Consumers National Federation. She served as chair of the federation from 1936 to 1941. Hall was the consumers' representative to the New York State Milk Advisory Committee and was a member of the Consumer Advisory Committee to the United States Office of Price Administration. In 1952 she joined the board of the Consumers Union.

During World War II, Hall took a year's leave of absence (1942–1943) from the Henry Street Settlement and rejoined the American Red Cross to organize service clubs and rest homes for American troops in the South Pacific and Australia. After the war, she supervised an investigation of the living conditions of families with annual incomes under $2,000 for the National Social Welfare Assembly. The data collected during this study was used in a congressional report entitled *Making Ends Meet on Less Than $2,000 a Year*.

Hall retired from the Henry Street Settlement in 1967. However, she maintained her ties to the settlement movement by serving as an observer to the United Nations for the National Federation of Settlements and the International Federation of Settlements.

Bibliography
Chambers, *Seedtime of Reform: American Social Justice and Social Action, 1918–1923*; Hall, *Unfinished Business in Neighborhood and Nation*; Trattner, *Biographical Dictionary of Social Welfare in America*, pp. 343–45; Trolander, *Settlement Houses and the Great Depression*.

Hamilton, Alice
physician, settlement resident, social activist, peace advocate
b. February 27, 1869; d. September 22, 1970.

The Chicago-based settlement **Hull House** provided Alice Hamilton with a base of operations for her long and varied career as a social reformer. Hamilton was a physician, a medical educator, an expert on industrial medicine, and a peace activist. In addition, she served as a consultant on labor-related issues for the federal government.

Hamilton and her sisters and brother grew up in a well-to-do, sheltered family enclave in

Fort Wayne, Indiana. Following family tradition, Alice Hamilton enrolled in Miss Porter's School in Farmington, Connecticut, when she was 17 years old. By the time she graduated two years

Alice Hamilton
The Schlesinger Library, Radcliffe College

later (1885), Hamilton was determined to become a doctor, a career that she believed was meaningful and that would free her from the traditional restraints on women. Returning to Indiana, she enrolled in science courses at the Fort Wayne College of Medicine before entering the University of Michigan in 1892. She earned her degree the following year having specialized in pathology, a field she found more interesting than general medical practice.

Hamilton accepted an internship at Northwestern Hospital for Women and Children in Minneapolis, but after only two months, she transferred to the New England Hospital for Women and Children in Roxbury, near Boston. Hamilton found her work with the poor of Roxbury's slums rewarding.

In 1895, Hamilton returned to Ann Arbor, Michigan, where she worked in a bacteriology laboratory. That same year she traveled to Europe with her sister, the classicist Edith Hamilton, to study bacteriology and pathology at the Universities of Leipzig and Munich before returning to the United States to complete a final year of training at the Johns Hopkins Medical School.

Shortly before leaving for Germany, Hamilton and her sister Norah attended lectures by **Jane Addams** at which she discussed her work at Hull House. Hamilton was so impressed with Addams and her work that she decided to combine her medical career with

settlement work. When she secured a position as a professor of pathology at the Woman's Medical School at Northwestern University in Chicago, Hamilton became a resident at Hull House. She established a well-baby clinic and participated in a number of health-related projects sponsored by the settlement including investigating the causes of a local typhoid epidemic

During the course of her work, Hamilton was able to observe the relationship between environment and disease among the residents of the crowded inner-city neighborhood around Hull House. She was especially sensitive to the health hazards that both parents and children were exposed to as a result of their jobs.

When the Woman's Medical School closed in 1902, Hamilton moved to the Memorial Institute for Infectious Diseases as a bacteriologist. She continued to live and work at Hull House. In September 1908, she contributed an article to the social welfare journal *Charities and The Commons* (*see* **the Survey**) about industry-related illness in America, one of the first studies to appear on the subject in the United States. That same year, Hamilton was selected by Governor Charles S. Deneen to serve on the Illinois Commission on Occupational Diseases. When the commission's initial investigation revealed the need for an in-depth examination of industry-related illness, the state legislature funded a two-year project to look into the situation. Hamilton resigned from the commission to become the medical investigator charged with overseeing the survey.

At first, she concentrated her efforts on the dangers of lead, which was the most widely used industrial poison at the time. Hamilton eventually went on to investigate a number of other dangerous materials and to serve as a special investigator for the Federal Bureau of Labor (1911–1912). She publicized her work about industrial disease by speaking at the annual meeting of the National Conference of Charities and Correction (*see* **National Conference on Social Welfare**), an influential organization composed of leaders from both public and private charitable relief organizations and correctional institutions.

By 1915, Hamilton had become the foremost authority on lead poisoning in the United States. That year she accompanied Addams to The Hague in the Netherlands, to attend the **International Congress of Women**, which was organized to protest the war in Europe. She also accompanied Addams on her peace mission to the capitals of several of the combatants.

Even after the United States entered the hostilities in 1917, Hamilton, like Addams, remained opposed to the war.

In 1919, Harvard University instituted a degree program in industrial hygiene. Hamilton was hired as an assistant professor of industrial medicine, becoming Harvard's first woman professor. She arranged to spend only six months per year at Harvard so that she could spend the remaining time at Hull House. She worked on a series of three-year appointments until her retirement in 1935.

In addition to her work at Harvard and at Hull House, Hamilton maintained an active interest in the women's reform network. She was a member of the League of Women Voters and the Chicago branch of the **Women's Trade Union League**. She was a vice president of the National **Consumers' League** and a national board member of the **Women's International League for Peace and Freedom**. Hamilton was also a member of the League of Nations Health Committee.

Following her retirement from Harvard, Hamilton accepted a position as a medical consultant to the Division of Labor Standards, a unit of the Department of Labor which was headed by the social reformer **Frances Perkins**. The division promoted uniform labor legislation and administrative practices, provided technical assistance to state labor departments, and sponsored special training programs for state officials. In the course of her work, Hamilton conducted surveys, attended conferences, and testified at congressional hearings.

By 1940, Hamilton had left the Division of Labor Standards. She continued to lecture on industrial standards and published her autobiography, ***Exploring the Dangerous Trades*** (1943).

Hamilton died in 1970 at the age of 101 after a productive career as a social reformer, physician, pioneer in industrial safety and health, labor reformer, and peace advocate.

Bibliography

Dictionary of American Biography, supl. 8, pp. 241–42; Sicherman, *Alice Hamilton: A Life in Letters*; Sicherman, *Notable American Women: The Modern Period*, pp. 303–06; Trattner, *Biographical Dictionary of Social Welfare in America*, pp. 345–47.

Handbook of Settlements (1911)

The reformers active in the settlement movement realized the value of sharing information, coordinating activities, and when possible, sharing resources. The *Handbook of Settlements* was an attempt to catalog the participants and accomplishments of the settlement movement in the United States up to the time of its publication.

The *Handbook* was the initial enterprise undertaken by the newly established **National Federation of Settlements**, which was a coalition of settlement houses that promoted cooperation and coordination among its members. It was intended to continue the *Bibliography of Settlements,* which had been published by the **College Settlements Association**, an organization started by a group of Smith College alumnae that was also intended to coordinate the activities of its member settlements. The material for the *Handbook* was compiled and edited by **Robert A. Woods** and **Albert J. Kennedy**, both residents of **South End House** settlement in Boston. The *Handbook* presents information on 413 settlements in 32 states, the District of Columbia, and the Hawaiian Islands.

The book is arranged alphabetically by state, then by city, and then by the name of the settlement. Entries for the individual settlements include the name and address of the house, date established and principal objectives, a description of the neighborhood and a list of the settlement's activities. Data on the number of residents and volunteers are listed as well as the name of the head residents. Each entry has a bibliography of authorized statements issued by the settlement, and many entries present a bibliography of articles and studies written by the settlement's residents. Information about the residents' publications was added to demonstrate the amount and kind of research and analysis undertaken by those active in the settlement movement.

In the course of preparing the manuscript, almost all of the settlements listed were visited, and interviews were conducted with their leading representatives. In addition to the entries for the individual houses, the *Handbook* also includes a brief listing of "Historical Antecedents in England and America" and a "General Bibliography" of books and articles, most of which were written by head workers or settlement founders. The book also has a listing of settlements in other countries and a section on discontinued settlements that includes brief summaries of those institutions that were no longer operating and their work.

The *Handbook of Settlements* was well received by settlement workers and served a dual purpose. It provided settlement workers with comprehensive information about the day-to-day staff, facilities, activities, and publications of the various settlements across the United States. At the same time, it presented a brief history of the American Settlement Movement which provided settlement workers at the time and present-day historians with a historical perspective of this multifaceted social reform effort.

Bibliography
Woods, *Handbook of Settlements*.

Hartley House

Although they may have had common goals, charity organization societies such as the New York **Association for Improving the Condition of the Poor** (AICP) had different missions and employed different methodologies than settlements. In the case of the New York AICP, these differences came together when the AICP established a settlement, Hartley House.

The man behind the Hartley House move was **James G. Phelps Stokes**, a member of a wealthy New York family whose interest in social reform led him to serve on the board of a number of social welfare-related organizations and institutions including the **New York Child Labor Committee**, the **Outdoor Recreation League**, and the New York **Association for Improving the Condition of the Poor** (AICP). He was also a resident at the **University Settlement**.

Stokes believed that charity organizations like the AICP should incorporate settlement work into their activities. In 1897, he persuaded the other AICP board members to establish a settlement which they named Hartley House, in honor of **Robert Hartley**, the founder of the New York AICP.

The settlement was located on West Forty-sixth Street in a crowded area populated primarily by Irish, German, and Italian immigrants. The house was originally established to provide housekeeping training and workrooms for unskilled women and children from the neighborhood, but it soon offered much more. Its residents conducted social surveys, helped organize the work of the local home and school visitors association, and ran a relief station and employment bureau on behalf of the New York AICP.

Like other settlements, Hartley House maintained a kindergarten and a public bath. It offered clubs and classes and sponsored a debating league. Additionally, Hartley House maintained two summer camps, Hartley Farm in Convent, New Jersey, and Weeburn Farm in Talmage Hill, Connecticut.

What may have begun as an experiment in combining the social reform techniques of the AICP and the settlement movement has proven to be a long-lasting community service. The Hartley House still serves its New York City community today, providing a variety of social services including a day care center.

Bibliography
Trattner, *Biographical Dictionary of Social Welfare in America*, pp. 693–95; Woods and Kennedy, *The Handbook of Settlements*.

Hartley, Robert Milham
reformer, social service agency founder and administrator
b. February 17, 1796; d. March 3, 1881.

As a young man, Robert Hartley had not intended to devote himself to a career as a social reformer, but he soon immersed himself in a variety of the social reform initiatives that were gaining momentum during the 1830s and 1840s. Most notably, he assumed a leadership role in the work of the New York **Association for Improving the Condition of the Poor** (AICP).

In 1820 at the age of 24, he entered Fairfield Academy in Herkimer County, New York, to study for the ministry. Forced to abandon his studies because of illness, he relocated to New York City and set himself up as a dry goods merchant. While pursuing his business interests, Hartley was also active in local Bible and tract societies, and he served as a lay reader in a neighborhood church.

In 1829, Hartley and a group of associates organized the New York City Temperance Society, and he served as the society's secretary. Hartley soon became a part-time businessman and a full-time reformer. In his position as secretary of the Temperance Society, Hartley started investigating all of the local distilleries, confronting the owners about the often devastating effects of their products. During the course of his investigations, Hartley discovered that cows were being fed distillery refuse and that in turn, their milk was consumed by infants living in inner-city tenements. Based on his research, Hartley concluded that the rise in infant mortality rates among these same children was directly related to their consumption of this contaminated milk.

Hartley joined the New York City Mission Society (1833), coming into contact with a group of civic-minded, wealthy Christian business owners and professionals. Like many of their social class, Hartley and his colleagues believed that poverty was a manifestation of a moral defect. However, at the same time, they believed that they had a Christian duty to improve the character of the poor. The economic distress that hit New York City following the Panic of 1837 provided Hartley and his associates with an opportunity to transform their convictions into actions. In 1843, they established the New York Association for Improving the Condition of the Poor (AICP), a citywide, nonsectarian organization that, among other objectives, sought to coordinate the city's public and private relief agencies.

Hartley served as the general secretary of the AICP until his retirement in 1876 and significantly influenced the organization's ideology and operations. In an attempt to identify and classify the principal causes of poverty, Hartley distinguished between the worthy and the unworthy poor, those who were willing to work but unable, and those who chose to live off the charity of others rather than work even though they were able. In ranking the major causes of poverty, Hartley listed intemperance, improvidence, and, curiously, extravagance. He also acknowledged the want of moral culture, lack of education, and a variety of environmental factors.

To coordinate the benevolent efforts of the many charitable agencies in New York at the time, Hartley and the AICP apportioned the city into 22 districts which were further subdivided into 278 sections. Each district was governed by an advisory committee that recruited and trained a corps of paternal guardians or **friendly visitors**. These volunteer visitors were each assigned a section, and it was the visitor's responsibility to investigate requests for assistance.

Hartley used the resources of the AICP to establish dispensaries and he cooperated with the New York City Board of Health to compel landlords to improve their buildings' sanitary conditions. He also supported the construction of model tenements. In addition, he lobbied the New York State Legislature to pass a truancy law and a compulsory school attendance law. In 1851, using a grant of $50,000 from New York State and a matching contribution of its own, Hartley and the AICP established the New York Juvenile Asylum. The asylum was intended to serve as a refuge for children from the dangerous streets.

Hartley was also instrumental in the formation of the Society for the Relief of the Ruptured and Crippled in 1863. The society provided surgical assistance as well as artificial limbs free of charge to the poor.

Hartley retired on his eightieth birthday in 1876. He died of pneumonia five years later. Hartley's career bridged the gap between the volunteerism of the private charity approach and the beginning professionalization of publicly funded social welfare programs. Many of the issues that Hartley considered were later taken up by settlement workers including the need for clean milk for children, the establishment of dispensaries, and the need to work with the municipal authorities to improve sanitary conditions. Hartley's contributions were further acknowledged when the AICP decided to name its settlement, **Hartley House**, in his honor.

Bibliography

Boyer, *Urban Masses and Moral Order in America: 1820–1920;* Brandt, *The Growth and Development of the AICP and COS: A Preliminary and Exploratory Review;* Lubove, "The New York Association for Improving the Condition of the Poor: The Formative Years"; Trattner, *Biographical Dictionary of Social Welfare in America,* pp. 357–60.

Henderson, Charles Richmond
clergyman, educator, social reformer
b. December 17, 1848; d. March 29, 1915.

Charles Henderson was a religious man who devoted himself to his ministerial work, to teaching, and to a variety of social welfare-related causes. He was a member of Chicago's active reform community, and he contributed to the development of social work education and to crusades such as prison and labor reforms.

Henderson graduated from the University of Chicago (1870) and earned a Bachelor of Divinity degree from the Baptist Union Theological Seminary in 1873. That same year he became the minister of the First Baptist Church of Terre Haute, Indiana. He also served as the first president of the Terre Haute Charity Organization Society.

In 1882, Henderson moved to Detroit, Michigan, to assume responsibility for the Woodward Avenue Baptist Church. He also became involved in social reform efforts in Detroit as a member of the local charity organization society and as an arbitrator during a strike against the Detroit Street Car Company. Henderson also became interested in the field of prison management at this time.

His work in Detroit brought Henderson to the attention of the administration of the University of Chicago, and in 1892, he was offered a position in the school's new Department of

Sociology. Within 12 years he became chair of the department.

In the fall 1903, Henderson joined with **Graham Taylor**, the founder and head resident of the **Chicago Commons** settlement house, to teach a 12-week evening course for a small group of men and women who were involved in various types of social welfare work in Chicago. The course, which examined dependency and social welfare agencies, was a successful venture. Taylor and Henderson expanded their offerings over the following years, and their pioneering work contributed to the establishment and growth of the Chicago School of Civics and Philanthropy. (*See* **Graduate School of Social Service Administration**.) In addition to his work with Taylor, Henderson taught a course in rural sociology at the University of Chicago. His use of the local survey method contributed to the growth of the "Chicago School" of sociology.

Henderson fostered a sense of cooperation between the university and various community-based social service organizations. He encouraged his students to work with local charitable agencies and in settlement houses. He was a frequent visitor at **Hull House**, the Chicago settlement founded by **Jane Addams** and **Ellen Gates Starr**, where he participated in a variety of activities, including lecture and discussion groups. Henderson also worked at Chicago Commons.

Like many social activists of the time, Henderson worked with a number of organizations on the local, state, and national levels. He served as president of the American Prison Association (1902) and was a representative to the International Prison Congress in 1909. Henderson served on the Illinois Occupational Disease Commission, and as president of the National Conference of Charities and Correction (*See* **National Conference on Social Welfare**) (1898–1899) and of the United Charities of Chicago (1913).

In addition to his teaching and social reform activities, Henderson wrote several books including *The Social Spirit of America* (1896), *Modern Methods of Charity* (1904), and *Citizens in Industry* (1915). In poor health due to overwork, Henderson died unexpectedly in 1915.

Bibliography

Trattner, *Biographical Dictionary of Social Welfare in America*, pp. 371–74; Wade, *Graham Taylor: Pioneer for Social Justice, 1851–1938*.

Henry Street Settlement

The Henry Street Settlement on New York City's Lower East Side served as a center of social reform on the local, state, and national levels. Through the work of its corps of visiting nurses, it was a pioneer in the field of public health nursing. In addition, the settlement's founder and guiding force, **Lillian Wald**, provided inspiration and leadership for a variety of reform crusades.

In July 1893, Lillian Wald and **Mary Brewster** established a **Visiting Nurse Service** to care for the residents of tenement neighborhoods on New York City's Lower East Side. At first the women operated the service out of the **College Settlement** on Rivington Street. A short time later, they relocated to a tenement on nearby Jefferson Street. In 1895, thanks to the generosity of the banker and philanthropist **Jacob Schiff**, the women moved into a house at 265 Henry Street and opened the Nurses' Settlement.

The Nurses' Settlement provided a home nursing service to the people in the surrounding neighborhood. Wald soon realized that providing only a nursing service was not enough to meet the varied needs of the community. In March 1903, she reorganized and renamed the Nurse's Settlement as the Henry Street Settlement. This new settlement provided a full range of social services in addition to the nursing service.

The residents of the Henry Street Settlement involved themselves in both research projects and reform activities. Numerous investigations of conditions in their neighborhood and in surrounding areas were undertaken, often in cooperation with their colleagues in other settlements such as the **University Settlement** and the **College Settlement**. They lobbied for better housing and for sanitary reforms. Wald and the other Henry Street residents were active in the campaign for public recreation facilities, and they established one of the earliest public play spaces in New York City. The residents also sponsored clubs and a kindergarten; offered dance and carpentry classes; and maintained a lending library, a gymnasium, and a savings bank.

The services of the Henry Street Nurses were available seven days a week, 24 hours per day. The nursing service continued to provide home care and expanded its program of convalescent houses outside the city with special facilities for tuberculosis patients. Additionally, the settlement sponsored medical inspections

Backyard of the Henry Street Settlement.
Museum of the City of New York

in the public schools and was active in the clean milk campaign and the baby hygiene movement.

When Wald and her colleagues first moved to Henry Street, the neighbors were primarily recent immigrants from Eastern and Central Europe. Over time, these groups were replaced by immigrants from Asia and Latin America. Eventually, the Henry Street Settlement included three branch locations. The uptown Nurses' Settlement on East Seventy-Ninth Street was established in 1896. In October 1906, a branch was opened in the Bronx on Cauldwell Avenue, and the Stillman Branch for black people was opened in December 1906.

Under Wald's leadership, the Henry Street Settlement earned a national reputation as a leading force in a variety of social welfare reforms including child labor, labor unions, and education. Residents such as the social reformer **Florence Kelley**, who lived at the house for many years, were active in the establishment of reform organizations, including the **Women's Trade Union League** and the **Consumers' League**. The Henry Street Settlement sponsored a scholarship program to encourage students to remain in school after age 14, and established Clinton Hall, which served as the headquarters of several trade unions in addi-

tion to supplying meeting space for community groups and lectures. The settlement even contributed to the arts through its support of the **Neighborhood Playhouse** and the Henry Street Music School. Wald wrote about her life and work in two autobiographical accounts, *The House on Henry Street* (1915) and *Windows on Henry Street* (1934).

When Wald retired in 1933, she was succeeded by **Helen Hall**, the former head worker at the University Settlement in Philadelphia and president of the **National Federation of Settlements**. During Hall's term as head of the Henry Street Settlement, the Nursing Service became a separate administrative unit in 1937. In 1944 it was incorporated as the Visiting Nurse Service of New York.

The Henry Street Settlement continues to serve its community on New York City's Lower East Side. It is a busy community center that sponsors a wide variety of social welfare and cultural programs and stands as a memorial to the vision and dedication of Lillian Wald and her colleagues.

Bibliography
Jackson, *Encyclopedia of New York City*, p. 540; Romanofsky, *The Greenwood Encyclopedia of American Institutions: Social Service Organizations*, vol. 1, pp. 345–51; Woods, *The Handbook of Settlements*.

Hill, Octavia

housing reformer, charity worker
b. December 3, 1838; d. August 13, 1912.

Octavia Hill's interest in improving the lives of London's poor inspired her to become a leader in housing reform efforts in England. Her methods of property management and development, which limited investors' profits and provided funding for property improvements, were adopted by American housing reformers.

Hill was the daughter of James Hill, a corn merchant and banker who was active in local municipal and education reform efforts. Octavia was especially influenced by her maternal grandfather, Dr. Thomas Southwood Smith, known for his work on fever epidemics and sanitation. Southwood Smith's work brought him into contact with the poorer class, and his work in East London sparked the public health movement in Britain in the 1840s. He shared his experiences and described the living conditions of the poor to young Octavia and her sisters.

When she was 14, Hill began working at the Ladies' Guild, a cooperative association in London that was managed by her mother and supported by the Christian Socialists. Within a short time, Hill assumed responsibility for a branch of the guild that taught school children how to make toys. While at the guild, she came under the influence of the prominent Christian Socialist **Frederick Denison Maurice**. Hill shared with him a desire to assist the poor in becoming economically independent.

In 1853, not long after she began working with the Ladies' Guild, Hill met John Ruskin who assisted her with her artistic training and employed her to copy his pictures for his book *Modern Painters*, an association that would eventually help her reform efforts. In 1856, Hill began working at the Workingmen's College in Great Ormond Street, which had been established in 1854 by Maurice and some associates. She served as secretary for the women's classes at the college and soon established a school of her own which she and her sisters operated. During this time, Hill spent a considerable amount of time visiting her poor neighbors, gaining firsthand knowledge of their living conditions.

In 1864, with Ruskin's assistance, she purchased a group of buildings in the Marylebone section of London which she remodeled into model flats to create what she referred to as an urban village for the poor. Hill believed that improving the environment in which people lived would eventually transform their character.

In addition to her efforts to provide adequate housing accommodations, Hill also purchased vacant lots and turned them into urban parks. She successfully managed the properties in her care, employing a large number of women trained as rent collectors who ensured that the tenants met their financial obligations promptly. Hill and her rent collectors were not only concerned with their tenants' fiscal habits and physical needs. They also sponsored sewing clubs and play groups to foster a sense of community. Hill invested a portion of the rents collected to pay for improvements requested by her tenants.

Hill proved to be a successful manager who earned her investors a profit of five percent, and over time, more properties were placed under her control. Additionally, some civic-minded investors donated substantial amounts of money to Hill to enable her to purchase and build homes for the poor. One of Hill's more significant property management responsibilities was her appointment by the Ecclesiastical Commissioners in 1884 to manage a substantial portion of the Southwark property holdings in London's slum areas.

Hill's housing work left her little time for her teaching and artistic pursuits. In 1874 as an expression of support, a group of her friends and supporters established a fund to allow her to pursue her interest in housing reform without having to earn a living.

In addition to her housing-related reform efforts, Hill was also active in other areas. She worked with the London Charity Organization Society and was one of the founders of the National Trust for Places of Historic Interest or Natural Beauty in 1895. Although she was reluctant to become involved in political activities, Hill worked for the passage of the Artisans' Dwelling Act (1875), which provided for an extensive slum clearance project in London's East End. She was a prominent member of the Commons Preservation Society, which worked to save common areas and open spaces in and near London. Hill was also a member of the Royal Commission on the Poor Laws (1905). Her housing reform methods were adopted by the city of Edinburgh and by many communities in the United States whose reform organizations used her concept of rent collectors as the inspiration for their corps of **friendly visitors**.

Hill maintained an active interest in housing reform activities up to her death in 1912.

Bibliography

Dictionary of National Biography, 1912–1921, p. 257–59; Meacham, *Toynbee Hall and Social Reform, 1880–1914: The Search for Community*, Seligman, *Encyclopedia of the Social Sciences*, vol. 7, pp. 350–51.

Hine, Lewis Wickes

photographer, child labor reformer
b. September 26, 1874; d. November 4, 1940.

Lewis Hine's photographs documented the work and accomplishments of some of the most significant reform crusades of the early twentieth century. His images of immigrants, children, and working men and women inspired many to become involved in social welfare campaigns either as active participants or as benefactors.

Hine was born in Oshkosh, Wisconsin, and he graduated from the local high school in 1892. That same year his father died unexpectedly, and Lewis was compelled to take a variety of low-paying jobs to help support his family. While working these jobs, he continued his education through extension courses. In 1900, Hine met Sara Ann Rich, a student at the Oshkosh Normal School, and they were married four years later. Rich introduced Hine to Frank A. Manny, an instructor in education and psychology at the Normal School. Manny persuaded Hine to enroll in the University of Chicago to earn a degree in education. When he graduated the following year (1901), Hine joined the faculty of the **Ethical Culture Society** school in New York City where Manny had recently been appointed principal.

Hine's early years in New York City were exciting ones. Manny encouraged him to take up photography to record the various academic and social functions at the Ethical Culture School, and Hine became an accomplished photographer. In addition to his teaching responsibilities and his interest in photography, Hine continued his education and earned a Ph.D. from New York University in 1905. He completed additional graduate work in sociology at Columbia University in 1907.

One of Hine's first photographic projects was documenting the arrival of new immigrants on Ellis Island. His straightforward, compelling images captured the fear and excitement of the immigrants' first experience with America. Hine soon began photographing the newly arrived in their homes and at their jobs. As a result of what he witnessed, he developed an interest in social reform work and soon became acquainted with many of the social reformers living and working in New York City at the time including **Paul U. Kellogg** and his brother **Arthur Kellogg** and **Florence Kelley**.

Lewis Hine Photo of a Few Boys Going to Work on the Night Shift in a Virginia Glass Factory
Museum of the City of New York

Through his connection with the Kelloggs, Hine joined the staff of *Charities and the Commons*, later the **Survey**, as a social photographer. Kelley helped him secure freelance photographic work for the **National Child Labor Committee** (NCLC). Hine also worked for the National **Consumers' League**. In addition, several volumes of the **Pittsburgh Survey**, a comprehensive social research project, include examples of Hine's work.

In 1908, Hine resigned from the Ethical Culture School to work for the National Child Labor Committee. During the next decade, he traveled across the United States investigating and photographing the unsafe and unsanitary living and working conditions of child laborers. The NCLC used Hine's photographs in its publications and news releases and in exhibitions organized by social welfare reformers. Hine's photographs were widely circulated and were instrumental in bringing about a number of significant reforms such as restricting children's working hours and the institution of minimum age restrictions.

Hine left the National Child Labor Committee in 1918 to join the staff of the American Red Cross as an assistant to **Homer Folks**, the director of the Department of Civil Affairs in France. During his year in Europe, Hine photographed civilians in central, eastern, and southern Europe. His work was used to illustrate Folks's book *The Human Costs of the War* (1920).

When he returned to the United States in 1919, Hine secured a position at the National Red Cross Headquarters in New York City photographing the organization's domestic projects and organizing exhibitions. He left the Red Cross in 1930 to pursue a career as a freelance photographer. When he was no longer using his camera to aid the work of investigative committees and other reform efforts, the focus of Hine's work changed. His photographs now displayed a more symbolic style. He celebrated the American worker in his images of assembly line workers and various craftsmen; however, these photographs were not commercially successful.

Hine's contacts in the reform community helped him to obtain other work. Paul Kellogg, editor of the *Survey*, assisted Hine in securing freelance assignments for the NCLC, the National Consumers' League, the Amalgamated Clothing Workers of America, and Western Electric. In 1930, the social reformer and political activist **Belle Moskowitz** persuaded former New York Governor **Alfred Smith** to hire Hine to photograph the construction of the Empire State Building. Hine's work was a day-by-day chronicle of the project. He even photographed the driving in of the final rivet while suspended from a crane.

Hine published two books during the 1930s, *Men at Work* (1932), a collection of industrial photographs, and *Through the Loom* (1933), a portfolio of photographs of textile mill workers. He also completed an assignment for the Tennessee Valley Authority and the Rural Electrification Administration. Through his association with the Photo League of New York City, Hine was able to convey his experience to a new generation of social photographers, and although he died a poor man, he left a significant photographic legacy.

Bibliography

Dictionary of American Biography, supl. 2, pp. 305–06; Jackson, *Encyclopedia of New York City*, p. 544; Trattner, *Biographical Dictionary of Social Welfare in America*, pp. 374–76.

Hiram House

Although the work of settlements in larger urban centers such as Chicago, New York, Boston, and Philadelphia seemed to dominate accounts of the American Settlement Movement, many other lesser-known houses served the needs of residents in smaller cities. One example is Hiram House, which offered assistance to the people of Cleveland, Ohio, for more than 50 years. Its programs and activities reflected the influence of its founder, **George Bellamy**.

Hiram House was established in July 1896 by Bellamy, a recent graduate of Hiram College for which the settlement was named. Bellamy served the settlement for 50 years, first as head resident and later as a member of the settlement's board of trustees. The settlement's first location, on Washington Street on the lower east side of Cleveland, was in a mixed tenement and factory neighborhood that was inhabited principally by Jews and later by Italians. The house moved several times before a permanent four-story brick building was constructed in 1900 on Orange Avenue.

The settlement maintained an auditorium and a gymnasium, and its playground provided the only play space in the surrounding district. Like settlement workers in other houses, Bellamy and his colleagues worked to improve housing and sanitary conditions in their neighborhood and to build public **baths**.

Hiram House maintained a kindergarten, a milk station, and a savings bank. The house also functioned as a branch of the Cleveland Public Library and as a branch of the Cleveland Visiting Nurse Association. It sponsored clubs for children, young people, and adults, and offered sewing, cooking, and music classes. In 1897, the settlement established Camp Hiram in Chagrin Falls, Ohio. The operation of the camp eventually became the house's primary activity as more and more of its services were taken over by the municipal authorities.

Although Hiram House eventually ceased operations in the early part of the twentieth century, its work and accomplishments illustrate the type of settlement work that was being carried out in smaller cities across the United States.

Bibliography
National Cyclopaedia of American Biography, vol. XLIX, pp. 29-30; Woods, *The Handbook of Settlements*.

Holland, Henry Scott
clergyman, social reformer
b. December 25, 1832; d. March 17, 1918.

Henry Scott Holland was instrumental in persuading the leaders of the Church of England to acknowledge that the church had a role to play in the social sphere as well as in the spiritual. He co-founded the Christian Social Union in 1889, which sponsored a settlement house, and he also founded and edited a Christian social reform magazine, the *Commonwealth*.

Educated at Oxford University, Holland served as Canon of St. Paul's Cathedral in London from 1884 to 1910. Holland participated in the resurgence of **Christian Socialism** which occurred in England in the late 1880s. This revival of Christian Socialism was more diffuse than the movement inspired by **Frederick Maurice** and **Charles Kingsley** in the 1840s. In his work, Holland outlined how the church and the labor movement could work together. By not identifying himself with socialism, Holland was able to persuade those who held more conservative church opinions to consider the views of the social idealists who advocated social reform. In this way, Holland contributed to the growth of friendly relations between the church and labor in England.

The revival of interest in Christian Socialism was dominated by high churchmen who exerted a considerable influence through the work of a number of organizations, the most powerful of which was the Christian Social Union (CSU). The CSU was founded in 1889 by Holland and Charles Gore. Under their leadership, the young high church clergymen who belonged to the CSU fused their interest in radical politics with their personal religious commitments.

The members of the Christian Social Union founded Oxford House, the second major English settlement. Oxford House was strongly denominational (Anglican), and the settlement's residents were very active in parish work.

In addition to his social reform work, Holland also founded and edited (1895–1912) the *Commonwealth*, a monthly magazine dedicated to the study of social conditions in the light of Christianity. Holland was appointed Regius Professor of Divinity at Oxford in 1910, a position he held until his death in 1918.

British and American social reformers were members of an active transatlantic intellectual community, and many young American settlement workers traveled to Europe to observe the work being accomplished by their British counterparts. In this way, they had first-hand knowledge of the influence that the Christian Socialist revival, which Holland spearheaded, exerted on the settlement movement in England. Through his writings and his work with the Christian Social Union, Holland helped to popularize the doctrines of Christian Socialism which were incorporated into the reform crusades of settlement workers and other social welfare reformers.

Bibliography
Dictionary of National Biography, supl. 3, pp. 260–62; Seligman, *Encyclopedia of the Social Sciences*, vol. 7, p. 415.

The House on Henry Street (1915)

Written in 1915, *The House on Henry Street* provides a picture of the people and events that **Lillian Wald** encountered during her first 20 years living and working in the settlement house at 265 Henry Street on New York City's Lower East Side. Much of the material in the book appeared in a series of six articles that ran in the *Atlantic Monthly* between March and August of 1915.

Wald's first experience with New York's crowded tenement neighborhoods came in 1893 when she was teaching a home health care class for new immigrants. This work led her to establish a **visiting nurse service** that provided nursing care to tenement dwellers in their homes. In 1893, Wald and a fellow nursing student, **Mary Brewster**, ran their nursing service from a tenement apartment on Jefferson

Street. Two years later they moved to the house on Henry Street and established the Nurses' Settlement, later incorporated as the **Henry Street Settlement**.

The *House on Henry Street* begins with Wald's account of her early experiences in which she relates her initial impressions of the neighborhood and the people who lived in it. Through a series of vignettes she provides the reader with a vivid account of the hardships and joys that she shared with her neighbors. She conveys her impressions of the squalor of tenement life and the numerous acts of kindness that she encountered as she won the trust of the people she sought to help. Although the book is primarily anecdotal, Wald does convey her philosophy of settlement work, which is based on the concept of mutual respect.

Like **Jane Addams**'s book, *Twenty Years at Hull-House* (1910), the *House on Henry Street* is part of the official history of the American Settlement Movement. Written by one of the movement's best known and most well-respected participants, it provides valuable insights into the philosophy and motivations of the women and men who were urban reform pioneers. Wald was a first generation settlement worker and her account of her experiences provided an opportunity for younger settlement workers to understand the context of their own work. For historians, the book provides a picture of a lost world seen through the eyes of an idealistic, yet realistic, young woman.

Bibliography

Wald, *The House on Henry Street*.

How the Other Half Lives: Studies among the Tenements of New York (1890)

Settlement workers were active in the prolonged crusade to improve housing conditions in the squalid tenement neighborhoods. They regularly worked with housing reformers collecting data and documenting conditions, and they also provided valuable insights into the needs of their immigrant neighbors. Although the settlement workers and their housing reform colleagues wrote graphic, accurate descriptions of the conditions they observed, they could only create word pictures in their reports and official accounts. With the publication of **Jacob A. Riis**'s *How the Other Half Lives: Studies among the Tenements of New York* in 1890, the public could see for itself.

Riis emigrated from Denmark in 1870 and worked at a variety of jobs before becoming a police reporter for the *New York Tribune*. He wrote human interest stories about people he encountered in the police courts and followed up leads from the police blotter. Riis generally began his pieces with a dramatic statement about the individual's situation. He then established a sense of the person's struggle for survival in the hostile urban slum environment and closed his account with an appeal to the reader's sense of justice.

Riis's first inspiration to write about the conditions he revealed in *How the Other Half Lives* came while covering the hearings of the Tenement House Commission of 1884. (*See* **New York Tenement House Commissions**.) During the hearings, Riis gained a certain respect for the people who lived in the slums. Unlike some of his contemporaries, Riis became convinced that these people were better than their environment. Over the next few years he covered other housing reformers' meetings calling attention to slum conditions. He soon found himself taking a personal interest in the housing reform movement.

Riis began delivering lectures about the slums, and he illustrated his talks with a series of lantern slides. In 1888, his photographs of the slums appeared in print in *The New York Sun*. An editor for *Scribner's Magazine* who attended one of his lectures invited Riis to write an article. The following year *Scribner's* published Riis's book-length manuscript, which he called *How the Other Half Lives: Studies among the Tenements of New York*.

In the book, Riis constructed a concept of the slum through a number of individual stories filled with picturesque details such as "Downtown Back Alleys," "The Problem of the Children," and "Pauperism in the Tenements." Although present-day readers may be offended by Riis's use of racial and ethnic stereotypes in his descriptive vignettes, they also reveal his personal compassion for the men, women, and children he encountered as well as his belief that they deserved a better life.

The book was well received by both the general public and the critics. It soon became required reading for settlement workers and other Progressive Era reformers.

Bibliography

Davis, *Spearheads for Reform: The Social Settlements and the Progressive Movement, 1890–1914*; Riis, *How the Other Half Lives: Studies among the Tenements of New York*.

Hudson Guild

The Hudson Guild was founded by **John Elliott** in March 1895 to teach the ethics of social organization and to prepare the recently arrived immigrants in its neighborhood for productive lives as American citizens.

Like **Stanton Coit**, Elliott had been inspired by **Felix Adler**, the founder of the **Ethical Culture Society**, to become involved in social reform activities. In establishing the guild under the auspices of the society, he attempted to apply some of Coit's ideas about community service and reform to his enterprise, although in modified form. Elliott called his establishment a guild, not a settlement, and his distinction was based on two principles. First, he believed that a guild should be as financially independent as possible, and second, he contended that clubs and activities should be self-governing and initiated by the people in the neighborhood. His watchwords were self-education and self-government, and every club was responsible for doing something either for the house or for the neighborhood.

The guild was run by the Clubs Council which included Elliott, who did not have a vote in council decisions but a veto; staff members; and representatives from all of the clubs and organizations that used the house. The council was responsible for apportioning and collecting rents from the clubs and for paying house expenses that exceeded $1,500 per year, such as lighting and heating. Elliott believed that encouraging the clubs to be fiscally responsible would make them more responsible in using the facility. In addition to club dues, funding was also provided by subscriptions and by donations from the **New York Ethical Culture Society**.

Located on the Lower West Side of Manhattan, initially at 252 and 254 West 26th Street and after 1908 at 436 and 438 West 27th Street, the guild served a local population of mostly Irish and German immigrants, although some Jews, Italians, and Swedes lived in the neighborhood. Like many of their settlement house counterparts, the Hudson Guild volunteers worked to secure a public park and a playground for the neighborhood, and the residents were involved in hygiene and housing reform efforts. The settlement published a monthly neighborhood newspaper, The *Chelsea*. It also maintained a printing shop and a savings bank, and provided nursing services, particularly for babies. In the summer, neighborhood children were provided with vacations at a summer camp run by the Ethical Culture Society.

Unique among the other settlements in Manhattan because it provided an opportunity for self governance on the part of the neighborhood residents, the Hudson Guild combined settlement work and the ideals of the Ethical Culture Movement regarding community service. Today, the Hudson Guild still provides a range of social welfare services to the community on the Lower West Side of Manhattan known as the Chelsea District.

Bibliography

Artera, *Living in Chelsea: A Study of Human Relations in the Area Served by the Hudson Guild*; Elliott, *The Hudson Guild: Founded 1895: A Brief Record of Twenty-Five Years of Service*; Melvin, *American Community Organizations: An Historical Dictionary*, pp. 84–86; Woods, *The Handbook of Settlements*.

Hull House

Established in Chicago by **Jane Addams** and **Ellen Gates Starr** in September 1889, Hull House was the best-known settlement house in the United States. It was the focus of social reform activity on the local, state, and national levels, and served as a training center for those interested in settlement work. Its residents participated in almost every major social welfare program undertaken during the first half of the twentieth century.

Located on South Halsted Street in Chicago, Hull House was intended "to provide a center for the higher civic and social life; to institute and maintain educational and philanthropic enterprises; and to investigate and improve the conditions in the industrial districts of Chicago" (Woods and Kennedy, *Handbook of Settlements*, p. 53). Addams served as head resident of Hull House from 1889 to 1935. Other well-known residents included **Julia Lathrop**, **Grace** and **Edith Abbott**, **Florence Kelley**, **Alice Hamilton**, and **Sophonisba Breckinridge**.

The settlement was supported by a small endowment and by subscriptions. The house, which had been the residence of Charles J. Hull, a wealthy businessman, was located in what had become a factory and tenement section of the city. The people in the immediate neighborhood were Greek, and large numbers of Italians and Russian and Polish Jews lived nearby. The most important local industry was clothing manufacturing.

Hull House sponsored many and varied activities, often in conjunction with local, state, and federal agencies. For example, in 1892 the residents investigated the sweating system for the Illinois State Bureau of Labor Statistics.

(The sweating system was a method of production that was used in factories or plants where numbers of workers were employed for long hours at low wages under poor working conditions. These places were referred to as sweatshops and were common in urban centers where large numbers of immigrants provided a plentiful and cheap source of labor.) In 1893, the Hull House residents conducted a dietary investigation for the United States Department of Agriculture.

The Hull House residents also worked to improve housing conditions and to secure better sanitary and health facilities. In 1893, they established the first public playground in Chicago and the first public bath. (*See* **Baths**.) Health issues were a particular concern for Addams and the others. Hull House offered a physician in residence and sponsored a number of clinics. The house provided a base of operations for the **Chicago Visiting Nurse Association** and operated a milk distribution center.

A number of organizations were supported by the settlement. Local unions used Hull House for meeting space, and the residents helped to organize a local branch of the Consumers' League (1898). In 1909 Addams and several other residents organized the **Immigrants Protective League**, which was intended to help ease the transition of newly arrived immigrants to their new environment.

The residents were involved in a wide range of other activities in and around Chicago. They offered art and bookbinding classes, sponsored a craft shop, and established a music school.

In addition to being active reform leaders in local and national organizations, the Hull House residents published numerous articles and books, including the *Hull-House Maps and Papers* (1895), a social study of the community around the settlement; they also testified before numerous committees.

Perhaps more than any other settlement in the United States, Hull House came to symbolize what was best about the American Settlement Movement. The physical building that Jane Addams and Ellen Gates Starr knew as Hull House was demolished in the 1960s and was replaced by a number of new settlement facilities located throughout Chicago. These facilities are now operated under the auspices of the Hull House Association, which provides an array of social services and music, theater, and arts programs.

Bibliography
Melvin, *American Community Organizations: An Historical Dictionary*, pp. 86-87; Romanofsky, *The Greenwood Cyclopedia of American Institutions: Social Service Organizations*, pp. 351–57; Woods, *The Handbook of Settlements*.

Hull-House Maps and Papers (1895)

Settlement workers were very interested in learning as much as possible about their neighbors to gain their confidence and acceptance and to provide them with the resources and services they needed. To accomplish these goals, they spent a considerable amount of time investigating the living and working conditions of the people they were living among. One of these studies was published as *Hull-House Maps and Papers: A Presentation of Nationalities and Wages in a Congested District of Chicago Together with Comments and Essays on Problems Growing out of the Social Conditions*.

In the fall of 1892, the social reformer **Florence Kelley** introduced the political economist **Richard Ely** to the other residents of **Hull House**. Ely encouraged Kelley and the other settlement workers to conduct scientific and systematic social investigations and to publish their findings. At the time, Kelley was working as a special agent for the Illinois State Bureau of Labor Statistics investigating the sweating trade (use of sweatshops) among garment workers in Chicago. Based on this work, she was invited by Carroll D. Wright, the United States Commissioner of Labor, to oversee the Chicago-related portion of a national investigation of urban slums.

Kelley's studies were the basis for the first Hull House publication, *Hull-House Maps and Papers*, which was modeled after **Charles Booth**'s systematic study of the poor, *Labour and Life of the People of London*. Almost every resident of Hull House participated in the project, which involved a comprehensive survey of the origins of every family living in the third of a square mile around the settlement. The investigators identified people of 18 different nationalities and transferred the survey results to multi-colored maps. The maps were supplemented with a series of articles including: "The Sweating System," "Wage Earning Children," "The Cook County Charities," and "The Settlement as a Factor in the Labor Movement."

Although some of the residents referred to the project as the "jumble book" because it included such a diverse selection of articles and data, it was a significant work with a wide range of useful data. Ely persuaded his publisher Thomas Y. Crowell to include the book in its series, the Library of Economics and Politics, which he edited. The book's publication was delayed at first because contributors were late in submitting their articles and then because Ely and Kelley disagreed about whether it was economically practical to include the many maps.

Even though it did not enjoy widespread distribution, the book was well received and served as a model for other scientifically based social surveys of Chicago and other American cities.

Bibliography

Carson, *Settlement Folk: Social Thought and the American Settlement Movement, 1885–1930*; Davis, *American Heroine: The Life and Legend of Jane Addams*; *Hull-House Maps and Papers: A Presentation of Nationalities and Wages in a Congested District of Chicago Together with Comments and Essays on Problems Growing out of the Social Conditions*.

Hunter, Niles Robert
social investigator, author, settlement worker
b. April 10, 1874; d. May 15, 1942

Robert Hunter began his career as a social reformer in Chicago, a city with a large, dynamic reform community. He lived and worked in the city's most famous settlement, **Hull House**, and was involved in a number of reform organizations. From Chicago he moved to New York to an equally dynamic reform community. Eventually, Hunter devoted his energies to writing, research, and supporting various political causes.

Niles Robert Hunter was born in Terre Haute, Indiana, where his father, William, was a successful carriage maker. The Hunters lived comfortably, and Robert, as he was known, was educated by private tutors in addition to attending the local public school. The depression of 1893 had a particularly significant effect on Hunter as he had witnessed firsthand the hardships endured by workers who had been laid off from his father's factory. This experience motivated him to pursue a career as a social worker. He earned a B.A. degree from Indiana University in 1896.

After graduating from college, Hunter moved to Chicago and became active in the settlement house movement there. During the next six years he worked with a number of Chicago-based social reform organizations. Hunter served as organizing secretary of the Chicago

Bureau of Charities (*see* **Chicago Relief Society**), director of Chicago's first free children's dental clinic, and founder and superintendent of the Municipal Housing Lodge for Vagrants. Between 1899 and 1902, Hunter was a resident at **Hull House**. During the summer of 1899, Hunter traveled to London to visit **Toynbee Hall**, the first English settlement that had been established by **Samuel Barnett** in London's East End.

In addition to his practical social reform activities, Hunter was also a researcher and writer. While serving as chair of the Investigating Committee of the City Homes Association in 1901, he published his first book, *Tenement Conditions in Chicago* (1901), a survey of working-class housing.

In 1902, Hunter moved to New York City to accept the position of head worker at the **University Settlement** and quickly joined the city's social reform community. He served as chair of the newly established **New York Child Labor Committee** and successfully led the group's campaign for a statewide child labor law that was enacted in 1903. The same year, Hunter married Caroline Margaretha Phelps Stokes, the daughter of New York civic leader Anson Phelps Stokes. His wife's social position and wealth permitted Hunter to resign from the University Settlement and to devote his time to writing and research.

Poverty (1904), Hunter's second book, was the first general statistical survey of the poor in America. In it, Hunter combined careful statistical analysis with the methodology of contemporary sociology, arguing that poverty was the result of social factors that required social solutions. The book generated extensive discussion and drew attention to the necessity for environmental reform.

Hunter made two more trips to Europe, in 1903 and again in 1906. Both times he met with leading European socialists. He subsequently joined the moderate American Socialist Party, rising rapidly through its ranks to represent the United States in Stuttgart, Germany, at the Third International in 1907. Hunter was a member of the party's central committee from 1909 to 1912. During these years he stood for office as a socialist candidate in New York and in Connecticut.

Hunter became disillusioned with socialism following the outbreak of hostilities in Europe in 1914. Four years later he moved from New York to Berkeley, California, where he lectured in economics and literature and served on the Berkeley Board of Charity. During the 1930s, Hunter gradually lost interest in social reform work as he became more and more involved in a variety of right-wing causes. He was a member of the National Economic League and an outspoken critic of Franklin Roosevelt and the New Deal.

Bibliography

Dictionary of American Biography, supl. 3, pp. 372–74; *National Cyclopaedia of American Biography*, vol. 14, pp. 353–54; Trattner, *Biographical Dictionary of Social Welfare in America*, pp. 413–15.

I

Illinois Immigrants' Protective League *See* Immigrants' Service League

Immigrants' Protective League *See* Immigrants' Service League

Immigrants' Protective League of Chicago *See* Immigrants' Service League

Immigrants' Service League

The late nineteenth and early twentieth centuries were a time of growth for many American cities. Rapid industrialization and urbanization placed an enormous strain on the physical and psychological resources of those who were experiencing these rapid changes. Added to this change was the unprecedented influx of immigrants, particularly from southern and eastern Europe. Some elements of American society reacted to the newcomers by advocating restrictive immigration laws. Others adopted a more humane approach that emphasized easing the transition to American life. The Immigrants' Service League was created to help immigrants to adjust to their new environment.

Large numbers of new immigrants either passed through or settled in Chicago, and settle-ment workers and other social reformers in the city were acutely aware of the hazards, both physical and moral, that confronted single immigrant women when they arrived in the United States. For example, unscrupulous baggage men often took all or most of the women's money, leaving them with little or nothing for food or shelter. Sometimes single women were waylaid at the train station and brought to brothels where they were forced to work as prostitutes. The Chicago branch of the **Women's Trade Union League** (WTUL) instituted an immigration committee to assist the newly arrived in adjusting to American life and to protect them from being exploited by unscrupulous employers. Eventually, the WTUL leadership realized they needed to establish an independent association that could assist all newcomers in adjusting to life in America.

In April 1908, a number of prominent social reformers and settlement workers established the League for the Protection of Immigrants. One of the league's principal objectives was to mobilize the social, philanthropic, and civic resources of Chicago to address the needs of new immigrants; to protect them from exploitation; and to assist in their integration into American society.

Soon after it was founded, the league changed its name to the Immigrants' Protective League. Among the founding members were **Margaret Dreier Robins**, president of the National Women's Trade Union League; **Julia Lathrop**, a **Hull House** resident and later director of the **United States Children's Bureau**; **Mary E. McDowell**, head resident of the **University of Chicago Settlement**; **Jane Addams**, founder of **Hull House**; and **Sophonisba Breckinridge**, professor of social economy at the University of Chicago. They were joined by Julius Rosenwald, chair of the board of Sears Roebuck and Company who, for several years, contributed almost 10 percent of the league's annual budget. **Grace Abbott**, a Hull House resident, served as executive secretary and was the principal guiding force of the league during most of its first two decades.

League representatives attempted to meet all new arrivals at Chicago's various railroad terminals and to ensure that they reached their destinations. Using information provided by the authorities on Ellis Island, league members met single women who were traveling to Chicago from New York. They followed up this initial contact with a personal visit during the course of the following year to determine if a woman needed additional assistance.

Besides providing food and clothing, the Immigrants' Protective League located relatives and traced lost baggage. It helped immigrants secure employment and provided assistance to those who were injured in industrial accidents. The league also secured legal assistance for new immigrants who were victimized by employment bureaus, bankers, or ticket agents.

In addition to the practical aid it dispensed, the staff of the Immigrants' Protective League applied a casework approach in their interaction with immigrants. They learned about their living and working conditions and collected data which they used to suggest programs that the local and federal governments could offer to assist newcomers. However, few of the league's suggestions were implemented.

In 1919, Illinois did act on one of the league's proposals when it established the Commission of Immigration, which was to assume responsibility for the league's programs. Grace Abbott served as the commission's executive secretary. However, the commission was disbanded in 1921 due to inadequate funding. The Immigrants' Protective League was reactivated in response, though on a reduced budget and with a new set of problems.

The restrictive immigration quota legislation of 1921 and 1924 marked the beginning of a series of laws and rulings that placed new demands on the league. These restrictive quota laws ended the period of mass immigration. Individuals wishing to enter the United States now had to work their way through a maze of legal documents and hearings. Members of the league now had to spend time helping immigrants complete forms and accompanying individuals to hearings. During the late 1920s, the league was able to provide additional services with funds from the Chicago Community Trust and the Young Men's Christian Association.

Despite some lean years in 1920s, the Immigrants' Protective League met the challenges of the Great Depression and World War II. It helped immigrants secure nationalization papers and traced relatives affected by the hostilities in Europe. In 1958, the Immigrants' Protective League changed its name to the Immigrants' Service League. Nine years later, it merged with the Travelers Aid Society of Metropolitan Chicago, maintaining its own identity but gaining financial stability and increased efficiency.

Bibliography

Abbott, *The Immigrant and the Community*; Buroker, "From Voluntary Association to Welfare State: The Illinois Immigrants' Protective League, 1918–1926; Leonard, "The Immigrants' Protective League of Chicago, 1908–1921"; Romanofsky, *The Greenwood Encyclopedia of American Institutions: Social Service Organizations*, vol. 1, pp. 357–60.

Industrial Relations Commission

The campaign waged by settlement workers and other reformers to form an industrial relations commission was only one element of their decades-long struggle to assist the worker and to encourage industrial peace. These reformers envisioned the commission as a research and fact-finding organization that would investigate and then report its findings to all concerned as a first step in working out appropriate reform solutions. They believed that the federal government had to be involved in investigating the condition of industrial relations in the United States and that by so doing, relations between management and labor would improve. They were confident that involving the federal government would ensure fewer strikes and other types of possibly violent industrial action.

The committee was actually formed in response to just such a violent act. The dynamiting of the *Los Angeles Times* building in October 1910 by a union official named John McNamara and his brother caused a flood of anti-labor publicity in the national press. The McNamara brothers were tried and convicted, and in December 1911, a few days before their sentences were handed down, a group of welfare reformers met in New York City to devise a plan of action to counteract the negative publicity and to try to prevent similar actions in the future. Present at the meetings were **Jane Addams**, founder of **Hull House**; **Lillian Wald**, founder of the **Henry Street Settlement**; **Mary K. Simkhovitch**, founder of **Greenwich House; Paul Kellogg**, a member of the **National Child Labor Committee** and editor of the social welfare journal the *Survey*; **Florence Kelley** of the National **Consumer's League**; the political reformer **Henry Moskowitz**; **Edward T. Devine** of the New York **Charity Organization Society**; **Owen Lovejoy**, a member of the National Child Labor Committee; and **James B. Reynolds**, former head resident of the **University Settlement** among others.

The proceedings of these gatherings were compiled and published in the *Survey* under the title, "The Larger Bearings of the McNamara Case." One of the recommendations that emerged from the discussion was the creation of an industrial relations commission. The reformers were confident that if they could gather complete and accurate knowledge about the problems that existed between management and workers, they could avoid strikes and the violence that often accompanied them.

A delegation of reformers sent a letter to President Taft in December 1911, in which they called upon him to create a commission empowered to investigate labor conditions and to make recommendations for a solution. Two months later Taft asked Congress to authorize the establishment of a Federal Commission on Industrial Relations.

The New York offices of the *Survey* served as headquarters for the lobbying effort to secure congressional passage of the legislation that would create such a commission. Devine served as chair of the campaign. He was assisted by Adolph Lewison, a New York businessman who served as vice chair and by Wald, who served as treasurer. They were joined by two former settlement workers, Allen T. Burns, secretary of the Pittsburgh Civic Commission, who sponsored the Washington-based lobbying effort, and **Graham Romeyn Taylor**, a member of the editorial staff of the *Survey*, who acted as secretary of the campaign. Addams mobilized support for the effort in Chicago.

The reformers drafted a bill that was introduced in the House of Representatives by Williams Hughes of New Jersey and in the Senate by William Borah of Idaho in March 1912. While the bill was being debated, the *Survey* ran a special series of articles on labor conditions and industrial relations. Concerned organizations such as the American Federation of Labor and the National Civic Federation endorsed the Hughes-Borah Bill.

After an aggressive lobbying effort, the bill was signed into law in August 1912. The commission that the new law provided for included three representatives from labor, three from industry, and three who would represent the public interest. Although the reformers were not entirely pleased with the selections made by either President Taft or his successor, Woodrow Wilson, they were confident that the new Industrial Relations Commission would prove to be a valuable mechanism for bringing about political change.

The commission was chaired by the labor activist Frank Walsh, and it adopted a two-prong approach in carrying out its work. Walsh conducted a long series of public hearings in cities across the United States. These hearings produced sensational headlines, but they did little to advance the cause of labor/management relations and within two years the commission was disbanded.

The commission's other tactic was to sponsor research conducted by experts. Charles McCarthy, director of the Wisconsin Legislative Reference Library, was hired to coordinate the research effort. He was assisted by **Crystal Eastman**, Selig Perlman, and Gertrude Barnum. When a disagreement with Walsh led to McCarthy's dismissal, most of the research work was abandoned. The commission's findings were published in 1916, but by this time most of its early supporters had abandoned all hope of its making a positive contribution to labor/management relations.

Bibliography

Davis, "The Campaign for the Industrial Relations Commission, 1911–1913"; Davis, *Spearheads for Reform: The Social Settlements and the Progressive Movement, 1890–1914*.

Institute of Social Science and

Arts *See* Graduate School of Social Service Administration (Chicago)

Intercollegiate Bureau of

Occupations *See* American Association of Social Workers

J

Juvenile Protective Association

During the late nineteenth and early twentieth centuries, social reformers working in urban centers were especially concerned about the impact that the overcrowded city had on young people who had been forced for economic reasons to work as long or longer than adults and had been deprived of their childhoods as a result. Besides the child labor problem, children living in cities were exposed to many temptations and often found themselves in trouble with the authorities. Treated as adults by the criminal justice system, they were provided with few opportunities for rehabilitation.

Reformers in Chicago, which was a densely populated city, were particularly aware of the problems encountered by young people, many of whom were left to their own devices while their parents worked. The Juvenile Protective Association began as the Probation Committee of the Chicago Women's Club, whose members were particularly concerned that no adequate program on either the state or local level was in place to deal with the large number of dependent and delinquent children. **Julia Lathrop**, a **Hull House** resident and a recognized expert on child welfare, was selected to serve as chair of the committee.

Working with other social reformers, the members of the Probation Committee helped to draft the Juvenile Court Act, which was signed into law in April 1898. This act estab-

lished the Cook County Juvenile Court, the first juvenile court system in the world. The law, however, included no provisions for salaries for personnel. Lathrop's committee had to raise the necessary funds to pay the first probation officers.

By the fall of 1903, the Probation Committee had separated from the Chicago Women's Club and was established as an independent agency known as the Juvenile Court Committee. Lathrop was selected to serve as chair, and she was assisted by **Louise DeKoven Bowen**, the treasurer of Hull House who later became chair of the committee. When the Juvenile Court Committee incorporated in 1904, Bowen became president and Lathrop vice president.

Following the establishment of the Cook County Juvenile Court, the Juvenile Court Committee united with other Chicago-area reformers to establish a federation of branch offices of the Juvenile Protective League. These smaller units were designed to assist the Juvenile Court by working in the community to advocate reform. However, they proved to be ineffective, and in 1909, the work of the League was taken over by the Juvenile Court Committee.

Two years later the Juvenile Court Committee changed its name to the Juvenile Protective Association (JPA). The JPA was based at Hull House, and from 1907 until the end of World War I in 1918, it functioned as one of the most aggressive child welfare agencies in the United States. It worked to improve social conditions harmful to children, lobbied for the passage of a state mother's pension law, and established the Juvenile Psychopathic Institute, the world's first child guidance clinic.

Jessie Binford, a Hull House supporter, led the JPA from 1916 to 1952. During this time the association worked to ensure the enforcement of child welfare laws and conducted research studies. Gradually, the work of the JPA began to focus more and more on social casework. The JPA was reorganized in 1952 under a new executive director, Lewis Penner.

Penner hired certified social workers and introduced a system of casework supervision.

In 1965, the JPA founded the Bowen Center, which at the time was the first comprehensive treatment center for neglected children and their families in the United States. This facility enabled the JPA to continue its work as one of the only social welfare agencies providing long-term care to neglected children and their families. *See also* **Child Welfare.**

Bibliography

Romanofsky, *The Greenwood Encyclopedia of American Institutions: Social Service Organizations*, vol. 1, pp. 391–96.

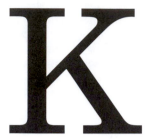

K

Kehew, Mary Morton Kimball
labor reformer, social welfare agency
administrator
b. September 8, 1859; d. February 13, 1918.

Like many women of her social class, Mary
Kehew, the wife of a wealthy Boston merchant,
devoted time to social reform crusades. Kehew
was more than just a well-meaning volunteer.
She was an organizer and a leader who made
significant contributions to the labor movement, to social welfare research, and to various
legislative campaigns. Realistic and astute,
Kehew's behind-the-scenes approach and skills
as an organizer and administrator enabled her
to bring together parties on both sides of an issue and to work toward a productive
compromise.

Mary Kimball came from a well-to-do family and enjoyed the benefit of a private school
education supplemented with two years of study
abroad in France, Germany, and Italy. In January 1880, Mary Kimball married a Boston oil
merchant, William Brown Kehew. Although
William Kehew was not active in social reform
crusades, he supported his wife's interests,
which developed soon after their marriage when
Mary became involved in the work of the
Women's Educational and Industrial Union of
Boston. The union, which was founded in 1877,
provided general assistance and employment
guidance to young girls from rural areas who
traveled to Boston in search of work.

Kehew joined the union in 1886. Within
four years she was a director, and in January
1892, she became president. She was involved
with the union for most of her adult life, resigning in 1913, but returning the following year
to serve as acting president and chair of the
board until her death in 1918.

During Kehew's tenure, the focus of the
union shifted. It became increasingly concerned
with educational efforts rather than philanthropic programs. In addition to offering women
legal aid and a site in which to sell their handi-
work, the union began to offer vocational training, and established schools for dressmaking,
sales, and housekeeping.

Kehew also involved the union in social
research and welfare legislation. She guided it
into a variety of humanitarian causes, and the
union was soon recognized as one of the most
important reform organizations in Boston. In
addition to its other work, in 1910 the union
established an Appointment Bureau to assist
college-educated women to find professional
careers.

Kehew herself was active in a number of
reform organizations including **Denison
House**, the **College Settlements Association**, the Milk and Baby Hygiene Association,
and the American Park and Outdoor Association. She also served as a trustee of Simmons
College, was a member of the Massachusetts
Association for promoting the Interests of the

Blind, and was a member of the Civil Service Reform Association.

Early in her career, Kehew became interested in the American labor movement. She realized that it had the potential to develop into a powerful agent for social reform. On the advice of her sister, Hannah Parker Kimball, Kehew invited former **Hull House** resident and American Federation of Labor organizer Mary Kenney (later **Mary Kenney O'Sullivan**) to come to Boston to encourage trade unionism among the city's working women. Building on the resources of the Women's Educational and Industrial Union, the two women founded the Union for Industrial Progress which by 1896 had succeeded in organizing Boston area women bookbinders and laundry workers. Three years later tobacco workers were unionized followed by garment-trade workers in 1901. When the National Women's Trade Union League of Boston formed two years later, Kehew was elected the organization's first president.

Kehew was also active in a number of successful campaigns to secure the passage of social-welfare-related legislation. She was well-armed in these crusades: first, because she had the backing of the many women workers whom she had successfully organized; and second, because she supported her efforts with solid, detailed research that was conducted by the research department of the Women's Educational and Industrial Union.

The research department was created in 1905 and benefited from the competent leadership of **Susan M. Kingsbury**, who served as director from 1907 to 1915. It prepared detailed reports about women's working conditions for the Massachusetts Bureau of Statistics of Labor. These and other studies that the Women's Educational and Industrial Union conducted provided a ground-breaking analysis of the living and working conditions of women in the Boston area.

Under Kehew's influence, the research department of the union stressed the need for protective legislation to ensure the economic and health rights of women workers. The union presented a series of bills to the Massachusetts State Legislature for consideration on a variety of issues including factory inspection and sanitation, old-age pensions, regulation of installment debt, and a minimum wage. Kehew was not satisfied with merely having a bill become a law. Her interest extended to campaigning for the laws' enforcement and on several occasions, serving on the commissions charged

with their administration. She remained active in reform movements right up to her death in 1918.

Bibliography

Dictionary of American Biography, vol. 5, pp. 287–88; *Notable American Women, 1607–1950*, vol. 2, pp. 313–14; Randall, *Improper Bostonian: Emily Greene Balch*.

Kelley, Florence
child labor reformer, social activist, settlement worker
b. September 12, 1859; d. February 17, 1932.

Florence Kelley was a committed and forceful woman who mobilized fellow reformers to investigate problems, to educate others regarding their existence, and to develop workable solutions. She was a tireless worker who at different times in her career lived at both **Hull House** in Chicago and the **Henry Street Settlement** in New York City. Kelley worked as a factory inspector and as a researcher and writer. She also played a significant role in the work of the **National Child Labor Committee** and the National **Consumers' League**.

Kelley earned a bachelor's degree from Cornell University in 1882. Refused admission to the University of Pennsylvania graduate school because she was a woman, Kelley began teaching evening classes for working-class girls at Philadelphia's New Century Club. While on a tour of Europe with her brother in 1883, Kelley enrolled at the University of Zurich in Switzerland, the first European university open to women. Kelley became a socialist, and in 1884, she married a Russian medical student, Lazare Wischnewetzky, who was also a socialist. Two years later, after the birth of their first child, the Wischnewetzkys moved to New York City.

During the next five years Florence gave birth to two more children and devoted herself to Socialist Party work. Lazare was unable to establish his medical practice and the family's debts mounted. Eventually the couple separated. Florence moved to Illinois where she took advantage of that state's more liberal laws to obtain a divorce. She resumed using her maiden name and was granted custody of her three children.

Toward the end of 1891, after making arrangements for her children to be cared for by her mother, Kelley became a resident at Hull House, the social settlement founded by **Jane Addams** and **Ellen Gates Starr**. In 1892, shortly after she arrived at the settlement,

Kelley was hired by the Illinois Bureau of Labor Statistics to investigate the garment trade. Later the same year Carroll D. Wright, the federal Commissioner of Labor, hired Kelley to take part in a survey of city slums.

Kelley's years at Hull House were productive ones. She was instrumental in lobbying the Illinois State Legislature for the passage of the 1893 Factory Act that limited women's working hours and prohibited the use of child labor in tenement sweatshops. She served as Illinois Chief Factory Inspector (1893–1897), and during the 1890s, she wrote a number of articles about labor and housing reform. She also arranged for the publication of the *Hull-House Maps and Papers* (1895), a detailed social survey of the neighborhood surrounding Hull House. In 1894, Kelley earned a law degree from Northwestern University night school.

In 1899, the labor reformer **John Graham Brooks** invited Kelley to become the general secretary of the newly established National Consumers' League. The league was organized to put pressure on the public to purchase only those goods that were manufactured under proper working conditions. Kelley accepted Brooks's invitation and moved her family to New York City to live at the **Henry Street Settlement**. Within six years, Kelley had established 64 local Consumers' Leagues in 20 states.

In addition to her crusade for the enactment of wage and hour laws, Kelley was also interested in eliminating child labor. In 1902, she and **Lillian Wald**, founder of the Henry Street Settlement, cooperated with other settlement workers to establish the New York Child Labor Committee. Two years later Kelley helped to organize the **National Child Labor Committee**. In her 1905 book, *Some Ethical Gains Through Legislation*, she proposed creating a national agency that would be responsible for child welfare. Her idea was implemented, after much work on her part and on the part of many others including Wald, with the establishment of the **United States Children's Bureau** in 1912.

Kelley's significance to the social welfare reform movement goes beyond the passage of specific legislation to protect women and children. She was a founding member of the National Association for the Advancement of Colored People (NAACP) in 1909, and she was a founding member of the **Women's International League for Peace and Freedom**.

Throughout the 1920s, Kelley continued to devote her attention to the child labor cause,

campaigning unsuccessfully for a child labor amendment to the U.S. Constitution. Dying in 1932 after a long illness, Kelley played a key role in a number of social reform crusades including the American Settlement Movement. Dedicated, forceful, and forthright, she mobilized the social reform communities of Chicago and New York City in generally successful campaigns to eliminate the worst child labor abuses, relieve overcrowding and unsanitary housing, and improve working conditions in factories and retail establishments.

Bibliography

Dictionary of American Biography, supl. 1, pp. 462–63; Goldmark, *Impatient Crusader: Florence Kelley's Life Story*; *Notable American Women, 1607–1950*, vol. 2, pp. 316–19; Trattner, *Biographical Dictionary of Social Welfare in America*, pp. 440–45.

Kellogg, Arthur Piper
editor, writer, social reformer
b. March 18, 1878; d. July 20, 1934.

Arthur Kellogg was a journalist who made an important contribution to the settlement movement in the United States and to other reform campaigns through his work on the New York **Charity Organization Society** periodical, *Charities*, which was later known as the *Survey*.

Kellogg was born and raised in Kalamazoo, Michigan, where his father ran the family lumber business until it failed sometime in the 1890s and the elder Kellogg abandoned his wife and two sons to start a new life for himself in Texas. In 1897, Arthur and his younger brother, **Paul U. Kellogg**, graduated from Kalamazoo High School and joined the staff of the Kalamazoo *Daily Telegraph*. Arthur started in the business office and later transferred to the editorial department. When he resigned in 1902, he had worked his way up to the position of city editor. While employed at the *Daily Telegraph*, Kellogg also worked as clerk of the Ways and Means and Railroad committees of the Michigan State Legislature, both of which were chaired by State Senator E.M. Dingley, owner of the *Daily Telegraph*.

Following a brief hiatus from newspaper work, during which time he worked at the Dunkley-Williams Transportation Company in South Haven, Michigan, Kellogg was hired as city editor of Kalamazoo's *Gazette-News*. Four months later, in April 1903, he left Kalamazoo to join his brother in New York City. That summer he completed the New York Charity Organization Society's Summer School of

Philanthropy course and secured a position on the editorial staff of *Charities*, an official publication of the Charity Organization Society founded in 1897 and edited by **Edward T. Devine**.

Over the next 31 years as *Charities* merged with *The Commons* (1905) and was renamed the **Survey** (1909), the Kellogg brothers worked together in a productive partnership that influenced the course of social welfare journalism. Between 1908 and 1934 Arthur alternated between the positions of managing editor and business editor. In 1920, he became the treasurer for the **Survey Associates**, the journal's publishing company.

To a significant degree, Arthur Kellogg was the driving force behind the *Survey* and its two spin-off publications, *Survey Graphic* and *Survey Midmonthly*. All manuscripts passed across his desk since he was responsible for editing, proofreading, layout, and illustrations. He also ensured that the publication went to press on time and was delivered to subscribers. In addition to his back office responsibilities, Arthur Kellogg was a regular contributor, authoring the "Gist" pages and the "Common Welfare" section, and providing reviews, captions, and editorial notes.

In 1927, Kellogg accompanied then-Secretary of Commerce Herbert Hoover and the acting director of the American Red Cross, James L. Fieser, on an inspection tour of flooded areas of the lower Mississippi from Vicksburg to New Orleans. Based on his observations, he published two substantial articles in the *Survey*, "Behind the Levees" (June 1927) and "Up from the Bottom Lands" (July 1927).

Kellogg died unexpectedly of a heart attack in 1934. His work as managing editor of the *Survey* provided reformers with a quality venue in which to publish their research and to share information.

Bibliography

Chambers, *Paul U. Kellogg and the Survey: Voices for Social Justice*; Trattner, *Biographical Dictionary of Social Welfare in America*, pp. 445–46.

Kellogg, Paul Underwood

editor, writer, social reformer

b. September 30, 1879; d. November 1, 1958.

Paul Kellogg combined his interest in social reform with his skill as a journalist to become a significant force in the American reform community during the first half of the twentieth century.

Born in Kalamazoo, Michigan, Kellogg attended the local high school where he edited the school newspaper with his older brother, **Arthur Kellogg**. After graduating from high school in 1897, he went to work as a reporter for the Kalamazoo *Daily Telegraph*. The following year he became city editor. Kellogg's interests and ambitions lay beyond Kalamazoo, and in the summer of 1901, he moved to New York City. That fall he enrolled in Columbia University as a special student. He completed a year (1901–1902) of full-time study and then continued to take classes on a part-time basis over the next several years.

In 1902, Kellogg enrolled in the New York **Charity Organization Society's** (COS) Summer School of Philanthropy. Based on his prior experience and editorial abilities, he was offered a position as assistant editor of the COS's publication, *Charities*. Arthur Kellogg joined his brother in New York and on the staff of *Charities* in 1903. Working together, the two brothers broadened the editorial profile of the journal, transforming it from a narrowly focused publication concerned with the delivery of charitable service to one that provided a forum for critical evaluation and discussion of contemporary social issues. The scope of *Charities* was further enlarged in 1905 when it merged with *The Commons*, the official publication of the settlement movement. Paul Kellogg became managing editor of the new publication, *Charities and The Commons*.

In 1907, Kellogg assumed responsibility for directing a project known as the **Pittsburgh Survey**. This was the first significant social survey of an American urban community which gathered data on all aspects of living and working conditions in Pittsburgh, Pennsylvania. Scholars, community leaders, and reformers, including settlement house workers, contributed to this comprehensive, cooperative research effort. The results of the survey were published in a series of articles in *Charities and The Commons* and in a six-volume series of books issued between 1910 and 1914.

In 1909, Kellogg resumed his editorial duties at *Charities and The Commons,* which was soon renamed the **Survey**. Three years later he became editor-in-chief, and his brother Arthur was named managing editor. Over the next 40 years Kellogg guided the *Survey* as it became a significant force in social reform and the leading journal of the developing profession of social work.

The editorial profile that Kellogg developed for the magazine reflected the belief of many reformers of the Progressive period that a well-informed corps of professional reformers could guide the United States in a direction that would lead to social progress and contribute to the creation of a more equitable America. Kellogg solicited experts to write articles for the *Survey* on the public housing situation, the need for playgrounds, the minimum wage/maximum hour crusade, the right of labor to organize, and the importance of education, among other topics.

Besides his editorial work, Kellogg was active in other areas. Although he opposed the United States' entry into World War I, Kellogg supported the war effort once the country was a combatant. From 1917 to 1918 he conducted field surveys for the Red Cross in Italy, France, and Belgium. After the war, Kellogg played a major role in creating the organization that became the American Foreign Policy Association and in the formation of the **American Civil Liberties Union**, serving on the boards of both groups for many years. He was also a member of the group that helped write the Social Security Act of 1935.

Kellogg was an editor, not an administrator. After the death of his brother in 1934, he attempted to oversee all aspects of the *Survey's* production, but he was unable to do so, sacrificing his own physical health and the financial well being of the journal. The *Survey* ceased publication on 1952.

Kellogg died in New York City where he lived with his second wife, **Helen Hall**, the director of the **Henry Street Settlement**.

Bibliography

Chambers, *Paul U. Kellogg and the Survey: Voices for Social Welfare and Social Justice*; *Dictionary of American Biography*, supl. 6, pp. 329–30; Trattner, *Biographical Dictionary of Social Welfare in America*, pp. 446–49.

Kellor, Frances (Alice)

reformer, social activist, advocate for the protection of immigrants
b. October 20, 1873; d. January 4, 1952.

Frances Kellor's concern with the effect that unemployment had on the adjustment and assimilation of migrants and immigrants entering urban centers was the focus of most of her work as a social reformer. She pursued this interest as a fellow of the **College Settlements Association**, as a member of the New York State Immigration Commission, and as a member of the North American Civic League for Immigrants.

A graduate of Cornell University, Kellor's first experience as a social investigator was her study of penal institutions and women prisoners conducted in 1902 while she continued her education at the University of Chicago. Her efforts resulted in the publication of her first book, *Experimental Sociology, Descriptive and Analytical: Delinquents*. The following year she moved to New York City and attended the New York Summer School of Philanthropy.

Based on her work at the school, Kellor secured a fellowship from the College Settlements Association which she used to study the practices of unethical employment agencies. These agencies guaranteed living accommodations and employment to young black women in the South who were willing to relocate and then failed to deliver what they had promised. Kellor later expanded the scope of her work to include newly arrived European immigrants who were similarly victimized.

Kellor's relationship with the College Settlements Association, the quality of her research, and her amiable personality helped her to become part of the New York social reform community. In 1904 she met **Mary Dreier**, a fellow reformer interested in woman suffrage and in labor issues. The two women became friends and eventually purchased a house in Brooklyn Heights where they lived until Kellor's death in 1952.

A consequence of Kellor's interest in the relationship between immigration and employment was her campaign to secure legislation that would regulate employment agencies and would protect the rights of their clients. In 1905, Kellor and some of her New York City colleagues cooperated with their Philadelphia counterparts to organize the Inter-Municipal League for Household Research and the Association for the Protection of Negro Women. These agencies were intended to protect black women migrants from exploitation.

The following year they expanded their efforts by establishing the National League for the Protection of Colored Women, which was designed to safeguard black women during their trip North and to assist them in securing employment when they arrived at their destinations. In 1911 the league merged with two other agencies with similar goals to form the National League on Urban Conditions among Negroes, which was better known as the National Urban League.

In addition to her work with North-bound migrants, Kellor also worked to protect European immigrants. She advocated their cause in her research and publications and sought legal safeguards for them through the work of the Inter-Municipal Bureau for Household Research. As a result of her efforts in this area, Kellor was appointed by Governor Charles Evans Hughes to the New York State Immigration Commission in 1908.

Lillian Wald, the founder of the **Henry Street Settlement,** was also a member of the Immigration Commission. For the next year, she and Kellor, who served as the secretary of the commission, undertook an intensive study of the living and working conditions of immigrants. Based on their findings, the women recommended that a permanent agency be established and that it be charged with ensuring the legal rights of immigrants and with providing oversight of their integration into their new environment. Acting on these recommendations, Governor Hughes and the New York State Legislature created the Bureau of Industries and Immigration. Kellor served as director of the bureau from 1910 to 1912.

Kellor supported the Immigration Commission's call for a permanent immigration agency by co-founding the New York branch of the North American Civic League for Immigrants in 1909. She was instrumental in having the New York branch adopt a program that called upon the federal government to implement a national plan for the protection of immigrants. When this policy caused friction with the Civic League's parent organization in Boston, the New York association was reorganized as the Committee for Immigrants in America. Kellor served as vice chair of this new organization. Determined to bring the issue of immigrants' assimilation to the attention of a national forum, Kellor resigned as director of the New York Bureau of Industries and Immigration in 1912 to work with the Progressive Party. She served as director of the party's publicity and research department and as head of the **National Progressive Service**.

Throughout her years of service, Kellor never lost sight of her primary goal, the integration of immigrants into American society. With the outbreak of World War I, she redirected her energies to emphasize the necessity for the foreign-born to acknowledge their allegiance to the United States while native-born Americans needed to continue to extend themselves to meet the needs of immigrants. Kellor believed that the workplace provided perhaps the most important site for the **Americanization** process to succeed. Toward the end of the war, she formed the Inter-Racial Council, which was supported by a number of corporations and was intended to counter any racial or nationalistic prejudice that had been inflamed by wartime propaganda.

In the post-war years Kellor's energies were channeled in a new direction. As a result of her research into intergroup understanding, Kellor was recognized as an authority on national and international arbitration issues. In the 1930s she served as an officer of the American Arbitration Association and wrote the American Arbitration Tribunal's Code of Arbitration.

Although her focus changed in these later years, Kellor's social reform career was grounded in the settlement movement; a fellowship from the College Settlement Association introduced her to the New York City reform community, and she was quickly acknowledged as an able and thorough researcher. Working in conjunction with settlement residents and other reformers, she tirelessly campaigned to protect immigrants from discrimination.

Bibliography

Davis, *Spearheads for Reform: The Social Settlements and the Progressive Movement, 1890–1914*; *Dictionary of American Biography*, supl. 5, pp. 380–81; Jackson, *Encyclopedia of New York City*, p. 633; Trattner, *Biographical Dictionary of Social Welfare in America*, pp. 449–53.

Kennedy, Albert Joseph
settlement leader, researcher, author
b. January 20, 1879; d. June 4, 1968.

Albert J. Kennedy
Social Welfare History Archives, University of Minnesota

Albert Kennedy began his more than 50-year career in the settlement movement as a research fellow at the **South End House** settlement in Boston. He went on to spend almost two decades at this settlement before moving to the **University Settlement** in New York City. Kennedy was also involved with settlement work on the national level, and along with **Robert Woods**, also of South End House, was the author of a number of important research studies.

Born in Rosenhayan, New Jersey, Kennedy graduated from the Marion Collegiate Institute in Marion, New York. He attended the University of Rochester where he earned an A.B. degree in 1901. At first, Kennedy was interested in a career in the church. He graduated from Rochester Theological Seminary in 1904 where he was exposed to the theories of the **Social Gospel** Movement.

After serving for one year (1904–1905) as a clergyman in Granite Falls, Minnesota, Kennedy decided to return to school. From 1905 to 1906 he was a Williams Fellow at Harvard University. He then spent two years studying sociology as a South End House Fellow (1906–1908), working on a national survey of settlements. During this fellowship, Kennedy also attended Harvard Divinity School, earning a Bachelor of Sacred Theology degree in 1907.

Kennedy was a resident at South End House for 17 years and was one of the few settlement workers who raised a family while living in the settlement. In 1908, he became director of investigations at South End House, and six years later he became associate head worker. During his tenure at South End House, Kennedy worked closely with the house's head resident, Robert Woods. The two men collaborated on a number of undertakings. Their first book, *Handbook of Settlements*, was an annotated guide to more than 400 settlements across the United States. Woods and Kennedy joined forces on two other publications, *Young Working Girls* (1913), a survey of working and living conditions of young women, and *The Settlement Horizon* (1922), which provided an account of the history and workings of the settlements.

Kennedy's contributions to social reform extended beyond his publications. In 1911, Woods and Kennedy were instrumental in the founding of the **National Federation of Settlements** (NFS). Woods served as the group's first executive secretary, and he was succeeded by Kennedy in 1923. In addition to his work at South End House, Kennedy lectured at the **Boston School for Social Workers** and at Simmons College and Harvard. Following Wood's death in 1925, Kennedy became the head

worker at South End House. Three years later he accepted the position of head worker at the University Settlement in New York City.

At times, Kennedy's colleagues were critical of his approach to settlement work. During his tenure as head of the NFS, Kennedy promoted the cultural role of the settlements, emphasizing their importance in the visual and performing arts. During the Depression years his enthusiasm for this aspect of settlement work put him at odds with other prominent reformers such as **Paul U. Kellogg** who believed that the settlements' social action role was more important. Kennedy's clashes with his social reform colleagues may have contributed to his being replaced as head of the NFS in 1934. He was succeeded by **Lillie M. Peck** who was his assistant at the University Settlement. Kennedy continued his research and remained active in the NFS. He retired from the University Settlement in 1944.

For Kennedy, retirement did not mean inactivity. Throughout his career in the settlement movement, Kennedy was committed to the promotion of cultural pluralism. Realizing the important role that blacks played in the settlement movement, Kennedy carried out a comprehensive study of race relations in settlements on behalf of the National Federation of Settlements in 1946. Regarded by some as the "elder statesman" of the settlement movement, Kennedy willingly shared his early experiences with younger reformers. In 1947 he taught a social work course for the City College of New York. During the 1950s he worked as a consultant, carrying out studies of settlements in Des Moines, Detroit, Evansville, and Sioux City.

Bibliography

Melvin, *American Community Organizations: An Historical Dictionary*, pp. 98–100; Trattner, *Biographical Dictionary of Social Welfare in America*, pp. 453–55.

Kingsbury, Susan Myra
social investigator, economist, educator
b. October 18, 1870; d. November 28, 1949.

Susan Kingsbury was an economist, teacher, and social science researcher. Her investigations and detailed reports were used by settlement workers and other social reformers to support their campaigns for legislation that would improve the living and working conditions of women and children during the opening decades of the twentieth century.

Kingsbury earned an M.A. in history in 1899 from Stanford University. The following year she left California for New York City where she enrolled in Columbia University. Before earning a Ph.D. in 1905, Kingsbury spent a year in England (1903–1904) as a fellow of the Women's Education Association of Boston and a year as a history instructor at Vassar (1904–1905).

After leaving Columbia, Kingsbury pursued an interest in researching industrial conditions. She conducted an investigation of children in industry for the Massachusetts Commission on Industrial and Technical Education from 1905 to 1906. In addition to teaching economics at Simmons College in this period, Kingsbury also served as director of the research department of the Women's Educational and Industrial Union of Boston (1907–1915) In this capacity, she came in contact with settlement workers and other social reformers such as **Mary Morton Kimball Kehew** who were involved in labor reform campaigns.

In 1915, Kingsbury became a professor of social economy and director of the Carola Woerishoffer Graduate Department of Social Economy and Social Research at Bryn Mawr, a position she held until her retirement in 1936. She was instrumental in establishing the first academic department dedicated to providing advanced training in social service.

In her work, Kingsbury examined the relationship between social forces and the community, a topic that was especially interesting to settlement workers. She was particularly concerned with the effect that women and child laborers had on working conditions both in the factory and in the home. She also investigated the economic impact of enforcing labor laws in factories. In addition, Kingsbury developed improved methodologies for conducting field studies and for reporting research results in a more constructive way so that reformers could more easily implement recommendations.

Besides her work as a scholar and teacher, Kingsbury served as vice president of the American Economic Association and the American Sociological Association. She also made two world tours (1911-1912 and 1921-1922) to observe the living and working conditions of women and children.

Even though she formally retired in 1936, Kingsbury maintained her interest in the economic and legal status of women through her participation in the American Economic Association and the American Sociological Association. Her work at Bryn Mawr helped develop the professional training of social welfare reformers and helped to raise the standard of social science field research.

Bibliography

Notable American Women, 1607–1950, vol. 2., pp. 335–36; Trattner, *Biographical Dictionary of Social Welfare in America*, pp. 461–64.

Kingsley, Charles
clergyman, social activist, author
b. June 12, 1819; d. January 23, 1875.

Charles Kingsley was an English clergyman who played a limited role in the **Christian Socialism** movement that emerged during the 1840s. This movement enjoyed a resurgence in the latter part of the nineteenth century and influenced a number of settlement workers. Kingsley's primary contribution to the original movement was his work as an author and editor of periodicals that helped to bring the Christian Socialists' ideas before the public.

Born in Devonshire, England, Kingsley attended Kings College, Cambridge, before deciding to take holy orders. As a young man he read widely and was particularly influenced by Thomas Carlyle, Samuel Taylor Coleridge, and **Frederick Denison Maurice**. Kingsley was ordained in 1842 and went to Eversley, Hampshire, as curate. Two years later he became Rector at Eversley.

In 1844, Kingsley met Maurice to whom he had written for advice about a parish matter. He admired Maurice very much, and he soon became closely associated with the group of Christian Socialists who recognized Maurice as their spiritual guide.

For a short time Kingsley held an appointment as a professor of English literature in the newly established Queens College, London, of which Maurice was president. His teaching and work in his parish at Eversley prevented Kingsley from taking part in many activities associated with the Christian Socialists. However, he contributed to the cause by writing about the condition of the poor and the church's responsibility for both the physical and spiritual well-being of the poor in a number of Christian Socialist publications such as *Politics for the People* and the *Christian Socialist: A Journal of Association*.

Kingsley also wrote novels that described the deplorable conditions of the working class, *Yeast* (1848) and *Alton Locke* (1850). In addition, Kingsley wrote a popular pamphlet, *Cheap Clothes and Nasty* (1850), in which he exposed the conditions of the sweating system (the use of sweatshops). Following the decline of the Christian Socialist movement, Kingsley devoted himself primarily to his parish duties at Eversley.

Although not a contemporary of other settlement workers, Kinglsey had an important though indirect influence on the American Settlement Movement. His works were influential during the Christian Socialism revival of the 1880s, and in this regard, he may be considered a spiritual and philosophical ancestor of the men and women who were active in settlement work both in England and in the United States.

Bibliography

Dictionary of National Biography, vol. 11, pp. 175–81; Seligman, *Encyclopedia of the Social Sciences*, vol. 8, pp. 567–68.

Kingsley House (Pittsburgh)

While not as well known as some of the larger settlements located in a major urban center like Chicago or New York, Kingsley House provided the citizens of two neighborhoods in Pittsburgh with a range of services. It also played an important role in the work of the **Pittsburgh Survey**, which was an in-depth study of all aspects of life in the city.

Kingsley House was established in December 1893 by the Reverend George Hodges in a neighborhood populated by German, Polish, Jewish, and Irish immigrants. The residents established a kindergarten, a resident-physician service, a bank, and a library. The house also offered a range of classes including art, sewing, mechanical drawing, and military drill, as well as social and cultural clubs.

In 1901, Kingsley House moved to the Hill District section of Pittsburgh where the neighborhood residents were Jewish, Italian, Irish, Syrian, and Arabian. The settlement residents continued their work at the new location, and in addition, began an aggressive campaign to secure better housing. From 1907 to 1908, William Matthews, the head resident of Kingsley House, opened the settlement to be used as a base of operations for the Pittsburgh Survey.

Charles Cooper, Matthews's successor as head of Kingsley House, demonstrated a strong interest in social action. Cooper was one of a small number of settlement workers who were married and raised their families in the settlement house. He was an outspoken critic of the Community Chest Movement, which provided funding for settlements in some cities. Cooper believed that the chests called for too much conformity and standardization on the part of the settlements. He maintained that this standardization led to a lack of initiative and innovation on the part of those houses that relied on chest funding.

Up until his untimely death in 1930, Cooper attempted to limit the influence that the Pittsburgh Community Chest had on the operations of Kingsley House. Toward this end, he attempted to increase the number of private donors who were willing to underwrite the settlement's activities. Eventually, Kingsley House was forced to accept chest funding, and in the years before the settlement closed, the chest exerted a considerable amount of control over its policies.

Bibliography

Carson, *Settlement Folk: Social Thought and the American Settlement Movement, 1885–1930*; Davis, *Spearheads for Reform: The Social Settlements and the Progressive Movement, 1890–1914*; Hall, *Unfinished Business In Neighborhood and Nation*; Trolander, *Settlement Houses and the Great Depression*; Woods, *Handbook of Settlements*.

Labor Laws and Their Enforcement (1911)

Labor Laws and Their Enforcement with Special Reference to Massachusetts is an authoritative and exhaustive work that is representative of the social research being carried out by social welfare reformers during the opening decades of the twentieth century. At the time of its publication, it was recognized as a significant contribution to the literature of labor legislation.

Susan Kingsbury served as editor of the volume. The research and the writing of the various chapters were undertaken by a number of social investigators who were either academics or former or present associates of the Women's Educational and Industrial Union. Some of the research was done under the auspices of a fellowship program sponsored by the Massachusetts Federation of Women's Clubs.

Kingsbury was a pioneer in the field of social investigation. From 1906 to 1915 she was the director of the research department of the **Women's Educational and Industrial Union** in Boston. Based on her knowledge of the methodology employed by social investigators in England, Kingsbury developed comparable methodologies for field studies in the United States. *Labor Laws and Their Enforcement* was one of the studies she published using this methodology while working at the Industrial Union.

Labor Laws and Their Enforcement is a history of factory legislation in Massachusetts, which was the first state to enact any significant factory legislation. The first part of the book relates to early history of this factory legislation in the state, drawing on original documents and ending with the passage of the tenement law in 1874. The book also includes chapters on unregulated conditions in women's work, the Massachusetts child labor law, and a discussion of the way in which Massachusetts administrated its labor law.

Bibliography

Kingsbury, *Labor Laws and Their Enforcement with Special Reference to Massachusetts*.

Lathrop, Julia Clifford

social reformer, settlement worker, women and children's advocate, social welfare agency administrator
b. June 29, 1858; d. April 15, 1932.

Julia Lathrop pursued a wide range of social reform interests including immigrants, delinquent children, infant and maternal health, and civil service reform. Her commitment to social justice and reform set an example for other social welfare workers, and she established a precedent for women serving in the federal government.

Lathrop graduated from Vassar College in 1880 and then went to work in her father's law office. She successfully invested her salary in two local manufacturing companies and was soon able to draw a private income.

During the winter of 1888–1889, Lathrop heard **Jane Addams** and **Ellen Gates Starr** speak in Rockford, Illinois, about their work at **Hull House**, the settlement they had established in Chicago. Inspired by what she heard, Lathrop became a resident at Hull House the following year. She quickly organized a Sunday afternoon discussion group, the Plato Group, and worked as a volunteer **friendly visitor** investigating requests for relief on behalf of the Cook County Charities. This experience convinced Lathrop of the inadequacy of the public assistance programs Chicago offered.

During the 1893 depression, Lathrop volunteered as a county agent to investigate relief applicants. That same year Illinois Governor **John Altgeld** appointed Lathrop to the Illinois Board of Charities, which supervised public institutions in the state.

Besides her charitable relief work, Lathrop was also interested in the treatment of the ill and insane. She traveled to Europe (1898–1900) to investigate how the insane were treated there, and when she returned home, she thoroughly investigated the treatment of inmates in Illinois state institutions. In her reports, Lathrop stressed the need for separate facilities for different ages and the need to separate the sick from the insane. She also spoke out against using untrained workers and political appointees as workers in state institutions. To ensure that workers were properly trained, Lathrop helped **Graham Taylor** of the **Chicago Commons** organize a series of training classes in 1903 that eventually became the Chicago School of Civics and Philanthropy. (*See* **Graduate School of Social Service Administration**.)

Lathrop lectured at the school, and in 1907, she worked with **Sophonisba Breckinridge**, a fellow reformer and an authority on child welfare and labor legislation, and **Edith Abbott**, a leader in social work research and education, to establish the school's research department. One of her most significant contributions was the development of occupational therapy courses for attendants who worked with the insane. Lathrop served on the board of trustees of the school until it was absorbed by the University of Chicago in 1920.

Juvenile delinquents and newly arrived immigrants benefited from Lathrop's interest and abilities as well. In 1899, she, Addams, the philanthropist and reformer **Lucy L. Flowers**, and other Hull House residents joined forces with the Chicago Women's Club and the Chicago Bar Association to secure legislation to establish the first juvenile court system in the United States. Through Lathrop's efforts, Chicago finally secured a juvenile court building with a detention home and psychopathic clinic in 1909. In 1908, Lathrop co-founded the Immigrants' Protective League (*see* **Immigrants' Service League**) which was organized by the residents of Hull House to help the newly arrived make the transition to American society. She served as a trustee of the league until her death in 1932.

Like many of her contemporaries, Lathrop was interested in child welfare. While on a world tour with her sister, Anna Lathrop, she prepared a study on the public schools in the Philippines. In 1913, President Taft was so impressed with her report and with her other accomplishments, that he appointed her head of the new **United States Children's Bureau**, which had been created by Congress within the Department of Commerce and Labor as a central agency responsible for collecting and distributing ideas and information on child welfare.

Lathrop and her staff of 15 investigators undertook a study of infant mortality in the United States and recommended a program for uniform birth registration procedures. Reappointed by President Woodrow Wilson, Lathrop expanded her study of infant mortality to include an examination of nutrition. She also marshaled the bureau's resources to work for child labor legislation and for mothers' pensions.

In 1916, Congress passed the country's first child labor law and the Children's Bureau was charged with coordinating this effort. Lathrop called upon another former Hull House resident, **Grace Abbott**, to head up the Children's Bureau Child Labor Division. Although the law was declared unconstitutional in 1918, the bureau continued its investigative efforts. Abbott remained, serving as Lathrop's assistant.

Lathrop had to retire from the United States Children's Bureau due to poor health, but not before the culmination of the Children's Bureau's efforts on behalf of mothers and infants was realized in 1921 with the passage of the **Sheppard-Towner Act**, which provided federal aid to the states. She was succeeded by Grace Abbott that same year. After her retirement, Lathrop returned to Rockford, Illinois, where she remained active in social reform work. From 1922 to 1924 she served as president of the Illinois League of Women Voters. President Calvin Coolidge named her to the commission investigating conditions on Ellis Island (1922). From 1925 to 1931 Lathrop served as an assessor on the Child Welfare Committee of the League of Nations.

Lathrop's wide-ranging social reform efforts were intertwined with those of the settlement movement in the United States. A long-time settlement resident, she mobilized the local Chicago and the national reform communities to work for better care for the mentally ill, a juvenile court system, and better health care for mothers and children. Her emphasis on casework and social research methods, particularly during her tenure at the Children's Bureau, set a standard for other reformers, and her appointments to the Illinois State Board of Charities and the United States Children's Bureau opened the way for other women to serve in similar capacities.

Bibliography

Addams, *My Friend, Julia Lathrop*; *Dictionary of American Biography*, supl. 1, pp. 484–86; James, *Notable American Women, 1607–1950*, vol. 2, pp. 370–72; Trattner, *Biographical Dictionary of Social Welfare in America*, pp. 478–81.

League for the Protection of Immigrants *See* Immigrants' Service League

Lee, Joseph
reformer, playground movement activist
b. March 8, 1862; d. July 28, 1937.

Joseph Lee was known as "The Father of American Playgrounds." A wealthy man, he devoted himself to social reforms in three broad areas: local government and social legislation initiatives, education-related initiatives, and efforts related to the cultivation of play and recreation.

Lee attended Harvard, earning an undergraduate degree in 1893 and an L.L.B. degree four years later. Although he was admitted to the bar, Lee never practiced law. Henry Lee, Joseph's father, was a successful banker who provided his son with an independent income. But the younger Lee spurned luxurious living and felt no sense of satisfaction from his personal wealth. Keenly aware of the miserable conditions of the poor, he lived modestly and devoted much of his time and money to various social reform efforts.

Lee's philanthropic endeavors targeted causes that emphasized ways to strengthen and develop both the community and the individual. Lee's interests in local government reform, edu-

cation improvement, and recreation brought him into contact with settlement workers and other social welfare workers who shared his concerns. In 1897, for example, Lee organized the Massachusetts Civic League, which played a significant role in influencing social legislation in the state. He served as president of the league until 1935.

As part of his efforts to improve education, Lee gave generously to Harvard's department of education and also served as an elected member of Boston's School Committee from 1908 to 1917. He and his wife Margaret, who was interested in the kindergarten movement, supported the School Visitors Association. Lee was interested in a number of education-related issues including school medical inspections, programs for both slow and gifted children, and the school center movement, which advocated the use of school buildings as community centers.

It was **Zilpha D. Smith**, a Boston social worker, who first stimulated Lee's interest in recreation. In the early 1890s, she recruited Lee's help with a survey of play areas in crowded inner-city neighborhoods. He was an enthusiastic investigator who carefully studied existing recreational facilities and programs as well as the difficulties encountered by those who oversaw their use. As a result of Lee's efforts, playgrounds were opened in both of the districts he investigated.

Lee published several articles based on his survey findings. His writings brought him a national reputation, and in 1906, he was elected vice president of the new Playgrounds Association of America. In 1910, Lee replaced Luther Halsey Gulick as president, a position he held until his death in 1937. During his tenure as president of the Playground Association, it evolved into the **National Recreation and Park Association**.

Lee did not go unrecognized for his work in promoting recreation. He was awarded the War Department's Distinguished Service Medal for his efforts in establishing an affiliate of the National Recreation Association, the War Camp Community Service, and for his role in developing recreational facilities for use by soldiers on leave. He remained active in his reform work throughout the rest of his life

Bibliography

Carson, *Settlement Folk: Social Thought and the American Settlement Movement, 1885–1930*; *Dictionary of American Biography*, supl. 2, pp. 374–75.

Lewisohn, Irene
settlement worker, art patron
b. September 5, 1892; d. April 4, 1944.

Settlement workers were not only concerned with their neighbors' health and safety at home and at work. Most settlements provided some type of recreational facilities and some sponsored music, dance, and drama classes. Thanks to the monetary contributions and the countless hours they devoted, Irene Lewisohn and her sister Alice helped the **Henry Street Settlement** to become a neighborhood center for drama and dance productions.

Lewisohn's father, Leonard, was a successful businessman who contributed to a number of philanthropic causes. One of the reform causes that he supported was the Henry Street Settlement, which had been founded by **Lillian Wald** and **Mary Brewster** in 1893. Alice Lewisohn worked at the settlement as a club leader and teacher. Irene, who had studied theater and dance as a child, soon followed her example, and the two sisters began offering acting and dancing classes to the surrounding community. They also organized amateur productions, staging their first dance performance in the Henry Street gymnasium in 1907.

Adults and children were attracted to the Lewisohn sisters' productions, which drew upon neighborhood talent and promoted pride in the immigrant's heritage by incorporating various ethnic songs, dances, and costumes into their performances. In 1912 the Lewisohns offered a dramatic performance by a group called the **Neighborhood Playhouse** in the Clinton Hall on the Bowery. The following year they organized a street pageant to commemorate the Henry Street Settlement's 20th anniversary.

Over the years Irene and Alice contributed more than a half million dollars to the Henry Street Settlement. In 1914 they donated an 80-acre farm called Echo Hill to the settlement to be used as a summer camp for neighborhood children. The same year they purchased a lot on Grand Street and built a theater, which they called the Neighborhood Playhouse after the group in the Clinton Hall. The Lewisohns donated the building to the settlement, and although it was legally part of the Henry Street Settlement, it functioned as an independent artistic entity. The playhouse started as a drama school that featured lectures and workshops offered by visiting actors. It also presented exhibits and workshop performances. However, by 1920 the amateur talent had been largely replaced by a resident professional company. In

recognition of its original mission to provide neighborhood residents with access to dramatic arts, in 1923 the playhouse instituted a popular annual satire review entitled Grand Street Follies.

Eventually, the Neighborhood Playhouse gained recognition as a center for experimental theater and the avant-garde. The Lewisohn sisters directed productions, scouted talent, and performed, Alice as an actress and Irene as a dancer. Over the years, a variety of esoteric productions were staged including Japanese Noh plays, Norse fairy tales, and medieval miracle plays. These performances reflected the Lewisohns' personal taste for Asian and Middle Eastern art forms. These regions were of particular interest to Irene and Alice who traveled extensively in both areas during two world tours that they undertook in 1910 and 1922.

During the 1920s, the Neighborhood Playhouse was unable to maintain subscribers, and it experienced severe financial difficulties. Alice married in 1925 and spent more and more time abroad. The theater closed in 1927, and the building reverted to the Henry Street Settlement. During the next few years, Irene mounted a series of orchestral dramas in which dancers interpreted the music performed by a full symphony orchestra. Performances were held in New York City, Cleveland, and Washington, DC.

In 1928, Irene Lewisohn and Rita Wallach Morgenthau founded the Neighborhood Playhouse School of the Theater. This enterprise occupied much of Irene's time for the rest of her life, though she continued to find time for reform activities including supporting the Loyalists during the Spanish Civil War and establishing the Spanish Child Welfare Association. In 1937, she founded the Museum of Costume Art to make her costume collection available for public exhibitions and as a resource for stage designers. Following Lewisohn's death, the museum's collection became the basis for the Costume Institute at the Metropolitan Museum of Art in New York City.

Bibliography

Crowley, *Alice Lewisohn: The Neighborhood Playhouse;* James, *Notable American Women, 1607–1950,* vol. 2, pp. 400–02; Trattner, *Biographical Dictionary of Social Welfare in America;* pp. 495–98; Wald, *The House on Henry Street;* Wald, *Windows on Henry Street.*

Lloyd, Henry Demarest
journalist, social activist
b. May 1, 1847; d. September 28, 1903.

Henry Demarest Lloyd was a crusading journalist and political activist who proved to be a valuable friend and ally to settlement workers at the Chicago-based settlement **Hull House**, giving generously of his fortune and his time to help advance the house's work.

A graduate of Columbia University and a member of the New York Bar, Lloyd moved to Chicago in 1872 where he secured a position as the financial editor and chief editorial writer for the *Chicago Tribune*. In 1885, thanks to his wife's inheritance, Lloyd retired from newspaper work and devoted his time to public affairs.

The year of the inheritance, Lloyd toured Europe, studying social conditions. While in Europe, he became acquainted with the English reform movements of the time including the Christian Socialist revival, which would prove to be very influential in the development of the settlement movement in the United States. When he returned to the United States in 1886, he joined with William Sulter of the Chicago **Ethical Culture Society** and others to call for clemency for the seven anarchists who had been sentenced to death following the Haymarket Riots.

The Lloyds were financial supporters of Hull House from the time of its founding in 1889. Lloyd introduced the settlement's founder and head resident **Jane Addams** and her colleagues to a wide variety of social activists and political figures. He funded research projects undertaken by Hull House residents, financed building projects, and lobbied politicians on behalf of the settlement. Lloyd often attended labor union meetings at the settlement. He supported the workers' cause during the Pullman Strike in 1894 and was active in the child labor crusade. In 1893, Illinois Governor **John P. Altgeld** offered Lloyd the newly created position of chief factory inspector for the state. Lloyd declined the offer, but he recommended **Florence Kelley**, whom he knew from Hull House. Lloyd was a frequent contributor to *The Commons* (*see* **the *Survey***), the social reform journal established by **Graham Taylor** of the **Chicago Commons** settlement.

In his writings, Lloyd advocated a variety of individual reforms including regulation of railroads and an end to industrial monopolies. The latter was the subject of his best-known work, *Wealth against Commonwealth* (1894), which attacked monopolies generally and the Standard Oil Company specifically.

Lloyd was active in public affairs up to the time of his death in 1903. In his writings he attempted to raise the public's consciousness regarding political and corporate corruption and the dangers of allowing these trends to go unchecked. In addition to contributing his ideas and his time, Lloyd was a generous financial contributor to the work of Hull House and to the many initiatives undertaken by the Chicago and national reform communities.

Bibliography
Carson, *Settlement Folk: Social Thought and the American Settlement Movement, 1885–1930*; Davis, *Spearheads for Reform: The Social Settlements and the Progressive Movement, 1890–1914*; Garraty, *Encyclopedia of American Biography*, pp. 693–94.

Loch, Charles Stewart
reformer, social service agency administrator
b. September 4, 1849; d. January 23, 1923.

Charles Loch's career in social welfare was inspired by his religious commitment to apply Christian principles to his daily life and to work for the good of society. He channeled his interests and energies into the London Charity Organization Society, whose work served as a model for similar organizations in the United States.

Born in Baghalpur, Bengal, while his father was serving as a judge of the High Court of Calcutta, Loch had hoped to enter the Indian Civil Service, but poor health prevented him from doing so. Instead, after obtaining his degree from Balliol College, Oxford, he became clerk to the Royal College of Surgeons in London in 1873.

While at Balliol, Loch had become interested in the increasingly popular growing social service movement that stressed the practical application of Christian principles to everyday life. He was particularly inspired by the teachings of one of his tutors, Thomas Hill Green, and by the social service work of another Oxford undergraduate, **Arnold Toynbee.** While working at the College of Surgeons, Loch stayed involved in reform work through the Islington branch of the **Charity Organization Society** (COS).

In 1875, Loch became secretary of the Charity Organization Society of London, marking the beginning of an association that was to continue for 40 years. Loch proved to be an able and enthusiastic administrator. Working with a small dedicated staff, he oversaw the investigation of each application for assistance. A permanent record was kept of each case, and every effort was made to avoid duplication of effort among the various public and private relief agencies. Loch employed a large number of educated men and women volunteers who spent a considerable amount of time investigating claims and visiting the recipients.

Loch believed that many of the problems of the poor were the result of the English poor law system, and he was an ardent critic of any form of government relief. He was critical of the social legislation enacted by the liberal government between 1906 and 1914 because he felt that this legislation did not sufficiently emphasize the responsibility of the individual in its approach to social problems. Loch also recognized that social service work was an international concern. To learn from his contemporaries, he spent three months in 1896 visiting associated charities groups in various cities in the United States. He also maintained contact with similar groups in France.

In addition to his administrative responsibilities, Loch published pamphlets about the work of the London COS and maintained an active public speaking schedule. He maintained good working relationships with the local authorities and with influential individuals who served on the society's various committees. He was influential in ensuring the passage of a number of Acts of Parliament related to social service concerns including the Mental Deficiency Act of 1913, and the Maternity and Child Welfare Act of 1918. In addition, Loch served on a number of royal commissions including those concerned with the aged poor (1893–1895) and the care and control of the feeble-minded (1904–1908). Besides his work with the COS, Loch was the Tooke Professor of economic science and statistics at King's College, London, between 1904 and 1908. He retired from the COS in 1914 and was knighted in 1915.

In his work with the London Charity Organization Society, Loch set an example for the COS movement in the United States and for the American Settlement Movement. His interest in coordinating the work of various social welfare agencies in a community and his early attempts to develop a case work approach were later adopted by settlement workers.

Bibliography

Dictionary of National Biography, 1922–1930; pp. 512–14; Seligman, *Encyclopedia of the Social Sciences*, vol. 9, p. 593.

Lovejoy, Owen
clergyman, child labor reformer
b. September 9, 1866; d. June 29, 1961.

Owen Lovejoy's career as a child labor reformer brought him into contact with many settlement workers and other social welfare activists.

A native of Grand Rapids, Michigan, Lovejoy earned B.A. (1891) and M.A. (1894) degrees from Albion College and was ordained a Methodist minister in 1891. Over the next seven years, he held pastorates at several Michigan churches. In 1898, he was called to the First Congregational Church in Mount Vernon, New York, a parish assignment that placed him in close proximity to the large and dynamic New York City-based reform community.

In 1902, at the request of a group of his Mount Vernon parishioners and other concerned citizens, Lovejoy went to observe conditions during the Pennsylvania anthracite coal strike. Two years later he was sent by the **National Child Labor Committee** (NCLC) to investigate child labor in the coal mines. At the coal mines, Lovejoy witnessed the extremely dangerous conditions in which young children were forced to work. In his report he described the work of the children called "breakers" who spent long hours bent over coal chutes sorting through the broken rubble to pick out usable pieces of coal. Lovejoy's experiences inspired him to become more directly involved in the crusade against child labor, and he soon became one of the two salaried, full-time assistant secretaries of the NCLC.

By 1907, Lovejoy had become the general secretary of the National Child Labor Committee. He proved to be an active and impassioned advocate, an effective public speaker, and an able administrator. He assembled a competent group of field investigators, board members, legislative agents, and fund raisers, and by the time he retired from the NCLC in 1926, Lovejoy had made significant progress in improving child labor conditions, including limiting the number of hours that children could work, raising the wages they received, and improving sanitary and safety reforms.

In addition to his work with the National Child Labor Committee, Lovejoy chaired the National Conference of Charities and Correction's Committee on Standards of Living and Labor (1912), and he was elected president of the National Conference of Social Work (*see* **National Conference on Social Welfare**) in 1920. He also served as secretary of the Children's Aid Society of New York (1927–1935).

Lovejoy retired in 1939 and went to live on a farm in Biglerville, Pennsylvania. During his long and productive career as a social reformer, Lovejoy made significant contributions to the child labor reform crusade and worked closely with many of the men and women of the American Settlement Movement.

Bibliography

Dictionary of American Biography, supl. 7, pp. 483–84; Trattner, *Crusade for the Children: A History of the NCLC and Child Labor Reform in America*.

Lowell, Josephine Shaw
charity organization society founder, reformer, social activist
b. December 16, 1843; d. October 12, 1905.

Lowell's career in social reform is noteworthy for the way in which she successfully combined the practical and the theoretical. An intelligent and energetic woman, Lowell transformed personal tragedy into positive change. She inspired many women of her social class to become active reformers and was instrumental in the formation of important social welfare reform organizations such as the New York **Charity Organization Society** and the National **Consumers' League**.

Born in West Roxbury, Massachusetts, in 1843, into a prosperous, well-connected family, an interest in social welfare concerns seemed to come naturally to the young Josephine whose parents were impassioned abolitionists and were involved in the establishment of the Freedmen's Bureau.

In 1847, the family moved to Staten Island, so that Josephine's mother, Sarah, whose eyesight was failing, could be near a New York City-based specialist. Beginning in 1851, the Shaw family traveled through Europe where the children studied in Paris and Rome. As a result, Josephine achieved proficiency in German, French, and Italian before returning to the United States to complete her formal education in schools in both New York and Boston.

The Civil War had a profound effect on Josephine and her family and provided the impetus for getting her involved in public affairs. Her first exposure to organized charity came when she and her sister joined the New York branch of the Woman's Central Association of Relief, an auxiliary of the United States Sanitary Commission (1862). It was the personal tragedies she endured during the Civil War, however, that galvanized her reform work. Her brother, Robert Gould Shaw, commanded the Massachusetts 54th, the first black regiment sent into combat by the free states. He was killed in action in 1863, the same year that Josephine married Colonel Charles Russell Lowell, the nephew of the poet James Russell Lowell. Colonel Lowell, who was attached to the 2nd Massachusetts Cavalry, was wounded at Cedar Creek and died a short time later. Six weeks after his death, Josephine gave birth to a daughter, Carlotta Russell. Following her husband's death, Lowell, who had accompanied him to Virginia, returned to New York where the home that she shared with her daughter eventually became a gathering place for social reformers and philanthropists.

Inspired by the memory of her husband and her brother, Lowell quickly immersed herself in social causes, including the movement for black relief and education, becoming the principal fund-raiser for the National Freedman's Relief Association in New York. In 1866 along with a charity worker colleague, Ellen Collins, Lowell inspected black schools in Virginia on behalf of the association.

As her post-war charity efforts began to wind down, Lowell became involved in the work of the New York Charities Aid Association, which had been founded in 1872 by Louisa Lee Schuyler to conduct regular inspections of state charity institutions. Lowell was a competent and able woman and her abilities were recognized when she was appointed head of the Staten Island committee of the Charities Aid Association. Because of her forthright reports of the filthy conditions in jails and almshouses that exerted no effort to rehabilitate inmates, she was selected in 1875 to conduct a statewide study of able-bodied paupers. The following year New York Governor Samuel J. Tilden appointed Lowell the first woman member of the State Board of Charities.

Over the next several years, Lowell established a reputation as a hardworking, competent commissioner for the state board. She conducted numerous personal inspections of almshouses, jails, hospitals, and orphanages, and she submitted reports that enumerated shortcomings and suggested improvements especially in relation to the rehabilitation of inmates. As a result of Lowell's efforts, the first custodial facility for feebleminded women was established in Newark, New York, in 1885, and in the following year, a House of Refuge for Women, which offered healthy surroundings and emphasized constructive activity, was established in Hudson, New York.

In 1881 the State Board of Charities commissioned Lowell to study waste and duplication among privately financed charitable institutions. As a result of her investigations, the New York Charity Organization Society was established to promote cooperation and efficiency among charitable organizations. Over the next 25 years, Lowell made the New York society one of the foremost associations of its kind in the United States.

Although she was active in the day-to-day work of social relief, Lowell also devoted a considerable effort to developing her own theories on the underlying purpose of state-sponsored charitable aid, which she believed was not the relief of immediate suffering but the fundamental reformation of the individual. She defined her theories of charitable aid in the articles, addresses, and official reports she wrote over many years. Perhaps her most significant work was *Public Relief and Private Charity* (1884). In this publication, she delineated her belief that the community should support only those individuals whom it could control and that it should offer rigorous rehabilitation programs designed to assist the truly needy to become useful citizens while at the same time discouraging the able-bodied from seeking charitable aid.

Although her writings appear to have a certain harshness, Lowell's daily exposure to poverty gradually turned her attention to the plight of the working poor who despite their best efforts could not earn a living wage. In 1889, she resigned from the State Board of Charities and began to devote more of her attention to labor problems. The following year she was one of the principal founders of the Consumers' League of New York, which was established to improve wages and working conditions of young women employed in retail stores by establishing a code of working conditions and encouraging consumers to boycott stores that did not honor the code. Lowell served as president of the league until 1896. In 1892, she actively supported the workers during the Homestead Strike, and during the winter of 1893–1894, she organized a committee to provide work relief for the unemployed living on New York's Lower East Side. A number of settlement workers, **Lillian Wald** among them, were involved in this program. The committee initiated a number of projects including street cleaning and the whitewashing of tenement buildings.

Always interested in politics, Lowell organized the Woman's Municipal League in 1894 as an anti-Tammany campaign effort. The league intended to promote humanitarian reform through political action. Three years later it was reorganized on a more permanent basis and became an important vehicle of urban reform during the Progressive period.

Lowell's political activism was manifested in other activities as well. In 1895, she founded the women's auxiliary of the Civil Service Reform Association of New York State and served as chair of the executive committee for many years. During the Spanish-American War she was active in the anti-imperialist movement, using her influence to secure prominent speakers such as William James and Charles William Eliot for rallies.

Lowell remained active in reform efforts until her death in 1905. An important participant in a number of social reform crusades, she worked closely with many of the women and men active in the American Settlement Movement.

Bibliography

Bremner, *From the Depths: The Discovery of Poverty in the United States*; *Dictionary of American Biography*, vol. 6, pp. 467–68; Jackson, *Encyclopedia of New York City*, pp. 695–96; James, *Notable American Women, 1607–1950*, vol. 2, pp. 437–39; Seligman, *Encyclopedia of the Social Sciences*, vol. 9, p. 621; Trattner, *Biographical Dictionary of Social Welfare in America*, pp. 511–18.

M

McDowell, Mary Eliza
settlement worker, labor activist
b. November 30, 1854; d. October 14, 1936.

Mary McDowell was almost 40 years old when she began a career as a settlement worker in earnest. On the recommendation of **Jane Addams**, the founder of the Chicago-based settlement **Hull House**, McDowell became the head resident of the **University of Chicago Settlement**. This position brought her into the center of Chicago's vibrant social reform community, and McDowell quickly became a leader among her peers as she fought relentlessly for health, sanitary, and labor reforms.

McDowell's first exposure to relief work came when she participated in the relief and rehabilitation work carried out after the Chicago Fire of 1871. After the McDowell family moved to Evanston, Illinois, several years later, Mary met Frances Willard, national president of the Women's Christian Temperance Union (WCTU), and she became involved in the work of the WCTU. She also taught Sunday school and headed the WCTU's kindergarten.

Deciding on a career as a social reformer, McDowell returned to Chicago in 1890 to live and work at Hull House, the settlement founded by Jane Addams and **Ellen Gates Starr**. She started a kindergarten and helped to organize the settlement's women's club. McDowell planned to remain a permanent resident and kindergarten worker at Hull House, but her mother's illness forced her to return to Evanston.

In 1894, Addams recommended McDowell as the director of the settlement that a group of faculty members at the University of Chicago established as a sociological laboratory in an industrial immigrant neighborhood behind the Chicago stockyards. Pleased with the opportunity to return to settlement work, McDowell lived in a small apartment in the neighborhood known as Packingtown for two years, spending her time getting to know the residents. In 1896, she and a group of settlement workers moved into more spacious accommodations over a feed store. By 1906, they were living and working in the newly constructed University of Chicago settlement house.

McDowell and her colleagues at the house worked tirelessly for better health and sanitary conditions. They continually petitioned the municipal authorities to clean up alleys and streets and to close the open garbage dumps that surrounded the neighborhood. They worked to have the sewers installed to eliminate the polluted streams that were used to carry away the waste from the packinghouses, and they secured a park and a public bathhouse for the neighborhood residents.

Like many other Chicago-based settlement workers, McDowell took an active interest in local ward politics and in labor issues. She encouraged local unions to meet at the settlement and was a strong supporter of the striking meat cutters in 1904. McDowell also campaigned on behalf of reform candidates in local elections, and in 1912 led a successful campaign that resulted in the creation of the City Waste Commission.

McDowell was also sensitive to racial issues. In response to the Chicago race riots in 1919, she helped to organize the International Cooperative Committee. She was also an active member of the National Association for the Advancement of Colored People, which was founded in 1909.

In addition to her settlement work, McDowell cooperated with other social reformers to establish the National **Consumers' League** (1899) and the National **Women's Trade Union League** (1903). She served as president of the latter's Chicago branch from 1904 to 1907. Her interest in women workers was a long-term one. She was an advocate of the Committee on Women in Industry, which monitored women's working conditions during World War I, and during the 1920s she played a major role in securing a Women's Bureau in the United States Department of Labor.

In 1923, McDowell was appointed Commissioner of Public Welfare by Chicago Mayor William Dever. As part of her responsibilities, she established a Bureau of Employment and a Bureau of Social Survey. McDowell continued her settlement work until she retired as head resident of the University of Chicago Settlement in 1929.

Bibliography

Dictionary of American Biography, supl. 2, pp. 407–09; James, *Notable American Women, 1607–1950*, vol. 2, pp. 462–64; Trattner, *Biographical Dictionary of Social Welfare in America*, pp. 525–28.

Madison House

Settlement houses were established for a variety of reasons: to assist a particular ethnic group, to advocate a religious doctrine, or to provide health care. Madison House was established to advance the social/ philosophical ideals of the Ethical Culture Movement, which advocated expressing personal virtue through social service. Like the **Neighborhood Guild** (later the **University Settlement**) and the **Hudson Guild**, which were also established by reformers associated with the Ethical Culture Movement, Madison House offered a range of services to the community, including social clubs, a savings bank, a sewing school, and an athletic program.

Felix Adler, the founder of the **Ethical Culture Society**, was interested in pursuing the society's work on New York City's Lower East Side. He believed that the venture would be successful only if it were carried out by neighborhood residents. The social and political activist **Henry Moskowitz** was just the sort of person Adler had in mind to carry out such a program. Moskowitz had grown up on the Lower East Side, and as a boy had participated in clubs sponsored by the University Settlement. While a student at City College, Moskowitz began attending Adler's lectures and was active in the Ethical Culture Society.

In 1898, Adler approached Moskowitz with his idea of establishing a settlement that would carry on the work of the Ethical Culture Society. That same year Moskowitz and 11 friends established a settlement on Madison Street, which they named the Down Town Ethical Society. Funding for the house was provided by the Ethical Culture Society. After several years, the name was changed to Madison House.

The founders of the new settlement, which was located in a neighborhood with a large population of Jewish immigrants, articulated three goals: to build character through ethical teaching, to Americanize the neighborhood residents while also maintaining strong family ties between immigrant parents and American-born children, and to teach the neighborhood residents self-governance skills.

The residents of Madison House had a broad range of interests. They were active in local ward politics and worked with other settlements to secure parks and playgrounds; they were also involved in the anti-prostitution crusade headed up by the Committee of Fifteen. As was the case with other settlements, Madison House offered a range of clubs for the people in the neighborhood and its workers were instrumental in organizing the Federation of Boys Clubs and the East Side Civic Club.

Although Madison House was originally founded under the auspices of the Ethical Culture Society, it offered its services to all community residents in the same way that the other Ethical Culture Society-sponsored settlements did. Today, Madison House, now known as the Madison Hamilton Settlement, still serves the local community, providing social activities such as clubs and athletic events as well as social services such as day care.

Bibliography
Davis, *Spearheads for Reform: The Social Settlements and the Progressive Movement, 1890–1914*; Woods, *The Handbook of Settlements*.

Marsh, Benjamin C.
urban planner, political activist
b. March 22, 1877; d. December 30, 1952.

Benjamin Marsh's interest in population density and land and tax reform brought him into contact with settlement workers and other social reformers. He frequently led the coalitions these various reformers established to reform taxes, create programs for more uniform population distribution, and initiate comprehensive city planning.

A graduate of Grinnell College in Iowa (1848), Marsh worked for a short time as the Iowa Assistant State Secretary for the Young Men's Christian Association. He enrolled in courses in political economy at the University of Chicago, and he then spent two years traveling around the United States raising funds for the Congregationalist Board of Commissions for Foreign Missions.

During his travels around the states, Marsh observed living and working conditions, and he came to know many of the problems faced by urban communities. He also became interested in the relationship between rents and taxes to population congestion. In 1902, he secured a fellowship at the University of Pennsylvania, under the direction of Simon Patten, to study homelessness. The following summer (1903), Marsh traveled in Europe investigating the treatment of beggars and the homeless in various countries.

When he returned to the United States, Marsh became more involved in the reform movement. He was named secretary of the Pennsylvania Society to Protect Children from Cruelty soon after his return. By 1906, he was living and working at **Greenwich House**, the settlement founded by **Mary K. Simkhovitch** on New York City's Lower West Side. Simkhovitch and some of her New York settlement colleagues were concerned with the effects of population density on the health and safety of New York City's tenement dwellers. To bring these concerns to the public's attention, the settlement workers formed a **Committee on Congestion of Population** and planned a public exhibition. Based on his experience, Marsh was selected to coordinate the exhibition. In preparation, he toured various European countries during the summer of 1907 to gather information about European city planning initiatives.

The so-called Congestion Exhibition was held at the American Museum of Natural History in March 1908. The exhibition was a success and generated a substantial amount of interest in the relationship between population density and city planning. Following the Congestion Exhibition, Marsh and some of the other reformers associated with it persuaded New York Governor Charles Evans Hughes to create the Commission on Distribution of Population to continue the research of the Committee on Congestion of Population. Marsh served as the secretary of this temporary state organization. The commission was primarily concerned with educating the public about the effects of overcrowding. Under Marsh's leadership it held hearings about population distribution, investigated housing projects, and advocated public control over the placement of industry in communities.

At the same time that he was working with the Commission on Distribution of Population, Marsh was also serving as the secretary of the Society to Lower Rents and Reduce Taxes on Homes in New York. This group advocated the transfer of taxes from buildings to land values. Marsh also worked to establish a City Commission on Congestion of Population, arranged public meetings, and supervised an exhibition open to the public on European and American city planning.

Marsh's activities reached beyond the local and state levels to the national arena. After the success of the New York Congestion Exhibition, he and the other organizers called for a National City Planning Conference. Marsh presided over the conference, which was held in Washington, DC, in May 1909. He was also executive secretary of the People's Lobby, an ad hoc reform coalition established in 1931 which called on the federal government to restore confidence during the economic crisis by providing relief, unemployment insurance, and public works jobs.

Marsh worked with the People's Lobby until shortly before his death in 1952. Marsh's expertise in city planning made him a valuable ally of settlement workers, especially in New York City where substandard housing and population congestion were serious problems. With his assistance, these reformers organized exhibitions and conferences that brought housing problems to the attention of local and national authorities.

Bibliography

Davis, *Spearheads for Reform: The Social Settlements and the Progressive Movement, 1890–1914*; Lubove, *The Progressives and the Slums: Tenement House Reform in New York City, 1890–1917*; Marsh, *Lobbyist For the People: A Record of Fifty Years*; Scott, *American City Planning Since 1890: A History Commemorating the Fiftieth Anniversary of the American Institute of Planners*.

Maurice, Frederick Denison
clergyman, social activist
b. August 29, 1805; d. April 1, 1872.

As a spiritual leader of the Christian Socialist movement that developed in England during the 1840s, Frederick Denison Maurice helped to popularize the group's idea that Christian principles should be applied to social reform efforts. (*See* **Christian Socialism**.) Although the original Christian Socialist movement was short-lived, it experienced a rebirth in the 1880s. This revival, with its emphasis on social action, appealed to many settlement workers and other social reformers.

Maurice's father, Michael, was a Unitarian preacher who wanted his son to follow him into the ministry. Frederick had other plans for himself, and in 1823, he entered Trinity College, Cambridge, to study law. He took a first-class degree in civil law in 1827. While still a student, Maurice contributed articles to several popular periodicals and eventually became editor of the *Athenaeum*. Family obligations compelled him to resign his editorship and return home to Southhampton.

Eventually, Maurice decided to take holy orders. He enrolled at Oxford in 1830 and was ordained a priest in the Church of England four years later. In 1836, he became chaplain to Guy's Hospital, and in 1840, he was elected professor of English Literature and History at King's College, London.

Throughout these years, Maurice took an avid interest in the religious and social debates of the time. He sympathized with the Chartists and radicals, who were calling for democratic social and political reform in England such as equal participation by all adult males in the affairs of state, but maintained that substituting Christianity for secularist doctrines was the only way to bring about a genuine reconstruction of society. Although he was not entirely comfortable with his role, Maurice became the spiritual leader of a group of like-minded individuals who were known as the Christian Socialists.

Maurice edited the group's short-lived publication, *Politics for the People*. His home became the site of weekly gatherings to discuss current events and the Bible. The Christian Socialists held meetings and established associations with various groups of workers to improve social relations between the classes. Maurice was joined in his work by **Charles Kingsley**, who shared his desire to do away with class differences. Although the initiatives sponsored by Maurice and his associates failed after a short time, Maurice remained committed to the idea of cooperation between the classes. Because of his activities, he was attacked as a radical and forced to resign his position at King's College in 1853, but he retained the Chaplaincy of Lincoln's Inn.

In 1854 Maurice drew up a plan for a Working Men's College to educate the artisan class which had been a goal of the Christian Socialist associations. Maurice served both as principal and as a lecturer. Many prominent men also delivered lectures at the college including John Ruskin, a professor of fine arts at Oxford University. Maurice maintained his connection with the college after his election to a professorship of philosophy at Cambridge.

Maurice's health gradually declined during the 1860s. However, he continued his church work and delivered occasional lectures. He died suddenly in April 1872.

A dedicated and devout clergyman, Maurice worked tirelessly on behalf of the poor during his career. His pioneering work in helping to define and popularize the philosophy of the early Christian Socialists established a legacy for social reformers, particularly settlement workers both in England and the United States.

Bibliography

Dictionary of National Biography, vol. 13, pp. 97–105; Seligman, *Encyclopedia of the Social Sciences*, vol. 10, p. 233.

Mitchell, Lucy Sprague
educational reformer
b. July 2, 1878; d. October 15, 1967.

Lucy Sprague Mitchell was a pioneer in education reform in the first half of the twentieth century. As a young woman living in Chicago, she had contact with settlement workers and other reformers who aroused her interest in social activism. She maintained her connection with the reform community when she moved to New York City and established the Bureau of Educational Experiments, which served as a laboratory for innovations in early childhood education.

Mitchell was born in Chicago where her father, Otho Sprague, was a partner in Sprague

Warner and Company, one of the largest wholesale grocery businesses in the world. Lucy was raised in an oppressive household that was dominated by Otho. He and Lucy's mother, Lucia, almost never expressed any affection for each other or for their children. Although the Sprague household was emotionally cold, it was not without intellectual stimulation. In addition to her father's extensive library, Lucy was exposed to the ideas of a variety of prominent guests who frequented her family's dinner table. These included faculty members at the University of Chicago such as John Dewey, who established the Laboratory School at the university; and Alice Freeman Palmer, the former president of Wellesley College who introduced Lucy to Marion Talbot, the Dean of Women at the University of Chicago; and the social worker and political activist **Sophonisba Breckinridge**. Otho Sprague supported the work of the Chicago settlement **Hull House**, and its founder and head resident **Jane Addams** was also a regular guest.

Her exposure to the ideas of Chicago's social welfare community opened Lucy Sprague's eyes to the work being accomplished by reformers. Gradually, Lucy acquired a sense of social responsibility and a desire to do something constructive to alleviate the suffering endured by those less fortunate than she. Her desire for an opportunity to assert herself was stifled by a series of family health problems that in 1893 caused the Spragues to move to the Sierra Madre region of California, which was believed to offer a more favorable climate for her father's recurrent hemorrhages from tuberculosis.

For the next year, Lucy served as her father's nurse. Although she was able to continue her education at the Marlborough School in Los Angeles, she was forced to resume her nursing responsibilities following her graduation. A reprieve was granted in the form of an invitation from family friends Alice Freeman Palmer and her husband George to stay with them and attend Radcliffe College back east. Although her father initially objected, Lucy accepted the Palmers' offer. She entered Radcliffe in 1896, graduating four years later with honors in philosophy.

After graduation, Lucy once again resumed her role as her father's nurse, and once again, the Palmers provided her a release. She accompanied them to Europe, and when Alice Palmer died unexpectedly in Paris, Lucy returned to Cambridge with George Palmer where she kept house for him for several years. During this time, she also became secretary to the dean of Radcliffe and took graduate courses at Harvard.

Then, in 1906, the president of the University of California at Berkeley, Benjamin Wheeler, invited Sprague to become the school's first dean of women. She also received an appointment as an assistant professor of English. Although initially concerned that she lacked sufficient formal training for the job, Sprague blossomed in her role as dean, introducing new courses, improving housing conditions for women, and strengthening the role of women's organizations on campus. In addition, Sprague encouraged students to expand their horizons and to learn about social conditions in San Francisco.

Her interest in developing new programs that would prepare women for careers other than teaching led Sprague to New York City in 1911 where she consulted with a number of women who had found careers for themselves outside the classroom including **Lillian Wald**, the founder of the **Henry Street Settlement**; **Mary Richmond** of the Baltimore Charity Organization Society; and **Florence Kelley** of the **National Child Labor Committee**. But it was her interaction with Julia Richman, the principal of a Manhattan high school, that had the most significant impact on Sprague's future direction. She now came to view public education as the most productive way to deal with social problems, and teaching became her new vocation. When she returned to California in 1912, Sprague resigned from the university. That same year she married Wesley Clair Mitchell, an economist whom she had known for some time.

In 1913, the Mitchells moved to New York City where Wesley joined the faculty at Columbia and pursued his research into business cycles. He also shared Lucy's interest in social and educational reform and supported her efforts to pursue an independent career in education reform. During the next few years, Lucy Mitchell took classes at Teachers College with John Dewey, worked as a volunteer teacher for the Public Education Association, and taught nursery school and kindergarten classes at the Play School.

One of Mitchell's primary objectives in education reform was to apply her research on learning to actual classroom situations. In 1916, with the assistance of her cousin Elizabeth Sprague Coolidge, Mitchell was able to make her dreams a reality. Coolidge offered to fund an educational venture for a period of 10 years.

With this funding, Lucy and Wesley Mitchell, along with Harriet Johnson of the Public Education Association, established a private educational corporation called the Bureau of Educational Experiments. The Mitchells designed the bureau to function as an experimental forum where educators could conduct research related to progressive education and be trained to conduct educational experiments in the classroom. In 1950, the bureau was chartered as the Bank Street College of Education. Mitchell served as president until her retirement in 1956.

Mitchell was the guiding force behind the bureau as it broke new ground in the field of early childhood education. As head of its governing board, she worked to ensure that the bureau remained a cooperative endeavor where professional women could come together to conduct research on child development and educational theory that had direct application in the classroom. The influence of Dewey and other Progressive educators was evident in Mitchell's belief that theory and practice were intertwined. The key was to train the "whole teacher" who could then provide a stimulating classroom environment that would promote the growth and development of the "whole child." This was a dynamic process that addressed the mental, emotional, and physical development of the child. Teachers were trained to employ all their resources to encourage children to participate in the education process and to learn, not to be passive recipients of the teacher's knowledge.

Mitchell took a special interest in the bureau's teacher training and writing programs. She wrote, edited, or co-authored six books for adults and 20 for children. In addition, she helped develop of a number of auxiliary programs and organizations. Along with some of her colleagues, she established the Cooperative School for Teachers (1931) in which she taught courses in children's language. In 1938, Mitchell inaugurated the Writers' Workshop, which was designed to assist the writers of children's books in understanding the developmental needs and interests of children.

Mitchell's long career united her two interests, social reform and education, and her work enabled countless women to pursue careers as professionally trained educators.

Bibliography

Antler, *Lucy Sprague Mitchell*; *Dictionary of American Biography*, supl. 8, pp. 442–43; James, *Notable American Women, 1607–1950*, pp. 484–87.

Moskowitz, Belle Linder Israels

labor activist, social reformer, political activist
b. October 5, 1877; d. January 2, 1933.

The work that Belle Moskowitz accomplished during her career helped to bridge the world of politicians with the world of social reformers. At various times she collaborated with settlement workers, labor reformers, and woman suffrage advocates. Additionally, she earned a strong reputation as a political advisor of some acumen.

Belle Linder spent a year of study (1894–1895) at Teacher's College, Columbia University where she studied dramatic arts. Between 1895 and 1900, Linder alternated between working in her father's shop and teaching drama at the Educational Alliance, which, much like the settlements, provided young people with cultural and educational opportunities. Most of its clients were recent Jewish immigrants living on New York City's Lower East Side. Linder found the work of helping the newly arrived immigrants who went to the alliance satisfying. She became a full-time worker in 1900 and remained there for three years. While working at the Alliance, she met and married Charles Henry Israels (1903).

Belle Israels was a talented, energetic woman. Following her marriage, she continued her involvement in social reform by joining voluntary associations such as the New York Council of Jewish Women and the New York **Charity Organization Society**. As a member of the council, she was instrumental in establishing the Lakeview Home for Wayward Girls. She also held an executive position on the New York State Conference of Charities and Correction. In 1908, she became the first woman vice president of the conference. Between 1908 and 1910, she was a staff member and editorial assistant for the social reform journal, the *Survey*.

As a result of her work with the troubled youth of the Lakeview Home, Israels turned her attention to the lack of recreational opportunities for children in the tenements. She formed the Committee on Amusement and Vacation Resources of Working Girls. The committee's investigations of East Side dance halls, which were frequented by young immigrant girls, revealed lax management procedures that encouraged gambling, drinking, and **prostitution**. In response to this discovery, her committee instituted a successful campaign that resulted in a

1911 law requiring state licensing of all dance halls.

That same year, Israels assumed a leadership role in the investigation prompted by the **Triangle Shirtwaist Company Fire** that resulted in the death of more than 140 young women. Later in 1911, Charles Israels died unexpectedly of a heart ailment, and Belle was forced to look for full-time employment to support herself and her family.

The first position she obtained was as a field secretary for the Playground Association of America (*see* **National Recreation and Park Association**), a committee of settlement workers and other reformers interested in providing adequate recreation facilities particularly in urban areas. In 1913, Israels was recommended as a grievance mediator for the dress and waist manufacturers' association. In this position, she was involved in negotiating agreements that avoided strikes in the garment industry.

In November 1914, Belle Israels married Dr. **Henry Moskowitz**, whom she had known from the Educational Alliance. Moskowitz had been an associate of **Felix Adler**, founder of the New York **Ethical Culture Society**, and he had been head resident of the society's settlement on New York City's Lower East Side, **Madison House**. Belle Moskowitz continued to work after her marriage, and from 1914 to 1916, she worked as a manager of the Manufacturers' Association's Labor Department. In this capacity she helped to settle thousands of grievances, and she gained a reputation as an expert on factory legislation. By 1916, the collective bargaining agreement that had been established by garment worker unions and the manufacturers had broken down. Moskowitz's supporters within the manufacturers' association were replaced by a faction that was not supportive of the agreement with the unions and Moskowitz lost her job. After she was fired by the Manufacturers' Association, Moskowitz renewed her connection with various voluntary associations. She worked for woman suffrage through the **New York Women's City Club** and for the suppression of prostitution through the work of the Committee of Fifteen.

Belle and Henry Moskowitz pursued parallel political careers beginning with their positions in the administration of New York City Mayor John P. Mitchell. Henry served as commissioner of public markets, and Belle was secretary of the Mayor's Committee of Women on National Defense during World War I. Beginning in 1917, the Moskowitzs collaborated as public relations counselors for a variety of clients.

In 1918, Belle Moskowitz was introduced to the Democratic candidate for governor of New York, **Alfred E. Smith**. This was the first time that women were voting in a state election, and Moskowitz proposed a special campaign on Smith's behalf directed toward women. As a result of her work, Smith came to consider Moskowitz a shrewd advisor. She worked closely with him during his eight years as governor (1919–1921, 1923–1929). Although she held no high political office, Moskowitz played an important role in Smith's administrations. She collected information on political and technical problems and served as a link between the governor's office and various technical experts. Additionally, Moskowitz served as executive secretary of the New York Legislative Reconstruction Commission (1919–1921).

Moskowitz supported Smith in both his unsuccessful bids for the presidency (1924 and 1928), and then served as his literary consultant and as the publicity agent for the Empire State Building, which Smith was in charge of building. During the time she worked with Smith, Moskowitz maintained her interest in many reform concerns such as the protection of working girls, housing reform, and labor relations.

After coordinating Smith's unsuccessful campaign for the Democratic presidential nomination in 1932, Moskowitz retired from politics. She died unexpectedly after a fall in 1933.

Moskowitz's career as a reformer involved her in a number of productive working relationships with settlement residents including the work to secure recreation and playground facilities, and her role in labor reform crusades.

Bibliography

Dictionary of American Biography, supl. 1, pp. 567–68; Jackson, *Encyclopedia of New York City*, p. 775; James, *Notable American Women, 1607–1950*, vol. 2, pp. 589–591; Perry, *Belle Moskowitz: Feminine Politics and the Exercise of Politics in the Age of Alfred E. Smith*; Trattner, *Biographical Dictionary of Social Welfare in America*, pp. 551–54.

Moskowitz, Henry
ethical culture leader, settlement worker, political activist, civil rights activist
b. September 27, 1880; d. December 17, 1936.

Henry Moskowitz was a leader in the New York **Ethical Culture Society** who began his career as a social reformer working in a settlement on New York City's Lower East Side. He combined this experience with a variety of social welfare crusades including the anti-prostitution campaign, the struggle for health and safety standards in factories, the movement for racial equality, and the fight to curtail the influence of political bosses in municipal affairs.

While he was growing up, Henry Moskowitz held a variety of jobs including working as an operator in East Side sweatshops, as a newsboy, and as an office boy in a law firm. He knew firsthand the difficulties of the working class. Henry attended public schools before enrolling in City College. He graduated in 1899 and then went to Columbia University for graduate work in philosophy, economics, and education. In his spare time, he was a member of the Social and Educational Improvement Club (SEI), which was sponsored by the **University Settlement** located on New York City's Lower East Side. This association with the settlement had a significant impact on Moskowitz's later life, not only because it provided him with a group of friends, but also because he gained intimate experience with settlement work.

While a student at City College, Moskowitz began attending **Felix Adler**'s Ethical Culture lectures on Sunday mornings. Adler and his associate **John Lovejoy Elliott** of the **Hudson Guild** settlement were interested in pursuing ethical work on the Lower East Side. They believed that the work could be successful only if it were taken up by neighborhood residents. In 1898, they approached Moskowitz and some of his University Settlement friends about establishing a Down Town Ethical Society. The young men rented rooms on Madison Street and began sponsoring clubs for neighborhood residents. The settlement, which was called the Down Town Ethical Society, was later renamed **Madison House**.

One of Moskowitz's first reform crusades was against **prostitution**. The **New York City Tenement House Commission**, which was investigating housing conditions, was aware that prostitution in crowded residential neighborhoods was a growing problem at the turn of the century. Eventually, protests against police protection of brothels in residential neighborhoods intensified and led to an outcry against Tammany Hall. In 1900, Moskowitz and **James Reynolds** of the University Settlement brought together settlement workers and other reformers to organize an investigation. As a result, a group of civic leaders formed the Committee of Fifteen to investigate the situation and to pressure the police authorities to stop providing protection to brothels.

The following year, Moskowitz became actively involved in the work of two other community groups. He founded and served as chair of the Federation of East Side Boys' Clubs, which coordinated social and moral uplift activities of boys' clubs in the area. In addition, he and Paul Abelson, a friend from the University Settlement SEI Club, established the East Side Civic Club, which mobilized public opinion on neighborhood issues. Moskowitz served as the club's first vice president and later as president.

In 1904, the Ethical Culture Society awarded Moskowitz its first fellowship to prepare scholars for ethical leadership. At Adler's suggestion, Moskowitz went to Germany to study, first at the University of Berlin and later at the University of Erlangen where he earned a Ph.D. in philosophy. When he returned to New York, Moskowitz was named associate leader of the Uptown Ethical Culture Society. At the same time, he also became the head resident at the downtown branch.

During the following years, Moskowitz spoke about social and industrial conditions before numerous groups and served on a number of reform committees. He was particularly interested in working conditions and began working as a labor mediator in New York City's garment district. In 1910, Moskowitz brought together workers and management in the ladies' cloak, suit, and skirt industry. He also served as secretary of the garment industry's Board of Arbitration. In addition, Moskowitz was the secretary of the Joint Board of Sanitary Control, which supervised a scientific and medical survey of factory conditions. He was also a member of the Committee of Safety that was established in 1911 after the tragic **Triangle Shirtwaist Company Fire**, and he spent a significant amount of time lobbying state lawmakers in Albany for adequate fire protection laws and for limited working hours.

Moskowitz was also active in a variety of other civic and social reform issues. Like many other social reformers, he was interested in politics. In 1912, he helped to organize the Lower East Side on behalf of the Progressive candidate for governor, Oscar Straus. He was a candidate for Congress for the Twelfth District himself and was a delegate to the Progressive Party's convention in Chicago. Like Straus, he was defeated, but he continued to be an active participant in the political process. In 1913 as a member of the Citizen's Municipal Committee, Moskowitz helped the fusion candidate John Purvoy Mitchell win the election for mayor of

New York City. As a reward, Mitchell appointed Moskowitz president of the Municipal Civil Service Commission. Political pressure eventually led Mitchell to remove Moskowitz from the commission and to appoint him New York's first markets commissioner.

In addition to political activities, Moskowitz also fought for racial equality. In 1909, Moskowitz was present at a meeting held in the New York City apartment of the reformer **William English Walling**. Walling had called for the creation of a practical movement to work for racial equality following the Springfield, Illinois, race riot in 1908. **Mary White Ovington**, a settlement worker engaged in an extensive study of black life, was also present. At this meeting initial plans were drawn up for the establishment of the National Association for the Advancement of Colored People (NAACP). Moskowitz remained involved in the work of the NAACP for many years, serving on a number of the organization's committees including those related to fund-raising and membership.

Over the years Moskowitz had grown away from Adler and the Ethical Culture Movement, and in 1914, he resigned as associate leader of the Ethical Culture Society. That same year Moskowitz married Belle Linder Israels (*see* **Belle Linder Israels Moskowitz**), a widow with three children whom he had known for several years. The two had much in common having worked in the settlements and in a variety of reform crusades, and they continued to pursue careers as social reformers and political activists.

Moskowitz and his wife served as social welfare advisors to New York Governor **Alfred E. Smith**. Henry Moskowitz wrote a biography of Smith, *Up from the City Streets: Alfred E. Smith* (1927) and organized a selection of Smith's papers in a volume entitled *Progressive Democracy—Speeches and State Papers of Alfred E. Smith*. Moskowitz also served on a variety of reform-related committees, an activity which frequently provided him with an opportunity to work closely with settlement workers. These committees were concerned with labor rights, housing, dance halls, and industrial safety. Moskowitz maintained his active interest in public affairs up to his death in 1936.

Bibliography

Davis, *Spearheads for Reform: The Social Settlements and the Progressive Movement, 1890–1914*; Jackson, *Encyclopedia of New York City*, p. 775; Perry, *Belle Moskowitz: Feminine Politics and the Exercise of Power in the Age of Alfred E. Smith*.

Mother's Pensions

The widow's pension or mother's pension movement was another public welfare cause of settlement workers. They and other social welfare reformers were acutely aware of the problems of needy children. The **White House Conference on Dependent Children** had been convened in 1909 largely because of the efforts of settlement workers such as **Lillian Wald** and **Florence Kelley**.

Delegates to the conference emphasized in their final report that whenever possible needy children should be cared for in their own homes, especially after the father has died. They believed that this arrangement would help to preserve the family unit and to curtail juvenile delinquency. The delegates did not want to encourage public relief to accomplish their goals. Rather, they advocated assistance in the form of private charity.

However, private charitable agencies, where they existed, were often not equipped to handle all the demands on their resources. Additionally, many agencies' policies prevented them from distributing funds if the women who requested assistance were considered to be capable of working. In many instances, this stipulation meant that widows had to give up their children for adoption or place them in institutions or foster homes because they could not care for them and go out to work.

Women's wages were generally lower than men's, which meant they had to work longer hours to earn the minimum required for subsistence. Those women who elected to keep their children with them had no support networks to rely upon, and so their families were left unsupervised for long periods while they were working, a situation that often resulted in the children becoming delinquents. Also, these women often became ill because of overwork and worry. Ultimately these individuals, despite their best efforts, became a burden on the state.

Confronted with the cycle of dependency, many social reformers, settlement workers among them, supported a program of widow's pensions to aid women with dependent children. They believed that this type of assistance would enable women to remain at home and keep their families intact. They reasoned that this system would ultimately prove to be less expensive and more efficient. Although some social welfare workers were opposed to the idea of providing aid to able-bodied women, the campaign for mother's pensions was successful.

The first widow's pension legislation was enacted in Missouri in 1911, and it provided for monetary assistance to mothers with dependent children. By 1935 only two states, Georgia and South Carolina, had failed to pass similar laws.

Bibliography

Leiby, *A History of Social Welfare and Social Work in the United States*; Trattner, *From Poor Law to Welfare State: A History of Social Welfare in America*.

N

Nathan, Maud

philanthropist, social reformer, labor activist, suffragist

b. October 20, 1862; d. December 15, 1946.

During her career as a social reformer, Maud Nathan worked closely with settlement workers and other reformers to draw attention to problems, to propose solutions, and to effect substantive change. Nathan's single-minded dedication to improving the working conditions of women in the garment trades and in retail department stores is reflected in her more than 20 successful years as the president of the New York branch of the National **Consumers' League**. She combined this concern for women workers with efforts on behalf of woman suffrage, which she believed would bolster women social activists' efforts to accomplish meaningful reform.

Born into a wealthy, close-knit family, Nathan was educated at private girls' schools in New York City until her father's business reverses forced him to sell his seat on the New York Stock Exchange and to move his family to Green Bay, Wisconsin, where he worked for four years as a railroad passenger agent. Maud Nathan completed her formal education at the local high school, graduating in 1876. Two years later, after the death of her mother, she and her siblings returned to New York City where they were cared for by relatives. In April 1880, at the age of 17, Nathan married her first cousin, Frederick Nathan, a successful stockbroker al-

most twice her age. The Nathans had one child, a daughter named Annette Florence, who was born in 1887.

Although she occupied a prominent place in New York social circles, Nathan wanted more out of life. Like many women of her social class, Nathan became involved with charitable work. Her father-in-law was one of the founders of Mount Sinai Hospital, and she was named a director of its nursing school. She was also involved on a limited basis with the Hebrew Free School Association, the New York Exchange for Women's Work, and the Women's Auxiliary of the Civil Service Reform Association. This work brought her into contact with a range of social reformers.

In 1890, Nathan was one of a number of women whom **Josephine Shaw Lowell**, a founding member of the New York **Charity Organization Society**, interested in forming the New York Consumers' League. The Consumers' League hoped to improve the working conditions of sales clerks employed in New York City department stores by organizing the public to use its purchasing power to pressure employers to treat employees more equitably. Her first experience with the league was as an investigator in retail stores.

While Nathan was interested in her work, her family remained the primary focus of her life. This changed when her daughter died unexpectedly in 1895. Lowell, who herself had been overcome by grief after her husband's death in the Civil War, persuaded Nathan to surmount her personal sense of loss by following Lowell's own example and becoming more involved in social reform work.

Responding to Lowell's suggestion, Nathan devoted more and more time to the Consumers' League. In 1897, she was elected president of the New York branch, a position she held for 20 years. She also served as a member of the executive committee of the National Consumers' League and in later years as a vice president. In addition to her work with the league, Nathan served as vice president of the Woman's Municipal League of New York (1894) and as chair of the industrial committee of the General Federation of Women's Clubs.

A persuasive speaker, Nathan's tenure as president of the Consumers' League was productive as she was able to change tactics to respond to evolving conditions. At first the league published a series of "white lists" that included the names of establishments it recommended to buyers based on how the proprietors treated their employees. Later, those firms that met league standards were permitted to attach a "consumers' label" to their goods. When this campaign failed to achieve results, Nathan guided the league in a more aggressive strategy to secure protective legislation and to ensure its enforcement. This strategy included holding public meetings to bring their cause before the public, lobbying state lawmakers in Albany to secure their support, and waging court battles to ensure that protective labor legislation was properly enforced.

As a result of her work as a lobbyist at Albany and her interactions with state legislators, Nathan realized that the league's cause would be strengthened if women had the vote. She began devoting her time to woman suffrage, serving as vice president of the New York Equal Suffrage League and as chair of Theodore Roosevelt's 1912 presidential campaign's Woman Suffrage Committee. Nathan's concern in her suffrage work was not merely to secure the vote for women but to demonstrate to women that with the vote they could become more effective social and industrial reformers. She was also active in the international suffrage movement, often scheduling holiday trips abroad with her husband to coincide with conferences of groups such as the International Woman Suffrage Alliance so that she could deliver speeches at these gatherings.

Besides her interests in various reform crusades, Nathan also was interested in spiritual matters. She was active in the New York section of the National Council of Jewish Women and was devoted to what she believed were Judaism's universal truths. Despite this strong belief, Nathan was not dogmatic and was personally committed to liberal religion and interfaith understanding. In 1897, she was invited to read a paper entitled "The Heart of Judaism" in place of a sermon during a service of worship at New York's Temple Beth-El.

Although she maintained a timely interest in social welfare issues, during the last 10 years of her life Nathan devoted more of her time to travel and to social affairs. Before her death in 1946, Nathan could look back on a productive career as a labor reformer. Her work with the New York and National Consumers' Leagues brought her into contact with many settlement workers who shared her concerns about the unhealthy and dangerous working conditions of women and children.

Bibliography

Dictionary of American Biography, supl. 4, pp. 622–24; Nathan, *The Story of An Epoch Making Movement*; *Notable American Women, 1607–1950*, vol. 2, pp. 608–09.

National Child Labor Committee

Settlement workers had firsthand knowledge of the dangers and abuses of the labor system that deprived the children in their neighborhoods of receiving even the most basic education or of enjoying the benefits of recreation. In short, these children were denied a childhood because they were forced to work in factories or in the street trades to support their families.

Although settlement workers and other social welfare reformers had been successful in securing the passage of legislation to regulate child labor in a number of states, these laws were frequently struck down by the courts or were subverted by the actions of unscrupulous inspectors. Reformers were gradually won over to the belief that a national organization that could work to secure the passage and enforcement of federal legislation was the only way to stop child labor abuses.

The impetus for adopting such a national approach to the problem of child labor came from Edgar Gardner Murphy, an Alabama clergyman and publicist who became involved in the child labor crusade after reading an investigation of Alabama textile mills that had been conducted by the American Federation of Labor. In 1901, Murphy organized the Alabama Child Labor Committee, which at the time was the only state committee of its kind.

Two years later, Murphy read a paper entitled "Child Labor as a National Problem" at the annual meeting of the National Conference of Charities and Correction (*see* **National Conference on Social Welfare**) in Atlanta, Georgia. This organization was composed of leaders from public and private charitable relief organizations and correctional institutions. **Florence Kelley**, then a resident at the **Henry Street Settlement** in New York City, and **Jane Addams**, founder and head resident of **Hull House** in Chicago, delivered papers on the problem of destitute children at the same conference session. While in Atlanta, Addams and Kelley spoke with Murphy about the feasibility of establishing a national organization concerned with child labor.

Later that year, Murphy traveled to New York City to consider the idea further with some members of the New York Association of Neighborhood Workers Subcommittee on Child Labor, which had been established in 1902. As a result of these discussions, an organizational committee was formed that in addition to Murphy included **Felix Adler**, founder of the **Ethical Culture Society**; William H. Baldwin, president of the Long Island Railroad; and Kelley.

The organizing committee's proposal recommending the formation of a national organization met with a favorable response. In April 1904, Murphy and the **New York Child Labor Committee** formed the National Child Labor Committee (NCLC), which would be headquartered in New York City. Adler was selected to serve as the group's first chair. Kelley, Addams, and **Lillian Wald** of the Henry Street Settlement were among the 30 child labor activists who were invited to become charter members of the National Child Labor Committee. Although members of the New York Child Labor Committee were instrumental in organizing the National Child Labor Committee, the New York group remained an independent entity, and in fact, the two groups frequently disagreed about policy matters and fund-raising.

Although the NCLC did much to eliminate the most blatant evils of child labor, it did not make steady progress and had to return to deal with many of the same issues again and again. It often faced formidable opposition to its appeals for federal legislation. The National Civic Federation, a business-oriented group that had been organized to promote better management-labor relations, attempted to counteract the NCLC's program by claiming that child labor was a "comparatively insignificant" problem that could be controlled with the passage of uniform state child labor laws.

Nevertheless, the NCLC continued to fight for a federal child labor law, and in 1906, it supported legislation introduced in Congress by Albert Beveridge. Although Beveridge's bill was defeated, the NCLC continued to campaign for federal legislation while at the same time working on other related issues.

One of these issues was the call for a federal children's bureau. Lillian Wald had devised a plan for such a bureau in 1904, but no action was taken at that time. In 1906, Wald and fellow NCLC board member Florence Kelley persuaded their colleagues to draft a bill for a children's bureau, but despite a nationwide publicity campaign, no action was taken. It was not until the issue of a children's bureau was raised at the 1909 **White House Conference on the Care of Dependent Children** that hearings were opened on the bill for a federal children's bureau. However, it would be another three years before President William Howard Taft signed the legislation and appointed the social reformer and researcher **Julia Lathrop** as the first director of the **United States Children's Bureau**.

Although the NCLC made some progress toward dealing with child labor, it was not until the passage of the Federal Child Labor Law of 1916 that children in all states enjoyed a high level of protection. Members of the NCLC had worked hard to ensure passage of this legislation and when the 1916 law was ruled unconstitutional by the U.S. Supreme Court on the grounds that Congress had exceeded its regulatory authority, the NCLC took up the fight again in 1918. Today, the NCLC continues its work of protecting the rights of child workers across the United States. *See also* **Child Welfare**.

Bibliography

Davis, *Spearheads for Reform: The Social Settlements and the Progressive Movement, 1890–1914*; Felt, *Hostages of Fortune: Child Labor Reform in New York State*; Goldmark, *Impatient Crusader: Florence Kelley's Life Story*; Trattner, *Crusade for the Children: A History of the NCLC and Child Labor Reform in America*.

National Civil Liberties Bureau

Settlement workers and other social reformers were active in the anti-preparedness and peace movements leading up to and continuing through World War I. Although they shared a common cause, these social activists were sometimes at odds when it came to agreeing on a strategy for accomplishing their goals. Such conflicts and compromises surrounded and contributed to the formation of the National Civil Liberties Bureau as settlement workers **Lillian Wald** of the **Henry Street Settlement**, **Jane Addams** of **Hull House**, and **Paul Kellogg** of the social welfare journal the *Survey* found themselves disagreeing with the tactics of younger social activists such as **Roger Baldwin**.

Shortly after the Selective Service Act was passed by Congress in May 1917, Roger Baldwin of the **American Union Against Militarism** (AUAM), a coalition of reformers which mounted an anti-preparedness crusade in the months before the United States entered World War I, organized a Bureau for Conscientious Objectors. Baldwin believed that since the AUAM was directing its energies toward securing peace, it was necessary to establish a separate sub-agency to deal with the issue of conscientious objectors. He appealed to pacifist groups to lend their endorsement to his venture.

Baldwin's supporters, however, recommended that the new bureau remain an agency within the AUAM and not declare itself independent. Baldwin became director of the new bureau and was joined on the executive committee by prominent social activists such as Joseph D. Cannon, Scott Nearing, Edmund C. Evans, Alice Lewisohn, Hollingsword Wood, John Haynes Holmes, and Norman Thomas.

Some members of the AUAM board, particularly Jane Addams, Lillian Wald, and Paul U. Kellogg, objected to the bureau's creation, believing that its activities could be viewed as antagonistic to the Wilson administration, and by extension, damaging to the work of the AUAM. When the AUAM board supported Baldwin over Kellogg and Wald, the latter two threatened to resign from the AUAM.

A compromise was offered by the social investigator and former settlement worker **Crystal Eastman**. Under Eastman's plan, the name of the Bureau for Conscientious Objectors would be changed to the Bureau for the Maintenance of Civil Liberties, which would broaden its charge to assist anyone whose rights were infringed on by wartime legislation. The compromise was accepted by all parties, and Baldwin changed the name of the organization to the Civil Liberties Bureau (CLB).

However, the formation of the CLB was not well received by the public. Further, when the board of the AUAM agreed to send representatives to a conference sponsored by the socialist,

antiwar People's Council, Wald once again expressed her displeasure. Rather than accept her resignation and the accompanying loss of stature for the organization, the AUAM board voted to formally separate from the Civil Liberties Bureau. In October 1917, the CLB became the National Civil Liberties Bureau, an independent organization under Baldwin's direction.

In an effort to reposition the NCLB in the years following World War I, a group of NCLB board members, including Roger Baldwin, proposed reorganizing and renaming the NCLB as the **American Civil Liberties Union** (ACLU). The ACLU continued to concern itself with many of the same issues including free speech, right of assembly, and a free press. It also expanded its activities into the area of labor relations, particularly in instances when employers attempted to restrict civil liberties.

Bibliography
Johnson, *The Challenge to American Freedoms: World War I and the Rise of the American Civil Liberties Union*; Walker, *In Defense of American Liberties: A History of the ACLU*.

National Conference of Charities and Correction *See*

National Conference on Social Welfare

National Conference of Social Work *See* National Conference on Social Welfare

National Conference on Social Welfare

The American Social Science Association (ASSA) had been founded in 1865 to consider questions related to sanitary conditions, crime prevention, education of the poor, and other matters of philanthropic interest. In 1873, the association expanded its membership to include delegates from state boards of charity. The following year, representatives from Massachusetts, New York, Connecticut, and Wisconsin founded the Conference of Boards of Public Charities (CBPC) in New York City. The CBPC changed its name to the Conference of Charities (CC) in 1875 and began sponsoring sessions of interest to its members at the American Social Science Association's annual meeting. Gradually, interest in its work increased.

In 1879, the members of the CC began to meet independently of the ASSA to discuss matters of interest to them, including immigration, child labor, delinquent children, and treatment of the insane. The membership realized that the CC shared many of the same concerns as the American Prison Association regarding the care and treatment of individuals in state institutions, and by 1884, the Conference of Charities had changed its name to the National Conference of Charities and Correction (NCCC).

The growth of charity organization societies in the late nineteenth century increasingly influenced the work of the NCCC, particularly in the field of child welfare. Evidence of this was the NCCC-sponsored conference on child welfare at the World's Columbian Exposition in Chicago in 1893, the proceedings of which were published as the *History of Child Saving in the United States*.

Representatives from the settlements began attending NCCC conferences during the 1890s. A special program on the social settlements and labor was held at the NCCC's 1896 annual meeting. **Julia Lathrop** of **Hull House** and **James Reynolds** of the **University Settlement** were among the speakers at this meeting. During the next several years, settlement workers delivered papers on a variety of topics at NCCC annual meetings, including ones on education and child labor. At the 1897 annual meeting, **Mary Richmond** of the Baltimore Charity Organization Society delivered an influential paper about the need for training charity workers which had a direct impact on the establishment of social work training schools in New York, Boston, and Chicago.

During the opening decades of the twentieth century, the NCCC established itself as the leading social service organization in the United States. A group of social welfare reformers appointed by the NCCC were responsible for developing the social and industrial planks of the Progressive Party's platform in the 1912 presidential election. By 1919, the NCCC had changed its name once again and was known as the National Conference of Social Work. A final name change was effected in 1956 when the organization became the National Conference on Social Welfare.

A number of individuals active in the American Settlement Movement were elected president of the National Conference of Charities and Correction or the National Conference of Social Work. They included **Jane Addams** of Hull House; **Jeffrey Brackett**, one of the founders of the **Boston School for Social Workers**; **Edward T. Devine** of the New York **Charity Organization Society**; **John M.**

Glenn of the **Russell Sage Foundation**; Julia Lathrop, head of the **United States Children's Bureau**; **Owen Lovejoy** of the **National Child Labor Committee**; **Graham Taylor** of the **Chicago Commons** settlement; and **Robert A. Woods** of the Boston-based **South End House** settlement.

Bibliography

Carson, *Settlement Folk: Social Thought and the American Settlement Movement, 1885–1930*; Davis, *Spearheads for Reform: Social Settlements and the Progressive Movement, 1890–1914*; Romanofsky, *The Greenwood Encyclopedia of American Institutions: Social Service Organizations*, vol. 2, pp. 484–88.

National Consumers' League

See Consumers' Leagues

National Federation of Settlements

In the late 1880s, settlement houses opened in large urban centers such as New York, Chicago, and Boston, and during the next several years, houses also opened in smaller cities. While the leaders of these institutions were primarily interested in their immediate neighborhoods, they recognized the importance of promoting cooperation and communication among their houses. Beginning in 1892, a small group of settlement leaders, including **Jane Addams** of **Hull House**, **Robert A. Woods** of **South End House**, and **Lillian Wald** of the **Henry Street Settlement**, began meeting informally to exchange information and share ideas. However, it would be several years before any attempt was made to regularize this arrangement.

In the meantime, settlements in Chicago, Boston, and New York began establishing citywide federations, a model that was followed by the settlement houses in smaller cities. The settlement workers recognized the value of sharing ideas, promoting cooperation, and when necessary, pooling resources. They knew that particularly when dealing with state and federal authorities, their voice would be heeded if they presented a united front. It did not take the leaders of the settlement movement long to build on the informal arrangement they had and to transform it into the National Federation of Settlements, a well-organized pressure group that represented the interests of its members and provided them a forum for exchanging ideas and developing solutions to shared problems.

Interest in a formal, national organization was aroused at the 1908 annual meeting of the National Conference of Charities and Correc-

The Founders of the National Federation of Settlements

Social Welfare History Archives, University of Minnesota

tions (NCCC) (*see* **National Conference on Social Welfare**), a coalition of social welfare and penal reformers whose meetings settlement workers had been attending since the 1890s. A proposal was made at the meeting that separate gatherings for settlement workers should be organized. In response to this proposal, settlement workers sponsored a number of sessions of interest to them at the 1910 NCCC annual meeting.

That same year, representatives from every known settlement were invited to a meeting that eventually led to the establishment of a new organization, the National Federation of Settlements (NFS). Before any organization was formally established, 10 representatives were selected from among those attending the 1910 gathering to collect information about individual settlements across the United States. Their research, which was compiled and edited by Robert Woods and **Albert Kennedy**, also of South End House in Boston, resulted in the publication of the *Handbook of Settlements* in 1911. This book presented detailed information about the history and activities of settlements across the country.

When the NCCC met in Boston in 1911, a platform was presented that called for united action by settlements throughout the United States. Almost 200 representatives were present at the meeting that officially organized the National Federation of Settlements. Addams and Woods were elected president and secretary respectively. At first, each settlement was required to pay a membership fee. Individuals interested in settlement work could enroll as corresponding members but would not be accorded voting privileges.

The federation's goals included developing policies regarding settlements issues, cooperating with other reform organizations to achieve common goals, and publishing the results of research studies undertaken by the NFS and its members. In addition, the NFS was committed to attracting college men and women to participate in the work of the settlements.

The National Federation of Settlements was conceived as a working organization, and it quickly began to work. Between 1911 and 1912, it conducted a comprehensive investigation of adolescent girls, which was published in 1913 under the title *Young Working Girls*. This publication quickly became a guidebook for settlements' youth programs. In addition to its independent research projects, the NFS cooperated in a variety of reform endeavors and made a significant contribution to the creation of the **United States Children's Bureau**, created in 1912 to serve as a federal agency overseeing the welfare of children.

Headquartered in Boston, the NFS had a critical impact on settlements all over the country. It sponsored an annual conference at which experienced leaders shared their knowledge with those who were new to the settlement movement. Throughout the rest of the year, the federation sponsored local and regional institutes that were attended by residents, contributors, and in some instances, by neighborhood residents.

Besides its work with the member settlements, the NFS was active in supporting a range of legislative initiatives such as the Smith-Hughes bill that provided federal support for vocational education, and the effort to establish a women's department within the National Bureau of Labor and Industry.

During World War I, the membership of the NFS was deeply divided over differences among pacifists such as Jane Addams and those who supported the Wilson administration's war efforts. After a great deal of discussion and soul-searching, the NFS eventually rallied to support America's entry into the war in 1917.

Through the 1920s, the NFS focused its attention on the housing situation in the United States. Wald chaired a committee charged with promoting public interest in better housing. The NFS membership supported the idea that housing was a government responsibility, and in 1922, the federation called for a model housing code and for the creation of a federal oversight organization that would coordinate the work of housing commissions on the state, municipal, and local levels.

The NFS continued its efforts even as the settlement movement itself evolved. It investigated the effect that the economic depression had on families during the 1930s and supported campaigns for old-age pensions and state compulsory unemployment insurance. Even though the number of local settlements declined during the 1930s and 1940s, the NFS remained an active force in the national social service movement. In recognition of the increasing number of neighborhood centers that were working in communities, the NFS changed its name to the National Federation of Settlements and Neighborhood Centers in 1949.

Bibliography

Chambers, *Seedtime of Reform: American Social Justice and Social Action, 1918–1923*; Romanofsky, *The Greenwood Encyclopedia of American Institutions: Social Service Organizations*, vol. 2, pp. 533–40; Trolander, *Settlement Houses and the Great Depression*; Woods, *The Settlement Horizon*.

National Housing Association

Housing reform was a priority for workers in virtually every settlement. This was especially true in New York City, which by the end of the first decade of the twentieth century was probably the most densely populated city in the world. Because of their city's unique problems, housing reformers in New York were forced to confront many serious issues more quickly than the rest of the country and to devise solutions that would provide both immediate and long-term relief. Settlement workers and housing reformers worked side-by-side to accomplish their goals. Because of this situation, New York City housing reformers established a well-organized local crusade and took a leadership role in the national housing reform crusade. The formation of the National Housing Association (NHA), which was headed up by the noted New York City housing reformer **Lawrence Veiller**, illustrates the type of concerted response that settlement workers and other reformers took to solve problems of mutual concern. The NHA's purpose was to improve housing conditions in every conceivable way, and under Veiller's leadership, it promoted local campaigns to fulfill its mission.

Even before the formation of the NHA, Lawrence Veiller was a central player in the New York City housing reform crusade and exerted a significant influence in encouraging efforts in other communities. For many years he lobbied for the establishment of a national agency to coordinate reformers' efforts. Eventually, Veiller persuaded **Robert W. DeForest**, president of the New York **Charity Organization Society** and a director of the **Russell Sage Foundation**, to provide the initial funding for such a national agency.

In January 1910, representatives from 20 cities across the United States met in New York City to establish the National Housing Association (NHA). DeForest served as president; **John M. Glenn**, general director of the Russell Sage Foundation, as treasurer; and Veiller as secretary and director. Many other housing reformers were also associated with the NHA including the Brooklyn-based builder **Alfred T. White**; **Jane Addams**, founder and head resident of **Hull House**; and **Frederic Almy**, secretary of the Buffalo, New York, Charity Organization Society.

Shortly after it was organized, the NHA began to publish a series of monographs concerned with housing reform issues. It also issued bibliographies and made available an extensive collection of reference materials related to housing reform in its corporate offices in the Charities Building in New York City. In 1912, the National Housing Association began publishing a journal, *Housing Betterment*. Veiller assumed editorial responsibilities for the publication in 1916, and in 1928, the publication was expanded and changed its name to *Housing*.

In addition to its publications, the NHA sponsored an extensive outreach program to assist local housing reformers. Except for two years, it sponsored annual conferences between 1911 and 1920, and the association frequently organized institutes and seminars, sometimes in cooperation with other organizations. Thanks to Veiller's efforts, the NHA was able to accomplish a substantial amount of work despite significant staff and budget limitations.

During World War I, the NHA worked with the federal government to establish housing standards for war workers and to ensure the completion of war-related housing projects under the auspices of the United States Housing Corporation. Despite the efforts of Veiller and others, interest in the NHA dissipated during the 1920s. Only three national conferences were held during the decade; membership declined, and the publication program was discontinued.

Even with the decline during the 1920s, the NHA remained an active force for change. Under Veiller's leadership in the 1930s, the NHA persuaded the participants of the White House Conference on Child Health to adopt a set of standards for housing children in the United States. Veiller's influence was also evident when the 1931 President's Conference on Home Building and Home Ownership issued a housing bill of rights. During the New Deal years, Veiller and the NHA resisted the trend toward government-built and government-owned housing. However, they soon realized they could not resist this new trend, and the NHA was disbanded in 1936.

During its tenure, the NHA was successful in galvanizing support to improve housing conditions within large cities and in smaller communities. It brought the national housing problem to the attention of ordinary citizens and elected officials, and it maintained interest in housing by organizing conferences, offering seminars, and providing relevant information to housing reformers.

Bibliography

Glenn, *Russell Sage Foundation*; Lubove, *The Progressives and the Slums: Tenement House Reform in New York City, 1890–1917*; Romanofsky, *The Greenwood Encyclopedia of American Institutions: Social Service Organizations*, vol. 2, pp. 550–53.

National Housing Conference

The growth and development of the organization that was ultimately known as the National Housing Conference (NHC) illustrates the way in which settlement workers assumed leadership roles in other social welfare coalitions designed to effect positive change on the state and national levels. The housing reform efforts of the NHC originated in New York City, which, because of its unique housing problems, served as a focal point in the housing reform movement in the United States in the twentieth century.

The City Affairs Committee (CAC) of New York City was a nonpartisan group founded in 1930. Its goal was to work for a better city through research and education. In 1932, members of the CAC's Housing Committee formed a pressure group called the Public Housing Conference (PHC), which brought together social reform workers and housing experts to lobby for housing legislation on the state and federal levels. The group's goal was clearly stated on its letterhead: "To Promote Slum Clearance and Low Rent Housing Through an Established Federal-Local Service." The founding members included the housing reformer **Edith Elmer Wood**; the social researcher **Edith Abbott**; **Lillian Wald**, founder of the **Henry Street Settlement**; **Mary K. Simkhovitch**, founder of **Greenwich House**; the settlement worker **Helen Alfred**; and the attorneys **Louis H. Pink** and Ira Robbins. Simkhovitch served as president and Alfred served as executive secretary.

On the state level, the PHC worked to extend the New York State housing laws permitting the financing of limited dividend or cooperative building projects funded by state bonds. The PHC also worked on the federal level to include housing as part of the public works construction program of the Federal Relief and Reconstruction Act of 1932. Although the PHC was not successful in its first attempt on the federal level, it was able to accomplish its goal the following year when housing construction was included in the public works program of the National Industrial Recovery Act of 1933.

The PHC's long-range plans included the establishment of a housing and slum clearance project that would be accomplished with funding from the federal government. Under this plan, local authorities would assume responsibility for constructing and managing new housing projects. Toward this end, Pink, a member of the PHC's special legislation committee, proposed a plan that would permit local housing authorities to substitute for regular housing commissions or city housing departments. Pink's plan was adopted by the New York State Legislature as the New York Municipal Housing Authorities Law of 1934. This legislation led to the establishment of a New York City public housing program.

During the 1930s, Senator **Robert F. Wagner** of New York was involved in the campaign for the institution of a national housing program. The members of the Public Housing Conference were also interested in a national-level program, and they were anxious to assist Wagner in his work. In July 1933, they changed their name to the National Public Housing Conference (NPHC) to reflect the new national focus of their work, and they joined with other housing groups such as the Labor Housing Conference and the National Association of Housing Officials to support Wagner's efforts. NPHC members worked closely with Wagner's legislative assistant Leon Keyserling to draft a bill and to line up support for its passage. After a three-year struggle, the **Wagner-Steagall Housing Act** of 1937 was passed.

Once the NPHC achieved this goal, its focus began to change. It no longer functioned as a pressure group but became an organized lobby. It now turned its attention to the implementation of the Wagner-Steagall Act, and in particular, to assuring that the act's provisions were carried out in New York State. Changes in key personnel hastened the organization's transformation.

In 1941, Alfred stepped down as the executive secretary. She was replaced by Alexander L. Crosby, a newspaper man who advocated broadening the organization's constituency base. Two years later, Mary Simkhovitch stepped down as president of the NPHC. She was replaced by Dr. Byrn J. Hovde, the chair of the Pittsburgh Housing Authority. In the meantime, Crosby began bringing in labor leaders and local housing authorities to serve on the NPHC's board of directors. Eventually he succeeded in merging the constituency of the NPHC with those of its former allies in the effort to pass the Wagner-Steagall bill, the Labor Housing Conference and the National Association of Housing Officials.

In recognition of the organization's truly national focus, the NPHC closed its headquarters in New York City and opened an office in Washington, DC, in February 1944. Although its members carried on, the NPHC was not as vibrant as it had been during the 1930s. This was due in part to the changes brought about by World War II and in part because the group's strongest public housing advocates were no longer active.

In 1949, the NPHC changed its name to the National Housing Conference (NHC). By dropping the word public from its name, the members hoped to demonstrate their desire to broaden the group's focus to include representation from the urban redevelopment and community planning fields.

During the time that settlement workers dominated the organization, the NHC's most significant contribution was the passage of the Wagner-Steagall Housing Act, which involved the federal government directly in the provision of low-cost housing. Today, the National Housing Conference brings together federal and state government officials, religious leaders, and civic groups in an effort to devise housing and community development programs and to explore ways to provide affordable and accessible housing for all Americans.

Bibliography

McDonnell, *The Wagner Housing Act: A Case Study of the Legislative Process*; Romanofsky, *The Greenwood Encyclopedia of American Institutions: Social Service Organizations*, vol. 2, pp. 553–55.

National Progressive Service

Following the presidential election of 1912 and the Progressive Party's strong third-party showing, many settlement workers and other social reformers were committed to remaining politically active, particularly on the national level. They believed that they could significantly contribute to the political process by doing what they believed was what they did best: investigating problems, suggesting solutions, and educating the public regarding what had to be accomplished. To realize this goal, they created the National Progressive Service, an organization that applied the techniques of social welfare reform to the political process.

Many settlement workers and other social reformers supported the Progressive Party in the 1912 presidential election because of the party platform's social and industrial planks, not because they favored Theodore Roosevelt. They viewed the Progressive Party's campaign as the zenith of their struggle for social reform and social justice. A number of settlement workers played a prominent role in the 1912 election including **Jane Addams**, founder of **Hull House**; **Henry Moskowitz**, former settlement resident and political activist; the social investigator **Frances Kellor**; **Paul U. Kellogg**, editor of the social welfare journal the *Survey*; the settlement worker and political activist **Raymond Robins**; **Margaret Dreier Robins**, president of the Chicago chapter of the **Women's Trade Union League**; and the labor reformer **Mary Dreier**.

Although these men and women worked long and hard, few of them were convinced that the Progressive Party would be victorious. Rather, they viewed their work in the 1912 campaign as an opening salvo in a new era of politics. So, once the election was decided, they turned their attention to creating an organization that would enable them to continue their campaign of educating the American public about what could be done to solve the nation's social and economic problems. Although they did not realize all they hoped to achieve, many of the reformers were energized by their participation in the political process. They believed that their efforts to develop a well-informed electorate could yield results in the form of legislative action that would right the various wrongs they had identified. The National Progressive Service (NPS) was formed to accomplish this goal.

The founders of the NPS hoped to apply the principles and techniques that they employed in their reform work to the organization of a political party. Although they knew that in an election the goal was to get their candidate elected, they were not interested in the more mundane aspects of getting out the vote. Rather, they saw their strength in educating voters about the issues, a process that included developing and writing political platforms and drafting bills for consideration.

Frances Kellor devised a plan for the National Progressive Service which was presented at a meeting of the National Executive Committee of the Progressive Party in December 1912. Although some committee members were skeptical, Jane Addams was able to persuade the group to support Kellor's plan.

Kellor was selected to serve as executive head of the NPS, which was headquartered in New York City. The service was divided into two bureaus—the Legislative Reference Bureau and the Speakers' Bureau. These bureaus were further subdivided into four departments: Social and Industrial Justice, Conservation, Popular Government, and Cost of Living and Corporation Control. Each department was divided into subcommittees of experts charged with conducting research and presenting their findings. George Record headed the Department of Popu-

lar Government, and Gifford Pinchot directed the Conservation Department.

Responsibility for the Department of Social and Industrial Justice was shared by Addams and Charles Bird. Settlement workers were active in the work of a number of subcommittees of this department including Henry Moskowitz and Raymond Robins (men's labor); **Mary McDowell**, **Edith Abbott**, and Margaret Dreier Robins (women's labor); **Emily Balch**, **Grace Abbott**, Kellor, and **Jacob A. Riis** (immigration); and Paul U. Kellogg and **Frederic Almy** (social insurance).

Information and data collected by the departments and various subcommittees was forwarded to the Legislative Reference Bureau, which was headed by Donald Richberg. The members of this bureau were responsible for synthesizing the materials and drafting bills for consideration on the state and national levels.

The members of the NPS believed that unless the public understood the meaning of the laws passed, effective enforcement would not be possible. Toward this end, the service maintained a Speakers' Bureau that operated year round and sent out lecturers to talk before various groups on a variety of legislative initiatives and to distribute literature in all parts of the country. In addition to this work, the NPS encouraged the establishment of progressive service organizations on the state and local levels, and by 1914 Progressive Service organizations had been established in 21 states.

Although settlement workers and like-minded reformers had successfully organized Progressive Service organizations on the state and local levels and had fulfilled their charge of educating voters about the issues, in the final analysis the NPS was not as successful as its founders had hoped it would be. Internal disagreements about the organization's rules and regulations as well as disagreements among reformers about the validity of the Progressive Party as a political force led to the demise of the NPS by 1917.

Bibliography

Addams, *The Second Twenty Years at Hull-House, September 1909 to September 1928 with a Record of a Growing World Order*; Davis, *Spearheads for Reform: The Social Settlements and the Progressive Movements, 1890–1914*.

National Public Housing Conference *See* National Housing Conference

National Recreation and Park Association

Many Progressive Era reformers believed that by improving the physical urban environment they would encourage people to become better citizens. After embarking on crusades for better housing and sanitary conditions, many settlement workers turned their attention to providing neighborhood residents, particularly children, with adequate recreation space. Settlement residents in many communities worked together to secure parks and playgrounds. In some cases, the settlements came together in more formal organizations whose larger numbers provided them with additional influence to bring to bear on the local authorities. For example, settlement workers in New York City organized the **Outdoor Recreation League**, which was able to secure public playgrounds.

In some cities, private philanthropists funded playgrounds, thereby supplementing the support that social reformers obtained from the local government. As was true with several of their other campaigns, settlement workers and other social reformers realized the benefits of coming together in a national organization. The various recreation-related coalitions eventually became known as the National Recreation and Park Association.

In 1906, a group of educators and social welfare workers met in Washington, DC, to explore ways to coordinate the efforts of reformers interested in the playground movement. **Charles Stover** and a number of his colleagues from the New York-based Outdoor Recreation League, including **Mary Simkhovitch** of **Greenwich House**; **Lillian Wald** of the **Henry Street Settlement**; **Felix Adler** of the New York **Ethical Culture Society**; Nicholas Murray Butler, president of Columbia University; **Elizabeth Williams** of the **College Settlement**; James K. Paulding of the **University Settlement**; and the housing reformer **Jacob Riis**, were present. They were joined by settlement workers from other cities including **Jane Addams** of **Hull House**. As a result of this meeting, the Playground Association of America (PAA) was founded. The officers of the new association were Luther Gulick, president; and **Joseph Lee**, vice president; Henry Curtis, secretary; and Seth Steward, chair of the Executive Committee.

The group's leaders were interested in coordinating the development of playgrounds and recreational facilities across the country. At first, the PAA relied on the support of private donors

and volunteers to carry out its plan for providing year-round recreational facilities nationwide. Shortly after it was founded in 1907, the **Russell Sage Foundation** agreed to finance the work of the association. This arrangement provided the PAA with a degree of financial security. The directors established the group's headquarters in New York City and hired a full time, professional executive secretary, Howard Braucher.

By 1910, the PAA had made significant progress. It was publishing a monthly periodical, *The Playground* (later called *Recreation*), it had succeeded in upgrading existing playgrounds, and it had organized a series of training institutes for social workers. Dissension among the PAA's leadership and the withdrawal of the Russell Sage Foundation's financial support led to Gulick's resignation in 1910. He was replaced by Lee, who guided the organization over the next 30 years. In recognition of its decision to broaden its mission and appeal, the PAA changed its name to the Playground and Recreation Association of America (PRAA) in 1911.

Lee believed that the most effective way for the PRAA to shape the direction of municipal recreation was to provide expert assistance in individual municipalities through a cadre of field workers. The PRAA encouraged its workers to devise individualized solutions to the problems they encountered in the cities they visited. Representatives of the PRAA encouraged local authorities to experiment with a variety of recreational activities including arts and crafts, community pageants, and athletic events. In addition, the PRAA continued to publish *Recreation* and to offer a training program.

In 1917, in response to American involvement in World War I and at the request of President Woodrow Wilson, the PRAA broadened its mission to include recreational activities for troops in training camps and for soldiers on leave from military facilities. These activities were coordinated by the War Camp Community Services, a subunit of the PRAA. After the war, the PRAA turned its attention to physical education programs in the nation's public schools. It established a pressure group, the National Physical Education Service, which lobbied state governments to pass laws to require physical education programs in schools. This undertaking proved to be a success, as 28 states enacted such legislation.

In 1920, Ernest T. Altwell was hired by the PRAA to expand its offerings and to coordinate efforts to establish recreation facilities for blacks. Other initiatives during the 1920s included the establishment of the National Recreation School, which offered systematic training of professional recreation workers, and the funding of scholarly research initiatives.

During the 1930s, the PRAA broadened its scope and activities and once again changed its name, this time becoming the National Recreation Association (NRA). The lack of adequate funding during the Depression years compelled the NRA to cut back on its programs and services. Its work was soon eclipsed by that of the Works Progress Administration and the United Service Organizations for National Defense Inc. Following World War II, the NRA continued to function as a clearinghouse for information on recreation problems, providing field services and publishing literature. In 1965, the NRA merged with a number of other professional recreation groups to form the National Recreation and Park Association.

From the beginning settlement workers recognized the need to provide the inhabitants of crowded urban neighborhoods with adequate play and recreation space. They made provision for small playgrounds in the backyards of their settlements or lobbied municipal authorities for larger park areas in the community. The national-level organizations that grew out of these early efforts were an acknowledgement that the settlement workers' demands for play and recreation space were legitimate and that such facilities contributed to their social reform efforts. Today, the National Recreation and Park Association is still working to fulfill this settlement movement goal.

Bibliography

Davis, *Spearheads for Reform: The Social Settlements and the Progressive Movement, 1890–1914*; *Dictionary of American Biography*, supl. 2, "Joseph Lee," pp. 374–75; Romanofsky, *The Greenwood Encyclopedia of American Institutions: Social Service Organizations*, vol. 2, pp., 587–92; Woods, *The Settlement Horizon*.

National Recreation Association *See* National Recreation

and Park Association

National Social Workers Exchange *See* American Association of

Social Workers

Neighborhood Guild *See* University

Settlement

Neighborhood: My Story of Greenwich House (1938)

Published in 1938, *Neighborhood: My Story of Greenwich House* is both an autobiography of **Mary Simkhovitch** and an account of the social experiment that she and her colleagues engaged in when they established a settlement called **Greenwich House** in the old ninth ward of New York City in 1902.

In many ways, Simkhovitch's book is reminiscent of accounts written by two of her contemporaries, **Jane Addams**'s *Twenty Years at Hull-House with Autobiographical Notes* (1910) and **Lillian Wald**'s *The House on Henry Street* (1915). Simkhovitch was one of a small number of settlement workers who raised a family while living and working in a settlement house, and her account makes frequent references to the idea of family and home and their relationship to reform work.

The book begins with an account of her early life in suburban Boston and her education both in the United States and in Europe. It goes on to discuss the process by which she became involved in social settlement work, and it recounts her earlier experiences at both the **College Settlement** and the Friendly Aid House.

Like Addams and Wald, Simkhovitch uses vignettes of her life at Greenwich House and her interaction with the people in the surrounding neighborhood to advance her theory of social settlement work, which is the cultivation of the concept of neighborhood as the primary social unit.

Besides presenting a colorful historical account of a unique New York City community and its residents, *Neighborhood: My Story of Greenwich House* provides a unique perspective to Progressive reform efforts as it recounts Simkhovitch's struggles to reconcile her commitment to her husband and children and her commitment to social reform work.

Bibliography

Simkhovitch, *Neighborhood: My Story of Greenwich House*.

The Neighborhood Playhouse

Settlement workers were not only concerned with providing for the health and safety of their neighbors. They realized that people needed a release from the long hours they spent working in factories or in the building or street trades. To meet this need for recreation, most settlements sponsored a playground or provided access to gymnasiums. Many houses had a music or art school, and some supplied facilities for amateur theatricals.

The Neighborhood Playhouse, which was associated with the **Henry Street Settlement**, was both unique and representative of settlement efforts; unique because it was a separate, distinct facility that enjoyed a generous amount of independent financial support; representative because like many settlement-sponsored theaters it exposed many local residents to live performances, either as participants or as spectators.

In 1914, Alice and **Irene Lewisohn,** two wealthy sisters who were active supporters of the Henry Street Settlement, purchased a lot on Grand Street on New York City's Lower East Side not far from the settlement. The following year they presented a theater, The Neighborhood Playhouse, to the settlement. The playhouse was one of the first "little theaters" in the United States. For more than a decade, the Lewisohns generously supported the endeavor as it developed into a major center of avant-garde and experimental theater.

Like other similar groups such as the Provincetown Players and the Washington Square Players, the Neighborhood Playhouse produced the works of playwrights that were not attractive to the proprietors of commercial uptown theaters including Bernard Shaw, James Joyce, and Sholem Asch. Although it was legally part of the Henry Street Settlement, the Neighborhood Playhouse, which at first featured amateur talent, eventually became an independent enterprise with a resident professional company.

The Lewisohns were involved in all aspects of the enterprise. They sought out new talent and directed productions. Alice frequently appeared in productions as an actress, while Irene's performances focused on dancing and stylized movement. The playhouse's offerings reflected the taste of the two women, particularly in their emphasis on the more esoteric forms of Asiatic and Middle Eastern drama.

Over the years, the Neighborhood Playhouse produced Burmese Pwe dramas, Norse fairy tales, Japanese Noh plays, and Chinese fantasies in addition to ballets and dance dramas. Two notable productions were a Hindu play, *The Little Clay Cart,* which was produced in 1924, and the *Dybbuk,* a Yiddish folk play, which ran the following year.

Even though Alice and Irene Lewisohn contributed more than a half million dollars to the theater during the 1920s, the Neighborhood Playhouse faced increasingly serious financial setbacks. Never able to reach its goal of securing a base of ten thousand subscribers, the Neighborhood Playhouse closed in the spring of 1927, but during its short existence it brought a different type of culture to the lives of people in its neighborhood.

Bibliography

Crowley, *The Neighborhood Playhouse: Leaves From a Theater Scrapbook*; Jackson, *Encyclopedia of New York City*, p. 804; *Notable American Women, 1607-1950*, vol. 2, "Irene Lewisohn," pp. 400–02.

Neighbourhood Guilds (1891)

Neighbourhood Guilds: An Instrument of Social Reform was published in 1891 and presents **Stanton Coit**'s guild system, a version of the ideal society in which the members of the community organize themselves into social units and assume responsibility for themselves.

Stanton Coit was an associate of **Felix Adler**, the founder of the New York **Ethical Culture Society**. Like Adler, Coit believed in the importance of expressing personal virtue through social service. In 1886, he founded the first American settlement house, which he named the Neighborhood Guild. (*See* **University Settlement**.) After only two years, Coit left the United States to assume the principal Ethical Culture ministry in England.

Neighbourhood Guilds: An Instrument of Social Reform was written after Coit left New York. In it, he describes the concept of the guilds and provides practical information about their establishment and functions.

Coit believed that the first step toward social reform was to create a system of community groups or guilds. Each guild would be made up of approximately 100 families, and from this unit, a leadership corps would emerge that would lead the group during a process of social reform.

Although Coit's book was read with interest at the time, the concept of establishing neighborhood guilds was not adopted in the United States, with the exception of the **Hudson Guild** in New York City, which was established by **John Elliott** in 1895. For the most part, the settlement model in which a group of reformers lived in the neighborhood and helped the local resident organize reform efforts was the preferred form.

Bibliography

Coit, *Neighbourhood Guilds: An Instrument of Social Reform.*

New York Charity Organization Society Tenement House Committee

Settlement workers in urban centers were acutely aware of the substandard and often dangerous conditions in which so many thousands of poor people lived. From the beginning, they formed productive alliances with local housing reformers as they formulated campaigns to arouse public interest and to pressure local and state authorities to improve conditions. Because New York City was so large and so densely populated, conditions there were often thought of as extreme, almost too much to control. However, New York settlement workers and housing reformers were particularly aggressive in dealing with the city's housing dilemma. The New York City Charity Organization Society Tenement House Committee was a productive alliance that these social reformers formed with existing charitable organizations to achieve their goals.

In 1898, housing reformer **Lawrence Veiller** suggested to the New York **Association for Improving the Condition of the Poor** and to the State Charities Aid Association that a permanent agency charged with overseeing housing conditions in New York City be established. When he received no support from either of these organizations, Veiller approached the president of the New York **Charity Organization Society** (COS), **Robert DeForest**, for assistance. After several months delay, DeForest and his COS colleagues saw the benefit of Veiller's suggestion, and the New York COS established a Tenement House Committee which over the next 20 years functioned as a pressure group that lobbied for housing reform and defended the rights of tenants.

Frederick W. Halls, a New York attorney, was appointed to chair the committee, and Veiller was selected to serve as secretary and executive officer. They were joined by other prominent social reformers including **Richard Watson Gilder**, George B. Post, **Felix Adler**, I.N. Phelps Stokes, **E.R.L. Gould**, Ernest Flagg, Constant A. Andrews, **Edward T. Devine**, John Vinton Dahlgren, and Robert DeForest.

Veiller was the committee's guiding force. Often, he was critical of the ways in which the municipal authorities responded to the city's housing crisis and used the committee to voice his concerns. One example of this came about in 1900 when, unhappy with the actions of the New York City Municipal Building Code Commission, he aroused the public sentiment about housing reform through the **New York Charity Organization Society Tenement House Exhibition**, which presented a graphic picture of the city's housing problems. The public outcry following the exhibition was instrumental in the formation of the **New York State Tenement House Commission of 1900**, which eventually succeeded in changing the housing laws.

Over time, the achievements of the Charity Organization Society Tenement House Committee were instrumental in the development of a national housing reform movement. One of the committee's most noteworthy contributions to this national movement was Veileer who, having gained valuable experience and connections within the reform community, went on to head the **National Housing Association**.

Bibliography

Lubove, *The Progressives and the Slums: Tenement House Reform in New York City, 1890–1917.*

New York Charity Organization Society Tenement House Exhibition

Settlement workers and other social welfare workers knew that they could not hope to achieve their goals unless they could gain the support of the middle and upper classes, those elements of the society who had the time, and most importantly, the money, to devote to reform campaigns. The photographs taken by the housing reformer **Jacob Riis** and others were one way to illustrate the squalid conditions of the slums to these groups. The members of the **New York Charity Organization Society Tenement House Committee** took these pictorial representations a step further when they organized a Tenement House Exhibition using photographs, maps, and scale models. This exhibition graphically portrayed terrible conditions in the slums.

The New York **Charity Organization Society** (COS) established a Tenement House Committee in 1898. Its members included **Robert DeForest, Richard Watson Gilder, E. R. L. Gould, Felix Adler**, and Jacob A. Riis. The noted housing reformer **Lawrence Veiller** served as the committee's secretary and executive officer. Concerned about the dangerous housing situation in New York City, the committee drew up a series of 15 tenement-related ordinances to supplement existing municipal housing laws. These ordinances were collected in a pamphlet that was distributed to the public in June 1899.

The committee's legislative proposals were favorably received by the New York City Chapter of the American Institute for Architects, the New York **Association for Improving the Condition of the Poor**, the **Boston Children's Aid Society**, the **University Settlement**, the **College Settlement**, the Nurses' Settlement (see **Henry Street Settlement**), as well as numbers of private citizens. However, none of the committee's suggestions were adopted by the municipal authorities.

Unable to achieve its goal of improving construction standards with the passage of the 1899 New York City Metropolitan Building Code, the COS Committee decided to prepare a public exhibition about conditions in the tenements which it hoped would draw attention to the city's housing crisis and encourage support for improvement.

Lawrence Veiller organized the exhibition, and many New York City settlement house workers participated in its preparation. The exhibition opened in February 1900 in the Sherry Building at Thirty-Eighth Street and Fifth Avenue. It ran for two weeks, and more than 10,000 people attended. Veiller's purpose in organizing this exhibit was to demonstrate that working-class families in New York City were housed in worse conditions than almost anywhere else on earth. In addition, they were forced to pay one fourth of their income in rent, which was more than was demanded of workers for better homes in other communities.

The exhibition included more than one thousand photographs and detailed maps of the city's slum districts and a variety of statistical tables and charts. These materials were supplemented by five papier-mâché scale models of tenement blocks. The settlement workers had collected information on the income and expenditures of their neighbors, and they used this information to demonstrate the correlation between pauperism, disease, and housing conditions.

The maps included in the exhibition showed population density, death rates in tenement house districts, and the distribution of various nationalities in tenement neighborhoods. A series of poverty and disease maps provided a striking picture of conditions and indicated the change that had taken place over time. Perhaps the most striking feature of the exhibition was a cardboard model of an entire block of tenements on New York City's Lower East Side. This model depicted the block that was bounded by Chrystie, Forsyth, Canal, and Bayard Streets and covered 80,000 square feet. Within this space, 39 different tenement houses collectively housed 2,781 people.

In addition to displays that illustrated that many tenement rooms lacked ventilation and air, the committee also displayed models of well-designed buildings as alternatives. Overall, Veiller orchestrated a comprehensive presentation that included studies of model tenements in Europe and the United States, suburban tenements and workingmen's cottages in the United States and Europe, and studies of public parks, playgrounds, libraries, and public baths and schools.

During the second week of the exhibition, the organizers arranged for a series of conferences to be held each evening. These presentations included talks by housing experts on a variety of topics including "Model Tenements," "The Tenements and Poverty," and "The People Who Lived in Tenements."

The data compiled for the exhibition was included in the ***Tenement House Problem*** (1903), a two-volume study written by Veiller and Robert DeForest.

As a result of the COS Tenement House Exhibition, a number of influential people became interested in New York City's housing situation. New York State Governor Theodore Roosevelt, for example, appointed a **New York State Tenement House Commission** in 1900, which was charged with investigating existing conditions and implementing improvements.

Veiller served as secretary of this commission, which relied on settlement workers to conduct investigations and to testify at hearings. Veiller and other members of the commission drafted a new housing code designed to eliminate the worst aspects of the tenements and to provide for ventilation and toilet facilities in each apartment. This new housing code was adopted in 1901 and provided for the creation of the **New York City Tenement House Department**, which was charged with enforcing the new code. The work of the COS Tenement House Exhibition and the passage of the 1901 code affected housing reform efforts in almost every industrial city in the United States.

This exhibition, which relied on the contributions of settlement workers and other social welfare reformers, served as a model for other exhibitions that were designed to call attention to substandard conditions and to pressure local authorities to correct the housing situation in their communities. The 1901 code that passed in part as a result of the exhibition was so effective that tenements built after this date were known as "New Law Tenements." *See also* **Committee on Congestion of Population**.

Bibliography

Davis, *Spearheads for Reform: The Social Settlements and the Progressive Movement, 1890–1914*; DeForest, *The Tenement House Problem*; Lubove, *The Progressives and the Slums: Tenement House Reform in New York City, 1890–1917*.

New York Child Labor Committee

The abusive child labor system that existed in the United States during the late nineteenth and early twentieth centuries was considered by many to be a national disgrace. Settlement workers witnessed the dangers and debilitating effect on the children in their neighborhoods of working long hours in factories, canneries, tenements, and in the street trades.

As was true in many other reform crusades, the New York-based settlement workers took the lead in working to eliminate child labor. Operating out of an existing reform coalition, the New York Association of Neighborhood Workers (*see* **United Neighborhood Houses**), settlement workers allied themselves with other social welfare reformers to form the New York Child Labor Committee, which worked for the passage of protective legislation and served as a model for the **National Child Labor Committee**.

The committee's origins can be traced to 1902, when some members of the New York City-based Association of Neighborhood Workers, including **Florence Kelley**, **Lillian Wald**, and **Felix Adler**, formed a subcommittee on child labor to investigate reports of the exploitation of children in various industries. **Robert Hunter**, the head resident of the **University Settlement**, served as chair of the group. In addition to Kelley and Wald, the other members of the subcommittee included **Mary K. Simkhovitch** of **Greenwich House** and **Pauline Goldmark** of the National **Consumers' League**. Hunter also recruited **James G. Phelps Stokes**, a resident of the University Settlement.

Hunter successfully raised $1,000 through an appeal letter and personal contacts to help finance the group's work. In August 1902, the subcommittee hired Helen Marot, later secretary of the New York **Women's Trade Union League**, as a full-time investigator. At first the members hoped to expose the terrible child labor conditions so that New York State would be obligated to appoint a permanent, official commission on child labor, but they soon expanded their focus.

Marot coordinated the work of settlement residents from all over the city who collected statistics on more than one thousand child labor cases. During the course of their research, the subcommittee members realized that immediate action was needed besides the more long-range investigations they were conducting. Toward this end, they prepared three model bills designed to strengthen New York State child labor laws. Kelley, Wald, and Marot assembled the statistical evidence for the report, and Hunter and Stokes headed the delegation that traveled to the state capital in Albany to testify and to lobby on behalf of the proposed bills. To arouse interest and support, copies of the proposed legislation were sent to the State Labor Bureau, the superintendent of the Board of Public Health, and the governor.

The subcommittee's work was a key factor in the passage of the New York State Child Labor Law of 1903, which became a model for other states. This law included a number of significant provisions such as the regulation of street trades and a reduction in the maximum number of hours a child could work to nine per day. The law also coordinated state factory and compulsory education laws. In addition, it included a new provision regarding the documentary evidence of age for children under 16. Under the new law, a parent's affidavit stating the age of the child was no longer sufficient. Instead, the state health officer had to obtain independent documentary proof of age such as a birth certificate or baptismal certificate prior to issuing a work permit.

The settlement workers in the subcommittee did more than just directly influence the passage of necessary legislation. They also aroused public opinion against child labor abuses and were instrumental in the establishment of the National Child Labor Committee. The public awareness these reformers generated along with Marot's final report convinced Hunter of the need for a permanent state-level child labor committee. The only other similar committee had been organized in Alabama in 1901 by Edgar Gardner Murphy, a clergyman and publicist.

Hunter realized that he would need to enlist the financial and personal support of a number of prominent New Yorkers to create such a committee. In addition to the members of the existing subcommittee, he obtained the assistance of William H. Baldwin, the president of the Long Island Railroad; **Jacob H. Schiff**, an attorney and philanthropist; **Lyman Abbott**, the editor of the social welfare journal the *Outlook*; **Felix Adler** of the **Ethical Culture Society**; **Jacob Riis**, the noted housing reformer; and Henry Codman Potter, the reform-minded Protestant Episcopal Bishop of New York City.

In 1905, this group was officially incorporated as the New York Child Labor Committee (NYCLC). Initially based in New York City, the NYCLC eventually broadened its scope to include the entire state. The NYCLC was the only organization in the state whose primary purpose was to do away with child labor through legislation. To accomplish its goals, it aroused public sympathy by promoting the idea that child labor was morally wrong and by proposing and lobbying for new laws.

In addition to its intensive campaign for regulatory legislation, the NYCLC was also concerned with the enforcement of laws once they were enacted. The NYCLC continued its work until 1942 and was eventually responsible for the passage of over 40 pieces of legislation, including the Finch-Hill Factory Act (1903), which made the employer responsible for illegally employed children; the Feld-Bretbart Bill (1935), which established 16 as the minimum age for leaving school; and the Factory Law of 1907, which limited children under 16 years of age to an eight-hour day and a 48-hour work week. *See also* **Child Welfare.**

Bibliography

Davis, *Spearheads for Reform: The Social Settlements and the Progressive Movement, 1890–1914*; Felt, *Hostages of Fortune: Child Labor Reform in New York States*; Goldmark, *Impatient Crusader: Florence Kelley's Life Story*; Woods, *The Settlement Horizon*.

New York City Tenement House Department

Once settlement workers and other reformers had successfully campaigned to have local, state, and federal authorities enact legislation that would correct housing or labor abuses, they realized that their fight was only half over. They also had to ensure that the laws were properly enforced. As was the case with the New York City Tenement House Department, this enforcement could involve the creation of a separate government organization.

While serving as secretary of the **New York State Tenement House Commission** of 1900, **Lawrence Veiller** recommended that the state legislature establish an agency responsible for ensuring that the builders and landlords obey the new housing code. At first, he proposed a permanent State Board of Tenement House Commissioners, but the other members of the commission suggested a city agency instead, and the New York State Legislature acted on the commission's recommendation by incorporating a Tenement House Department into the New York City Charter.

Robert W. DeForest, president of the New York **Charity Organization Society**, was appointed by New York City Mayor Seth Low to head the new department. But it was Veiller, whom DeForest appointed as his first deputy commissioner, who was the driving force behind the work of the department. Veiller established three divisions within the Tenement House Department. The Buildings Division was charged with inspecting plans for proposed tenement construction and for examining the buildings during the construction process. The Inspection Division assumed the tenement-related responsibilities of the Board of Health and was responsible for supervising the conditions in completed housing units. The Records Division collected information and compiled statistics about the completed buildings and their occupants.

The Tenement House Department was also empowered to license tenements and to ensure that structural violations committed by builders did not become the responsibility of the landlord who purchased the completed house. The department issued licenses to builders certifying that houses met all legal requirements, thus ensuring that no house could be occupied until it met the department's criteria.

Veiller's tenure with the department was brief. When the Tammany-backed George B. McClellan became mayor of New York City in 1902, both Veiller and DeForest resigned. T.C.F. Crain, a political appointee became commissioner of the Tenement House Department, but the department practically collapsed within a year. Unwilling to permit the work of the department to be abandoned, Veiller showed Mayor McClellan that Crain was unqualified and secured his dismissal in late 1904. Crain was replaced by Edmond J. Butler who served as commissioner until 1909. Butler was succeeded by John J. Murphy whose term of office spanned the years 1910 to 1917.

As changes occurred in city government, the work of the Tenement House Department was assumed by the City Housing Authority. During its tenure, the Tenement House Department did make progress in cleaning up the tenements. Windows were installed in interior rooms, water closets replaced hall sinks, and fire prevention measures were more strictly enforced. *See also* **Dumbell Tenements; Tenement Houses**.

Bibliography
Lubove, *The Progressives and the Slums: Tenement House Reform in New York City, 1890–1917.*

New York Consumers' League

See Consumers' Leagues

New York School of Philanthropy *See* Columbia University Graduate School of Social Work

New York School of Social Work *See* Columbia University Graduate School of Social Work

New York State Factory Investigating Commission

The New York State Factory Investigating Commission, which was formed following the **Triangle Shirtwaist Company Fire** in 1911, was a cooperative effort that settlement workers engaged in with other reformers to initiate change. In this instance, the social welfare workers formed a coalition with key political figures who provided valuable experience in the political system and established key working relationships with these influential, reform-minded legislators.

Following the Triangle Shirtwaist Company Fire on March 25, 1911, in which 146 young women were killed, a number of public protest meetings were held around New York City. Large crowds gathered in assembly halls such as the Cooper Union and Chickering Hall and at the Metropolitan Opera House to draw attention to the fire and to garner public support for remedial legislation to prevent similar tragedies in the future.

Reform organizations such as the New York branches of the **Women's Trade Union League** and the **Consumers' League** joined forces with various trade unions and with settlement workers and other reformers to pressure the New York State Legislature to enact remedial legislation.

On June 30, 1911, three months after the Triangle fire, and in response to the public outcry, the New York State Legislature created a special Factory Investigating Commission. State Senator **Robert F. Wagner** served as chair; **Alfred E. Smith**, the leader of the State Assembly was vice chair. Other members of the commission included Samuel Gompers, president of the American Federation of Labor and **Mary Dreier**, president of the New York Women's Trade Union League. The labor activist **Rose Schneiderman** and the social reformer **Frances Perkins** worked as investigators for the commission.

At first, only $10,000 was appropriated by the legislature to finance the work of the commission. The members agreed that they wanted to do more than just investigate the fire at the Asch Building where the Triangle Shirtwaist Company had been located. In their preliminary report, the committee members emphasized the need for a more thorough investigation into the general conditions of the factory life in New York State.

Wagner and Smith succeeded in having the Factory Investigating Commission's charge expanded, and they began to inspect factories and to hold hearings. The commission was empowered to compel witnesses to appear, and it could require the production of books and other papers. Two prominent attorneys, Abram L. Elkins and Bernard L. Shientag, donated their services as chief and assistant legal counsel. In the first year of the commission's operations, its representatives inspected 1,836 industrial establishments in various cities across the state. More than 220 witnesses offered testimony.

The Factory Investigating Commission did deal effectively with its original charge to look into the causes of the Triangle Shirtwaist Company Fire, but what it went on to accomplish was much more important to the cause of long-term reform. Wagner and Smith were skilled politicians and legislators. Due in large measure to their efforts, more than 30 new laws were passed during the three years that the commission existed. Legislation was adopted that eliminated fire hazards and regulated sanitary conditions in factories. New York State adopted a "one-day-of-rest-in-seven-law" as well as laws prohibiting women from working in factories from 10 PM until 6 AM, and banning children from working in tenements and cannery sheds. The commission also contributed to the passage of a Workmen's Compensation Act (1913) and a Widowed Mother's Pension Bill (1915).

The work of the Factory Investigating Commission provided settlement workers and other reformers in New York City with an important opportunity to become involved in many aspects of the reform process. They were also able to establish working relationships with Wagner and Smith, two politicians who would prove to be important allies in other reform crusades of the early twentieth century.

Bibliography

Huthmacher, *Senator Robert F. Wagner and the Rise of Urban Liberalism*; Jackson, *The Encyclopedia of New York City*, p. 387; Josephson, *Al Smith: Hero of the Cities*; Stein, *The Triangle Fire*.

New York State Tenement House Commissions (1884, 1894, 1900)

Settlement workers and other social reformers drew attention to the problems they encountered such as unsafe working conditions, substandard housing, or unsanitary living conditions by writing articles or speaking at public gatherings. If the public outcry was significant enough, municipal or state authorities might respond by establishing a commission to conduct an official investigation of the problem under consideration. Settlement workers often contributed to these commissions either by conducting research and supplying statistics or by testifying at public hearings.

New York State Tenement House Commission of 1884

Following the *Sanitary Engineer*'s 1878 competition for a design of a tenement on a 25 by 100 foot lot, housing reformers rallied to protest the adoption of the magazine's winning design, the so-called **dumbbell tenement**. But their concerns were not heeded, and dumbbell-style tenements appeared in many city neighborhoods.

Housing conditions in New York City were so extraordinarily bad that in 1884 the state legislature enacted the first in a series of Tenement House Commissions, which were charged with investigating conditions and recommending improvements. The driving force behind the calling of this first commission came when **Felix Adler**, founder of the New York **Ethical Culture Society**, delivered a series of lectures condemning the conditions in New York City's tenement house neighborhoods. As a result of Adler's lectures, the New York State Legislature appointed the first of a series of official state tenement house commissions to investigate conditions and to make recommendations for improvements.

A number of prominent reformers and civic leaders served on the New York State Tenement House Commission of 1884, including Adler, Charles F. Wingate, Joseph W. Drexel, S.O. Vanderpoel, Oswald Ottendorfer, Moreau Morris, Anthony Reichardt, Joseph J. O'Donohue, Abbott Hodgman, and William P. Esterbrook.

Based on the commission's reports, in 1887 a number of amendments were added to the **New York State Tenement House Law of 1879**. Most of these amendments were not substantive and did little to improve housing conditions. They included an increase in the number of sanitary police from 30 to 45, the establishment of a standing tenement house commission composed of the mayor of New York City and the heads of several city government departments, and a requirement that the owners of tenement houses file their names and addresses annually with the New York City Board of Health. In addition, tenement landlords were required to provide running water on every floor and one water closet for every 20 residents.

New York State Tenement House Commission of 1894

Because the 1884 committee had been largely ineffective, the housing problems just worsened. The New York State Tenement House Commission of 1894 was convened following a series of articles that appeared in the *Press*, a local newspaper, which were intended to focus the attention of both the general public and the politicians on the deplorable housing conditions in many areas of New York State.

The magazine editor and social activist **Richard Watson Gilder** chaired the 1894 committee. He was assisted by a group of concerned citizens that included Edward Marshall, Sunday editor of the *Press*; Dr. Cyrus Edison, sanitary superintendent of the New York Board of Health; lawyers Roger Foster and John P. Schuchman; William D'H Washington, a civil engineer; George B. Post, an architect; and Solomon Moses of the United Hebrew Charities.

Under Gilder's guidance, the committee conducted a detailed, thorough investigation of housing conditions. During the course of their research they concentrated on three aspects of tenement houses: the high incidence of sickness and death among tenement dwellers due to structural and sanitary defects of the buildings; the problem of population congestion in tenement neighborhoods; and the lack of adequate recreation facilities such as parks and playgrounds in tenement neighborhoods.

Based on their investigations, the members of the Tenement House Committee of 1894 prepared a number of bills for consideration by the New York State Legislature. Much of their proposed legislation was concerned with establishing minimum standards for light, ventilation, sanitation, and fire prevention. The committee recommended restricting the size of tenements to no more than 70 percent of the lot and requiring the installation of a window opening to the open air in every room.

Although its members expressed outrage over the deplorable sanitary conditions they observed, the committee did not place the responsibility for providing adequate facilities on landlords and builders. Instead, it called upon municipal authorities to provide public baths (see **Baths**) and toilets.

A number of bills relating to fire prevention were also brought forward. Although little was done to prohibit the continuing construction of dumbbell tenements, the 1894 committee did urge that the Municipal Board of Health be given authority to demolish buildings that were designated unfit for human habitation.

Besides these efforts, the New York State Tenement House Committee of 1894 put forward a number of recommendations to control overcrowding in tenements such as stricter enforcement of minimum per-person space allotments. The committee also drew attention to the high rents that some immigrants were forced to pay. Unable to meet the rent, many families took in lodgers, a situation that only exacerbated the overcrowding problem. The committee approved the idea of model tenements as another way to ease overcrowding.

Despite the positive work of the 1894 commission, it still left most of the worst housing problems unsolved.

New York State Tenement House Commission of 1900

The deplorable housing conditions that had led to the formation of the housing commissions of 1884 and 1894 were still plaguing New York City by 1900, forcing reformers to go to greater lengths to reveal these conditions and have them resolved. The New York State Tenement House Commission of 1900 was established in response to such an effort, the **New York Charity Organization Society Tenement House Exhibition,** which settlement workers and other reformers staged in an attempt to once again bring before the public the terrible housing conditions that existed in New York City's slums. The work of this commission was significant because it contributed to the passage of a more comprehensive Tenement House Law in 1901. (*See* **New York State Tenement House Laws.**)

The **New York Charity Organization Society Tenement House Committee** organized an exhibition in February 1900 which was designed to graphically portray the relationship between disease, poverty, and population density. The exhibition, which was possible in large measure to the efforts of New York City-based settlement workers and other social reformers, aroused the public's interest in the housing problem in New York.

In response to all the uproar the exhibit caused, **Lawrence Veiller**, secretary and executive officer of the Charity Organization Society committee, succeeded in having the New York State Legislature appoint another Tenement House Commission in 1900, which, like its predecessors, was charged with investigating the tenement house situation and making recommendations for improvements. New York State Governor Theodore Roosevelt appointed Veiller secretary of the New York State Tenement House Commission of 1900. Veiller's colleagues on the 1900 commission were lawyers, architects, builders, settlement workers, and city officials; they included William A. Douglas, Williams Lansing, Otto M. Eidlitz, Myles Tierney, **Alfred T. White**, Charles S. Brown, I.N. Phelps Stokes, Raymond T. Almirall, Paul D. Cravath, F. Norton Goddard, **James B. Reynolds**, Dr. George B. Fowler, Hugh J. Bonner, William J. O'Brien, and **Robert W. DeForest**, who served as chair.

Veiller was responsible for planning and implementing most of the commission's work. The members held a series of eight public hearings devoted to the incidence of tuberculosis among tenement dwellers to demonstrate the relationship between population overcrowding and the spread of disease. As part of the commission's efforts, Veiller prepared a detailed history of tenement house legislation in New York City. The commission made a number of recommendations to the New York State Legislature regarding regulations, including the adoption of a new tenement house code and the creation of a separate **New York City Tenement House Department** that would be responsible for enforcing the new code. Veiller was instrumental in seeing that the commission's bills passed through the legislature successfully as the Tenement House Law of 1901.

Perhaps the major accomplishment of the new law was the elimination of the narrow dumbbell airshaft in the construction of all future tenements. Instead, it called for the inclusion of a courtyard between buildings which would vary in size depending on the height of the surrounding structures. Two other significant reforms were the requirement that for all future construction, each apartment be equipped with a separate water closet and that stricter fire-protection measures be enacted. Tenements constructed after 1901 were referred to as "New Law Tenements."

The commission also established a subcommittee on the Moral and Social Influence of Tenement House Life. This group was concerned with a number of quality-of-life issues such as parks and schools, and the elimination of gambling and **prostitution** in residential neighborhoods. The Committee of Fifteen was organized in December 1900 to support the commission in its efforts to eliminate prostitution in the tenements and saloon-centered prostitution, also known as Raines-Law Hotels.

Although the deplorable housing conditions had led reformers to form tenement commissions as early as 1884, it wasn't until the public got behind the work of the commissions through the congestion exhibit of 1900 that any real progress was made to ease New York City's housing crisis.

Bibliography

DeForest, *The Tenement House Problem*; Lubove, *The Progressives and the Slums: Tenement House Reform in New York City, 1890-1917*.

New York State Tenement House Laws of 1867, 1879, and 1901

During the late nineteenth and early twentieth centuries as thousands and thousands of immigrants entered the United States, housing conditions in urban centers, particularly in ports of entry such as New York City, became congested, unsanitary, and dangerous. Settlement workers cooperated with housing reformers to bring these conditions to the attention of municipal and state authorities and to lobby for corrective legislation. The New York State Tenement House Laws of 1867, 1879, and 1901 illustrate the type of legislative reform these social welfare workers were able to accomplish.

Public attention was drawn to housing conditions in New York City following the 1863 Draft Riots. These disturbances highlighted the sub-standard housing of the poor and led many prominent citizens to take steps to improve sanitary conditions in the city. In 1864, a Council of Hygiene was created, and this agency conducted a thorough investigation of housing conditions. Two results of this effort were the formation of the Metropolitan Board of Health in 1866 and the enactment of the first tenement house law the following year.

The Tenement House Law of 1867 defined a tenement as any building occupied as a residence by more than three families living independently of one another and doing their own cooking, or by two families living on the same floor and having common access to halls, stairways, water closets, or privies. The law provided for minimum fire protection standards and for ventilation of interior bedrooms. It set no limit on the percentage of the lot that a building could occupy, however. Nor did it compel the landlord to supply more than one water tap either in the house or in the yard, or more than one water closet or privy per 20 residents.

The Tenement House Law of 1879 corrected some of the deficiencies of the 1867 legislation. It stipulated a set amount of space that must be left at the rear of the lot on which a tenement was constructed, and it mandated that the tenement house could occupy no more than 65 percent of the lot. The new law also required rooms used for sleeping to have at least one window of a minimum of 12 square feet which opened directly onto a street or yard. In addition, the law provided for a force of 30 sanitary police officers who were charged with conducting sanitary inspections under the supervision of the Board of Health. As was true with the 1867 law, discretionary clauses appeared in the 1879 legislation, and their inclusion resulted in the virtual nullification of certain aspects of both laws.

A number of The **New York State Tenement House Commission** of 1900's recommendations were enacted by the state legislature. These changes, which were introduced in the Tenement House Law of 1901, included the elimination of the use of the narrow airshaft within buildings in new construction. The airshaft was a 28-inch wide indentation that was enclosed on all sides. Although it was originally intended to provide light and air, it was actually more of a health and safety hazard. It was used as a garbage container and when fires broke out, the shaft functioned like a flue, carrying the deadly flames from one story to another. The shaft was to be replaced by a courtyard that varied in size according to the height of the building. The 1901 law also required that new buildings have a separate water closet in each apartment, called for the fireproofing of halls and stairs, and regulated the construction and location of fire escapes. Cellar floors had to be waterproofed, lighting was required for dark hallways, and interior rooms had to be ventilated.

The 1901 law was the most influential of the three tenement laws because it called for significant changes in the construction of new buildings and then enforced these changes. It was so successful that structures built according to its provisions became known as "New Law Tenements."

Bibliography

DeForest, *The Tenement House Problem*; Lubove, *The Progressives and the Slums: Tenement House Reform in New York City, 1890–1917*.

New York Working Women's Society

The New York Working Women's Society was an early example of middle-class and working-class women cooperating to bring about better working conditions for women. The accomplishments of this coalition provided the model for other cooperative reform organizations such as the **Women's Trade Union League**.

The growth of the American Settlement Movement coincided with the development of trade unionism among women. In recognition of the large number of women in the workforce, the Knights of Labor appointed Mary Kenney (later **Mary Kenney O'Sullivan**) as the first paid woman member of its executive staff in 1886 with responsibility for investigating women's working conditions. Kenney also spoke at meetings about the terrible conditions she encountered and persuaded many settlement workers and middle-class women to become involved in the effort to improve working women's lives.

In February 1888, a group of women formed the New York Working Women's Society. Their purpose was to encourage cooperation between middle-class and working-class women in the fight for better labor laws. Toward this end, the society advocated establishing trade unions for women and supported efforts to increase women's wages while decreasing their working hours at the same time.

Within two years, the members of the society won approval for an amendment to the New York State Factory Act which provided for the appointment of female factory inspectors. That same year, 1890, Alice Woodbridge, the secretary of the New York Working Women's Society, investigated working conditions in a number of New York City retail stores. Woodbridge's report, which detailed the long hours and unsafe working environment that young shop girls endured for little pay, came to the attention of **Josephine Shaw Lowell**, founder of the New York **Charity Organization Society**.

Shocked by what she learned from Woodbridge's report, Lowell encouraged public discussion of the working conditions in retail stores, and in May 1890, a mass meeting was held in Chickering Hall to discuss the issue. Many middle-class women were present at the gathering and a number of them joined with the members of the Working Women's Society to form a committee to investigate retail establishments and to prepare a list of those stores that treated their employees fairly. The committee published this list to encourage consumers to patronize only those stores that had been approved by the society. This committee formed the nucleus for the New York **Consumers' League**, which was formally organized in 1891 and proved to be one of the most potent and effective reform organizations of its time.

As the predecessor to the New York Consumers' League, the New York Working Women's Society drew attention to the working women's plight and was a model for later reform organizations.

Bibliography

Daniels, *Always a Sister: The Feminism of Lillian D. Wald*; Lubove, *The Progressives and the Slums: Tenement House Reform in New York City, 1890–1917*; Woods, *The Settlement Horizon*.

Northwestern University Settlement

Settlement houses were established for a variety of reasons: to serve a religious purpose, to advance a particular social or personal cause, or to improve race relations. The Northwestern University Settlement in Chicago was opened to provide a focal point for studying the interactions among various ethnic communities in a particular Chicago neighborhood. Once established, it developed a distinctive character as a politically active settlement.

Located in the northwest section of Chicago, the Northwestern University Settlement was founded in December 1891 by the social gospel minister and civic reformer Charles Zueblin, his school friend Clark Tisdale, and Tisdale's wife. Zueblin and the Tisdales appealed to the faculty and students of the men's alma mater, Northwestern University, for funds to open and maintain the settlement. Zueblin hoped that the settlement would serve as a laboratory to study the surrounding neighborhood and to bring the diverse ethnic groups represented together as a community.

Like their colleagues in other settlements, the residents at the Northwestern University Settlement were involved in housing and sanitary reform campaigns; some residents even served as sanitary inspectors for the city. The settlement opened a playground, secured a public bath (see **Baths**) for the community, and operated a dispensary, a food station, and a day nursery.

Providing a supply of clean milk, particularly for infants, was a concern for many settlement workers and for health reformers. In 1897, the house installed equipment for pasteurizing milk and supplied other Chicago settlements with clean milk. As part of a citywide campaign for infant health in Chicago in 1905, the Northwestern University Settlement cooperated with the **Chicago Relief Society** and the Chicago **Visiting Nurse Association** to establish an outdoor educational clinic at the settlement.

During its early years, the Northwestern University Settlement had several head residents. One particularly active and well-known individual was **Raymond Robins**, whose wife, **Margaret Dreier Robins**, was a leader in the National **Women's Trade Union League** and in the Chicago branch of the same organization. Raymond Robins was particularly interested in local politics and was an associate of reform Mayor William Dever.

While he was head resident, Robins established a Civic Club that was modeled after the Community Club of the **Chicago Commons** settlement, which had been founded by **Graham Taylor**. Working in tandem, the Northwestern University Settlement and Chicago Commons cooperated in many Chicago-based reform campaigns. They were particularly active in politics on the ward level and regularly sponsored candidates in aldermanic campaigns. The settlement's involvement in various political contests provided a focus for reform-minded voters and helped to control the balance of power in the ward.

As was true with many other houses, the Northwestern University Settlement did not survive into the second half of the twentieth century. During its operation it provided a valuable service to a local community by working to improve health and sanitary conditions and by actively participating in local politics. *See also* **Ward Politics.**

Bibliography

Davis, *Spearheads for Reform: The Social Settlements and the Progressive Movement, 1890–1914*; Woods, *Handbook of Settlements*; Woods, *The Settlement Horizon*.

Nurses' Settlement *See* Henry Street Settlement

On Journey (1937)

Some settlement workers and social reformers were prolific writers who published many articles and books about their work and their reasons for becoming involved in various reform crusades. **Vida Scudder** was one of the founders of the **College Settlements Association**, and she combined a career in higher education with one in social activism. Her autobiography, *On Journey,* provides descriptions of the many facets of her life and work as well as insights into the motivation behind her involvement in a variety of causes.

Written in 1937, this autobiography provides an account of Vida Scudder's work both in the settlement movement and as a professor of English literature at Wellesley. *On Journey* begins with a discussion of Scudder's early life and education, particularly her time at Oxford University where she discovered the writings of the English art critic and social reformer John Ruskin.

In the book, Scudder provides insights into the establishment of the College Settlements Association and of her years as a resident at the Boston-based settlement **Denison House**. *On Journey* provides useful and enlightening descriptions of many of the early leaders of the settlement movement in the United States including **Helena Dudley** and **Emily Balch** of Denison House, **Jane Addams** of **Hull House** in Chicago, and **Lillian Wald** of the **Henry Street Settlement** in New York City.

On Journey reflects the broad range of causes and subjects that attracted Scudder's attention and personal commitment. In addition to providing an examination of her interest in socialism and feminism, Scudder also discusses her religious convictions and her scholarly research into the lives of Saint Francis of Assisi and Saint Catherine of Sienna.

Although *On Journey* came out too late to have much influence on the American Settlement Movement, it does provide important insights into the life and work of those who shared Scudder's commitment to social change.

Bibliography
Scudder, *On Journey.*

O'Sullivan, Mary Kenney
settlement worker, labor reformer
b. January 8, 1864; d. January 18, 1943.

Settlement houses often served as a base of operations for reformers who were interested in a variety of causes. In the case of the labor organizer Mary Kenney O'Sullivan, settlements in Chicago and Boston provided her with connections to the social reform networks and enabled her to organize women in a variety of trades into labor unions.

Born and raised in Hannibal, Missouri, Kenney attended the local public school. Her formal education ended in the fourth grade when she was apprenticed to a dressmaker. After her father's death in 1878, Kenney assumed responsibility for the care of her invalid mother. To support her family, she took a job with a printing and binding company, becoming profi-

Mary Kenney O'Sullivan
The Schlesinger Library, Radcliffe College

cient in all aspects of the trade that were open to women. Within four years, Kenney became a forewoman, and when the company moved to Keokuk, Iowa, in 1882, Kenney followed. Four years later the firm closed, and Kenney moved with her mother to Chicago in search of employment.

Kenney was shocked by the living and working conditions she encountered in the city. After working in several different binderies, she became convinced that women workers must organize to secure better working conditions and adequate compensation. Through her association with a girls' social club, Kenney came in contact with the Women's Federal Union #2703 of the American Federation of Labor (AFL), and she organized the Chicago Women's Bindery Union. In addition, she was elected a delegate to the Chicago Trades and Labor Assembly, and she soon assumed a leadership role in that organization.

Jane Addams, the founder of **Hull House**, proved an important ally. She invited the women bookbinders to hold their meetings in the settlement, and she financed the printing and oversaw the distribution of circulars for the union. In addition, Addams assisted Kenney in organizing a boarding club for working girls. While working at Hull House, Kenney met **Florence Kelley**. The two women cooperated with the Chicago Trades and Labor Assembly on an investigation of sweatshops, and their research was instrumental in the establishment of the Illinois Factory Inspection Department in 1893.

Kelley was appointed the chief inspector of the department, and Kenney served as one of her deputies.

While with the Women's Bindery Union, Kenney met Samuel Gompers, the president of the American Federation of Labor. In 1892, Gompers appointed her the AFL's first woman organizer. Kenney spent five months organizing women garment workers in New York City, shirtwaist makers in Troy, New York, and printers, binders, shoe workers, and carpet weavers in Massachusetts. While in Boston, Kenney met and became engaged to John F. O'Sullivan, the labor editor of the *Boston Globe*.

By October 1893, Kenney was back in Chicago. Although she was not re-appointed by the Executive Council of the AFL, she remained active in Hull House-sponsored labor activities and continued to organize women garment workers in Chicago.

The following year, Kenney married John O'Sullivan. They lived in Boston, and John O'Sullivan encouraged his wife to pursue her interest in labor. Mary O'Sullivan soon became active in the Boston reform community. She and John lived for a short time at the Boston settlement **Denison House** when their own home was destroyed by fire. She organized the Union for Industrial Progress, and as the organization's executive secretary, she studied working conditions in Boston's factories and workshops. With the help of **Mary Morton Kehew** and the Women's Educational and Industrial Union, O'Sullivan organized women rubber makers and laundry workers.

In 1902, John O'Sullivan was killed in a train accident. To support herself and her four children, Mary secured a job as a rent collector and property manager with a Boston real estate association. In addition, she managed a model tenement sponsored by the local Improved Dwelling Association. O'Sullivan also taught English and housekeeping skills to newly arrived immigrants and operated a summer camp for working girls on behalf of Denison House.

Throughout these years, O'Sullivan never abandoned her labor work, and in 1903, she joined with the labor activist **William English Walling** to organize the National **Women's Trade Union League**. She served as the league's secretary and vice president. Although she was committed to cooperative efforts, O'Sullivan was not afraid to exert her independence. When the Boston branch of the Women's Trade Union League failed to support the

Lawrence textile strike, she went to the aid of the strikers, bringing together the major parties involved and thereby hastened the resolution of the strike.

In 1914, O'Sullivan became a factory inspector for the Massachusetts Department of Labor and Industries, a position she held until her retirement in 1934.

Bibliography
Davis, *Spearheads for Reform: The Social Settlements and the Progressive Movement, 1890–1914*; *Dictionary of American Biography*, supl. 3, pp. 575–77; Henry, *Women and the Labor Movement*; *Notable American Women, 1607-1950*, vol. 2, pp. 655–56.

Out of Work (1904)

Out of Work is a good example of the way in which social investigators in the opening decades of the twentieth century applied scientific principles to the field of social investigation. **Frances Kellor**, the author, was a social investigator with a particular interest in the problems encountered by black migrant women as they relocated to the North. She was also concerned with the parallel situation faced by European immigrants once they arrived in the United States. Kellor's research emphasized the significant role that environment played in the adjustment of the newly arrived, both migrants and immigrants, to their new homes.

Kellor was a fellow of the **College Settlements Association**, an organization that sponsored settlements in various cities and provided funding for men and women to spend time in settlements and to conduct research projects. As a part of her fellowship, she investigated employment agencies, and the results were published in 1904 under the title, *Out of Work*.

In this study, Kellor investigated the policies and procedures used by a network of employment agencies in New York, Chicago, Philadelphia, and Boston. During the course of her research, Kellor uncovered the graft and corrupting influence that marked the activities of many employment agencies in operation at the time. These agencies were supposed to help young black women from Southern states to find safe, legitimate employment once they arrived in Northern cities. Instead, in many instances, they exploited the women by taking their money and in some instances forcing them into **prostitution**.

Out of Work drew attention to this serious situation and contributed to the efforts to curb these exploitative practices. It also served as an example for other reformers of the power of using carefully conducted research to effect social change.

Bibliography
Kellor, *Out of Work*.

Outdoor Recreation League

In congested, overpopulated cities where men, women, and children worked long hours under unsafe conditions and lived in equally unsafe tenements, access to adequate play and recreation space was particularly important. Settlement workers were especially aware of this need, and they formed working coalitions with other social reformers to convince local officials to set aside areas for parks and play spaces. As was true with many other reform crusades, the New York City settlement workers were among the first to be active in this campaign, and the Outdoor Recreation League that they established was an approach that reformers adopted in other cities.

In 1887, New York City passed a park act that acknowledged the need to establish small parks around the city and to equip these areas with play apparatus. Although some parks were created, no provisions were made to designate portions of them for use as playgrounds for the city's children.

Charles Stover, the head resident of the **University Settlement**, knew from firsthand experience that children in crowded city neighborhoods needed somewhere safe to play. In 1890, he recruited the support of the former mayor of New York City, Abram S. Hewitt, and the **Social Reform Club**, a group of New York City-based settlement workers and social activists, to found the Society for Parks and Playgrounds in New York. One of the society's goals was to work with municipal authorities to set aside portions of public parks to be used exclusively for children's recreation. For a short time, the Society for Parks and Playgrounds operated a large playground at Ninety-Second Street and Second Avenue, but Stover and his group found it difficult to maintain momentum for their cause.

In 1895, interest in public playgrounds was renewed when a committee chaired by **James B. Reynolds** of the University Settlement worked with representatives from the New York City mayor's office to select sites for two parks on the Lower East Side of Manhattan. Although the city purchased the property and tore down the tenements on it, the parks were never constructed.

Despite these setbacks, Stover did not lose interest in the crusade for adequate play space. In 1898, to obtain support for his convictions about the importance of recreation space, he called together settlement workers, philanthropists, social reformers, and community leaders to form the Outdoor Recreation League.

In addition to Stover, the other founding members were **Mary K. Simkhovitch** of **Greenwich House**, **Elizabeth Williams** and **Jane Robbins** of the **College Settlement**, and **Lillian Wald** of the **Henry Street Settlement**. The league's Advisory Board was composed of well-known reformers and philanthropists such as **Jacob A. Riis**, **Felix Adler**, Nicholas Murray Butler, and **Richard Watson Gilder**. The College Settlement served as headquarters for the league.

One of the Outdoor Recreation League's first projects was to induce the municipal authorities to clear a lot at Canal and Jefferson Streets on New York's Lower East Side. Wald was instrumental in convincing the Commissioner of Health to persuade the appropriate officials to clean up the lot and to put a fence around it. Stover and his associates then outfitted the lot with playground equipment that they purchased with funds collected from private donors. This first league-sponsored playground opened on June 3, 1899, and became known as Seward Park.

After this initial success, the Outdoor Recreation League channeled its energies into the campaign to convince municipal authorities of the need to create city-owned playgrounds outfitted with recreation equipment, basketball courts, and sandboxes. The group achieved a degree of success, and in recognition of his work and contributions to the parks and playground movement, Stover was appointed Parks Commissioner of New York City in 1910.

The Outdoor Recreation League's work was re-created on the national level by organizations such as the **National Recreation and Park Association**. The league continued to function in New York City into the second decade of the twentieth century. Gradually, its work was taken over by the New York City municipal authorities.

Bibliography

Davis, *Spearheads for Reform: The Social Settlements and the Progressive Movement, 1890–1914*; Klein, *Prisoners of Progress: American Industrial Cities, 1850–1920*; Woods, *The Handbook of Settlements*.

The Outlook

Social welfare workers realized the importance of exposing the problems they encountered, particularly in urban centers, and of suggesting possible reforms. One way for them to accomplish this task, was to write articles for the many periodicals that enjoyed substantial circulation during the late nineteenth century in the United States. One of the publications that many settlement workers published in was *The Outlook*, edited by **Lyman Abbott**. *The Outlook* had begun as a religious periodical but had gradually modified its editorial profile to become a journal of social and political trends.

In 1869, the J.B. Ford & Company gained control of the *Church Union*, a Baptist paper that had been established by Henry E. Childs in 1867. Ford & Company were the publishers of the clergyman and lecturer Henry Ward Beecher's *Life of Christ* and of *Plymouth Pulpit*, a weekly periodical that published Beecher's sermons. Beecher had been editor of another Ford publication, the *Independent*, and Ford decided to make him the editor of the *Church Union*. Beecher accepted and suggested that the publication's name be changed to the *Christian Union*, which he believed would broaden its appeal. This new name was adopted, and gradually, the paper changed from a religious journal to a general family periodical.

Beecher contributed a regular column to the *Christian Union* entitled, "Lecture Room Talks." Other popular attractions included serials and essays from Beecher's sister, Harriet Beecher Stowe, and contributions from Louisa May Alcott, George MacDonald, Edward Eggleston, and Edward Everett Hale. Within a short time, the *Christian Union* included features for everyone: old, young, men, women. In addition to Beecher's "Lecture Room Talk," the other departments included "The Outlook," a collection of shorter, informative editorials; "Public Opinion," which were extracts from popular periodicals and books; and "Inquiring Friends," a theological question and answer feature.

By the end of the 1870s, Ford & Company had suffered a number of setbacks that forced the firm into bankruptcy. Additionally, Beecher was involved in a public marital scandal. In the ensuing reorganization, **Lyman Abbott**, a disciple of Beecher and an accomplished religious journalist, became managing editor of the *Christian Union*.

Abbott set about transforming the paper into a journal of opinion. Some of the older contributors remained, including Harriet Beecher Stowe, and a number of new ones were brought in, including the Episcopal clergyman **Phillips Brooks**, who contributed religious essays, and John Burroughs, who wrote nature studies. Circulation increased steadily during the 1880s. Over time, correspondents from Boston, Chicago, and Washington were added to the staff. In 1891, the *Christian Union* became know as *The Outlook*, which had been the name of an editorial comment department for the past 20 years.

This name change marked a shift from an emphasis on religious subjects to a broader scope that also included public affairs and arts and letters. Charles B. Spahr joined the staff of *The Outlook* during the 1890s and contributed pieces on industrial and social subjects. During the opening years of the twentieth century, coverage of political topics expanded. *The Outlook* published **Jacob Riis**'s "Theodore Roosevelt the Citizen" (1903), and Roosevelt's own work, "The Man with the Muck Rake" (1906). Three significant autobiographies also appeared in the pages of *The Outlook*. They were *Up from Slavery* by Booker T. Washington, *The Making of an American* by Jacob Riis, and *Memories of a Hundred Years* by Edward Everett Hale.

By 1902, under Abbott's editorship, circulation for *The Outlook* reached 100,000, and it remained steady for the next 20 years. During this time Riis and Spahr wrote frequently about immigration, and Abbott continued to publish book reviews, poetry, and travel pieces. In 1908, Theodore Roosevelt became a contributing editor, publishing two series, "Nationalism and Progress" and "The American Workers." Settlement workers and other social welfare reformers were frequent contributors. Over time, more photographs were included in the pages of *The Outlook*.

Lyman Abbott died in 1923, and his son, E.H. Abbott, a Congregationalist Minister who had been his father's assistant for 20 years, became editor of *The Outlook*. Circulation declined despite a program that offered the journal to schools as a record of current events.

In 1927, *The Outlook* was sold to Francis A. Bellamy, a journalist and author who eventually merged it with another publication, the *Independent*. The new title was *The Outlook and Independent*. In 1932, *The Outlook and Independent* became a monthly, but it suspended publication after only a few months. It re-emerged in September 1932 as *The New Outlook* with former New York Governor **Alfred**

E. Smith as editor. Smith remained with the journal for only 18 months. In June 1935, *The New Outlook* ceased publication.

Bibliography

Mott, *A History of American Magazines*, vol. 3, pp. 422–35.

Ovington, Mary White
social researcher, settlement worker, civil rights advocate
b. April 11, 1865; d. July 15, 1951.

For the most part, the mainstream American Settlement Movement largely ignored the needs of black city dwellers. In some instances, this snub reflected the personal bias of the settlement workers. Other settlement workers were responding to the prevailing prejudice of the society at large, and they feared losing the support of their benefactors who often would not support charity for black people. Although some settlements such as **South End House** in Boston had separate satellite houses for black neighbors, little effort was made to integrate the settlements' programs and services. (*See* **Robert Gould Shaw House**.) In regard to her attitudes about race and her efforts to provide settlement services to blacks, Mary White Ovington was an exception among her settlement colleagues.

Ovington's sensitivity to the matter of race was nurtured by her parents who were ardent abolitionists. Throughout her career as a social reformer, she was dedicated to improving the living and working conditions of blacks. She believed that it was the isolation between blacks and whites that created racial tension. As a social reformer working within the settlement movement, she was confident that if the races could live together in an integrated, model tenement that much of the racial tension would be dispelled. Her work in the settlement movement provided Ovington with an opportunity to pursue this goal.

A Brooklyn native, Ovington attended the Brackett School and the Parker Institute before spending two years, 1891–1893, at Radcliffe College. There she maintained an interest in social causes, particularly the economic conditions of both blacks and whites. After leaving Radcliffe, Ovington became the registrar at the Pratt Institute. From 1896 to 1903, she served as the head resident at the Greenpoint Settlement, which was located on Twenty-Third Street in New York City and was operated by the Pratt Institute Neighborhood Association. Her work at the settlement brought her face-to-face with the difficulties experienced by the white working class, but more important, she witnessed firsthand the tragic life that blacks endured.

In 1903, Ovington attended a lecture by the educator and lecturer Booker T. Washington at a meeting of the **Social Reform Club** in New York City. Washington's speech galvanized her feelings about the plight of blacks and inspired her to take immediate positive action. That same year she left the Greenpoint Settlement to take a position as a fellow at the recently established **Greenwich House**, a settlement on the Lower West Side of Manhattan. Here she undertook an economic and social survey of every income level of the 60,000 black people living in New York City at the time. She interviewed people, inspected tenements, and worked with boys' and girls' clubs to gain insight into working and living conditions. Ovington's goal was to establish an integrated settlement house, although she knew that this idea would not be well received.

In 1904, Ovington contacted Dr. W.E.B. DuBois and told him of her research and her plan for an integrated settlement. DuBois was supportive, and this initial contact marked the beginning of a 30-year personal and professional relationship during which the two cooperated on a number of undertakings.

In 1904 at DuBois's invitation, Ovington attended the Atlanta Conference where she saw firsthand the racially segregated Southern society. Two years later while working as a reporter for the *New York Evening Post,* Ovington attended a meeting of DuBois's Niagara Movement which was held in Harper's Ferry; she then toured the South researching a series of articles about the condition of blacks under the Jim Crow Laws. When she returned to New York City, Ovington continued to work on her survey. She lived in the Tuskegee Apartments, a model housing project for blacks which she helped establish.

On February 12, 1909, the centennial of Abraham Lincoln's birth, Ovington, settlement worker and political activist **Henry Moskowitz**, and social activist **William English Walling** met in New York City and organized a national "Conference on the Status of the Negro in the United States." The participants adopted a platform recognizing the fundamental rights of blacks and calling for the end of forced segregation, the right to vote, the extension of educational advantages, and the enforcement of the fourteenth and fifteenth amendments. In addition, the conference established a permanent committee charged with defending the rights of blacks across the United States. This committee eventually evolved into the National Association for the Advancement of Colored People (NAACP).

Until her retirement in 1947, Ovington's career was closely aligned with the work of the NAACP. For 10 years she served as the chair of the board of the association. She was active in the fight for anti-lynching legislation, worked to alleviate the racism and prejudice faced by black soldiers in World War I, and raised money to hire attorneys who represented NAACP-supported clients fighting housing segregation and other injustices.

In 1911, Ovington published the results of her survey in a book entitled *Half a Man: The Status of the Negro in New York*. Based on comprehensive research that included an examination of 1900 Census records, juvenile court records, church visits, and extensive in-depth interviews, Ovington's study began with a brief history of race relations in the United States. It then went on to describe the current state of housing conditions, the discrimination in the workplace, the condition of women and children, and the segregation in public places that Ovington had uncovered during the course of her research.

During the 1930s, Ovington worked to secure equal access to government work projects and to eliminate literacy tests for voters. She took up the fight against segregation and discrimination in the armed forces once again during World War II. A tireless fighter for racial equality, Ovington retired in 1947 and died at her home in Massachusetts in 1951.

Ovington's interest in racial issues was relatively unique among the men and women who worked in the American Settlement Movement. Before she started working at the Greenpoint Settlement she had little contact with black people, but seeing their difficult lives, she was moved to action. Ovington dedicated her life to the struggle for racial equality, which earned her the name "The Mother of the New Emancipation."

Bibliography

Jackson, *Encyclopedia of New York City*, p. 870; Lasch-Quinn, *Black Neighbors: Race and the Limits of Reform in the American Settlement House Movement, 1880–1945*; Trattner, *Biographical Dictionary of Social Welfare in America*, pp. 578–81.

P

Paine, Robert Treat
attorney, philanthropist, reformer
b. October 28, 1835; d. August 11, 1910.

Robert Treat Paine was a wealthy philanthropist who gave more than just money to social welfare causes. Like many people of his social class, he was not interested in merely distributing relief to the poor. He wanted to provide people with an opportunity to help themselves. Although his interest in housing reform occupied a good deal of his time and talents, Paine also devoted himself to children's causes and to providing educational opportunities for both working men and for college students who wanted to pursue social reform work.

Paine was educated at the Boston Latin School and graduated from Harvard in 1855. After spending a year at Harvard Law School, Paine toured Europe for two years before being admitted to the Massachusetts bar in 1859. For the next 11 years, he enjoyed a successful career as an attorney accumulating a substantial fortune in railroad, real estate, and mining ventures.

At the age of 35 in 1870, Paine retired from the law to begin a second career as a philanthropist and reformer. The first cause he took up was housing reform. His work with various relief agencies gave Paine firsthand knowledge of the squalid housing conditions endured by the poor. He recognized the relationship between adequate housing and the improvement of people's social and economic condition and believed that home ownership would help solve the housing problem of the inner city.

In his philanthropic work, Paine sought to assist what he described as the "substantial workers," who despite their best efforts at hard work and thrifty living were unable to rise above their poverty, the people whom other reformers characterized as the "worthy poor." To achieve his plan for home ownership, Paine built a few brick row houses in the inner Tremont Street district in Boston. A few years later he invested in a building project in Roxbury, Massachusetts, that between 1886 and 1890 built a development of small, two-story brick houses. Each single-family unit was outfitted with plumbing. Several years later Paine was involved in another construction project that provided larger detached houses in the Tremont Street district. These units were financed in a somewhat creative manner that involved amortizing the mortgages, a process that permitted the gradual payment of the mortgages by prorating, proportionately distributing the expense of the mortgage over a fixed period of time.

To further his housing reform work, Paine established the Workingmen's Building Association in 1888, which supervised the planning and financing of his housing projects. Using $25,000 of his own money, he also organized the Workingmen's Loan Association in 1888 to provide mortgages at one percent, one and one-half percent lower than the average rate.

One of Paine's most significant contributions to the social reform efforts of the time, though, was his work with the **Boston Associated Charities**, which he co-founded in 1879. Paine served as president of this organization from 1879 to 1907 and is credited with devising its motto, "Not Alms but a Friend."

In addition to his work in housing reform and with the Associated Charities, Paine served as a director of both the American Prison Association and the **Boston Children's Aid Society**. He was also active in the peace movement, serving as president of the American Peace Society from 1891 until his death in 1910. In 1893 Paine lead the World's Fair Peace Congress at the World's Columbian Exposition in Chicago.

One of Paine's most original undertakings was the Wells Memorial Institute for Workingmen that he organized in 1879. He funded the cost of a building to house the institute two years later. The institute was similar to the Workingmen's Center that Paine had seen during his travels in England. It functioned as a central gathering place for Boston's working men. Trade school classes were held in the building, which also served as a meeting hall for organized labor groups and as the site of a cooperative bank. Paine took an active interest in the institute, often attending meetings and participating in discussions.

Paine was also forward-thinking in his sponsorship of the Robert Treat Paine Fellowship, which he and his wife, Lydia, established with a $10,000 grant in 1887. This fellowship was awarded to Harvard students interested in applying the scientific method to the study of social problems. In 1890, Robert and Lydia Paine established a $200,000 trust, the Robert Treat Paine Association, to encourage the physical, spiritual, and moral welfare of working men and women. The association sponsored a number of agencies including the Working Girls' Club and the Windsor Home for Aged People.

Besides his reform work, Paine was also active in his church. He has been described as one of the most prominent laymen in the Episcopal Church in the United States. Raised a Unitarian, he began attending Trinity Church in Boston in 1870 and enjoyed a long and close friendship with **Phillips Brooks**, the Rector of Trinity Church. Paine was a delegate to the General Convention on several occasions, served as a vestryman or warden of Trinity Church, and was chairman of the Trinity Church Building Committee.

Paine had a long and productive life and maintained an active interest in social welfare and religious work up to his death in 1910. Like the men and women who worked in the settlement movement, Paine realized the relationship between adequate housing and the social and economic conditions of the poor, and he devoted his time and his fortune to providing affordable housing for the poor. Paine also financed scholarships to encourage young women and men to seek professional training as social researchers and as settlement or social workers.

Bibliography

Dictionary of American Biography, vol. 7, pp. 158–59; Trattner, *Biographical Dictionary of Social Welfare in America*, pp. 583–85; Warner, *Streetcar Suburbs: The Process of Growth in Boston, 1870–1900*.

Peck, Lillie M.
settlement worker and administrator, reformer
b. December 28, 1888; d. February 21, 1957.

Lillie Peck's settlement career spanned the local, national, and international arenas. She believed strongly in the principle of the neighborhood as the basic social unit, and she spent almost 20 years as a settlement resident immersing herself in all aspects of the work. But Peck also understood the advantage of reaching beyond the local level to interact and cooperate with other settlement workers. This understanding is reflected in her work both with the **National Federation of Settlements** (NFS), the coalition of settlement houses from across the United States, and with the International Federation of Settlements, which encouraged cooperation between American and European houses.

While she was an undergraduate at Simmons College, Peck volunteered at the **South End House** settlement in Boston. Following her graduation in 1913, Peck went to live and work at South End House where she gained valuable experience in all aspects of settlement work over the next 17 years.

Peck's interests extended beyond South End House, though. Between 1918 and 1924, she was secretary of the **Boston Social Union**, a coalition of Boston area settlements, and from 1921 to 1922 she worked with Ellen Coolidge, another resident of South End House, to establish the International Federation of Settlements. During the 1920s Peck traveled in Europe cultivating a communications network between American and European settlements.

In 1928, Peck became the assistant head worker at South End House, sharing this responsibility with **Albert J. Kennedy**, who was also serving as executive secretary of the National Federation of Settlements. In 1930, Kennedy moved the NFS's headquarters from Boston to New York City. At the time, Peck became assistant secretary of the federation, and four years later, she replaced Kennedy as the head of the NFS.

During the 1930s and through World War II, Peck lived at the **Henry Street Settlement** on New York City's Lower East Side, a testimony to her belief in the fundamental settlement principle of sharing in the life of a neighborhood. Peck retired as head of the National Federation of Settlements in 1947.

Peck became especially interested in social work at the international level in her later years. She received the Barnett Fellowship, a research grant named in honor of **Samuel Barnett**, the founder of **Toynbee Hall**, the first English settlement. Between 1946 and 1949 she used the fellowship to study the British community center movement. In 1949, during the Berlin Blockade, Peck worked with the United States military government to re-establish neighborhood centers in Germany. She returned to Germany in 1951 to establish a settlement house in Bremen. Peck also served as the NFS representative to UNESCO in 1952. Four years later she was elected honorary president of the International Federation of Settlements in recognition of her contributions to the organization over 30 years.

Peck remained active in the International Federation of Settlements right up to her death in 1957. Her emphasis on human relationships in settlement work and her ability to work cooperatively with settlement workers on all levels were important contributions to the American Settlement Movement.

Bibliography

Trattner, *Biographical Dictionary of Social Welfare in America*, pp. 587–89.

Perkins, Frances

social worker, reformer, cabinet secretary
b. April 10, 1880; d. May 14, 1965.

During Frances Perkins's career as a social welfare advocate, New York State Industrial Commissioner, and U. S. Secretary of Labor, she developed a number of close working relationships with settlement workers and other social reformers.

Born in Boston, Perkins graduated from Worcester Classical High School in 1898 and received a B.A. from Mount Holyoke College four years later. While still a student at Mount Holyoke, Perkins heard the labor reformer **Florence Kelley** speak about the National **Consumers' League**'s efforts to eradicate sweatshops and child labor. She was so moved by Kelley's presentation that she joined the league and decided to devote her life to social service.

Unsuccessful in her attempt to secure a position as a family visitor for the New York **Charity Organization Society**, Perkins spent two years (1902–1904) teaching at various girls' schools in New England. Between 1904 and 1907, she taught at Ferry Hall, a fashionable school in Lake Forest, Illinois. During these years, she pursued her interest in social reform by working weekends and during school vacations at two Chicago Settlements: **Chicago Commons** and **Hull House**. Her settlement experience helped Perkins galvanize her commitment to social service and helped her obtain a position as executive secretary of the Philadelphia Research and Protective Association, which had been organized in 1907 to protect newly arrived young girls.

In 1909, Perkins won a fellowship to study at the New York School of Philanthropy. (*See* **Columbia University Graduate School of Social Work.**) Her social survey of malnutrition among children in the Hell's Kitchen slum district helped her to earn a M.A. from Columbia University in 1910. That same year Perkins became executive secretary of the New York Consumers' League, where she worked with Kelley and other national settlement leaders. In addition to working as the league's lobbyist in Albany, Perkins developed expertise in the sanitary regulation of bakeries and fire prevention in factories. The passage of the league-sponsored 54-hour work week bill for women and children in 1912 marked Perkins's first experience with the legislative process.

Beginning in 1912, Perkins spent five years as a member of the New York Committee on Safety, a citizen's group formed in the aftermath of the **Triangle Shirtwaist Company Fire** in which more than 140 young women were killed on March 25, 1911. She served as the committee's representative to the **New York State Factory Investigating Commission** that had been established as a result of the fire to look into working and sanitary conditions. Based on her work, Perkins was acknowledged by her peers as an expert in industrial and labor conditions.

Her work with the Factory Investigating Commission allowed Perkins to renew an important professional working relationship with the leader of the New York State Assembly, **Alfred E. Smith**. The two had first worked together when Perkins was a lobbyist in Albany. When Smith became governor of New York in 1918, he appointed Perkins to the New York State Industrial Commission, the agency charged with administering the state's labor laws. Perkins served as a commission member from 1923 to 1926 and as chair from 1926 to 1929, all the while gaining valuable administrative and political skills.

Smith's successor as governor, Franklin Delano Roosevelt, appointed Perkins State Industrial Commissioner in 1929, making her the first woman responsible for the administration of the New York State Labor Department. During the Depression, Perkins worked to expand the Labor Department's role in dealing with the economic crisis. She stressed the need to collect reliable statistics and enhanced the resources of the state's employment agencies. In addition, she acquired a useful knowledge of unemployment insurance.

Following his election as president of the United States in 1932, Roosevelt appointed Perkins secretary of labor. She reorganized the Labor Department, which included establishing the Division of Labor Standards that was charged with providing assistance to state labor departments. Additionally, Perkins served as chair of the Presidential Committee on Economic Security, which was responsible for developing a national social security program. Perkins pushed the committee beyond its initial charge to provide for, among other items, maternal and child health care, child welfare services, and assistance to the blind. The committee's work resulted in the passage of the Social Security Act of 1935.

Perkins served as secretary of labor during the 12 years of Roosevelt's presidency (1932–1945). President Truman appointed her to the United States Civil Service Commission in 1946. She served on the commission until 1953. After leaving government service, Perkins was a visiting professor at the Cornell University School of Industrial Relations.

Bibliography

Dictionary of American Biography, supl. 7, pp. 606–10; Jackson, *Encyclopedia of New York City*, p. 894; Martin, *Madame Secretary: Frances Perkins*; Sicherman, *Notable American Women: The Modern Period*, pp. 535–39; Trattner, *Biographical Dictionary of Social Welfare in America*, pp. 589–91.

Perry, Clarence
teacher, school center activist, recreation reformer
b. March 4, 1872; d. September 5, 1944.

Clarence Perry's career in social welfare reform was centered around the **Russell Sage Foundation**, a private philanthropic foundation that provided funding for many research projects and reform crusades. Perry focused his energies on the school center movement and on recreation projects. Like many reformers at the time, he recognized the importance of providing adequate recreation equipment and space for people living in congested urban centers.

Poverty deprived Perry of many happy childhood memories. Born in Truxton, New York, where his father worked as a farmer and a teamster, Perry sold newspapers to help support the family. Lack of money caused him to postpone attending college until he was in his twenties. He spent two years (1893–1894 and 1896–1897) at Stanford University before transferring to Cornell where he earned a B.S. degree in 1899.

Perry then secured a job as a teacher. He spent two years teaching in the Philippines before enrolling in graduate courses at Teachers College, Columbia University in the summer of 1904. He spent the 1904–1905 academic year as a high school principal in Ponce, Puerto Rico. There he met Leonard P. Ayres, the general superintendent of schools who was later secretary of the Russell Sage Foundation's investigation of backward children.

In 1907, the Russell Sage Foundation established a committee on Playground Extension. Two years later this committee became the Division of Recreation in the foundation's Department of Child Hygiene. That same year, on Ayres's recommendation, Perry was appointed to the staff of the Russell Sage Foundation. When the Division of Recreation became a separate Department of Recreation in 1913, Perry became associate director, a position he held until his retirement in 1937.

Perry considered the public school to be a more important focus for providing social unity than the settlement. As a result, he became involved in the school center movement, which advocated expanding the after-hours use of public school buildings for recreation, social, civic, and educational purposes. Many settlement residents were also active in the school center movement, particularly those from smaller houses that could not provide extensive meeting space or access to gymnasiums and other recreational facilities for neighborhood residents.

In 1911, Perry attended the first meeting of the National Conference on Civic and Neighborhood Center Development, which was held in Madison, Wisconsin. He found it invigorating. During the next decade, he advocated the school center movement through the Division of Recreation at the Russell Sage Foundation in cooperation with the extension division of the University of Wisconsin and the National Community Center Association.

Perry was most interested in supervised group recreation, which he believed would have a positive impact on community residents by building character and providing citizenship training. His most important contribution to the school center movement was promotion. The Russell Sage Foundation's Division of Recreation published three books and 20 pamphlets that provided instructions on techniques for establishing school centers. Although he had devoted a considerable amount of time and energy to the school center movement, by late 1921 Perry had come to the conclusion that the movement was a failure because for a variety of reasons, it had never been fully established in any communities.

During the 1920s, Perry was active in the development of the Playground and Recreation Association's Training School for Recreation Workers. At about this time, he also began to turn his attention to the fields of housing and planning and became identified with the neighborhood unit concept. For Perry, the neighborhood unit was the equivalent of a traditional village in which each person took an active interest in the lives of his neighbors. Interpersonal relationships were encouraged by planning the physical environment around a central community space. Perry's concept of the neighborhood unit was based in part on his own experience of living as an adult in Forest Hills Gardens, a model garden suburb on Long Island that had been planned by the Russell Sage Foundation.

In 1929, Perry was asked to contribute to the Social Division of the Russell Sage Foundation's Regional Plan of New York and its environs. He was also a member of the **New York City Tenement House Department**'s Slum Clearance Committee. Perry served on the Community Action Committee of the New York City Housing Authority, and he participated in the 1931 President's Conference on Home Building and Home Ownership.

Perry's participation in these committees occupied a substantial amount of his time during his final years. He died at home in New Rochelle, New York, after a long illness. During his career as a reformer, Perry had a good deal in common with the men and women of the American Settlement Movement. He shared their concern for providing adequate play and recreation facilities for urban dwellers and recognized the value of the neighborhood and the identification with one's neighbors as an important component of the social welfare reform process.

Bibliography
Dictionary of American Biography, supl. 3, pp. 600–01; Glenn, *Russell Sage Foundation, 1907–1946*.

Pink, Louis Heaton
attorney, settlement worker, housing reformer, insurance reformer
b. December 4, 1882; d. May 18, 1955.

Although Louis Pink was initially interested in a career as a settlement worker, he chose to become a lawyer. However, he never abandoned his interest in what settlement workers and other reformers were accomplishing. Nor did he sever his professional ties to the New York reform community. Instead, Pink managed to combine his legal and social welfare interests to play a significant part in the establishment of New York State's social welfare system as a housing reformer and as a member of the State Insurance Department.

Pink graduated from St. Lawrence University in 1904, and the following year he enrolled in New York Law School. At this time, he also joined the **University Settlement**, which was located on New York's Lower East Side. While a resident at the settlement, Pink studied New York City's so-called Old Law Tenements, houses built before the **New York Tenement House Law of 1901**. Although he was particularly interested in settlement work, Pink chose a career in the law, which he believed offered him better prospects for the future. After graduating law school, he clerked in the law office of Judge William J. Gaynor in Brooklyn.

By 1910, Pink had returned to social reform work, becoming the head worker at the United Neighborhood Guild Settlement in Brooklyn, New York. There he established lodging houses for men and boys and became interested in the school center movement. However, after three years, Pink resumed his legal practice, this time concentrating on insurance litigation and bankruptcy cases with the New York State Insurance Department.

New York established a State Board of Housing in 1926, which was charged with investigating incentives for limited-dividend housing projects. Pink was appointed to this board by Governor **Alfred E. Smith**, most likely at the suggestion of Smith's advisor, **Belle Moskowitz**, whom Pink had known from his time at the University Settlement. He approached his new responsibilities enthusiastically, overseeing the construction of more than a dozen housing projects. In 1927, Pink published *The New Day in Housing*, a review of model tenement construction in Europe and the United States.

During the early 1930s, Pink began to reconsider his commitment to the state's housing program, which was based on tax incentives for limited-dividend builders. He began to lobby for the creation of a state housing authority that was authorized to raise funds for construction through the sale of tax-exempt bonds. In addition, he allied himself with a group of settlement workers and housing reformers who lobbied for the creation of a municipal housing authority that would assume responsibility for slum clearance and new construction.

To accomplish his goals, Pink joined with **Mary K. Simkhovitch**, founder and head resident of **Greenwich House**, and **Helen Alfred**, a resident of **Madison House**, as charter members of the **Public Housing Conference** (PHC). As a member of the PHC, Pink submitted a plan for the creation of an independent housing authority that had the power to condemn property and to construct and operate new housing. When the New York City Housing Authority was created in 1934, Pink was appointed to serve on this body. Two years later he was re-appointed to the State Board of Housing.

During the 1930s, Pink also pursued a parallel interest in insurance. In 1932, he joined the New York State Insurance Department and was responsible for reorganizing bankrupt title and mortgage guarantee companies. Three years later, he became state insurance superintendent. Over the next seven years, Pink was involved in a number of insurance-related initiatives including establishing low-cost savings bank life insurance, permitting insurance companies to invest in limited dividend housing, and re-codifying New York State's insurance laws.

When he resigned as state insurance superintendent in 1942, Pink turned his attention to the field of health insurance, becoming president of the Associated Hospital Service (AHS) of New York, also known as Blue Cross. Pink concentrated his efforts on signing up corporate employers and unions, and by 1949, 4.2 million people received health coverage under AHS.

Before his death in 1955, Pink was developing an interracial cooperative housing project that was to be called Queensview. Pink's career as a housing reformer was firmly grounded in the settlements, and his experience as a settlement worker inspired him to provide affordable housing and health insurance. His reform efforts formed the basis for New York State's social welfare system.

Bibliography
Trattner, *Biographical Dictionary of Social Welfare in America*, pp. 594–97.

The Pittsburgh Survey

In the opening decades of the twentieth century, settlement workers and other reformers continued to study many different facets of urban life to find ways to improve living conditions. The Charities Publication Committee of the social welfare journal *Charities and the Commons* (*see* **the Survey**) was organized in 1905 to sponsor these types of social investigations. The success of the committee's first two undertakings, a study of living conditions in Washington, DC, and an examination of the treatment of blacks in a number of Northern cities, inspired a more ambitious study that came to be known as the Pittsburgh Survey.

In 1906, the publication committee provided an initial appropriation of $1,000 to explore the feasibility of conducting a systematic examination of all aspects of life in an industrial city. The city of Pittsburgh, Pennsylvania, was selected, and in 1907, the work began.

Paul U. Kellogg, editor of *Charities and The Commons,* was selected to direct the work of the Pittsburgh Survey. **The Russell Sage Foundation** (RSF) provided an original grant of $7,000, which was predicated on the assumption that the work would be completed within three months. In the end, the study took 18 months to complete. The RSF appropriated an additional $30,000 to complete the research and another $20,000 to cover the costs of publishing the results.

Kellogg assembled a team of social welfare workers and researchers who over the course of almost two years investigated all aspects of life in Pittsburgh—health, housing, sanitation, and industry among other things. The researchers examined the consequences of low wages and the lack of urban planning. They looked into industrial health and safety issues and documented the cost of industrial accidents in both human and economic terms. During the course of their investigation, the researchers were assisted by William Matthews, the head resident at **Kingsley House**.

The initial results of the survey were published in three issues of *Charities and the Commons*. Between 1909 and 1914, the full results were published in six hardcover volumes that were illustrated with graphs, charts, and photographs, some of which had been taken by the photographer **Lewis Hine** who had done memorable work for the **National Child Labor Committee**. The Pittsburgh Survey series included Elizabeth Beardsley Butler, *Women and the Trades, Pittsburgh* (1909); **Crystal Eastman**, *Work Accidents and the Law* (1910); Margaret F. Byington, *Homestead: The Household of a Mill Town* (1910); Paul U. Kellogg, editor, *The Pittsburgh District Civic Frontage* (1914), and *Wage-earning Pittsburgh* (1914).

The impact of the Pittsburgh Survey was far reaching. It inspired similar investigations in other cities. Some communities organized their own studies, and the Russell Sage Foundation sponsored six in cities across the United States including Atlanta, Georgia, and Topeka, Kansas. In acknowledgement of the survey's influence, in 1909 *Charities and the Commons* changed its name to the ***Survey***.

Bibliography

Carson, *Settlement Folk: Social Thought and the American Settlement Movement, 1885–1930*; Chambers, *Paul U. Kellogg and the Survey*; Trattner, *Biographical Dictionary of Social Welfare in America*, "Paul U. Kellogg," pp. 446–49; Trattner, *From Poor Law to Welfare State: A History of Social Welfare in America*.

Playground and Recreation Association of America *See*

National Recreation and Park Association

Playground Association of America *See* National Recreation and

Park Association

Poverty (1904)

Poverty was **Robert Hunter**'s attempt to define poverty and estimate its extent in the United States, to describe its effects, and to offer suggestions for remedial action. Written in 1904, it was Hunter's second book. Hunter had lived and worked in settlement houses for almost eight years, first at **Hull House** in Chicago and then as the head resident of the **University Settlement** in New York City. He resigned from the University Settlement in 1903 to pursue his interests in social research and political activism.

In *Poverty*, Hunter presents a bleak view of child labor and the degrading struggle that the poor must wage each day. The book contains seven chapters. The first is a general discussion of poverty and its causes and effects. The other chapters are concerned with the pauper, the vagrant, the child, and the immigrant. Hunter presents some of his suggestions for a solution to poverty in the conclusion.

Hunter defines poverty as deprivation relative to a standard of normal living that was necessary for industrial efficiency. To estimate the percentage of the population living in poverty, he used an absolute definition of poverty, which he established as $460 per year for a family of five in Northern industrial areas and $300 for a family of the same size in rural areas of the South. Based on his definition, Hunter estimated that 20 percent of the population in the Northern industrial areas and 10 percent in the Southern rural areas of the United States were poor in 1900.

The text is supplemented with statistics and a map. The appendixes include statistics and charts on a variety of topics including housing and child labor, tuberculosis rates, and wage rates.

When it was published, *Poverty* was considered the most objective study of its kind up to that time. Using a scientific approach in his examination of the subject, Hunter presented a thorough analysis that captured the attention of the public and of social reformers and forced them to re-evaluate their ideas about the nature of poverty in the United States and what could be done to alleviate it.

Bibliography

Hunter, *Poverty*; Patterson, *America's Struggle against Poverty, 1900–1985*.

Prohibition

During the late nineteenth and early twentieth centuries, the saloon was the natural social center for the neighborhood in many parts of the city. It provided a place, particularly for men, to escape from the crowded tenements and to share the company of others. Most settlement workers were not opposed to saloons. In fact, in

1904 the New York Association of Neighborhood Workers (*see* **United Neighborhood Houses**), which was a coalition of settlement workers and other reformers in New York City, opposed closing the saloons on Sundays because they recognized that they functioned as social centers.

What settlement workers did find troubling was the overindulgence that these establishments encouraged. Many city dwellers found it difficult to cope with their poverty and substandard living conditions. Compelled to work in meaningless jobs for long hours and for low wages, they could find little escape from their drudgery in an overcrowded apartment. The saloon provided an escape from these unhappy realities. But as the settlement workers and other reformers knew, it was the families who often suffered the consequences in the form of domestic violence and the inability to buy food or pay the rent once the family's income had been spent on alcohol.

To counter what they believed were the negative effects of the saloon, settlement residents were involved in a variety of moral purity crusades. They believed that the saloon and its associated vices such as drunkenness, **prostitution**, and political corruption, destroyed family life and encouraged juvenile delinquency, public disorder, crime, and other forms of vice. They worked to establish neighborhood social centers, public gymnasiums, and school center recreation facilities and parks to offer alternative gathering places for neighborhood residents.

Although many settlement workers supported the saloons as necessary social environments, some workers believed that just providing alternatives to saloons did not go far enough. Many of the social investigations that settlement residents conducted about their neighborhoods as far back as the 1890s had denounced the neighborhood saloon as a center of crime and vice. What many of these reformers wanted was legislation that would prohibit the sale of alcoholic beverages.

Robert Woods of the **South End House** settlement in Boston was one of the most enthusiastic supporters of national prohibition. Woods was a teetotaler. While living and working at South End House, he served as chair of the Board of Trustees of the Foxboro State Hospital for Dipsomaniacs (1907). Six years later, Woods secured an appointment to the Massachusetts State Licensing Board, and during his term of office, he was particularly troublesome to the liquor interests.

In 1917 the National Conference of Charities and Correction (*see* **National Conference on Social Welfare**), an influential organization composed of leaders from both public and private charitable relief associations and correctional institutions, supported the campaign for national prohibition. Many settlement workers welcomed the passage of the Eighteenth Amendment to the Constitution, which made national prohibition the law of the land in 1920.

For the most part, settlement workers were not as fanatical about prohibition as were their colleagues in the temperance crusade. Settlement workers viewed prohibition as a method of social reform, and as had been true in the past, they sought out ways to provide their neighbors with alternatives to the saloon and dance halls as social centers by offering more family-centered recreation opportunities.

Lillian Wald, the founder of the **Henry Street Settlement** on New York's Lower East Side, was the chair of the **National Federation of Settlements**' Prohibition Committee. During the mid-1920s, some settlement workers and other social reformers were concerned that the enforcement of national prohibition was breaking down. **Paul Kellogg**, the editor of the social welfare journal the *Survey*, and Bruno Lasker, a social critic and one-time resident of the Henry Street Settlement, called upon Wald to initiate an investigation on behalf of the National Federation of Settlements into the social effects of prohibition.

At the suggestion of Kellogg and Lasker, the writer and artist Martha Bensley Bruere was recruited to supervise the survey, which was financed by the National Federation of Settlements. Using data supplied by workers in settlement houses in cities across the United States, the study concluded that the benefits to society that advocates of prohibition had hoped for had been achieved in some places, and that even though national prohibition was not an overwhelming success, it should be continued. In short, the settlement workers viewed the prohibition as a mixed blessing—drunkenness and public disorderliness had declined in many of their neighborhoods even though bootlegging and corruption were widespread across the nation.

National prohibition was repealed with the ratification of the Twenty-first Amendment to the U.S. Constitution in December 1933. As had happened when prohibition began in 1920, settlement workers had mixed feelings about its demise. They acknowledged that prohibition had helped to curtail prostitution and vice in some areas, but they were also aware that enforcement of the law had been inconsistent and ineffective.

Bibliography

Carson, *Settlement Folk: Social Thought and the American Settlement Movement, 1885–1930*; Davis, *Spearheads for Reform: The Social Settlements and the Progressive Movement, 1890–1914*.

Prostitution

Prostitution thrived in urban centers during the nineteenth and early twentieth centuries for a number of reasons. During this time, the number of single young women living and working in cities increased dramatically; some of these women had come from rural areas and some were immigrants. These women worked long hours for little pay, and they frequently became prostitutes to supplement the money they earned in their legitimate employment.

Settlement workers were aware of the red-light districts and prostitution rings that operated in their neighborhoods, and they mounted frequent campaigns to close brothels, saloons, and dance halls that served as havens for prostitutes and their clients. The anti-prostitution campaign was part of the larger effort on the part of settlement workers and other social reformers to prevent the exploitation of women and children.

Settlement workers realized that economic conditions often drove young girls to become prostitutes. As part of the effort to control prostitution in their neighborhoods, they cooperated with labor reformers to secure better working conditions and a minimum wage. A related concern for settlement workers was the way in which newly arrived immigrants, particularly single women, were taken advantage of and lured into the white slave trade. In cooperation with other reformers, settlement workers established organizations such as the **Immigrants' Protective League** to draw attention to the needs of this vulnerable segment of the population and to offer various social services to them.

As was the case with other issues of concern to them, settlement workers formed committees and undertook social investigations to support their demands for reform. In New York City, settlement workers **Henry Moskowitz** and **James Reynolds** were instrumental in the creation of the Committee of Fifteen, which functioned between 1900 and 1902 and investigated vice in the city. Settlement workers were joined in this effort by wealthy business owners, capitalists, and other reformers. The Committee of Fifteen served as the prototype for the vice commissions that were created in cities across the United States at this time. For example, **Graham Taylor**, the founder of the **Chicago Commons** settlement, served on the Chicago Vice Commission which was established in 1910 to investigate prostitution in that city.

The anti-prostitution crusade moved on to the national stage in 1909. As a result of the work of the United States Immigration Commission, the Mann Act was passed in 1910. This law prohibited the transportation of women across state lines for immoral purposes.

Settlement workers frequently wrote about their concerns and their work in the popular magazines of the day. In 1911 **Jane Addams**, the founder of the Chicago settlement **Hull House**, published a series of articles about the white slave trade in *McClure's Magazine*. Drawing on the case records of the Chicago-based Juvenile Protective Association, she related the stories of young women who had been lured into prostitution. The following year, Addams gathered the *McClure* articles into a book which she published under the title *A New Conscience and an Ancient Evil*.

Bibliography

Carson, *Settlement Folk: Social Thought and the American Settlement Movement, 1885–1930*; Davis, *Spearheads for Reform: The Social Settlements and the Progressive Movement, 1890–1914*; Wade, *Graham Taylor: Pioneer for Social Justice, 1851–1938*.

Public Housing Conference *See*

National Housing Conference

R

Reynolds, James Bronson
settlement worker, social and political
reformer
b. March 17, 1861; d. January 1, 1924.

James Reynolds began his social welfare reform
career working for the Young Men's Christian
Association (YMCA). He spent some time living and working at the **University Settlement**
in New York City and became active in local
politics. This interest inspired him to attend law
school, and he eventually devoted himself full-
time to a career in politics. However, Reynolds
never lost touch with his social welfare roots,
and he served as a member of a variety of committees and organizations with settlement
workers and other reformers.

While an undergraduate at Yale, Reynolds
was a class deacon in addition to working for a
New Haven church mission and the Yale branch
of the YMCA. Following his graduation in 1884,
Reynolds traveled abroad for a year before returning to Yale to study in the Divinity School.

Although he earned his degree in 1888,
Reynolds was never ordained. Instead, he accepted a position as the representative of the
College YMCA of the United States to European
Universities, with the responsibility of promoting cooperation among Protestant student associations. For the next two and a half years,
Reynolds visited schools in almost every country in Europe. He was particularly impressed
with the interest students in England had in
social reform efforts. Illness forced Reynolds to
return home in 1892.

Two years later he was invited to replace
Stanton Coit as the head resident of the University Settlement on New York City's Lower
East Side. Along with the other residents of the
settlement, Reynolds was involved in a variety
of social improvement efforts including serving
as a public school trustee. He eventually supported the effort to replace the trustee system
with a central school board. He was also a member of the **Outdoor Recreation League** and
of the **Tenement House Commission** of 1900.

Like many other reformers at the time,
Reynolds believed that if people were presented
with adequate information about the existence
of social problems and with suggestions for ways
to solve them, improvements could be achieved.
Toward this end, he and other workers at the
University Settlement conducted research studies and testified before special investigative commissions and legislative bodies.

Besides his investigating, Reynolds was one
of the first settlement workers to try to effect
social change by becoming involved in local political campaigns. His battles with the machine
politicians of Tammany Hall turned him into a
sophisticated political activist, and he encouraged other settlement workers to follow his example by cooperating to defeat local political
bosses. Reynolds was also involved in other
municipal government reform efforts as a member of two other local associations, the Committee of Seventy (1893) and the Citizen's Union
(1897).

Reynolds's life and career began to move in new directions in 1898. That year he married Florence Blanchard Dike and entered New York University to study law. In 1900, Reynolds was admitted to the New York State Bar. The following year he resigned his position at the University Settlement and turned his attention full-time to politics.

In 1901, Reynolds played a significant role in Seth Low's successful campaign for mayor of New York City. He went on to serve in Low's reform-minded administration as the mayor's secretary, and in this position, he was instrumental in expanding the city's public welfare programs. Reynolds's political involvement moved beyond the municipal level when he served as an informal advisor to President Theodore Roosevelt, who appointed him a special advisor on municipal affairs for Washington, DC. Reynolds was also a member of special commissions that were concerned with various issues such as labor conditions in Panama and the American Immigration Service.

Throughout his years as a settlement worker and a political advisor, Reynolds was active in many Progressive Era organizations. He co-founded the National Playground Association of America and the National Vigilance Association. He was a vice president of the Immigration Restriction League and on the executive board of the National Prison Association.

Reynolds remained active in social reform and political circles until shortly before his death in 1924. He was one of the earliest settlement workers to take an active interest in local politics and used the political connections he made to both secure neighborhood improvements and further his own career. In addition to his work on the local level, Reynolds also made significant contributions to the efforts of a number of national reform groups.

Bibliography

The National Cyclopaedia of American Biography, vol. 10, pp. 235–36; Stover, *James Bronson Reynolds, March 17, 1861–January 1, 1924: A Memorial*; Trattner, *Biographical Dictionary of Social Welfare in America*, pp. 620–22.

Richmond, Mary Ellen

researcher, author, social work administrator
b. August 5, 1861; d. September 12, 1928.

Mary Richmond's career in the **Charity Organization Society** movement had a significant impact on the work accomplished by settlement house workers and other social reformers. Her ideas about standardized training, the application of the scientific method, and the coordination of community relief resources helped to professionalize social welfare reform in the United States.

Born in Belleville, Illinois, Richmond was orphaned when young and was raised by her maternal grandmother and two maiden aunts in Baltimore, Maryland. During her lonely and unhappy childhood, she was frequently ill. She was also an avid reader, and in spite of the fact that she had no formal schooling until she was 11 years old, Richmond graduated from the academically demanding Baltimore Eastern Female High School in 1878.

Over the next 11 years she worked first as a proofreader in New York City and then as a bookkeeper in Baltimore. In 1889, Richmond became the assistant treasurer of the Baltimore Charity Organization Society. On a visit to Boston to observe the work of the **Boston Associated Charities**, she met **Zilpha D. Smith**, its director. Smith introduced Richmond to the charity organization movement in more detail, and the two women became lifelong friends.

Back in Baltimore, Richmond volunteered as a **friendly visitor** to witness firsthand the work accomplished by the Baltimore Charity Organization Society. As assistant treasurer, Richmond was also involved in the public relations and fund-raising aspects of the society's work. Based on her accomplishments, she was promoted to general secretary within two years.

At this stage of her career, Richmond still subscribed to the widely held belief that the poor could only be reformed by means of stringent measures that placed little or no emphasis on the individual and that prohibited the dispensing of funds to those in need. Instead, she believed the relief worker should exhort the poor to improve and should serve as a good example. However, she gradually modified her views to the point that she acknowledged that the judicious dispensing of funds did not encourage pauperism.

This departure from the prevailing wisdom of social reform led Richmond in a new direction. She began to explore the feasibility of augmenting the cadre of volunteer friendly visitors with salaried workers who were professionally trained to conduct systematic investigations, to scientifically evaluate circumstances, and to make recommendations regarding methods of treatment, especially in more difficult cases. Richmond began offering training sessions for the society's workers and established a cooperative program with the Johns Hopkins Medical School to offer specialized professional instruction for charity workers who believed that personality disorders were at the root of the pauperism they encountered.

Richmond's adoption of the casework approach reflected the growing emphasis in the organized charity movement, both in America and abroad, that individual causes of poverty could be discerned and that specific self-help solutions could be designed and implemented. In 1897 in a speech delivered at the annual meeting of the National Conference of Charities and Correction. An influential organization composed of leaders from both public and private charitable relief organizations and correctional institutions, she advocated establishing a professional training school for charity workers based on the casework method that had been introduced by the London Charity Organization Society. The following year she taught this methodology in the newly established New York Charity Organization Summer School of Philanthropy. (*See* **Columbia University Graduate School of Social Work**.)

Richmond's ideas about training and the use of detailed investigations to establish the best use of community resources for assisting individual families were put forth in her book, *Friendly Visiting Among the Poor* which was published in 1898. Her ideas gained a wider audience through the articles she contributed to the *Baltimore Charities Record* and through her participation in the National Conference of Charities and Correction.

In 1900, Richmond left Baltimore to take on the task of bringing order to the confusing state of affairs at the Philadelphia Society for Organizing Charity. While at Philadelphia, she established a program to train district staff leaders, and she abolished the practice of independent district fund-raising. Her work in Philadelphia led to Richmond's writing a column in the social welfare journal *Charities,* in which she engaged in the regular exchange of ideas with other charity workers about, among other things, fund-raising, casework, and training programs. Eventually, Richmond served as editor of the Field Department of the social work journal *Charities and the Commons* (later the **Survey**). In 1907, she published *The Good Neighbor in the City* setting forth her ideas about how cities could benefit from the establishment of a network of social service agencies.

Richmond entered the final phase of her career when she moved to New York in 1909 to become the director of the Charity Organization Department of the **Russell Sage Foundation**. There she directed research on social problems and on methodologies for bringing about solutions. The results of her research were distributed to charity organizations throughout the United States that were employing the casework approach.

Her book, *Social Diagnosis*, which was published in 1917, was an authoritative analysis of the theory and methodology of social casework. Applying a medical model to social work, she set forth a logical, orderly process of investigation, diagnosis, prognosis, and treatment. As a result of Richmond's book, the philosophy and methodology of the casework approach became predominant in the field of social work.

Between 1910 and 1922, Richmond conducted training institutes for caseworkers and supervisors. She developed her ideas even further through the classes she taught in the new social work schools that had been established in New York, Boston, and Philadelphia. Additionally, she exerted a significant influence on social work education by combining classroom instruction with practical field experiences.

Some of Richmond's strongly held beliefs, such as her opposition to public relief for families and to the Community Chest Movement generated disagreement within the social work community and ultimately cost her the presidency of the National Conference of Social Work (*see* **National Conference on Social Welfare**) in 1922. But this setback did not diminish her influence on the profession as she worked in later years to develop a standardized vocabulary and a code of ethics for social workers. Richmond remained active until shortly before her death in 1928.

Bibliography

Jackson, *Encyclopedia of New York City*, p. 1004; Lubove, *The Professional Altruist: The Emergence of Social Work as a Career, 1880–1930*; James, *Notable American Women, 1607–1950*, vol. 3, pp. 152–54; Trattner, *Biographical Dictionary of Social Welfare in America*, pp. 622–25; Trattner, *From Poor Law to Welfare State: A History of Social Welfare in America*.

Riis, Jacob Augustus
journalist, photographer, housing reformer, social activist
b. May 3, 1849; d. May 26, 1914.

The journalist and photographer Jacob Riis provided settlement workers and other social reformers with the verbal and visual pictures of the squalid conditions of tenement life they needed to obtain the financial backing from middle- and upper-class supporters of reform efforts.

Born in Ribe, Denmark, Riis was educated at home by his father who was a senior master at Ribe Latin School. In 1865, at the age of 16, the younger Riis was apprenticed to a carpenter in Copenhagen, but when he returned to his

Jacob A. Riis, c. 1903
Museum of the City of New York

hometown four years later, he discovered few opportunities for work. After two years, he emigrated to the United States (1870) and spent some time traveling through the Northeast and Midwest working in a variety of jobs: farming, coal mining, peddling, and brick-making.

In 1875, Riis returned to Denmark to marry his childhood sweetheart, Elisabeth Nielsen. By 1877, the couple were living in New York City where Riis had secured a position as a police reporter for the *New York Tribune.* For more than a decade he covered stories about crime and accidents for the *Tribune,* which led him deeper and deeper into the city's tenement districts. He witnessed both the spiritual and physical degradation of the inhabitants of the squalid neighborhoods that he entered at all hours of the day and night.

What he saw moved Riis beyond the journalistic boundary of reporting what he observed. He felt compelled to do something to improve the conditions he saw, and not content with just writing about it, Riis began to illustrate his articles with photographs to force his readers to see what he saw and to inspire them to action.

In *How the Other Half Lives: Studies among the Tenements of New York* (1890), Riis describes the environment of the immigrant colonies. His account captured the public imagination, and his appeal to the conscience of the middle class did much to incite reformers to

action. In *The Children of the Poor* (1892), the sequel to *How the Other Half Lives,* Riis once again used his dramatic, anecdotal style of writing to dramatize the problems of the tenement neighborhoods. This book inspired reformers to expand the idea of housing reform to consider the quality of all aspects of neighborhood life.

In addition to his publications, Riis was active in a variety of social welfare reform efforts. He served on various city and state tenement house commissions and on the boards of directors of several settlements, providing not only the cache of his reputation, but also the benefit of his knowledge, enthusiasm, and commitment to genuine social reform.

Throughout his career Riis was a tireless worker on behalf of the poor. In addition to his work as a journalist and photographer, he was in demand as a lecturer and was often called upon to lend his support to various reform campaigns. Diagnosed with heart disease in 1904, Riis did not heed his doctors' advice and continued with his rigorous schedule during the next decade. He died at his country home in Massachusetts in 1914.

Bibliography

Dictionary of American Biography, vol. 8, pp. 606–08; Jackson, *Encyclopedia of New York City,* p. 1005; Lubove, *The Progressives and the Slums: Tenement House Reform in New York City, 1890–1917*; Trattner, *Biographical Dictionary of Social Welfare in America,* pp. 625–27.

Robbins, Jane Elizabeth
teacher, physician, settlement worker
b. December 28, 1860; d. August 16, 1946.

Jane Robbins successfully combined a career as a physician with her commitment to the settlement movement. As the head resident of the New York City-based **College Settlement**, she inspired her colleagues to pursue a variety of issues including labor, housing, and health reform. Robbins shared her experience and expertise with reformers in other settlements as well as with those involved in the work of the International Red Cross.

Robbins attended Smith College for one year (1879–1880), and then spent the next five years teaching in various schools in New Jersey and Kentucky. Eventually, she settled on a career as a physician, which she believed would enable her to assist the poor in a meaningful way. In 1887, Robbins moved to New York City where she enrolled in the Woman's Medical College of the New York Infirmary. At the same time, she became involved in a number of social reform causes including teaching Sunday school classes at the Five Points Methodist Mission.

Along with **Jean Fine**, a friend from Smith College, Robbins organized a children's sewing club at the **Neighborhood Guild**, the first social settlement in the United States which had been organized by **Stanton Coit** in 1886. Robbins soon felt that her biweekly visits were not enough time to spend in the settlement, and she moved into an apartment house on Forsyth Street where the guild was located to devote more time to social welfare work.

The following year Robbins helped the **College Settlements Association** establish its first settlement house in New York City, the College Settlement, and she became one of the house's first residents. After graduating from medical school in 1890, Robbins completed a year's internship at the New York Infirmary before opening her own practice near Mott Street in the center of New York City's Italian community.

In 1894, Robbins became the head worker at the College Settlement. Her training as a physician gave her a unique insight into the lives of her immigrant neighbors, which she used to good advantage as she and her settlement colleagues mounted an extensive campaign for social reform during the 1890s. She viewed the settlement both as a gathering place for the neighborhood residents and as a tool of social investigation. In addition to sponsoring social clubs and working for housing reform, the College Settlement supported striking garment workers in their effort to obtain a 10-hour day and a minimum wage. The settlement's residents also testified before various state investigating committees looking into working conditions of women and children. Robbins herself testified before the **New York State Tenement House Commission** of 1894 to recommend stricter enforcement of the tenement house laws as well as to lobby for public baths and playgrounds.

Besides her settlement work, Robbins was a strong supporter of public education. She believed that the public school could play an important role in Americanizing new immigrants, and she advocated adopting an augmented curriculum that emphasized each child's interests and abilities. While head resident at the College Settlement, Robbins also worked as a public school inspector. In addition to her interest in the daily functioning of the schools, Robbins was a strong supporter of the popular school

center movement that advocated using public school buildings after hours as neighborhood centers.

In 1897, Robbins resigned from the College Settlement to resume her private medical practice. The following year she entered yet another phase of her career. Over the next 30 years she traveled from place to place providing medical care to those in need. In Chickamauga Park, Georgia, she treated typhoid patients during the Spanish-American War. She also worked as head resident at several settlements including Normal College Alumnae House, New York (1901); Alta House, Cleveland (1902); Little Italy Settlement, Brooklyn (1911); and the Jacob A. Riis Neighborhood Settlement, New York (1914). From 1905 to 1911, Robbins served as executive secretary of the Public Education Association in New York.

In addition to her work in various communities across the United States, Robbins was involved in various international social reform crusades. For example, following World War I, she worked for the Red Cross in Italy, and as a member of the Medical Women's International Association, she organized hospitals in Greece. Beginning in 1927, Robbins spent two years assisting Greek refugees during the conflict with Turkey. In her work in Europe, Robbins displayed the same sense of commitment and dedication that she brought to her work in the American Settlement Movement.

Robbins maintained her interest in social reform work all her life, although she did begin to curtail her schedule during the 1930s as she entered her seventies. She died after a long illness in 1946. Her pioneering work at the College Settlement set an example for other young college-educated women. As a physician she was unique among the first generation of American settlement workers.

Bibliography
Davis, *Spearheads for Reform: The Social Settlements and the Progressive Movement, 1890–1914*; James, *Notable American Women, 1607–1950*, vol. 3, pp. 172–74; Woods, *The Settlement Horizon*.

Robert Gould Shaw House

The mainstream American Settlement Movement largely ignored the needs of the significant number of black people who lived and worked in urban centers. To some degree, this reflected the bias of the society at large and of the individual men and women who worked in the settlements. However, some settlements were established specifically for blacks in what were predominantly black neighborhoods. Some settlements operated a branch house; **South End House** in Boston was one of these, operating the nearby Robert Gould Shaw House.

Established as a branch of the South End House in Boston in February 1908, this settlement was named in honor of Robert Gould Shaw, the commander of the Massachusetts 54th, the first black regiment sent into action from the free states. The settlement was located on Hammond Street in a predominantly black neighborhood, but it welcomed people of all races.

The Shaw House offered a full range of settlement activities including classes in cooking, sewing, and millinery. It also sponsored clubs for women and children, athletic clubs, and choral groups.

When it was established, the Robert Gould Shaw House primarily served the needs of the black community. The house continued to offer services during the first half of the twentieth century, and over time more whites began to take advantage of the settlement's offerings.

See also **Frederick Douglass Center**

Bibliography

Woods, *The Handbook of Settlements.*

Robins, Margaret Dreier
reformer, labor activist
b. September 6, 1868; d. February 21, 1945.

Margaret Dreier Robins's work with the **Women's Trade Union League** was her primary contribution to the Progressive reform efforts of the early twentieth century. In addition to her accomplishments as a labor organizer, Robins was closely allied to the settlement movement through her marriage to the settlement worker and political activist **Raymond Robins**, and she worked with him and other Chicago-based reformers on a variety of municipal reform crusades.

Margaret Dreier's parents instilled a sense of personal and civic responsibility in their five children. Margaret, who was the eldest, was educated at small private schools, and although her formal education ended when she graduated from the Brackett School in Brooklyn Heights, she pursued a private, independent study in history and philosophy. When she was 19 years old, Dreier obtained a position as secretary-treasurer of the women's auxiliary of the Brooklyn Hospital. Her visits to the wards and her work on developing a new nutrition program marked her first foray into social welfare work.

Starting in 1901, Dreier became active in a number of reform causes and organizations. She joined the New York State Charities Aid Association's committee for visiting state institutions for the insane that same year and became an advocate for better treatment of the mentally ill. She was so successful as an advocate that she was encouraged to speak on behalf of social welfare reforms by established reformers such as **Homer Folks**. Two years later, Dreier accepted a position on the legislative committee of the Women's Municipal League. The league had been founded in 1901 to mobilize women on behalf of the reform-minded Seth Low's candidacy for mayor of New York City. After Low's election, Dreier was instrumental in transforming the league into a force for social legislation. One of her first priorities was to assist the social investigator **Frances Kellor** in an inquiry into the mistreatment of women by employment agencies. Dreier went on to spearhead a lobbying effort that resulted in the enactment of a state law regulating private employment agencies.

At the invitation of the social activist **William English Walling** and the labor reformer Leonora O'Reilly, Dreier and her sister Mary Elizabeth (*see* **Mary Dreier**) became founding members of the New York **Women's Trade Union League** in 1904. The league was a coalition of middle-class and working-class women who strove to unionize women workers. Dreier was elected president of the league the following year. Trade unionism now became the focus of Dreier's professional life. She believed that working women had to be given every opportunity to provide for their own welfare. Toward this end, Dreier worked to unionize women workers, lobbied to secure the passage of protective legislation, and provided training for future labor union leaders.

In June 1905, Margaret Dreier married Raymond Robins, the head resident at **Northwestern University Settlement** in Chicago. Robins had made a fortune in the Klondike and was using his wealth to benefit various social, political, and economic reform efforts. The Robinses set up housekeeping in a tenement in Chicago's west side. While her husband carried on his settlement work, Margaret Robins soon assimilated herself into the Chicago reform community.

From 1907 to 1914, Robins served as president of the Chicago chapter of the Women's Trade Union League; during this same period, she was also president of the national organization (1907–1922). Her major focus was always organization of workers, although she did occasionally fight for the passage of legislation that would benefit labor. When she was not traveling around the country mobilizing strikers or cultivating supporters, Robins opened her home in Chicago as a meeting place for like-minded reformers.

During her tenure as president, the league made significant progress. Representatives lobbied for protective legislation, educated the public about labor conditions and the need for union activity, and provided leadership training to working women at a special school based in Chicago. The league also organized new branches in several cities.

Robins was also active in the American Federation of Labor (AFL) as a member of the national education committee and as a member of the executive board of the Chicago organization. She favored conforming with the American Federation of Labor's policies as a way to secure a place for the Women's Trade Union League in the mainstream of union activity. However, Robins was never able to overcome the AFL's lack of interest in organizing women workers. Nor was she willing to compromise her belief in the importance of protective legislation as the primary method of labor reform.

During World War I, Robins and other trade unionists were active in government service through the work of the Women in Industry Service department of the U. S. Department of Labor. In the post-war period, she began to focus on international labor issues. Robins convened the first International Congress of Working Women in Washington, DC, in 1919 and served as its president for the next four years.

In addition to her work with the Women's Trade Union League, Robins worked with her husband on a variety of municipal reform efforts. She also actively crusaded for woman suffrage, campaigned for Theodore Roosevelt during the 1912 presidential election, and served as vice chair of the National Conference of Charities and Correction in 1912. (*See* **National Conference on Social Welfare**.)

Although she retired in 1924 and moved to Florida with her husband, Robins maintained an interest in the league. She served on the planning committee for the 1929 White House Conference on Child Health and Protection. In Florida she also was a supporter of various local charities, such as the Red Cross and the Young Women's Christian Association until her death in 1945.

Bibliography

Davis, *Spearheads for Reform: The Social Settlements and the Progressive Movement, 1890–1914*; *Dictionary of American Biography*, supl. 3, pp. 638–39; Dreier, *Margaret Dreier Robins*; *National Cyclopaedia of American Biography*, vol. 33, p. 584; James, *Notable American Women, 1607–1956*, vol. 3, pp. 179–81; O'Neill, *Everyone Was Brave: A History of Feminism in America*; Trattner, *Biographical Dictionary of Social Welfare in America*, pp. 630–32.

Robins, Raymond
settlement worker, social evangelist, political activist
b. September 17, 1873; d. September 26, 1954.

Raymond Robins had a varied career as a social reformer. While working as the head resident of the **Northwestern University Settlement** in Chicago, he was actively involved in campaigns to defeat corrupt local ward politicians. His interest in politics also extended to the national and international arenas. He combined this interest in politics and reform with a strong religious commitment and worked in a variety of spiritual crusades both in the United States and abroad. He was married to the labor organizer **Margaret Dreier Robins**, and they were active members of the dynamic Chicago reform community.

Born in Staten Island, New York, Robins was raised by relatives in Ohio and Kentucky before moving in with cousins in Florida. There he was educated in country schools. Robins hated being poor. When he was 18, he organized a phosphate mine and then sold it to a Wall Street banking establishment. Two years later he traveled across the Southwestern United States supporting himself by working in various lead and coal mines.

Robins embraced the Populist Movement and was determined to make his mark in the reform efforts of the day. Toward this end he earned a law degree in 1896 from Columbian (later George Washington) Law School in Florida. After graduation, Robins moved to San Francisco where he worked as a lawyer and campaigned for William Jennings Bryan during the 1896 presidential campaign.

Robins was especially fond of his sister Elizabeth who was an actress in England. When she would not join him in San Francisco in 1897, Robins left California for the gold, fields of Alaska. During the first year, Robins was bitterly disappointed. He did not find gold, he could not accustom himself to the harsh climate, and he felt physically and spiritually isolated. With the assistance of a local Jesuit priest, Robins rediscovered his Christian faith. He moved to the city of Nome where he became a lay preacher and reentered the political and reform arenas.

In 1900, Robins's sister Elizabeth persuaded him to leave Alaska. Although he claimed to be penniless when he left Alaska, Robins appears to have amassed a substantial fortune, either while there or immediately upon his reentering the United States. Shortly after he returned to Florida, he purchased a large estate near Brooksville. Robins deeded the entire estate, which he called Chinsegut Hill, to Elizabeth. However, she returned half of it to her brother when he married Margaret Dreier in 1905.

At the time of his marriage, Robins was a leading member of the settlement house movement in Chicago. He was both superintendent of the Chicago Municipal Lodging House (1902–1905) and the head resident of the Northwestern University Settlement (1903–1905). Robins was very active in reform politics, and at one point his opposition to the local ward bosses in Chicago led to his being savagely beaten and left for dead.

After leaving the Northwestern University Settlement, Robins turned his attention to religion once again. He played a prominent role in the activities of the Men and Religion Forward Movement, and he participated in its world tour in 1911. Robins was also a speaker with the National Christian Evangelistic Camp that traveled around to various college campuses during 1915 and 1916.

Although he was committed to his spiritual work, politics still exerted a strong attraction for Robins. In 1914, he became chair of the Progressive Party's Illinois State Central Committee. This position provided him with an entree into the national political arena. Robins supported Theodore Roosevelt's candidacy for the presidency and served as the chair of the 1916 Bull Moose Convention.

Robins's interest in reform was not limited to the domestic sphere. He opposed counterrevolutionary intervention in the Soviet Union after Lenin and the Bolsheviks assumed control. Robins held a high-level position in the Red Cross mission to Russia in 1917. After returning to the United States, Robins remained active in politics serving as a member of the Executive Committee of the Republican National Committee. President Harding offered him a place in his cabinet as secretary of labor, but Robins declined.

Instead, Robins turned his attention to the campaigns for outlawing war and for local option prohibition. He traveled extensively across the United States on behalf of the latter cause. In 1932, Robins suffered a psychological breakdown while on a prohibition-related speaking tour, but he enjoyed a swift recovery.

During this period, Robins once again became interested in the Soviet Union, this time as part of a mission that led to the exchange of ambassadors between Moscow and Washington. Based on his participation in this venture, Robins was under the impression that he would be appointed the American envoy to the Soviet Union, but he was mistaken. Following this disappointment he withdrew from the national political scene. However, he remained active in local and state politics in Florida where he had retired during the 1920s, and he was also involved with a number of local charitable causes such as the Red Cross.

Bibliography

Davis, *Spearheads for Reform: The Social Settlements and the Progressive Movement, 1890–1914*; *Dictionary of American Biography*, supl. 5, pp. 578–80; Dreier, *Margaret Dreier Robins*, Williams, *American-Russian Relations, 1781–1947*.

Roosevelt, (Anna) Eleanor
political and social reformer, human rights activist
b. October 11, 1884; d. November 7, 1962.

Eleanor Roosevelt began her long, impressive career as a social welfare activist by volunteering at the **College Settlement** on New York City's Lower East Side. This work not only brought her into contact with the city's poor, but it also provided her access to New York's active network of social reformers. This connection proved to be long-lived and very useful, both for Roosevelt and for the reformers who benefited from her insights and her position of influence.

As a young child, Eleanor Roosevelt enjoyed all the social advantages of being a member of New York's social elite. Yet this was not a happy time for her. By the time she was 10 years old, both of her parents and one of her brothers were dead. Roosevelt and her younger brother, Hall, were sent to live with their maternal grandmother, Mrs. Valentine Hall in New York City. There, Roosevelt was educated at private schools before attending Allenswood, a finishing school outside London. When she returned to the United States in 1902, Eleanor entered the New York social world, but she was not interested in the carefree lifestyle adopted by many other young women of her class.

Instead, Eleanor turned her attention to the world of social reform. She joined the National **Consumers' League** and through this association gained firsthand knowledge of the

Eleanor Roosevelt (center) and Alice Hamilton (right) (woman on the left is not identified)

The Schlesinger Library, Radcliffe College

working conditions in factories and sweatshops. Her volunteer work with the Junior League and at the College Settlement introduced her to the city's poor, and she developed a lifelong interest in their welfare.

In 1905, Eleanor married her cousin Franklin Delano Roosevelt. During the next decades, her life revolved around her five children and her husband's political career, although she did find some time for her reform work. For example, like many women of her social class, Roosevelt was involved in Red Cross-related activities during World War I.

The 1920s were a critical decade in Roosevelt's development as a social reformer as she became increasingly active in social welfare activities. In later years, she made use of the knowledge and experience she gained at this time and of the social and professional relationships she established with other reformers. Roosevelt became a member of the **Women's City Club of New York** and of the League of Women Voters. Through these organizations she met many of the women who were involved in the New York City settlement movement including **Lillian Wald**, founder of the **Henry Street Settlement**, and **Mary Simkhovitch**, founder of **Greenwich House**. She joined the **Women's Trade Union League** in 1922 and formed a close personal and political friendship with

Rose Schneiderman, the head of the New York branch of the league. The friendships and professional alliances with social welfare reformers that Roosevelt cultivated during the 1920s blossomed into a dynamic women's reform network in the 1930s.

Roosevelt made the most of her position as first lady as she traveled across the United States to visit factories, mines, schools, and other sites witnessing firsthand the suffering endured by the disadvantaged. During the 1930s and 1940s, she was at the center of a significant women's reform network and often channeled information and requests for assistance from reformers to President Roosevelt. Through her influence, a number of women social welfare reformers secured positions in the New Deal where they worked to realize their reform-related goals and objectives.

Roosevelt continued to work to alleviate the problems of the disadvantaged during World War II. In the post-war years, she broadened the scope of her work to include war victims living in other countries. A high point of her career occurred when the General Assembly of the United Nations adopted the Universal Declaration of Human Rights in December 1948, a document to which she had devoted a considerable amount of energy. Roosevelt remained active in a variety of political and social welfare concerns during the 1950s. In December 1961, she was appointed chair of President Kennedy's Commission on the Status of Women. This was to be her last official responsibility. Roosevelt died from tuberculosis in November 1962. A capable and committed social welfare advocate, Roosevelt was also an astute politician who used her influence to further the cause of social reform.

Bibliography

Dictionary of American Biography, supl. 7, pp. 658–62; Jackson, *Encyclopedia of New York City*, pp. 1018–19 ; Kearney, *Anna Eleanor Roosevelt: The Evolution of a Reformer*; Trattner, *Biographical Dictionary of Social Welfare in America*, pp. 639–43.

Russell Sage Foundation

Russell Sage was not known as a philanthropist during his lifetime, but in the years following his death in 1906, his widow, **Margaret Olivia Sage**, succeeded in altering that reputation. At the time of his death, Sage left his wife a fortune of almost $65 million with no conditions attached. At first, in a spirit of generosity, Mrs. Sage gave away moderate sums to a variety of charitable causes and to individuals. When it came to disposing of larger sums, though, she consulted her attorney **Robert DeForest**, the president of the New York **Charity Organization Society** and a prominent member of the New York City social reform community.

Drawing on the advice and support of his reform connections, DeForest proposed that Mrs. Sage establish a philanthropic foundation. In April 1907, the Russell Sage Foundation (RSF) was incorporated with a mandate to improve social and living conditions in the United States. Mrs. Sage's initial endowment for the foundation was $10 million. An additional $5 million was added when she died. The foundation proved beneficial for settlement workers and many other reformers.

DeForest served as the first chair of the Russell Sage Foundation's Board of Trustees. The other original board members included Louise Lee Schuyler, founder of the New York Charities Aid Association; **John Glenn** of the Baltimore Charity Organization Society; Gertrude Rice of the New York Charity Organization Society; and the social activist Helen M. Gould.

Under the guidance of Mrs. Sage and the Board of Trustees, the foundation became a leading force in a variety of Progressive reform crusades. The first recipient of a Russell Sage Foundation Grant was the New York Charity Organization Society, which used the money to subsidize the publication of its social work journal, *Charities and The Commons,* which later became the **Survey**. Grants were also made to the State Charities Aid Association, to various tenement house reform crusades, to the playground movement, and to numerous consumer leagues. The Russell Sage Foundation also provided funding for the development of social work schools in Boston, Chicago, New York, and St. Louis.

The first extensive project that the RSF funded was the **Pittsburgh Survey**, the first significant social survey of an American urban community which gathered data on all aspects of living and working conditions in Pittsburgh, Pennsylvania. Settlement workers and many others involved in social reform work participated in this undertaking. Supervised by **Paul U. Kellogg**, the project helped to establish the social survey method as an authentic research tool. Other communities conducted similar surveys, and the foundation funded six of these projects.

Shortly after the RSF was established, its Board of Trustees created departments charged with pursuing various projects such as women's work, child welfare, recreation, and charity organizations. In addition to working with social reform agencies and organizations on a variety of crusades, the various departments published books and studies that brought important issues to the attention of the general public.

Although the RSF continued to support a number of reform causes in the years following World War I, its most significant project during the 1920s was its support of the Committee on the Regional Plan of New York and its Environs. Between 1921 and 1933, the foundation donated $1.2 million to the work of the Regional Plan Committee, which, with the assistance of social workers and other reformers, conducted a comprehensive survey of the New York metropolitan region. Once the committee's report was completed, the foundation contributed an additional $500,000 to publicize its recommendations.

During the 1930s and 1940s, the RSF conducted surveys and studies of the social and economic impact of the Depression and World War II.

Bibliography

Glenn, *Russell Sage Foundation, 1907–1946*; Jackson, *Encyclopedia of New York City*, p. 1029; Romanofsky, *The Greenwood Encyclopedia of American Institutions: Social Service Organizations*, vol. 2, pp. 649–52.

S

Sage, Margaret Olivia Slocum
philanthropist
b. September 8, 1828; d. November 4, 1918.

A spirited, self-assured individual, Olivia Sage was the wife of the successful entrepreneur Russell Sage. She believed that a woman's first duty was to her home, but she also believed that she had an equal responsibility to work for social improvement. During his lifetime, Russell Sage was known as a frugal man, and it was Olivia who was the driving force behind his charitable works. After her husband's death, Olivia Sage was able to give free rein to her charitable impulses, and she did so generously. Settlement workers and other social reformers benefited from the funds she provided for research and for the support of churches, schools, hospitals, and a variety of other organizations and institutions.

Although she never gained a national reputation, Olivia Slocum Sage emerged as the leading female philanthropist in the United States during the opening decades of the twentieth century. In 1846, at the age of 18, Slocum, known as Olivia, left her family's home in Syracuse, New York, intending to enter Mount Holyoke Seminary. When she fell ill during her journey, an uncle in Troy, New York, persuaded her to enroll in the Troy Female Seminary from which she graduated in 1847. Family financial difficulties compelled Slocum to accept a teaching position at the Chestnut Street Seminary in Philadelphia. Although she resigned her position within two years because of ill health, she maintained an interest in women's education and taught intermittently over the next 20 years.

In November 1869, at the age of 41, Olivia Slocum married Russell B. Sage, a widower who had been married to one of her close friends from Troy Seminary. Russell Sage was a former U.S. congressman who rose rapidly through the New York business community earning a fortune from money lending and from investments in railroads and the stock market. During the 1870s, Sage's fortune increased substantially as he skillfully speculated in various railroad and telegraph companies. In the 1880s, he was best known as a money lender.

The couple had no children, and Olivia Sage expended a great deal of time and energy in various social reform causes. She maintained that women were men's intellectual equals and that they were morally superior. Sage channeled her energies into a number of popular social causes such as the crusade against tobacco and vice, the fight for woman suffrage, and the milk inspection campaign. She also supported a number of Presbyterian Church-sponsored causes such as home and foreign missions and the Woman's Christian Temperance Union.

Although her husband was not a generous man, Sage persuaded him to fund a number of charitable causes during his lifetime including financing the education of 40 Native American children, paying for the construction of a dormitory at the Troy Seminary, and donating

$50,000 to the Woman's Hospital of the State of New York. When he died in 1906, Russell Sage left an estate of $63 million. The following year, at the age of 79, Olivia Sage embarked on a new career in philanthropy.

With the assistance and guidance of her attorney and financial advisor **Robert W. De Forest**, president of the New York **Charity Organization Society**, one of Sage's first acts was to establish the **Russell Sage Foundation** with an endowment of $10 million. The purpose of the foundation was to improve living conditions in the United States with an emphasis on research and education. The first extensive research project that the foundation supported, with grants totaling more than $50,000, was the **Pittsburgh Survey**, the first significant social survey of an American urban community which gathered data on all aspects of living and working conditions in Pittsburgh, Pennsylvania. Churches, schools, hospitals, and the YMCA and YWCA also benefited from Sage's generosity. In addition, she contributed a dormitory to Harvard University and established the Russell Sage College.

Sage also made generous bequests in her will. In addition to adding more than $5 million to the Russell Sage Foundation's endowment and giving gifts in excess of a million dollars to the Children's Aid Society and the New York Charity Organization Society, 15 colleges and the New York Public Library each received gifts of $800,000. Substantial bequests were made to the Metropolitan Museum of Art, the New York Botanical Garden, and the Museum of Natural History as well as to various Bible and tract societies. In all, Olivia Sage gave away between $75 and $80 million.

Bibliography

Dictionary of American Biography, vol. 8, pp. 291–92; Jackson, *Encyclopedia of New York City*, p. 1032; James, *Notable American Women, 1607–1950*, vol. 3, pp. 222–23.

Schiff, Jacob Henry
financier, philanthropist
b. January 10, 1847; d. September 25, 1920.

Jacob Schiff's principal contribution to the American Settlement Movement was the initial funding and continuing financial support he provided to **Lillian Wald** and **Mary Brewster** when they established the Nurses' Settlement in New York City. He was the type of philanthropist on whom settlement workers and other social welfare workers relied to support their work.

Schiff was born in Frankfurt-am-Main and educated in the local schools. In 1861, at the age of 14 he was apprenticed to a business firm. Four years later, he emigrated to the United States, where he secured employment in a brokerage firm. In 1866, he was licensed as a broker, and the following year he joined the firm of Budge, Schiff, & Company. In 1870, Schiff became a citizen of the United States.

When Budge, Schiff, & Company ceased operations in 1872, Schiff returned to Germany. He served as manager of the Hamburg Branch of the London & Hanseatic Bank for a short time, but in 1874, Schiff returned to New York to accept a position at the firm of Kuhn, Loeb, and Company. In 1885 Schiff became head of the firm. During his career, Schiff was concerned with financing railroad companies and with insurance firms.

In 1893, Schiff financed Lillian Wald and Mary Brewster's visiting nurse service on New York City's Lower East Side. Two years later, he donated the house that became the **Henry Street Settlement**. Schiff was also a supporter of the **National Child Labor Committee**, the Red Cross, and the National Employment Exchange.

Schiff took a special interest in Jewish philanthropies. In 1909, he funded a new translation of the Bible under Jewish auspices. He also financed the Schiff Library of Jewish Classics, which published a collection of 20 volumes. In 1906, Schiff helped organize the American Jewish Committee, which provided funds to meet emergencies among Jews in other countries. He was also a supporter of the Jewish Theological Seminary of New York and of the Hebrew Union College in Cincinnati, Ohio.

Schiff remained active in social reform work until shortly before his death in 1920. His generous support was vital to the work of the Henry Street Settlement, and he also contributed to other reform groups organized by settlement workers.

Bibliography

Adler, *Jacob H. Schiff: His Life and Letters*; *Dictionary of American Biography*, vol. 8, pp. 430–32; Jackson, *Encyclopedia of New York City*, p. 1047.

Schneiderman, Rose
labor organizer, reformer, political activist
b. April 6, 1882; d. August 11, 1979.

Rose Schneiderman began her career as a piece worker in the garment trade and went on to become a federal labor official and advisor to President Franklin D. Roosevelt. Over the years

Rose Schneiderman
Museum of the City of New York

she established herself as a respected member of both the New York and national reform communities, and she relied on her professional and personal relationships to organize unions and reform labor.

Rose Schneiderman's family emigrated to New York City from Poland when she was eight years old in 1895. Within two years her father, Samuel, was dead, and Schneiderman had to leave school to stay at home and care for her younger sister while their mother worked in the fur trade. After a short stay in a Jewish orphanage, during which time she resumed her education, Schneiderman's formal education ended, and she was forced to find work to support her family. At the age of 13, she found work as an errand girl and later became a cashier, earning $2.25 per week. By 1898 Schneiderman was working as a lining maker in a cap factory where she eventually earned six dollars a week as a sample maker. She realized that these working conditions were inadequate, but she saw no other option. Her perception would soon change.

In 1902, the Schneiderman family lived for a year in Montreal so that Rose's mother could be close to her sister. There Schneiderman became acquainted with the Kellerts, a family with socialist leanings who introduced her to organized labor. When she returned to New York

City, Schneiderman aligned herself with Bessie Braunt, an anarchist who assisted her in organizing the first women's local of the Jewish Socialist capmakers union. Schneiderman was aware of the differences between the treatment of men and women workers, and she came to believe that organization was the best way to get more money and better working conditions for women. Schneiderman's persistence eventually overcame the union leadership's resistance, and within a short time, they chartered Local 23 of the United Cloth Hat and Cap Makers.

Schneiderman quickly rose through the labor ranks, and she was elected secretary of the union and served as its delegate to the New York City Central Labor Union. In 1904, Schneiderman became the first woman to be elected to a union executive board. Although she was suspicious of the middle-class women who ran the New York branch of the **Women's Trade Union League** (WTUL), Schneiderman was soon won over when the WTUL offered its support to the striking capmakers in 1905. The following year, she became vice president of the New York WTUL, and two years later, thanks to the financial assistance of a league backer, she was able to leave her job to attend the Rand School of Social Science while working part-time as a union organizer.

By the opening decades of the twentieth century, Schneiderman was a well-known labor organizer on New York City's Lower East Side. The fact that she spoke Yiddish made it easy for her to win the confidence of the Jewish immigrant women in the needle trades. She also played a central role in the shirtwaist makers strike (1909–1910).

By 1910, Schneiderman was working full-time as a labor organizer. She helped form Local 62 of the International Ladies' Garment Workers' Union and was the union's first president and the driving force behind its 1913 general strike.

An internal dispute within the leadership of the New York WTUL over which groups of women would be the better candidates for unionization led Schneiderman to resign her position. It did not take her long to find a new cause. Convinced that the vote would enable working women to achieve better wages and working conditions, she now offered her assistance to the woman suffrage campaign. In the summer of 1912, Schneiderman was hired by the National American Woman Suffrage Association to encourage trade unionists to support woman suffrage. Although she remained active in the work of the association over the next several years, Schneiderman's real interest was still organized labor. She returned to the New York WTUL in 1914. The following year she became a national organizer for the International Ladies Garment Workers' Union.

Schneiderman withdrew from the suffrage movement during the 1920s after its supporters advocated the passage of the Equal Rights Amendment. Her decision was based on her belief that such an amendment would undermine the effectiveness of the protective legislation for women that she and others had fought for. Nevertheless, Schneiderman learned many valuable lessons from her involvement in the suffrage campaign. When she refocused her attention on labor organization, Schneiderman applied the strategy of securing protective legislation for minimum wage and maximum hour legislation. These causes occupied her attention while she was president of the New York WTUL (1918–1949) and president of the national WTUL (1926–1950).

During the 1920s, Schneiderman began to look to the state for assistance in solving many of labor's problems. Although she had been a member of the Socialist Party, Schneiderman was gradually drawn toward the Democratic Party, partly as a result of her personal friendship with Eleanor and Franklin Roosevelt.

In 1933, President Roosevelt appointed Schneiderman to the National Recovery Administration's (NRA) Labor Advisory Board. She was the only woman on the board, and she was responsible for overseeing NRA codes as they affected workers, with special responsibility for women. In addition to her work with the NRA, Schneiderman was also a member of Roosevelt's brain trust.

From 1937 to 1944, Schneiderman was the secretary of the New York State Department of Labor. She never abandoned her interest in organized labor, and as president emeritus, Schneiderman attended meetings of the New York WTUL until the organization disbanded in 1955.

Bibliography
Dictionary of American Biography, supl. 9, pp. 705–06; Endelman, *Solidarity Forever: Rose Schneiderman and the Women's Trade Union League*; Trattner, *Biographical Dictionary of Social Welfare in America*, pp. 660–62.

Scudder, Julia Vida Dutton
settlement worker, social reformer, educator, author
b. December 15, 1861; d. October 9, 1954.

Vida Scudder's life and career combined scholarship and social activism. Like many college-educated young women of her generation, she possessed a strong social conscience that was inspired to action by the doctrines of socialism and the writings of the Christian Socialists. (*See* **Christian Socialism**.) Scudder began her career as a settlement worker and went on to combine this commitment to social activism with a parallel career as a university professor and religious scholar.

Julia Davida Scudder was born in Madura, India, in 1861 where her father, David Coit Scudder, was a Congregationalist minister and missionary. She returned to Boston the following year with her mother, Harriet Louisa Dutton Scudder, after her father accidentally drowned. The Duttons and the Scudders were prominent Boston families, and young Vida enjoyed a privileged upbringing which included extended European travel before she was enrolled at the private Miss Sanger's School in Boston in 1881. Education and Christian duty were valued above money in the Scudder household, and Vida was encouraged to pursue her religious and literary interests. She was a member of the first graduating class of the Boston Girl's Latin School in 1880, and she graduated from Smith College in 1884. The following year, she and Clara French were the first two American women admitted to Oxford University to pursue graduate study in literature.

When she returned to Boston at the end of 1885, Scudder spent two unsettled years reading extensively about history, religion, and the new social thought. Her social conscience was stirred by the writings of the English artist and critic John Ruskin as was her interest in socialism by the work of the Christian Socialists **Charles Kingsley** and **Frederick Denison Maurice**, and the Russian novelist Leo Tolstoy. Scudder also began to explore her interest in religion. Although her family was Congregationalist, she and her mother both joined **Philips Brooks**'s Episcopalian Trinity Church. Additionally, in 1888 she joined a semi-monastic group of Episcopalian women called the Companions of the Holy Cross, which was dedicated to intercessionary prayer and social reconciliation. Scudder also developed an interest in the life and works of St. Francis of Assisi and of St. Catherine of Sienna. Many of her later writings were an attempt to reconcile Franciscan and Marxist tenets.

In 1887, Scudder received a master of arts degree from Smith and accepted a position teaching English at Wellesley College. This same year she returned to Smith for a meeting of the Association of College Alumnae, where she and two friends, **Jean Fine** and Helen Rand, were instrumental in the establishment of the **College Settlements Association**. In 1893, Scudder took a leave of absence from Wellesley, where she was now an assistant professor, to assist **Helena Dudley** in establishing the association's Boston-based settlement, **Denison House**.

Scudder was never entirely convinced that the settlements could effectively eliminate poverty. She chose instead to focus on the role that the houses could play in providing educated women with an opportunity for public service. During this time, Scudder taught college extension courses at Denison House and lectured for the Society of Christian Socialists, which had been founded by **William Dwight Porter Bliss**.

After she resumed teaching, Scudder maintained her ties to Denison House and its neighborhood. She encouraged her students at Wellesley to develop an interest in social action. Scudder was also active in the Boston labor movement, serving as a delegate at the Boston Central Labor Convention (1893), helping to organize women workers, and writing about labor issues. In 1903, Scudder helped found the Boston branch of the **Women's Trade Union League** and became director of the Circolo Italo-Americano, a social/cultural group for immigrants at Denison House. In 1910, amid much controversy, Scudder supported the striking textile workers in Lawrence, Massachusetts, a gesture that almost cost her her teaching position.

Over the next few years, she became more and more critical of what she considered were the limitations of settlement work. Convinced that the settlements were willing to betray the working classes to placate their rich benefactors, she gave up active participation in the work of Denison House in 1912. She maintained an interest in the settlement's work, but her militancy alarmed both her family and her friends. Finally, Scudder's dissatisfaction led to her break her connection with Denison House in 1918, when she resigned from its Board of Directors and turned her attention to her writing and teaching.

In 1920, Scudder left Boston and moved to Wellesley. Eight years later she retired from teaching but continued to write, exploring ways in which she could reconcile her interests in religious thought, social idealism, and the new industrial society. Her writings reflect her lifelong struggle to reconcile her cultured life as a professor of literature with her equally important commitment to social justice.

Bibliography

Davis, *Spearheads for Reform: The Social Settlements and the Progressive Movement, 1890–1914*; *Dictionary of American Biography*, supl. 5, pp. 616–17; Scudder, *On Journey*; Trattner, *Biographical Dictionary of Social Welfare in America*, pp. 667–71.

The Second Twenty Years at Hull-House (1930)

Jane Addams worked on the sequel to her autobiography, ***Twenty Years at Hull-House with Autobiographical Notes* (1910)**, during most of the 1920s. When it was finally published in 1930, *The Second Twenty Years at Hull-House* presented a picture that was markedly different from its predecessor. Addams's life had changed during the intervening 20 years as had life at **Hull House** and the lives of people all over the world.

As she points out in the book's introduction, the 20-year period that Addams is concerned with can be conveniently subdivided into two decades. The first decade may be further subdivided into two five-year components—one of peace and one of war. The second decade was a time of rapid and far-reaching change.

Addams discusses the various reform efforts that were pursued and accomplished from 1909 to 1914, including the work of the **Pittsburgh Survey**, the first significant social survey of an American urban community; the creation of the **United States Children's Bureau**, a central government agency formed to collect and exchange ideas and information on child welfare; and the activities of the National Conference of Charities and Correction (*see* **National Conference on Social Welfare**), an influential organization composed of leaders of both public and private charitable relief organizations and correctional institutions. It also includes a discussion of the Progressive Party and the 1912 presidential candidacy of Theodore Roosevelt.

Addams's narrative of these years also examines the woman's movement and the suffrage crusade, the impact of World War I on Hull House, and the activities of the Peace Movement during the years of the conflict.

In her discussion of the activities of the second decade under consideration, 1919–1929, Addams writes of her awareness of a growing new world consciousness. She acknowledges that the work of Hull House must be seen as a single element in a larger picture. This last portion of *The Second Twenty Years at Hull-House* examines **prohibition**, immigration quotas, juvenile delinquency, and education reform.

Like many of her reform colleagues, Addams supported prohibition, believing that alcohol contributed to the decline of morals, particularly in working-class neighborhoods. Addams was especially concerned with juvenile delinquency. She acknowledged that the city held many temptations for young people and was concerned that even small indiscretions could lead to severe consequences. Addams's discussions of these and other issues in *The Second Twenty Years at Hull-House* provide a picture of the various social issues that settlement workers confronted during the early decades of the twentieth century. Additionally, the book gives insights into Addams's personal growth and development.

Bibliography

Addams, *The Second Twenty Years at Hull-House, September 1909 to September 1928, with a Record of a Growing World Consciousness*; Davis, *American Heroine: The Life and Legend of Jane Addams.*

The Settlement Horizon (1922)

Settlement residents frequently conducted detailed investigations on a variety of topics such as housing, health, or working conditions. These projects were undertaken to provide information about the communities the settlements were located in, and the results were evaluated to suggest new programs to assist the community and its inhabitants. From time to time, the men and women who were active in the settlement movement took the opportunity to examine and evaluate their own work.

Published in 1922, *The Settlement Horizon* appraised the American Settlement Movement up to the time. It was written by **Robert Woods** and **Albert Kennedy**, both of whom were associated with the **South End House** settlement in Boston. In addition, the two men had served as joint secretaries of the **National Federation of Settlements** (NFS) during the decade preceding the book's publication. The NFS was the coalition of settlement houses that promoted cooperation and coordination among its members nationwide. Woods and Kennedy were assisted in their work by a number of their colleagues, particularly those associated with settlements in New York and Boston.

The Settlement Horizon begins with a discussion of both the English antecedents of the American Settlement Movement and the growth and development of the network of settlement houses in the United States. This discussion is followed by chapters on the various activities and services offered by the settlements such as clubs, summer camps, schools, and health care. The development of local and national settlement federations is also covered. The appendixes provide information about specific projects and programs that were undertaken by various settlement houses. These include details about efforts to secure protective legislation, training classes, festivals, and the activities of settlement governing boards. A bibliography of works written by men and women active in the settlement movement provides information on the stages of development of the movement, particularly in the United States.

Although *The Settlement Horizon* provides a fairly detailed account of the accomplishments and activities of the settlements up to that time, it does little to illuminate the tensions that had developed within the ranks of settlement workers as they were called upon to respond to the ever-changing needs of American society during the opening decades of the twentieth century.

Bibliography

Woods, *The Settlement Horizon.*

Sheppard-Towner Act

Settlement workers realized the value of securing protective legislation and the means for seeing that it was enforced. The care of women and children were always a high priority for settlement workers, and they entered into a number of productive alliances with other social welfare reformers to aid these vulnerable portions of the population. Over the years a number of laws protecting women and children were passed—thanks in large measure to the efforts of settlement workers. One example was the Sheppard-Towner Act that provided funds for health care for women and children. The Sheppard-Towner Act demonstrated the federal government's interest in the well-being of children, something that settlement workers and other social reformers believed was a critical step in securing adequate funding and support for child welfare legislation.

Among her many accomplishments, **Julia Lathrop** was appointed in 1913 by President William Howard Taft to head the newly created **United States Children's Bureau**. The bureau was intended to serve as a central agency responsible for collecting and distributing ideas and information on child welfare. As head of the bureau, one of Lathrop's first initiatives was to undertake a thorough study of infant mortality in the United States. During the course of their research, she and her staff examined the relationship between infant and maternal health and mortality. As a result of their investigations, Lathrop and her colleagues were able to document that infant and maternal mortality rates in the United States were unusually high and that many women received no prenatal care. Based on these findings, Lathrop recommended in 1917 that the federal government supply aid to states to provide health care for mothers and children. The bill that Lathrop prepared was introduced in Congress by Representative Jeanette Rankin in 1918, but it was not acted upon. Lathrop and her colleagues did not abandon their fight, though. The bill was re-introduced by Senator Morris Sheppard and Representative Horace Towner and was passed in 1921.

The Act for the Promotion of the Welfare and Hygiene of Maternity and Infancy, popularly known as the Sheppard-Towner Act, provided for an appropriation of $1.47 million to be distributed among states on a matching basis. Under the terms of the act, states had to agree to expend the money they received on hygiene instruction for mothers and infants.

This instruction was to be carried out by doctors and nurses in homes or in health centers, through conferences, and through the distribution of literature. The act also provided for the training of health care professionals who would then qualify to train the public.

The act called for annual appropriations to be made to cooperating states for a term of five years. The states were responsible for designating a state child hygiene or child welfare division that would assume responsibility for administering the act's provisions. In 1927, the life of the Sheppard-Towner Act was extended for two years with the understanding that it would lapse after June 30, 1929. At the time that the act expired, 45 states and Hawaii were cooperating. The decision to continue the services that the Sheppard-Towner Act financed was left to the discretion of the states.

The Sheppard-Towner Act proved successful, and during its life, infant and maternal mortality rates declined significantly. As a result of the monies it provided, more than 3,000 health centers were established, primarily in rural areas. The act helped to bolster state health departments and led to the development of county health care systems. The act also aroused public interest in the area of health care, and as the first statute to provide federal grants-in-aid to states for noneducational programs, it established a precedent for future cooperative federal-state programs under the Social Security Act of 1935. *See also* **Child Welfare**.

Bibliography

Axinn, *Social Welfare: A History of the American Response to Need*; Chepaitis, "Federal Social Welfare Progressivism in the 1920s"; Lemons, "The Sheppard-Towner Act: Progressivism in the 1920s"; Trattner, *From Poor Law to Welfare State: A History of Social Welfare in America*.

Simkhovitch, Mary Melinda Kingsbury

settlement founder, social reformer, housing expert
b. September 8, 1867; d. November 15, 1951.

A religious-minded young woman, Mary Kingsbury was inspired by **William Dwight Porter Bliss** and the doctrines of **Christian Socialism** to apply her personal piety to the prevailing reform movements by becoming involved in church-related social reform efforts. She was personally acquainted with **Vida Scudder** and the other founders of the **College Settlements Association**, and she became involved in their work at the Boston settlement **Denison House**.

This early settlement experience provided Kingsbury with a connection to the active Boston-area social reform network. Using this network as a foundation, she eventually moved to

Mary K. Simkhovitch
The Schlesinger Library, Radcliffe College

New York City where she became a respected leader in that city's reform community. Unlike most of her colleagues, she raised two children while living and working in the settlement she founded, **Greenwich House**. Gradually, she focused her attention on the housing issue, and she became a leader in the national movement to secure low-cost public housing.

Like many of her contemporaries, Kingsbury took advantage of opportunities for higher education for women to prepare herself for a career outside the home. After graduating from Boston University (1890), she taught Latin in the Somerville High School before pursuing graduate study at Radcliffe College in economics and sociology. In 1894, she was awarded a scholarship by the Women's Industrial Union of Boston, and she used the funds to study at the University of Berlin for a year. It was here that she met her future husband, Vladimir Simkhovitch, a fellow student. After returning to the United States, Kingsbury enrolled in graduate classes at Columbia University.

In 1897, she abandoned her studies to become the head resident at the **College Settlement** on New York City's Lower East Side. The following year she became the head resident at the Friendly Aid House, a Unitarian-sponsored settlement in New York City. Kingsbury spent three years at the Friendly Aid House. During this time she married Simkhovitch, who had

secured a position as a professor of history at Columbia University. Mary Simkhovitch was increasingly frustrated with her position at the Friendly Aid House. She had serious philosophical differences with the settlement's sponsors, and finally in 1902, she, her husband, and a group of like-minded associates established a settlement, Greenwich House, in the old ninth ward on New York's Lower West Side.

Simkhovitch used Greenwich House to foster her personal settlement philosophy which centered on the importance of the neighborhood concept. She encouraged others who were interested in settlement work to use Greenwich House as a base of operations for their social research. For example, **Mary White Ovington** was a Greenwich House Research Fellow when she began her groundbreaking study of New York City's black community.

Simkhovitch participated in social reform efforts on the local, state, and national levels. She was active in school reform, campaigns for parks and playgrounds, and a variety of public health initiatives. She was one of the founders of the New York City-based Association of Neighborhood Workers (*see* **United Neighborhood Houses**) and of the **Outdoor Recreation League**, and was a member of the New York and national branches of the **Women's Trade Union League** and the **National Child Labor Committee**. Simkhovitch served as president of the **National Federation of Settlements** during World War I, leading that coalition through a difficult period of its history.

Eventually, Simkhovitch concentrated her energies in the campaign to secure low-cost public housing, and she was recognized as a housing reform expert. As president of the National Public Housing Conference (*see* **National Housing Conference**), she worked with **Helen Alfred** and **Louis Pink** to secure passage of the **Wagner-Steagall Housing Act** in 1937. She also served as vice chair of the New York City Housing Authority.

Retiring as director of Greenwich House in 1946, Simkhovitch and her husband continued to live at the settlement and remained active in the work of the house and in the life of the surrounding neighborhood up to her death in November 1951.

A dynamic force within the American Settlement Movement for more than 50 years, Simkhovitch had a wide range of reform interests including recreation, women and children workers, women's rights, and health and safety issues. Her primary concern was housing, and she worked on both the local and national levels to secure adequate, safe housing for the poor.

Bibliography

Dictionary of American Biography, supl. 5, pp. 630–31; Simkhovitch, *Neighborhood: My Story of Greenwich House*, Trattner, *Biographical Dictionary of Social Welfare in America*, pp. 673–76.

Smith, Alfred Emanuel
politician, social reformer
b. December 30, 1873; d. October 4, 1944.

Al Smith was a skilled politician who combined his political expertise with an interest in social reform. During his career, Smith forged a number of long-term, productive working relationships with settlement workers and other social welfare workers. These alliances resulted in the passage of numerous legislative acts that enabled social reformers to realize their goals of providing safe and clean working and living conditions for the poor.

When Smith was 12 years old, his father died unexpectedly, leaving the family in a precarious financial position. Two years later, Smith left school to help support his mother and sister. Over the next several years, he held a number of jobs including working as an errand boy, selling fish to merchants and restaurants at New York City's Fulton Fish Market, and working in a boiler manufacturing plant.

While in his early twenties, Smith was befriended by the owner of the local neighborhood saloon, Tom Foley. He ran political errands for Foley, a Democratic precinct leader and Tammany Hall supporter. As a result of Foley's political connections, Smith secured an appointment as a process server in 1895. With Tammany backing, Smith was elected to the New York State Assembly in 1903. He learned the rudiments of state government and gradually assumed leadership positions, serving as majority leader, chair of the ways and means committee, and finally, speaker of the Assembly in 1913. During this time, Smith balanced his allegiance to Tammany with a program of social reform.

In 1911, Smith served as vice chair of the **New York State Factory Investigating Commission**, which had been established following the **Triangle Shirtwaist Company Fire** in which 146 women died. New York State Senator **Robert F. Wagner** chaired the commission, which was charged with looking into working conditions in factories across the state. Smith and Wagner were assisted in their investigations by a number of settlement workers and other social reformers. Due in large measure to the political acumen of Smith and Wagner, more than 30 bills dealing with the improvement of health and safety standards were enacted into law by the New York State Legislature.

Smith moved steadily through the political ranks. In 1915, he was elected sheriff of New York City. Two years later he became president of the Board of Aldermen, and in 1918 he received the Democratic nomination for governor of New York, winning the election. Defeated in 1920, Smith was re-elected governor in 1922, 1924, and 1926. During his tenure, Smith was responsible for the passage of a number of reform initiatives related to housing, public health, jobs development, and child labor. Smith retained his connection to the New York reform community, and a number of social reformers worked closely with Smith's administration at this time including **Frances Perkins** and **Belle Moskowitz**.

Smith was a candidate for the Democratic presidential nomination in 1924, but lost to John W. Davis. Four years later, Smith led the party's ticket, but he was defeated by Herbert Hoover in the general election. Following the election, Smith entered private business, serving as president of the Empire State Building Corporation and overseeing the construction of that building, which was completed in 1931. During this time he also served as chair of a trust company and as editor of a periodical called the *New Outlook*. (*See* **The *Outlook***.)

After an abortive campaign to win the Democratic nomination for president in 1932, Smith grew increasingly critical of Franklin Roosevelt and the New Deal, and his political power gradually diminished during the 1930s. ***See also* Ward Politics**.

Bibliography

Dictionary of American Biography, supl. 3, pp. 716–21; Jackson, *Encyclopedia of New York City*, pp. 1079–80; Olson, *Historical Dictionary of the New Deal*, pp. 457–58.

Smith, Zilpha Drew
social reformer, social work educator
b. January 25, 1852?; d. October 12, 1926.

One of the first women to establish a professional career for herself within the **Charity Organization Society** movement, Zilpha Smith was instrumental in the social welfare-related educational reform efforts that transformed the nineteenth-century friendly visitor (*see* **Friendly Visitors**) into the twentieth-century professional social worker. Smith remained a lifelong advocate of the ideal of volunteer personal service. Her attitude reflected her parents' dedication to social causes such as temperance, woman suffrage, and religious tolerance and their belief in the indispensability of social service.

After graduating from Boston's Girls' High and Normal School in 1868, Smith eschewed her teacher training for a job as a telegrapher in the Commercial Telegraph Office in Boston. At the same time, she served as a volunteer in the Co-operative Society, a Boston-based relief organization. A perfectionist who demonstrated a partiality for accuracy in detail, Smith applied her classification and analytical skills to the task of reorganizing the index of the Probate Court of Suffolk County. The successful completion of this project, along with her relief work contributions following the Boston Fire of 1872, enhanced Smith's reputation with the Boston reform community and led to her appointment as registrar of the newly established **Boston Associated Charities** (BAC) in 1879.

Smith was responsible for the registration bureau, or confidential exchange, which maintained a central file of every individual who benefited from the various agencies affiliated with the Associated Charities. In 1886, she was named general secretary of the BAC. Under her leadership, the BAC became one of the most successful organizations of its type, known for the large number of volunteers it enlisted and for the careful training that Smith provided to volunteers and paid agents.

Through this training, Smith became a pioneer in social work education. She advocated formal training for charity workers so they could not only reform the needy individual but also educate the general public and their elected and appointed officials about the need for effective social reform policy. Her course of training prepared volunteers and paid BAC workers to function as professional investigators, applying the objectivity and precision of the social scientist to their work. Smith instituted study classes for relief workers, and in 1888, along with Charles Birtwell of the **Boston Children's Aid Society**, founded the Monday Evening Club, a social work discussion group that anticipated later social work professional associations.

As a result of her work in Boston, Smith became a central figure in the National Conference of Charities and Correction (*see* **National Conference on Social Welfare**), the influential organization composed of leaders of both public and private charitable relief organiza-

tions and correctional institutions. She lectured at the New York School of Philanthropy (*see* **Columbia University Graduate School of Social Work**), and served as a mentor to many young women who selected social work as a profession.

Smith retired from the Boston Associated Charities in 1903. The following year, she became assistant director of the newly established **Boston School for Social Workers**, which had a branch for women at Simmons College and one for men at Harvard University. The school's program provided students with an opportunity for fieldwork experience and studying social problems by using actual case studies. **Florence Kelley** and **Lillian Wald** were among the social reformers who lectured at the school during its first year. Smith retired from the Boston School for Social Workers in 1918.

Bibliography

James, *Notable American Women, 1607–1950*, vol. 3, pp. 321–23; Lubove, *The Professional Altruist: The Emergence of Social Work as a Career, 1880–1930*; Trattner, *Biographical Dictionary of Social Welfare in America*, pp. 681–83.

Social Gospel

Before the rise of large urban centers, people living in rural areas or in smaller towns and villages tended to look after each other during times of economic or social distress. Individuals felt a sense of commitment to the community, and in turn, the community felt a sense of responsibility to its individual members. The economic expansion and rapid industrialization that characterized the latter part of the nineteenth century altered these social interactions and responsibilities. The acceptance and growth of the doctrine of the Social Gospel, also known as Social Christianity or Applied Christianity, particularly in the decade of the 1890s, was one response to the changing times.

The Social Gospel Movement was an effort on the part of Protestant clergy to apply the teachings and doctrines of Christianity to the social, economic, and political problems they encountered in their parishes, particularly those located in urban centers. Although the Social Gospel advocates were theologically diverse, they shared a common goal, which was to counteract the alienation of the working class from organized religion and to make the middle class aware of its responsibility for the prevailing social injustice.

Within the Social Gospel Movement, opinions differed regarding the best way to achieve its goals. The Social Christians advocated a more moderate approach, while those who identified themselves as Christian Socialists called for a more comprehensive revision of the existing social order.

The Social Gospel Movement of the 1890s may be distinguished from earlier church movements by its underlying assumption that rather than individual shortcomings, it was a prevailing social injustice that contributed to poverty, vice, and urban social dislocation. Its advocates called on individuals to assume responsibility and to challenge the prevailing social order.

In their attempts to apply Christian principles to their everyday lives, those who subscribed to the Social Gospel doctrine generally supported labor unions' efforts to secure higher wages and better working conditions. They favored tax reform, dissolution of monopolies, and more state control of the economy. Additionally, Social Gospel adherents supported political reform including an end to rule by machine politicians and more direct participation in the democratic process, such as the direct election of senators.

A number of influential clergy who advocated the doctrines of the Social Gospel Movement taught in colleges and universities. This affiliation provided them with an opportunity to bring their ideas to the attention of young men and women who were looking for meaningful careers after completing their formal education. William Jewett Tucker, for example, was a Congregational minister who taught at the Andover Theological Seminary in Massachusetts. Tucker was a strong advocate of finding ways to enlarge the function of the church in modern society. One of Tucker's students was **Robert Woods**, who at Tucker's suggestion traveled to England to study the settlement movement there, and who, after returning to the United States, helped Tucker to establish a settlement in Boston. This settlement, Andover House, was later known as **South End House**, and its work served as an example for other Boston-area settlements and for settlements across the United States.

The doctrines of the Social Gospel Movement, which stressed the need for individuals to assume responsibility for bringing about positive change within the existing social order, were infused in the work of literally every settlement house whether the workers consciously articulated them or not. In this way, the Social Gospel was incorporated into the philosophy of the settlement movement. *See also* **Christian Socialism**.

Bibliography
Axinn, *Social Welfare: A History of the American Response to Need*; Bremner, *From the Depths: The Discovery of Poverty in the United States*; Davis, *Spearheads for Reform: The Social Settlements and the Progressive Movement, 1890–1914*; Leiby, *A History of Social Welfare and Social Work in the United States*.

Social Reform Club

In the early 1890s, groups of social welfare reformers who were living and working on New York City's Lower East Side often came together informally to discuss the economic, social, and political issues of the day which had a direct impact on their everyday lives. Often, these discussions developed into lively debates on how to best change the world. One such discussion group was the Social Reform Club.

The club counted among its members an impressive group of intellectuals, social reform professionals, and labor leaders such as **Mary Simkhovitch**, founder of **Greenwich House**; **Felix Adler** of the **Ethical Culture Society; Charles Stover** and **Edward King** of the **Neighborhood Guild;** Charles P. Spahr of the *Outlook*; and **Lillian Wald** of the **Henry Street Settlement**. In 1894, the group asked Leonora O'Reilly, an energetic and articulate labor organizer, to join them. She eventually became vice president of the club.

The discussions of the Social Reform Club were primarily concerned with improving the condition of the laboring class in New York City and with encouraging the growth of trade unionism. Other pressing social reform causes such as housing and immigration were also considered.

The Social Reform Club provided more than just intellectual exercise for its members. It was a municipal reform organization. The members were aware of the potential influence they could exert, and from time to time, they used this leverage to speak out either in favor of or against various issues, especially those related to labor issues and to the housing situation in New York City.

A number of social reform efforts were initiated as a result of the discussions of the members of the Social Reform Club. These efforts included the establishment of the **Women's Trade Union League**, the New York branch of the **Consumers' League**, and the **Committee on Congestion of Population**.

Bibliography
Daniels, *Always a Sister: The Feminism of Lillian D. Wald*; Siegel, *Lillian Wald of Henry Street*.

Social Service Center for Practical Training in Philanthropic and Social Work *See* Graduate School of Social Service Administration (Chicago)

Social Union of the North and West Ends *See* Boston Social Union

Social Work (1922)

Edited by **Edward T. Devine,** this book was the first in a series entitled The Social Welfare Library. Devine was the general secretary of the New York **Charity Organization Society** for 21 years. He started and edited the society's publication, *Charities* (*see* **the *Survey***), and he was director of the New York School of Philanthropy. (*See* **Columbia University Graduate School of Social Work**.) In addition, he was involved in many social welfare initiatives including housing and child labor reform.

Social Work was intended as a classroom text that could also be used by the general reader who was interested in the basic concepts of social reform work. It examines the history and meaning of social work as well as its scope and significance. Chapters are devoted to the family, dependent adults, children, the sick, the handicapped, and crime and the courts. Devine also discusses preventive case work, coordination and supervision of social work efforts, and preparation and training required. He concludes with a discussion of the future of the social work professionals.

In addition to being used as a textbook, *Social Work* attempted to make the theory behind the field of social welfare work accessible to the general public. In this way, Devine hoped to gain the support of the community for the work being done by professional social workers and at the same time to attract more men and women to the field.

Bibliography

Devine, *Social Work*.

Some Ethical Gains through Legislation (1905)

Written in 1905 by **Florence Kelley** when she was general secretary of the National **Consumers' League**, *Some Ethical Gains through Legislation* presents and interprets legislation and judicial decisions that affected the rights of children and women workers. Some of the material included in the book was taken from articles that Kelley had previously published and from speeches she had delivered as she traveled across the United States lecturing on college campuses on behalf of the National Consumers' League.

The first chapters are concerned with children and their employment in a number of different trades including domestic work, the street trades, retail trade, and the glass bottle industry. Kelley also discusses the need to ensure that children do in fact enjoy the benefits of childhood, a home, adequate food, an education, and recreation, which she believed would make them better citizens. She then outlines the basic requirements of an effective child labor law which included safeguards for the child, such as regulating the age of child workers and the hours they could be employed; responsibilities of parents, and guidelines for employers.

Kelley discusses the need to establish a national agency to protect the children. This agency would be concerned with all aspects of the physical, mental, and moral condition of children in the United States. This call for action was finally realized in 1912 with the creation of the **United States Children's Bureau**.

Kelley next examines the condition of women workers. She argues that women need leisure time, which she believes could be guaranteed by legislation that would restrict the numbers of hours that women could work. Other chapters examine the issue of woman suffrage and the effect that having the vote would have on women's everyday lives.

Finally, Kelley examines the negative effects of the factory system and the potentially positive effect that groups such as the National Consumers' League could have on regulating the means of production to protect workers' rights. The appendixes provide detailed discussions of selected court cases that affected the passage of protective legislation.

Although her contemporaries in the social reform community read Kelley's book with interest and used it as a reference in their efforts to secure political labor legislation, *Some Ethical Gains through Legislation* is probably more valuable today as an historical record of the conditions of women and children workers at the beginning of the twentieth century and of the efforts of Kelley and her colleagues to bring about substantive positive change.

Bibliography
Kelley, *Some Ethical Gains through Legislation*.

South End House

William Jewitt Tucker was a Congregationalist minister who taught at Andover Theological Seminary and who had been influenced by the **Social Gospel** movement. He was interested in applying his ideas in a practical setting and was determined to establish a settlement. In 1890, he sent **Robert A. Woods**, one of his students, to England to study the settlement movement there.

In 1891, Tucker appointed Woods head resident of his new settlement in Boston's South End, Andover House. Four years later, Woods changed the name of the settlement to South End House in acknowledgment of the district in which it was located. The settlement was situated in a congested factory and tenement neighborhood. Most of the residents were Irish, although a significant number of Jews and Italians also lived there.

Like other settlements, South End House was established to improve the lives of the people in the surrounding neighborhood. In addition to their work to better the housing and sanitary conditions of the area, the residents secured a playground, worked with the local public school to develop an industrial education program, and established an anti-tuberculosis campaign and a dispensary. The residents also helped to organize several women's trade unions and were active in the campaign to establish a juvenile court. In 1910 an independent music school was organized.

South End House also sponsored a branch for blacks called the **Robert Gould Shaw House,** which was named in honor of the Commander of the Massachusetts 54th, the first black regiment sent into action from the free states during the Civil War.

South End House counted a number of leaders of the American Settlement Movement among its residents. In addition to Woods, **Albert J. Kennedy** and **Lucy Peck** also worked at South End House. The residents of South End House also produced a number of important research studies that served as models for other settlement workers including *Americans in Process* (1902) and *The City Wilderness* (1898).

Bibliography
Woods, *The Handbook of Settlements*; Woods, *The Settlement Horizon*.

South End Social Union *See*

Boston Social Union

Starr, Ellen Gates
settlement founder, social reformer, labor activist
b. March 19, 1859; d. February 10, 1940.

Although **Jane Addams** was the principal force in the long-lived success of the Chicago-based settlement **Hull House**, her successes were due in large measure to the support and encouragement of Ellen Gates Starr, whom she met when they were students at Rockford Seminary in the late 1870s. During the 40 years that she was associated with Hull House, Starr was responsible for many of the settlement's cultural programs, including literature and art appreciation classes that were intended to inspire the neighborhood residents and to encourage their assimilation.

Starr's father, Caleb Allen Starr, could only afford to send his daughter to Rockford Seminary for one year beginning in the fall of 1877. However, during her short stay at Rockford, Starr formed a significant attachment to Addams, who was 18 months her junior. Starr left Rockford to teach in a country school in Mount Morris, Illinois, for one year. In 1879, she accepted a position at the fashionable Miss Kirkland's School for Girls in Chicago where she taught art appreciation and other subjects.

Starr's relationship with Addams was maintained through the exchange of numerous letters and occasional visits. In 1888 while the two women were touring Europe together, Addams confided her desire to found a settlement house. Starr was an enthusiastic supporter from the start, and she used her reputation with the parents of her students to secure the trust and patronage of influential members of Chicago society.

A central principle of Starr's life was her quest for religious truth, but until she found the answers she sought, she strove to improve the lives of others. She was deeply concerned about the decline of art, particularly folk art, within the context of an industrial society. At Hull House, Starr organized reading clubs and art history classes to infuse the lives of her neighbors with an appreciation of classical literature and art. In 1891, she secured a $5,000 donation from Edward Butler, a wealthy Chicagoan, to build an art gallery for Hull House. Three years later she founded and served as president of the Chicago Public School Art Society. Although her effort to establish a book bindery at Hull House was less than successful, Starr was instrumental in the establishment of the Hull House Labor Museum in 1900, which was intended to help preserve the traditional weaving skills of the Italian immigrants who lived in the neighborhood around the settlement.

Gradually, Starr's concern with the aesthetic elements of her neighbors' lives was overshadowed by her alarm over the negative economic consequences that rapid industrialization had had on the lives of the working class. She assumed a more confrontational stance than that of Addams and many of the other Hull House residents in regard to the working conditions of the poor, and she became a leading advocate of unionization. In the 1890s, Starr worked with **Florence Kelley**, another Hull House resident, to promote an eight-hour day for women workers and to reform working conditions for children.

During the opening decades of the twentieth century, Starr became increasingly active in the labor movement. In 1903, she became a charter member of the National **Women's Trade Union League**. She supported striking textile workers on a number of occasions by organizing meetings, collecting money, and walking picket lines. To reward her efforts, the Amalgamated Clothing Workers of America made Starr a lifetime member in 1915.

In 1920, Starr's personal spiritual quest was realized when she was received into the Roman Catholic Church. From this time forward, she spent most of her time writing and speaking about Catholic worship and art and was only an occasional visitor at Hull House. Starr was paralyzed below the waist as a result of an operation to remove a spinal abscess in 1929, and the following year she moved to the Convent of the Holy Child in Suffern, New York, where she pursued her writing and remained until her death in 1940.

Bibliography

Addams, *Twenty Years at Hull-House with Autobiographical Notes*; Davis, *American Heroine: The Life and Legend of Jane Addams*; Davis, *Spearheads for Reform: The Social Settlements and the Progressive Movement, 1890–1914*; *Notable American Women, 1607–1950*, vol. 3, pp. 351–53; Trattner, *Biographical Dictionary of Social Welfare in America*, pp. 686–88.

Stevens, Alzina Parsons

settlement worker, social reformer, factory inspector, juvenile parole officer
b. May 27, 1849; d. June 3, 1900.

A childhood accident introduced Stevens to the dangerous conditions faced by children working in factories and gave her a heightened awareness of the pressing need for child labor reform. This personal tragedy, coupled with the positive experience she had as a resident at **Hull House**, prepared her for a productive career as a member of the Chicago reform community and as a pioneer in the field of juvenile delinquency.

Alzina Parsons's father was a prosperous farmer and small manufacturer in Parsonfield, Maine. When he died, 13-year-old Alzina was forced to go to work in a textile factory to help support the family. Not long after she started working, Alzina lost her right index finger in an industrial accident. This accident served as a constant reminder of the harshness of the child labor system. Alzina was married when she was quite young and was divorced soon after. Although she never spoke about her husband to anyone, she kept his name, Stevens.

Alzina Stevens was an ambitious young woman. She made her way to Chicago in 1871 in search of a better life, and despite the fact that she had little formal education, she became a newspaper proofreader and typesetter. While in Chicago, she joined Typographical Union No. 16. This was her introduction to the labor movement, and this association eventually brought her into contact with the active Chicago-based reform network. A few years later in 1877, she organized a women's labor group, Working Woman's Union Number 1, and served as the group's first president.

In 1882, Stevens relocated to Toledo, Ohio, and found work as a proofreader and compositor for the *Toledo Bee*. Between 1885 and 1891, Stevens worked as a correspondent and editor for the newspaper. While living in Toledo, Stevens maintained her ties to organized labor through the local branch of the Knights of Labor. She also organized the Joan of Arc assembly and became its first president.

Stevens rose steadily within the Knights of Labor, and in 1890, she was elected chief officer of District 72, which was made up of 22 local assemblies. That same year, Stevens was nominated to be director of woman's work for the Knights of Labor, but declined. Two years later she represented the northwestern Ohio labor organizations at the Populist Party national convention.

Shortly after the convention, Stevens returned to Chicago. After working on a weekly reform newspaper for a year, she went to work for the American Federation of Labor, helping to organize several new unions. At this time she was living at Hull House and was active in many of the settlement's reform campaigns.

Based on her reputation in labor circles, Stevens was named to the post of assistant state factory inspector in 1893 by Illinois Governor **John P. Altgeld**. In this position, she was under the supervision of **Florence Kelley**, another Hull House resident who had recently been named to the position of Chief Factory Investigator. During the next four years, Stevens and Kelley researched child labor conditions in the tenements and factories in Chicago. The two women were assisted in their work by deputy inspector Mary Kenney (later **Mary Kenney O'Sullivan**) and by the residents of Hull House. In addition to their research, Kelley and Stevens also lobbied the Illinois State Legislature for passage of additional protective legislation.

When Altgeld left office in 1897, his successor did not reappoint Kelley and Stevens. Stevens now turned her attention to a related social welfare crusade that was occupying the attention of a number of Hull House residents. Along with **Jane Addams** and **Julia Lathrop**, Stevens began to investigate the growing problem of juvenile delinquency in Chicago. (*See* **Juvenile Protective Association**.) She started to attend the courts regularly and to speak on behalf of delinquent boys, often taking responsibility for them. Alarmed by the large number of children held in the Chicago House of Correction, Addams and Lathrop solicited the aid of the Chicago Woman's Club to establish a school for boys that they could attend while they were in jail. Meanwhile, Stevens provided the legislature with material she had gathered during a fact-finding trip to Boston to investigate that city's truant schools and its judicial treatment of children. She and a number of other reformers persuaded the Chicago Bar Association to take up the cause of establishing a juvenile court, and eventually the bill was signed into law. Due to these efforts, a separate juvenile court building was located on Halsted Street, diagonally across from Hull House.

Although the new juvenile court law provided for the services of probation officers, it included no provision for their salaries. Lathrop helped to organize a private Juvenile Court Committee that raised the necessary funds. The first probation officer hired was Alzina Stevens. Although she died within a year of her appointment, Stevens successfully defined the role of a juvenile court probation officer and trained a staff to carry on the work.

Bibliography

Blumberg, *Florence Kelley: The Making of a Social Pioneer*; Davis, *Spearheads for Reform: The Social Settlements and the Progressive Movement, 1890–1914*; *Notable American Women, 1607–1950*, vol. 3, pp. 368–69; Trattner, *Biographical Dictionary of Social Welfare in America*, pp. 688–90.

Stokes, James Graham Phelps
philanthropist, reformer
b. March 18, 1872; d. April 8, 1960.

James Stokes was from a prominent New York family whose members were interested in a number of philanthropic activities. Following in this tradition, he donated funds for social reform campaigns and was active in settlement work as a labor reformer.

Stokes attended the Berkeley School in New York City before entering Yale, graduating from its Sheffield Scientific School in 1892. While he was a student at Yale, Stokes served on the board of the YMCA and as director of the Cooperative Society, a community relief organization sponsored by the college. After finishing school, he decided to combine his interest in social reform with a career in medicine, and toward that end, he enrolled in the College of Physicians and Surgeons at Columbia University in New York City. While he was in medical school, Stokes worked as an ambulance surgeon for Roosevelt Hospital, and in this capacity, he gained firsthand knowledge of the lives of the residents of one of New York City's worst neighborhoods, Hell's Kitchen.

Stokes graduated from medical school in 1892, but was unable to pursue his career because his father's illness compelled him to enter the family business. Eventually, he spent a year studying political science at Columbia and also became involved in settlement work, working as a resident and as a member of the board of directors of the **University Settlement** on New York City's Lower East Side.

When he returned from a tour of military duty during the Spanish-American War, Stokes devoted most of his time to social reform work. He served on the board of a number of social reform-related coalitions that had been established by settlement workers and other social reformers such as the **Outdoor Recreation League**, the New York State Conference of Charities and Correction, and the **New York Child Labor Committee**.

Stokes was also on the board of the New York **Association for Improving the Condition of the Poor** (AICP). He persuaded the organization to expand its activities to include sponsoring a settlement house. In 1897 he cofounded **Hartley House**, a settlement established under the auspices of the AICP and named for that organization's founder, **Robert Hartley**.

In 1902, Stokes married Rose Harriet Pastor, a militant reporter for the *Jewish Daily News* and a former cigar factory worker. He now turned his attention to labor issues, and the two became active in the work of the Socialist Party. Stokes's decision to support America's entry into World War I lead him to split with the Socialists, and following the war he focused once again on philanthropic matters. Stokes donated funds to a variety of cultural causes such as museums and to programs that sponsored educational reform efforts. He supported the social welfare programs of the New Deal.

Although it appears paradoxical, Stokes maintained an interest in business even while he was active in the Socialist Party. Toward this end, he served as president of the Nevada Central Railroad and was on the board of directors of his family's firm, the Phelps-Dodge Company. Stokes's business career provided him with the money he needed to continue making donations to various social causes during his lifetime.

Bibliography

Davis, *Spearheads for Reform: The Social Settlements and the Progressive Movement, 1890–1914*; Trattner, *Biographical Dictionary of Social Welfare in America*, pp. 693–95.

Stover, Charles B.

recreation reformer, settlement worker
b. July 14, 1861; d. April 24, 1929.

Although he became a pioneering recreation reformer and was a long-time resident at several settlement houses, Charles Stover had intended to become a Presbyterian minister following in the footsteps of his uncle, the Reverend Henry Bunstein.

Intent on emulating his uncle's example, Stover attended the same schools, graduating from Lafayette College (1881) and Union Theological Seminary (1884). As a seminary student, he did fieldwork preaching in the Dakota Territory and working in the city missions on the Bowery in New York City. This activity was followed by a year of study at the University of Berlin, where Stover left the ministry as a result of a personal spiritual crisis.

Back in New York in 1885 with no official affiliation with any religious sect, Stover found it difficult to secure church-related work. However, while a student in Berlin, Stover had visited **Toynbee Hall** in London's East End where he had witnessed the work of the emerging English Settlement Movement. This experience benefited him when, for a short time, he served as the director of the **Ethical Culture Society**'s Cherry Street model tenement. This building had been based on the English social reformer **Octavia Hill**'s experimental urban village in the Marylebone section of London. Drawing on the English settlement model, Stover organized clubs and held classes for the tenement's residents. This practical experience proved beneficial when in February 1887 the Reverend **Lyman Abbott**, a leading Congregationalist minister, introduced Stover to **Stanton Coit**, founder of America's first settlement, the Neighborhood Guild.

Stover joined Coit and his associate, Edward King, at the Neighborhood Guild and was soon drawn into the New York City reform community. Like Coit, he believed that the poor residents of inner-city neighborhoods had hidden resources that could be cultivated to enable them to improve their neighborhoods. Stover immersed himself in the work of the guild, using the money from his inheritance to pay bills and to finance reform projects. As a result of his generosity, Stover exhausted his inheritance long before he died.

In 1887, Coit accepted an Ethical Culture ministry in England, leaving Stover and his other associates to carry on the work of the Neighborhood Guild. Stover served as a director of the guild for a few years, but the enterprise did not prosper without Coit's direct participation, and in 1891, Stover and King reorganized the settlement under a new name, the **University Settlement**. That same year, Stover and a few colleagues established the Chadwick Civic Club in the tenement where he lived, across the street from the University Settlement. The group's principal accomplishment was its successful lobbying effort in favor of public ownership of New York City's mass transit system.

In addition to his work with the Chadwick Club, Stover was also involved with the East Side Civic Club, which led the opposition to elevated trains in New York City, and the **Social Reform Club,** which had been founded by **Felix Adler** in 1894 to effect municipal and national social improvements.

Stover gained a national reputation through his efforts for public recreation. In 1887, he wrote a bill that called upon New York City to fund small parks and play equipment. When the New York City Council was unwilling to fund parks, claiming that it was beyond the scope of the city's responsibility to provide recreation facilities, Stover and a group of like-minded reformers formed the Society for Parks and Playgrounds in New York in 1890. The society operated a few parks at its own expense, but did not generate sufficient involvement among the members of the city's reform community, and plans for two parks on the Lower East Side were never completed.

In 1898, Stover successfully obtained the cooperation of a number of the city's settlement leaders including **Lillian Wald** of the **Henry Street Settlement**, **Mary Simkhovitch** of **Greenwich House**, and James K. Paulding of the University Settlement in forming the **Outdoor Recreation League,** which he hoped would accomplish what the Society for Parks and Playgrounds could not, namely, the establishment of public parks on the city's Lower East Side. That is exactly what happened, and in June of the following year, Seward Park was opened. Stover and the league won a major victory in 1900 when they persuaded the city to assume financial responsibility for improving and maintaining this park. Not content with his local victories, Stover formed the National Playground Association in 1906, which was organized to coordinate local movements to secure playgrounds and other recreation facilities in cities across the United States.

From 1910 to 1914, Stover served as park commissioner of Manhattan and Richmond (Staten Island) counties. Among his accomplishments were the creation of the Bureau of Recreation, the planting of more than 250 trees along Delancy Street, and the establishment of Jacob A. Riis Park. However, Stover's administration was marred by controversies that included interdepartmental policy disputes and an uneasy relationship with the press. Inadequate administrative skills, his inability to speak effectively in public, and periodic bouts of depression added to Stover's woes. At one time Stover disappeared for almost three months, prompting a nationwide search that culminated in his resignation from the Parks Commission.

Destitute, Stover returned to the University Settlement. His friends established a fund for his benefit and Stover devoted his remaining years to various reform efforts, including the summer camp program that the University Settlement sponsored at Beacon, New York.

Bibliography

Jackson, *Encyclopedia of New York City*, p. 1126; Paulding, *Charles B. Stover, July 14, 1861-April 24, 1929: His Life and Personality* ; Scheuer, *Legacy of Light: University Settlement's First Century*; Trattner, *Biographical Dictionary of Social Welfare in America*, pp. 695–97.

The *Survey*

Social welfare workers founded journals such as the *Survey* to publicize their work, to keep their colleagues informed about their activities, and to encourage research and investigations into a variety of issues. To some degree, these journals provided a rationale for the professionalization of social work. The New York **Charity Organization Society**'s (COS) official organ, *Charities Review*, was launched in 1891. It was a scholarly journal that was popular among social welfare reformers. Several years later, in response to a perceived need for a more practical publication, the New York COS's president, **Robert W. DeForest**, approached the organization's general secretary, **Edward Devine**, about publishing a second official organ for the COS. With DeForest's support, Devine began publishing *Charities: A Monthly Review of Local and General Philanthropy* in December 1897.

At first, *Charities* consisted of 16 pages, about one-third of which were advertisements. An annual subscription cost one dollar. By the end of its first year, *Charities* boasted 4,750 subscribers, and it had become a weekly publication. Almost from the beginning, *Charities* was more than a house organ. It reported meetings and conferences and published abstracts of speeches of interest to social reform workers across the United States. It also included short articles about many areas of social reform.

In March 1902, *Charities* absorbed *Charities Review,* Edward Evertt Hale's Boston-based monthly which was devoted to similar causes such as unemployment, strikes and labor, housing, and recreation. Following the 1902 merger, *Charities* modified its format. The first issue each month was a magazine that consisted of longer, full-length articles as well as a review of other magazines and books of interest to social workers. The remaining three or four issues each month were shorter bulletins of news and information of interest to social reformers and their organizations. From time to time, shorter articles appeared in the issues. Eventually, these issues became departmentalized and focused on issues of interest to workers in different social service professions.

As the circulation increased, Devine was assisted by W. Frank Parsons and Paul and **Arthur Kellogg**. Devine contributed a regular editorial feature, "Social Forces," and the magazine occasionally published special issues. For example, the October 1905 issue was devoted to blacks and included contributions by Booker T. Washington and W.E.B. DuBois.

In 1905, *Charities* absorbed **Graham Taylor**'s Chicago-based magazine, *The Commons,* which had been started by Taylor and John Palmer Gavitt as a bulletin for Taylor's settlement, **Chicago Commons**, in 1896. The publication now became known as *Charities and the Commons*. Taylor joined the staff and contributed articles about the social service of the church in addition to pieces on a variety of other topics.

DeForest headed up a new Charities Publications Committee, which included many prominent social reformers including **Jane Addams**, **Jacob Riis**, **Joseph Lee**, and **Robert Treat Paine**. Other reformers joined the staff of the magazine as writers or editors including **Florence Kelley** and **Mary Richmond**. **Paul Kellogg** was named managing editor, and his brother Arthur became business manager. Graham Taylor's son, **Graham Romeyn Taylor**, who was based in Chicago, was appointed assistant business manager.

The magazine gained recognition as a result of a series of special issues that examined such topics as the care of the blind (February 1906), visiting nurses (March 1906), and child labor (October 1907). *Charities and The Commons*'s most significant project during this time, however, was the social survey of the city of Pittsburgh, Pennsylvania, which was undertaken with funding from the **Russell Sage Foundation**. This project, which was directed by Paul Kellogg, was known as the **Pittsburgh Survey**. It was the first significant social survey of an American urban community which gathered data on all aspects of living and working conditions. The results appeared in an illustrated series in *Charities and the Commons* in 1909. Later, they were also issued by the Charities Publication Committee in a six-volume series. Based on the success of the Pittsburgh Survey, the Publications Committee turned its attention to similar social surveys. In recognition of this new focus and format, in April 1909, the name of the magazine was changed to the *Survey*.

Circulation increased substantially at this time, but it never achieved huge numbers. The staff of the *Survey* was active in many areas and

investigated jail conditions, strikes, and industrial relations. Articles and editorials that appeared in the *Survey* provided the impetus for many reform crusades that were headed up by editors of the magazine.

Although the magazine was well-regarded, the circulation was less than 20,000 subscribers. To cope with the continuing deficit, in 1912 the **Survey Associates** was established as a financing organization. Readers were asked to contribute money in addition to their annual subscription cost. This type of contribution earned them a designation as an Associate. DeForest served as president of the Survey Associates until his death in 1931, when he was succeeded by Lucius R. Eastman.

In 1912, Paul Kellogg became editor-in-chief of the *Survey*. Devine, Graham Taylor, and Addams were named associate editors and were regular contributors. The first issue each month was the magazine issue, and it gradually broadened its scope to include more in-depth coverage of politics, socialism, child welfare, health issues, and labor concerns.

Although it generally avoided partisan alliances, the *Survey* supported the Progressive Party in 1912. It took a strong pacifist stand when the war broke out in Europe; however, when the United States entered the conflict, it rallied to the war effort. Paul Kellogg served with the Red Cross in France and Italy in 1917 and 1918, and he sent back a number of articles. The *Survey* also supported the League of Nations.

Post-war inflation almost brought about the demise of the *Survey*, and in October 1921, it became a semimonthly publication. The weekly bulletin issues were consolidated into a "mid-monthly number," and the magazine issue was called the "graphic number" because it was illustrated. Subscribers could elect to receive either or both numbers. However, the *Survey* still had to rely on the generous financial support of the Survey Associates.

During the 1920s, the *Survey* remained a visually attractive publication, with many of its articles illustrated with drawings and with photographs by noted social photographers such as **Lewis Hine**. The *Survey* also published a number of special reports during the decade including ones on coal mines and miners (April 1921) and on family life in America (December 1927).

The graphic number became a separate monthly magazine with the name *Survey Graphic* during the 1930s. The mid-monthly number retained the title the *Survey* and continued as a monthly professional journal for social workers. Early in 1949 the two magazines merged again with the name the *Survey,* which continued to be published until 1952.

The *Survey* was one of the most important social welfare journals of the twentieth century. Its pages provided settlement workers and other reformers with a forum in which to share ideas and debate issues and concerns, and it contributed to the growth of the literature of social work and to the professionalism of the field. Today, its pages provide a record of the work accomplished by settlement workers and other social welfare reformers.

Bibliography

Chambers, *Paul U. Kellogg and the Survey: Voices for Social Welfare and Social Justice*; Mott, *A History of American Magazines.*

Survey Associates

Settlement workers and other social reformers recognized the benefits of publishing the results of their investigations. These publications–newsletters, both scholarly and popular periodicals, and books—allowed them to share their research and methodologies with their colleagues and to keep the public informed and interested in their various reform campaigns. These publications could be costly to produce and distribute, and those responsible had to find ways to offset their expenses. The Survey Associates was a cooperative publishing society dedicated to conducting investigations and to publishing books, pamphlets, and periodicals that could contribute to the advancement of constructive philanthropy.

Although the Survey Associates financed numerous publishing ventures, its primary purpose was to support the *Survey,* a magazine that chronicled the work of the numerous organizations and agencies engaged in various social welfare campaigns during the first half of the twentieth century. The *Survey* evolved as a result of the merger of several other reform-minded journals, some of which were published by the New York **Charity Organization Society** (COS). *Charities Review,* the COS's first publication was absorbed by the COS house organ, *Charities,* which in turn merged with *The Commons*, the magazine of the Chicago Commons settlement, to become *Charities and the Commons.*

In 1905 **Edward T. Devine**, the general secretary of the New York COS, formed a Charities Publication Committee (CPC) to investigate the possibility of making *Charities and The Commons* a magazine that would provide a forum for the discussion of social work and reform on a broader level. **Jane Addams**, the founder of **Hull House**; **Jacob Riis**, author and social reformer; **John M. Glenn** of the **Russell Sage Foundation**; and **Robert DeForest**, chair of the New York Charity Organization Society, agreed to serve on the committee.

In 1909, *Charities and The Commons* changed its name to the *Survey*, recognizing the importance of the **Pittsburgh Survey**, the 1907–1908 social study of the economic and social conditions of Pittsburgh, Pennsylvania, and emphasizing the more scientific approach to the process of social welfare reform. Three years later, in an effort to guarantee editorial independence, the CPC severed its relationship with the COS and established the Survey Associates, an independent publishing organization.

As a nonprofit organization, the Survey Associates relied on voluntary contributions to offset deficits not covered by its publishing revenues. Anyone contributing at least 10 dollars per year was classified as an Associate. In its first year, the group had 600 members who earned this designation, most of whom were professional social workers or business owners.

The Survey Associates held annual meetings at which they elected a slate of officers including a president, chair of the board, vice presidents, secretary, treasurer, and editor. DeForest served as president from 1912 until his death in 1931. He was succeeded by Lucius R. Eastman (1931–1938); Richard B. Scudder (1938–1948), and chairs of the board Julian W. Mack (1938–1943) and Joseph P. Chamberlain (1943–1952). The Survey Associates published the *Survey* until the journal's demise in 1952.

Bibliography

Chambers, *Paul U. Kellogg and the Survey: Voices for Social Welfare and Social Justice*; Romanofsky, *The Greenwood Encyclopedia of American Institutions: Social Service Organizations,* vol.2, pp. 677–84.

T

Taylor, Graham
clergyman, settlement founder, social and labor activist, social work educator
b. May 2, 1851; d. September 26, 1938.

Graham Taylor
Social Welfare History Archives, University of Minnesota

The underlying motivation of Graham Taylor's reform career was his deep faith in Social Christianity. Although he was not a trailblazer like some of his colleagues in the dynamic reform community of Chicago, he was quick to recognize, modify, and champion new ideas. During Taylor's career he avoided a narrow focus and was involved in a number of crusades including labor reform and municipal government reform. Additionally, he was a leader in social work education.

Born in Schenectady, New York, Taylor spent his childhood in Philadelphia and in New Brunswick, New Jersey. He graduated from Rutgers College in 1870. Intent on becoming a Dutch Reform Minister like his father, Taylor then entered the Theological Seminary of the Reformed Church in America. He was ordained in 1873 and accepted the pastorate of the Dutch Reform Church of the village of Hopewell in Dutchess County, New York. That same year he married Leah Demarest with whom he would eventually have four children.

Taylor remained in the rural community of Hopewell for seven years. He organized prayer meetings and regularly visited the homes of poor families. Eventually he found it difficult to reconcile the gulf that separated the wealthy landowners and the tenant farmers, and his work with the poor began to alienate some of the more prosperous members of the congregation. Afterward, he claimed that his experience in Hopewell represented a turning point for him, marking a progression in his spiritual outlook from one that emphasized individual responsibility to one that stressed community consciousness.

In 1880, Taylor moved to the Fourth Congregational Church in Hartford, Connecticut. This debt-ridden urban environment contrasted sharply with his previous assignment, but Taylor blossomed under the more liberal atmosphere of Congregationalism. Although his older colleagues were critical of his efforts to save souls among the inhabitants of the waterfront district, Taylor eventually earned their support as he increased church membership, paid off all the debt, and built a new facility to provide services for wayward men.

Inspired by an 1883 canvass conducted by the Connecticut Bible Society, Taylor enlisted the aid of other Congregationalist pastors nearby to begin a missionary program at the Fourth Church. The success of this program, coupled with his emergence as an inspirational leader to others, led to his appointment as professor of Practical Theology at the Hartford Theological Seminary. Taylor used his appointment to train students in the urban missionary techniques he had developed at the Fourth Church, involving them in the work of city missions, the YMCA, and local temperance societies.

In 1892, Taylor moved his family to Chicago, where he had been offered a position with the Chicago Theological Seminary. He was given a free hand to head their newly established department of Christian Sociology, and over the next 30 years he functioned as a teacher, administrator, and principal fund-raiser. Taylor was an inspired teacher who encouraged students to gain practical experience of the church in the inner cities by living the **Social Gospel** theology.

Taylor believed there must be a connection between Christianity and the solving of urban problems. He wanted his seminary students to come to know about this connection by experiencing industrial conditions firsthand. For Taylor, the settlement represented the marriage of the church and the city. From 1911 to 1912, he wrote a series of articles for the social welfare journal the *Survey* about the practice of Social Christianity. Next, he set about creating an opportunity to put his theories into practice.

Taylor knew about **Toynbee Hall** in London and the **Neighborhood Guild** in New York City. As a resident of Chicago, he was also aware of the work being done at **Hull House**, the settlement that had been established by **Jane Addams**. In 1894, he and his family, along with four graduate students, moved into a house, which he called **Chicago Commons**, on the west side of Chicago in the 17th ward. The Taylors were the first family to reside in a settlement. Graham started a kindergarten and offered some classes and clubs to the local residents. His efforts were well-received. Within five years, 25 residents lived at Chicago Com-

mons, and in 1901, a specially designed L-shaped building was constructed to house the settlement's activities.

The staff of Chicago Commons proved to be very adaptable as a continuous stream of different ethnic groups came to live in the surrounding neighborhood including Germans, Irish, Poles, Greeks, and Russians. Taylor and his staff were active in nonpartisan municipal reform activities. A branch of the Municipal Voters' League met at the house, and the residents' efforts did much to improve the political situation of the 17th ward.

Taylor recognized the need for trained community service workers in part because at times it was difficult for him to get and keep residents at Chicago Commons. In 1903, he studied the training methods employed in English settlements and returned to Chicago with a plan to institute a similar program. With the support of President William Rainey Harper of the University of Chicago, Taylor and a colleague, **Charles Richmond Henderson**, offered the first course for social workers through the university's extension program. The following year, a full-time course of study was offered. In 1908, the Social Work Training School was incorporated as the Chicago School of Civics and Philanthropy. The school's research department was endowed by the newly established **Russell Sage Foundation**, and Taylor, who served as president and lecturer, enlisted many of his colleagues from the Chicago settlement movement to serve as faculty including **Jane Addams**, **Julia Lathrop**, **Mary McDowell**, **Edith Abbott**, and **Sophonisba Breckinridge**. Faced with fund-raising setbacks, the school was absorbed into the University of Chicago as the **Graduate School of Social Service Administration** in 1920.

In addition to his teaching and his daily responsibilities at Chicago Commons, Taylor was involved in a number of other activities. He worked with the Chicago Civic Federation and with the Municipal Voters' League, mediated labor disputes, and served on city and state commissions. Additionally, he wrote about religion, education, labor, and political and social reform. In 1896 along with John Palmer Gavitt, Taylor started a small monthly magazine, *The Commons*, which became the unofficial publication of the settlement movement. In later years *The Commons* merged with another important social reform journal, *Charities*, to form *Charities and The Commons*, which was eventually reorganized as the *Survey*. Beginning in 1902 and continuing until shortly before his death, Taylor wrote a weekly column about reform issues for the *Chicago Daily News*.

Through his work with the Chicago Commons, Taylor developed a national reputation. In 1894 along with Jane Addams and Mary McDowell, he started the Chicago Federation of Settlements, which was the forerunner of the **National Federation of Settlements**. Taylor served as president of the latter organization in 1918. He also served a president of the National Conference of Charities and Correction (*see* **National Conference on Social Welfare**) in 1914. This influential organization was composed of leaders from both public and private charitable relief organizations and correctional institutions. Although he turned over the daily operations of Chicago Commons to his daughter **Lea Taylor** in 1921, Taylor maintained an active role in fund-raising and policy decisions until his death.

Bibliography

Dictionary of American Biography, supl. 2, pp. 654–56; Melvin, *American Community Organizations: An Historical Dictionary*, pp., 173–74; Trattner, *Biographical Dictionary of Social Welfare in America*, pp. 707–10; Wade, *Graham Taylor: Pioneer for Social Justice, 1851–1938*.

Taylor, Graham Romeyn

settlement resident, journalist

b. March 17, 1880; d. August 30, 1942.

Men and women became involved in the settlement movement for a variety of reasons. For most, the commitment to this type of reform movement meant leaving one's home to move to a house in a crowded city neighborhood and sharing in the lives of people who started as strangers but who soon became neighbors. Graham Romeyn Taylor's career was a variation on this theme. **Chicago Commons**, the settlement founded by his father, **Graham Taylor**, had been his home since he was a teenager. The career he chose was essentially an extension of his daily life.

When Graham Romeyn Taylor was 14 years old, he and his three sisters went to live in Chicago Commons. After graduating from Harvard in 1900, the younger Taylor returned to live and work in the settlement.

Taylor became a reporter for *The Commons*, the publication that his father and John Palmer Gavitt had established four years earlier, and which functioned as the unofficial publication of the settlement movement. When *The Commons* merged with the New York Charity Organization Society's (COS) publication *Charities* in 1905, Taylor served as the chief western

correspondent of the new publication, *Charities and the Commons*. In 1909, Taylor moved to New York City to assume a position as a staff member for the successor to *Charities and the Commons*, the social welfare journal the ***Survey***.

Taylor's interest in social welfare extended beyond the boundaries of the United States. In 1915, Taylor and **Edward T. Devine** of the New York COS traveled to Russia on a humanitarian mission to assist interned German and Austrian civilians. Taylor spent the following year working in the Office of the American Consul General in Moscow.

After returning to the United States, Taylor was selected to serve as one of two executive secretaries of the Chicago Commission on Race Relations. This group had been formed in the aftermath of the 1919 Chicago race riot to investigate the events leading up to the unrest. The commission's report, *The Negro in Chicago*, was published in 1922. Following his work with the commission, Taylor accepted a position in New York City as executive director of the Commonwealth Fund's task force on juvenile delinquency. In 1927, he was named director of the fund's publications division, which issued reports dealing with child welfare, health issues, and education.

Taylor was still actively involved in the Commonwealth Fund when he died in 1942. During his career Taylor used his skills as a journalist to contribute to the work being accomplished by the men and women working in the American Settlement Movement and in related social reform crusades.

Bibliography

Trattner, *Biographical Dictionary of Social Welfare in America*, pp. 710–11; Wade, *Graham Taylor: Pioneer for Social Justice, 1851–1938*.

Taylor, Lea Demarest

settlement worker, social reformer

b. June 24, 1883; d. December 3, 1975.

Lea Taylor was 11 years old when she and her family went to live in **Chicago Commons**, the settlement her father, **Graham Taylor**, established on the northwest side of Chicago. As a child, she witnessed firsthand the difficulties her neighbors endured in their overcrowded tenements. At the same time, she was also aware of the work that Graham Taylor and his colleagues were accomplishing. Although she was very much influenced by her father's approach to settlement work, Taylor developed her own personal style and philosophy of reform work, which not only helped her to continue Graham Taylor's legacy, but to build on it.

Lea attended the local public schools and the Lewis Institute before graduating from Vassar College (1904). Following her graduation, Taylor returned to live and work at Chicago Commons as her brother, **Graham Romeyn Taylor,** had done. Lea eventually assumed responsibility for the girls' program at the settlement. During World War I, Taylor worked with her father to run the local draft board, which was headquartered in the auditorium of Chicago Commons. She served as assistant secretary and organized the office staff.

In 1917, Taylor became assistant head resident of the settlement. Five years later, she replaced her father as head resident, a position she held until her retirement in 1954. In addition to her work at Chicago Commons, Lea Taylor was also active in local and national reform organizations. She served as president of the Chicago Federation of Settlements from 1924 to 1937 and again from 1939 to 1940. From 1930 to 1934 and from 1950 to 1952, Taylor was president of the **National Federation of Settlements**. She used her position in these two organizations to work for relief for the unemployed and for jobs. Taylor was concerned with the same issues when she was vice president of the **American Association of Social Workers** (1934–1935) and when she held leadership positions in the National Conference of Social Work (*see* **National Conference on Social Welfare**) as a member of the executive committee from 1932 to 1934 and as vice president in 1945.

Carrying on the family tradition of settlement work, Lea Taylor also moved in new directions to keep the work of the settlements meaningful in the rapidly changing post-World War II environment. When the number of black residents in the neighborhood around the settlement increased, for example, she instituted interracial clubs and focused the settlement efforts on race relations. Although she retired as director of Chicago Commons in 1954, Taylor continued to take an active interest in the settlement's work up to her death in 1975.

Bibliography

Trattner, *Biographical Dictionary of Social Welfare in America*, pp. 711–12; Trolander, *Settlement Houses and the Great Depression*; Wade, *Graham Taylor: Pioneer for Social Justice, 1851–1938*.

The Tenement House Problem (1903)

Housing reformers and their settlement colleagues realized the importance of conducting social investigations to learn about the existing conditions and to recommend sound solutions to the problems they uncovered. In 1900, New York Governor Theodore Roosevelt appointed a State Tenement House Commission to study the condition of housing in city tenement neighborhoods and to make recommendations for improvements. *The Tenement House Problem* presents the results of the investigation of the **New York State Tenement House Commission of 1900**. This two-volume study was edited by **Robert DeForest** and **Lawrence Veiller**, members of the commission who were both active in New York City housing and social welfare reform circles.

The book begins with a detailed discussion of tenement reform in New York City between 1834 and 1900. It also examines housing conditions and tenement laws in leading American and European cities. Chapters on parks and playgrounds, public **baths**, and foreign immigration are also included. The text is supplemented by extensive statistics, tables and charts, as well as by photographs and detailed maps. The appendixes include the text of various tenement house acts and the testimony of officials and others who appeared before the Tenement House Commission of 1900.

The Tenement House Problem provided widespread access to the various reports that were issued by the New York State Tenement House Commission of 1900, including a copy of the Tenement House Law as amended up to the time of publication. The book fulfilled a dual purpose. It reported on the progress that had been made to improve housing conditions and it presented information that could be used to guide individuals and communities interested in improving local housing conditions.

Bibliography

DeForest, *The Tenement House Problem*.

Tenement Houses

Rapid industrial growth and the influx of large numbers of immigrants produced unprecedented housing problems in many American cities during the nineteenth century. Settlement workers lived in these crowded urban centers and were intimately acquainted with the problems of overcrowding: unsanitary and unsafe housing, filthy streets, and high disease rates.

York Street, Family in Courtyard, 1903
Museum of the City of New York

As the primary port of entry for hundreds of thousands of immigrants, New York City experienced these problems on a massive scale. The tremendous increase in the number of urban dwellers resulted in overcrowding as one-family houses were quickly converted during the 1830s to accommodate two or more families, and warehouses, stores, and other nonresidential structures were crudely adapted to provide shelter.

These small, cramped, and poorly ventilated rookeries were soon supplemented by barrack-style tenant houses or tenements that were built by speculators to meet the demand for housing by the large number of families who could only afford cheap rents. The buildings were constructed on standard lots that measured 25 feet by 100 feet. They were generally four stories high and had four apartments on each floor. Only the front and rear rooms had windows. The configuration of the interior rooms, which were connected like railroad cars, led to these dwellings being called railroad flats or railroad apartments. These interior rooms had no light or ventilation. Most of the tenements had no indoor running water and only a single, shared privy located either in the backyard or in the cellar. In many instances, the small area at the back of the house was taken up by a second tenement called a double house.

Families were crowded into two, or more likely, one room, and they often shared this small space with boarders.

By the mid-nineteenth century, many people began to view the tenements as a danger to the health and safety of the entire city. Although a number of commissions and committees were formed to investigate the problem and to propose solutions, it was not until 1867 that the first legislative action was taken in regard to tenement houses. The **New York State Tenement House Law of 1867** defined a tenement as a building that served as a home for more than three families living independently of each other. It provided that every sleeping room must have either a window, a ventilator, or a transom window; that fire escapes be provided; and that there be at least one water closet for every 20 occupants. The law also established the maximum percentage of the lot that the building could occupy. Although this law sought to remedy many of the most flagrant problems, it did little to require that builders and speculators satisfy more than minimum requirements.

During the late nineteenth century, many social reform organizations such as the New York **Association for Improving the Condition of the Poor** were actively involved in campaigns to improve housing and maintain health and safety standards. At the same time, many architects, builders, and landlords were equally committed to developing plans that would allow them to meet the steady demand for cheap accommodations. In December 1878, Henry C. Meyer, a housing reformer and the proprietor of the newspaper *Sanitary Engineer*, sponsored a competition for the best architectural design for a tenement house on an ordinary city lot. Architects from the United States, Canada, and Britain submitted 206 plans for tenement houses which were placed on free exhibition and viewed by many interested parties. Meyer reproduced the 10 leading plans in the *Sanitary Engineer* and included discussions of the merits of each design.

A jury of award, which included an architect, the president of the Board of Health, and a number of prominent clergy, awarded the first prize of $500 to the architect James E. Ware for his design of a double-decker **dumbbell tenement**. Ware's tenement was basically a double house, front and rear, separated in the middle by a hallway and water closets. A narrow airshaft between buildings made the outline of the structure resemble the handle of a dumbbell, hence the name.

The winning design was not met with universal approval, and with just cause. One of the worst problems was the shaft between buildings, which was between 50 and 60 feet long and only 28 inches wide. It was enclosed on all four sides and was the full height of the building, between 60 and 70 feet high. The shaft was intended to provide light and air, but no space was provided for the intake of air at the bottom and very little light penetrated from the top to the bottom of the long shaft. Additionally, the shaft was used as a rubbish dump by residents, collected the cooking smells from the kitchens of the surrounding apartment units, and acted like a flue when fires broke out, spreading the flames from one floor of the tenement to another.

Contemporary newspaper editorials warned that construction of the winning design would only serve to increase the evils of the present tenement house system ten-fold. In spite of these warnings, almost 20,000 tenements were constructed in already crowded areas all over New York City. By 1900, New York, the only city to adopt this design, was the site of possibly the worst housing conditions in the world.

During the 1880s housing reformers continued their efforts to establish health and safety standards and to correct the most fla-

grant abuses. However, conditions worsened steadily. By 1890, five-story houses designed for 20 families were being occupied by as many as 100 residents, many of whom were boarders. Contemporary surveys revealed that only one third of New York City's tenements had running water and only three percent of the people living on the Lower West Side had bathrooms in their apartments.

In 1898, the New York Charity Organization Society formed a Tenement House Committee composed of a number of prominent housing reformers including **Felix Adler** of the **Ethical Culture Society**; the journalist and housing reformer **Jacob A. Riis**; **Robert DeForest**, president of the New York **Charity Organization Society** (COS); and **Edward Devine**, executive secretary of the New York COS to address the conditions in the city's tenements. When the municipal authorities failed to act on any of the committee's recommendations, the members resolved to take their case to the people. In 1900, with the assistance of the housing reformer **Lawrence Veiller,** they organized a Tenement House Exhibition that used models, photographs, and charts to graphically portray the city's housing problems. Settlement workers and other reformers made significant contributions to this effort. Thousands of people viewed the exhibit, and municipal authorities were ultimately moved to act. As a result, a new law, the **New York State Tenement House Law of 1901**, was enacted by the New York State Legislature.

Tenements built according to the standards established by this legislation were referred to as "New Law Tenements" and were eagerly sought out as housing. Among other provisions, the 1901 act required that a tenement occupy no more than 72 percent of a standard lot. This law also established the **New York City Tenement House Department**, which was charged with enforcing the new law's standards and with improving conditions in older structures.

Bibliography
DeForest, *The Tenement House Problem*; Jackson, *The Encyclopedia of New York City*, pp. 1161–63

The Tenements of Chicago, 1908–1935

The Tenements of Chicago, 1908–1935 presents the history and development of the tenement neighborhoods of Chicago. This study represents a series of studies conducted over a 25-year period by faculty members and students at the **Graduate School of Social Service Admin-**

istration at the University of Chicago. The studies were undertaken at the request of Charles B. Ball, former chief sanitary inspector of Chicago, and were supervised by **Edith Abbott,** dean of the Graduate School of Social Service Administration and part of the dynamic circle of reformers who used the Chicago settlement **Hull House** as a base of operations. In part, the studies were intended to introduce graduate students to the methods of social statistics and social research.

The Tenements of Chicago provides information on the growth and development of the city of Chicago and on the history of tenement house-related legislation there. As in New York City, large numbers of new immigrants either settled in or passed through Chicago, and the city was severely overcrowded, with large numbers of people living in substandard housing. These problems are reflected in chapters on riots, population congestion, and tenement landlords. The text is supplemented with detailed maps and charts and with photographs. In addition, the authors provide suggestions for improvement including the development of slum clearance programs and the hiring of an adequate number of trained housing inspectors.

At the time of its publication, *The Tenements of Chicago* drew attention to the poor housing conditions that existed in Chicago and helped reformers win support for their efforts for improvements. This type of detailed social investigation was an important aspect of settlement work, and it and other such detailed studies were signs that social work was maturing as a profession.

Bibliography

Abbott, *The Tenements of Chicago, 1908-1935*.

Toynbee Hall

The American Settlement Movement drew its inspiration from a dedicated group of social activists living and working in England's industrial centers, particularly London. One of the most influential of these groups was centered at Toynbee Hall. Established in 1884 under the auspices of the **Universities Settlements Association**, Toynbee Hall was the first English social settlement.

The Universities Settlements Association, a coalition of Oxford University tutors and members of Parliament, was formed in 1884 to investigate the condition of the poor and to develop plans to promote their social and economic well-being. Its program was designed to bring recent college graduates together with the residents of working-class neighborhoods for their mutual benefit. The leaders of the association believed that educated young men living among the poor could re-establish a sense of community and at the same time exercise a degree of social control over the poor.

To accomplish its plan, the association purchased a building that had once housed a boys' industrial school in the parish of St. Jude's in the Whitechapel area of London's East End. Canon **Samuel Barnett** was selected as director of the enterprise, which came to be known as a settlement because these social reformers had actually settled in the area, intent on sharing in all aspects of the lives of their neighbors. The building was converted into a residence for the young college graduates and a social center for the neighborhood residents. It was named Toynbee Hall in honor of Arnold Toynbee, an Oxford undergraduate who, following the example of **Edward Denison,** had lived and worked among the poor of London. Toynbee was a close friend of Barnett and his wife, Henrietta Rowland Barnett, and he had worked with them in St. Jude's before his untimely death in 1883 at the age of 32.

Barnett conceived of Toynbee Hall as an outpost of culture and education in the East End. The settlement workers became involved in the life of the community and lobbied the local politicians to provide better housing, cleaner streets, and recreation facilities. Today, Toynbee Hall functions as a community center, providing a variety of services for the local residents.

Besides the people it helped in London, Toynbee Hall served as an inspiration for a number of the leaders of the American Settlement Movement. **Jane Addams**, **Ellen Gates Starr**, **Vida Scudder**, **Robert Woods**, **Charles Stover,** and **Stanton Coit** all visited the house prior to establishing settlements in the United States.

Bibliography

Carson, *Settlement Folk: Social Thought and the American Settlement Movement, 1885–1930*; Meacham, *Toynbee Hall and Social Reform, 1880–1914: The Search for Community*.

Triangle Shirtwaist Company Fire

Even though New York City settlement workers and their labor reformer colleagues conducted investigations, organized unions to protect workers, and lobbied municipal and state officials to improve the sanitary and safety conditions of factories, it was not until authorities were confronted with a terrible disaster and the resulting public outcry that significant steps were taken to protect the health and safety of factory workers in the early twentieth century. The Triangle Shirtwaist Company Fire had far-reaching consequences and the legislative initiatives it inspired benefited workers far beyond the confines of New York City.

Saturday, March 25, 1911, was a warm spring day. Shortly before 4:40 PM, a fire broke out on the eighth floor of the Asch Building at the northwest corner of Greene Street and Washington Place just east of Washington Square Park in lower Manhattan. The Triangle Shirtwaist Company, one of the largest manufacturers of the women's shirtwaist popularized by Charles Dana Gibson's Gibson Girl, occupied the eighth, ninth, and tenth floors of this building. Almost 500 women were working that Saturday; most were Jewish immigrants between 13 and 23 years old. The fire reportedly began among the remnants under the cutting tables on the eighth floor and spread rapidly.

Although many of the women on the eighth and tenth floors escaped, dozens on the ninth were trapped, unable to open the fire door that had been locked by the proprietors to prevent the workers from leaving before their shift was over. When too many of the women climbed onto the rear fire escape, it collapsed, killing most of those who were on it and eliminating an escape route for others. As spectators and rescue workers looked on, many women, their hair and clothing alight, jumped from the windows to their deaths. More were killed as they jumped, some two or three at a time, hitting the safety nets and tearing through them. Although the fire department responded within minutes, the fire fighters were unable to position their equipment close to the building because of the bodies on the sidewalk. In addition, their ladders went no higher than the sixth floor, well beyond the reach of the women who were clinging to the window frames and ledges before plunging to their deaths.

Within 10 minutes, 146 women died, identifying this tragedy as the worst factory fire in New York City history. A year before, the Triangle Company workers were among the thousands of shirtwaist workers around the city who walked picket lines fighting for safer and more sanitary conditions including unlocked doors and adequate fire escapes in factory buildings. Although the women returned to work, their demands were unmet. Now in the aftermath of the blaze, a sense of rage spread over New York City as individual citizens and social reformers tried to come to terms with the tragedy.

A protest meeting was held at the headquarters of the New York **Women's Trade Union League** the day after the fire. Those present called for the formation of a citizens' committee to gather information about the fire which could provide a basis for drafting remedial legislation. Over the next few days, other public meetings were held around the city, at the Grand Central Palace, at the Cooper Union, and at the Metropolitan Opera House.

On June 30, 1911, the New York State Legislature created a special nine-member **New York State Factory Investigating Commission**. The chair, **Robert F. Wagner,** and the vice-chair, **Alfred E. Smith**, were assisted by a number of social reformers and labor leaders including Samuel Gompers, president of the American Federation of Labor, and **Mary Dreier**, president of the New York Women's Trade Union League. The commission was empowered to compel witnesses to attend and to produce books, papers, and other relevant documents. During its four-year term, it was responsible for the passage of more than 30 new laws to the New York State labor code. Although it had been formed in response to the Triangle fire, the commission's legislative accomplishments covered a number of other labor concerns including limiting hours and abolishing night shifts for women and children.

Although the Factory Investigating Commission was responsible for passing much useful legislation, the Triangle fire victims and their families received little in the way of justice and compensation. Eight months after the fire, Isaac Harris and Max Blanck, the owners of the Triangle Shirtwaist Company, were tried for manslaughter. They were acquitted. In 1914, Harris and Blanck were ordered by a judge to pay damages of 75 dollars to each of the families of 23 victims who sued them for damages.

Bibliography

Stein, *The Triangle Fire.*

Twenty Years at Hull-House with Autobiographical Notes (1910)

The reformers who lived and worked in **Hull House** in Chicago were involved in most of the major reform crusades waged during the early twentieth century including juvenile law reform, child labor reform, and labor reform for women. At the center of this group was **Jane Addams**, founder and head resident of the settlement.

In *Twenty Years at Hull-House with Auto-biographical Notes,* which was published in 1910, Addams describes what she and her co-founder, **Ellen Gates Starr**, hoped to accomplish when they opened Hull House in 1889. Addams discusses what her work meant, explains the meaning of the settlement movement, and uses her experience to illustrate the hard work and perseverance that were required to achieve one's goals.

It took Addams five years to write *Twenty Years at Hull-House.* By the time it was published, she had already written three other books, *Democracy and Social Ethics* (1902), *Newer Ideals of Peace* (1907), and *The Spirit of Youth and the City Streets.* Initial reviews of *Twenty Years at Hull-House* were favorable, and the book went through six printings in its first year.

The first five chapters are concerned with Addams's life, including her years at Rockford Female Seminary and her travels in Europe where she observed the new English Settlement Movement firsthand. The sixth chapter, "The Subjective Necessity for Social Settlements" is critical. It describes Addams's ideas about the need for the settlement in American society and the benefits the work provided to young women of her generation. The remaining 12 chapters are devoted to an account of the activities of Hull House.

Twenty Years at Hull-House provided important insights into Addams's motivations for becoming involved in settlement work and a record of the work that was being accomplished at what was probably the best known settlement in the United States at the time. Other reformers such as **Lillian Wald** and **Mary Simkhovitch** used this book as a model when they wrote their own autobiographical accounts of the settlement movement years later. Additionally, the book may have also encouraged other young women and men to become involved in reform work.

Bibliography

Addams, *Twenty Years at Hull-House with Autobiographical Notes*; Davis, *American Heroine: The Life and Legend of Jane Addams*.

U

United Neighborhood Houses

Settlement workers and other reformers quickly recognized that they could accomplish more if they came together in working coalitions to present a more powerful and unified front when dealing with local, state, and national authorities. Social welfare workers in larger urban centers such as New York, Boston, and Chicago formed associations in their respective cities like the group that became known as the United Neighborhood Houses.

On December 11, 1900, **Mary Simkhovitch** of **Greenwich House** and **John Elliott** of the **Hudson Guild** called together representatives from a variety of social service agencies in New York City—settlements, organized charities, child welfare agencies, housing and public health workers—to unite in a new organization that would coordinate its efforts and resources to work for social change. The result of this meeting was the founding of the Association of Neighborhood Workers, whose purpose was to "effect cooperation among those who are working for neighborhood and civic improvement, and to promote movements for social progress" (Woods and Kennedy, *Handbook of Settlements,* p. 188). This association later evolved into the United Neighborhood Houses organization.

The Association of Neighborhood Workers met monthly in various settlement houses and other offices around the city. Much of its work was accomplished through committees, some of which were especially active and productive. For example, the Housing Committee worked with the local authorities to secure enforcement of the existing tenement house laws and to ensure the passage of new laws. Simkhovitch was a member of this committee when it organized the so-called Congestion Exhibit at the American Museum of Natural History which graphically illustrated the dangers of overcrowding and congestion in neighborhoods all over the city. (*See* **Committee on Congestion of Population**.) The Labor Committee organized a Child Labor Subcommittee to lobby for protective legislation for working children. This group served as the nucleus for both the New York and **National Child Labor Committees**. The Association of Neighborhood Workers was also active in labor reform initiatives and worked closely with the **Women's Trade Union League**. Simkhovitch was a member of the association's Parks Committee that worked with members of the **Outdoor Recreation League** and with the New York City authorities to establish a number of small parks and public playgrounds at various sites throughout New York City.

The leadership corps was eager to involve community residents in the work of the Association of Neighborhood Workers, and it employed some of the same techniques to their citywide organization that were used in individual neighborhoods. For example, many New York settlements sponsored a Mother's Club for neighborhood residents which served both social and educational functions. Realizing that the women in these clubs represented a potentially powerful interest group, the Association of Neighborhood Workers called together the 26 existing clubs from settlements in 1912 to join a League of Mothers' Clubs with the purpose of "promoting legislative action for improved living conditions, gaining a better understanding of various social movements and increasing their personal opportunities for friendship, education, and recreation" (Woods and Kennedy, *Handbook of Settlements*, p. 189). As the Association of Neighborhood Workers' second decade of operations began, the League of Mothers' Clubs became active in a number of causes such as public dance hall supervision, the construction of model tenements, the establishment of a minimum wage for women workers, and the enactment of laws to regulate child labor. By sponsoring the growth of Mother's Clubs and the League of Mothers' Clubs, the Association of Neighborhood Workers encouraged the residents to become part of the local leadership corps that **Stanton Coit** had championed under his neighborhood guild system.

The association was active in a broad range of other causes as well. The association's Arts and Festivals Committee formed the Guild of Settlement Industries in 1911 to conserve and develop the skills of foreign-born women and to help them market their products. Over the next several years, various association committees cooperated with city officials on a city planning exhibit and fought for public health controls over working hours in grocery stores. Association members were also active in the school center movement and campaigned for the use of schools as social centers after regular school hours.

In 1919, the Association of Neighborhood Workers was reorganized as the United Neighborhood Houses (UNH). This new organization was more structured than its predecessor, and only settlement houses were included. The UNH was governed by a council composed of six delegates from each member house: two members of the house's staff, two members of the house's board of directors, and two neighborhood residents. The head residents from all the member houses and the chairs of all the standing committees of the old Association of Neighborhood Workers made up the Executive Committee of the United Neighborhood Houses.

The committees of the United Neighborhood Houses carried on much of the work begun by the committees of the Association of Neighborhood Workers. The membership in the League of Mothers' Clubs also expanded, and in 1923 the United Neighborhood Houses Executive Committee added a staff worker whose sole responsibility was the running of the league. During the 1920s and 1930s, the United Neighborhood Houses was a guiding force in the movement for housing reform in New York City. It served as a clearinghouse for information for housing reformers in other communities across the United States. The United Neighborhood House still provides services to the residents of various neighborhoods in New York City.

Bibliography

Jackson, *Encyclopedia of New York City*, pp. 61–62; Woods, *The Settlement Horizon*; Woods, *Handbook of Settlements*.

United States Children's Bureau

Settlement workers quickly learned the value of organizing themselves into working coalitions as a way to draw attention to social problems and to pressure authorities to bring about positive change. They also understood that it was not enough to secure protective legislation; the uniform enforcement of the new laws had to be ensured. Many reformers, particularly those interested in the welfare of women and children, were wary of the ability of local and state authorities to protect these more vulnerable groups in society, and they looked to the federal government to provide the necessary structure and support to guarantee protection.

The idea of creating a central agency that was responsible for coordinating child welfare efforts across the United States was advanced by the social reformer **Florence Kelley** as early as 1900 in relation to her work as the chief factory inspector of Illinois. Kelley witnessed firsthand the hardships that children endured as they were compelled to support their families by working long hours in dangerous occupations. She also realized that the problem was so widespread and the opposition from factory owners would be so strong that her goal could only be achieved with the support of the federal government. In 1904, Kelley and some of her social reform colleagues, including **Lillian Wald** of the **Henry Street Settlement** and **Edward T. Devine** of the New York **Charity Organization Society,** met with President Theodore Roosevelt to discuss the creation of a federal bureau charged with protecting the welfare of children. Although Roosevelt expressed interest in their proposal, no concrete action was taken at the time.

Wald and Kelley were not deterred. As members of the executive board of the **National Child Labor Committee** (NCLC), they persuaded the leadership of the NCLC to draft a bill in 1906 calling for the creation of a federal agency for child welfare. The bill was introduced in Congress, but it met with considerable opposition. Business interests feared that such an agency would eliminate child labor and rob them of a substantial source of cheap labor. Despite the publicity campaign mounted by the NCLC, the bill died in committee.

Settlement workers and other reformers continued to press for a national children's agency, however. Wald was one of the organizers of the **White House Conference on Dependent Children** in 1909, which was held to draw attention to the needs of dependent children. One of the most significant outcomes of this conference was the recommendation that Congress reconsider and pass the NCLC bill that called for the creation of a national children's bureau. Because of the national attention generated by the White House Conference, the social workers were able to exact a promise from President Theodore Roosevelt that he would lend his support to the bill's passage. As a result, Roosevelt sent a special message to Congress recommending passage of the NCLC bill. His support and the attendant publicity forced Congress to open hearings at which many settlement residents and other social welfare workers testified. After three years, the reformers' efforts were rewarded when President Taft signed the law establishing the United States Children's Bureau on April 9, 1912.

Julia Lathrop, a member of the Illinois State Board of Charities and a former **Hull House** resident, was selected to head up the bureau, which received an initial appropriation of $25,640 to accomplish its work. At first the bureau was placed under the auspices of the Department of Commerce and Labor. The following year it was transferred to the newly created Department of Labor, where it became part of the Department of Health, Education, and Welfare.

The Children's Bureau was charged with investigating all matters relating to the condition and treatment of children. However, it had no administrative power; it was basically a research agency. Despite its limited function, the bureau played a significant role. By virtue of its existence, the federal government recognized the rights of children, and the bureau soon became a clearinghouse of authoritative information about children across the country.

Perhaps the biggest achievement of the United States Children's Bureau was its role in the passage of the **Sheppard-Towner Bill**. This success and other positive changes were due in large measure to the leadership provided by Lathrop, an active member of a large national network of social reformers. Based on her experience, Lathrop believed that her best chance of success was to avoid controversy. Rather than incite her powerful opponents, Lathrop concentrated the bureau's effort at first on an infant health and hygiene campaign, not on child labor. Toward this end, the Children's Bureau not only collected information on the number and causes of infant deaths, but it also examined the high death rate among mothers and the effect that this mortality rate had on their surviving children.

As a result of this study, the bureau's 1917 annual report called on the federal government to assist the states in improving health facilities for women and children by providing grants-in-aid. Lathrop and her agency colleagues included this concept in the bill they drafted, which became known as the Infancy and Maternity or the Sheppard-Towner Bill. After a bitter fight this bill was signed into law on November 19, 1921, by President Harding. The Sheppard-Towner Act was significant because it provided funding to strengthen state health services on the local level. It also marked the first time that federal grants-in-aid were distributed to states for social welfare programs other than education.

After the passage of the Sheppard-Towner Act, the Children's Bureau continued to research the social and economic conditions of children in the United States and to lobby for special welfare programs and legislation. In 1946, the bureau was placed under the auspices of the Social Security Administration.

Today, the programs and work of the Children's Bureau have been incorporated into the United States Department of Health and Human Services, Administration for Children and Families. *See also* **Child Welfare**.

Bibliography

Davis, *Spearheads for Reform: The Social Settlements and the Progressive Movement, 1890–1914*; Trattner, *From Poor Law to Welfare State: A History of Social Welfare in America*.

Universities Settlements Association

The Universities Settlements Association was the driving force behind the founding of the **Toynbee Hall** settlement that influenced many American settlement workers. The association was established in 1884 and registered as a joint-stock undertaking by a group of tutors of Balliol College, Oxford, who included Sidney Ball and the liberal member of Parliament James Bryce among their number. Although the association was primarily an Oxford-based undertaking, members of Cambridge University also offered support, including the participation of the historian J.R. Seeley. Among the association's objectives were to inquire into the condition of the poor; to devise and advance plans to promote the welfare of the poor, and to provide education and the means of recreation and enjoyment for the poor.

The leadership of the association established an elaborate committee structure that it employed to generate funding and to secure volunteers to carry out its programs of having college-educated young men settle, or live and work among the poor. To accomplish its objectives, the directors of the Universities Settlements Association decided to purchase property and to erect a building to house these settlers. They established a trust to receive and disburse the funds donated, and they selected the Reverend **Samuel Barnett,** who at the time was the vicar of St. Jude's Parish in Whitechapel in London's East End, to direct the settlement. Barnett suggested that rather than erect a building the association should purchase the boys' industrial school that was adjacent to St. Jude's. The association purchased the building, and by Christmas Eve 1884, the first settlers were in residence.

This settlement became known as Toynbee Hall. It was the first English social settlement and served as the model for many of the settlements established in the United States.

Bibliography

Meacham, *Toynbee Hall and Social Reform, 1880–1914*: *The Search for Community*.

University of Chicago School of Social Work *See* Graduate School of Social Service Administration (Chicago)

University of Chicago Settlement

Settlement houses were established in communities across the United States for a variety of reasons. Some were founded by religious organizations, others were the outgrowth of a philosophical movement. There were settlements opened to provide services to particular racial or ethnic groups or to provide a service, such as health care, to the needy. And as was the case with the University of Chicago Settlement, some were established to train future social workers.

Hoping to create a laboratory of social service that would benefit students interested in social welfare and the community, a number of faculty members at the University of Chicago established a settlement house in 1894 in the area known as the "Back of the Yards," west of the Union Stockyards in Chicago. Two graduate students, William Johnson and Max West, took up residence in the neighborhood in January of that year. The following September **Mary McDowell** was recruited to serve as the settlement's head resident, and she rented a small apartment in a tenement on Gross Avenue.

The neighborhood where McDowell established herself was isolated from the rest of Chicago. The streets were unpaved and were filled with uncollected garbage. The sewers were open, and the air was heavy with the acrid smell of the refuse from the stockyards. The neighborhood residents were primarily Slavs, Poles, and Lithuanians.

From the beginning, McDowell and the other settlement residents organized the people in the neighborhood into civic clubs that lobbied municipal authorities to provide regular garbage collection. They also called on City Hall and the Health Department to improve neighborhood conditions. These efforts yielded modest results as gradually streets were paved, sewer connections were made to houses, and some street lighting was provided.

In addition to their work to improve housing and sanitary conditions, the settlement workers maintained a playground and provided the services of a resident nurse. They worked with the local public school to open a special facility for deaf children and to provide meeting space for public lectures. The settlement residents also offered clubs for men, women, and children as well as cooking, sewing, metal work, and music classes. Through the efforts of the settlement's Woman's Club, a public bath and a public park were secured.

The University of Chicago Settlement was particularly active in the labor movement in the Chicago area. The residents worked with labor reformers to unionize both men and women workers, and they supported striking neighbors during the meat cutters' strike in 1904. Additionally, McDowell encouraged local labor unions to meet regularly at the settlement house.

The University of Chicago Settlement continued to serve the local community through the first half of the twentieth century. Because of its involvement with local labor unions and its success in working with local municipal authorities to bring about health and sanitary improvements, the settlement played an important role in the Chicago reform community and the American Settlement Movement.

Bibliography

Davis, *Spearheads for Reform: The Social Settlements and the Progressive Movement, 1890–1914*; *Dictionary of American Biography*, supl. 2, "Mary McDowell," pp. 407–09 ; Woods, *Handbook of Settlements*.

The University Settlement

The beginning of the American Settlement Movement may be traced to the founding of the **Neighborhood Guild**, which was later reorganized as the University Settlement, on New York City's Lower East Side. In the summer of 1886, a young American named **Stanton Coit** had recently returned from graduate study in Germany and from a short residence at the first English settlement, **Toynbee Hall** in London. Coit had been influenced by the teachings of **Felix Adler,** the founder of the **Ethical Culture Society**, and he was anxious to put Adler's ideas about the relationship between ethical work and social reform to a practical test. He decided that an undertaking similar to what he had observed at Toynbee Hall would provide him with an opportunity to do so.

Even though Coit was impressed by Toynbee Hall and its work, he took its model of a settlement a step further. He believed that the best way to accomplish any meaningful social reform work was to work through a system of neighborhood guilds, which would take on some of the functions previously performed by the village unit. Each guild consisted of approximately one hundred families. Coit was confident that leaders would emerge from within each guild to guide the others in the group in their attempts to accomplish various reforms.

In August 1886, Coit moved to New York City's Lower East Side and took up residence on Forsyth Street. His first contact with the neighborhood residents was to encourage local clubs to meet in his apartment. The following year, Coit acquired a building on nearby Eldridge Street, and he invited a group of like-minded reformers to join him in his enterprise, which he now called the Neighborhood Guild, the first social settlement established in the United States. **Charles B. Stover** and Edward King, a young Englishman with an interest in social reform, were among the first to join him.

Although Coit was interested in social reform work, his first priority was his commitment to the Ethical Culture Movement. In 1887, Coit left the Neighborhood Guild to live in England and work in the Ethical Culture Movement there. Without him, the Neighborhood Guild soon collapsed. However, Stover and King were committed to the idea of social settlement work, and in May 1891, they reorganized the guild as the University Settlement. Stover became the settlement's head resident, and under his guidance and that of his successors, the University Settlement played a significant role in social reform efforts in New York and the United States in the late nineteenth and early twentieth centuries.

The neighborhood around the University Settlement was populated primarily by Jewish immigrants, most of whom lived in overcrowded, substandard tenements. One of the first campaigns launched by the settlement residents was for better housing. The residents also cooperated with various municipal commissions that were investigating housing conditions, often testifying at hearings or providing written reports of their investigations. They also worked to clean up the neighborhood streets and to provide safe, adequate play space for children. Stover was particularly active in the playground movement, and the University Settlement served as the headquarters of the **Outdoor Recreation League**, which was a citywide organization devoted to securing parks and recreation space for city dwellers.

The University Settlement's residents were active in a number of other causes as well. Several residents were particularly interested in public school reform, and they served as local school trustees. The settlement workers also helped to organize several unions, and they made the house available for use as a meeting place for union functions. In addition, the residents of the settlement were particularly active in the crusade to identify and close down neighborhood sweatshops.

Like their colleagues in other settlements, the residents at the University Settlement maintained a kindergarten, a public bath, a gymnasium, and a savings bank. For several years they operated a public library. The settlement sponsored art exhibits, public lectures, and concerts as well as a full-range of clubs for men, women, and children.

As the first settlement in the United States, the University Settlement served as a model for other houses, particularly for those that served communities in New York City. Its residents led a number of reform initiatives including the playground movement, school reform, and labor reform. The University Settlement still serves the residents of the Lower East Side neighborhood.

Bibliography

Jackson, *The Encyclopedia of New York City*, p. 1217; Scheuer, *Legacy of Light: University Settlement's First Century*; Woods, *The Handbook of Settlements*.

V

Van Kleek, Mary Abby
social reformer, social researcher
b. June 26, 1883; d. June 8, 1972.

Mary Van Kleek's work as a researcher of labor-related issues was interwoven with the work of the American Settlement Movement. Her initial research was funded by the **College Settlements Association**, and during her career she interacted with a number of reformer coalitions, was employed by the **Russell Sage Foundation,** and served on numerous local and national committees.

Van Kleek earned an A.B. degree from Smith College in 1904. The following year she received a College Settlements Association fellowship. She used her grant to research the overtime work of girls employed in New York City factories and to study child labor in New York City tenements.

Van Kleek's studies were very influential and won her the support of the reform community. Based on her reports, the Alliance Employment Bureau, a philanthropic organization that helped girls to find jobs, established a department of industrial investigations. In 1907, Van Kleek was named director of the department. The following year she received financial support for her research from the **Russell Sage Foundation**. By 1910, Van Kleek's studies on women's employment and the relationship between wages and the standard of living were an established part of the Russell Sage Foundation's research program. In 1916, the

foundation named Van Kleek director of its newly established Department of Industrial Studies, a position she held until her retirement in 1948.

Van Kleek's work at the Russell Sage Foundation represented only one aspect of her commitment to social welfare reform. She taught courses on industrial conditions and industrial research at the New York School of Philanthropy (*see* **Columbia University Graduate School of Social Work**) from 1914 to 1917. During this time, she was also president of the Intercollegiate Bureau of Occupations and was active in the National Social Worker's Exchange.

In 1918, Van Kleek was appointed director of the women's branch of the Federal Government Ordnance Department Industrial Service Section. She served on the War Labor Policies Board (1918–1919) and helped develop standards for the employment of women in war industries. In the summer of 1918, Van Kleek was named director of the Department of Labor's Women in Industry Service. In this capacity, she established guidelines for women's employment and developed the investigative research methodology that was employed by the service and its successor, the United States Women's Bureau.

During the 1920s, Van Kleek turned her attention to the area of employer-employee relations. Under her guidance, the Russell Sage Foundation financed a number of studies in this area. In addition to her research, Van Kleek was active in the work of a number of groups involved in social work including the President's Conference on Unemployment (1921) and the Committee on Unemployment and Business Cycles.

In 1933, Van Kleek was appointed to the Federal Advisory Council of the United States Employment Service. However, she resigned after one day, citing her opposition to the policies of the National Recovery Administration. She became an outspoken critic of the New Deal, which she believed restricted workers' liberties and supported industrial monopolies.

Van Kleek was also active in international reform circles. She served as an associate director of the International Industrial Relations Institute (1928–1948); chaired the World Social Economic Congress program committee in 1931; and was president of the Second International Conference of Social Work in 1932. In addition to these activities, Van Kleek extended her research to the international arena when she undertook a study of the impact of technological change on employment and wages for the International Industrial Relations Institute.

Van Kleek retired from the Russell Sage Foundation in 1947 and moved to Woodstock, New York. She maintained an interest in social and political issues until her death in 1972.

Van Kleek got her start in social reform with a fellowship from the College Settlements Association and throughout her career she maintained a connection to the American Settlement Movement. Her reports on working conditions were used by settlement workers and labor reformers to win better working conditions and higher wages.

Bibliography

Glenn, *Russell Sage Foundation, 1907–1946*, vol. 1; Sicherman, *Notable American Women, The Modern Period*, pp. 707–09; Trattner, *Biographical Dictionary of Social Welfare in America*, pp. 725–28.

Veiller, Lawrence Turnure
housing expert, political activist
b. January 7, 1872; d. August 30, 1959.

Unlike many other social reformers, it was not a strong religious fervor that drew Lawrence Veiller to the field of social welfare, but a more secular conviction regarding individual social responsibility. His particular concern was providing adequate housing, which he believed was the touchstone of all social reform.

While a student at the City College of New York, Veiller's interest in social activism was stimulated by his reading of John Ruskin and Thomas Carlyle. Unlike many of his reform-minded contemporaries, Veiller did not believe in the inherent goodness of humans, nor did he subscribe to a belief in the inevitability of progress. But this cynicism served him well as he operated in the political arena lobbying for housing reform causes, organizing pressure groups, and writing legislation.

Veiller began his career as a social reformer with the East Side Relief Work Committee in New York City during the depression of 1893. Two years later he secured a position as a housing plan examiner in the Building Department during Mayor William L. Strong's administration. His work with the Building Department provided Veiller with a firsthand view of the city's principal housing problem: the tenements. As a result of the problems he saw in that capacity, Veiller persuaded the New York **Charity Organization Society** (COS) to establish a Tenement House Committee on which he served as executive officer and secretary. For the next quarter century, the **New York Charity Organization Society Tenement House Committee** played a leading role in housing reform efforts in New York City and served as a model for similar committees in other communities.

In 1899, the New York State Legislature passed what Veiller considered to be an inadequate residential building code. In response, the following year he organized a exhibition on behalf of the New York Charity Organization Society which was displayed at the Sherry Building in New York City. The exhibition was designed to illustrate the below-average living conditions of the working class and to mobilize public opinion regarding the need to eliminate slums. Local settlement house workers were enthusiastic collaborators, and Veiller benefited from their firsthand knowledge of urban living conditions. They provided him with information about the income and expenditures of the people in their neighborhoods and assisted him in constructing scale models and in obtaining photographs that depicted the dark, overcrowded neighborhoods of the inner city. More than 10,000 people viewed the exhibition during the two weeks it was on display in New York City. Thousands more saw it as it traveled to cities across the United States and to the 1900 Paris Exposition. (*See also* **New York Charity Organization Society Tenement House Exhibition**.)

Armed with the public indignation he aroused with the exhibition, Veiller was able to persuade New York Governor Theodore Roosevelt to organize a **New York State Tenement House Commission**. Veiller served as secretary of this 15-member body, which was charged with revising the 1899 law. Their efforts resulted in the passage of the **New York State Tenement House Law of 1901** that outlawed construction of so-called **dumbbell tenements** in undeveloped areas of New York City, mandated separate water closets in each apartment, and called for comprehensive fire prevention measures.

Veiller's work on the local and state levels quickly established him as a preeminent campaigner in the growing housing reform movement. In 1902, he was appointed first deputy commissioner of the **New York City Tenement House Department**, which functioned as an autonomous city agency charged with implementing the provisions of the 1901 law. Two years later both he and the department's commissioner, **Robert W. DeForest**, who was president of the New York Charity Organization Society, resigned when Tammany-backed George McClellan replaced the more reform-minded Seth Low as mayor of New York City. Years later, when a more sympathetic administration won control of city hall, Veiller once again offered his services to the Tenement House Department, this time as an unofficial advisor.

Unhappy with the COS Tenement House Committee's support of certain housing legislation, Veiller resigned from the committee and gradually turned his attention away from the local, municipal arena toward the growing national housing movement that was steadily gaining momentum. In 1910, he co-founded the **National Housing Association** and served as its director from 1911 to 1936. Under Veiller's guidance, this organization helped transform housing reform into a national movement managed by professionals.

Having achieved success on the local level with his strategy of restrictive legislation, Veiller employed the same approach in the national arena. He wrote several books on drafting and implementing tenement house legislation, which were used by reformers across the nation, including *Housing Reform: A Hand Book for Practical Use in American Cities*.

In the years following World War I, many American housing reformers became disillusioned with the restrictive legislative approach. They were inspired by the more constructive European model that was based on government subsidized housing for the working class. As the

ideas of model tenements and government-built and government-subsidized housing grew more popular in the United States, Veiller grew defensive regarding his belief in restrictive legislation. Eventually he became one of the most antagonistic critics of the New Deal federal housing projects of the 1930s.

As his influence in housing reform circles waned, Veiller turned his attention to a related cause. In 1916, he helped to formulate New York City's, and the nation's, first comprehensive zoning law. Five years later he prepared the Standard Zoning Law of 1921 for the United States Department of Commerce, which over the next decade was adopted by most communities in the country. In 1928 Veiller was named to Commerce Secretary Herbert Hoover's Advisory Committee on City Planning and Zoning.

In addition to his lifelong interest in housing, Veiller was also involved in criminal law and court reform. For more than 20 years he served as secretary of the New York Charity Organization Society's Committee on Criminal Courts. During the 1920s, he served as an unofficial advisor to the Baumes Crime Commission campaigning against lenient parole standards. In the late 1930s, he became president of the New York Citizens Crime Commission.

Veiller had a long and productive career as America's first professional housing reformer. An advocate of restrictive housing legislation, he formed a number of important alliances with settlement workers and housing reformers that resulted in the passage of stricter housing laws in New York City and in communities across the United States. Although his approach to housing reform lost favor during the 1930s when many reformers turned to public housing, Veiller maintained an interest in urban planning and zoning laws. Veiller died of a heart aliment in 1959.

Bibliography

Jackson, *Encyclopedia of New York City*, p. 1227; Lubove, *The Progressives and the Slums: Tenement House Reform in New York City, 1890–1917*; Trattner, *Biographical Dictionary of Social Welfare in America*, pp. 731–33.

Visiting Nurse Association (Chicago)

The health of their neighbors was always of concern to settlement workers. They realized the danger of living in unsanitary, overcrowded tenements. At the same time, many settlement workers and other reformers knew that newly arrived immigrants often could not pay for health care, nor were they anxious to seek assistance from strangers in what must have appeared to them to be large, impersonal hospitals. Neighborhood-based health care professionals such as visiting nurses helped to meet the needs of these urban dwellers. They were known to the neighborhood residents, and they provided health care in the home, often at no cost. In some cities, visiting nurse services had strong ties to the local settlements and provided an important link between the reformers and the community residents.

The Chicago Visiting Nurse Association (VNA) was founded in 1889. Its professed goals included democratizing quality medical care by providing assistance to the poor in their homes, instructing family members in the correct care of the sick, and fostering the importance of cleanliness and good living. From its inception, the association enjoyed the support of an active and prominent board that included **Jane Addams**, founder of **Hull House**, and two prominent Chicago philanthropists, **Louise DeKoven Bowen** and Florence Pullman, wife of the industrialist and inventor George Pullman.

The nurses of the Chicago Visiting Nurse Association were not associated with a particular settlement house, as was the case with the Henry Street Visiting Nurse Association in New York City, and because of this, they received most of their calls via public telephone. Addams allowed Hull House to be used as a call station, and she let the nurses use the settlement's kitchen. The nurses' work took them to most of Chicago's poorest neighborhoods. They were careful to approach their patients in a non-threatening manner, hoping to win their confidence and cooperation. Many of the visiting nurses' patients were chronically ill or incurable, and the nurses made every effort to provide care for them in their homes. The nurses' observations of their patients' living conditions were passed on to settlement workers and other reformers engaged in a number of crusades including the pure milk campaign and a variety of sanitary and housing reform efforts.

In addition to their home visits, the nurses of the VNA also assisted during citywide emergencies. They provided and staffed a pesthouse during the 1893 smallpox epidemic and aided victims of the Iroquois Theater fire in 1903.

The VNA provided a vital service for the poorer residents of Chicago who could not afford to pay for medical attention or who were afraid to go to a hospital for assistance. The nurses formed a crucial working relationship with the city's settlement workers and together they fought for sanitary and housing reforms that would improve the health of the community. Today, the Visiting Nurse Association still provides quality skilled nursing care to the citizens of Chicago.

Bibliography

McCarthy, *Noblesse Oblige: Charity and Cultural Philanthropy in Chicago, 1849–1924*; Woods, *The Settlement Horizon*.

Visiting Nurse Service (New York)

The Visiting Nurse Service of New York, which was operated by the **Henry Street Settlement**, served as a model for similar services in other cities. As visiting nurse associations were established in other urban centers, they often maintained a similar connection with their city's settlements.

From the beginning, settlement residents and other social reformers recognized the urgent need to address the health problems of the thousands of immigrants living in crowded cities. They realized the interrelationship between housing and health and launched numerous campaigns for better housing and better sanitation as well as for the provision of basic health care. Toward this end, many settlements established clean milk stations and clinics and dispensaries. In some cities, settlements were able to pay the salary of a doctor and/or a nurse who were available at the house at specified times to see patients.

One of the most significant contributions that the settlements made to the field of public health care was the provision and support of a visiting nurse service. One of the best-known of these was established by **Lillian Wald** and **Mary Brewster,** the founders of the **Henry Street Settlement** on New York City's Lower East Side. Eventually, their service was duplicated in communities across the United States until by 1890, 21 visiting nurse services had been established in the United States.

Wald, the driving force behind the formation of the Visiting Nurse Service, got involved in nursing in her early twenties after becoming dissatisfied with her circumscribed life. Like many other young women of her generation, she longed to find meaningful work. Inspired by the nurse who had cared for her sister during a serious illness, Wald enrolled in nursing school. Following her graduation, she was disappointed with her experience at New York City's Juvenile Asylum and decided to enroll at the Women's Medical College for additional training.

When Mrs. Solomon Loeb, a prominent philanthropist, sponsored a home health care and hygiene class for immigrants at the Louis Technical School on Henry Street on New York's Lower East Side, Wald volunteered to act as an instructor. Called away from the class one day to tend to the needs of a gravely ill woman, she resolved to become involved in the lives of the poor and assist them by providing much-needed health care.

Wald persuaded a classmate from the Medical College, Mary Brewster, to join her. The two women went to live among the poor and to provide them with health care in their homes. Wald and Brewster were not the first trained nurses to work among the poor on New York City's Lower East Side. As early as 1877, trained nurses from the women's branch of the New York City Mission were working in the area. In 1879, trained nurses under the auspices of the **Ethical Culture Society** were working in neighborhood dispensaries, but Wald and Brewster were not interested in charity work. Their plan marked a different approach to health care.

At first, the two women lived at the recently established **College Settlement** on Rivington Street. Dressed in dark blue uniforms, each morning they set out to visit patients in the tenements. They cared for the neighborhood residents in their homes and when necessary made arrangements for patients to be taken to the hospital, keeping careful records of each patient. Wald and Brewster soon realized that their goals were more narrowly focused than those of the other women at the College Settlement. By September 1893, the two nurses were renting a small apartment on nearby Jefferson Street.

Over time, other young women joined Wald and Brewster in their work, using the Jefferson Street apartment as a base of operations. During the course of their work, the nurses encountered resistance both from their patients and from the local doctors. Many immigrants were afraid to seek medical assistance. Others were ashamed to accept charity. Doctors were alarmed by the existence of a free nursing service, which they feared would be a threat to their incomes. In an effort to professionalize their service and to set them apart from other nursing services offered by religious or charitable organizations, Wald and Brewster charged a fee of 10 cents per visit. Those who could not afford even this modest fee were not turned away, though.

As they went about their work, Wald and Brewster enjoyed the financial assistance of Mrs. Loeb's son-in-law, **Jacob Schiff**, a wealthy New York banker who took an interest in their work. Schiff introduced the nurses to a group of doctors from the United Hebrew Charities who provided them with professional assistance when needed. By 1895, Schiff had purchased a house at 265 Henry Street and the women had established the Nurses' Settlement, which was conceived as an independent professional service that assisted persons in need of home care. (*See* **Henry Street Settlement**.)

Brewster died shortly after the settlement opened, but Wald continued the work, assisted by an ever-growing number of trained nurses. By 1913, 92 nurses were working in the Henry Street Visiting Nurse service, completing 200,000 visits annually. In addition to the Henry Street headquarters, branches were established on West Seventy-Ninth Street in Upper Manhattan in 1896 and in the Bronx on Cauldwell Avenue in 1906.

In response to the needs of the community, Wald steadily increased the scope of the nursing service. Aware that many children missed school because of illness, she arranged for one of the Henry Street nurses to spend a month in a local public school in 1902. This program was so successful that the New York City Board of Health established a public school nursing program, the first of its kind in the United States.

Wald applied the same health care principles to the parents of the school children. In 1909, she suggested to the Metropolitan Life Insurance Company that it provide its industrial policyholders with a professional nursing service. Once again Wald set a standard. Within 18 months insurance companies in 1,200 cities and towns across the United States had instituted a similar service.

By 1912, Wald saw the need for a visiting nurse service that extended beyond the city limits. She persuaded the American Red Cross to establish a rural public health nursing service that eventually became known as the Town and Country Nursing Service.

In 1944 following Wald's retirement from the settlement, the Henry Street Visiting Nurse Service became a separate organization, changing its name to the Visiting Nurse Service of New York.

Bibliography

Carson, *Settlement Folk: Social Thought and the American Settlement Movement, 1885–1930*; Siegel, *Lillian Wald of Henry Street*; Woods, *The Settlement Horizon*.

W

Wagner, Robert Ferdinand
politician, social reformer
b. June 8, 1877; d. May 4, 1953.

Settlement workers and other social reformers sometimes formed very productive working relationships with politicians who shared their interest in social welfare reform. One such productive alliance was that of Robert F. Wagner and the New York-based reform community which functioned during the first half of the twentieth century.

Reinhardt and Magdalene (Schmidt) Wagner arrived in the United States in 1886 from Nastatten, Germany, when the youngest of their seven children, Robert, was nine years old. The family settled in New York City. Robert Wagner attended City College and New York Law School. While a student at City College, Wagner became interested in local politics and joined the neighborhood Tammany political organization. The social and political connections he made enabled him to gain election to the New York State Assembly in 1904, where during his first term of office he demonstrated his loyalty to Tammany.

Defeated for re-election in 1905, Wagner was returned to office the following year. Tempering his Tammany allegiance with an interest in the crusade for municipal reform, he rose steadily through the legislative ranks, becoming president pro tem of the New York State Senate in 1911.

That same year Wagner was selected to head the **New York State Factory Investigating Commission,** which had been established to look into working conditions in factories in the wake of the **Triangle Shirtwaist Company Fire** in which 146 women died. New York State Assemblyman **Alfred E. Smith** served as vice-chair of the commission. He and Wagner were assisted in their extensive investigations by a number of settlement workers and other social welfare reformers. Thanks in large measure to the political acumen of Smith and Wagner, more than 30 bills dealing with industrial health and safety standards were passed by the New York State Legislature.

After his work with the Factory Investigating Commission was complete, Wagner was elected to a 14-year term on the First District Supreme Court in 1918, and he was responsible for a number of innovative initiatives in the field of labor law. After only eight years on the bench, Wagner returned to the legislative arena when he was elected to the United States Senate in 1926.

In Washington, Wagner turned his attention to the problem of unemployment. He devised a comprehensive approach that in many ways anticipated the programs enacted during the New Deal. During the 1930s, Wagner assumed a leadership role in helping to draft and later sponsoring the National Industrial Recovery Act, the Railroad Retirement Act, and various Social Security-related legislation.

During this time, Wagner worked with a number of reformers on a variety of health, labor, and social welfare issues. He drafted the National Labor Relations Act in 1935 which outlawed unfair labor practices on the part of employers and was instrumental in the formation of the National Labor Relations Board. Wagner worked with settlement workers **Mary K. Simkhovitch**, **Helen Alfred**, and other members of the **National Public Housing Conference** to secure passage of the **Wagner-Steagall Housing Act** in 1937. During World War II, Wagner continued to work for social welfare programs, sponsoring legislation for full employment and national health insurance. Wagner remained in the Unites States Senate until 1949. He died four years later.

The productive working relationships that Wagner formed with settlement workers and other social reformers resulted in the passage of significant social welfare legislation, particularly the Wagner-Steagall Housing Act. *See also* **Ward Politics**.

Bibliography

Dictionary of American Biography, supl. 5, pp. 717–19; Garraty *Encyclopedia of American Biography*, pp. 1157–58; Huthmacher, *Senator Robert F. Wagner and the Rise of Urban Liberalism*; Jackson, *Encyclopedia of New York City*, p. 1231.

Wagner-Steagall Housing Act

Housing reform was a priority for many social welfare reformers during the nineteenth and early twentieth centuries. Although some progress had been achieved by the end of the 1920s, more than 40 years of working for better housing conditions had not really improved the situation as much as settlement workers and housing reformers had hoped. The debate over the advisability of the federal government's becoming directly involved in the housing business, and specifically in the provision of single-family dwellings, was renewed in the early years of the Depression.

During the Progressive Era and into the 1920s, settlement workers and housing reformers often adopted a high moral tone in their reform crusades. Efforts during the New Deal were characterized by a very different tone. The subjective, moral focus of the earlier campaigns was replaced by a more objective, pragmatic approach. While they acknowledged the continuing existence of the problems of the cities and their residents, New Deal reformers were, at first, primarily concerned with the practical issue of reviving the economy of the United States.

When he assumed the presidency in 1933, Franklin D. Roosevelt was committed to economic recovery. The flurry of legislation that was passed during the 100-day session, including the creation of the National Recovery Administration and the Agricultural Adjustment Administration, was designed to bring about a quick, national economic turnaround. Legislation that was enacted in later Roosevelt administrations involved the federal government more directly in the lives of individuals and was concerned with the more social-oriented issues of welfare, housing, and labor.

The National Housing Act of 1934, for example, established the Federal Housing Administration, which insured private lending institutions that made long-term loans for the construction and sale of housing. Gradually, the number of housing starts increased and individual homeowners realized the benefits the 1934 act was designed to provide, but they did so at the expense of those living in the slums.

It was apparent to many settlement workers and housing reformers that these federally sponsored recovery efforts were primarily intended to benefit individual homeowners. No provisions were being made for the large number of working-class Americans who could not afford their own homes. In many instances, the housing constructed by limited-dividend corporations during the early twentieth century had been beyond the reach of the poor. It now seemed that scenario was being repeated. Many housing reformers were convinced that the only hope for slum dwellers was direct assistance from the federal government in the form of low-cost, government-financed housing.

The push for this federal assistance started even before the Housing Act of 1934 was passed. In 1931, a group of New York City-based settlement workers and housing reformers formed a pressure group called the Public Housing Conference (PHC), later known as the National Public Housing Conference (1933) and then the **National Housing Conference** (1949). This organization brought together social reform workers and housing experts to lobby for housing legislation on the state and federal levels. Its objective was to promote low-cost housing through public construction and government funding. **Mary K. Simkhovitch**, the founder and head resident of the **Greenwich House** settlement, served as president of the PHC, and the New York City-based settlement worker **Helen Alfred** was executive secretary.

This coalition of housing reformers faced formidable opposition from the real estate and construction interests who were opposed to government involvement in the housing industry. However, they had a powerful ally in the United States Congress in the person of Senator **Robert F. Wagner** of New York to represent their case. Members of the Housing Conference worked with Wagner's staff to draft bills that would provide for government-financed housing.

Wagner introduced three housing bills in Congress. His efforts in 1935 and 1936 were unsuccessful. However, by the time he came forward with his third attempt in 1937, Wagner had secured the support of President Roosevelt, and he was victorious. The Wagner-Steagall Housing Act became law on September 1, 1937. Under the terms of this law the United States Housing Authority was created and provided with $500 million for loans for low-cost housing. Loans could be advanced for up to 90 percent of the cost of the construction.

By 1941, more than 500 housing projects were either under construction or had been completed under the auspices of the United States Housing Authority. During World War II, the Housing Authority was engaged in planning and building defense housing projects. Although the provisions of the Wagner-Steagall Housing Act did not cure all of the nation's housing problems, it did set a precedent for government-sponsored public housing. It also served as an example of what could be accomplished when settlement workers formed working relationships with other reformers and reform-minded politicians.

Bibliography

Hutchmacher, *Senator Robert F. Wagner and the Rise of Urban Liberalism*; McDonnell, *The Wagner Housing Act: A Case Study of the Legislative Process.*

Wald, Lillian D

public health nurse, settlement founder, social reformer
b. March 10, 1867; d. September 1, 1940.

Although many considered Lillian Wald's most noteworthy contribution to social welfare to be in the area of public health nursing, she had a significant impact on a variety of reform efforts on the local, state, and national levels. The visiting nurse service she established on New York City's Lower East Side served as a model for similar services in other cities across the United States, and based in large measure on the force of Wald's personality and strong sense of commitment, the **Henry Street Settlement**, which she founded, became a center for social welfare reform.

Max Wald, Lillian's father, was a prosperous optical goods dealer whose business took the family from Cincinnati, Ohio, where Lillian was born, to Dayton and finally to Rochester,

Lillian D. Wald
Social Welfare History Archives, University of Minnesota.

New York. Lillian grew up in a well-to-do, warm household. After attending Miss Cruttenden's English-French Boarding and Day School, she applied to Vassar College, but she was refused admission because at 16 she was considered too young. During the next few years Wald, like many other attractive young women of her social class, enjoyed an active social life. When a trained nurse was employed by the family to care for her sister, Lillian was inspired to pursue a career in nursing herself.

In 1889, when she was 22 years old, Wald enrolled in the New York Hospital Training School for Nurses. Two years later she graduated and found a position as a nurse at the New York Juvenile Asylum. Wald disliked her work at the asylum, in part because she felt that she had been inadequately trained. To remedy this situation, she entered the Woman's Medical College in New York. In 1893, while still a student at the Medical College, Wald was invited to teach home nursing classes to new immigrants on New York's Lower East Side. Called from her classroom to attend a sick woman in a nearby tenement, Wald witnessed the wretched living conditions endured by slum residents. She immediately resolved to leave medical school to offer her nursing skills to the poor. Along with her nursing school colleague **Mary Brewster**, she established the first independent public health nursing service in the United States.

Wald and Brewster settled in temporary quarters at the **College Settlement** on New York's Lower East Side. Realizing that their objectives were more narrowly focused than those of the other young women living and working in the settlement, Wald and Brewster decided to establish quarters of their own. In September 1893, they moved to the top floor of a tenement on nearby Jefferson Street. The women soon won the confidence of neighborhood residents and their Visiting Nurse Service grew rapidly. Intelligent and personable, Wald began a fund-raising campaign to assist in a program of expansion. First, she secured the backing of Mrs. Solomon Loeb, who had provided the funding for the home nursing course Wald had taught. Then, Mrs. Loeb's son-in-law, **Jacob H. Schiff**, a banker and philanthropist, contributed to the work. As a result of Schiff's generosity, Wald and Brewster were able to acquire larger quarters at 265 Henry Street in 1895 and to establish the Nurses' Settlement with a staff of 11 residents.

Wald conceived of the Nurses' Settlement as an independent professional service that assisted persons in need of home care. Fees were charged in accordance with the patient's ability to pay. By 1913, 92 nurses were working in the Henry Street Visiting Nurse Service, making 200,000 visits annually. In addition to the Henry Street headquarters, branches were established in Upper Manhattan and in the Bronx.

Wald enlarged the scope of the nursing service in response to community need. She realized that many children missed school because of poor health, and in 1902, Wald arranged for Lina L. Rogers, a Henry Street Nurse, to spend a month working in a nearby public school. This experiment was so successful that it prompted the New York City Board of Health to establish a public school nursing program, the first of its kind in the United States.

In 1909, Wald suggested to the Metropolitan Life Insurance Company that it provide a nursing service for its industrial policyholders. This arrangement was so successful and so well received by the insurance industry that within 18 months companies in 1,200 cities and towns across the country had instituted a similar service.

Wald's commitment to supplying nursing care extended beyond the city. In 1912 she persuaded the American Red Cross to begin a rural public health nursing service that eventually became known as the Town and Country Nursing Service. That same year Wald was among the founding members of the National Organization for Public Health Nursing, and she served as the organization's first president. Wald was also instrumental in the establishment of the Nursing and Health Department at Teachers College of Columbia University (1910).

The Nurses' Settlement housed two separate social service institutions, the nursing service and a social settlement. Nursing was at the core of Wald's social welfare work. However, the house on Henry Street also functioned as full-blown settlement, and Wald's influence was central to its success. Her introduction to the many social, economic, and physical needs of her neighbors came during the first winter (1893–1894) that she and Brewster lived on the Lower East Side. At the time she served on a committee with **Josephine Shaw Lowell**, the founder of the New York **Charity Organization Society** that provided work relief for the unemployed. Other community outreach initiatives followed, and the Nurses' Settlement soon changed its name to the Henry Street Settlement as the medical services that the house provided were eclipsed by a full range of social welfare services.

Like their counterparts in other settlement houses, Wald and her colleagues at Henry Street worked to improve their neighbors' housing and sanitary conditions. They organized clubs for boys and girls and opened a playground in the backyard of the settlement house. Wald also organized sewing and cooking classes for mothers and established a scholarship program to enable children to stay in school until they were 16 years old. The settlement also provided a range of cultural opportunities. In 1915, two patrons of Henry Street, Alice and **Irene Lewisohn**, established the **Neighborhood Playhouse**, and in 1927, a music school was opened.

Wald played a significant leadership role in the many child welfare campaigns of the time. In 1904, along with other reformers including **Felix Adler** of the **Ethical Culture Society**, **Jane Addams** of the Chicago-based settlement **Hull House**, and **Florence Kelley**, a resident at Henry Street for more than 20 years, Wald helped to establish the **National Child Labor Committee** which worked to secure legislation to control child labor abuses.

In 1905, Wald and Kelley proposed to President Theodore Roosevelt that a federal agency be established to ensure adequate protection for children. Although it took seven years, their suggestion was finally implemented when President Taft established the **United States Children's Bureau** in 1912 and appointed **Julia Lathrop**, a former Hull House resident, to direct it.

Like many of her reformer colleagues, Wald was hopeful that neutral nations could prevail upon the combatants and force an end to the hostilities of World War I. In 1914, she and other settlement workers, including Addams and Kelley, organized the **American Union Against Militarism**. The union, of which Wald was president, lobbied the Wilson administration to pressure neutral countries to end the fighting.

After the United States became involved in the hostilities, Wald refocused her attention on health-related issues, serving as head of the Council of National Defense's Home Nursing Committee. The Henry Street nurses, whose number more than doubled between 1913 and 1918, were especially active during the influenza epidemic of 1918. During the epidemic, Wald was chair of the Nurses' Emergency Council and coordinated the effort to recruit volunteer nurses. She also oversaw the efforts of private and public nursing agencies. Following World War I, Wald helped to establish the League of Free Nations Association, which was an offshoot of the American Union Against Militarism.

During the 1920s, Wald maintained her busy schedule as both the nursing service and the settlement work at Henry Street continued to grow. Wald was active on the local and national levels in a variety of health and labor-related reform efforts. In 1933, she resigned as head resident of the Henry Street Settlement after 40 years having chosen her successors—**Helen Hall** to oversee the settlement work and Marguerite Wales to head the Visiting Nurse Service.

Bibliography

Dictionary of American Biography, supl. 2, pp. 687–88; Duffus, *Lillian Wald: Neighbor and Crusader* ; Jackson, *Encyclopedia of New York City*, p. 1232; James, *Notable American Women, 1607–1950*, vol. 3, pp. 526–29; Trattner, *Biographical Dictionary of Social Welfare in America*, pp. 735–37.

Walling, William English

settlement worker, labor activist, civil rights advocate

b. March 14, 1877; d. September 12, 1936.

William English Walling's career as a social reformer was grounded in the American Settlement Movement. A member of both the New York and Chicago reform communities, his interests were diverse and included the protection of women and children workers, international affairs, and race relations in the United States.

Walling was educated in private schools in his hometown of Louisville, Kentucky, and in Edinburgh, Scotland, where his father served as U.S. Consul for four years. In 1897, Walling graduated from the University of Chicago with a B.S. degree. He spent the following year at Harvard Law School and then took graduate courses in economics and sociology at the University of Chicago.

Walling worked as a factory inspector for the State of Illinois (1900–1901), and during this time, he lived in Chicago in a tenement neighborhood where he witnessed the social and economic conditions of the poor firsthand. While living in Chicago, he became acquainted with the leaders of the city's settlements, **Jane Addams** of **Hull House**, **Mary McDowell** of the **University of Chicago Settlement**, and **Graham Taylor** of **Chicago Commons**.

When he moved to New York City in 1902, Walling became a resident at the **University Settlement** on the city's Lower East Side. During the next four years, he was an active member of the city's reform community. In 1902, he was one of the organizers of the **New York Child Labor Committee**, which worked to secure protective legislation to combat child labor abuses, and along with Addams, **Mary Kenney O'Sullivan**, and others, he founded the **Women's Trade Union League**, a coalition of reformers and working women dedicated to unionizing women workers.

As a result of his interaction with Russian immigrants on New York's Lower East Side, Walling became interested in the Russian revolutionary movement. He spent two years in Russia (1905–1907) studying the movement and interviewing many of the principal participants. In 1908, he published a book based on his inquires, *Russia's Message*.

By the time he returned to the United States in 1907, Walling had become a socialist and had married Anna Strunsky, a socialist and writer he met in Europe. The Wallings settled in New York City, and their apartment became a gathering place for the city's social reformers. During this time, Walling devoted much of his time to writing and lecturing about conditions in Russia.

While on a trip to Chicago in 1908, Walling and his wife witnessed a race riot in Springfield, Illinois. Both of them wrote articles about what they observed, and although they continued their Russia-related lecture tour, race relations in the United States began to occupy more of their attention.

At the suggestion of **Mary White Ovington**, a New York settlement worker who was conducting a research study on blacks in New York City, Walling called a meeting in December 1908 to discuss the possibility of organizing a movement that would work for racial equality. In addition to Walling and Ovington, **Henry Moskowitz**, then the head resident at the **Madison House** settlement, was present. By the time they adjourned, the three had laid out the initial plans for the establishment of the National Association for the Advancement of Colored People (NAACP), which eventually became the foremost organization of its kind in the United States.

Walling maintained an active interest in the Socialist Party until 1917, when he resigned in protest over its antiwar stance. He was also a supporter of the American Federation of Labor, and after World War I, he worked full time for that organization writing articles and speeches. He was appointed executive director of the Labor Chest of the Relief and Liberation of Workers of Europe and died while on a fact-finding mission for that organization in 1936.

Bibliography

Davis, *Spearheads for Reform: The Social Settlements and the Progressive Movement, 1890–1914*; *Dictionary of American Biography*, supl. 2, pp. 689–90; Trattner, *Biographical Dictionary of Social Welfare in America*, pp. 739–40.

Ward Politics

Even though urban centers such as New York, Chicago, and Boston expanded during the nineteenth and early twentieth centuries, they were still composed of smaller districts or units that possessed distinct characteristics, perhaps because of the nationalities that settled there or because of the type of housing or industry that dominated the area. The smallest political unit within the larger cities was designated a ward. Wards varied in size, some encompassing only a few city blocks while others extended over much larger areas. New York City's system of wards was similar to systems that functioned in smaller urban centers. One of the key features of the ward system as far as settlements were concerned was the development of the ward boss, a political leader who dominated local politics. Many settlement workers viewed these ward bosses as direct obstacles to their goals of reform.

The first six wards in New York were established in 1686 and were clustered around the southern tip of Manhattan. By the middle of the nineteenth century, the city was divided into 19 wards, and by 1873 there were 23, which in total extended as far north as lower Westchester County. Each ward elected an alderman and an assistant alderman to serve on the city's common council. Prior to 1800, wards also elected other minor officials such as tax assessors and constables.

As New York City grew, particularly with the influx of new immigrants, the wards developed into centers of political power. The same was true of other cities such as Boston, Chicago, and Philadelphia. By 1850, the Tammany political organization was firmly established in New York City, and the ward boss had become a powerful figure in city politics. Ward bosses in other cities filled a similar role.

To settlement workers and other social reformers, the ward boss, in most cases, was viewed as a corrupt political organizer who traded favors for votes. The boss was usually a local businessman, often the saloonkeeper. He knew the neighborhood, and he knew his neighbors. The ward boss might help a family pay its rent or secure legal assistance for a newly arrived immigrant. The boss could find a patronage job for someone in need or expedite the process for having a sick family member admitted to the hospital. Since the ward boss lived in the neighborhood, many of those in need felt more comfortable going to him for assistance. Unlike charity organization reformers, the ward boss did not distinguish between the deserving and the undeserving. He helped anyone who could one day help him, usually by voting for a particular candidate.

By the late nineteenth century, many reformers blamed the ward boss for the corruption and inefficiency that characterized municipal government. Ward politicians were considered by many to be too parochial, putting the needs of their neighborhoods before those of the city as a whole.

To counter the influence of the ward bosses, settlement workers became involved in local politics either by running for office or by supporting reform candidates. **Graham Taylor** and many of the other residents of the **Chicago Commons** settlement were particularly active in municipal politics as were **Raymond Robins** of the **Northwestern University Settlement** in Chicago and **James Reynolds** of the

University Settlement in New York City. *See also* **Alfred Smith; Robert Wagner**.

Bibliography

Davis, *Spearheads for Reform: The Social Settlements and the Progressive Movement, 1890–1914*; Jackson, *Encyclopedia of New York City*, pp. 1236–37; Wade, *Graham Taylor: Pioneer for Social Justice, 1851–1938*.

Warner, Amos Griswold

social planner and author
b. December 21, 1861; d. January 17, 1900.

Although Amos Warner's career as a social welfare reformer was brief, he made a significant contribution to the **Charity Organization Society** movement through his work with the Baltimore Charity Organization Society. Additionally, with the publication of his book, *American Charities*, Warner articulated an important theory regarding the cause of poverty, namely that social factors were more significant in bringing about dependency than were individual character deficiencies.

Warner entered the preparatory department of the University of Nebraska in 1878. While a student, he became interested in the economic roots of the social welfare problems of the time. Instead of returning to his family's farm, following graduation he enrolled in Johns Hopkins University in Baltimore to study economics in 1885.

Two years later, Warner was invited by the philanthropist **John Glenn** to become the secretary of the Baltimore Charity Organization Society (COS). Warner subscribed to the prevailing COS tenet of the time that poverty was a direct reflection of a character flaw and that the best way to assist those in need was to subject them to a strict character-building program.

Warner earned a Ph.D. in economics in 1888, and the following year he accepted a position as head of the Department of Economics at the University of Nebraska. Warner now turned his attention to applying the scientific method to the study of industrial corporations. He was particularly interested in the growth and development of railroad companies.

Warner took a practical approach to teaching. In his courses, he examined the relationship between contemporary economic theory and social problems. In addition, he encouraged his students to visit social welfare-related institutions such as jails, police courts, and almshouses to observe firsthand the impact that these institutions had on society.

In 1891, Warner was named the first Superintendent of Charities for Washington, DC, charged with coordinating the efforts of the many charitable agencies that had been established in the nation's capital, most of which solicited congressional funds to carry out their work. Warner's experience with the Baltimore COS proved a valuable asset in this new position. He developed an efficient program for overseeing agency requests for funds that helped to avoid the costly duplication of effort. At the same time, he was active in the campaign to secure legislation that established a Board of Children's Guardians in 1892, the first public agency in the District of Columbia devoted to providing social services to children.

In 1893, Warner left Washington and joined the faculty at Stanford University, teaching courses in administration and engineering problems. This appointment was especially attractive to Warner because Stanford had recently acquired the Hopkins Railway Library, and with access to this resource, Warner could pursue his interest in the railroad industry.

The following year, Warner published *American Charities*, which was the first significant attempt to identify a scientific approach to the problem of poverty in the United States. In this study, Warner adheres to the COS doctrine that the deterioration of character was a direct cause of poverty. However, he also develops a parallel argument which holds that it is possible to identify objective environmental factors, such as unemployment and illness, as contributing factors to the rise of poverty. This new argument reflected a shift in thinking that many of the reformers and settlement workers of this era made.

Poor health compelled Warner to abandon his teaching career, and he died in 1900. Even though Warner's career was not a long one, *American Charities* did have an impact on the course of social welfare reform in the United States. Warner's thorough and systematic approach in investigating the causes of poverty drew attention to the fact that social factors were more significant than personal deficiencies in causing poverty and dependence.

Bibliography

Trattner, *Biographical Dictionary of Social Welfare in America*, pp. 740–42; Trattner, *From Poor Law to Welfare State: A History of Social Welfare in America*.

White, Alfred Tredway

housing reformer, philanthropist
b. May 28, 1846; d. January 29, 1921.

Alfred Tredway White believed that poor housing was a major factor in the many social problems that existed in cities—crime, poverty, disease. Like many of his contemporaries, White realized that the problems of the poor were everyone's problems. To protect the social order and ensure social justice, something needed to be done to provide adequate housing. His interest in housing brought him into contact with settlement workers and other reformers as he combined a successful business career with a productive career as a housing reform advocate.

The son of a wealthy businessman, White was born in Brooklyn, New York, and attended the Brooklyn Collegiate and Polytechnic Institutes. Shortly after graduating from Rensselaer Polytechnic Institute in 1865, he entered his father's importing firm, W.A. & A.M. White. He eventually became a partner, and he maintained an active interest in the firm until his death.

While still a young man, White became interested in social reform work, especially in relation to housing. He began to study housing in the United States, particularly in urban centers. In 1872, after returning from a visit to England where he had studied improved housing schemes, White constructed the Tower and Homes buildings on the Brooklyn waterfront. The units he built offered well-lighted rooms, separate entrances, and space for gardens and playgrounds. The homes were made available to working-class families at moderate rates on a financial plan that gave White a five-percent return on his investment.

In fact, White's housing philosophy was sometimes referred to as "philanthropy and five percent." He realized that commercial builders would not be interested in providing housing for the poor unless they could be sure that the venture would be a profitable one. At the same time, he believed that to make it affordable the return on their investment, their dividend, should be limited to five percent.

Under White's scheme, both parties benefited. White also thought that such limited-dividend homes should be well-designed, structurally sound, and easily managed. In this way, commercial builders would be encouraged to join in the effort. White believed that eventually his approach would pressure slumlords into improving their properties and keeping their rents reasonable to maintain high occupancy rates.

White's significant role in the housing reform movement went beyond rhetoric and ideas. Through his family-owned business, which he called the Improved Dwellings Company, White built 300 one- and two-family homes in Brook-

lyn. White published two pamphlets that contained information about his efforts: *Improved Dwellings for the Laboring Class* (1877) and *Better Homes For Working Men* (1885).

In 1896, White joined with **E.R.L. Gould** and a number of others to form the City and Suburban Homes Company. White served as a director of the firm. This organization became one of the most successful limited-dividend housing companies in the United States. By the 1920s, it was providing accommodations to more than 12,000 tenants. However, these housing efforts were not an overwhelming success since few investors were willing to limit the return on their capital investment to a maximum of five percent. Based on his housing reform efforts, White was appointed to the **New York State Tenement House Commission** of 1900.

White did not limit his interest in social welfare reform to housing. In 1878, he cofounded the Brooklyn Bureau of Charities and served as president of the bureau for more than 20 years. White was particularly interested in children and was a trustee of the Brooklyn Children's Aid Society for over 50 years. In connection with this organization, he built the Seaside Home for Children (1876) and the Seaside Home for Children in Coney Island (1910). White was also a director of the Brooklyn Society for the Prevention of Cruelty to Children and was its vice president from 1894 until his death. He was a director of the **Russell Sage Foundation** (1901–1921), the Brooklyn Institute of Arts and Sciences, and the Brooklyn Academy of Music.

In addition to these activities and his business dealings, White was a generous supporter of education. He donated substantial sums of money to the Hampton Institute and the Tuskegee Institute. In 1906, as a result of a donation from White, Harvard University established a Department of Social Ethics, which offered courses on the ethical and technical aspects of social work.

White combined his social welfare work with a full-time business career. He had a wide range of reform interests including housing, child welfare, and education, and he gave generously of both his time and his money to all these causes. White remained active in reform crusades up to his death from drowning in 1921.

Bibliography

Birch, "The Seven-Percent Solution: A Review of Philanthropic Housing, 1870–1910" ; Lubove, *The Progressives and the Slums: Tenement House Reform in New York City, 1890–1917*; National Cyclopaedia of American Biography, vol. 23, pp. 301–02; Trattner, *Biographical Dictionary of Social Welfare in America*, pp. 751–53.

White House Conference on Dependent Children

Settlement workers and other social welfare reformers were especially sensitive to the needs of children, particularly those who were orphaned and those whose parents were unable to care for them. Under different circumstances, many of these children would probably have been cared for through the informal support networks that existed in small towns and villages. However, these kinds of social safety nets did not exist in large urban centers, and many children were left to their own devices or cared for in impersonal institutions.

James E. West was an orphan who had been raised in an institution. As an adult he became a lawyer and was a close friend of President Theodore Roosevelt. Because of his background, West had an interest in the way dependent children were cared for in the United States. He knew that his concerns were shared by many social welfare reformers, but he also realized that unless the plight of these children was brought to the attention of the public in a forceful way, no real progress could be made to assist them.

West secured the support of a number of prominent settlement workers and other social reformers including **Lillian Wald**, **Jane Addams**, **Homer Folks**, and **Florence Kelley**. With their help, he persuaded Roosevelt to call a national conference to investigate the care of dependent children.

In January 1909, 200 prominent men and women met in Washington, DC, for two days to examine the existing programs for providing assistance to dependent children and to formulate plans for expanding and improving care. The conference brought the work of child welfare workers into the national spotlight. By calling the participants together, Roosevelt acknowledged the importance of their work, and he lent the power and prestige of the presidency to their cause. The gathering was also significant because through his actions Roosevelt acknowledged that the federal government was in some respects responsible for the social welfare of America's younger citizens.

One outcome of the conference was the publication of an official report that included a number of recommendations for the future. For example, the participants recommended that children who were delinquent or homeless or who needed to be removed from their homes be cared for in family settings rather than in institutions. This recommendation helped to strengthen the foster care system and to encourage the development of an adoption agency system. The conference participants also called for the states to become more involved in the process of institutional care of dependent children. Recommendations were forwarded regarding the need for state licensing of child care institutions and for regular inspections of these facilities.

Another significant outcome of the White House Conference on Dependent Children was the creation of the **United States Children's Bureau** in 1912. The idea for a central agency that was charged with collecting information about child welfare had been put forward almost a decade earlier by Kelley in relation to her work on child labor reform, but the national attention that was focused on the plight of children because of the 1909 conference helped accelerate the creation of the Children's Bureau. *See also* **Child Welfare.**

Bibliography

Trattner, *From Poor Law to Welfare State: A History of Social Welfare in America.*

Williams, Elizabeth Sprague

educator, settlement resident, education advocate

b. August 31, 1869; d. August 19, 1922.

Elizabeth Sprague Williams was introduced to settlement work as a college student. At first, she combined a teaching career with settlement work, but eventually she devoted her full attention to social reform work and became an integral part of the New York City social reform community, concentrating her efforts on public school reform and club work.

Williams's interest in social reform was awakened as a student at Smith College. After graduating in 1891, she returned to her hometown, Buffalo, New York, to establish a library and to teach. She also worked in a social settlement there supported by her Unitarian congregation.

After a few years, Williams moved to New York City, where she attended Columbia University, earning an A.M. degree in 1896. She spent the following year teaching at Barnard College, where she was selected a fellow. Anxious to supplement her academic training with practical experience, Williams went to live at the **College Settlement** on Rivington Street on New York's Lower East Side.

In October 1898, Williams succeeded **Mary** Kingsbury (later **Simkhovitch**) as head resident, a position she held until 1919. Williams immersed herself and her colleagues in the various crusades that characterized the Progressive Era. Under her guidance, the College Settlement's residents were encouraged to join, among other organizations, the New York **Consumers' League**, the New York **Charity Organization Society**, the **Outdoor Recreation League**, the Public Education Association, and the Manhattan Trade School for Girls. In addition, Williams encouraged the settlement residents to work on a variety of programs with their colleagues in other New York City settlements.

Like other settlement workers, Williams was involved in many housing and public health initiatives. In particular, she encouraged other residents of the College Settlement to be particularly active in assisting the **New York Charity Organization Society Tenement House Committee** to prepare its landmark Tenement House Exhibition in 1900. Later that same year, Williams testified before the **New York State Tenement House Commission** about housing conditions in the congested neighborhoods on the Lower East Side. Williams also opened the College Settlement to serve as the headquarters of the East Side Recreation Society, which along with the Outdoor Recreation League worked to secure playgrounds and parks for the residents of inner-city neighborhoods.

Education, though, was the cause that most appealed to Williams. She was committed to improving the educational facilities available to recent immigrants, viewing the public schools as an integral component in the **Americanization** process. Williams's service as a member of the local school board is just one example of her commitment to public education. She also established and maintained libraries in schools, organized night classes for working men and women, and helped to establish kindergartens.

Besides education, Williams stressed the importance of clubs and group work at the College Settlement, believing that by cooperating to achieve common goals, neighborhood residents could learn the discipline and skills they needed to function effectively in society. In addition to a variety of social and athletic clubs, the College Settlement sponsored a summer camp and farm, Mount Ivy, in Rockland County, New York. Williams thought the cooperative skills acquired in the country could be put to good use once neighborhood residents returned to their homes.

When Williams resigned from the College Settlement in 1919, it was not to enjoy her retirement but to enter into a new arena of social service work. That year she traveled to Serbia to open an orphanage in Veles, a town near the Albanian border. Over the next two years, Williams not only built an orphanage, but she also secured a locomotive for the local railroad so that supplies could reach the war-torn area. When she left, the Serbian government assumed responsibility for the orphanage. Williams died of cancer a year after she returned to the United States. The Serbian government awarded her a posthumous royal decoration in recognition of her accomplishments.

Bibliography

James, *Notable American Women, 1607–1900*, vol. 3, pp. 619–20; Trattner, *Biographical Dictionary of Social Welfare in America*, pp. 769–71; Woods, *The Settlement Horizon*.

Windows on Henry Street (1934)

Lillian Wald wrote *Windows on Henry Street* in 1934 while in Connecticut recuperating from a protracted illness. Her first book, ***The House on Henry Street***, which was written in 1915, related the story of the first 20 years of her life and work at the **Henry Street Settlement**, the settlement house she established at 265 Henry Street in 1895. This second volume takes up the story of the next 20 years spent with her neighbors on New York City's Lower East Side.

Wald is emphatic in the opening pages of *Windows on Henry Street* that she has not written an autobiography. This is not her story. Rather, she views it as an account of the place of a settlement in the context of the social movements of the time. The book is an attempt on her part to illustrate the "harmonies built up in the community by the many little groups, through their sympathetic relations with other groups" (Wald, *Windows on Henry Street*, p. 5).

The 20 years that Wald considers in this volume were years of change and upheaval for her and for her neighbors as they experienced war and peace, economic boom and depression, prohibition, and the influx of new immigrant groups into the neighborhood. As she did in *The House on Henry Street*, Wald uses vignettes of the people and events she encountered to advance the narrative, but as was true in her earlier work, the subjects are carefully chosen to illustrate her central theme: the encouragement of the art of humanity.

For example, Ward was proud that racial tensions in the neighborhood around the Henry Street Settlement were few, and she recounts an experience she had one Christmas night when she stopped in at the nearby All Saints Church, which had a predominantly black congregation. While she was there, she listened to the choir and recognized most of the choir members as having been trained at the Henry Street Settlement Music School. Using her experience as an illustration of racial harmony in the neighborhood she concludes, "At Henry Street it is a long time since we had any fear of embarrassment over the typically American 'race problem' . . . The coming of the Negro Colony to our neighborhood has often given us very rare delights" (Wald, *Windows on Henry Street*, pg. 28).

The world that Wald entered in 1895 as a young visiting nurse had changed dramatically by 1934, when she was an acknowledged leader of the American Settlement Movement. Yet, she maintains that one constant endured as she looked back on her accomplishments: her hope that young people will learn from her experience the importance of participating in the process of living by becoming involved in a cause that will help others, whether social or political.

Windows on Henry Street recounts the changes that occurred at the Henry Street Settlement since the publication of Wald's first book, *The House on Henry Street* (1915). For the current historian or modern reader, *Windows on Henry Street* provides a firsthand account of life on New York City's Lower East Side during the first half of the twentieth century.

Bibliography

Duffus, *Lillian Wald: Neighbor and Crusader*; Wald, *Windows on Henry Street*.

Woerishoffer, Emma Carola

philanthropist, settlement resident, social reformer, labor advocate

b. August [n.d.] 1885; d. September 11, 1911.

Carola Woerishoffer was a wealthy young woman with a strong social conscience. She not only donated her money to various social reform crusades, but she also was a settlement resident and an active participant in a number of reform efforts related to labor and women's working conditions.

Emma Carola Woerishoffer, who was known as Carola, inherited more than one million dollars from her father, Charles Frederick, a Wall Street banker and New York Stock Exchange broker who died the year after she was born. Woerishoffer's interest in social reform was fostered by her mother, Ann, who was active in a variety of charitable activities in New York City, and by her maternal grandfather, Oswald Ottendorfer, the editor and manager of a liberal German-language daily newspaper *New Yorker Staats-Zeitung,* and an active participant in Democratic reform politics.

Woerishoffer graduated from Bryn Mawr College in 1907 having studied economics, philosophy, politics, psychology, and languages. She immediately immersed herself in a number of the reform efforts that were underway in Manhattan's immigrant neighborhoods. Her participation in the New York City reform community was almost paradoxical. An intelligent young woman with a vigorous personality, she avoided public recognition of her significant contributions, both personal and monetary.

Woerishoffer began her social reform work as a part-time resident and member of the board of managers of **Greenwich House**, the settlement on Manhattan's Lower West Side founded by **Mary Simkhovitch**. With the settlement serving as a base of operations, Woerishoffer became active in various social welfare and labor organizations including the New York **Consumers' League**, the New York Association for Labor Legislation, and the woman suffrage crusade. Her willingness to explore all possible avenues of reform was illustrated by her becoming a member of the board of directors of the Taylor Iron and Steel Company, because it was interested in establishing a model industrial village.

In 1908, Woerishoffer provided financial backing for the Congestion Exhibition at the American Museum of Natural History which was sponsored by the New York City Tenement House Committee's **Committee on Congestion of Population** whose members included Simkhovitch and **Florence Kelley**, then a resident at the **Henry Street Settlement**. The following year, Woerishoffer undertook a grueling investigation of the New York City laundry industry. Concealing her identity, she worked 15 hours a day as a laundress in several different laundries over a period of four months. Then, she reported on her experiences to the New York Consumers' League and to the Wainwright Commission, which was charged with investigating the treatment of injured employees by their employers and with enacting employers liability legislation. The Wainwright Commission was instrumental in the passage of the New York State Workers' Compensation Act of 1914, which created the Workers' Compensation Fund insuring employers against occupational injury suffered by their employees.

As part of her crusade to improve labor conditions, Woerishoffer also supported union movements and strikers. She joined the New York **Women's Trade Union League** (WTUL) in 1908 and served as an executive committee member and as treasurer. She was also president of the WTUL's label shop, where only those goods that were made under approved conditions were offered for sale. In 1909, when the striking women shirtwaist makers were jailed in New York City, Woerishoffer put up a $75,000 property bond to secure their release. In addition, she donated $10,000 to establish a permanent strike fund. Although the press was eager to report on these actions, Woerishoffer insisted on protecting her privacy.

Like many of her reformer colleagues, Woerishoffer came to believe that government regulation was required to significantly improve working conditions. Toward this end, she became a member of the executive committee of the New York State Association for Labor Legislation. In 1910 when the State Department of Labor established the Bureau of Industries and Immigration, Woerishoffer became a special investigator for the bureau. She also served as benefactor for the bureau and donated significant sums of money to supplement its budget.

In 1911 while on an inspection tour of immigrant labor camps across New York State on behalf of the New York State Department of Labor, Woerishoffer was killed in an automobile crash. Part of the $750,000 legacy she left to Bryn Mawr was used to fund the college's Carola Woerishoffer Graduate Department of Social Economy and Social Research, which was the first school of its kind to be affiliated with an institution of higher learning.

Bibliography

Bryn Mawr College Class of 1907, Carola Woerishoffer: Her Life and Work; James, *Notable American Women, 1607–1950,* vol. 3, pp. 639–41; Simkhovitch, *Neighborhood: My Story of Greenwich House;* Trattner, *Biographical Dictionary of Social Welfare in America,* pp. 787–89.

Women's City Club of New York

The Women's City Club of New York was a voluntary association formed in July 1915 by suffragists who believed that once women gained the vote, they should have an environment in which they could study and debate political issues. The club's founders intended it to fulfill two functions: to educate the city's citizens about the political process and to use the political process to improve the quality of life of all residents.

Soon after the club was organized, its board of directors established committees that were charged with studying issues and reporting back to the membership with policy recommendations. From time to time, committees published the results of their investigations. Club leaders organized lobbying efforts for legislation and other reforms based on the information collected by the committees. Among the issues that the club concerned itself with were industrial and labor relations, especially as they related to women and children; housing; recreational facilities; education; and government finance and planning.

In addition to educating the voting public, the Women's City Club provided its members with a means of exerting political influence. A number of women connected with the settlement movement were founding members of the Women's Club including **Katherine B. Davis**, **Mary E. Dreier**, **Lillian Wald** and **Mary Simkhovitch**. In addition to these women, several prominent reformers who worked closely with the settlement movement occupied leadership positions in the club including **Eleanor Roosevelt**, **Belle Moskowitz**, and **Frances Perkins**.

Over the years, settlement workers had joined together with other social reformers to form voluntary organizations. These organizations often functioned as pressure groups and gave the members an opportunity to influence local authorities. In this respect, the Women's City Club was no different from other organizations that New York City settlement workers joined, such as the New York branches of the **Consumers' League** or the Child Labor Committee. What made the Women's City Club unique was that only women were eligible for membership.

During its years of operation, the Women's City Club of New York actively promoted women's issues such as the provision of maternal and infant care by the state, minimum wage and protective labor legislation for women and children, and the election and appointment of women to public offices. The club also fought for economic and civil rights of minorities and for housing for low- and middle-income city residents. The club successfully lobbied for a revised city charter, improved tenant relocation process, special treatment for youthful offenders, and improved city personnel practices. Today, the Women's City Club of New York continues to provide women with an opportunity to make their voices heard in the political process.

Bibliography
Jackson, *Encyclopedia of New York City*, p. 1269 ; Perry, *Women's Political Chances after Suffrage: The Women's City Club of New York, 1915–1990."*

Women's International League for Peace and Freedom

Many of the women who were involved in the American Settlement Movement were active in national and international women's organizations. One cause that attracted the attention of a number of prominent settlement workers was the international peace movement.

During the first decade of the twentieth century, women demanding suffrage organized the International Woman Suffrage Alliance (IWSA), which was headquartered in London. With the outbreak of war in 1914, the membership of the IWSA was divided over whether the group should support the war effort or declare itself for peace. Many IWSA members believed that the campaign for suffrage should be allied with the peace movement, and to pursue this connection, some members of the IWSA called for an international conference.

In April 1915, the International Congress of Women convened at The Hague, The Netherlands, to express its opposition to the war in Europe and to consider ways of ending the conflict. Representatives of more than 150 organizations from 12 countries were in attendance. **Jane Addams**, the founder of the Chicago settlement **Hull House,** agreed to preside at the congress. She brought a strong American delegation with her that included a number of prominent settlement workers such as **Emily Balch**, **Grace Abbott**, and **Alice Hamilton**.

The delegates at The Hague Congress passed two resolutions. One called for the formation of two delegations to visit the capitals of the 13 warring and neutral countries to meet with their leaders and to urge them to seek an immediate end to the hostilities. The second resolution called for the establishment of a new organization called the International Committee of Women for Permanent Peace. It was decided that this second group would reconvene during the peace talks after the war ended. When the International Committee met again at the peace talks in 1919, it changed its name to the Women's International League for Peace and Freedom (WILPF). The league established its international headquarters in a small house in Geneva which was called Maison Internationale.

Shortly after World War I, women in the United States and many European countries gained the vote. Some women felt that the vote granted them the equality they sought when they originally formed the IWSA, and the international women's movement lost momentum. Others believed that there was still much to be done, and these women who remained active in the work of the WILPF refocused their attention on the peace movement and international relations.

The membership of the WILPF was pleased with the formation of the League of Nations and worked with the league to ensure peace, particularly through the use of nonviolent means. The work of the women of the WILPF did not go unrecognized as evidenced by the fact that Jane Addams and Emily Balch, two of the founding members, were awarded the Nobel Peace Prize in 1931 and 1946, respectively.

Bibliography
Bussey, *Women's International League for Peace and Freedom, 1915–1965: A Record of Fifty Years' Work*; Foster, *Women for All Seasons: The Story of the Women's International League for Peace and Freedom*.

Women's Trade Union League

Many settlement workers, particularly those in large urban centers such as Boston, Chicago, and New York, were actively involved in organizing women into labor unions. They often encouraged unions to hold their meetings in the settlement houses and helped striking workers by providing money and food as well as moral support, which sometimes included walking on picket lines. Although individual organizers met with some success, they soon realized that genuine progress could be achieved if they combined in a more concerted effort.

A Women's Trade Union League (WTUL) had been formed in England in 1874 and had enjoyed considerable success in organizing women to win shorter hours and better working conditions. After investigating the work of the English league, **William English Walling**, a New York City settlement worker, was convinced that women workers in the United States could benefit from a similar organization. In November 1903, during the annual meeting of the American Federation of Labor (AFL) in Boston, Walling approached **Mary Kenney O'Sullivan**, a union organizer and a former resident of **Hull House**, with his idea for a trade union league. O'Sullivan pledged her support, as did the president of the AFL, Samuel Gompers, and a national Women's Trade Union League (WTUL) was established.

Headquarters of the Women's Trade Union League of New York during the Shirt Waist Strike of November 22, 1909–February 15, 1910 (Jan. 10)
Museum of the City of New York

From the beginning, settlement workers from Boston, Chicago, and New York took a leadership role in the work of the WTUL, and local branches of the WTUL were formed in these cities. **Robert Woods**, **Helena Dudley**, **Vida Scudder**, **Jane Addams**, **Lillian Wald**, **Mary Morton Kehew**, and **Mary McDowell** participated in the national organizational meetings. Kehew was elected president; Addams, vice president; O'Sullivan, secretary; and Mary Donovan of the Lynn, Massachusetts, Central Labor Union was elected treasurer. Wald, McDowell, and **Leonora O'Reilly**, a union organizer, were selected as members of the executive board.

The leaders of the national WTUL realized that they must win the support of organized labor, especially the AFL, if they were to accomplish their goals. Despite initial resistance and suspicion, the national WTUL leadership was able to secure this cooperation. Over the years, **Margaret Dreier Robins**, the president of the national league from 1907–1922, and other labor reformers also worked to enlist the support, both moral and monetary, of upper- and middle-class women who were sympathetic to their cause. Although these leisured women were sometimes considered too domineering by

their working-class associates, the WTUL managed to accomplish a great deal and attracted support from women of different social classes. It organized women into unions in a variety of trades, sponsored educational and training programs for working women, and fought for the passage and enforcement of protective legislation.

In 1905, **Rose Schneiderman** was recruited as a member of the WTUL, and she made significant progress toward organizing women into unions, particularly in the garment industry. The WTUL led a strike by shirtwaist makers in 1909–1910, the largest strike by American women up to that time. Settlement workers from several New York City settlement houses actively supported this labor action, which was popularly known as the "uprising of the thirty thousand."

In the years following World War I, the league began to concentrate its efforts on educating workers and on securing protective legislation. Toward these ends, the WTUL operated a school for working women from 1923 to 1955, offering classes in literature, economics, and labor history, and it used New York State as a testing ground for securing labor legislation. The WTUL helped pass minimum wage, maternity insurance, and fire safety laws during the 1920s and 1930s. During the 1940s the WTUL concentrated its efforts on protecting women employed in war-related industries. Due to lack of financial support, the WTUL disbanded in 1955.

Bibliography

Davis, *Spearheads for Reform: The Social Settlements and the Progressive Movement 1890–1914*; Dye, *As Equals and as Sisters: Feminism, Unionism, and the Women's Trade Union League in New York*; Jackson, *Encyclopedia of New York City*, pp. 849–850; O'Neill, *Everyone Was Brave: A History of Feminism in America*.

Wood, Edith Elmer
housing reformer
b. September 24, 1871; d. April 29, 1945.

Edith Elmer Wood became involved in the national campaign for low-cost public housing after witnessing the relationship between substandard housing and the high incidence of diseases such as tuberculosis. Although she worked with settlement workers and other social reformers, Wood's own interest was consistently focused on housing reforms rather than on the broader issues of social and economic planning.

Wood's father, Horace Elmer, was an officer in the United States Navy, and because of his military assignments, Edith and her family lived in a variety of places both in the United States and abroad. As a result, Wood received her early education from tutors and governesses. In 1890, she graduated from Smith College with a B.L. degree. Three years later she married Albert Norton Wood, who, like her father, was a naval officer. Once again, Wood traveled, living where her husband was stationed.

After graduating from Smith, and during the early years of her marriage, Wood wrote romantic fiction and travelogues. But in 1906, while the family was living in Puerto Rico, Wood's life underwent a dramatic change. A household servant was diagnosed with tuberculosis, and Wood discovered while trying to assist her that the island had no appropriate treatment facilities. This state of affairs inspired her to abandon her fiction writing and to undertake a crusade to improve health care facilities in Puerto Rico. Among her accomplishments was the founding of the Anti-Tuberculosis League of Puerto Rico, of which she served as president until 1910.

Following her husband's reassignment to Washington, DC, Wood became active in local public health initiatives including a campaign to clean up the housing in the congested slum area where many of the capital's black residents resided. By now, Wood was convinced of the relationship between substandard housing conditions and the high incidence of tuberculosis. In 1913, she helped draft a bill that would have permitted the District of Columbia to issue low-interest loans to limited dividend companies to finance the construction of better housing. Although the bill was defeated, Wood did not abandon her crusade, and she spent the next two years investigating the housing situation in the nation's capital. She had found her life's work in the campaign for government-financed housing and became the first woman housing economist.

Although she had significant firsthand practical experience, Wood lacked formal training in the fields of social economy and housing reform. Her husband's retirement in 1915 made it possible for Wood to move to New York City, where she enrolled in a joint program at the New York School of Philanthropy and Columbia University.

During this time, Wood prepared a study of the **New York City Tenement House Department**'s Vacation Bureau for the Bureau of Municipal Research. She also served as a advisor on housing legislation for the Women's Municipal League of Boston(1917–1919), and in 1917, she became chair of the American Association of University Women's national committee on housing, a position she held for the next 12 years. In 1919 Wood earned a Ph.D., writing a dissertation that considered housing conditions on the national level. She later published her research as a book entitled *The Housing of the Unskilled Wage Earner* in which she discussed the state of the housing available to the urban working class, reviewed the history of the housing reform movement, and commented on its future course. Wood was also critical of the restrictive legislation approach to housing reform, a theme that she returned to in her writings and speeches during the next several years.

During the 1920s, Wood wrote and lectured about the housing problem in the United States, arguing that decent housing was an essential right of all American citizens. Although Wood acknowledged the need for the restrictive housing legislation to establish minimum housing standards favored by the New York City housing reformer **Lawrence Veiller**, among others, she contended that a more constructive approach would be more economical and, in the long run, would benefit a larger percentage of the population. She argued that housing was essentially an economic issue and that private philanthropic efforts had proved inadequate. Wood called on the federal government to lend money to municipalities for slum clearance and for constructing government-owned housing projects. She also advocated establishing a national housing agency to administer a joint program of low-interest loans and public housing. Wood believed that such an agency could also enforce minimum housing standards nationwide and disseminate information on housing and city planning to communities. Her argument for government aid to housing was based on the model of government financing and construction that had been developed in western Europe as early as the 1890s.

Wood was active in the work of a number of housing reform-related organizations. During the 1920s, she became a member of the Regional Planning Association of America. In 1932, Wood served as vice president of the National Public Housing Conference (*see* **National Housing Conference**), a well-organized lobby of social reformers founded by **Mary K. Simkhovitch**, the founder and head resident of the New York settlement **Greenwich House**. The National Public Housing Conference provided vital assistance to New York Senator **Robert F. Wagner** by mobilizing support, especially within the reform community, for the **Wagner-Steagall National Housing Act** (1937), which marked the beginning of federal support for public housing.

Between 1933 and 1937, Wood entered government service as a consultant to the housing division of the Public Works Administration and to its successor, the United States Housing Authority from 1938 to 1942. On the state level Wood also served as a commissioner of the New Jersey State Housing Authority from 1934 to 1935.

Wood's most significant contribution to the housing reform efforts was her advocacy of government-sponsored housing. She did not believe that housing legislation that set minimum standards of light, ventilation and fire protection could guarantee an adequate supply of decent housing for the poor and argued that the government needed to become involved in providing affordable housing. Wood died in 1945 after a long illness.

Bibliography

Dictionary of American Biography, supl. 3, pp. 837–39; James, *Notable American Women, 1607–1950*, vol. 3, pp. 644–45; Trattner, *Biographical Dictionary of Social Welfare in America*, pp. 789–92.

Woods, Robert Archey

settlement worker, social reformer, writer, editor

b. December 9, 1865; d. February 18, 1925.

Pragmatic and practical, Robert Woods was instrumental in shaping the ideas and goals of the settlement movement in the United States. He served as a role model for his contemporaries, weaving together the ideals of the **Social Gospel** Movement with the practical goals of the Progressive reformers' campaigns for social reconstruction. In his work, he emphasized cooperative efforts among social reformers and was a leader in the movement to establish local and national settlement house federations. As a researcher and author, Woods emphasized the value of conducting scientifically based social investigations as a methodology for identifying problems and promoting solutions.

Born and raised in Pittsburgh, Pennsylvania, Woods enrolled in Amherst College where he came under the influence of Charles Edward Garman, a professor of philosophy and psychology who was also a proponent of the Social Gospel Movement, the social theory that emphasized the individual's moral obligation to society. After graduating from Amherst in 1886, Woods enrolled in Andover Theological Seminary. There, the Reverend William Jewett Tucker became his mentor after Woods registered for Tucker's new courses in sociology and economics. A short time later, Woods abandoned his plans to enter the ministry. He resolved to pursue a career in social reform, and toward this end, he decided to live and work in a settlement house.

As part of his course work at the seminary, Woods traveled to New York City in 1888 to interview labor leaders such as Samuel Gompers, Henry George, and representatives from the Knights of Labor regarding labor's relation to the church and the state. Two years later, Tucker awarded Woods a traveling fellowship to study English reform efforts. For six months in 1895 Woods lived at **Toynbee Hall**, the settlement founded by **Samuel Barnett** in London's East End. When he returned to Andover in 1891, Woods delivered a series of lectures on the new English Settlement Movement which were published as a book entitled, *English Social Movements,* in 1891. That same year, Tucker decided to test the settlement idea in the United States by establishing Boston's first settlement, which was named Andover House and was located in an overcrowded area in the city's South End. Tucker appointed

Woods to serve as head resident, a position he held until 1925.

Under Woods's leadership, Andover House, which was renamed **South End House** in 1895 to acknowledge the connection with the neighborhood, became one of the leading settlements in the United States. Woods viewed the settlement as a "social science laboratory" and advocated the scientific method of observation and analysis by settlement residents when conducting research. In his writings such as *The City Wilderness* (1898), *Americans in Process* (1902), *Neighborhood in Nation-Building* (1923), and *The Settlement Horizon* (1923), Woods established the concept of the neighborhood as the primary community unit out of which social reconstruction would evolve. The role of the settlement was to provide the impetus to build a strong, cohesive neighborhood. Through their service to the settlement and the neighborhood, residents were contributing to the larger crusade of providing an opportunity for the classes to come together to form a new, stronger society.

Woods and the residents of South End House were involved in many of the same reform crusades that their colleagues in other houses in Boston and in settlements in other cities such as Chicago and New York were waging. He believed that public **baths** and gymnasiums were important for the health and hygiene of the community, and he chaired the Boston Committee on Public Baths and Gymnasiums, which was responsible for the establishment of the Dover Street Bath in the city's South End. Working with **Joseph Lee**, the well-known advocate of playgrounds and recreation, Woods established the South End Playground in 1904.

He and other settlement residents worked with the municipal board of health to improve the health of neighborhood residents. Toward this end, Mary Strong was appointed to serve as a resident nurse at South End House. She established a milk station and later initiated baby clinics and a prenatal care service. Another settlement-owned building was used as a call station for the district nurse and a physician from the Boston Dispensary.

Woods was also involved in other reforms, including education-related initiatives and temperance efforts. He chaired the Citizens Committee to Promote a State System of Industrial Education and was secretary of the State Committee to Establish Industrial Schools. Woods also believed that alcohol abuse impeded the process of social regeneration in urban neighborhoods, and for many years he lobbied for a hospital to treat alcoholics. In 1907 in recognition of his efforts, the governor of Massachusetts appointed him chair of the State Hospital for Inebriates. He was associated with the State Hospital until 1914, when he was appointed to the Boston Licensing Board and worked to limit the number of saloons in tenement districts. In 1918, Woods chaired the Massachusetts Committee to Secure Ratification of the Eighteenth Amendment, which prohibited the sale and manufacture of alcohol.

In 1899, Woods applied the concept of cooperative effort to the work of the various settlements in Boston when he organized the South End Social Union, a federation of 10 settlement houses. He served as president of the organization until 1908, and during his term of office, the federation, which had been renamed the **Boston Social Union**, included 26 Boston-based settlement houses. Woods's efforts to promote a more comprehensive consolidation of settlement efforts resulted in the formation of the **National Federation of Settlements** in 1911. He served as secretary of the organization from 1911 to 1923, and then served as president until 1925.

In many ways, Woods set a standard for his fellow settlement workers. Hardworking and realistic, he merged the ideals of the Social Gospel Movement with the practical reform work that he accomplished at South End House and in other social welfare reforms. In addition to his research and reform work on the local level, Woods was active in the work of the National Federation of Settlements which provided him an opportunity to work cooperatively with his peers nationwide. Woods died unexpectedly in 1925 after a brief illness.

Bibliography

Dictionary of American Biography, vol. 10, pp. 503–04; Melvin, *American Community Organizations: An Historical Dictionary*, pp. 196–98; Trattner, *Biographical Dictionary of Social Welfare in America*, pp. 792–97.

Woolley, Celia Parker

minister, social reformer, settlement worker, civil rights advocate
b. June 14, 1848; d. March 9, 1918

Celia Parker Woolley became involved in settlement work after pursuing careers as a fiction writer and as an ordained Unitarian minister. She distinguished herself as a settlement worker by establishing a house dedicated to promoting racial harmony and cooperation.

Woolley was a member of the first graduating class of the Coldwater Michigan Female

Seminary in 1867. The following year she married Jefferson H. Woolley, a dentist who was 10 years her senior. After her marriage, Woolley began to write poetry and short stories. Like other women of her social class, she also became involved in local civic affairs and was a founding member of the Ladies Library Association. In 1869, she was elected secretary of the Branch County Suffrage Association.

In 1896, the Woolleys moved from Michigan to Chicago. While Jefferson's career advanced, Celia continued to write. Over the next several years, she published articles and stories in a variety of magazines and wrote three novels. During this time, Woolley became a member of the exclusive Chicago Women's Club, which was originally a social organization but eventually became a leading philanthropic agency. She served as president from 1888 to 1890 and was active in the work of its reform committee. She was also a member of the Fortnightly Club, another prestigious women's group.

Religion also played a central role in Woolley's life, and in 1894, she was ordained into the Unitarian Fellowship. She served as pastor of the Unitarian Church in Geneva, Illinois from 1893 to 1896, and as pastor of the Independent Liberal Church in Chicago from 1896 to 1898.

In addition to her church-related responsibilities, Woolley maintained an interest in social reform work, and in 1904 she established a settlement on the south side of Chicago in a predominately black neighborhood, which she named the **Frederick Douglass Center**. **Jane Addams**, the founder of Chicago's most well-known settlement, **Hull House**, was instrumental in raising funds for this center that promoted ethical and friendly relations between the races by providing assistance to both blacks and whites. Woolley lived and worked at the settlement for the next 14 years, providing services to the community and working to make the settlement a symbol of interracial cooperation.

Like **Mary Ovington**, Woolley's most distinctive contribution to the American Settlement Movement was her effort to extend the services of the settlement house to the black community. Woolley made a conscious effort to integrate the activities of the Frederick Douglass Center, a policy that truly set her apart from her social reformer colleagues. Woolley was active in the programs offered by the center up to her death in 1918.

Bibliography

Dictionary of American Biography, vol. 10, p. 575.

Y

Young Working Girls: A Summary of Evidence from Two Thousand Social Workers (1913)

Young Working Girls was the first major research effort of the **National Federation of Settlements**. Published in 1913, the study was based on evidence gathered from 2,000 settlement house girls' club leaders between 1911 and 1912. The data was collated and analyzed by **Robert A. Woods** and **Albert J. Kennedy** of **South End House** in Boston. The book included an introduction by **Jane Addams**, founder of **Hull House.**

Settlement workers viewed girls, especially those between 17 and 20 years of age, as more vulnerable than their male counterparts. In their crowded, urban, industrial environment these young women were faced with a variety of dangers and temptations both in the workplace and in their personal lives. Reformers were concerned that after spending long hours working at monotonous factory jobs young women would be attracted to the festive atmosphere of the local dance hall or saloon, which seemed to offer a refreshing change of pace. Additionally, they were concerned that in the factory system young women often worked in a close proximity with men, a situation that would probably not have occurred in a rural setting. Reformers realized that society set a different moral standard for young women and that once a woman violated the expected moral code, she had little hope of reclaiming her reputation.

In *Young Working Girls*, Woods and Kennedy contend that it is the responsibility of the settlement to mitigate these conditions. One way to do so was for the settlement to develop a high-quality girls' club program that could build character through constructive activity. By participating in well-run, settlement-sponsored clubs, girls could develop their individual talents and self-esteem while also learning to work cooperatively. Many settlements used this information as a basis for establishing girls clubs in their neighborhoods or for modifying the activities of those they were already offering to residents. In addition, *Young Working Girls* served as a model for later National Federation of Settlements studies which combined scientifically based analysis with scholarly research.

Bibliography

Carson, *Settlement Folk: Social Thought and the American Settlement Movement, 1885–1930*; Woods, *The Settlement Horizon*; Woods, *Young Working Girls: A Summary of Evidence From Two Thousand Social Workers*.

Bibliography of Resources

Abbott, Edith. *The Tenements of Chicago, 1908–1935*. New York: Arno Press and the New York Times, 1970.

Abbott, Grace. *The Immigrant and the Community*. New York: Century Company, 1907.

Addams, Jane. *My Friend Julia Lathrop*. New York: Macmillian Company, 1935.

———. *The Second Twenty Years at Hull-House, September 1909 to September 1928, with a Record of a Growing World Consciousness*. New York: Macmillan Company, 1930.

———. *Twenty Years at Hull-House with Autobiographical Notes*. Urbana, IL: University of Illinois Press, 1990.

Adler, Curtis. *Jacob H. Schiff: His Life & Letters*. 2 vols. New York: Doubleday Doran, 1928.

Antler, Joyce. *Lucy Sprague Mitchell: The Making of a Modern Woman*. New Haven, CT: Yale University Press, 1986.

Artera, Rhetta M. *Living in Chelsea: A Study of Human Relations in the Area Served by the Hudson Guild*. New York: Center for Human Relations Studies, 1934.

Axinn, June and Herman Levin. *Social Welfare: A History of the American Response to Need*. 2nd ed. New York: Harper & Brothers Publishers, 1982.

Barnard, Harry. *"Eagle Forgotten": The Life of John Peter Altgeld*. Indianapolis, IN: The Bobbs-Merrill Company Publishers, 1938.

Birch, Eugenie Landner and Deborah S. Gandner, "The Seven-Percent Solution: A Review of Philanthropic Housing, 1870–1910." *Journal of Urban History* (August 1981): 403–38.

Blackham, Harold J. *Stanton Coit, 1857–1944: Selections from His Memoir*. London: Faxill Press, 1944.

Bliss, William Dwight Porter, and Rudolph M. Binder, eds. *The New Encyclopedia of Social Reform*. New York: Arno Press and The New York Times, 1970.

Blumberg, Doris. *Florence Kelley: The Making of a Social Pioneer*. New York: Augustus M. Kelley Publishers, 1966.

Boyer, Paul. *Urban Masses and Moral Order in America: 1820–1920*. Cambridge, MA: Harvard University Press, 1978.

Brandt, Lilian. *The Growth and Development of the AICP and COS: A Preliminary and Exploratory Review*. New York: Community Service Society of New York, 1942.

Bremner, Robert H. *From the Depths: The Discovery of Poverty in the United States*. New York: New York University Press, 1956.

Brown, Ira V. *Lyman Abbott: Christian Evolutionist: A Study in Religious Liberalism*. Cambridge, MA: Harvard University Press, 1953.

Brown, James. *The History of Public Assistance in Chicago, 1833 to 1893*. Chicago: University of Chicago Press, 1941.

Browne, Waldo Ralph. *Altgeld of Illinois: A Record of His Life and Work*. New York: B.W. Huebsch, Inc., 1924.

Bryn Mawr College. Class of 1907. *Carola Woerishoffer, Her Life and Work*. New York: Arno Press, 1974.

Buroker, Robert L. "From Voluntary Association to Welfare State: The Illinois Immigrants Protective League, 1908–1926." *The Journal of American History*, 58, 3 (December 1971): 643–63.

Bushman, Richard L. and Claudia L. Bushman. "The Early History of Cleaniness in America." *The Journal of American History*, 74, 4 (March 1985): 1213–38.

Bussey, Gertrude C. and Margaret Tims. *Women's International League for Peace and Freedom 1915–1965: A Record of Fifty Years' Work*. London: George Allen and Unwin Ltd., 1965.

Carson, Mina. *Settlement Folk: Social Thought and the American Settlement Movement, 1885–1930*. Chicago: University of Chicago Press, 1990.

Chambers, Clarke A. *Paul U. Kellogg and the Survey: Voices for Social Welfare and Social Justice*. Minneapolis, MN: University of Minnesota Press, 1971.

———. *Seedtime of Reform: American Social Justice and Social Action, 1918–1923*. Minneapolis, MN: University of Minnesota Press, 1963.

Chepaitis, Joseph B. "Federal Social Welfare Progressivism in the 1920s." *Social Service Review*, 46(June 1972): 213–19.

Coit, Stanton. *Neighbourhood Guilds: An Instrument of Social Reform*. New York: Arno Press and the New York Times, 1974.

The College Settlement of Philadelphia: A History. Horsham, PA: The College, 1989.

Costin, Lila B. *Two Sisters for Social Justice: A Biography of Grace and Edith Abbott*. Urbana, IL: University of Illinois Press, 1983.

Crowley, Alice Lewisohn. *The Neighborhood Playhouse: Leaves from a Theater Scrapbook*. New York: Theater Arts Books, 1959.

Daniels, Doris Groshen. *Always a Sister: The Feminism of Lillian D. Wald*. New York: The Feminist Press at the City University of New York, 1989.

Davis, Allen Freeman. *American Heroine: The Life and Legend of Jane Addams*. New York: Oxford University Press, 1973.

———. "The Campaign for the Industrial Relations Commission, 1911–1913." *Mid-America*, 45 (October 1903): 211–28.

———. *Spearheads of Reform: The Social Settlements and the Progressive Movement 1890–1914*. New York: Oxford University Press, 1967.

DeForest, Robert K. and Lawrence Veiller, eds. *The Tenement House Problem*. 2 vols. New York: Arno Press and The New York Times, 1970.

Devine Edward T. *Social Work*. New York: Macmillan Company, 1922.

Dictionary of American Biography. New York: Charles Scribner and Sons, 1930–.

Dictionary of National Biography. London: Oxford University Press, 1930–.

Dreier, Mary E. *Margaret Dreier Robins: Her Life, Letters, and Work*. New York: Island Press Cooperative, 1950.

Duffus, R.L. *Lillian Wald: Neighbor and Crusader*. New York: Macmillan Company, 1938.

Dye, Nancy Y. Schrom. *As Equals and as Sisters: Feminism, Unionism, and the Women's Trade Union League of New York*. New York: Columbia University, 1983.

Elliott, John L., ed. *The Hudson Guild, Founded 1895: A Brief Record of Twenty-Five Years of Service*. New York: The Hudson Guild, [n.d.]

"Encouraging Opening of the Boston School for Social Workers." *Charities*, 13 (November 5, 1904): 112–13.

Endelman, Gary Edward. *Solidarity Forever: Rose Schneiderman and the Women's Trade Union League*. New York: Arno Press, 1982.

Felt, Jeremy P. *Hostages of Fortune: Child Labor Reform in New York State*. Syracuse, New York: Syracuse University Press, 1965.

The Fiftieth Anniversary of the Ethical Movement, 1876–1926. New York: D. Appleton and Company, 1926.

Foster, Catherine. *Women for All Seasons: The Story of the Women's International League for Peace and Freedom*. Athens, GA: The University of Georgia Press, 1989.

Garraty, John A. and Gerome L. Steinstein, eds. *Encyclopedia of American Biography*. 3rd ed., New York: Harper Collins Publishers, 1996.

Glenn, John M, Lilian Brandt, and F. Emerson Andrews. *Russell Sage Foundation 1907–1946*. 2 vols. New York: Russell Sage Foundation, 1947.

Goldmark, Josephine Clara. *Impatient Crusader: Florence Kelley's Life Story*. Urbana, IL: University of Illinois Press, 1953.

Guttchen, Robert S. *Felix Adler*. New York: Twayne Publishers, 1974.

Hall, Helen. *Unfinished Business in Neighborhood and Nation*. New York: Macmillan Company, 1971.

Hamilton, Alice. *Exploring the Dangerous Trades*. Boston: Northeastern University Press, 1943.

Handen, Ella. "In Liberty's Shadow: Cornelia Bradford and Whittier House," *New Jersey History* (Fall/Winter, 1982), 49–69.

Henry, Alice. *Women and the Labor Movement*. New York: George H. Doran Company, 1923.

Huggins, Nathan Irvin. *Protestants against Poverty: Boston's Charities, 1870–1900*. Westport, CT: Greenwood Publishing Corporation, 1971.

Hull-House Maps and Papers: A Presentation of Nationalities and Wages in a Congested District of Chicago Together with Comments and Essays on Problems Growing Out of the Social Conditions, by Residents of Hull-House a Social Settlement. New York: Arno Press Inc. and The New York Times, 1970.

Hunter, Robert. *Poverty*. New York: Grossett & Dunlap, 1934.

Huthmacher, Joseph. *Senator Robert F. Wagner and the Rise of Urban Liberalism*. New York: Atheneum, 1968.

Jackson, Kenneth T., ed., *Encyclopedia of New York City*. New Haven, CT: Yale University Press, 1995.

James, Edward T. and Janet Wilson James, eds. *Notable American Women 1607–1950: A Biographical Dictionary*. 3 vols. Cambridge, MA: The Belknap Press of Harvard University Press, 1971.

Johnson, Donald. *The Challenge to American Freedoms: World War I and the Rise of the American Civil Liberties Union*. Lexington, KY: University of Kentucky Press for the Mississippi Valley Historical Association, 1963.

Josephson, Matthew. *Al Smith, Hero of the Cities: A Political Portrait Drawing on the Papers of Frances Perkins*. London: Thames & Hudson, 1970.

Kearney, James. *Anna Eleanor Roosevelt: The Evolution of a Reformer*. Boston: Houghton Mifflin, 1968.

Kelley, Florence. *Some Ethical Gains through Legislation*. New York: Arno Press and The New York Times, 1969.

Kellor, Frances A. *Out of Work*. New York: G.P. Putnam, 1905.

Kingsbury, Susan M. *Labor Laws and Their Enforcement*. New York: Arno Press and the New York Times, 1971.

Klein, Maury. *Prisoners of Progress: American Industrial Cities*. New York: Macmillan Company, 1976.

Kusmer, Kenneth L. "The Functions of Organized Charity in the Progressive Era: Chicago as a Case Study," *The Journal of American History*, 60: 3(Dec. 1972), 657–78.

Lamson, Peggy. *Roger Baldwin, Founder of the American Civil Liberties Union: A Portrait*. Boston: Houghton Mifflin, 1976.

Lasch-Quinn, Elisabeth. *Black Neighbors: Race and the Limits of Reform in the American Settlement House Movement, 1890–1945*. Chapel Hill, NC: The University of North Carolina Press, 1973.

Leiby, James. *A History of Social Welfare and Social Work in the United States*. New York: Columbia University Press, 1978

Lemons, J. Stanley. "The Sheppard-Towner Act: Progressivism in the 1920s." *Journal of American History*, 55 (March 1969): 776–86.

Leonard, Paul. "The Immigrants' Protective League of Chicago, 1908–1921," *Illinois State Historical Society Journal*, 66: 3(1973), 271–79.

Lubove, Roy. "The New York Association for Improving the Condition of the Poor: The Formative Years." *New York Historical Society Quarterly*, 11 (1959): 307–27.

———. *The Professional Altruist: The Emergence of Social Work as a Career, 1880–1930*. Cambridge, MA: Harvard University Press, 1965.

———. *The Progressives and the Slums: Tenement House Reform in New York City, 1890–1917*. Pittsburgh, PA: University of Pittsburgh Press, 1962.

McCarthy, Kathleen D. *Noblesse Oblige: Charity and Cultural Philanthropy in Chicago, 1849–1929*. Chicago: University of Chicago Press, 1982.

McDonnell, Timothy L., S.J. *The Wagner Housing Act: A Case Study of the Legislative Process*. Chicago: Loyola University Press, 1957.

Marsh, Benjamin. *Lobbyist for the People: A Record of Fifty Years*. Washington, DC: Public Affairs Press, 1953.

Martin, George Whitney. *Madam Secretary, Frances Perkins*. Boston: Houghton Mifflin, 1976.

Meacham, Standish. *Toynbee Hall and Social Reform, 1880–1914: The Search for Community*. New Haven, CT: Yale University Press, 1987.

Melvin, Patricia Mooney, ed. *American Community Organizations: An Historical Dictionary*. New York: Greenwood Press, 1986.

Mott, Frank Luther. *A History of American Magazines*. 5 vols. Cambridge, MA: Harvard University Press, 1936.

Nathan, Maud. *The Story of an Epoch Making Movement*. Garden City, NY: Doubleday, Page & Company, 1926.

The National Cyclopaedia of American Biography. New York: James T. White and Company, 1927–

O'Day, Rosemary and David Englander. *Mr. Charles Booth's Inquiry: Life and Labour of the People in London Reconsidered*. London: The Hambledon Press, 1993.

Olson, James S., ed. *Historical Dictionary of The New Deal: From Inauguration to Preparation for War*. Westport, CT: Greenwood Press, 1985.

O'Neill, William. *Everyone Was Brave: A History of Feminism in America*. New York: Quadrangle/The New York Times Book Company, 1971.

Ovington, Mary. *Half a Man: The Status of the Negro in New York*. New York: Longman's Green & Company, 1911.

Pacey, Lorene M., ed. *Readings in the Development of Settlement Work*. Freeport, New York: Books for Libraries Press, 1971.

Patterson, James T. *America's Struggle against Poverty, 1900–1985*. Cambridge, MA: Harvard University Press, 1986.

Paulding, James. *Charles B. Stover, July 14, 1861–April 24, 1929: His Life and Personality Together with Some Tributes from his Friends*. New York: The International Press, 1938.

Perry, Elisabeth Israels. *Belle Moskowitz: Feminine Politics and the Exercise of Power in the Age of Alfred E. Smith*. New York: Oxford University Press, 1987.

——— . "Women's Political Choices after Suffrage: The Women's City Club of New York 1915–1990," *New York History* (Oct. 1990), 416–34.

Rader, Benjamin G. *The Academic Mind and Reform : The Influence of Richard T. Ely in American Life*. Lexington, KY: University of Kentucky Press, 1968.

Randall, Hercules Moritz. *Improper Bostonian: Emily Greene Balch*. New York: Twayne Publishers, Inc., 1964.

Riis, Jacob August. *How the Other Half Lives: Studies among the Tenements of New York*. Sam Bass Warner, Jr., ed. Cambridge, MA: The Belknap Press of Harvard University Press, 1970.

Romanofsky, Peter. *The Greenwood Encyclopedia of American Institutions: Social Service Organizations*. 2 vols. Westport, CT: Greenwood Press, 1986

Scheuer, Jeffrey. *Legacy of Light: University Settlement's First Century*. New York: University Settlement, 1985.

"The School for Social Workers, Boston." *Charities* 14 (June 3, 1905): 783–84.

Scott, Mel. *American City Planning Since 1890: A History Commemorating the Fiftieth Anniversary of the American Institute of Planners*. Berkeley, CA: University of California Press, 1969.

Scudder, Vida Dutton. *On Journey*. New York: E.P. Dutton and Company, 1937.

Seligman, Edwin R.A., ed. *Encyclopedia of the Social Sciences*. 12 vols. New York : Macmillan Company, 1923.

Sicherman, Barbara. *Alice Hamilton: A Life in Letters*. Cambridge, MA : Harvard University Press, 1984.

——— and Carol Hurd Green, eds. *Notable American Women: The Modern Period: A Biographical Dictionary*. Cambridge, MA: The Belknap Press of Harvard University Press, 1980.

Siegel, Beatrice. *Lillian Wald of Henry Street*. New York: Macmillan Publishing Co., Inc., 1983.

Simkhovitch, Mary Kingsbury. *The City Worker's World in America*. New York: Arno Press and the New York Times, 1971.

——— . *Neighborhood: My Story of Greenwich House*. New York: Norton & Company, Inc., 1938.

Small, Albion W. "The Civic Federation of Chicago, A Study in Social Dynamics," *American Journal of Sociology*, I (July 1895), 80–91.

Stein, Leon. *The Triangle Fire*. Philadelphia, PA: J. B. Lippincott Company, 1962.

Stover, Charles B. *James Bronson Reynolds, March 17, 1861– January 1, 1924: A Memorial*. New York: University Settlement, 1927.

Sutherland, Douglas. *Fifty Years on the Civic Front*. Chicago: University of Chicago Press, 1943.

Trattner, Walter, ed. *Biographical Dictionary of Social Welfare in America*. New York: Greenwood Press, 1986.

———. *Crusade for the Children: A History of the NCLC and Child Labor Reform in America*. Chicago: Quadrangle Books, 1970.

———. *From Poor Law to Welfare State: A History of Social Welfare in America*. 4th ed. New York: The Free Press, 1989.

———. *Homer Folks: Pioneer in Social Welfare*. New York: Columbia University Press, 1968.

Trolander, Judith Ann. *Professionalism and Social Change: From the Settlement House Movement to Neighborhood Centers, 1886 to the Present*. New York: Columbia University Press, 1987.

———. *Settlement Houses and the Great Depression*. Detroit, MI: Wayne State University Press, 1975.

Tryon, Warren Stenson. *Parnassus Corner: The Life of James T. Fields Publisher to the Victorians*. Boston, MA: Houghton Mifflin Company, The Riverside Press Cambridge, 1963.

Wade, Louise E. *Graham Taylor: Pioneer for Social Justice, 1851–1938*. Chicago: University of Chicago Press, 1963.

Wald, Lillian. *The House on Henry Street*. New York: Dover Publications, 1971.

———. *Windows on Henry Street*. Boston: Little, Brown and Company, 1934.

Walker, Samuel. *In Defense of American Liberties: A History of the ACLU*. New York: Oxford University Press, 1990.

Warner, Sam Bass Jr. *Streetcar Suburbs: The Process of Growth in Boston, 1870–1900*. 2nd ed. Cambridge, MA: Harvard University Press, 1978.

Williams, Beryl. *Lillian Wald: Angel of Henry Street*. New York: Julian Messner, Inc., 1948.

Williams, Marilyn Thornton. *Washing "The Great Unwashed" Public Baths in Urban America, 1840–1920*. Columbus, OH: Ohio State University Press, 1991.

Williams, William A. *American-Russian Relations, 1781–1947*. New York: Rinehart, 1952.

Woods, Robert Archey, ed. *Americans in Process: A Settlement Study*. New York: Arno Press and the New York Times, 1970.

———. *The City Wilderness: A Settlement Study by Residents and Associates of the South End House*. New York: Garrett Press, Inc., 1970.

———. and Albert J. Kennedy, eds. *The Handbook of Settlements*. New York: Arno Press and The New York Times, 1970.

———. *The Settlement Horizon*. New York: Arno Press and The New York Times, 1970.

Index

by Francine Cronshaw

Boldface page numbers indicate presence of a main entry.

Abbott, Edith, **1–2**
  Sophonisba Breckinridge, 36
  Julia Lathrop, 118
  National Progressive Service, 144
  Public Housing Conference, 142
  Tenements of Chicago, 1908–1935, The, 208
Abbott, E.H., 4, 162
Abbott, Grace, **2–3**
  child welfare, 45, 118
  immigrants, 13
  Immigrants' Service League, 104
  International Congress of Women, 234
  Julia Lathrop, 118
  National Progressive Service, 144
Abbott, Lyman, **4**
  New York Child Labor Committee, 151
  Outlook, The, 161–62
  Charles B. Stover, 198
Abelson, Paul, 132
Adams, Annie. *See* Fields, Annie Adams (Mrs. James T.)
Addams, Jane, **4–6**
  Grace Abbott, 2, 3
  American Union Against Militarism, 10, 11, 12
  Anita Blaine, 25
  Louise DeKoven Bowen, 31, 32
  Charities Publication Committee (CPC), 201

Civic Federation of Chicago, 47
  Katherine Coman, 55
  John L. Elliott, 70, 71
  Frederick Douglass Center, 77, 239
  Hull House, 5, 99, 100
  Immigrants' Service League, 104
  Industrial Relations Commission, 104–05
  International Congress of Women, 234
  juvenile delinquency, 197
  Mary McDowell, 125
  National Child Labor Committee, 137, 225
  National Civil Liberties Bureau, 137
  National Conference of Charities and Correction, 139
  National Federation of Settlements, 139, 140
  National Housing Association, 141
  National Progressive Service (NPS), 143
  New Conscience and an Ancient Evil, A (1912), 172
  Nobel Peace Prize, 5
  On Journey (1937), 158
  Mary Kenney O'Sullivan, 159
  prostitution, 172
  Second Twenty Years at Hull-House, The (1930), 187–88

Summer School of Applied Ethics, 6
  Twenty Years at Hull-House with Autobiographical Notes (1910), 209–10
  United Charities of Chicago, 43
  White House Conference on Dependent Children, 45, 230
  Women's Trade Union League, 235
  Young Working Girls (1913), 240
Adler, Felix, **6–7**
  Stanton Coit, 50, 147
  John L. Elliott, 70
  Ethical Culture Society, 72
  Helen Goldmark, 82
  Greenwich House, 85
  guild system, 147
  Madison House, 126
  Henry Moskowitz, 131, 132
  National Child Labor Committee, 137, 225
  National Recreation and Parks Association, 145
  New York Charity Organization Society Tenement House Committee, 148, 207
  New York Child Labor Committee, 150, 151
  New York State Tenement House Commission of 1884, 153

Adler, Felix *(continued)*
  Outdoor Recreation League, 161
  Social Reform Club, 193
African Americans, ix
  Chicago Commons, 205
  Conference on the Status of the Negro in the United States, 163
  Frederick Douglass Center, 77
  Half a Man: The Status of the Negro in New York (1911), 86, 163
  Frances Kellor, 112
  Albert Kennedy, 114
  Henry Moskowitz, 163
  Out of Work (1904), 160
  Mary White Ovington, 162–63
  Pittsburgh Survey, 169–70
  race riot of 1919, 204
  Robert Gould Shaw House, 177–78
  Josephine Shaw, 123
  Stillman Branch Settlement, 93
  Survey, 200
  Lea Taylor, 205
  William English Walling, 163
Alcott, Louisa May, 161
Alfred, Helen, **7**, 142, 143
  Louis H. Pink, 169
  Wagner-Steagall Housing Act, 223, 224
Alliance Employment Bureau, 217
Almirall, Raymond T., 154
Almy, Frederic, **7–8**
  National Housing Association, 141
  National Progressive Service, 144
Altgeld, John Peter, **8–9**
  Julia Lathrop, 118
  Alzina Stevens, 197
Alton Locke (1850), 115
Altwell, Ernest T., 145–46
Amalgamated Clothing Workers of America, 96, 196
American Arbitration Association, 113
American Association of Group Workers, 10
American Association of Medical Social Workers, 10
American Association of Old Age Security, 7
American Association of Social Workers (AASW), **9–10**
  George Bellamy, 24
  Lea Taylor, 205
American Association of University Women, 236
American Charities, 228

American Civil Liberties Union (ACLU), **10–11**
  Roger Baldwin, 19, 138
  Crystal Eastman, 70
  Paul Kellogg, 112
  National Civil Liberties Bureau, 138
American Economic Association, 1, 71, 115
American Federation of Labor (AFL)
  child labor, 136–37
  Helena Dudley, 67
  Federal Labor Union, 17
  Industrial Relations Commission, 105
  Mary Kenney O'Sullivan, 158–60
  Margaret Dreier Robins, 179
  Alzina Stevens, 197
  William English Walling, 227
American Foreign Policy Association, 112
American Immigration Service, 174
American Institute for Architects, 149
American League for the Limitation of Armament (ALLA), 11
American Park and Outdoor Association, 108
American Prison Association, 92, 139
  Robert Treat Paine, 165
American Society of Extension of University Teaching, 63
American Sociological Association, 115
American Syndicalism (1913), 38
American Union Against Militarism (AUAM), 10, **11–12**
  anti-preparedness crusade, 138
  Roger Baldwin, 138
  rally in St. Louis, 19
  Lillian Wald, 226
American Union Commission, 4
Americanization, **12–13**
  athletics, 16
  Catherine Bauer, 23
  George Bellamy, 23
  Cornelia Bradford, 35
  clubs, 49
  Denison House, 63
  Frances Kellor, 113
  Elizabeth S. Williams, 231
Americanization Committee for New York State, 66
Americans in Process (1902), **13–14**, 195
  Robert A. Woods, 238

Andover House, 46, 193. *See also* South End House
  Robert A. Woods, 238
Andrews, Constant A., 148
anti-immigration, 12–13
anti-imperialist movement, 124
Anti-Preparedness Committee, 11–12, 138
Anti-Tuberculosis League of Puerto Rico, 236
arbitration issues, 113
Artisan's Dwelling Act (England), 20, 94
Asacog House, 65
assimilation, of immigrants, 12
Association for Improving the Condition of the Poor (AICP), **14–15**
  baths, 22
  Charity Organization Society, 40–41
  Congestion Exhibition, 56
  Elgin R.L. Gould, 83
  Robert M. Hartley, 90, 91
  Hartley House, 90
  New York COS Tenement House Committee, 148, 149
  James G. Phelps Stokes, 90, 198
  tenement houses, 206–07
Association for Promoting Technical Education (England), 20
Association for the Protection of Negro Women, 112
Association of Neighborhood Workers (Chicago), **15**
Association of Neighborhood Workers (New York). *See also* United Neighborhood Houses
  creation, 211
  Mary Simkhovitch, 190
Athenaeum, 128
Athletics, **15–16**
  clubs, 49
Atlanta Conference, 163
Atlantic Monthly, 97
Ayres, Leonard P., 167
Ayres, Philip W., 54

Babies' Hospital, 34
Balch, Emily Greene, **17–18**
  Katherine Coman, 54–55
  Helena Dudley, 66, 67
  International Congress of Women, 234
  National Progressive Service, 144
  On Journey (1937), 158
Baldwin, Roger, **18–19**
  National Civil Liberties Bureau, 11, 137
  peace movement, 12

Baldwin, William H., 18, 137, 151
Baltimore Central Relief
    Association, 33
Baltimore Charities Record, 175
Baltimore Charity Organization,
    33, 228
Baltimore Charity Organization
    Society, 80–81
    Graduate School of Social
        Service Administration
        (Chicago), **84**
Baltimore Department of
    Charities and Correction, 33
Bank Street College of Education,
    130
Baptist church, 91
Barnett, Henrietta Rowland, 208
Barnett, Samuel Augustus, viii,
    20–21
    Barnett Fellowships, 166
    Edward Denison's influence,
        62
    Toynbee Hall, 208
    Universities Settlements
        Association (England),
        214
Barnum, Gertrude, 105
Bates, Katherine Lee, 53, 55
baths, **21–22**
    Helena Dudley, 66
    Jean Fine, 75
    Greenwich House, 85
    Hartley House, 90
    Hiram House, 96
    Hull House, 100
    New York State Tenement
        House Commission of
        1894, 154
    Northwestern University
        Settlement, 157
    Tenement House Problem, The
        (1903), 61, 205
    Robert A. Woods, 238
Bauer, Catherine Krouse, **22–23**
Bedford Hills women's reforma-
    tory, 59
Beecher, Henry Ward, 4, 161
Bellamy, Francis A., 4, 162
Bellamy, George Albert, **23–24**
    Hiram House, 96–97
Bellevue-Yorkville Health
    Demonstration, 64
Belmont, August, 79
Berkeley Board of Charity, 102
Berlin Blockade, 166
Better Homes for Working Men
    (1885), 229
Beveridge, Albert, 137
Bibliography of Settlements, 89
Binford, Jessie, 107
Bing, Alexander Maximilian, **24–
    25**
Bird, Charles, 144

birth control, 65, 70
Birtwell, Charles W., 17, 29, 44,
    192
Bitter Cry of Outcast London, The
    (1883), 27
Blacks. *See* African Americans
Blaine, Anita Eugenie
    McCormick, **25**
    United Charities of Chicago,
        43
Bliss, William Dwight Porter, **26–
    27**
    Christian Socialism, 46, 187
    Richard Ely, 71–72
    garden cities, 79
    Vida Scudder, 187
    Mary Simkhovitch, 189
Board of Supervisors of City
    Charities (Baltimore), 33
Bonner, Hugh J., 154
Booth, Charles, **27–28**, 100
Borah, William, 105
Boston Associated Charities, 13,
    28–29, 33
    Robert Treat Paine, 165
    Mary Richmond, 174
    Zilpha Smith, 192
Boston Central Labor Union, **67**,
    187
Boston Children's Aid Society
    Emily Balch, 17
    Boston School for Social
        Workers, 30
    foster care, 44
    New York Charity Organiza-
        tion Society Tenement
        House Committee, 149
    Robert Treat Paine, 165
    Zilpha Smith, 192
Boston Cooperative Society of
    Visitors. *See* Boston
    Associated Charities
Boston School for Social Workers,
    29–30
    Jeffrey R. Brackett, 33
    Florence Kelley, 192
    Albert Kennedy, 114
    Zilpha Smith, 192
    Lillian Wald, 192
Boston Settlement Committee, 55
Boston Social Union (BSU), **30–
    31**, 165, 238
Boston Trade Union, 63
Bowen Center, 107
Bowen, Louise DeKoven, **31–32**
    Juvenile Protective Associa-
        tion, 106
    United Charities of Chicago,
        43
boys' clubs, **49–50**
Brace, Charles Loring, **32–33**
Brace Memorial Farm (Valhalla,
    New York), 32

Brackett, Jeffrey Richardson, 30,
    33–34
    National Conference of
        Charities and Correction,
        139
Bradford, Cornelia Foster, **34–35**
Brandeis, Louis D., 18, 81
Brandt, Lilian, **35**
Braucher, Howard, 145
Braunt, Bessie, 185
Breckinridge, Sophonisba
    Preston, **35–37**
    Edith Abbott, 1–2
    Grace Abbott, 3
    Graduate School of Social
        Service Administration
        (Chicago), 84
    Immigrants' Service League,
        104
    Julia Lathrop, 118
    professional organizations, 10
Brewster, Mary Maud, **37**, 48, 92,
    97–98
    Jacob Schiff, 184
    Visiting Nurse Service (New
        York), 220, 221
Brooklyn Bureau of Charities, 229
Brooklyn Children's Aid Society,
    229
Brooklyn Society for the Preven-
    tion of Cruelty to Children,
    229
Brooks, John Graham, **37–38**
    Florence Kelley, 110
Brooks, Phillips, **38–39**
    Katherine Coman, 54
    Outlook, The, 162
    Robert Treat Paine, 165
    Vida Scudder, 187
Brown, Charles S., 154
Bruere, Martha Bensley, 171
Bryan, William Jennings, 179
Bull Moose Convention, 180
Bumpus, Herman C., 56
Bureau for Conscientious
    Objectors, 12, 138
Bureau of Associated Charities,
    43–44
Bureau of Educational Experi-
    ments, 128, 130
Bureau of Labor Commission, 83
Bureau of Social Hygiene, 60
Bureau of Social Research, 82
Burns, Allen T., 105
Burroughs, John, 162
Butler, Edmond J., 152
Butler, Edward, 195
Butler, Elizabeth Beardsley, 170
Butler, Nicholas Murray, 145
    Nobel Peace Prize, 5
    Outdoor Recreation League,
        161
    peace movement, 11
Byington, Margaret F., 170

Cabot, Richard C., 30
Cannon, Joseph D., 138
Carlyle, Thomas, 115, 218
Carr, Charlotte, 32
Casa Revello, 52
Case Studies of Unemployment,
    87
casework approach to social work,
    8, 28
    Frederic Almy, 8
    Boston Associated Charities,
        28
    Jeffrey R. Brackett, 33
    immigrants, 104
    Charles Loch, 121–22
    Mary Richmond, 174–75
    Social Work (1922), 194
Cellar Players, 71
Central Labor Union, 63
Chadwick Civic Club, 198
Chalmers, Thomas, 40
Chamberlain, Joseph P., 201
Chandrel, Charles F., 67
charitable aid, theories of, 124
Charities. See also *Survey,* the
    Edward Devine, 63–64
    Arthur Kellogg, 110, 111
    Mary Richmond, 175
    Graham Romeyn Taylor, 204
Charities Review, 199, 201. See
    also *Survey,* the
Charities and the Commons. See
    also *Survey,* the
    funding, 200, 201
    industrial medicine, 88
    Paul Kellogg, 111
    Pittsburgh Survey, 169, 170,
        200, 201
    reformers on staff, 200
    Mary Richmond, 175
    Russell Sage Foundation, 182
Charity Organization Society
    (COS), **40–41**
    Frederic Almy, 7–8
    Association for Improving the
        Condition of the Poor, 14
    Jeffrey R. Brackett, 33
    Lilian Brandt, 35
    Chicago, 43
    as concept, ix
    John L. Elliott, 70
    friendly visitors, 77
    John Glenn, 80
    Kellogg brothers, 111
    Charles Loch, 121–22
    London, 94, 121
    Maud Nathan, 135
    Frances Perkins, 166
    Mary Richmond, 174
    School of Philanthropy, 54
    Zilpha Smith, 191–92
    Amos Warner, 228
Cheap Clothes and Nasty (1850),
    115

Chelsea District, New York, 99
Chicago Association of Neighbor-
    hood Workers. *See* Associa-
    tion of Neighborhood
    Workers
Chicago Bar Association, 197
Chicago Board of Charities, 76
Chicago Board of Education, 76
Chicago Bureau of Charities. *See
    also* Chicago Relief Society
    Anita Blaine, 25
    Robert Hunter, 101
Chicago Central Relief Associa-
    tion, 43. *See also* Chicago
    Relief Society
Chicago Civic Federation. *See*
    Civic Federation of Chicago
Chicago Commission on Race
    Relations, 204
Chicago Commons, **42**
    Association of Neighborhood
        Workers, 15
    Charles R. Henderson, 92
    journals, 200
    Northwestern University
        Settlement, 157
    Frances Perkins, 166
    Graham Taylor, 203
    Lea Taylor, 204
    Taylor, Graham Romeyn, 204,
        205
Chicago Community Trust, 104
Chicago Daily News, 203–04
Chicago Federation of Settle-
    ments, 104
    Lea Taylor, 205
Chicago Fire of 1871, 125
Chicago Institute, 25
Chicago Institute of Social
    Science, 84. *See also*
    Graduate School of Social
    Service Administration
    (Chicago)
Chicago Juvenile Court, 44
Chicago Juvenile Court Commit-
    tee, 31, 44
Chicago Municipal Lodging
    House, 180
Chicago Public Library, 42
Chicago Public School Art Society,
    196
Chicago Relief and Aid Society
    (CRA), 43. *See also* Chicago
    Relief Society
Chicago Relief Society, **42–44**
    Northwestern University
        Settlement, 157
Chicago School of Civics and
    Philanthropy, 35, 84. *See also*
    Graduate School of Social
    Service Administration
    (Chicago)
    Edith Abbott, 2, 84
    Grace Abbott, 3

Charles R. Henderson, 92
Julia Lathrop, 118
origins, 203
"Chicago School" of sociology, 92
Chicago Trades and Labor
    Assembly, 159
Chicago Visiting Nurse Associa-
    tion. *See* Visiting Nurse
    Association of Chicago
Chicago Women's Bindery Union,
    159
Chicago Women's Club, 44, 197,
    239
child labor
    John Peter Altgeld, 9
    Lilian Brandt, 34
    consumers' leagues, 57–58
    Lewis Hine, 96
    Robert Hunter, 101
    Florence Kelley, 110
    Susan Kingsbury, 115
    Julia Lathrop, 118
    Henry Demarest Lloyd, 121
    Owen Lovejoy, 122–23
    National Child Labor
        Committee (NCLC), 136–
        37
    New Jersey, 34
    New York Child Labor
        Committee (NYCLC),
        150–51
    Poverty (1904), 101, 170
    *Some Ethical Gains Through
        Legislation* (1905), 194–
        95
    Alzina Stevens, 196, 197
Child Labor Act, 3
child welfare, **44–45**
    Emily Balch, 17–18
    Boston Children's Aid Society,
        29
    Charles Loring Brace, 32
    Lucy Flower, 75–76
    Homer Folks, 76–77
    infant mortality, 189
    Juvenile Protective Associa-
        tion, 31, 106–07
    Florence Kelley, 44
    Mother's Pensions, 133–34
    National Conference of
        Charities and Correction,
        139
    Sheppard-Towner Act, 189
Children of the Poor, The (1892),
    176
Children's Aid Society, 32, 184
Children's Aid Society of New
    York, 122
Children's Aid Society of
    Pennsylvania, 44, 76–77
Children's Protective League, 34
Childs, Henry E., 161
Christian Social Union (CSU), 46,
    71–72
    Henry Holland, 97

Christian Socialism, **45–46**
William Bliss, 26–27
Phillips Brooks, 38
Richard Ely, 71–72
Henry Holland, 97
Charles Kingsley, 115
Ladies Guild (London), 94
Henry Demarest Lloyd, 121
Frederick Denison Maurice, 128
origins, 26
Vida Scudder, 186
Mary Simkhovitch, 189
Society of Christian Socialists, 26
Christian Socialist: A Journal of Association, 115
Christian Socialist Union, 26
Christian Union, 4
Church Association for the Advancement of the Interests of the Poor, 26
Church of England, 97, 128
Church Union, 161
Cigar Makers' Union, 17
Circolo Italo-Americano, 63, 187
Citizens Committee to Promote a State System of Industrial Education, 238
Citizens in Industry (1915), 92
Citizen's Municipal Committee, 132
Citizen's Union, 83, 173
City Affairs Committee (CAC) of New York, 142
City and Suburban Homes Company, 79
Elgin R.L. Gould, 83, 229
Alfred T. White, 229
City Homes Association, 25
City Housing Corporation (New York), 24
city planning, 56
City Wilderness, The (1898), 13, **46–47**, 195
Robert A. Woods, 238
City Workers' World in America, The (1917), **47**
Civic Federation of Chicago, 43, **47**
Graham Taylor, 203
Civil Liberties Bureau, 12, 138
Civil Service Reform Association, 109
Maud Nathan, 135
of New York State, 124
Civil War
Lyman Abbott, 4
John Peter Altgeld, 8
Josephine Shaw, 123, 135–36
class conflict, 41, 46
clean milk campaigns, 48, 90
Northwestern University Settlement, 157

Cleveland Public Library, 97
clinics and dispensaries, **48–49**
Robert M. Hartley, 91
clubs, **49–50**
Co-operative Society, 192
coal strikes, 122
Coit, Stanton, **50–51**
College Settlement, 75
Hudson Guild, 99
local leadership, 212
Neighborhood Guilds: An Instrument of Social Reform (1891), 147–48
James B. Reynolds, 173
Charles B. Stover, 198
University Settlement, 215–16
Coleridge, Samuel Taylor, 115
College Settlement (New York), **51–52**
Edith Abbott, 1
Mary Brewster, 37, 221
College Settlements Association, 53
Jean Fine, 75
girls' clubs, 49
Neighborhood: My Story of Greenwich House (1938), 85, 146
New York Charity Organization Society Tenement House Committee, 149
Jane Robbins, 176–77
Eleanor Roosevelt, 180
Mary Simkhovitch, 190
Visiting Nurse Service, 221
Lillian Wald, 225
Elizabeth S. Williams, 230–31
College Settlement (Philadelphia), **52–53**, 66
College Settlements Association, 53
College Settlements Association, **53**
College Settlement (New York), 51
College Settlement (Philadelphia), 52–53
Katherine Coman, 54–55
Denison House, 17, 53, 62–63
Helena Dudley, 66, 67
fellowships program, 160
Mary Kehew, 109
Frances Kellor, 112
Jane Robbins, 177
Vida Scudder, 187
Collegiate Anti-Militarism League, 18
Collins, Ellen, 123
Columbia University Graduate School of Social Work, **53–54**
Edward Devine, 63
Intercollegiate Bureau of Occupations, 9
origins, 63

Columbia University School of Social Work, 35
Coman, Katherine, **54–55**
College Settlements Association, 53
Commission of Employer's Liability and Causes of Industrial Accidents, Unemployment and Lack of Farm Labor, 69
Commission on Distribution of Population, 127
Commission on Status of Women, 182
Committee against Militarism, 18
Committee for Immigrants in America, 113
Committee of Fifteen, 126
Roger Baldwin, 18
Henry Moskowitz, 132
prostitution, 172
Tenement House Commissions, 155
Committee of Seventy, 173
Committee on Amusement and Vacation Resources of Working Girls, 130
Committee on Congestion of Population (CCP), **55–56**
College Settlement, 51
Benjamin Marsh, 127
Social Reform Club, 193
Committee on the Regional Plan of New York and Its Environs, 61, 182
Committee on Training Camp Activities, 24
Committee on Unemployment and Business Cycles, 218
Committee on Women in Industry, 126
Commons, The. See also Survey, the
Henry Demarest Lloyd, 121
origins, 200, 203
Graham Taylor, 203
Graham Romeyn Taylor, 204
Commons Preservation Society, 94
Commonwealth Fund, 204
Commonwealth magazine, 97
Community Chest Movement, 116, 175
Compulsory Insurance in Germany (1893), 38
Conference of Boards of Public Charities. *See* National Conference on Social Welfare
Conference of Charities (CC), 138. *See also* National Conference on Social Welfare
Conference of Labor Women, 70
Conference on the Status of the Negro in the United States, 163

Congestion Exhibition, 56, 211. *See also* Committee on Congestion of Population
Benjamin Marsh, 127
Carola Woerishoffer, 232
Congregationalist church, 4, 26, 122, 193, 202–03
conscientious objectors, 12, 19, 137–38
Consumers' Leagues, **57–58**
Sophonisba Breckinridge, 36
John Graham Brooks, 38
Katherine Coman, 55
Committee on Legislation and Legal Defense of Labor Laws, 81
Congestion Exhibition, 56
Josephine Goldmark, 81
Pauline Goldmark, 82, 83
Helen Hall, 87
Alice Hamilton, 89
Lewis Hine, 96
Hull House, 100
Illinois, 36
Florence Kelley, 44, 109, 110
Josephine Shaw Lowell, 57, 123, 124, 156
Mary McDowell, 126
Maud Nathan, 135–36
New Jersey, 34
Frances Perkins, 166
Eleanor Roosevelt, 180–81
Social Reform Club, 193
Some Ethical Gains Through Legislation (1905), 194–95
Triangle Shirtwaist Company Fire (1911), 152
Women's City Club of New York, **233**
Consumers' National Federation, 87
Cook County Juvenile Court, 106
Coolidge, Elizabeth Sprague, 129–30, 165
cooperative movement, 238
Cooperative School for Teachers (1931), 130
Cooperative Social Settlement Society, 85
Cooperative Society of Visitors (Boston), 28. *See also* Boston Associated Charities
Annie Fields, 74–75
corruption, political, 47
Coues, Lucy. *See* Flower, Lucy Louisa
Crain, T.C.F., 151
Cravath, Paul D., 154
Crosby, Alexander L., 143
cultural pluralism, 13, 114
Curtis, Henry, 145
Cutting, Robert Fulton, 83

Dahlgren, John Vinton, 148
Davis, John W., 191
Davis, Katherine Bement, 52, **59–60**
Women's City Club of New York, 233–34
Dawn, The, 26
DeForest, Robert Weeks, **60–61**
Charities Publication Committee (CPC), 201
National Housing Association, 141
New York Charity Organization Society Tenement House Committee, 148
New York City Tenement House Department, 151, 219
New York State Tenement House Commission of 1900, 154
Russell Sage Foundation, 182
Margaret Olivia Sage, 184
Tenement House Problem, The (1903), 205
DeKoven, Louise. *See* Bowen, Louise DeKoven
Democracy and Social Ethics (1902), 210
Democratic Party, 186
Denison, Edward, **61–62**
Charity Organization Society, 41
Mary Simkhovitch, 189
Denison House, **62–63**
College Settlements Association, 53
Katherine Coman, 55
Helena Dudley, 66–67
Edward Denison, 62
founding, 17
Mary Kehew, 109
On Journey (1937), 158
Mary Kenney O'Sullivan, 159
Vida Scudder, 187
Department of Labor, 89, 126
Dever, William, 126, 157
Devine, Edward Thomas, **63–64**
Lilian Brandt, 35
Charities: A Monthly Review of Local and General Philanthropy, 199
Charities Publication Committee (CPC), 201
Industrial Relations Commission, 104–05
National Conference of Charities and Correction, 139
New York Charity Organization Society Tenement House Committee, 148, 207

professional organizations, 9
Social Work (1922), 194
Summer School of Philanthropy, 54
trip to Russia, 204
United States Children's Bureau, 212–13
Dewey, John, 25
Lucy Sprague Mitchell, 129, 130
Diet Kitchen, 34
Dike, Florence Blanchard, 174
disaster services, 64
disease, 64
Anti-Tuberculosis League of Puerto Rico, 236
Alice Hamilton, 88
influenza epidemic of 1918, 226
National Association for the Study and Prevention of Tuberculosis, 64
Dock, Lavinia Lloyd, **64–65**
Doty, Madeline, 19
Douglas, William A., 154
Down Town Ethical Society, 126, 132. *See also* Madison House
Draft Riots (1863), 155
drama, 71
Dreier, Mary Elizabeth, **65–66**
Frances Kellor, 112
National Progressive Service, 144
New York State Factory Investigating Commission, 152, 209
Women's City Club of New York, 233
Women's Trade Union League, 178
Drexel, Joseph W., 153
DuBois, W.E.B., 163
Dudley, Helena Stewart, 17, 52, **66–67**
College Settlements Association, 53
Denison House, 62, 63
On Journey (1937), 158
Vida Scudder, 187
Women's Trade Union League, 235
dumbbell tenements, **67–68**
design, 207
outlawed, 219
protested, 153, 155, 207
Dutch Reform church, 202

early childhood education, 130
East Side Civic Club, 126, 132, 198
East Side Relief Work Committee, 218
Eastman, Crystal, **69–70**
Roger Baldwin, 19

conscientious objectors, 138
Industrial Relations Commis-
    sion, 105
Work Accidents and the Law
    (1910), 170
World War I, 11
Eastman, Lucius R., 201
Eastman, Max, 11
education, **76**
Educational Alliance, 130
educational reform
    Samuel Barnett, 20–21
    Anita Blaine, 25
    industrial education, 238
    Joseph Lee, 119
    Lucy Sprague Mitchell, 128–30
    Jane Robbins, 177
    teacher training, 25
    Elizabeth S. Williams, 231
Eggleston, Edward, 161
Eidlitz, Otto M., 154
eight-hour day, 58
Eliot, Charles William, 124
Elkins, Abram L., 152
Elliott, John Lovejoy, 49, 50, **70–
    71**
    Hudson Guild, 99
    Henry Moskowitz, 132
    United Neighborhood Houses
        (UNH), 211
Ellis Island Commission (1922),
    119
Elmer, Edith. *See* Wood, Edith
    Elmer
Ely, Richard Theodore, **71–72**,
    100, 101
Emergency Relief Bureau (Long
    Island), 64
Emerson, Ralph Waldo
    Felix Adler, 6
    Stanton Coit, 50
Empire State Building Corpora-
    tion, 191
Encyclopedia of Social Reform
    (1897), 27
English Settlement Movement,
    viii
    Jane Addams, 5
    Samuel Barnett, 20–21
    Charles Booth, 27–28
    Cornelia Bradford, 34
    College Settlements Associa-
        tion, 53
    Edward Denison, 61–62
    Octavia Hill, 94–95
    Henry Holland, 97
    Charles Kingsley, 115–16
    Charles Loch, 121–22
    Frederick Denison Maurice,
        128
    Charles B. Stover, 198
    Toynbee Hall, 208

Universities Settlements
    Association (England),
    21, 214
    Robert A. Woods, 237
English Social Movements (1891),
    46, 237
Episcopal church, 26, 33, 38–39,
    71–72, 151, 165, 187
Epworth House, 15
equal opportunity, 77
Equal Rights Amendment, 58
Espionage Act (1917), 19
Esterbrook, William P., 153
Ethical Culture Society, **72**
    Felix Adler, 6–7
    Emily Balch, 17
    Cherry Hill model tenement,
        198
    Stanton Coit, 50–51
    John L. Elliott, 70, 71, 99
    Lewis Hine, 95, 96
    Hudson Guild, 99
    Henry Demarest Lloyd, 121
    Henry Moskowitz, 131, 132,
        133
    nursing services, 221
    Charles B. Stover, 198
Evans, Edmund C., 138
Exploring the Dangerous Trades
    (1943), **72–73**, 89

Factory Law of 1907, 151
Fatigue and Efficiency (1912), 81
Federal Child Labor Law of 1916,
    137
Federal Labor Union, 17
Federation of Boys Clubs, 126
Federation of East Side Boys'
    Clubs, 132
Federation of Social Settlements
    Association of Neighborhood
        Workers (Chicago), 15
    Hull House, 15
Feld-Bretbart Bill (1935), 151
Fellowship of Reconciliation, 18,
    67
fellowships programs
    Barnett Fellowships, 166
    College Settlements Associa-
        tion, 53, 160
    Greenwich House, 85, 86
    Henry Moskowitz, 132
    Robert Treat Paine, 165
    Frances Perkins, 166
    Mary Simkhovitch, 190
    Women's Industrial Union,
        190
Fields, Annie Adams (Mrs. James
    T.), **74–75**
    Cooperative Society of
        Visitors, 28, 74
Fields, James Thomas, 74
Finch-Hill Factory Act (1903), 151

Fine, Jean, 49, **75**
    College Settlement, 51
    College Settlements Associa-
        tion, 53, 55
    Jane Robbins, 177
    Vida Scudder, 187
Flagg, Ernest, 148
Flower, James Monroe, 76
Flower, Lucy Louisa, **75–76**
    Central Relief Association, 43
    Julia Lathrop, 118
folk art, 195
Folks, Homer, **76–77**
    Human Costs of the War, The
        (1920), 96
    professional organizations, 9
    Margaret Dreier Robins, 178
    White House Conference on
        Dependent Children, 230
Ford, George, 56
Fortnightly Club, 239
foster care, 44
Foster, Roger, 153
Foundation for World Peace, 25
Fowler, George B., 154
Foxboro State Hospital for
    Dipsomaniacs, 171
Frederick Douglass Center, **77**
    Jane Addams, 239
    Celia Parker Woolley, 239
Free Religious Association, 6
Freedmen's Bureau, 123
Freemantle, W.H., 20
French, Clara, 75
Friendly Aid House, 85, 146, 190
Friendly Visiting Among the Poor
    (1898), 175
friendly visitors, **78**
    Association for Improving the
        Condition of the Poor, 14
    Charles Loring Brace, 33
    Charity Organization Society,
        40–41
    Cooperative Society of
        Visitors, 28
    *Friendly Visiting Among the
        Poor* (1898), 175
    Robert M. Hartley, 91
    Octavia Hill, 94
    Julia Lathrop, 118
    Zilpha Smith, 191–92
    United Charities of Chicago,
        43

Gage, Lyman J., 47
Galen, George W., 48
garden cities, **79–80**
Garden Cities of Tomorrow
    (1902), 79
Garden City Association of
    America, 79
Garman, Charles Edward, 237
garment workers' strike, 3

Gavitt, John Palmer, 200, 203
Gaynor, William J., 168
General Federation of Women's
Clubs, 136
Giddings, Franklin H., 17, 63
Gilder, Richard Watson, **80**
New York Charity Organiza-
tion Society Tenement
House Committee, 148
New York State Tenement
House Commission of
1894, 153–54
Outdoor Recreation League,
161
girls' clubs, **49–50**
Glenn, John M., **80–81**
Charities Publication
Committee (CPC), 201
National Conference of
Charities and Correction,
139
National Housing Association,
141
Russell Sage Foundation, 182
professional organizations, 9
Amos Warner, 228
Goddard, F. Norton, 154
Goldmark, Helen, 82
Goldmark, Josephine Clara, **81–
82**
Goldmark, Pauline Dorothea, 81,
82–83
New York Child Labor
Committee, 150
Gompers, Samuel, 152, 159, 209
Women's Trade Union League,
234
Good Neighbor Commission, 71
Good Neighbor in the City, The
(1907), 175
Gore, Charles, 97
Gould, Elgin Ralston Lovell, 79,
83
City and Suburban Homes
Company, 229
New York Charity Organiza-
tion Society Tenement
House Committee, 148
Gould, Helen M., 182
Graduate School of Social Service
Administration (Chicago),
83–84
Grace Abbott, 3
Sophonisba Breckinridge, 36
origins, 203
*Tenements of Chicago, 1908–
1935, The,* 207–08
Grand Street Follies, 120
Great Depression
National Federation of
Settlements, 141
People's Lobby, 127
Frances Perkins, 167
Russell Sage Foundation, 182

Green, Thomas Hill, 121
Greenpoint Settlement, 162–63
Greenwich House, **85**
Frederic Almy, 8
athletics, 16
Edward Devine, 64
Crystal Eastman, 69
founding, 190
Benjamin Marsh, 127
*Neighborhood: My Story of
Greenwich House* (1938),
85, 146
Mary White Ovington, 85, 86,
163
Mary Simkhovitch, 190
Carola Woerishoffer, 232
Greenwich Village Improvement
Society, 85
guild concept, 50–51
Guild of Settlement Industries,
212
Gulick, Luther Halsey, 119, 145
Gurteen, S. Humphries, 40
gymnasiums
athletics, 15–16
Helena Dudley, 66
Robert A. Woods, 238

Haiti, 18
Hale, Edward Everett, 161, 162,
199
*Half a Man: Status of the Negro
in New York* (1911), 85, **86**,
163
Hall, Helen, **87**
John L. Elliott, 70, 71
Henry Street Settlement, 93
Paul Kellogg, 112
Hall, John, 67
Halls, Frederick W., 148
Hamilton, Alice, **87–89**
*Exploring the Dangerous
Trades* (1943), 72–73, 89
International Congress of
Women, 234
Hamilton, Edith, 88
Handbook of Settlements (1911),
89–90, 114
National Federation of
Settlements, 140
Handbook of Socialism (1895), 27
Harper, William Rainey, 25, 84,
203
Harper's Magazine, 4
Hartford Theological Seminary,
203
Hartley House, **90**, 91
James G. Phelps Stokes, 198
Hartley, Robert Milham, **90–91**
Association for Improving the
Condition of the Poor, 14
Hartley House, 90, 91

Harvard University, industrial
hygiene program, 89
Hatfield, R.S., 67
Haymarket Riot (1886)
John Peter Altgeld, 8
Henry Demarest Lloyd, 121
health care
Association for Improving the
Condition of the Poor, **15**
baths, 21–22
Mary Brewster, 37
clinics and dispensaries, 48–49
Hull House, 100
Sheppard-Towner Act, 189
Hebrew Free School Association,
135
Henderson, Charles Richmond,
84, **91–92**, 203
Henry Street Group, 11
Henry Street Music School, 93
Henry Street Settlement, **92–93**
consumers' league, 57
Lavinia Dock, 64–65
Helen Hall, 87
Florence Kelley, 109, 110
Alice Lewisohn, 120
Irene Lewisohn, 120
Leonard Lewisohn, 120
Neighborhood Playhouse, 120,
146–47
Lillie M. Peck, 166
Jacob Schiff, 184
Lillian Wald, 224
Hewitt, Abram S., 160
Hill, Octavia, **94–95**
Samuel Barnett, 20
Charles Booth, 27
Charity Organization Society,
41, 74
Annie Fields, 74
Hine, Lewis Wickes, **95–96**
Pittsburgh Survey, 169–70
Survey, the, 200
Hiram House, **96–97**
George Bellamy, 23
*History of Child Saving in the
United States,* 139
Hodges, George, 116
Hodgman, Abbott, 153
Hoe, Robert, 67
Hold, Hamilton, 11
Holland, Henry Scott, **97**
Christian Socialism, 46
Holmes, John Haynes, 11, 138
homelessness, 127
children, 32
Homestead Strike, 124
Hoover, Herbert, 111
House of Refuge for Women, 123
House on Henry Street, The
(1915), 93, **97–98**, 231
Housing and Home Finance
Agency, 23

Housing Association of New York, 64
Housing Betterment, 142
Housing Committee of the City Affairs Committee (New York), 6
Housing of the Unskilled Wage Earner, The, 236
Housing of the Working Poor, The (1895), 83
housing reform
  Felix Adler, 6
  Helen Alfred, 7
  Catherine Bauer, 22–23
  Alexander Bing, 24–25
  Robert DeForest, 60–61
  dumbbell tenements, 67–68
  Richard Gilder, 80
  Elgin R.L. Gould, 83
  Octavia Hill, 94
  housing code, New York, 149, 150
  National Federation of Settlements, 141
  National Housing Association (NHA), 141–42
  New York Charity Organization Society Tenement House Exhibition, 148, 148–50
  New York State Tenement House Laws of 1867, 1879, and 1901, 155–56
  Robert Treat Paine, 164–65
  Louis H. Pink, 168–69
  Mary Simkhovitch, 190
  Tuskegee Apartments, 163
  United Neighborhood Houses, 212
  Lawrence Veiller, 218–19
  Wagner-Steagall Housing Act, 223, 223–24
  Alfred T. White, 228–29
  Edith Elmer Wood, 236–37
Housing Reform: A Hand Book for Practical Use in American Cities, 219
Hovde, Bryn J., 143
How the Other Half Lives: Studies among the Tenements of New York (1890), **97**
  Jacob Riis, 176
How to Help the Poor (1883), 74
Howard, Sir Ebeneezer, 79
Howe, Frederic C., 11
Hudson Guild, **99**
  Felix Adler, 6
  Alexander Bing, 24
  John L. Elliott, 49, 50, 70–71
  Ethical Culture Society, 72
  Madison House, 126
  Neighborhood Guilds: An Instrument of Social Reform (1891), 147–48

Hughes, Charles Evans, 69, 113
  urban overcrowding, 127
Hughes, William, 105
Hull, Charles J., 99
Hull House, **99–100**
  Edith Abbott, 1, 2
  Grace Abbott, 2
  Jane Addams, 5, 99
  Anita Blaine, 25
  Sophonisba Breckinridge, 36
  Exploring the Dangerous Trades (1943), 72–73
  Lucy Flower, 75–76
  Alice Hamilton, 87–89
  Charles R. Henderson, 92
  Robert Hunter, 101, 170
  Juvenile Court Committee, 29, 44
  Juvenile Protective Association, 106
  Florence Kelley, 109, 110
  Julia Lathrop, 118
  Henry Demarest Lloyd, 121
  Frances Perkins, 166
  Second Twenty Years at Hull-House, The (1930), 187–88
  Ellen Gates Starr, 99, 195–96
  Graham Taylor, 203
  Tenements of Chicago, 1908–1935, The, 208
  Twenty Years at Hull-House with Autobiographical Notes (1910), 209–10
Hull House Labor Museum, 196
Hull House Woman's Club, 31
Hull-House Maps and Papers, **100–101**
  Richard Ely, 71
  Florence Kelley, 110
Human Costs of the War, The (1920)
  Homer Folks, 96
  Lewis Hine, 96
Hunter, Niles Robert, **101–02**
  New York Child Labor Committee, 150
  Poverty (1904), 170
hygiene. *See* baths

Illinois Commission of Immigration, 104
Illinois Factory Act (1893), 9, 110
Illinois Factory Inspection Department, 159
Illinois Immigrants' Protective League. *See* Immigrants' Service League
Illinois League of Women Voters, 118
Illinois Occupational Disease Commission, 92
Illinois State Bureau of Labor, 8

Illinois State Bureau of Labor Statistics
  Hull House, 99–100
  Florence Kelley, 110
Illinois Training School for Nurses, 76
Illustrated Christian Weekly, The, 4
immigrants
  Grace Abbott, **3**
  abuses of, 2–3, 13, 103
  amateur performances, 120
  Americanization, 12–13
  Mary Brewster, 37
  casework approach, 104
  Chicago Commons, 42, 203
  Chicago Relief Society, 42–44
  clinics and dispensaries, 48–49
  Committee on Congestion of Population (CCP), 55
  cultural and educational opportunities, 130
  Robert DeForest, 60
  Denison House, 62–63
  dumbbell tenements, 67–68
  Greenwich House, 85
  Hartley House, 90
  Henry Street Settlement, 93
  Hine's photography, 95–96
  Hudson Guild, 99
  Hull House, 100
  Immigrants' Service League, 103–04
  Frances Kellor, 112–13
  Kingsley House (Pittsburgh), 116
  Julia Lathrop, 118
  Madison House, 126
  Belle Moskowitz, 130
  Outlook, The, 162
  Philadelphia, 52
  prostitution, 172
  restrictive legislation, 104
  Rose Schneiderman, 186
  settlement worker attitudes, 12
  stereotypes of settlement workers, ix
  tenement houses, 205–07
  University Settlement, 215
  values studied, 47
  ward politics, 227
  Whittier House, 34
Immigrants' Protective League of Chicago. *See* Immigrants' Service League
Immigration Restriction Acts, 12
Immigration Restriction League, 174
Immigrants' Service League, **103–04**
  Grace Abbott, 2, 3
  Americanization, 13

Immigrants' Service League
(continued)
Sophonisba Breckinridge, 36
Hull House, 100
Julia Lathrop, 118
prostitution, 172
Impatient Crusader: Florence
Kelley's Life Story (1953), 82
Improved Dwelling Association,
159
Improved Dwellings Company,
229
Improved Dwellings for the
Laboring Class (1877), 229
Independent, 162
Lyman Abbott, 4
industrial medicine
Exploring the Dangerous
Trades (1943), 73
Alice Hamilton, 88–89
Industrial Relations Commission,
64, **104–05**
Industrial Workers of the World,
67
industrialization
Christian Socialism, 45
clinics and dispensaries, 48–49
Committee on Congestion of
Population (CCP), 55
Mary Dreier, 66
England, viii, 27
garden cities, 79–80
Graduate School of Social
Service Administration
(Chicago), 83–84
Immigrants' Service League,
103–04
Social Gospel, 4, 192, 203
Ellen Gates Starr, 196
substandard conditions, 41
tenement houses, 205–07
infant mortality, 118
Ingersoll, Robert, 70
Institute for Research in Land
Economics, 72
Institute of Social Science and
Arts, 84. See also Graduate
School of Social Service
Administration (Chicago)
Intercollegiate Bureau of
Occupations (IBO), 9, 217.
See also American Associa-
tion of Social Workers
(AASW)
Inter-Municipal League for
Household Research, 112,
113
International Bill of Rights, 19
International Congress of Women
Grace Abbott, 3
Emily Balch, 18
Alice Hamilton, 88–89

Women's International League
for Peace and Freedom,
234
International Congress of
Working Women (1919), 179
international cooperation, 66
International Council of Nurses,
65
International Federation for
Housing and Town Planning,
24
International Federation of
Settlements, 165, 166
International Industrial Relations
Institute, 218
International Journal of Ethics, 7
International Labor Organiza-
tion, 3
International Ladies' Garment
Workers' Union, 186
International League for the
Rights of Man, 19
International Prison Congress, 92
International Woman Suffrage
Alliance (IWSA), 136, 234
Inter-Racial Council, 113
interracial issues
Roger Baldwin, 18–19
Chicago Commission on Race
Relations, 204
Conference on the Status of
the Negro in the United
States, 163
Frederick Douglass Center, 77
Half a Man: The Status of the
Negro in New York
(1911), 86, 163
Mary McDowell, 126
Henry Moskowitz, 133
Negro in Chicago, The (1922),
204
Mary White Ovington, 162–63
race riots of 1919, 204
William English Walling, 226–
27
Windows on Henry Street
(1934), 231–32
Celia Parker Woolley, 239
Israels, Belle. See Moskowitz,
Belle Linder Israels
Israels, Charles Henry, 130, 131

Jackson, John, 20
James, Edmund, 63
James, William, 6, 124
Japan, 19
Japanese-Americans, 18
J.B. Ford & Company, 161
Jewish Socialist capmakers union,
185
Jim Crow laws, 163
Johnson, Harriet, 130

Joint Board of Sanitary Control,
132
Joint Committee for Social
Service among Colored
People, 18
Journal of Home Economics, 7
journalism
Lyman Abbott, 4
Richard Gilder, 80
How the Other Half Lives:
Studies among the
Tenements of New York
(1890), 98
Arthur Kellogg, 110–11
Paul Kellogg, 111–12
Henry Demarest Lloyd, 120–
21
Outlook, The, 161–62
Jacob Riis, 175–76
Juvenile Court Act (1898), 106
Juvenile Court Committee, 29,
197
juvenile court movement, 36
Lucy Flower, 76
juvenile delinquents
Boston Children's Aid Society,
29
Louise DeKoven Bowen, 31
child welfare, 44, 45
Lucy Flower, 75–76
Homer Folks, 76–77
Robert M. Hartley, 91
Hull House, 197
Julia Lathrop, 118
Mother's Pensions, 133–34
Philadelphia, 52
Alzina Stevens, 197
Juvenile Protective Association
(JPA), 31, **106–07**
prostitution, 172
Juvenile Psychopathic Institute,
107

Kehew, Mary Morton, **108–09**
Helena Dudley, 67
Susan Kingsbury, 115
Mary Kenney O'Sullivan, 159
Women's Trade Union League,
235
Kelley, Florence, **109–10**
biography, 82
Boston School for Social
Workers, 30, 192
child welfare, 44
consumers' league, 57
Richard Ely, 71
factory inspection, 9
Josephine Goldmark, 81
Lewis Hine, 95–96
Hull-House Maps and Papers,
100–01
Industrial Relations Commis-
sion, 104–05

National Child Labor Committee, 137, 225
National Consumers' League, 38
New York Child Labor Committee, 150
Mary Kenney O'Sullivan, 159
peace movement, 11
Frances Perkins, 166
Some Ethical Gains Through Legislation (1905), 194–95
Ellen Gates Starr, 196
Alzina Stevens, 197
United States Children's Bureau, 212–13
White House Conference on Dependent Children, 230
Kellogg, Arthur Piper, **110–11**
Lewis Hine, 95–96
Survey, the, 200
Kellogg, Paul Underwood, **111–12**
American Union Against Militarism, 10, 11, 12
Lilian Brandt collaboration, 35
John L. Elliott, 70, 71
Espionage Act, 19
Helen Hall, 87
Lewis Hine, 95–96
Industrial Relations Commission, 104–05
Albert Kennedy, 114
National Civil Liberties Bureau, 137
National Progressive Service (NPS), 143–44
Pittsburgh District Civic Frontage, The (1914), 170
Pittsburgh Survey, 169, 170, 182
Prohibition, 171
Survey, 200
Wage-Earning Pittsburgh (1914), 170
Kellor, Frances (Alice), **112–13**
National Progressive Service (NPS), 143, 144
Out of Work (1904), 160
Margaret Dreier Robins, 178
Kennedy, Albert Joseph, **113–14**
Handbook of Settlements (1911), 89
National Federation of Settlements, 140
Lillie M. Peck, 165–66
Settlement Horizon, The (1922), 188
South End House, 195
Young Working Girls (1913), 240
Kennedy, John F., 182
Keyserling, Leon, 143
King, Edward, 51, 198

Social Reform Club, 193
University Settlement, 215
Kingsbury, Mary. *See* Simkhovitch, Mary K.
Kingsbury, Susan Myra, 109, **114–15**
Labor Laws and Their Enforcement (1911), 117
Kingsley, Charles, **115–16**
Christian Socialism, 26, 45–46, 97
Richard Ely, 71
Frederick Denison Maurice, 128
Vida Scudder, 187
Kingsley House (Pittsburgh), **116**
Kingsley, Sherman, 43
Kitchen Garden Association, 31
Knights of Labor
William Bliss, 26
Richard Ely, 72
Mary Kenney O'Sullivan, 156
Alzina Stevens, 196

Labor Chest of the Relief and Liberation of Workers of Europe, 227
Labor Housing Conference, 143
Catherine Bauer, 23
Labor Laws and Their Enforcement (1911), **117**
labor, rights/protection of
Grace Abbott, 3
John Peter Altgeld, 8–9
American Civil Liberties Union, 11
Emily Balch, 17
Roger Baldwin, 19
Charles Booth, 27
John Graham Brooks, 38
Chicago Women's Bindery Union, 159
Civic Federation of Chicago, 47
College Settlement, 51
Katherine Coman, 55
Denison House, 63
Mary Dreier, 65–66
Helena Dudley, 66–67
Richard Ely, 72
England, 27
of Free Nations Association, 226
free speech, 18
Josephine Goldmark, 81–82
Pauline Goldmark, 82
Elgin R.L. Gould, 83
Charles R. Henderson, 91
Henry Street Settlement, 93
Hine's photographs, 96
Hull House, 99–100
industrial medicine, 88–89
Industrial Relations Commission, 64, 104–05

Mary Kehew, 109
Labor Laws and Their Enforcement (1911), 117
Henry Demarest Lloyd, 121
Mary McDowell, 125–26
Frederick Denison Maurice, 128
Belle Moskowitz, 131
Henry Moskowitz, 132
New York Working Women's Society, 156
Mary Kenney O'Sullivan, 158–60
Frances Perkins, 166–67
Philadelphia, 52
Jane Robbins, 177
Rose Schneiderman, 184–86
Vida Scudder, 187
Secretary of Labor Frances Perkins, 167
Social Gospel, 192
Social Reform Club, 193
Some Ethical Gains Through Legislation (1905), 194–95
Ellen Gates Starr, 196
Alzina Stevens, 196–97
James G. Phelps Stokes, 198
University of Chicago Settlement, 215
Carola Woerishoffer, 232–33
women and consumers' leagues, 57–58
Women's Trade Union League (WTUL), 234–36
Robert A. Woods, 237
Labor's Challenge to the Social Order (1920), 38
Labour and Life of the People of London (1889–1891), 27, 100
Ladies' Guild (London), 94
Ladies Library Association, 239
Lake Geneva Fresh Air Association, 76
Lakeview Home for Wayward Girls, 130
Lansing, Williams, 154
Lasker, Bruno, 171
Lathrop, Anna, 118
Lathrop, Julia Clifford, **117–19**
Graduate School of Social Service Administration (Chicago), 84
Immigrants' Service League, 103–04
Juvenile Court Committee, 31, 44, 45
juvenile delinquency, 197
National Conference of Charities and Correction, 139
Sheppard-Towner Act, 189

Lathrop, Julia Clifford *(continued)*
United States Children's Bureau, 137, 213
Laughlin, James L., 1
Lawrence textile strike, 159–60, 187
lead poisoning, 88
League for Political Education, 38, 83
League for the Protection of Immigrants. *See* Immigrants' Service League
League of Mother's Clubs, 50, 212
League of Nations
Grace Abbott, 3
George Bellamy, 24
Anita Blaine, 25
Helena Dudley, 67
Alice Hamilton, 89
Julia Lathrop, 119
Survey, 200
Women's International League for Peace and Freedom, **234**
League of Neutral American Nations, 11–12
League of Women Voters, 181
Alice Hamilton, 89
Julia Lathrop, 118
Lee, Joseph, **119**
Playground Association of America, 145
Robert A. Woods, 238
Lee, Margaret, 119
Lewisohn, Alice, 120
American Union Against Militarism, 138
Neighborhood Playhouse, 147–48, 225
peace movement, 11
Lewisohn, Irene, **120**
Neighborhood Playhouse, 147–48, 225
Life and Labour of the People in London (1903), 27–28
Lincoln's Inn, 45, 128
Linder, Belle. *See* Moskowitz, Belle Linder Israels
Lloyd, Henry Demarest, **120–21**
factory inspection, 9
Loch, Charles Stewart, **121–22**
Lochner, Louis P., 11
Loeb, Mrs. Solomon, 37, 221, 225
London Charity Organization Society, 94, 121
London Society for Organizing Charitable Relief and Repressing Mendicancy (1869), 40
London Society for the Relief of Distress, 61–62
Longshoremen, The (1915), 82

Los Angeles Times bombing, 104–05
Lovejoy, Owen, **122–23**
Industrial Relations Commission, 104–05
National Conference of Charities and Correction, 139
professional organizations, 9, 10
Low, Seth, 151, 174, 178
Lowell, Charles Russell, 123
Lowell, Josephine Shaw, **123–24**
consumers' leagues, 57, 123, 124, 156
Maud Nathan, 135–36
Lillian Wald, 225
Ludlow, John Malcolm, 26, 45–46

McCarthy, Charles, 105
McClellan, George B., 151
McClure's Magazine, 172
McCormick, Anita. *See* Blaine, Anita Eugenie McCormick
McCormick, Cyrus Hall, 25
MacDonald, George, 161
McDowell, Mary Eliza, **125–26**
Boston School for Social Workers, 30
Immigrants' Service League, 104
National Progressive Service, 144
University of Chicago Settlement, 15, 214–15
Women's Trade Union League, 235
Mack, Julian W., 201
McNamara, John, 104–05
McNeill, George E., 38
Madison Hamilton Settlement, 126. *See also* Madison House
Madison House, **126–27**
Helen Alfred, 7
Ethical Culture Society, 72
Henry Moskowitz, 131, 132
Manhattan Trade School for Girls, 231
Mann Act (1910), 172
Manny, Frank A., 95
Mansfield House, 34
Manufacturers' Association, 131
Marot, Helen, 150
Marsh, Benjamin C., **127–28**
Committee on Congestion of Population (CCP), 56
Marshall, Edward, 153
Massachusetts Association for Promoting the Interests of the Blind, 108–09
Massachusetts Board of Public Welfare, 33
Massachusetts Civic League, 119

Massachusetts Commission on Industrial and Technical Education, 115
Massachusetts Department of Labor and Industries, 160
Massachusetts State Board of Charity, 33
Massachusetts State Commission on Industrial Education, 18
Mather, Mary H., 75
Matthews, William, 116, 170
Maurice, Frederick Denison, **128**
Phillips Brooks, 39
Christian Socialism, 26, 39, 45–46, 97
Richard Ely, 71
Octavia Hill, 94
Charles Kingsley, 115
Vida Scudder, 187
Maxwell Street Settlement, 15
Medical Women's International Association, 177
Men and Religion Forward Movement, 180
Men at Work (1932), 96
mentally ill, 118
Mercantile Inspection Law (1896), 57
Metropolitan Life Insurance Company, 221, 225
Metropolitan Museum of Art, 120, 184
Meyer, Henry C., 207
migrants, 112
Milk Advisory Committee (New York State), 87
Milk and Baby Hygiene Association, 108
milk, pure, campaigns for, 48, 90
Mill, John Stuart, 27
Miller v. *Oregon,* 81
minimum wage laws, 58
Mitchell, John Purvoy, 131, 132–33
Mitchell, Lucy Sprague, **128–30**
Mitchell, Wesley Clair, 129, 130
Modern Methods of Charity (1904), 92
Modern Painters, 94
Monday Evening Club, 192
monopolies, industrial, 121
moral guardians, 77
morality, 72
Morgenthau, Rita Wallach, 120
Morris, Moreau, 153
Moses, Solomon, 153
Moskowitz, Belle Linder Israels, **130–31**
Lewis Hine, 96
Henry Moskowitz, 133
Louis H. Pink, 169
Alfred E. Smith, 191

Women's City Club of New York, 233
Moskowitz, Henry, **131–33**
African Americans, 163
Industrial Relations Commission, 104–05
Madison House, 126
Belle Moskowitz, 131
National Progressive Service (NPS), 143, 144
prostitution, 172
mother's clubs, 49, 50, 211–12
Mother's Pensions, **133–34**
Widowed Mother's Pension Bill (1915), 153
Mount Ivy summer camp and farm, 231
Mumford, Lewis, 23
Municipal Civil Service Commission, 133
Municipal Housing Authorities Law (1934), 143
Municipal Housing Lodge for Vagrants, 101
Municipal Voter's League, **42**, 203
Murphy, Edgar Gardner, 136–37, 150–51
Murphy, Franklin, 34
Murphy, John J., 152
Museum of Costume Art, 120
Museum of Natural History, 184
Music School Settlement, 51

Nassau County (Long Island) Emergency Work Bureau, 64
Nathan, Maud, **135–36**
consumers' league, 57
National American Woman Suffrage Association
Jane Addams, **5**
Sophonisba Breckinridge, 36
Rose Schneiderman, 186
National Association for the Advancement of Colored People (NAACP)
Sophonisba Breckinridge, 36
founding, 163
Florence Kelley, 110
Mary McDowell, 126
Henry Moskowitz, 133
Mary White Ovington, 163
William English Walling, 227
National Association for the Study and Prevention of Tuberculosis, 64
National Association of Housing Officials, 143
National Association of Housing Reformers, 23
National Child Labor Committee (NCLC), **136–37**
Felix Adler, 6–7
Roger Baldwin, 18

Edward Devine, 64
Homer Folks, 77
Lewis Hine, 96
Florence Kelley, 110
Owen Lovejoy, 122
Pittsburgh Survey, 169–70
Jacob Schiff, 184
Mary Simkhovitch, 190
United Neighborhood Houses, 211
United States Children's Bureau, 213
Lillian Wald, 225
National City Planning Conference, 127
National Civic Federation, 105
child labor, 137
National Civil Liberties Bureau (NCLB), 10, **137–38**. *See also* American Civil Liberties Union
Roger Baldwin, 19
National Civil Liberties Union, 10. *See also* American Civil Liberties Union
National Conference of Charities and Correction, 139. *See also* National Conference on Social Welfare
Jane Addams, 5
Jeffrey R. Brackett, 33
child labor, 137
Columbia University Graduate School of Social Work, 53–54
Robert DeForest, 61
Crystal Eastman, 69–70
Homer Folks, 76–77
John Glenn, 80
Graduate School of Social Service Administration (Chicago), 84
Alice Hamilton, 88
Charles R. Henderson, 92
Owen Lovejoy, 122
National Federation of Settlements, 139–40
Prohibition, 171
Mary Richmond, 175
Margaret Dreier Robins, 179
Second Twenty Years at Hull-House, The (1930), 188
Zilpha Smith, 192
Graham Taylor, 204
National Conference of Social Work, 122. *See also* National Conference on Social Welfare
Mary Richmond, 175
Lea Taylor, 205
National Conference on City Planning, 56
National Conference on Civic and Neighborhood Center Development, 168

National Conference on Social Welfare, **138–39**. *See also* National Conference of Charities and Corrections
National Consumers' Leagues. *See* Consumers' League
National Council of Jewish Women, 136
National Defense Bill (1915), 11–12
National Economic League, 102
National Employment Exchange, 61, 184
National Federation of Settlements (NFS), **139–41**
Jane Addams, 5
George Bellamy, 24
child welfare, 44
John L. Elliott, 71
Helen Hall, 87
Handbook of Settlements (1911), 89
Albert Kennedy, 114
Lillie M. Peck, 165
Prohibition, 171
Settlement Horizon, The (1922), 188
Mary Simkhovitch, 190
Graham Taylor, 204
Lea Taylor, 205
Robert A. Woods, 238
Young Working Girls (1913), 240
National Federation of Settlements and Neighborhood Centers, 141. *See also* National Federation of Settlements
National Freedman's Relief Association, 123
National Housing Act of 1934, 223
National Housing Association (NHA), **141–42**,
Lawrence Veiller, 61, 141, 148, 219
National Housing Conference, (NHC), 23, **142–43**. *See also* National Public Housing Conference (NPHC)
Wagner-Steagall Housing Act, 223–24
National Labor Relations Act, 223
National League for the Protection of Colored Women, 112
National Physical Education Service, 145
National Playground Association of America
athletics, 15–16
James B. Reynolds, 174
Charles B. Stover, 199
National Prison Association, 174

National Probation Association, 18

National Progressive Service (NPS), **143–44**
  Katherine Coman, 55
  Frances Kellor, 113

National Public Housing Conference (NPHC), 143. *See also* National Housing Conference
  Mary Simkhovitch, 190
  Wagner-Steagall Housing Act, 223
  Edith Elmer Wood, 237

National Recreation and Park Association, **145–46**
  Outdoor Recreation League, 161

National Recreation Association (NRA), 146. *See also* National Recreation and Park Association

National Recreation School, 146

National Social Reform Union, 27

National Social Welfare Assembly, 87

National Social Workers Exchange (NSWE), 10, 217. *See also* American Association of Social Workers (AASW)

National Trust for Places of Historic Interest or Natural Beauty, 94

National Urban League, 18, 112

National Vigilance Association, 174

National War Fund Campaign, 24

National Woman's Party, 70

Native Americans, 183

nativism, 35

naturalization, 12

Nearing, Scott, 138

Negro in Chicago, The (1922), 204

neighborhood concept, 79
  Neighborhood Guilds: An Instrument of Social Reform (1891), 147–48
  Mary Simkhovitch, 190
  Robert A. Woods, 238

Neighborhood Guild. *See also* University Settlement
  Stanton Coit, 50–51
  Madison House, 126
  Jane Robbins, 177
  Charles B. Stover, 198
  University Settlement, 215–16

Neighborhood Guilds: An Instrument of Social Reform (1891), **147–48**

Neighborhood in Nation-Building (1923), 238

Neighborhood: My Story of Greenwich house (1938), 85, **146**

Neighborhood Playhouse, 120, **146–47**, 225

Neutral Conference for Continuous Mediation, 18

New Conscience and an Ancient Evil, A (1912), 172

New Day in Housing, The (1927), 169

New Deal
  Edith Abbott, 2
  Grace Abbott, 3
  critics, 102
  Edward Devine, 64
  federal role, 36
  housing reform, 223–24
  Public Housing Conference, 142
  Eleanor Roosevelt, 181
  Rose Schneiderman, 186
  James G. Phelps Stokes, 198

New Jersey Conference for Social Welfare, 34

New Jersey Neighborhood Workers' Association, 34

New Jersey Tenement House Commission, 34

New Law tenements, 155, 156, 207

New Outlook, The, 162, 191

New Republic, The, 7

New World Foundation, 25

New York Association for Labor Legislation, 232, 233

New York Association of Neighborhood Workers, 50. *See also* United Neighborhood Houses (UNH)
  John L. Elliott, 71
  National Child Labor Committee, 137
  New York Child Labor Committee, 150
  Prohibition, 170–71

New York Botanical Garden, 184

New York Building Congress, 24

New York Charities Aid Association, 123

New York Charity Organization Society
  Committee on Criminal Courts, 219
  Congestion Exhibition, 56
  Edward Devine, 63
  Elgin R.L. Gould, 83
  Margaret Olivia Sage, 184
  Josephine Shaw, 123–24
  Survey, 199-201
  Survey Associates, 201
  Tenement House Committee, 83, 207, 218
  Lawrence Veiller, 218–19
  Lillian Wald, 225
  Elizabeth S. Williams, 231

New York Charity Organization Society Tenement House Committee, **148**
  members, 148
  Elizabeth S. Williams, 231

New York Charity Organization Society Tenement House Exhibition, **148–50**, 154

New York Child Labor Committee (NYCLC), 137, **150–51**
  Congestion Exhibition, 56
  consumers' league, 57–58
  Pauline Goldmark, 82
  Florence Kelley, 110
  James G. Phelps Stokes, 90, 197
  United Neighborhood Houses, 211
  William English Walling, 226

New York Child Labor Law of 1903, 150

New York City Commissioner of Corrections, 59

New York City Council of Social Agencies, 71

New York City Housing Authority, 168

New York City Metropolitan Building Code (1899), 149

New York City Tenement House Commission
  College Settlement, 51
  Moral and Social Influence of Tenement House Life, 155
  Henry Moskowitz, 132

New York City Tenement House Department, 56, **151–52**
  creation, 149, 151, 207
  New York State Tenement House Commission of 1900, 155
  Clarence Perry, 168
  Lawrence Veiller, 219
  Edith Elmer Wood, 236

New York Committee of 1,000, 64

New York Consumers' League. *See also* Consumers' Leagues founding, **57–58**.
  Josephine Goldmark, 81
  Pauline Goldmark, 82
  Elizabeth S. Williams, 231
  Carola Woerishoffer, 232

New York Council of Jewish Women, 130

New York Equal Suffrage League, 136

New York Exchange for Women's Work, 135

New York Hospital Training School for Nurses, 224

New York Juvenile Asylum, 224

New York School of Philanthropy, 54. *See also* Columbia University Graduate School of Social Work
  Mary Dreier, 65
  Pauline Goldmark, 82
  Frances Perkins, 166
  Zilpha Smith, 192
  Mary Van Kleeck, 217
New York School of Social Work. *See also* Columbia University Graduate School of Social Work
  Robert DeForest, 61
New York Society for Ethical Culture, 72
New York State Charities Aid Association
  Homer Folks, 76, 77
  New York Charity Organization Society Tenement House Committee, 148
  Margaret Dreier Robins, 178
  Russell Sage Foundation, 182
New York State Charities Association, 61
New York State Committee on Education, 71
New York State Conference of Charities and Corrections
  Belle Moskowitz, 130
  James Stokes, 197
New York State Department of Labor, 186, 233
New York State Factory Act, 156
New York State Factory Investigating Commission, 65–66, 81, **152–53**
  Pauline Goldmark, 82, 83
  Frances Perkins, 166–67
  Alfred E. Smith, 191
  Triangle Shirtwaist Company Fire (1911), 209
  Robert F. Wagner, 222
New York State Immigration Commission, 112
New York State Industrial Commission, 167
New York State Tenement House Commission
  Felix Adler, 6, 153
  Robert DeForest, 60–61
  New York Charity Organization Society Tenement House Committee, 148
  Lawrence Veiller, 219
New York State Tenement House Commission of 1884, **153**
New York State Tenement House Commission of 1894, **153–54**
  Jane Robbins, 177
New York State Tenement House Commission of 1900, **154–55**
  laws passed, 155–56

James B. Reynolds, 173
Tenement House Problem, The (1903), 205
Alfred T. White, 229
New York State Tenement House Law of 1879, 153
New York State Tenement House Law of 1901, 83, 155, 207
  Lawrence Veiller, 219
New York State Tenement House Laws of 1867, 1879, and 1901, **155–56**
  tenement defined, 206
New York State Woman Suffrage Party, 66
New York Tenement House Committee of 1894, 80
New York Tenement House Law of 1901, 168
New York Visiting Nurse Service, 82
New York Women's City Club, 131
New York Women's Trade Union League, consumers' league, **57–58**
New York Working Women's Society, **156**
Newer Ideals of Peace (1907), 210
Niagara Movement, 163
Nielsen, Elizabeth, 176
Nobel Peace Prize
  Jane Addams, 5, 234
  Emily Balch, 18, 234
North American Civic League for Immigrants, 35, 112
Northwestern University Settlement, **156–57**
  clean milk campaign, 48
  Federation of Social Settlements, 15
  Margaret Dreier Robins, 178
  Raymond Robins, 179, 180
nurses
  Visiting Nurse Service of Chicago, 31, 219–20
  Visiting Nurse Service (New York), 220–21
Nurses' Settlement. *See also* Henry Street Settlement
  coordinated health care, 48
  New York Charity Organization Society Tenement House Committee, 149
  origins of Henry Street Settlement, 92
  Jacob Schiff, 184, 221
  Lillian Wald, 225
nursing
  Louise DeKoven Bowen, 31
  Mary Brewster, 37, 92
  Lavinia Dock, 64
  Henry Street Settlement, 92–93
nursing education

Lavinia Dock, 64
Lucy Flower, 76
Josephine Goldmark, 82

O'Brien, William J., 154
occupational therapy, 118
O'Donohue, Joseph J., 153
Office of Price Administration, U.S., 87
Old Age Pensions Act (London, 1906), 28
Old Law tenements, 168
On Journey (1937), **158**
O'Reilly, Leonora, **65**, 178
  Social Reform Club, 193
  Women's Trade Union League, 235
orphanages, 44, 45
O'Sullivan, John F., 159
O'Sullivan, Mary Kenney, **158–60**
  Helena Dudley, 67
  factory inspection, 9
  Knights of Labor, 156
  Alzina Stevens, 197
  Union for Industrial Progress, 109
  Women's Trade Union League, 234
Ottendorfer, Oswald, 153
Out of Work (1904), **160**
Outdoor Recreation League, 145, **160–61**
  athletics, 15–16
  James B. Reynolds, 173
  Mary Simkhovitch, 190, 211
  James G. Phelps Stokes, 90, 197
  Charles B. Stover, 199
  University Settlement, 215
  Elizabeth S. Williams, 231
Outlook and Independent, The, 162
Outlook, The, **161–62**
  Lyman Abbott, 4, 161–62
  Charles B. Spahr, 75, 162
Ovington, Mary White, **162–63**
  Greenwich House, 190
  Half a Man: Status of the Negro in New York (1911), 85, 86, 163
  NAACP, 133
Oxford House, 97

pacifism
  Jane Addams, 5
  Emily Balch, 18
  Cornelia Bradford, 34
  Crystal Eastman, 70
  National Civil Liberties Bureau, 10–11
  Raymond Robins, 180
  Survey, the, 200

Paine, Robert Treat, *See also* Consumers' Leagues
Boston Children's Aid Society, 29
Palmer, Alice Freeman, 129
Palmer, George, 129
Palmer, Mrs. Potter, 47
Pan-American Congress of Women, 31
Parker, Celia. *See* Woolley, Celia Parker
Parker, Colonel Francis Wayland, 25
Parks Commission, 199
parks. *See* playgrounds
Parsons, Alzina. *See* Stevens, Alzina Parsons
Parsons, W. Frank, 200
Pastor, Rose Harriet, 198
Patten, Simon Nelson, 63, 127
Paulding, James K., 145, 199
peace movement
    Jane Addams, 5
    American Union Against Militarism, 10, 11–12
    Emily Balch, 18
    Anita Blaine, 25
    Lavinia Dock, 65
    Mary Dreier, 66
    Alice Hamilton, 88–89
    Paul Kellogg, 112
    Women's International League for Peace and Freedom, 234
Peck, Lillie M., **165–66**
    Albert Kennedy, 114
Peck, Lucy, 195
penal reform
    Katharine Davis, 59–60
    Frances Kellor, 112
    National Conference on Social Welfare, 139
Penner, Lewis, 107
Pennsylvania Society to Protect Children from Cruelty, 127
pensions, 28
People's Bath, 15
People's Council, antiwar movement, 12, 138
People's Lobby, 127
People's Palace, 34
Perkins, Frances, **166–67**
    New York State Factory Investigating Commission, 152
    Alfred E. Smith, 191
    Women's City Club of New York, 233
Perlman, Selig, 105
Perry, Clarence, **167–68**
Philadelphia Society of Organizing Charity, 175
philanthrophy

applied training, 29–30
    Anita Blaine, 25
    Louise DeKoven Bowen, 31–32
    Charity Organization Society (COS), 40–41
    Robert Treat Paine, 164–65
    Margaret Olivia Sage, 183–84
    Jacob Schiff, 184
    Alfred T. White, 228–29
philanthropy and five percent, philosophy, 229
Photo League of New York City, 96
photography
    Lewis Hine, 95–96
    Jacob Riis, 175–76
physicians
    Alice Hamilton, 87–89
    Jane Robbins, 176–77
Pinchot, Gifford, 144
Pink, Louis Heaton, 142–43, **168–69**
Pittsburgh Civil Commission, 105
Pittsburgh Survey, **169–70**
    Addams's narrative, 188
    Robert DeForest, 61
    Crystal Eastman, 69
    Lewis Hine, 96
    Paul Kellogg, 111
    Russell Sage Foundation, 182
    Margaret Olivia Sage, 184
Plato Group, 118
Play School, 129
Playground, The, 145
Playground and Recreation Association of America (PRAA). *See also* National Recreation and Park Association
    George Bellamy, 24
    origins, 145
    Clarence Perry, 168
Playground Association of America (PAA). *See also* National Recreation and Park Association
    Joseph Lee, 119
    Belle Moskowitz, 131
    origins, 145
playgrounds
    athletics, 15-16
    George Bellamy, 24
    Hull House, 100
    Joseph Lee, 119
    National Recreation and Park Association, 145–46
    Outdoor Recreation League, 145, 160–61
political economy, 71–72
political reform
    John Peter Altgeld, 8–9
    Louise DeKoven Bowen, 31
    Chicago Commons, 42, 203

Elgin R.L. Gould, 83
    Joseph Lee, 119
    Henry Demarest Lloyd, 121
    Mary McDowell, 126
    Madison House, 126
    Henry Moskowitz, 133
    National Progressive Service (NPS), 143–44
    New York State Factory Investigating Commission, 152–53
    Northwestern University Settlement, 156–57
    James B. Reynolds, 173–74
    Margaret Dreier Robins, 179
    Raymond Robins, 180
    Josephine Shaw, 124
    social investigations, 14
politicians
    Belle Moskowitz, 131
    Alfred Emanuel Smith, 191
    Robert F. Wagner, 66, 143, 222–23
Politics for the People, 115, 128
Poor Law Commission (1905), 28, 94
poor laws criticized, 122
Populist Movement, 179, 196–97
positivism, 50
Post, George B., 148, 153
Potter, Henry Codman, 67, 79, 151
poverty
    causes of, 41
    character building, 41
    as character flaw, ix, 14
    child welfare, 44–45
    defined, 170
    economic origins, 33
    employment and, 27, 28
    friendly visitors, 78
    as individual failing, 174
    London, 27
    as moral defect, 91
    as moral deficit, 77
    moral regeneration, 61
    moralizing about, 14
    poor law system, 122
    Prohibition, 171
    social forms producing, 101
    substantial works, 164
    worthy vs. unworthy poor, ix, 14, 78, 164
Poverty (1904), 101, **170**
Pratt Institute Neighborhood Association, 162–63
Presbyterian church, 183
President's Conference on Home Building and Ownership, 142, 168
President's Conference on Unemployment, 217
Press, 153

Preston, W.C., 27
Prison Association, 61
Probation Committee of the
    Chicago Women's Club, 106
probation officers, 197
*Progressive Democracy—Speeches
    and State Papers of Alfred E.
    Smith,* 133
Progressive Era, vii–viii
Progressive movement
    antiwar movement, 12
    child welfare, 45
Progressive Party
    Frederic Almy, 8
    Louise DeKoven Bowen, 31
    Sophonisba Breckinridge, 36
    Katherine Coman, 55
    Katharine Davis, 60
    Frances Kellor, 113
    Henry Moskowitz, 132
    National Conference of
        Charities and Correction,
        139
    National Progressive Service
        (NPS), 143–44
    Raymond Robins, 180
    *Second Twenty Years at Hull-
        House, The* (1930), 188
    Survey support, 200
Prohibition, **170-72**
    Raymond Robins, 180
    *Second Twenty Years at Hull-
        House, The* (1930), 188
    Robert A. Woods, 238
prostitution, **172**
    Civic Federation of Chicago, 47
    Katharine Davis, 60
    Lavinia Dock, 65
    immigrants, 13
    investigated, 18, 47
    Madison House, 126
    Belle Moskowitz, 130–31
    Henry Moskowitz, 132
    Out of Work (1904), 160
    Prohibition, 171
    Tenement House Commis-
        sions, 155
Protestant clergy, 192. *See also*
    individual churches
Providence resolution, of AASW,
    10
public baths. *See* baths
public education, 177, 231
Public Education Association,
    129, 130, 177
    Elizabeth S. Williams, 231
Public Health Nursing, 7
public housing
    Lawrence Veiller, 219
    Edith Elmer Wood, 237
Public Housing Conference
    (PHC), 7, 142. *See also*
    National Public Housing
    Conference (NPHC)

Louis H. Pink, **169**
    Wagner-Steagall Housing Act,
        223–24
Public Housing Progress, 7
Public Relief and Private Charity
    (1884), 124
public school nursing programs,
    221, 225
public works construction, New
    Deal, 142
Puerto Rico, 236
Pullman, Florence, 220
Pullman strike, 121
    John Peter Altgeld, **8**
pure food campaign, 58

Raines-Law Hotels, 155
Rand, Helen C., 53, 55
    College Settlements Associa-
        tion, 75
    Vida Scudder, 187
Rand School of Social Science,
    185
Record, George, 144
Recreation, 145
recreation
    athletics, 15–16
    George Bellamy, 24
    Joseph Lee, 119
    Irene Lewisohn, 120
    Madison House, 126
    Belle Moskowitz, 130
    National Recreation and Park
        Association, 145–46
    Neighborhood Playhouse, 120,
        146–47
    Outdoor Recreation League,
        145, 160–61
    Clarence Perry, 167–68
    Charles B. Stover, 199
Red Cross
    Jeffrey R. Brackett, 33
    Edward Devine, 64
    Homer Folks, 76, 77
    Helen Hall, 87
    Lewis Hine, 96
    Arthur Kellogg, 111
    Paul Kellogg, 112
    nursing service, 221
    Jane Robbins, 177
    Margaret Dreier Robins, 179
    Raymond Robins, 180
refugees, 18, 71
Regional Planning Association of
    America, 23, 237
Reichardt, Anthony, 153
Reynolds, James B., 132, 154,
    173–74
    Industrial Relations Commis-
        sion, 104–05
    National Conference of
        Charities and Correction,
        139

Outdoor Recreation League,
    160
prostitution, 172
ward politics, 227
Rice, Gertrude, 182
Rich, Adena Miller, 32
Rich, Sara Ann, 95
Richberg, Donald, 144
Richmond, Mary Ellen, **174–75**
    applied philanthropy, 29–30
    Graduate School of Social
        Service Administration
        (Chicago), 84
    Lucy Sprague Mitchell, 129
    National Conference of
        Charities and Correction,
        139
    professional organizations, 9
Riis, Jacob Augustus, **175–76**
    Charities Publication
        Committee (CPC), 201
    Greenwich House, 85
    *How the Other Half Lives:
        Studies among the
        Tenements of New York*
        (1890), 98
    National Progressive Service,
        144
    National Recreation and Parks
        Association, 145
    New York Charity Organiza-
        tion Society Tenement
        House Committee, 148,
        207
    New York Child Labor
        Committee, 151
    Outdoor Recreation League,
        161
    Outlook, The, 162
Rivington Street Settlement. *See*
    College Settlement (New
    York)
Robbins, Ira, 142
Robbins, Jane Elizabeth, **176–77**
    College Settlement, 51, 75
    College Settlements Associa-
        tion, 53
    Jean Fine, 75
    girls' clubs, 49
    Outdoor Recreation League,
        161
Robert Gould Shaw House, **177–
    78**
Robins, Elizabeth, 179–80
Robins, Margaret Dreier, 65, **178–
    79**
    Immigrants' Service League,
        103–04
    National Progressive Service,
        144
    Northwestern University
        Settlement, 157
    Raymond Robins, 179

Robins, Margaret Dreier,
(continued)
Women's Trade Union League,
235
Robins, Raymond, 144, 157, 178,
179–80
ward politics, 227
Rockefeller Foundation, 82
Rockefeller, John D., Jr., 59
Rogers, Lina L., 225
Roman Catholic church, 196
Roosevelt, (Anna) Eleanor, **180–
82**
Rose Schneiderman, 186
Women's City Club of New
York, 233
Roosevelt, Franklin D.
Homer Folks, 76, 77
housing reform, 223
Frances Perkins, 167
Eleanor Roosevelt, 181
Rose Schneiderman, 186
Roosevelt, Theodore
Jane Addams, 5
"Man with the Muck Rake,
The" (1906), 162
New York State Tenement
House Commission, 149
New York State Tenement
House Commission of
1900, 154
James B. Reynolds, 174
Margaret Dreier Robins, 179
Raymond Robins, 180
tenements, 205
United States Children's
Bureau, 212–13
Woman Suffrage Committee,
136
Rosenwald, Julius, 104
Rowland, Henrietta, 20
Rural Electrification Administra-
tion, 96
Ruskin, John
William Bliss, 27
Octavia Hill, 94
Frederick Denison Maurice,
128
Vida Scudder, 158, 187
Lawrence Veiller, 218
Russell Sage Foundation, **182**
American Association of Social
Workers, 9–10
Lilian Brandt, 35
Chicago School of Civics and
Philanthropy, 203
Robert DeForest, 61
Department of Industrial
Studies, 217
John Glenn, 80, 81
Graduate School of Social
Service Administration
(Chicago), 84

National Recreation and Parks
Association, 145
New York School of Philan-
thropy, 54
Clarence Perry, 167–68
Pittsburgh Survey, 169, 170
Mary Richmond, 175
Margaret Olivia Sage, 184
Mary Van Kleeck, 217–18
Alfred T. White, 229
Russia's Message (1908), 226
Ryerson, Eleanor, 31

safety, Wainwright Commission,
232
safety standards, 38
Crystal Eastman, 69–70
*Exploring the Dangerous
Trades* (1943), 72–73
Josephine Goldmark, 81–82
Triangle Shirtwaist Company
Fire (1911), 208–09
Sage, Margaret Olivia Slocum,
183-84
Robert DeForest, 61, 184
Russell Sage Foundation, 182,
184
Sage, Russell, 183
St. Louis Civic League, 18
St. Louis Juvenile Court, 18
Sanitary Engineer, 67, 153, 207
Sayles, Mary, 34
Schiff, Jacob Henry, **184**
New York Child Labor
Committee, 151
Visiting Nurse Service, 37, 92,
221, 225
Schiff Library of Jewish Classics,
184
Schneiderman, Rose, **184–86**
New York State Factory
Investigating Commis-
sion, 152
Eleanor Roosevelt, 181
Women's Trade Union League,
235
scholarship programs, 93
school center movement, 167–68
Jane Robbins, 177
United Neighborhood Houses,
212
School Visitors Association, 119
Schuchman, John P., 153
Schuyler, Louisa Lee, 123, 182
Scudder, Richard B., 201
Scudder, Julia Vida Dutton, **186–
87**
Christian Socialists, 26, 39,
186
College Settlements Associa-
tion, 53, 75
Katherine Coman, 54–55
Denison House, 63

On Journey (1937), 158
Mary Simkhovitch, 189
Women's Trade Union League,
235
Seaside Home for Children, 229
*Second Twenty Years at Hull-
House, The* (1930), **187–88**
Seeley, J.R., 214
segregation, 163
Selective Service Act (1917), 138
Serbia, 231
Settlement Horizon, The (1922),
114, **188**
Robert A. Woods, 238
settlement houses. *See* Chicago
Commons; College Settle-
ment; Greenpoint Settle-
ment; Henry Street
Settlement; Hull House;
Hudson Guild; Kingsley
House; Madison Hamilton
Settlement; Maxwell Street
Settlement; Music School
Settlement; Northwestern
University Settlement;
Nurses Settlement; Stillman
Branch Settlement; United
Neighborhood Guild
Settlement; University of
Chicago Settlement;
Universities Settlement;
University Settlement
settlement movement, vii–ix
attitudes to immigrants, 12
Christian Socialism, 46
settlement workers, ix
child welfare, 45
techniques used, 41
Young Working Girls (1913),
240
Seventeenth Ward Civic Federa-
tion, **42**
Seward Park, 161, 199
Shaw, Robert Gould, 123
Robert Gould Shaw House,
177–78
Sheppard-Towner Act, **189**
Grace Abbott, 3, 45, 118
Julia Lathrop, 118
United States Children's
Bureau, 137, 213
Shientag, Bernard, 152
shirtwaist makers' strike, 65, 233,
235
Simkhovitch, Mary Melinda
Kingsbury, **189–91**
Christian Socialists, 26, 39
*City Workers' World in
America, The* (1917), 47
College Settlement, 51
Committee on Congestion of
Population (CCP), 55–56
John L. Elliott, 70, 71

Greenwich House, 85
Industrial Relations Commission, 104–05
Benjamin Marsh, 127
National Recreation and Parks Association, 145
Neighborhood: My Story of Greenwich House (1938), 85, 146
New York Child Labor Committee, 150
Outdoor Recreation League, 161, 199
Louis H. Pink, 169
Public Housing Conference, 7, 142, 143
Eleanor Roosevelt, 181
Social Reform Club, 193
United Neighborhood Houses (UNH), 211
Wagner-Steagall Housing Act, 223, 224
Women's City Club of New York, 233
Simkhovitch, Vladimir, 85, 190
Slavic Fellow Citizens, Our, (1910), 18
Smith, Alfred Emanuel, **191**
Lewis Hine, 96
industrial conditions study, 66
Belle Moskowitz, 131
Henry Moskowitz, 133
New Outlook, The, 162
New York State Factory Investigating Commission, 152, 209, 222
Frances Perkins, 167
Louis H. Pink, 169
Progressive Democracy— Speeches and State Papers of Alfred E. Smith, 133
Up from the City Streets: Alfred E. Smith (1927), 133
Smith, Zilpha D., **191–92**
Boston Associated Charities, 28
Boston School for Social Workers, 30, 33
Joseph Lee, 119
Mary Richmond, 174
Social and Educational Improvement Club (SEI), 132
"Social Aspects of Tuberculosis" (1903), 35
Social Christianity. *See also* Social Gospel
Denison House, 63
Graham Taylor, 202
social control, 14, 208
Social Diagnosis (1917), 175
Social Gospel, 4, 71, **192–93**

Albert Kennedy, 114
South End House, 195
Graham Taylor, 203
Robert A. Woods, 237, 238
social insurance
Grace Abbott, 2
Helen Alfred, 7
Frederic Almy, 8
European, 55
social investigation
Americans in Process, 13–14
Charles Booth, 27–28
child welfare, 44
Crystal Eastman, 69
friendly visitors, 78
John Glenn, 81
Elgin R.L. Gould, 83
Henry Street Settlement, 92
homelessness, 127
Hull-House Maps and Papers, 100–01
Robert Hunter, 101
industrial conditions, 66
Industrial Relations Commission, 105
infant mortality, 189
Mary Kehew, 109
Frances Kellor, 112–13
Albert Kennedy, 113–14
Susan Kingsbury, 114–15
laundry industry, 232
Joseph Lee, 119
Benjamin Marsh, 127
National Federation of Settlements, 140
Pittsburgh Survey, 169–70
James B. Reynolds, 173
Mary Richmond, 174–75
South End House, 195
Tenement House Problem, The (1903), 205
unemployment, 51
Mary Van Kleeck, 217–18
Carola Woerishoffer, 232
Edith Elmer Wood, 236
Social Reform Club, 86, 160, 163, **193**
Charles B. Stover, 198
Social Science Club, 66
Social Security Act, 87, 112
Frances Perkins, 167
Social Service Center for Practical Training in Philanthropic and Social Work. *See* Graduate School of Social Service Administration (Chicago)
Social Service Club (Boston), 63
Social Service Review
Grace Abbott, 3
Edith Abbott, 2
Sophonisba Breckinridge, 37

Social Spirit of America, The (1896), 92
Social Union of the North and West Ends (Boston), 30. *See also* Boston Social Union
Social Unrest, The (1903), 38
social work
American Association of Social Workers (AASW), 9–10
casework approach, 8, 28, 174–75
Helen Hall, 87
homeless children, 32
Juvenile Protective Association, 107
National Conference on Social Welfare, 138–39
national prominence, 45
professional establishment, ix
Second International Conference, 218
Survey, the, 199–201
Social Work (1922), **194**
social work education
Edith Abbott, 2
Grace Abbott, 3
American Association of Social Workers (AASW), 9–10
Roger Baldwin, 19
Boston Associated Charities, 28
Boston School of Social Work, 54
Boston School for Social Workers, 29–30
Jeffrey R. Brackett, 33
Lilian Brandt, 35
Sophonisba Breckinridge, 36–37
Columbia University Graduate School of Social Work, 53–54
Robert DeForest, 61
Pauline Goldmark, 82
Graduate School of Social Service Administration (Chicago), 83–84
Charles R. Henderson, 92
medical social work, 30, 54
National Conference on Social Welfare, 138–39
professionalization, 33
Mary Richmond, 53–54, 174–75
Russell Sage Foundation, 182
Zilpha Smith, 192
Social Diagnosis (1917), 175
Social Work (1922), 194
Graham Taylor, 203
socialism
John Graham Brooks, 37
Katherine Coman, 54–55
Robert Hunter, 101

socialism *(continued)*
    Florence Kelley, 109
    On Journey (1937), 158
Socialist Party
    Helena Dudley, 67
    Rose Schneiderman, 186
    James G. Phelps Stokes, 198
    William English Walling, 226–27
    World War I, 11, 12, 198
Society for Parks and Play-grounds, 160, 199
Society for the Relief of the Ruptured and Crippled (1863), 91
Society of Christian Socialists, 26, 187
Society to Lower Rents and Reduce Taxes on Homes in New York, 127
Some Ethical Gains Through Legislation (1905), 110, **194–95**
Some Folks Won't Work, 87
South End House, **195**
    African Americans, 162
    The City Wilderness (1898), **46**
    Helena Dudley, 66
    Albert Kennedy, 113–14
    Lillie M. Peck, 165–66
    Robert Gould Shaw House, 177–78, 195
    Social Gospel, 193
South End Social Union, 30, 238. *See also* Boston Social Union
Southwood Smith, Thomas, 94
Soviet Union, 180
Spahr, Charles B., 75, 162
    Social Reform Club, 193
Spanish Child Welfare Association, 120
Spanish Civil War, 120
Spanish-American War, 124
Spirit of Youth and the City Streets, The, 210
sports. *See* athletics
Sprague, Lucy. *See* Mitchell, Lucy Sprague
Standard Zoning Law of 1921, 219
Starr Center. *See* College Settlement (Philadelphia)
Starr, Ellen Gates, **195–96**
    Hull House, 5, 99
    Twenty Years at Hull-House with Autobiographical Notes (1910), **210**
State Board of Charities, Aids, and Corrections (New Jersey), 34
State Board of Charities, New York, 123

State Board of Children's Guardians (New Jersey), 34
Stevens, Alzina Parsons, **196–97**
    factory inspection, 9
Steward, Seth, 145
Stokes, Caroline Margaretha Phelps, 101
Stokes, I.N. Phelps, 148, 154
Stokes, James Graham Phelps, **197–98**
    Hartley House, 90
    New York Child Labor Committee, 150
Stover, Charles B., **198–99**
    Stanton Coit, 51
    National Recreation and Parks Association, 145
    Outdoor Recreation League, 145, 160–61
    Social Reform Club, 193
    University Settlement, 215
Stowe, Harriet Beecher, 161
Straus, Nathan, 48
Straus, Oscar, 132
Strong, Mary, 238
Strong, William L., 218
Strunsky, Anna, 226
Sulter, William, 121
Summer School of Applied Ethics, 6
Summer School of Philanthropy
    Frederic Almy, 8
    Edward Devine, 63
    Kellogg brothers, 111
    Mary Richmond, 175
Survey, the, **199–201**
    Roger Baldwin, 19
    Alexander Bing, 24
    Robert DeForest, 61
    Edward Devine, 63–64
    Lewis Hine, 96
    Industrial Relations Commission, 105
    Arthur Kellogg, 111
    Paul Kellogg, 111–12
    Belle Moskowitz, 130
    name change, 201
    social insurance articles, 55
    Graham Taylor, 203
    Graham Romeyn Taylor, 204
Survey Associates, **201**
    Alexander Bing, 24
    Robert DeForest, 61
    Arthur Kellogg, 111
    origins, 200
Survey Graphic, 111, 200–01
Survey Midmonthly, 111
sweating system, 99–100
    England, 115
sweatshops
    John Peter Altgeld, 9
    University Settlement, 215–16

Taft, William Howard, 105, 137
Talbot, Marion, 129
Taylor, Graham, **202–04**
    Anita Blaine, 25
    Chicago Commons, 42
    Graduate School of Social Service Administration (Chicago), 84
    Julia Lathrop, 118
    National Conference of Charities and Correction, 139
    National Social Workers Exchange, 10
    prostitution, 172
    relief measures in 1894, 43
    ward politics, 227
Taylor, Graham Romeyn, **204**
    business manager of *Charities and the Commons,* 200
    Industrial Relations Commission, 105
Taylor, Lea Demarest, **204–05**
temperance movement, 74
    Robert M. Hartley, 90
    Mary McDowell, 125
    Prohibition, 170–72
    Margaret Olivia Sage, 183
    Robert A. Woods, 238
Tenement Conditions in Chicago (1901), 101
Tenement House Building Company, Felix Adler, **6**
Tenement House Commission of 1884, 98
Tenement House Exhibition, Lawrence Veiller, **218–19**
Tenement House Law of 1901, 67–68
Tenement House Problem, The (1903), 61, 149, **205**
Tenement House Protective League, 34
tenement houses, **205–07**
    airshafts, 155–56
    Boston, 74
    Sophonisba Breckinridge, 36
    Stanton Coit, 50–51
    commission created, 60–61
    Committee on Congestion of Population (CCP), 55–56
    defined, 155, 206
    dumbbell tenements, 67–68
    Ethical Culture Society, 72
    Annie Fields, 74
    Richard Gilder, 80
    Robert M. Hartley, 91
    Henry Street Settlement, 92
    How the Other Half Lives: Studies among the Tenements of New York (1890), 98
    Benjamin Marsh, 127

New York Charity Organization Society Tenement House Exhibition, 148, 148–50
New York City Tenement House Department, 151–52
New York State Tenement House Laws of 1867, 1879, and 1901, 155–56
Louis H. Pink, 168–69
Jacob Riis, 175–76
Tenement House Problem, The (1903), 205
Lawrence Veiller, 218–19
Tenements of Chicago, 1908–1935, The, **207–08**
Tennessee Valley Authority, 96
theater, 120
Neighborhood Playhouse, 120, 146–47
Thomas, Norman, 138
Thomas Y. Crowell, publisher, 101
Through the Loom (1933), 96
Thursday Evening Club, 55
Tierney, Myles, 154
Tilden, Samuel J., 123
Tisdale, Clark, 157
Tolstoy, Leo, 187
Tomorrow: The Peaceful Path to Real Reform (1898), 79
Town and Country Nursing Service, 221, 225
Toynbee, Arnold, 20, 62
Charles Loch, 121
Toynbee Hall, 208
Toynbee Hall, viii, **208**
Jane Addams, 5
Samuel Barnett, 20
Cornelia Bradford, 34
Stanton Coit, 50
College Settlement (New York), 51
Jean Fine, 75
founding, 21
Robert Hunter, 101
Charles B. Stover, 198
Universities Settlements Association (England), 21, 214
Robert A. Woods, 237
trade unionism. *See* labor, rights/protection of
Transcendentalists, 6
transit system ownership, 198
Travelers Aid Society of Metropolitan Chicago, 104
Triangle Shirtwaist Company Fire (1911), 65–66, **208–09**
Josephine Goldmark, 81
investigating commission, 152–53
Belle Moskowitz, 131

Henry Moskowitz, 132
Frances Perkins, 166
Alfred E. Smith, 191
Trusdale, Charles, 43
Tucker, William Jewett, 193, 195, 237
Tuskegee Apartments, 163
Twenty Years at Hull-House with Autobiographical Notes (1910), **209–10**
Typographical Union No. 16, 196

unemployment
College Settlement (New York), 51
delinquency, 29
England, 27, 28
Helen Hall, 87
Frances Kellor, 112
London, 62
Mary Van Kleeck, 218
Robert F. Wagner, 222
unemployment among college-educated women, ix
Emily Balch, 17
Boston Social Union, 30
College Settlements Association, 53
Jean Fine, 75
Intercollegiate Bureau of Occupations (IBQ), 9
Mary Kehew, 109
Vida Scudder, 187
Twenty Years at Hull-House with Autobiographical Notes (1910), 210
Unemployment Insurance: A Summary of European Systems (1918), 55
Union for Industrial Progress, 109, 159
Unitarian church, 37–38, 128, 230, 239
United Charities, 25. *See also* Chicago Relief Society
Louise DeKoven Bowen, **32**
United Charities of Chicago, 43–44, 92
United Cloth Hat and Cap Makers Union, 185
United Garment Workers, 55
United Nations
Helen Hall, 87
Universal Declaration of Human Rights, 181
United Neighborhood Guild Settlement, 168
United Neighborhood Houses (UNH), **211–12**
athletics, 16
United States Bureau of Labor, 27
United States Children's Bureau, **212–13**

Grace Abbott, 2, 3
Sophonisba Breckinridge, 36
creation, 45, 194
Homer Folks, 77
Florence Kelley, 110
Julia Lathrop, 118, 137
National Federation of Settlements, 140–41
Second Twenty Years at Hull-House, The (1930), 188
Sheppard-Towner Act, 189
Lillian Wald, 225–26
White House Conference on Dependent Children, **230**
United States Civil Service Commission, 167
United States Coal Commission, 64
United States Housing Authority, 23
United States Railroad Administration, 82
United States Sanitary Commission, 123
United Workers, 64
Universities Settlements Association (England), 21, **214**
Toynbee Hall, 208
University of Chicago School of Social Work. *See* Graduate School of Social Service Administration (Chicago)
University of Chicago Settlement, 15, **214–15**
Mary McDowell, 125
University Settlement, **215–16**
Frederic Almy, 8
Edward Devine, 64
Albert Kennedy, 114
New York Charity Organization Society Tenement House Committee, 149
Louis H. Pink, 168–69
James B. Reynolds, 173
Social and Educational Improvement Club (SEI), 132
James G. Phelps Stokes, 90, 197
Charles B. Stover, 198, 199
William English Walling, **226**
University Settlement Association, 25
University Settlement, Philadelphia, 87
Up from the City Streets: Alfred E. Smith (1927), 133
Uptown Ethical Culture Society, 132
urban land studies, 72
urban overcrowding
Association for Improving the Condition of the Poor, 14–15

urban overcrowding *(continued)*
Alexander Bing, 24–25
City Wilderness, The, 47
Civic Federation of Chicago, 47
Committee on Congestion of
Population (CCP), 55–56
Congestion Exhibition, 56
garden cities, 79–80
Richard Gilder, 80
Elgin R.L. Gould, 83
health-related programs, 49
juvenile delinquency, 106
Benjamin Marsh, 127
New York, 51
New York Charity Organiza-
tion Society Tenement
House Exhibition, 148,
148–50
New York State Tenement
House Commission of
1894, 154
Outdoor Recreation League,
145, 160–61
tenement houses, 205–07

Van Kleek, Mary Abby, 9, **217–18**
Vanderpoel, S.O., 153
Veblen, Thorstein, 1
Veiller, Lawrence Turnure, **218–
19**
Congestion Exhibition, 56
National Housing Association,
141–42
New York Charity Organiza-
tion Society Tenement
House Committee, 148
New York Charity Organiza-
tion Society Tenement
House Exhibition, 148,
149
New York City Tenement
House Department, 151
New York State Tenement
House Commission of
1900, 154–55
Tenement House Exhibition,
207
Tenement House Problem, The
(1903), 61, 205
Villard, Oswald Garrison, 11
Visiting Nurse Association of
Chicago (VNA), Northwest-
ern University Settlement,
157
Visiting Nurse Service (New
York), **220–21**, 225. *See also*
Henry Street Settlement
Visiting Nurse Service of Chicago,
31, **219–20**
Jane Addams, 220
Louise DeKoven Bowen, 220
Mary Brewster, 37, 92
Chicago Commons, 42

Henry Street Settlement, 93,
97–98
Hull House, 100
visiting nurses
Cleveland, 97
clinics and dispensaries, 48–49
Lavinia Dock, 64–65
Ethical Culture Society, 72
Hiram House, 97
New York, 82
Visiting Nurse Service (New
York), 220–21
Visiting Nurse Service of
Chicago, 219–20

Wagner Act, 11
Wagner, Robert Ferdinand, 66,
143, **222–23**
National Public Housing
Conference, 237
New York State Factory
Investigating Commis-
sion, 152, 191, 209
Wagner-Steagall Housing Act,
224, 237
Wagner-Steagall Housing Act,
223–24, 237
Wagner-Steagall Housing Bill, 23,
143
Mary Simkhovitch, 190
Wainwright Commission, 232
Wald, Lillian D, **224–26**
American Union Against
Militarism, 10, 11, 12
Boston School for Social
Workers, 192
child welfare conference, 32
Committee on Congestion of
Population (CCP), 55–56
Lavinia Dock, 64–65
John L. Elliott, 70, 71
Espionage Act, 19
Henry Street Settlement, 92–
93, 97–98
House on Henry Street, The
(1915), 97–98
Industrial Relations Commis-
sion, 104–05
Frances Kellor, 113
Lucy Sprague Mitchell, 129
National Child Labor
Committee, 137
National Civil Liberties
Bureau, 137
National Federation of
Settlements, 139
National Recreation and Parks
Association, 145
New York Child Labor
Committee, 150
On Journey (1937), 158
Outdoor Recreation League,
161, 199

professional organizations, 9
Prohibition, 171
Public Housing Conference,
142
Eleanor Roosevelt, 181
Jacob Schiff, 184
Josephine Shaw, 124
Social Reform Club, 193
United States Children's
Bureau, 212–13
Visiting Nurse Service, 37, 48
Visiting Nurse Service (New
York), 220–21
White House Conference on
Dependent Children, 45,
230
Windows on Henry Street,
231–32
Women's City Club of New
York, 233
Women's Trade Union League,
235
Walling, William English, **226–27**
African Americans, 163
Helena Dudley, 67
Henry Moskowitz, 133
Mary Kenney O'Sullivan, 159
Margaret Dreier Robins, 178
Women's Trade Union League
(WTUL), 234
Walsh, Frank, 105
*War-Time Strikes and Their
Adjustment* (1921), 24
ward politics, **227–28**. *See also*
political reform; politicians
Ware, James E., 67, 207
Warner, Amos Griswold, **228**
Warren, Cornelia, 53
Washburn, Helen Lawrence, 38
Washington, Booker T., 86, 162,
163
Washington, William D'H, 153
Wealth against Commonwealth
(1894), 121
Webb, Beatrice and Sidney, 1
Welfare Council of New York, 35
Wells Memorial Institute for
Workingmen, 165
West Side Studies (1914), 82
White, Alfred Tredway, **228–29**
National Housing Association,
141
tenement housing commission,
154
White, Gaylord, 55
White House Conference on Child
Health, 142
White House Conference on Child
Health and Protection, 179
White House Conference on
Dependent Children, 230
Charles Loring Brace, 32
Homer Folks, 77

Mother's Pensions, 133
National Child Labor
    Committee, 137
United States Children's
    Bureau, 213
white lists, 136
Whittier House, 34–35
Widowed Mother's Pension Bill
    (1915), 153
Willard, Frances, 125
Williams, Elizabeth Sprague,
    230–31
College Settlement, 51
National Recreation and Parks
    Association, 145
Outdoor Recreation League,
    161
Wilson, Woodrow, 105
Windows on Henry Street (1934),
    93, **231–32**
Windsor Home for Aged People,
    165
Wingate, Charles F., 153
Wise, Stephen S., 11
Woerishoffer, Emma Carola, **232–
    33**
woman suffrage
    Louise DeKoven Bowen, 31
    Katharine Davis, 60
    Lavinia Dock, 65
    Mary Dreier, 66
    Crystal Eastman, 70
    Belle Moskowitz, 131
    Maud Nathan, 135, 136
    New York Equal Suffrage
        League, 136
    Margaret Dreier Robins, 179
    Rose Schneiderman, 186
    Women's International League
        for Peace and Freedom,
        234
    Celia Parker Woolley, 239
Woman's Central Association of
    Relief, 123
Woman's Medical College, 176,
    177, 221
Woman's Medical School, 88
Woman's Municipal League, 124
Woman's Municipal League of
    New York, 136
Woman's Peace Party, **5**
Woman's Roosevelt Republican
    Club, 31
Woman's World Fairs, 31–32
women, immigrant, 2–3
Women in Industry (1910), 1
women workers
    consumers' leagues, 57–58
    Pauline Goldmark, 82
    hours, 81
    Mary Kehew, 109
    Susan Kingsbury, 115
    Mary McDowell, 126

Belle Moskowitz, 131
Mother's Pensions, 133–34
Maud Nathan, 135–36
New York State Factory
    Investigating Commis-
    sion, 152–53
New York Working Women's
    Society, 156
Mary Kenney O'Sullivan, 158–
    60
Out of Work (1904), 160
Frances Perkins, 166
prostitution, 172
Margaret Dreier Robins, 178–
    79
Rose Schneiderman, 184–86
Triangle Shirtwaist Company
    Fire (1911), 208–09
Women's Trade Union League
    (WTUL), 234–36
Young Working Girls (1913),
    240
Women's City Club of New York,
    181, **233–34**
women's clubs, 49
Women's Educational and
    Industrial Union of Boston,
    108, 109
    Susan Kingsbury, 115
Women's Industrial Union, 190
Women's International League
    for Peace and Freedom, **234**
    Jane Addams, 5
    Cornelia Bradford, 34
    Helena Dudley, 67
    Alice Hamilton, 89
    Florence Kelley, 110
Women's Municipal League, 178
Women's Municipal League of
    Boston, 236
Women's Trade Union League
    (WTUL), **234–36**
    Edith Abbott, 1
    Association of Neighborhood
        Workers, 211
    Emily Balch, 17
    Boston, 109
    Sophonisba Breckinridge, 36
    Katherine Coman, 55
    Mary Dreier, 65–66
    Helena Dudley, 67
    Alice Hamilton, 89
    immigrants, 103
    Mary Kehew, 109
    Mary Kenney O'Sullivan, 159–
        60
    Margaret Dreier Robins, 178–
        79
    Eleanor Roosevelt, 181
    Rose Schneiderman, 185, 186
    Vida Scudder, 187
    Mary Simkhovitch, 190
    Social Reform Club, 193

Ellen Gates Starr, 196
Triangle Shirtwaist Company
    Fire (1911), 152, 208–09
William English Walling, 226
Carola Woerishoffer, **233**
Wood, Edith Elmer, 142, **236–27**
Wood, Hollingsword, 11, 138
Woodbridge, Alice, 57, 156
Woods, Robert A., **237–38**
    Americans in Process (1902),
        13–14
    Andover House, 46–47
    Boston School for Social
        Workers, 30
    Helena Dudley, 66
    Handbook of Settlements
        (1911), 89
    Albert Kennedy, 114
    National Conference of
        Charities and Correction,
        139
    National Federation of
        Settlements, 139, 140
    professional organizations, 10
    Prohibition, 171
    Settlement Horizon, The
        (1922), 114, 188
    Social Gospel, 193
    South End House, 195
    Women's Trade Union League,
        235
    Young Working Girls (1913),
        240
Woolley, Celia Parker, **238–39**
    Frederick Douglass Center, 77
Woolley, Jefferson H., 239
Work Accidents and the Law
    (1910), 69
worker's compensation, 69
Working Girls' Club, 165
Working Women's Society, 57
Working Women's Union Number
    1, 196
Workingman's School, 6
Workingmen's Building Associa-
    tion, 164
Workingmen's College (London),
    94, 128
Workingmen's Loan Association,
    164
Workmen's Compensation Act
    (1913), 153
World Social Economic Congress,
    218
World War I
    Jane Addams, 141
    black soldiers, 163
    William Bliss, 27
    Louise DeKoven Bowen, 31
    Cornelia Bradford, 34–35
    Chicago Commons, 205
    conscientious objectors, 137–
        38

World War I (*continued*)
Lavinia Dock, 65
Mary Dreier, 66
free speech, 19
Josephine Goldmark, 81–82
Pauline Goldmark, 82
Helen Hall, 87
housing, 142
Robert Hunter, 101–02
immigrants, 12, 113
industrial problems, 24
Inter-Racial Council, 113
Paul Kellogg, 112, 200
Frances Kellor, 113
labor regulations, 58
Mary McDowell, 126
National Civil Liberties
Bureau (NCLB), 137–38
National Federation of
Settlements, 141

Playground and Recreation
Association of America,
145
political support, 131
preparedness issue, 11
recreation, 119
Margaret Dreier Robins, 179
Eleanor Roosevelt, **181**
James G. Phelps Stokes, 198
Lea Taylor, 205
trade unions, 179
troop recreation, 24
Mary Van Kleeck, 217
Lillian Wald, 226
William English Walling, 227
Women in Industry Service
Department, 179, 217
World War II
Helen Hall, 87
public housing, 143
Eleanor Roosevelt, 181
Russell Sage Foundation, 182

Wright, Carroll D., 83, 100, 110
Writers' Workshop, 130
Wynbladh, Sigrid V., 9

Yeast (1848), 115
Young Men's Christian Associa-
tion, 104
Benjamin Marsh, 127
James B. Reynolds, 173
Young Women's Christian
Association, 179
*Young Working Girls: A Summary
of Evidence from Two
Thousand Social Workers*
(1913), 44, 49, 140, **240**
Albert Kennedy, 114

Zueblin, Charles, 157